W9-BZJ-899

Friday, April 6th:
Blackboard Unit Response

onday April 9th
iday April 13th:
atch Blackboard
Video (LINK)
espond to question
n Blackboard
londay April
6th: Discussion
eader (OUFR)
Vednesday May
2nd: Unit Response
Friday May 4th:
Take Home Final
Due

Postcolonial Plays

Discussion: Monday April 9th
    Once Upon A...
Develop + consider three to four points of
inquiry

This collection of contemporary postcolonial plays demonstrates the extraordinary vitality of a body of work that is currently influencing the shape of contemporary world theatre. The anthology, the first of its kind, includes both internationally admired 'classics' and previously unpublished texts. It draws upon work from Canada, the Caribbean, South and West Africa, Southeast Asia, India, New Zealand, Hawai'i and Australia.

Dealing with imperialism and its aftermath, the plays use a wide range of dramaturgical techniques drawn from Western theatre and local performance traditions. Agit-prop dialogue, musical routines, storytelling, ritual incantation, epic narration, dance, multimedia presentation and puppetry are among the many ways through which individuals and groups express their concerns. The plays dramatise issues as diverse as:

- globalisation
- political corruption
- race and class relations
- slavery
- gender and sexuality
- media representation
- nationalism

Postcolonial Plays: An Anthology includes a general introduction that outlines key issues relevant to the study of postcolonial theatre. Individual introductions to plays include biographical information on the author, an overview of the play's main thematic concerns and performance features, and a summary of its performance history.

Helen Gilbert lectures in Drama and Theatre Studies at the University of Queensland. She is author of *Sightlines: Race, Gender and Nation in Contemporary Australian Theatre*, and co-author of *Post-colonial Drama: Theory, Practice, Politics*.

Editoral Advisers: Susan Bennett, Sudipto Chatterjee, J. Ellen Gainor, Gareth Griffiths, Liz Gunner, Jacqueline Lo, Howard McNaughton, Tejumola Olaniyan, Martin Orkin, Lionel Pilkington, Elaine Savory, Jyotsna Singh and Jerry Wasserman.

- All three plays deal with the possession of others' bodies.
  ↳ people searching for autonomy in a society that won't
    allow it without sacrifice - is that really autonomy?
  ↳ Anowa: Kofi Ako is a slave owner
  ↳ gender roles: woman can't bear a strong breed ; it's
    Anowa's job to bear children; Joyd is wanted because
    she can bear children
  ↳ post-colonialism: power structure between men + wom

Unit Response 3 Notes: Princess Poconantas + the Blue Spot
                        Details cannot Body wants
                        QPH

3 essay questions : open from 7am to 12am on
Friday, April 6th, 2018

Postcolonial Plays

An anthology

Edited by Helen Gilbert

Unit Response Notes: Writing about the Strong Breed, Anowa,
and Harvest

- a list of concepts from plays / discussions
  - ↳ could be multiple choice
  - ↳ could be True or false
  - ↳ could be short answer

- All three plays deal with the effects of colonialism
  - ↳ Anowa ends with a suicide of Kofi Ako + Anowa
  - ↳ the Strong Breed ends with Eman dying to redeem
    the actions of others
  - ↳ Harvest ends in a science fiction utopian narrative
    that there are no winners or losers, only partners!
    Jaya wants to meet Virgil in person before having a kid

- All three plays <u>also</u> deal with the ideas of <u>choice +
  freedom</u>.

  - ↳ The Strong Breed: they tell him he has the choice to leave
    and not be the sacrifice; but does he really? What is his role
    in the world?
  - ↳ Anowa: does Anowa go with her own family or do her own
    thing? She does her own thing (choice?) and it ends in her
    down fall.

  - ↳ Harvest: Om <u>chooses</u> to give up the parts of his body; Jaya
    <u>chooses</u> to be defiant; Jeetu <u>chooses</u> to be a
    prostitute — BUT is anything a choice?

Routledge
Taylor & Francis Group
LONDON AND NEW YORK

First published 2001 by Routledge
2 Park Square, Milton Park, Abingdon, Oxon OX14 4RN

Simultaneously published in the USA and Canada
by Routledge
270 Madison Ave, New York, NY 10016

Reprinted 2007 (twice)

Transferred to Digital Printing 2008

Routledge is an imprint of the Taylor & Francis Group, an informa business

Typeset in Veljovic by Keystroke, Jacaranda Lodge, Wolverhampton

British Library Cataloguing in Publication Data
A catalogue record for this book is available from the British Library

Library of Congress Cataloging in Publication Data
A catalogue record for this book has been requested

ISBN10: 0–415–16448–6 (hbk)
ISBN10: 0–415–16449–4 (pbk)

ISBN13: 978–0–415–16448–1 (hbk)
ISBN13: 978–0–415–16449–8 (pbk)

To the playwrights whose unforgettable works are gathered here and those reluctantly passed over this time

Contents

Illustrations

Acknowledgements

First and foremost, I wish to acknowledge a tremendous debt to Marguerite Nolan, whose extensive input into this project has undoubtedly ensured its completion. As well as approaching routine editing tasks with faultless dedication and professionalism, she also contributed significantly to the intellectual content of this book by substantially writing the individual play introductions for Wole Soyinka, Briar Grace-Smith, Girish Karnad, Maishe Maponya and Ama Ata Aidoo. I am ever in her debt for this generosity. Heartfelt thanks also to Simone Murray, who bailed me out at a bad time and whose initial work on all of the introductions proved invaluable, leaving an indelible print throughout the anthology. To Jacqueline Lo, equal gratitude for coming to the rescue with ideas on paper when I needed them and for listening to my grumbles over a very long time. Without the support of each of these friends and colleagues, I would have surely given up in despair long ago.

For assistance with research, permissions and sundry other tedious tasks, I am indebted to Ursula Dauth, Amanda Lynch, Carrie Dawson and Mary Ann Hunter. Particular thanks also to Joan Ward for general support for the project and for help with life's practicalities. To my partner, Cameron Browne, I owe special gratitude for ignoring my stress and always keeping a sense of humour.

I would like to thank my Board of Advisers: Susan Bennett, Sudipto Chatterjee, J. Ellen Gainor, Gareth Griffiths, Liz Gunner, Jacqueline Lo, Howard McNaughton, Tejumola Olaniyan, Martin Orkin, Lionel Pilkington, Elaine Savory, Jyotsna Singh and Jerry Wasserman. Their suggestions and feedback, especially in the initial stages of the project, proved invaluable. While some have been required to do more than others, all have given willingly and generously of their time. I may have truculently ignored some of their advice on occasions, but I am nonetheless deeply grateful for it. David Bradby also deserves thanks for his comments on the initial proposal for this project.

Some people have done more than they should ever have been asked to do, especially for a relative stranger. For their extraordinary generosity in helping with permissions, textual preparations and research material, and for their patience in dealing with my requests, I owe significant debts to Miki Flockemann, Honor Ford-Smith, Claudia Harris and Gawrie du Toit.

Many of the dramatists whose works are featured here have communicated with me directly or indirectly. This book is enriched by their assistance with queries as well as by their extraordinary plays. In this respect, I wish to thank William Kentridge, Jane Taylor, Hertencer Lindsay, Kee Thuan Chye, Manjula Padmanabhan, Girish Karnad, Louis Nowra, Victoria Kneubuhl, Guillermo Verdecchia, Femi Osofisan, Chin Woon Ping, Ama Ata Aidoo and members of Sistren.

For general input at various points throughout this project, I owe gratitude to Christopher Balme, Jim Hoffman, Marc Maufort, Jennifer Harvie and Denis Salter. For specialist advice and help with obtaining permissions and references, I am deeply grateful to a great number of other academics, theatre practitioners and publishing personnel. In relation to South African plays, I wish to thank Rose Meny-Gibert, Glenda Younge, Hyreath Anderson, Aziza Solomons, Marcia Blumberg, Geoffrey Davis and Loren Kruger; West African plays: David Moody, Martin Banham, Ben Halm, Derek Wright and Celia Ely; plays from the Caribbean region: Rhonda Cobham, Joy Scott, Eugene Williams and Lana Finikin; Indian plays: Anuradha Roy and Erin B. Mee; plays from Southeast Asia: William Peterson, K.K. Seet, Shirley Lim and Shirley Hew; Australian plays: Veronica Kelly, Andrew

Ross, Glenice Allen, Raena Lea-Shannon, Kim Green, Jill Walsh, Kandese Garston, Margaret Leask, Rachel Fensham and Magabala Books; plays from New Zealand: Hone Kouka, Roma Potiki, Carol Stevenson and Huia Publishing; Hawaiian plays: Rebecca Howard and the Native American Women Playwrights Archive; Canadian plays: Alan Filewod, Bruce Barton, Mark Shackleton, Sheila Rabillard, Karl Seigler, Joh Hartog, Fraser Seely, Carolyn McCarthy, Canadian Broadcasting Commission and the Playwrights Union of Canada; and for advice concerning plays from Ireland: Ann Saddlemeyer, Helen Lojek, Rebecca Pelan, Colin Smythe, Shaun Richards, Mary Trotter and Maria Doyle.

Thanks also go to photographers Rouphin Coudzer, David Wilson and Jeff Busby. Their work, like William Kentridge's wonderful illustrations, adds life and colour to this book. Angela Tuohy, Sandra Gough and Cathy Squirrell deserve thanks for helping with secretarial tasks and showing extraordinary patience with my demands. Finally, I would like to acknowledge Routledge staff Talia Rodgers, Jason Arthur, Sophie Powell, Kate Trench and Rosie Waters for their support for this project. Early research was done with the assistance of an Australian Research Council grant from the University of Queensland, for which I am also deeply grateful.

Acknowledgements for play texts ─────────

Production or public reading rights to the plays must be requested from the individual playwrights or copyright holders.

Pink © Judith Thompson 1989. Reprinted with the permission of Playwrights Union of Canada from *The Other Side of the Dark: Four Plays by Judith Thompson*, first published in 1989 by Coach House Press, Toronto, Canada.

The Hungry Earth © Maishe Maponya 1993 & 1995. Reprinted from *Doing Plays for a Change: Five Works Introduced by Ian Steadman*, by permission of the Witwatersrand University Press on behalf of Maishe Maponya. Applications to perform this work should be addressed to the Dramatic and Literary Rights Organisation (DALRO). Fax: 27-(0)11-404-1934

Ubu and the Truth Commission © Jane Taylor and UCT Press 1998. First published in 1998 by the University of Cape Town Press, P.O. Box 14373, Kenwyn, Cape Town, South Africa.

The Strong Breed © Wole Soyinka 1973. Reprinted from *Wole Soyinka: Collected Plays Vol. I* with permission of Oxford University Press, Great Clarendon Street, Oxford, OX2 6DP, United Kingdom.

Once Upon Four Robbers © Femi Osofisan 1980. Reprinted with the permission of Femi Osofisan. First published BIO Educational Services, Ibadan, Nigeria, 1980.

Anowa © Ama Ata Aidoo 1965, 1970 & 1985. Reprinted with the permission of Ama Ata Aidoo. First published in *The Dilemma of a Ghost* and *Anowa*, Longman, United Kingdom, 1987.

Pantomime © Derek Walcott 1980. Reprinted from *Remembrance and Pantomime*, with permission of Farrar, Straus and Giroux, 19 Union Square West, New York, New York 10003, USA.

Caution: Professionals and amateurs are hereby warned that *Pantomime* by Derek Walcott, being fully protected under the Copyright Laws of the United States of America and all other countries of the Berne and Universal Copyright Convention, is subject to a royalty. All rights including, but not limited to, professional, amateur, recording, motion picture, recitation, lecturing, public reading, radio and television broadcasting, and the rights of translation into foreign languages are expressly reserved. All inquiries concerning rights should be addressed to the author's agent, Farrar, Straus and Giroux, 19 Union Square West, New York, New York 10003, USA.

QPH © Sistren Theatre Collective 1981 & 1999. Published with the permission of Sistren Theatre Collective and Hertencer Lindsay. Original text developed by members of Collective and scripted by Hertencer Lindsay with assistance from Honor Ford-Smith. Revised by Hertencer Lindsay in 1999.

Hayavadana © Girish Karnad 1971. Reprinted from *Girish Karnad, Three Plays*: *Ngā-Mandala, Hayavadana* and *Tughlaq*, with permission of Oxford University Press, YMCA Library Building, Jai Singh Rd, New Delhi, India.

Harvest © Manjula Padmanabhan 1997 & 1999. Reprinted with the permission of Manjula Padmanabhan. First published by Kali for Women, New Delhi, India, 1997.

Revised by the author in 1999 for current edition.

1984 Here and Now © Kee Thuan Chye 1987 &1999. Reprinted with the permission of Kee Thuan Chye. First published by K. DAS INK, Selangor, Malaysia, 1987. Revised by the author in 1999 for current edition.

Details Cannot Body Wants © Chin Woon Ping 1993. Reprinted with the permission of Chin Woon Ping. First published in *The Naturalisation of Camellia Song and Details Cannot Body Wants*, Times Books International, Singapore, 1993.

Inside the Island © Louis Nowra 1981. Reprinted from *Inside the Island/The Precious Woman*, with permission of Currency Press, P.O. Box 2287, Strawberry Hills, NSW, Australia.

Bran Nue Dae © Jimmy Chi, Mick Manolis, Steve Pigram, Garry Gower, Pat Bin Amat and Bran Nue Dae Productions 1991. Reprinted with the permission of Jimmy Chi on behalf of Bran Nue Dae Publications. First published in 1991 by Currency Press, P.O. Box 2287, Strawberry Hills, NSW, Australia, and Magabala Books Aboriginal Corporation, Broome, WA, Australia.

Ngā Pou Wāhine © Briar Grace-Smith 1997. Reprinted with the permission of Huia Publications, 27 Pipitea St, P.O. Box 17–335, Wellington, Aotearoa/New Zealand.

The Conversion of Ka'ahumanu © Victoria Nalani Kneubuhl 1988. Reprinted with the permission of Victoria Nalani Knuebuhl. First published in *But Still Like Air, I'll Rise: New Asian-American Plays*, edited by Velina Houston, Temple University Press, 1997.

The Rez Sisters © Tomson Highway 1988. Reprinted, with permission, from *The Rez Sisters*, published by Fifth House Ltd, Calgary, Canada, 1988.

Fronteras Americanas (American Borders) © Guillermo Verdecchia 1993 & 1997. Reprinted with the permission of Talon Books Ltd, Burnaby, BC, Canada. All rights reserved.

Somewhere Over the Balcony © Marie Jones, Eleanor Methven, Carol Moore and Peter Sheridan, 1988 & 2000.

General Introduction _____

Against the inert silence which autocrats
seek to impose upon their subjects, the
dissenting artist can triumph through the
gift of metaphor and magic, parody and
parable, masking and mimicry.

(Osofisan 1998: 11)

Femi Osofisan's assessment of theatre's
particular capacity to beguile autocratic
systems of power, giving expression to the
hopes and concerns of the dispossessed, aptly
conveys the achievement of some of the most
exciting dramatic work performed across the
world in recent decades. A great deal of this
work, developed within nations formerly
colonised by Western imperial powers,
exhibits a strong urge to recuperate local
histories and local performance traditions,
not only as a means of cultural
decolonisation but also as a challenge to the
implicit representational biases of Western
theatre. At the same time, there has been a
widespread engagement with Western texts
and performance idioms, to the extent that
critics have often categorised theatre in
postcolonial cultures as inherently syncretic
(see Balme 1999). Vibrant, energetic and
often provocative, this diverse and powerful
body of work, segments of which have long
been the subject of critical study in the
regions from which they derive, has now
reached a critical mass that demands broader
acknowledgement, both in academic and
theatrical realms.

To assemble any body of creative work
under the descriptor 'postcolonial', as this
anthology does, is to enter into contentious
but productive debates, not only about which
texts should be accorded some kind of
canonical value but also about the
constitution of the critical field in which they
are intended to circulate. Although a
relatively new force in academic circles,
postcolonialism has rapidly expanded its

conceptual reach over recent years so that
it now describes, in Stephen Slemon's words,
'a remarkably heterogeneous set of subject
positions, professional fields, and critical
enterprises' (1994:16). In many contexts, the
term indicates a degree of agency, or at least
a programme of resistance, against cultural
domination; in others, it signals the existence
of a particular historical legacy and/or a
chronological stage in a culture's transition
into a modern nation-state; in yet others, it is
used more disapprovingly to suggest a form
of co-option into Western cultural economies.
What is common to all of these definitions,
despite their variant implications, is a central
concern with cultural power.

For those less interested in staking out
disciplinary boundaries, 'postcolonial' has
become a convenient (and sometimes useful)
portmanteau term to describe any kind of
resistance, particularly against class, race and
gender oppressions. My particular take on
the field is considerably more specific,
focusing on cultural practices which have
both a historical *and* a discursive relationship
to Western imperialism, whether that
phenomenon is treated critically,
ambivalently or collusively. Hence, the
following plays, as well as deriving from
cultures which have been colonised by
European or American powers, respond in
demonstrable ways to the legacy of that
experience. Their responses – whether
passionate, angry, detached, cynical,
humorous, celebratory, ambivalent or even
whimsical – may be manifest in thematic
motifs, narrative structures and/or
performative features, all of which are coded
in culturally specific ways, taking into
account the resources available in a
particular theatrical milieu.

My positioning of Western imperialism as
one of the common historical denominators
of postcolonial studies may (justly) beg

debate for some readers. As Gary Boire argues in relation to the British Empire, 'The superficial crime of superimposition may have been the same in all colonies, but given the specificities of history, ethnicity, gender, culture and geography, there are significant and subtle variations between each repetition and amongst the multiple reactions to it' (1990: 306). Boire's caution against homogenisation is well heeded, particularly given the ongoing inequities between, and within, formerly colonised nations; yet his view is premised on the assumption that those interpreting cultural artefacts (fictional or historical) will not sufficiently attend to their particularised locations. Although this has sometimes been the case, the best broad-based postcolonial projects inevitably entail a careful accounting of differences and divisions even in the service of comparative analysis. The plays gathered here tend to insist on such processes of differentiation even while they are brought together in ways that allow opportunities for fruitful dialogue. Deeply embedded in specific cultures and historical circumstances, these texts elicit curiosity and challenge ignorance, encouraging readers to do the intellectual legwork necessary to generate an informed response.

Anthologising a range of plays under the broad umbrella of postcolonial theatre necessarily involves some narrowing of a potentially enormous field. In this instance, I have selected texts deriving from geographical areas directly affected by the British imperial project and circulated within English-language theatre, either in their own countries or internationally. This excludes significant and exciting bodies of work from the French- and Spanish-speaking postcolonial regions, whose study would add particular inflections to an understanding of the field. The time-span from which the chosen plays are drawn is restricted to the recent era of decolonisation, even though some compelling arguments have been made for applying a postcolonial analysis to pre-independence texts. These exclusions are driven by the need to provide such a massive project with some coherence.

By focusing on theatre inflected by a broadly comparable set of historical circumstances, I hope to enable productive analysis of both similarities and differences, parallels and divergences, and lines of continuity and disjunction. Hence, the indigenous plays drawn from Canada, Australia, New Zealand and Hawai'i might be examined as products of dispossessed minorities in various stages of struggle to attain agency within 'Western' settler cultures. On a very different tack, one might trace connections between specific African performance idioms and their diasporic transformations in Caribbean theatre. Alternatively, it is possible to consider the effect of global developments such as the Black Consciousness Movement on both of these groupings. Nationalism, communalism and multiculturalism are also issues that cut across regional boundaries; likewise, the recent implementation of official reconciliation processes designed to deal with histories of cultural genocide in, for example, South Africa, Australia and Canada. The legacy of Western orientalism, itself enmeshed with the British imperial project in India as well as in Malaysia and Singapore, suggests another possible area for comparative analysis.

How questions of chronology intersect with postcoloniality is also a relevant consideration, though it is not possible (or desirable) to establish complex postcolonial chronologies with the limited number of texts that can be represented in one book. The actual date of independence from British colonial rule is not the only issue here, especially since various countries have approached that event and experienced its aftermath in very different ways, sometimes peacefully, sometimes in the ravages of war. In terms of theatre, it seems that explicitly anti-imperial texts emerged earlier in Africa and the Caribbean than in the settler nations, probably because it was only in the aftermath of the 1960s to 1970s transnational civil-rights movements that majority groups in Canada and Australia, for instance, began to seriously debate issues relating to indigenous sovereignty. Earlier nationalist, and often aggressively masculinist, texts that (arguably) might be studied within postcolonial frameworks in these countries are not included here because they tend to ignore the internal racial divisions on which their cultures have been founded.

The geographical, social and racial limits of postcolonialism continue to shift depending on the perspectives of particular scholars and commentators. Some critics argue, for instance, that Northern Ireland, as a Western nation implicated in British systems of power, does not fall under the ambit of postcolonial inquiry, while others accept this categorisation but caution against simplistic interpretations of Irish nationalism as driven by anti-colonial impulses. The Irish play included here, Charabanc's **Somewhere Over the Balcony**, adds complexity but also clarity to such debates by anchoring them firmly in the lived reality of a Belfast community. There is also much argument about whether settler cultures in Canada, Australia or South Africa should be considered within postcolonial studies, given their past and ongoing role in the colonisation of indigenous populations. Yet it is evident that such oppressions trouble both settler and indigenous playwrights alike, though their perspectives on colonial history are necessarily charged by the politics of their particular communities, sometimes in surprising ways. For instance, Jimmy Chi and Kuckles' Aboriginal musical, **Bran Nue Dae**, is far more forgiving in its treatment of Australia's past and current race-relations than many recent white-authored plays. My inclusion of works drawn from the contested 'settler' groupings is based on a belief that their engagement with imperialism, however ambivalent, is none the less valuable to an understanding of the field. Moreover, to exclude these texts would be to suggest that colonial relations impact only on the dispossessed, which, judging by the wealth of settler theatre that engages critically with imperialism, is clearly not the case. Louis Nowra's haunting account of colonial Australian society and Jane Taylor's multimedia tour de force investigating post-apartheid politics in South Africa are powerful examples to the contrary. In a different way, Guillermo Verdecchia's **Fronteras Americanas**, a Canadian 'settler' text of sorts, adds immeasurably to a sense of the cultural and racial complexities of this increasingly multi-ethnic nation.

While this anthology brings together a broad-ranging selection of texts from the particular field as outlined, there are many other excellent postcolonial plays that could not be included, whether through lack of space, copyright difficulties, limited access to texts preserved in publishable forms, or the simple failure of communication technologies. Kenya,

Uganda, Zimbabwe and Zambia have all produced topical contemporary theatre that might be studied in tandem with the plays in this collection. Texts from these areas on my wider 'wish list' include Alex Mukulu's *30 Years of Bananas* (Uganda), Ngugi wa Thiong'o's *I Will Marry When I Want* (Kenya) and Andrew Whaley's *The Nyoka Tree* (Zimbabwe). Equally, Shamsul Haq's historical drama, *Nuraldeen's Life* (Bangladesh), Anton Juan's *Princess of the Lizard Moon* (Philippines) or Marianne Ackerman's *L'Affaire Tartuffe* (Québec) would enrich a study of the field. Readers are also encouraged to engage with the works of Athol Fugard and Brian Friel, whose reputations in the postcolonial field should have guaranteed a place in this collection, except that I was unable to gain permission to reprint any of their plays in full. Other dramatists prominent within their specific regions but not featured here include Jack Davis, widely lauded as the 'father' of Aboriginal theatre in Australia; Dennis Scott, whose influential work as a writer and director has been central to the development of Jamaican performance idioms; Michel Tremblay, the first Québecois playwright to challenge Canada's predominantly Anglo-centric canon; Vijay Tendulkar, author of *Ghasiram Kotwal*, a stunning allegory of political corruption in India; and Hone Kouka, currently a driving force in contemporary Māori theatre.

Such omissions, however regrettable, opened up exciting possibilities for alternative texts. Some were already targeted for this project; others, brought to my notice by experts in the field, demanded attention because of their arresting theatricality or their bold interventions in topical debates. The final selection does not attempt to deliver an in-depth survey of the field or to represent only paradigmatic texts/authors from each region – both futile projects in an anthology of this kind – but rather to suggest the vast range of work that might be considered under the rubric of postcolonial theatre. To this end, I have put together both high-profile and lesser known plays that vary not only in scale and subject matter but also in style, processes of authorship, and modes of production and consumption. In many cases, these are also texts that speak to key political struggles; in others, they express more subtle, and sometimes surprising, concerns.

The effort to represent a wide variety of genres within a field of theatre that tends to eschew narrow conceptions of dialogue-dependent performance has presented problems of its own. Some of the most vibrant and popular postcolonial performances are not easily textualised without extensive pictorial documentation not possible within the parameters of this project. Hence, I have chosen works such as **Ubu and the Truth Commission** and **Bran Nue Dae** with some trepidation, hoping that the few illustrations supplied or other available audiovisual resources might help to convey a little of their theatrical magic. In most other cases, a sense of the performance style can be gleaned from a careful reading of the script in tandem with relevant research on the conventions invoked. Understanding at least the basics of particular styles and their local articulation, whether through storytelling, folk forms, ritualised enactments, agit-prop theatre, performance art, farce or Western-style realism, is crucial to a complex engagement with many of the texts. It is also important to remember that the mode in which any kind of art is (re)produced is crucially affected by the demographics of its consumption. In this respect, particular performance styles have been fashioned to speak to specific audiences, many of whom may not participate in a literary culture. The work of popular theatre proponents such as Jamaica's Sistren Theatre Collective falls into this category.

Language itself is a crucial issue in postcolonial theatre, raising questions about which texts might be anthologised and how their particular languages are to be presented for audiences outside the societies for which they were originally produced. Because of its colonial legacy and its ongoing role in maintaining neo-colonial hierarchies through foreign education, the English language (or any language, for that matter) can never be a neutral medium. However, dramatists such as Wole Soyinka and Derek Walcott maintain that this fact should initiate not a paralysis but a newly invigorated sense of the complexities of the linguistic sites from which postcolonial artists speak. For Soyinka, one of the key dramaturgical tasks is thus to forge a culturally matrixed language adapted to particularised local circumstances:

When we borrow an alien language to sculpt or paint in, we must begin by co-opting the entire properties in our matrix of thought and expression. We must stress such a language, stretch it, impact and compact, fragment and reassemble it with no apology, as required to bear the burden of experiencing.

(Soyinka 1988: 107)

In some postcolonial regions, such a project has led to the formation of Creole and Pidgin variants of English that now claim status as separate languages and indeed function as such in many contexts. As Edward Brathwaite says of 'nation language' in the Caribbean, 'English it may be in terms of some of its lexical features. But in its contours, its rhythm and timbre, its sound explosions, it is not English, even though the words, as you hear them, might be English to a greater or lesser degree' (1984: 13).

Collectively, the plays gathered here demonstrate the malleability of the English language as well as suggesting some of its biases and limitations. With the exception of Girish Karnad's **Hayavadana** (first written in Kannada and then translated by the author), all have been written predominantly in some version of English, though many incorporate other languages to better convey certain culturally specific concepts, or, alternatively, to subvert the hegemony of the imperial tongue. For those playwrights born (or forcibly resettled) into monolingual English-speaking communities, working in/with this language is more or less a given; for others, it has been a strategic choice, governed by factors such as target audience. Soyinka and Ama Ata Aidoo, for instance, have been part of a conscious effort to forge an English-language theatre in West Africa while also attempting to gain the ear of a Western audience. Also hoping to circulate her work internationally, Manjula Padmanabhan, who speaks several languages, deliberately wrote **Harvest** in English despite the lack of a suitable English-language theatre culture through which to showcase the play in her home country, India. Karnad, on the other hand, produced his play in two Indian languages as well as in English, each translation involving a different kind of 'play-making' exercise. A slightly different situation pertains to Kee Thuan Chye, whose choice of English reflects its position as the lingua franca for communication between different cultural groups within a multi-ethnic nation.

If the use of English is a strategic choice for many of the playwrights, so too is the switch to other languages, which, in some cases, are meant to exclude part of the audience from their linguistic reach. This has raised complex questions about translations and glosses, particularly since theatre is a medium that often relies on intonation, pitch and gesture to communicate across language barriers. While postcolonial critics may feel that any kind of glossing is a Eurocentric practice, it has seemed necessary to annotate some of the texts included here in order for them to effectively cross cultural boundaries. I have attempted to gloss in accordance with the 'spirit' of each text, opting for minimal translations and explanations when a play has been written for a particular constituency different from the likely readership of this book. No glosses are supplied when the specific project of the dialogue is to make a point about language usage or where authors felt that their meaning could be gleaned with a little extra interpretive effort. While most explanatory material has been adopted from original publications or compiled in consultation with the respective playwrights, or experts in their field, these glosses are not intended to be exhaustive or to replace the textual and/or performative functions of the given languages. Among other things, such languages remind us that the scripts themselves are ineluctably inscribed with the oral traces of their performance.

The following plays are not grouped thematically or stylistically, on the grounds that readers will find their own connecting motifs. I have, however, loosely ordered them according to region, beginning with works that speak to African political issues, followed by those drawn from cultures occupied but not predominantly settled by Britain, then moving to indigenous and non-indigenous plays from 'Western' settler nations, to end with a fascinating example from Northern Ireland, often positioned as Britain's oldest colony, albeit contentiously. One of the features of the collection as a whole is the predominance of plays that tend to work either wholly or partly in non-naturalistic modes. This should not be surprising given that many of the cultures represented have powerful indigenous performance traditions/rituals that are antithetical to Western-style realism, which, in any case, is increasingly viewed as unsuitable for political theatre because of its tendency to reproduce the status quo. While I have deliberately chosen a mix of texts that might provoke readers to consider how stylistic devices can articulate postcoloniality, the bias against naturalism is, in fact, fairly typical of the broader field from which these scripts are drawn. While non-naturalistic modes are often chosen to facilitate criticism of particular regimes, as in farce, satire or agit-prop theatre, they may also be a response to the available theatrical resources, as, for instance, in monodrama and other kinds of theatre modelled on storytelling techniques. Above all, non-naturalistic theatre presumes a specific kind of relationship with its audience, one that avoids illusionism in favour of more explicit engagement with its interpretive community. All but a few of the following plays explicitly acknowledge their audiences, whether by telling them stories, inviting them to discuss philosophical problems, confronting them directly with controversial material, exhorting them to participate in the action, or suddenly transforming them into 'players' as Tomson Highway's **The Rez Sisters** does in its climactic Bingo fantasia.

The most extreme versions of explicit audience address, as evident in the closing scenes of Osofisan's **Once Upon Four Robbers** and Kee's **1984 Here and Now**, would seem to align with techniques derived from Brazilian director and theorist Augusto Boal, whose model of an organic 'forum theatre' firmly contextualises theatrical practice within community structures and current political struggles, so that performance becomes one kind of 'rehearsal' for social change. It is important to consider, however, that the precise degree of political leverage gained by this type of theatre may be compromised in countries where mass poverty prevents the vast majority of the population from participating in paid theatre activities, and where the status of English as the tongue of the highly educated lends certain kinds of experimentalism a distinctly coterie air. Osofisan has worked against these limitations by translating his plays into Yoruba and touring them outside the metropolitan areas. The issue of audience reception entails different kinds of traps for readers of this anthology. As Alan Filewod cautions in relation to mainstream productions of native Canadian plays, it can be dangerous to isolate particular texts from their 'inter-productive' communities, which 'constitute a discourse of material practice' that can 'absorb and synthesise contradictions' (1994: 372). This is a valid point that reiterates the importance of studying not just the texts represented here but also their production histories and particular cultural contexts.

This brief introduction can suggest only a few of the different reception issues, thematic concerns and performative strategies manifest in the plays collected here. Individual readers, teachers and students will undoubtedly develop their own ideas about various texts' treatment of tradition, religion, politics, gender, race, identity, class, history, myth, sexuality and cultural location, to point to some of the recurrent motifs in the field. This project has proceeded on the assumption that an anthology cannot and should not do the bulk of the cognitive work for its readers but rather supply basic information and interpretive cues that will entice them to find out more (and more again). In bringing together plays which generally lie outside the purview of Euro-American theatrical canons, my aim has been to assemble a teaching text that will be flexible enough to serve a range of pedagogical needs even though it is undeniably marked with my subjective imprimatur. The following plays confirm that postcolonial theatre, though differently configured in different places, is currently a major force reshaping the ways in which we can think about performance as social praxis. In this respect, it may be the exemplary art form through which to understand patterns of identity, oppression, migration, political negotiation, economics and global communication in the new millennium.

General notes

In this anthology, dates given in parentheses after plays refer to the first performance except in those few cases where publication preceded the script's premiere production. Orthography for each of the scripts follows the original publication unless otherwise requested by the playwright. Hence, in some instances, I have omitted various diacritics

that might be used customarily in local contexts. Yoruba words, for example, are not accented, while Māori and Hawaiian terms are. Apparent inconsistencies in the spelling of various Jamaican Creole words in Sistren's play generally reflect the subtle inflections of their usage.

Select bibliography

Ashcroft, B., Griffiths, G. and Tiffin, H. (eds) (1995) *The Post-Colonial Studies Reader*, London: Routledge.

Balme, C. (1999) *Decolonizing the Stage: Theatrical Syncretism and Post-Colonial Drama*, Oxford: Clarendon Press.

Banham, M., Hill, E. and Woodyard, G. (eds) (1994) *The Cambridge Guide to African and Caribbean Theatre*, Cambridge: Cambridge University Press.

Boire, G. (1990) 'Sucking Kumaras', *Canadian Literature* 124/125: 301–6.

Boon, R. and Plastow, J. (eds) (1998) *Theatre Matters: Performance and Culture on the World Stage*, Cambridge: Cambridge University Press.

Brathwaite, E. (1984) *History of the Voice: The Development of Nation Language in Anglophone Caribbean Poetry*, London: New Beacon.

Breitinger, E. (ed.) (1994) *Theatre and Performance in Africa: Intercultural Perspectives*, Bayreuth: Bayreuth University African Studies Series.

Childs, P. and Williams, P. (1997) *An Introduction to Post-Colonial Theory*, London: Prentice Hall.

Connolly, L.W. (ed.) (1995) *Canadian Drama and the Critics*, rev. edn, Vancouver: Talon.

Crow, B. with Banfield, C. (1996) *An Introduction to Post-Colonial Theatre*, Cambridge: Cambridge University Press.

Davis, G.V. and Fuchs, A. (eds) (1996) *Theatre and Change in South Africa*, Amsterdam: Harwood Academic.

Dunton, C. (1992) *Make Man Talk True: Nigerian Drama in English since 1970*, London: Zell.

Filewod, A. (1994) 'Receiving Aboriginality: Tomson Highway and the crisis of cultural authenticity', *Theatre Journal* 46, 3: 363–73.

Gainor, J.E. (ed.) (1995) *Imperialism and Theatre: Essays on World Theatre, Drama and Performance*, London: Routledge.

Gilbert, H. (ed.) (1999) *(Post)Colonial Stages: Critical and Creative Views on Drama, Theatre and Performance*, Hebden Bridge, UK: Dangaroo.

Gilbert, H. and Tompkins, J. (1996) *Post-Colonial Drama: Theory, Practice, Politics*, London: Routledge.

Gunner, L. (ed.) (1994) *Politics and Performance: Theatre, Poetry and Song in Southern Africa*, Johannesburg: Witwatersrand University Press.

Kelly, V. (ed.) (1998) *Our Australian Theatre in the 1990s*, Amsterdam: Rodopi.

King, B. (ed.) (1995) *Post-Colonial English Drama: Commonwealth Drama since 1960*, London: Macmillan.

Murray, C. (1997) *Twentieth Century Irish Drama*, Manchester: Manchester University Press.

Plastow, J. (1996) *African Theatre and Politics: The Evolution of Theatre in Ethiopia, Tanzania and Zimbabwe*, Amsterdam: Rodopi.

Olaniyan, T. (1995) *Scars of Conquest/Masks of Resistance: The Invention of Cultural Identities in African, African-American, and Caribbean Drama*, New York: Oxford University Press.

Orkin, M. (1991) *Drama and the South African State*, Johannesburg: Witwatersrand University Press.

Osofisan, F. (1998) '"The revolution as muse": drama as surreptitious insurrection in a post-colonial, military state', in R. Boon and J. Plastow (eds) *Theatre Matters: Performance and Culture on the World Stage*, Cambridge: Cambridge University Press, 11–35.

Slemon, S. (1994) 'The scramble for post-colonialism', in C. Tiffin and A. Lawson (eds) *De-scribing Empire: Post-Colonialism and Textuality*, London: Routledge, 15–32.

Soyinka, W. (1988) *Art, Dialogue and Outrage: Essays on Literature and Culture*, Ibadan: New Horn.

Stone, J. (1994) *Theatre: Studies in West Indian Literature*, London: Macmillan.

1 Judith Thompson

Pink
Canada

Introduction

Born in 1954 and raised in suburban Kingston, Ontario, Judith Thompson had an early introduction to theatre through her mother's work as a director and writer. Her first stage role at age 11, followed by several others during her teens, initially appeared to predict a career as a performer, but within a year of completing actor training at the National Theatre School in Montreal, Thompson decided that she would rather *write* plays. Her performance work, however, has proved invaluable to her efforts as a dramatist, especially in the creation of intense and often volatile characters whose internal drives and outward habits she seems to know intimately. Such characters are drawn from all walks of life, but they are essentially ordinary people driven to the extreme edge of experience. Across a range of plays that explore crumbling relationships within families, between lovers and among friends, this facility for creating unforgettable stage figures has earned Thompson many plaudits, including Canada's most prestigious prizes for excellence in drama, the Governor-General's Award (1984, 1990) and the Chalmers Award (1988, 1991). Her ability to convey the dark and turbulent inner worlds of her characters through voices fashioned to the rhythms of everyday life also constitutes a major achievement in extending the reach of naturalistic dialogue, which so often limits other playwrights' penetration of the spiritual crises that underpin human actions.

At first glance, Thompson's short monologue, *Pink*, written in 1986 for the Toronto Arts Against Apartheid Benefit, may seem to have little in common with the densely allusive and often mythic works that have established her reputation as one of Canada's most exciting contemporary dramatists. The brevity of the play, combined with its specific political focus as an anti-apartheid piece, allows minimal space for the kind of complex characterisation that drives Thompson's theatre; yet *Pink* delivers a poignant and evocative character portrait that gains in power by its very compact construction. Part of the play's appeal derives from its use of the monologue as a device through which to stage in concentrated form the raw pain and contradictory emotions of its young protagonist. This is a common strategy in Thompson's work, particularly in *The Crackwalker* (1980), *I Am Yours* (1987) and the recently premiered *Perfect Pie* (2000), where monologues, styled variously as dreams, reveries or confessional outbursts, often constitute the structural matrix around which other narrative fragments are juxtaposed. The result is a dramaturgical practice in which the voice takes on a particular materiality that provides an index to both personal and social worlds. As Thompson states, 'I believe that the voice is the door to not only the soul of an individual, but the soul of a nation, and within that, the soul of a culture, a class, a community, a gender' (1993: 658).

In *Pink*, a white child's voice becomes the narrative aperture through which the brutality of the recently dismantled South African apartheid system comes into focus. Lucy's emotional monologue to her dead Nanny, Nellie, reveals not only the poisoning of a loving adult–child relationship by government ordinance and a coercive social system but also the seemingly minor (to Lucy) yet immensely significant acts of discrimination through which the black populace is denied human rights. In the familiar tradition of the naive, unreliable narrator – often figured by children, mentally disabled people, and social or racial outcasts in Thompson's drama – Lucy unwittingly tells the audience much more than she herself can understand. This narrative perspective is designed to implicate the adult world in Lucy's racism as she parrots, in her own simple terms, glib theories of separate development and apparent white liberal tolerance. In the play's climax, her outraged diatribe against Nellie thus channels a society's racial hatred through a child's wilful tantrum to portray with chilling effect the easy movement from cruel words to violent actions. Lucy's subsequent penitence provides an uneasy resolution since it derives simultaneously from a childish desire to return everything to the way it was and a nascent maturity that allows her to recognise that she is somehow responsible for Nellie's death.

Thompson has admitted in interviews to being obsessed with the figure of the child and the nature of parenting. Such plays as *I Am Yours* and *Lion in the Streets* (1990) present children as idealised innocents through whom spiritual redemption may be offered to those who have violated others or compromised their own humanity. In *Pink*, the child's 'natural' purity – in Thompson's terms – has been irrevocably tainted by a corrupt social system that Lucy, positioned at the cusp of puberty, must now willingly choose or reject. The breaking of the maternal bond becomes critical at this point. Nellie's severing remark, 'You're not a child anymore, Lucy, you're a white person now', marks the child's expulsion from the maternal dyad and her initiation into the realities of a political system to which she has been beneficiary for her entire life.

Through the nanny–child relationship sketched so deftly in *Pink*, Thompson examines parenting in a broader context than the merely familial. Her interest in the parent role as a social and psychological contract is taken up in the radio drama, *Tornado* (1987), which twins natural and surrogate mothers in order to investigate primal maternal urges. But whereas this and most of Thompson's other plays dramatise motherhood through intensely personal perspectives, *Pink* maintains a more distanced view that takes account of the ways in which an oppressive political regime affects even the closest of interpersonal bonds. In the world of apartheid South Africa, as in the antebellum American South and other places where slaves nurtured the children of their oppressors, racial divisions inevitably taint other social bonds. While the play attempts to show the arbitrary construction of racial categories based on skin colour, it also conveys, through the suggestive title and recurrent motif of 'pink', that perceptions of colour take on their full resonances only when invested with a political reading. The pink innocence of Lucy's cake cannot be real in a world blinkered by the racially marked categories of black and white.

Production history

Pink was first performed by Clare Coulter for the Arts Against Apartheid Benefit in Toronto in the spring of 1986.

Select bibliography

Adam, J. (1992) 'The implicated audience: Judith Thompson's anti-naturalism', in R. Much (ed.) *Women on the Canadian Stage: The Legacy of Hrotsvit*, Winnipeg: Blizzard, 21–9.

Bessai, D. (1992) 'Women dramatists: Sharon Pollock and Judith Thompson', in B. King (ed.) *Post-Colonial English Drama: Commonwealth Drama since 1960*, New York: St Martin's Press, 97–117.

Kareda, U. (1989) 'Introduction', in J. Thompson, *The Other Side of the Dark: Four Plays*, Toronto: Coach House, 9–13.

Nunn, R. (1989) 'Spatial metaphor in the plays of Judith Thompson', *Theatre History in Canada* 10, 1: 3–29.

Thompson, J. (1989) *The Other Side of the Dark: Four Plays*, Toronto: Coach House.

—— (1990) Interview, in J. Rudakoff and R. Much (eds) *Fair Play: 12 Women Speak: Conversations with Canadian Playwrights*, Toronto: Simon & Pierre, 87–104.

—— (1993) Author's statement, in K. Berney (ed.) *Contemporary Dramatists*, 5th edn, Detroit: St James, 658.

Toles, G. (1988) '"Cause you're the only one I want": the anatomy of love in the plays of Judith Thompson', *Canadian Literature* 118: 116–35.

Wachtel, E. (1991) 'An interview with Judith Thompson', *Brick* 41: 37–41.

Zimmerman, C. (1994) 'Judith Thompson: voices in the dark', *Playwrighting Women: Female Voices in English Canada*, Toronto: Simon & Pierre, 177–209.

Pink

Judith Thompson

LUCY, *a 10-year-old white girl talking to her dead black nurse, Nellie, shot in a march, in her open coffin.*

LUCY   NELLIE I want you to come back, to shampoo my hair and make a pink cake and we can sit in the back and roll mealie pap in our hands see, I told you not to go in those marches and I told you, I told you that what you guys don't understand, what you didn't see, is apartheid's for YOU. IT'S FOR YOUR GUYS FEELINGS, see, like we got separate washrooms cause you like to spit, and if we said, 'Eww yucch, don't spit', it would hurt your feelings and we got separate movies, cause you like to talk back to movie stars and say 'amen' and 'that's the way' and stuff and that drives us crazy so we might tell you to shut up and then you might cry and we got separate bus stops cause you don't like deodorant cause you say it smells worse than people and we might tell you you stink and the only thing I don't get is how come you get paid less for the same job my Mummy says it's because you people don't like money anyway, you don't like TVs and stereos and all that stuff cause what you really like to do is sing and dance. And you don't need money to sing and dance I just . . . I don't understand why you weren't happy with us, Mummy let you eat as much sugar as you wanted, and we never said anything to you, some days, Mummy says it was up to a quarter-pound, but we know blacks like sugar so we didn't mind, and we even let you take a silver spoon, I heard Mummy say to her friends, 'there goes another silver spoon to Soweto' but she never called the police . . . and you had your own little room back there, and we even let your husband come once in a while, and that's against the law, Mummy and Daddy could have gone to jail for that, so how come you weren't grateful? How come you stopped singing those Zulu songs in the morning, those pretty songs like the one that was about love and kissing, you stopped singing, and you stopped shampooing my hair, you said I could do it myself, and and your eyes, your eyes used to look at me when I was little they would look at me like they were tickling me just tickling me all the time, like I was special, but they went out, they went out like a light does and you stopped making my cakes every Tuesday, every Tuesday morning I would ask you to make me a pink cake and you would always say, 'you ask your mummy' and then you'd make it, but you stopped making them, you told me I was too old for pink cakes, that the pink wasn't real, it was just food colour anyway and then, and then, you hardly ever came anymore, and when I saw you that day . . . when I saw you downtown with your husband and four children all . . . hanging off your arms, I just couldn't stand it! I wanted to yell at your children and tell them you were mine that you were more mine than theirs because you were with me more much more so you were mine and to let go of you to get off you and I hated the way you looked without your uniform, so brown and plain, not neat and nice anymore, you looked so pretty in your uniform, so pretty, but we didn't even mind when you didn't want to wear it.

We didn't mind, but you were still unhappy, and when I saw you in town looking so dusty and you didn't even introduce me to your kids and one of them, one of them did that rude thing that 'Amandilia' thing that means black power I saw you slap his hand but you didn't say anything, so you must have hated me too, I saw that you hated me too and I'd been so nice to you, I told you my nightmares and you changed my bed when I wet it and now you didn't even like me and it wasn't my fault it wasn't my fault it just when I asked you why that day, you were cleaning the stove and I said Nellie why . . . don't you like me anymore, and you said, 'you're not a child anymore, Lucy, you're a white person now' and it wasn't my fault I couldn't help it I couldn't help yelling

SLAVE, SLAVE, DO WHAT YOU'RE TOLD, SLAVE OR I SLAP YOUR BLACK FACE, I SLAP YOUR BLACK FACE AND I KICK YOUR BLACK BELLY I KICK YOUR BLACK BELLY AND KICK IT TILL IT CAVES RIGHT IN AND IT CAN'T HOLD MORE BABIES EVER AGAIN. NO MORE UGLY BLACK BABIES THAT YOU'LL . . . that you'll like more than me. Even though I'm ten years old I made you die. I made you go in that march and I made you die. I know that forever. I said I was sorry, I'm sorry, I'm sorry, I'm sorry, I'm sorry, but you never looked at me again. You hated me. But I love you, Nellie, more than Mummy or Daddy and I want you to come back, and sing those songs, and roll mealie pap and be washing the floor in your nice uniform so I can come in and ask you to make a pink cake and your eyes will tickle me. And you will say 'yes'.

'Yes, I'll make a pink cake . . . '

2 Maishe Maponya

The Hungry Earth
South Africa

Introduction

When Maishe Maponya first conceived and workshopped *The Hungry Earth* in 1978, reactions to the play's blatant political content, and its explicit criticism of South Africa's apartheid regime, led him to seek legal advice. His attorney's opinion confirmed his fears: 'I am of the view that the play would constitute a contravention of the laws relating to racial incitement and the Publications Act and, in addition, the presentation would result in the severe harassment of both the author and the performers' (quoted in Maponya 1995: vii). In response, Maponya cancelled the production but then, after much deliberation, he and the Bahumutsi Drama Group, which he had co-founded a year earlier, decided to perform and 'be damned'.

Maponya, like all black South Africans, had been personally affected by the discriminatory practices of the apartheid system. Born in 1951 in Alexandra Township in Johannesburg, he was forcibly resettled, with his family, in Soweto in 1962. There, he developed an increasing interest in the political theatre that emerged in the 1970s and became actively involved in the Black Consciousness Movement. A combination of socialist and essentialist ideology, this movement owed as much to black American cultural politics as it did to third-world theories of liberation inspired by such scholars as Frantz Fanon. For the African Black Consciousness Movement, political and cultural liberation were inextricable. Black Consciousness theatre, like the poetry, prose, music and art associated with the movement, was highly politicised and inherently confrontational, calling for urgent militancy in response to the ravages of apartheid. The central role that such art forms played in the dissemination of ideas threatening to the apartheid state's zealously guarded racial hierarchies can be seen in the prominence of cultural organisations as objects of state repression. In the Treason Trial of 1974–5, for instance, two of the five organisations prosecuted were theatre groups.

Very much a product of its times, Maponya's theatre shows the hallmarks of the Black Consciousness Movement in a number of ways. It owes a particular debt to revolutionary student leader Steve Biko, who was also a member of Bahumutsi and a Black Consciousness activist. Maponya's first play, *The Cry* (1976), was inspired by Biko's writings, while his 1984 work, *Gangsters*, explores aspects of Biko's interrogation, torture and death in detention. Its 'inflammatory' nature led to Maponya's harassment by security forces, who, fearing the play might incite political unrest, prevented it from being staged in the townships. By this time, Maponya was a familiar target of political censorship, having been interrogated earlier about his involvement with the Health Workers Association after he wrote *Umongikazi/The Nurse* (1983), an indictment of racism in the hospital sector. Among Maponya's other plays, *Dirty Work* (1984), a monologue revealing the malice of a paranoid security officer, and *Jika* (1986), an exploration of the difficulties inherent in political activism, also reflect their author's commitment to the consciousness-raising project of black artists and intellectuals of the period.

At the time Maponya wrote *The Hungry Earth*, the Black Consciousness Movement had been officially banned, and, because of widespread arrests following defiant and bloody insurrections that culminated in the Soweto uprising of 1976, many prominent activists chose to leave South Africa to continue the struggle from abroad. For those who stayed, including Maponya and fellow theatre practitioners Matsemala Manaka and Zakes Mda, producing plays in the townships became increasingly difficult. There was an absence of theatres, of capital and of rehearsal spaces, and many performances targeted at black audiences were permitted only in liberal, predominantly white venues such as the Market Theatre in Johannesburg. Maponya did, however, stage the premiere production of *The Hungry Earth* in Soweto in 1979. With a reduced cast due to difficulties obtaining passports and sufficient finances, the play later toured to Britain, where, advertised as 'a mirror and a voice of the dispossessed', it was critically acclaimed.

For Maponya, collaboration is central to theatre and he continually restructures his plays through the rehearsal process, using the script as a performative guide. Accordingly, *The Hungry Earth* underwent numerous metamorphoses before being presented in the form in which it would eventually be published in 1980. This version implicitly records the conditions under which township drama operated in the apartheid era; hence, the set design is extremely minimal to cut costs and aid mobility of productions, and the actors use only essential props, which are deposited in piles on the stage in the full view of the audience when not in use. The emphasis on a non-naturalistic performance style not only is driven by economics, but also underlines the play's demand for political transparency in South Africa. This transparency is also gestural: words are combined with iconic gestures, such as the clenched fists of Black Power salutes, that have overt political symbolism.

The play focuses on the social, economic and cultural effects of the South African migrant labour system and its relationship to the gold-mining industry, a subject that had become increasingly visible in the revisionist historiography of Southern African Studies throughout the 1970s. Under the apartheid regime, the black populace was seen as a ready supply of cheap labour power for various industries, resulting in considerable traffic of migrant workers from rural areas and neighbouring states to the gold mines of the Witwatersrand. After the 1976 Uprising, the government embarked on divisive strategies, including industrial relations reform, that attempted to privilege urban dwellers over outside migrant labourers.

The Hungry Earth explores these issues using an episodic structure that allows the development of the story from historical antecedents, through a description of rural plantation labour, to a portrayal of migrant labour. Each of the loosely linked, almost abstract vignettes, a prologue and five scenes, focuses on a different aspect of apartheid's oppression, showing its many faces: child labour and poverty, family breakdown, dangerous working conditions, state-sanctioned and legally enshrined racism, and the ruthless quelling of strikes. Overall, the play reveals apartheid as a servant of capital that supports an ideology of racial superiority to justify industrial exploitation and human subjugation. Maponya also dramatises the personal consequences of the migrant labour system: the destruction of families and communities that results from the demographic distortions produced by absent fathers and sons who are forced to abandon their communities in the face of poverty. In this respect, *The Hungry Earth*, like much political theatre, is both a lament for the dehumanisation of workers, and a call for resistance to, and rejection of, the oppressive state apparatus.

Theatrically, an important model for Maponya's early work was Bertolt Brecht's *The Measures Taken*, which he encountered while at the University of Leeds on a British Council scholarship. This influence is discernible in *The Hungry Earth*'s formal style, as well as in its vision of theatre as a potent tool for political demystification. The play's brief scenes, direct presentation of character, simple props, explicit reference to external political realities and disavowal of aesthetic attachment, all owe something to Brechtian dramaturgy. Like Brecht, Maponya does not concern himself with the moral or psychological complexities of individual characters. The construction of abstract figures such as Matlhoko (Sufferings), Usiviko (Shield), Beshwana (Loincloth) and Sethotho (Imbecile) works against a focus on interiority and directs critical audience thinking towards factors of social and economic determinacy. Similarly, the play's songs, along with a prologue in which the audience is directly addressed by the actors who introduce the Bahumutsi Drama Group, interrogate the encompassing political factors that shape the lives of the characters, and those of the target audience.

This emphasis on environment – physical, social and political – takes on a symbolic meaning through the play's repeated anthropomorphism, which casts the mines as living, hungry earth that swallows up people's lives.

Maponya's theatrical technique derives only partly from Brecht. It also has much in common with traditional African theatre's desire to ritualise key moments for presentation to an audience, the idea being to stimulate debate and to encourage community scrutiny. This kind of project is evident in early anti-apartheid protest plays such as Mthuli ka Shezi's *Shanti*, a call for racial unity that was dramatically structured around short episodes and visual tableaux, and produced by the People's Experimental Theatre before being banned. (Shezi was killed shortly after writing the play in 1972, making him, like Biko, a symbol of the struggle against white oppression.) In contrast to earlier Black Consciousness theatre, which was usually entirely in English, *The Hungry Earth* uses Zulu in some of its songs and dialogue as an affirmation of black South Africans' cultural heritage. This tactic must have had a powerful resonance at a time when the country's two official languages were English and Afrikaans, and Zulu was banned in educational contexts. As part of the recuperation of indigenous culture, the play also incorporates a 'traditional' gumboot dance, which evolved in the mines as a means of communication between black workers who were not allowed to speak to one another. The dance in Scene Four can thus be read as a powerful act of resistance; yet this interpretation is turned on its head when the miners are subsequently 'requested' to perform the dance for tourists on a Sunday. Here, Maponya delivers a subtle caution to privileged white audiences against turning acts of resistance into fetishised objects of interest, whereby the oppression the play seeks to critique becomes commodified and performed as entertainment.

The Hungry Earth has been criticised for its portrayal of an idyllic and harmonious pre-colonial society, as suggested in the early references to Mother Afrika. Such a romanticised vision is seen to simplify post-contact history into a reductive black–white dichotomy, an inadequate formulation for understanding the complexities of contemporary South Africa. Maponya's anti-apartheid theatre, with its overtly politicised essentialism, may, in the new millennium, 'appear formulaic and dated' (Steadman 1995: xiii), especially since recent political change has meant that black activists are no longer bound to the unambiguous morality of the 1970s and 1980s. Maponya himself has recognised the need to forge new post-apartheid dramaturgies:

> In the past, those opposed to apartheid could easily identify the 'enemy' and deal with relations between the struggle and art decidedly. Today the 'enemy' is no longer easily identifiable. What remains is how and from what perspective can practitioners deal with reconstruction.
>
> (Maponya 1998: 253)

Recent developments, particularly in theatre about the reconciliation process, suggest that this reconstruction will provide equally fertile ground for innovative performance. Maponya, who in 1985 was awarded the prestigious Standard Bank Young Artist Award for his contribution to theatre, deserves recognition for helping to make possible the transition to a more open political and cultural system. In spite of the perceived limitations of his specific brand of art, he is, as Ian Steadman notes, a key figure in the formative years of contemporary South African theatre and a precursor of its new voice (1995: xxii).

Production history

The Hungry Earth was first performed by a cast of five in May 1979 at the Donaldson Orlando Community Centre, Soweto, with Maishe Maponya as director. A short season at the Box Theatre of the University of the Witwatersrand, Johannesburg, followed. In 1981, with the cast reduced to three actors, one of whom was Maponya, the play toured to Britain, France and Germany before returning to South Africa for a commercial engagement in the Laager at the Market Theatre from January 1982.

Select bibliography

Anon. (1977) 'A new wave of cultural energy: Black theatre in South Africa', *Theatre Quarterly* 7, 28: 57–63.

Fuchs, A. (1992) 'The new South African theatre: beyond Fugard', in B. King (ed.) *Post-Colonial English Drama: Commonwealth Drama since 1960*, New York: St Martin's Press, 165–80.

Gray, S. (ed.) (1993) 'Introduction', *South African Plays*, London: Nick Hern, vi–xiv.

Holloway, M. (1991) '"Black" South African theatre: the conscience of a country', in C. Schumacher and D. Fogg (eds) *Small is Beautiful: Small Countries Theatre Conference Glasgow 1990*, Somerset: Castle Press, 165–73.

Kavanagh, R.M. (1985) *Theatre and Cultural Struggle in South Africa*, London: Zed Books.

Maponya, M. (1995) 'Preface', *Doing Plays for a Change*, Johannesburg: Witwatersrand University Press, vii–xi.

—— (1998) 'New challenges facing theatre practitioners in the new South Africa', in D. Attridge and R. Jolly (eds) *Writing South Africa: Literature, Apartheid and Democracy, 1970–1995*, Cambridge: Cambridge University Press, 249–56.

O'Brien, A. (1994) 'Staging whiteness: Beckett, Havel, Maponya', *Theatre Journal* 46, 1: 45–61.

Orkin, M. (1991) *Drama and the South African State*, Johannesburg: Witwatersrand University Press.

Peterson, B. (1994) 'Apartheid and the political imagination in Black South African theatre', in L. Gunner (ed.) *Politics and Performance: Theatre, Poetry and Song in Southern Africa*, Johannesburg: Witwatersrand University Press, 35–54.

Steadman, I. (1992) 'Performance and politics in process: practices of representation in South African theatre', *Theatre Survey* 33: 188–210.

—— (1995) 'The theatre of Maishe Maponya', in M. Maponya, *Doing Plays for a Change*, Johannesburg: Witwatersrand University Press, xiii–xxiii.

—— (1998) 'Race matters in South African theatre', in R. Boon and J. Plastow (eds) *Theatre Matters: Performance and Culture on the World Stage*, Cambridge: Cambridge University Press, 55–75.

The Hungry Earth

Maishe Maponya

As the house lights fade to blackout, the actors take position and sing:

> Wake up Mother Afrika
> Wake up
> Time has run out
> And all opportunity is wasted.
> Wake up Mother Afrika
> Wake up
> Before the white man rapes you.
> Wake up Mother Afrika.

As the song ends, the lights come up for:

Prologue

ALL   We are about to take you on a heroic voyage of the Bahumutsi Drama Group.

ONE   It seems as though some people are without feeling.

TWO   If we would really feel, the pain would be so great that we would stand up and fight to stop all the suffering.

THREE   If we could really feel it in the bowels, the groin, in the throat and in the breast, we would go into the streets and stop the wars, stop slavery, destroy the prisons, stop detentions, stop the killings, stop selfishness – and apartheid we would end.

FOUR   Ah, we would all learn what love is.

FIVE   We would learn what sharing is.

ONE   And, of course, we would live together.

ALL   (*singing*) Touched by our non-violent vibrations.

ONE   We will rise up.

ALL   (*singing*) We will sing while we crawl to the mine.

TWO   We will rise up.

ALL   (*singing*) Bleeding through the days of poverty.

THREE   We will fight hard.

ALL   (*singing*) Pulsing in the hot dark ground.

FOUR   We will rise up.

ALL   (*singing*) Dying in the stubborn hungry earth. (*speaking*) We will fight hard.

ALL   (*singing*)
   We will rise up
   And we will sing loud
   Against the hungry earth
   It is our sweat and our blood
   That made Egoli what it is today.

(The lights fade, and the actors take up position for:)

Scene One: The hostel

A hostel room. Four men are asleep. One of them is restless. He mumbles and groans and talks incoherently. He tosses about and finally cries out wildly. One of the inmates wakes him. They all wake up.

MATLHOKO [Sufferings]   For God's sake, I've been trying to wake you up while you twisted and turned and yelled, 'No, No, No!' like a Salvation Army lass being dragged into a brothel. Do you always have nightmares at dawn?

USIVIKO [Shield]   An evil nightmare has been torturing me. My whole body shivers. I wonder if this is real.

BESHWANA [Loincloth]   What is it, mngani [friend], tell us quickly.

USIVIKO   I dreamt I saw umlungu [the white man].

SETHOTHO [Imbecile]   But we see abelungu [whites] every day of our lives! Why do you behave like a child seeing a ghost when you just dream of umlungu? Don't make dreams your master.

USIVIKO   You are right. This umlungu was far different from them all in a way. This one has divided me against myself. He has tinted my colour. I can no longer distinguish between right and wrong.

BESHWANA   What did this strange umlungu do to you? What did he want?

(*The lights fade, leaving only* MATLHOKO *lit.*)

MATLHOKO   When this land started giving birth to ugly days, things started going wrong from the moment of dawning and peace went into exile, to become a thing of the wilderness. Yes, we experienced the saddest days of our lives when umlungu first came to these shores called Africa, a total stranger from Europe. We received him kindly. We gave him food. We gave him shelter. We adopted his ideas and his teachings. Then he told us of a god and all black faces were full of smiles. When he said love your neighbour we clapped and cheered for we had a natural love. Suddenly we drifted back suspiciously when he said you must always turn the other cheek when you are slapped. He continued to say love those who misuse you. We grumbled inwardly, smiled and listened hard as he was quoting from the Holy Book, little knowing we would end up as puppets on a string, unable to control our own lives. And whilst we were still smiling, he set up laws, organised an army and started digging up the gold and diamonds; and by the time our poor forefathers opened their eyes, umlungu was no more – he had moved to Europe. He has only left his army behind to 'take care of the unruly elements that may provoke a revolution'.

USIVIKO   We will repeat the incident as told by our forefathers.

(*The lights come up.*)

MATLHOKO   Men and women of Afrika: umlungu has left us secretly. He has taken with him a great wealth of property, our sheep and cattle, our men and women as servants, gold and silver and all precious stones.

USIVIKO   Let us give chase and get back what he has taken from us. Those riches belong to us, the aborigines of this land.

BESHWANA   Umlungu deserves to die. Let us set out to catch him and when we catch him we will hang him from the nearest tree. His servants must also be killed, they betrayed us. Let us kill the whole lot.

SETHOTHO   You speak of being robbed, you bastards? How can you say such things about umlungu? Before he came you were savages swinging onto trees and eating bananas. You deserted your culture and allowed the hides and wood to rot in the fields. Umlungu taught you how to make leather and how to make furniture. Today you can even make money. You lived like wild animals; now you live like human beings. But no, you ungrateful creatures, you are not satisfied with the things you got from umlungu. Does it surprise you that he has run away?

BESHWANA   How dare you curse my people like that! We blew horns, we beat the drums and we sang the song 'Ngelethu Mawethu' [it is ours, my people], when this land was unknown to the white skins! Shit! We gave culture to the world, we built the pyramids. No! (*Pointing a finger at* SETHOTHO) This man is trying to mislead us! You are obviously a great friend of umlungu. (*Clutching him*) Well, don't worry, we will not separate you from him. You will both be hung from the same tree . . . (*they all lift him above their heads*) and on your combined tombstone we will write:

ALL   In memory of the oppressor
And his oppressed spy
And to their love-hate
They were inseparable
In life and in death.
Find no peace.

USIVIKO   We gave chase in thousands. And when we got hold of him his army had received word that we meant to kill umlungu. We first wanted to tell him why we wanted to kill him.

UMLUNGU   What have I done to deserve your enmity? During the two hundred years I dwelt with you I taught you to live a better life. I brought you the wisdom and fertility of Europe. Why is it then that you are after my blood, that you want to kill me and my family?

BESHWANA   You are a stranger, a foreigner. By your labour you merely repaid your debt to our country, your debt to the country that extended its hospitality to you for two hundred years.

UMLUNGU   And why do you want to kill us today? What right have you to look upon yourselves as citizens and upon me as a foreigner?

USIVIKO   You are about to leave this country with all the wealth we sweated our lives for. You underpaid us and celebrated when we were starving. You gave us mirrors and knives in exchange for cattle. You never set foot on those vast tracts of land that are still in their virgin state. You did not want to get to them because you had no slaves to do the sweating for you.

(*During the next speech and the song the lights fade to half-light, and the actors mime the battle of spears against guns.*)

BESHWANA   We were still arguing when the army attacked from all sides. The spear matched the cowards' weapons from the West and only the crying tone of the singing warrior could be heard.

(*As the other actors chant softly,* BESHWANA *speaks.*)

Stand up all ye brave of Afrika
Stand up and get to battle,
Where our brothers die in numbers
Afrika you were bewitched
But our black blood will flow
To water the tree of our freedom.

BESHWANA   Our brave stormed the bullets to protect their motherland from the cruel umlungu. One–two–ten hundreds of our brave never flinched, yet they knew they were heading for death.

Mother Afrika wake up
And arm yourself,
Wipe the tears of your brave
Mother Afrika wake up,
Lest umlungu rapes you
Lest umlungu rapes you

MATLHOKO   Those were ugly days lived by our great-grandfathers, the days of Isandlwana and the days of Umgungundlovu. The days when our forefathers fought hard for what was theirs, for Mother Afrika.

(*The lights fade to blackout. A song – children singing at work – begins, and the lights come up for:*)

Scene Two: *The plantation*

Three child-workers seated. THE VISITOR, *an investigator, has just entered the compound.*

VISITOR   I am the man who visited Doringkop, owned by Illovo. (*Wandering about, talking to himself*) Ah! So many stables. This man must be very rich to afford so many horses. Let me just peep and see how many horses he has in each.

No! This cannot be true. I see people inside. Or maybe they did not look after the cattle well and that's why he locked them inside. Let me just find out. (*He knocks. There is a reply and he goes inside.*) Sanibonani.

ALL   Yebo!

VISITOR   I am looking for my son, Sizanani [Help one another].

SETHOTHO   USizanani is staying in B Compound. This is A.

VISITOR   Do you all stay in this stable? Why is it that there is no furniture?

ALL   Asazi [We do not know].

VISITOR   How old are you?

MATLHOKO   Mina [Me]?

VISITOR   Yes, wena [you].

MATLHOKO   I am twelve years old and will be thirteen next month.

VISITOR   You? How old are you?

BESHWANA   I am thirteen.

VISITOR   You?

USIVIKO   Twelve.

VISITOR   And you?

MATLHOKO   He is fourteen.

VISITOR   And you?

SETHOTHO   They lie, they are all thirteen years old, I know.

VISITOR   Do you go to school?

BESHWANA   No. We don't go to school. We work for Baas Phuzushugela [Sugardrinker] the whole year.

VISITOR   What does he pay you?

SETHOTHO   He gives me 50c.

BESHWANA   He gives me 70c – I started working last year.

USIVIKO   He gives us all 50c – he is lying. Ubaas Phuzushugela a soze a ku nike i70c [will never give you 70c].

VISITOR   Till when do you work?

BESHWANA   We start at five o'clock in the morning and knock off at three in the afternoon.

VISITOR   When is your lunch?

SETHOTHO   We don't go to lunch. Baas Phuzushugela gives us amageu [sour porridge] and bread at ten o'clock. And once a week we receive rations of mealie meal, beans, salt and meat.

VISITOR   Do you work on Saturdays?

USIVIKO   Yes. Siphumula ngesonto nje [We rest on Sundays].

VISITOR   How far is the sugar field from here?

BESHWANA   Six miles only.

VISITOR   And how do you travel there?

SETHOTHO   We wake up very early and walk.

VISITOR   Tell me, where do you come from?

USIVIKO   We are all from Transkei.

VISITOR   Now how did you come here?

SETHOTHO   Size nge Joini. We are on contract. Will you excuse us, we want to sleep, it is already late.

VISITOR   Where do you sleep?

USIVIKO   Silala lapha [We sleep here].

VISITOR   I immediately went out and eventually ended up in the compound where married men and their wives were staying. Some women told me they earned R1,10 a day and some men said they earned R2 a day after working nine hours. I slept there for a night. I went into the field and was chased because they said I was causing trouble.

(*The child-workers sing 'A Song of Rejection of Trouble-makers'.*)

> Here comes a man
> To cause trouble in my home,
> Bring that stick
> And I will discipline him . . .

(*The lights fade as the song ends. The actors move upstage to collect their props, except* MATLHOKO *who moves downstage left. Lights up on* MATLHOKO *only, for:*)

Scene Three: The train

MATLHOKO   Just how I wish I were a spectator of the scenes of the amagoduga [migrant labourers]. I would follow them about and just watch every little thing they do and listen to their newly found lingo, Fanagalo. Unfortunately, blacks can never be spectators of white creations, but victims. (*Lights full up.*) Yes, my wish was misplaced for I was one of the Basotho who were driven by hunger and drought from the confines of their rugged mountains. In those days it seemed as though the god of the white man from over the sea had stamped his feet in anger upon this land for the first time since its creation. Obviously many of us were coming to the mines for the first time. The talk in the crammed compartments was all of the hunger that had fallen in Lesotho. The older men put the blame on the younger generation that had put their faith in the mystical gods of Europe, foolishly forgetting the old and safe ways of the nation's ancestors, and I will never forget what happened on that ugly day in the train . . .

(*The men, who have been waiting at the station, are now infuriated and angered by the endless waiting. Finally we see four actors occupying chairs which are placed in two parallel rows – the train.*)

SETHOTHO   (*sniffing and looking about and eventually standing to look underneath the seat*) Hey man! There is a dangerous odour here. (*Nobody takes notice. He sits down. Then he repeats the same movements.*) Hey, man! I know we all want money but this odour is going to land us in shit!

(*While he ponders absent-mindedly, the compartment door is flung open and a ticket examiner enters, his uniform cap pushed well back from his forehead.*)

EXAMINER   Kaartjies! Tickets! Come on you black bastards. Hurry up! (*Standing in the doorway he surveys everybody and wrinkles his nose in disgust. He sniffs the air tentatively three or four times, quickly punches the tickets, and, before leaving, gives them another hard look.*)

SETHOTHO   (*calling out*) Men of the chief, kere ho a nkga mona [there is a smell here]. I can smell matekoane [marijuana]. The white man smelled it too. You saw his nose twitching like a jackal's.

BESHWANA   (*interrupting*) O nkgella masepa' mmae fela. Mosima'e towe!

SETHOTHO   I tell you, someone had better throw the matekoane out of the window. At the next station he will inform the police. Will someone please hide the stuff very far lest the police arrest the innocent together with the guilty?

(*No one moves.*)

BESHWANA   (*imitating the ticket examiner*) Maak gou [be quick], maak gou, you black skelms!

(*Laughter.*)

SETHOTHO   (*warning them*) Hey, my father lived in the City of Gold and he told me there are so many crimes against the law of the white man of which black people might unwittingly be guilty. You will end up in jail if you are found in the streets of the city and can't produce a pass any time and anywhere the police demand it – even in the toilet – I tell you, they sometimes hide in there. If you drink too much you may be arrested for over-indulgence in alcohol. Do you know detention without trial? Section Ten? Or Six? Do you know you can be arrested for being at the wrong place at the wrong time? Do you know house arrest? Do you know Robben Island? Makana? My father knows them all! Pasop banna! (*Warningly*) Hlokomelang! I don't want to repeat my father's experience. Lahlang matekoane ono [Throw it away]!

(*Realising that his warning is falling on deaf ears, he collects his few belongings to search for another place somewhere in the crowded train. Seeing that he cannot find a place elsewhere, he returns amidst jeers and laughter. They are still laughing when a white sergeant bursts noisily into the compartment with the ticket examiner at his heels. The travellers freeze in sullen silence.*)

EXAMINER (*eyeing them coldly*) Come! You black bastards! Where's the dagga? (*No one answers.*) All right! Out onto the platform, you baboons! (*He slaps and kicks the slow ones. Outside, he searches them thoroughly and, finding nothing, he pushes his cap to the very back of his head and turns into the compartment to start his search again. Finally he comes out swelling like a bullfrog in anger, holding a bag in his hand. He lifts it up and asks*) Wie se sak is hierdie [Whose bag is this]?

ALL We do not know, Sir.

EXAMINER Go! All into the police vans.

(*They all end up in the vans, after putting up some resistance during which one is threatened with a bullet in the head. 'Interrogation' and sentencing follow. The lights slowly fade except for the narrator's area downstage right.*)

USIVIKO Most of us were 'requested' to produce passes and permits. Those who failed to produce spent two weeks in jail and were deported to their respective homes on their release. This is the inhuman and unjust procedure to endorse the unjust laws that make another a stranger in the land of his birth and rob him of his freedom to move wherever he wants. Is freedom not the law of nature? Then what?

(*The lights come up for:*)

Scene Four: The mine

MATLHOKO (*from the window of his room*) Hey, Mzala [cousin]!

BESHWANA (*responding through his window*) Kuyabanda namhlanje, Mzala [It is cold today, cousin].

MATLHOKO Yes Mzala! The wind . . . It's freezing today.

BESHWANA The gods are angry.

MATLHOKO Yes, but their anger can't go beneath this earth. It is quiet there.

(*A traditional gumboot dance with song. A siren sounds. The lights fade for scene underground. The mineworkers gather at the cage to begin their night shift. The cage descends. It slows to a shuddering halt, and they swarm out like ants to their various places of work. They stoop low, twist and turn to avoid the wooden props which pit their strength against the full weight of the rocky roof that presses down on their crouching heads. Jannie, a white miner, inspects a work face and gives orders.*)

JANNIE Tonight I want holes to be drilled here . . . and here . . . and here . . . and here.

BESHWANA (*after a short while*) Sorry, master, this area may not be suitable, and besides the rock seems wet.

JANNIE I did not ask your opinion. Do you want to argue with me when I tell you to work?

BESHWANA I am sorry makhulubaas [big boss], I'm sorry.

(*They drill at the rock.*)

BAASBOY (*fuming*) Hei! Wena! Why tell makhulubaas and not me? Do you want to take my job?

BESHWANA (*apologetic*) I'm sorry, Baasboy.

BAASBOY Next time you'll be fired! Pasop, jong [watch out, boy]!

JANNIE Baasboy! Wat gaan aan daarso, jong [What's going on there boy]?

BAASBOY Makhulubaas, this one thinks he knows too much!

JANNIE Werk, julle bliksems!

BESHWANA and BAASBOY Dankie [Thank you], makhulubaas.

BAASBOY (*pointing a finger at* BESHWANA) Jy moet werk, jong!

(*Suddenly there is a great explosion. The miners collapse. Smoke and coughing. Again*)

*and again the miners scream in pain and
fright.*)

SETHOTHO   Without even considering the
weight of the risk, I stood up, passing the
dead bodies of my brothers just to save this
sole white skin.

(*As* JANNIE *screams again and again*
SETHOTHO *comes to his rescue.*)

MATLHOKO   And when the first two
ambulances arrived we limped towards
them but only the makhulubaas was
allowed into one. The other turned back
because the two ambulances were for the
white people only. I looked back into the
tunnel where my brothers were being
eaten by this hungry earth. I cursed the
white man and questioned the very
existence of God, for it was my sweat and
bones and blood that made Egoli what it is
today.

BESHWANA   This is actual fact. Two years
after this horrible accident I was
transferred to Carletonville where we
staged a strike . . .

(*The actors change positions and start milling
around, ignoring the siren that beckons them
to work.*)

BESHWANA   (*pointing a finger at* SETHOTHO,
the induna [headman]) Wena, induna, you
side with the white man today, you must
pack your belongings and go to stay with
him in the city. We are sick of this induna
business!

SETHOTHO   (*reassuring them*) I'm behind
you in everything!

COMPOUND MANAGER   Look at these fools!
Didn't you hear the machine? (*The miners
all keep quiet as he goes to them one by one.*)
Hey, wena. Yini wena haikhona sebenza
[Hey man, you don't want to work]?

SETHOTHO   Haikhona baas, thina aiyazi
sebenzela lo pikinini mali fana ga so [No
boss, we can't work for so little money]!

BESHWANA   Baas wena haikhona yipha thina
lo insurance, manje thina haikhona
sebenza [You refuse to insure us, now we
won't work]!

COMPOUND MANAGER   Wena yini ga lo
sikhalo ga wena [What is your complaint]?

MATLHOKO   Lo mali wena ga lo yipha thina,
thina haikhona satisfied. Kudala lo thina
sebenza lapha mgodi. Kodwa wena
haikhona yipha lo thina increase. Lo room

thina hlala, fana ga lo toilet [We are not
satisfied with the salary. We have long
been working in the mine yet you refuse to
give us an increase. The room we stay in is
as small as a toilet]!

COMPOUND MANAGER   You! What is your
complaint? What? No complaint? Now, all
of you, listen to me very carefully because
I'm not going to repeat myself! The first
thing: you get free lodging. The second
thing: you get free food. (*A sudden murmur
of discontent.*) The third thing: you get free
overalls, free gumboots . . .

(*A wave of angry protest: he pushes them
forward to work, they push him back.*)

COMPOUND MANAGER   Madoda! Skathi nina
haikhona hamba sebenza, mina biza lo
maphoisa [Men! If you refuse to go to work
I'll go and call the police].

ALL   (*threatening him with their hats*) Hamba
[Go]! Hamba!

(*The* COMPOUND MANAGER *can be heard
from his office talking to the police.*)

COMPOUND MANAGER   Yes sir, anything
may happen – they are about to destroy
everything, they are wild, come quickly!

ALL   The police won, but not without
declaring themselves enemies of the
people!

COMPOUND MANAGER   We shall not be
intimidated.

(*There is the sound of a machine-gun and as
some miners fall down, some raise their
hands, surrendering to go down into the mine.*
MATLHOKO *continues relating what
happened.*)

MATLHOKO   Yes, we were forced to go
down in Carletonville though we knew
that this earth was hungry. Who would
listen to our cries? Yes, never will I forget
that bloody Sharpeville for I was there in
1960 when an anti-pass campaign was
opened.

(*They produce passes and interact with each
other as they express their anger and disgust
at the pass system.* BESHWANA *throws his
pass away, but is advised not to do so.*)

USIVIKO   Hei Beshwana, not here! At the
police station. Come, everybody, let us go
to the police station.

BESHWANA   Let us throw stones then. We
must put up a fight.

(*They stop him from throwing stones.*)

USIVIKO You are giving them a wrong impression of us. We are not violent people. And this is a peaceful demonstration. Come everybody . . .

(*A procession and the burning of passbooks, with a song.*)

Senze ntoni na?	What have we done?
Senze ntoni na?	
Nkosi mthetheleli	God, our spokesman
Si bhekisa kuwe	We put all our faith in You
Yini na? Ukuba sibenjana?	Why have we to live this way?
Sikhulule kuwo lamatyatanga	Release us from these shackles
Sikhulule kuwo lamatyatanga	
Senze ntoni na?	
Senze ntoni na?	

(*As they put their passes on the fire, the lights fade until only the fire remains. The song continues.*)

USIVIKO The police panicked at the sight of the massed though unarmed innocent black faces. . . .

ALL We were all of the same frame of mind . . .

USIVIKO And they opened fire! (*Mimes firing at the protestors as they fall to the ground.*) I went to the funeral and was shocked to see how hungry this earth is, for it had opened to swallow the black man. Those who survived were arrested and charged with incitement to violence under the Public Safety Act . . . Someone somewhere did not understand 'peaceful' and 'violent' . . . Anyhow, let's forget about that because some very rich white women and some elite black women have formed 'Women for Peace' and I hope they will forget their elitism and their socialising process and be equally dedicated to peace in Afrika.

(*Saluting with a clenched fist, he stretches and flexes his body like a person who's just woken up from a sleep.*)

Scene Five: The compound

Sunday morning activity inside a compound room.

BESHWANA (*waking up from a sleep and calling out to* USIVIKO) We mgani wami.

Come here . . . I went to the biggest shebeen in the township yesterday.

USIVIKO Kuphi lapho [Where's that]?

BESHWANA At Rose's place.

USIVIKO Rose's shebeen?

BESHWANA Ngathenga ugologo mngani wami . . . ngathi laca . . . laca . . . laca . . . [I bought liquor and had so much to drink].

USIVIKO You must have been drunk.

BESHWANA Yebo mngani wami . . . ngas ngi lala la – here on the floor.

USIVIKO So you slept here, hey! That's not good for your health. You must stop drinking . . . And who was burning papers on the floor?

BESHWANA Where?

USIVIKO Behind you.

BESHWANA I don't know.

USIVIKO You will know when this place goes up in flames . . . ga!

BESHWANA (*angered*) I said I don't know . . .

USIVIKO Okay! You don't have to shout at me!

BESHWANA Fuck off!

USIVIKO You must count your words when you talk to me. Ga!

BESHWANA (*emphasising each word*) Go to hell!

USIVIKO (*as he removes the ash, frustrated*) Okay! I will meet you there!

(*There is tension between the two. Silence.*)

BESHWANA (*a little later*) Hey, my friend! Did you hear the latest news? (*Silence.*) The manager has requested us to do the traditional dance for the tourists.

USIVIKO When will we ever have a Sunday of our own? You're used to dancing every Sunday. Are you going to do it again today in that drunk state?

BESHWANA No, I've grown old, Sonnyboy. I can't dance anymore . . . (*Silence.*) Hey, can you see out there!

USIVIKO What?

BESHWANA The bus, my friend . . . (*He looks out of the window.*) Can you see it . . . there!

USIVIKO Look . . . SAR Tours. It's the tourists. Look, they've got cameras aimed at us. They are taking a picture of us.

(*They pose for a picture. They are in a happy mood as they run out of the room.*)

BESHWANA There it stops, my friend. They've got tape recorders . . . (*They walk towards the dance area.*) Hey, another picture . . . (*They hug and pose.*)

ALL Hi! Hello, beautiful tourists . . .
Welcome to sunny South Africa! Hello . . .

BESHWANA Another picture. (*Pose.*)
They're taking their seats. Come closer.
(*Talks softly to him.*) Can you see that man
over there?

USIVIKO Which one?

BESHWANA The one with small eyes . . . He
looks like eh . . .

USIVIKO He looks like . . . Mao Tse Tung.

BESHWANA But I'm scared, my friend. Can
you see the two men beside him? They
look like the Security Branch.

USIVIKO Oh, pity he's escorted.

BESHWANA (*sudden excitement*) My friend,
my friend, look . . .

USIVIKO I see . . .

BESHWANA That bearded one . . . what do
you think?

USIVIKO Yeh! He looks like Karl Marx!

(*They seem to have fun with their
explorations. They point at a lady in the
arena whom they agree looks 'like Lady
Diana!' Finally . . .*)

BESHWANA Can you see that black man
sitting alone there? He looks like . . .

USIVIKO Shame . . . that one, simple . . .

BOTH He is the bus driver! Ha ha ha!

(*They call out to* MATLHOKO, *whom they've
nicknamed Manikiniki.*)

BOTH We Manikiniki! Manikiniki!

BESHWANA Come out!

USIVIKO The tourists are here!

MATLHOKO What? Just leave me alone.

BESHWANA Come out! Come and see for
yourself. Tourists!

MATLHOKO Terrorists?

USIVIKO No, tourists!

(MATLHOKO *comes out dressed in traditional
garb and finally they dance and entertain the
tourists, drumming and singing and posing
for pictures until they are exhausted.*)

Scene Six: *The compound*

*Everyday activity. A gramophone plays a Zulu
tune, gambling, cooking, finally fighting.*

MATLHOKO Heje, I read a true statement in
the Bible last week: it says we shall live by
the sweat of our brows.

SETHOTHO Oh, how true that is, mngani –
it's amazing. (*Starts coughing.*) But it's time
I go on pension. I'm old and my chest

seems to be dry or maybe I have run out of
blood. I'm scared.

MATLHOKO Ja we must; you remember
when we started here way back in the
fifties. We were still young boys. Then you
could hardly speak Sesotho, only Xhosa. Of
course I did not trust you. Yooo! Who could
trust a Xhosa lad anyway? (*They laugh.*)
You remember we thought we would work
ourselves up, bring our families down here
and buy a 'Buick master road'. But here we
are now, still struggling and about to die,
no Buick and wives still far away.

SETHOTHO Hey, you remind me of the
houses outside the perimeter of this
compound. Hey man, the scene is pathetic
. . . there are women there!

MATLHOKO What are you talking about?

SETHOTHO I mean, have you not seen
those rusted, corrugated iron huts mixed
with pieces of wood and petrol drums?

MATLHOKO J-jaa, I saw them.

SETHOTHO Did you know people stay
there?

MATLHOKO Yes, I went there several times.
In fact let's get down there now, I feel
thirsty.

(*The lights fade as they exit singing.*)

WOMAN My name is Chirango. This is my
only home. I came here some five years
after my husband had written to me to
come and join him in this city of gold. To
my dismay, I was not permitted to stay
with him. I could not go back to Rhodesia
because I had no money. He took me into
his room at night. Later when a wall was
erected around the compound it became
risky to sneak in. Once I was arrested and
fined R90 or 90 days. He did not have the
money and I went to jail. When I came
back I was told that his contract had
expired and since then I have never seen
or heard of him. Today I manage to live
and feed my two fatherless children out of
the beers and indambola [liquor] I sell. And
when the beers don't sell I become every
man's woman. What else can I do? I can't
get permits to work here.

(*Sings 'The Woman's Song',*)

I'll never get to Malawi
I'll never get to Transkei
I'll never get to Bophuthatswana

(*The lights come up as men enter, singing.
They tease her, eventually settling down.*)

MATLHOKO Sisi, is Chirango your name or your husband's?

WOMAN It is my husband's. Why?

SETHOTHO Yes I thought as much. Your name rings a bell. I worked with a Chirango some two years ago in the Western Transvaal gold mine near Orkney. He was tall, dark, hefty – and wore a moustache . . .

WOMAN Where is he? He is the father of my children! He is my husband! I want him.

SETHOTHO This is a very sorry state of affairs. I even fear to talk about it.

WOMAN (anxious) Tell me! Where is my husband?

SETHOTHO (relating in a rather pathetic tone) Your husband was among the forty-one black miners trapped underground in a raging fire who were left to die when mine authorities gave the order to seal off the passageways. I was among the 233 mine workers who were affected by the fumes and were treated in hospital.

WOMAN (hysterical and crying) Oh, how cruel this earth is. Our men will never stop dying to feed this hungry earth. Today I have no place to stay. Today I am a widow. Today my children are fatherless yet I do not know. How many more have vanished like that without the knowledge of immediate relatives? My husband has died digging endlessly for gold which would help to prop up the apartheid system. My man is dead! My man is eaten by the hungry earth! He is dead!

(The lights fade slowly. Group song.)

ALL S'thandwa s'thandwa
    S'thandwa se nhliziyo yam
    [Beloved one of my heart]
    Beloved one, dry your tears
    Daughter of Afrika
    Somandla! Somandla!
    Uphi na Qamatha?
    [Almighty! Where art thou?]
    When this hungry earth
    Swallows, swallows
    Thy children
    Somandla! Somandla!
    Sikelela Insapho, ye Afrika
    Nkosi Sikelela thina lusapholwayo
    [Bless the family of Afrika]
    Sikelela insapho, ye Afrika
    Nkosi Sikelela thina lusapholwayo.

Epilogue

ALL (singing)
    Where have all our men gone?
    They have all gone down into the mines
    They will never return again
    They have been swallowed up by this hungry earth!

(Lights fade to blackout.)

3 Jane Taylor, with William Kentridge and the Handspring Puppet Company ———————

Ubu and the Truth Commission

<u>South Africa</u>

*[handwritten: * Real witness testimonies through these puppets * we can't only use one language because we are multilingual]*

Introduction

The controversial work of South Africa's Truth and Reconciliation Commission (TRC) has spawned a number of bold and imaginative theatrical ventures in the post-apartheid period. Among them, Jane Taylor's *Ubu and the Truth Commission* (1997), lauded as the 'touchstone for artful, affecting political engagement' in the 'new' South Africa (Gevisser 1997: 4), has attracted the most critical attention, both locally and internationally. Written in collaboration with artist, film-maker and animator William Kentridge, along with Basil Jones and Adrian Kohler of the Handspring Puppet Company, this multimedia text par excellence deals primarily with those who perpetrated atrocities during the apartheid regime. In doing so, the play enters a politically volatile terrain, asking difficult questions about the moral value and social effectiveness of 'reconciliation' as an official nation-building strategy, but refusing to provide easy answers.

Set up in 1995 with Archbishop Desmond Tutu as its chairman, the TRC was an independent body designed to facilitate a 'truth recovery process' by holding public hearings to determine the extent of gross human-rights violations in the three decades leading up to South Africa's first multiracial elections in 1994. As well as taking witness statements from victims and their families and friends, the Commission considered applications for amnesty by those admitting to politically motivated crimes. Its broader task was to lay foundations for the reconstruction of South African society by addressing, in ways that stressed reparation rather than retaliation, the legacies of hatred and violence undergirding the apartheid system. That this monumental task was fraught with difficulties from its very inception is widely acknowledged, not only by the TRC's detractors but also by its supporters. Journalist and poet Antjie Krog, whose complex and moving accounts of the Commission's work provided source material for Taylor's play, succinctly registers the painful compromises required for 'reconciliation' when she muses on the meaning of the word: 'Understand. Tolerate. Empathize. Endure . . . Without it, no relationship, no work, no progress is possible. Yes. Piece by piece we die into reconciliation' (Krog 1998: 50).

A number of commentators have pointed to the inherent theatricality of the TRC's work. In his director's note to *Ubu and the Truth Commission* (included in the handsomely illustrated script published by the University of Cape Town Press), Kentridge argues that the Commission proceedings were 'exemplary civic theatre, a public hearing of private griefs which are absorbed into the body politic as part of a deeper understanding of how the society arrived at its present position' (1998: ix). The lines of connection – and disjunction – between the theatricality of the Commission hearings and that of re-enacted testimonials embedded in a consciously crafted dramatic text are most poignantly expressed in another TRC-inspired theatre project, the Khulumani Support Group's workshop play, *The Story I'm about to Tell* (1997), in which torture victims tell their own stories. While this play differs markedly from *Ubu and the Truth Commission* in style and purpose, both works, like other recent post-apartheid plays such as Paul Herzog's *The Dead Wait* (1997) and André Brink's *Die Jogger* (1997), speak to a need to make sense of the incomprehensible 'raw material' that the TRC has unearthed.

The concept for *Ubu and the Truth Commission* has a complex genesis, arising partly out of Kentridge's artwork for an exhibition marking the centenary of the first production of Alfred Jarry's *Ubu Roi*, and partly from his earlier collaborations with Handspring puppeteers on performance projects such as *Woyzeck on the Highveld* (1993) and *Faustus in Africa* (1996), each a localised, multimedia adaptation of its 'classic' European counterpart. Looking for a new project to develop with Handspring, Kentridge found in the TRC hearings the kind of oral testimonials he had wanted to theatricalise, and decided to combine this material with Ubu animations he was developing at the time. He approached Taylor, a writer and academic who had initiated a series of cultural activities addressing war crimes, reparation and mourning, to script the play. Workshops with performers, puppets and animations followed, providing Taylor with material that helped to shape the eventual text.

As its name suggests, *Ubu and the Truth Commission* is textually indebted to Jarry's iconoclastic theatre. Grotesque, ambitious and remorseless, Taylor's Ma and Pa Ubu are modelled after Jarry's characters, their dialogue carrying echoes of his mannered and bombastic language, which is itself a parody of the 'grand' tradition of French classical tragedy. The narrative of Taylor's text also borrows from Jarry's plays, especially *Ubu Roi*, which, in its audacious account of rampant greed and violence, lends itself well to adaptation as satire of a variety of dictatorial regimes. In 1994, for instance, the Romanian theatre group Teatrul National of Craiova used elements of *Ubu Roi* in a production darkly satirising the Ceauçescu era. What distinguishes such experiments from Jarry's original play is the politicising of Ubu's world, its transformation into a domain where actions have recognisable, indeed catastrophic, consequences. In this respect, Taylor notes that her purpose in juxtaposing Pa Ubu's criminal exploits with witness testimonials drawn from the Truth and Reconciliation Commission hearings was to take the Ubu characters out of Jarry's burlesque context where their actions ultimately have no measurable effects because the world itself is represented as farcical (Taylor 1998: iv).

As an erstwhile agent of the state in contemporary South Africa, Pa Ubu is invested with traces of various real-life figures and, at times, speaks in voices reminiscent of those heard among amnesty seekers at the TRC hearings. Taylor explains, however, that Ubu is designed to suggest a more abstract concept, 'the failure of moral imagination' behind many people's refusal to accept responsibility for their roles in perpetuating the apartheid system. In Taylor's terms, 'Rather than represent[ing] any particular figure from South African history, Ubu stands for an aspect, a tendency, an excuse' (Taylor 1998: iv). This is neatly conveyed by the play's treatment of his testimony before the Commission. Accused of heinous crimes, Ubu feigns complete ignorance, casting the blame on those above him, those below him and those beside him. Ma Ubu similarly evades the truth, choosing to cast Pa's 'work' in a heroic light and remaining more concerned with her own sensual needs than with the brutalities that surround her. She is, nonetheless, the more complex character, oscillating between positions of power and vulnerability. Lesley Marx argues that she 'reflects those sturdy Afrikaner politicians' wives who stand by their men . . . only to find that they have been betrayed . . . both sexually and politically' (Marx 1998: 215). As played in Kentridge's production by a black actress in whiteface, Ma also suggests those blacks who were complicit in their own oppression. At another level, this costuming technique speaks back to the profoundly raced tradition of minstrelsy, as well as disrupting precisely the kind of racial essentialism on which apartheid itself was based.

Ubu and the Truth Commission is consciously constructed as a multimedia text combining human actors, puppets, animated etchings, myriad sound effects, and documentary press footage. That Ma and Pa Ubu are the only characters played by actual actors compels viewers to acknowledge, however uncomfortably, a shared humanity that implicates them in Ma and Pa's cynical world. Kentridge's animations, disarmingly crude in style, fill in the dramatic portrait of Pa Ubu by depicting his many barbarous acts as well as visually alluding to his infantile prototype in Jarry's *Ubu Roi*. Animated images of the eye and the camera, along with the projection of a disembodied 'Screen Ma' during her television interview, function more obliquely to comment on the mediatisation of the Commission hearings and the ways in which this process impacts upon notions of truth and reconciliation. As visual motifs, the eye and the camera are double-coded to suggest the importance of 'witnessing' (as a means of facing past atrocities) and, simultaneously, to call into question the reliability of vision itself. The eye also evokes the sense of an omniscient presence, which begs a complex reading of the final animated image of Ma and Pa sailing towards a giant eye that morphs into the setting sun. Although the pair beguile the Commission and avoid censure, the eye/gaze of a higher 'truth' than their own seems to oversee their getaway and may eventually even prick their consciences.

The puppetry that gives *Ubu and the Truth Commission* so much of its visual appeal amplifies the play's multilayered engagement with the reconciliation process. As animal puppets, the vulture, Brutus and Niles enable the presentation of symbolic acts or concepts that would be difficult to achieve with human actors. The vulture, as Jones and Kohler explain,

> acts as a single chorus, providing sardonic commentary throughout the action of the play. It has a limited range of actions and a set of electronic squawks interpreted on the screen as proverbs. Thus it is a form of manipulation: like gears driven by motors which in turn are driven by a remote technician – which is appropriate to its function in the play – an apparently authorless automaton spewing forth programmed truisms.
>
> (Jones and Kohler 1998: xvi)

Brutus, for his part, is Pa's canine henchman, a chilling reminder of the dogs trained to victimise black South Africans during the apartheid era. This puppet's three heads represent different but indivisible types: the foot soldier, the general and the politician. Though each is equally culpable for carrying out Pa's orders, when found guilty of gross human-rights violations they are given sentences that reflect their access to social privilege. The choice of a crocodile puppet as Pa's adviser and cover-up man draws on more abstract parallels between the dramatic function of the Niles character and the animal on which it is based. With a mouth large enough to swallow the evidence of Pa's crimes, the crocodile provided a solution to Kentridge's urge to stage some kind of

shredding machine, which for him is a potent image of a society asked to confront its crimes.

If the animal puppets seem to be extensions of the police state, and, in Brutus's case, a bleak commentary on the amnesty seekers' oft-heard (Nuremburg) defence that they were 'just obeying orders', the witness puppets, representing apartheid's victims, poignantly 'capture complex relations of testimony, translation and documentation apparent in the processes of the Commission itself' (Taylor 1998: vii). These puppets were developed as a practical solution to the ethical question of how stories of real-life testimonials could be staged. As Kentridge notes,

> There seemed to be an awkwardness in getting an actor to play the witnesses – the audience being caught halfway between having to believe in the actor for the sake of the story and also not believe in the actor for the sake of the actual witness who existed out there but was not the actor. Using a puppet made this contradiction palpable. There is no attempt to make the audience think the wooden puppet or its manipulator is the actual witness. The puppet becomes a medium through which the testimony can be heard.
>
> (Kentridge 1998: xi)

Using puppets to represent black characters is potentially a risky manoeuvre, as it could suggest white ventriloquism at its most basic level. However, the play minimises this risk by insisting on theatrical (and political) transparency; thus, the puppeteers remain highly visible at all times, while the role of the translator is foregrounded.

The consciously anti-naturalistic style of Taylor's text reflects the instability of any concept of truth. Because of the rapid shifts in action, and the tendency of one level of the narrative to comment ironically on another, no discourse is privileged with absolute dramatic authority. As soon as the audience becomes accustomed to one configuration of theatrical 'truth', it is fractured, inverted or shown to be artifice, as in the sequence in which the puppeteers break the carefully constructed 'humanity' of their puppets to reveal that they are inanimate assemblages of wood and cloth. Such depictions of truth as something elusive and yet continually manifest in different

✱ Marcel Duchamp
urinal (Dada)

ways and through different perspectives are consistent with what Krog sees as the proper mandate of the formal reconciliation process: to conceive 'truth as the widest possible compilation of people's perceptions, stories, myths, and experiences', and thus 'to restore memory and foster a new humanity' (Krog 1998: 21–2). *Ubu and the Truth Commission* situates itself firmly within this project.

Production history

Ubu and the Truth Commission was first showcased at The Laboratory, The Market Theatre, Johannesburg on 26 May 1997, directed by William Kentridge. The play received its world premiere at the Kunstfest in Weimar, Germany, on 17 June 1997, and was staged shortly afterwards at the National Arts Festival in Grahamstown. It toured to Italy, France and the United States (New York, Washington and Los Angeles) in 1998 and featured at the London International Festival of Theatre in 1999.

Select bibliography

Blumberg, M. (2000) 'Re-membering history, staging hybridity: *Ubu and the Truth Commission*', in H. Wylie and B. Lindfors (eds) *Multiculturalism and Hybridity in African Literatures*, Lawrenceville, NJ: Africa World Press, 309–18.

Coetzee, Y. (1998) 'Visibly invisible . . . the creation of theatrical meaning in *Ubu and the Truth Commission*', *South African Theatre Journal* 12, 1: 35–51.

Davis, G.V. (1999) 'Addressing the silences of the past: the legacy of race in contemporary South Africa', in B. Reitz (ed.) *Race and Religion in Contemporary Theatre and Drama in English*, Trier: Wissenschaftlicher Verlag, 119–34.

Gevisser, M. (1997) 'Setting the stage for a journey into SA's heart of darkness', *Independent on Sunday* [supplement] 10 August: 4.

Jones, B. and Kohler, A. (1998) 'Puppeteers' note', in J. Taylor, *Ubu and the Truth Commission*, Cape Town: University of Cape Town Press, xvi–xvii.

Kentridge, W. (1998) 'Director's note', in J. Taylor, *Ubu and the Truth Commission*, Cape Town: University of Cape Town Press, viii–xv.

Krog, A. (1998) *Country of My Skull: Guilt, Sorrow, and the Limits of Forgiveness in the New South Africa*, Johannesburg: Random House.

Maree, C. (1998) 'Resistance and remembrance: theatre during and after dictatorship and apartheid', *South African Theatre Journal* 12, 1/2: 11–32.

Marx, L. (1998) 'Slouching towards Bethlehem: *Ubu and the Truth Commission*', *African Studies* 57, 2: 209–20.

Rush, M. (1998) 'The enduring avant-garde: Jean-Luc Goddard and William Kentridge', *Performing Arts Journal* 20, 3: 48–52.

Taylor, J. (1998) 'Writer's note', in J. Taylor, *Ubu and the Truth Commission*, Cape Town: University of Cape Town Press, ii–vii.

Walder, D. (1998) 'Spinning out the present: narrative, gender and the politics of South African theatre', in D. Attridge and R. Jolly (eds) *Writing South Africa: Literature, Apartheid, and Democracy, 1970–1995*, Cambridge: Cambridge University Press, 204–20.

Ubu and the Truth Commission _____

Jane Taylor

Act One: 1

When the scene opens, there is a puppet near centre stage, making soup. Music in the background is tender, quiet. For several minutes the soup-making is undertaken, from cutting of vegetables, to stirring, to salting. The soup is tasted twice in this process. On the second tasting, the scene changes abruptly.

Act One: 2

The shift in scene is inaugurated by a change in music. The earlier piece is abruptly replaced by a brash, harsh, cartoonish piece. We find ourselves in the UBU home. There is a vulture-puppet on a stick (which stays on stage for much of the action, as it is the source of the axioms which will emerge on the projection screen throughout). The vulture is the only mechanically-operated puppet in the production. It functions as a detached commentator, rather like a chorus. There is also a small column upon which a witness-puppet is making a pot of soup. As PA UBU strides on stage, he kicks over the soup-maker, with no evident sense of what it is that he has done. The puppet drops, and is carried off by one of the two puppeteers. The other puppeteer is transformed into MA UBU, who proceeds with the scene. PA UBU strikes a pose, holding his injured foot, as if he has stubbed it on a stone.

PA UBU Pschitt!!

MA UBU Oooh! What a nasty word. Pa Ubu, you're a dirty old man.

(MA UBU and PA UBU begin a dance-like chase: they alternately pursue each other, snarling with rage, then are triggered into dance poses and smiling freezes. After several such moments, MA UBU and PA UBU flounce away from each other, begin a fight-dance.)

Act One: 3

At the back of the stage is a large projection screen. Images of various kinds are projected onto this surface, and the performers at times interact with and at times seem oblivious of the visual field which is behind them. In the opening sequence, several of the major motifs are introduced: the UBU mannekin, the camera tripod, and the all-seeing eye. The first credits appear on the projection screen.

Act One: 4

PA UBU (*holding his foot, which has been hurt by the kick*) And bugger, and damn! Our favourite foot has taken a mortal blow, because our wife cannot keep the house clean. I am dying!

MA UBU Your trotters can't kill you, unless that's where you keep your brains!

PA UBU Madam, we do not spend all day taking care of the affairs of state, to be insulted in our own castle!

MA UBU You shouldn't worry about the affairs of state, but the state of your affairs!

PA UBU And what, you old cow, do you mean by that?

MA UBU Just this – if you spend another night with your bitches, you can sleep in the shed with your dogs!

PA UBU We are offended by your accusations, Mother.

MA UBU And I am offended by your nocturnal activities, which have addled your brain, so that you see no further than your nose.

PA UBU By my green candle . . .

MA UBU Which is a miserable little organ, as I know.

PA UBU Ma, you go too far. I will bash your head in and never say sorry.

MA UBU I go too far? Let's go one step further. Where were you last night?

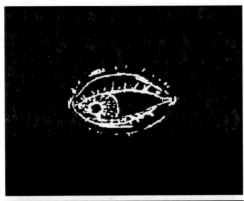

Figure 1 Animation fragment: eye/camera motif. *Ubu and the Truth Commission*, directed by William Kentridge, 1997. Artist: William Kentridge.

PA UBU Madam, we were busy with our business. The precise nature of our – undertaking – is classified.

MA UBU Pooh, as to that! The signs of your lust have given you away. I've seen the red on your collar, and tufts of hair on your sleeve.

PA UBU It is regrettable that our wife has chosen to fix her attentions on the domestic laundry when she would have found a more appropriate activity in tidying our house, so that at our day's end our corpulent self could enter at ease,

instead of stumbling over the furniture. We demand that you take more care over securing a safe passage for our nimble self.

MA UBU Pfarrt and Pshitt! Keep your secrets, then. But if you come back to me with the smell of your women upon you, I'll find you out, do you hear me! And when I find you out, I'll cut you out and throw you out.

PA UBU Damn you, Madam. We will not be accused by you!

MA UBU Who has more right to accuse than I?

PA UBU Question dismissed! Next!

MA UBU Who do you see each night?

PA UBU Question dismissed! Next!

MA UBU Who owns your heart?

(*Lights out.* MA UBU *exits. Lights up.* PA UBU *is standing alone.*)

PA UBU (*To himself, facing the audience, smelling into the palm of his hands, a look of horror and disgust. Pause. Collects himself.* PA UBU *sweeps up the vegetables which were scattered across the stage by his kick.*) My good lady wife would not complain if she understood the work that takes me out at night. Once I was an agent of the state, and had agency and stature. The country's money was in my safe-keeping, as I had blown up the safe and its keeper. I administered the funds to myself, to save the nation the burden of doing so. Now, after my years of loyal service, I find myself cast aside without thanks. My enemies are everywhere, and we therefore have to cover our back while at the same time protecting our strumpot, so that we are always defended.

(*The vulture puppet on a stick squawks, and the first vulture text appears on the screen:* **After the third fire on the roof, keep a bucket on the stairs.**)

Act One: 5

A table is wheeled on stage, with BRUTUS, *the three-headed dog. The dog enters, sniffs the air, begins howling.* PA UBU *enters.*

PA UBU Shut up, you pack of lies, or I'll split you end to end and feed you to Ma's kitty. Holy sherbert! How is a man to maintain his dignity if he cannot even control his dogs?

(*The dogs rub affectionately against* PA UBU.)

HEAD ONE   (*panting with excitement*) So, boss, where to tonight, boss? What's in it for us? Some little bone, eh? A tiny cartilaginous morsel, still fragrant and warm?

HEAD TWO   As for me, I'm of another breed: I don't want to bite, but I do long to lead.

HEAD THREE   While these brutes can carry out raids for the nation, diplomacy needs more informed conversation. What secret, special and covert activities are to be executed tonight? We only need to know, so that we know what to deny.

PA UBU   We will tell you what you need to know. Remember, we are the tail that wags the dog.

DOGS   (*together*) Right, captain. You're the boss. We're your creature.

(*At this point* PA UBU *and the dogs sing a scat quartet together.*)

PA UBU

Not any old dog is a man's best friend
Who'd service and obey as I intend.
To get what I need
I selectively breed
'Til his parts make the whole in a singular blend.

With razor-like teeth and with steel-sprung jaw
I've found myself a weapon that evades the law.
He'll attack when he's told
And submit when I scold
For I've now made a pet of the dogs-of-war.

DOGS

Not any old dog is a man's best friend
Who'd service and obey as he'd intend.
To get what he needs
He selectively breeds
'Til our parts make the whole in a singular blend.

With razor-like teeth and with steel-sprung jaw
We now provide a weapon that evades the law.
We'll attack when we're told
And submit should he scold
For we're old Pa Ubu's dogs-of-war.

PA UBU   Okay, enough of that. Come on boys.

(PA UBU *whistles for the dogs as he exits. The whistle should be distinctive, a four or five note whistle. This whistle will recur throughout the play, at points at which the audience should be reminded of the dogs' activities in the world. The whistle will thus serve as a kind of 'leitmotif', signalling a collaboration between* PA UBU *and his dogs. On the screen, we see images suggesting the dogs' evening walk. As they stop looking for direction, he speaks into an imaginary radio transmitter in his underpants.*)

PA UBU   Hello? Ja Generaal. Ja, Generaal. Nee, seker nie. Alles is in order. Presies, ja. Ja Generaal. Over and out.

(*They continue until they reach their destination at which point we hear an explosion.*)

Act One: 6

Back home in the UBU *household.* MA UBU *is brought on stage, in her armchair. On screen is the caption:* **Ma Ubu Dreams of Love and Money**. *She engages in a solo tap dance full of fantasies of unattained riches and adoration.*

MA UBU *collapses exhausted onto her armchair. A moment or two of silence. Then off-stage sounds of barking; noises off as* PA UBU *returns home: key in lock, etc.*

PA UBU *switches on a light. He is to one side of the stage, in the glass booth which is used as a shower.* MA UBU *lies in her armchair. A soft spotlight comes on, to show* PA UBU *in the shower.*

MA UBU   Is that you, Pa? PAAA? (*Her voice in the background while* PA UBU *showers.*) Washing, washing, washing. Every night it's the same. You come back home, used up and tired. And I must say nothing. What is it, Pa Ubu, that you wash away?

CAPTION ON SCREEN   **The Smell of Blood and Dynamite**

MA UBU   It's sex, isn't it? It's sex.

(*Drawings of* PA UBU*'s fantasies appear on the screen.* PA UBU *sings 'Hier's ek weer'. As he emerges from the shower,* MA UBU *pursues him.*)

MA UBU   Just because I've stood it till now doesn't mean I will take it for ever, you know! I'm telling you, I'll make you pay!

Act Two: 1

Sound of someone tapping a live microphone. Overhead, a voice speaks.

VOICE OF TRC   Can you hear my voice clearly? Good. Can you hear the translator?

(Puppeteer enters with witness puppet and microphone. To the left, MA UBU *as translator in the booth, also with microphone.)*

CAPTION ON SCREEN   **A Bath**. This quickly morphs to **A Bloodbath**

WITNESS

Queenstown yajika yaba yindawo yemfazwe.
Queenstown became a battleground.

Amapolisa ayenyuka esehla ezintratweni bedubula wonke umntu.
The police drove up and down the streets, shooting at anyone and everyone.

Wathi akungabuyi unyana wam, kwathwa mandiyokumbuza kwi mortuary polisa.
When my son didn't come home, they said I should ask at the police mortuary.

Kulapho kwafuneka ndifanise isidumbu sonyanam.
It was there that I had to identify my son.

Zazininzi izidumbu, zibaxakile.
There were so many bodies, they couldn't cope.

Salinda phambi kwe mortuary, uthotho lwegazi lwalubaleka lusuka phantsi komnyango, luvale idrain engaphandle.
We waited in front of the mortuary – a thick stream of blood was running from under the door – blocking the outside drain.

Ngaphakathi, ivumba lalilibi.
Inside, the smell was terrible.

Izidumbu zipakene esinye phezu kwesinye.
Bodies were stacked upon each other.

Igazi lalise lijike laba luhlaza.
The blood was already turning green.

Ndazixelela ukuba, noba bangabe benzentoni emntaneni wam, ndizakumbona ngophawu esilvini.
I said to myself, no matter what they have done to my child, I can identify him because of the mark on his chin.

Ndaya e mortuary.
I went to the morgue.

Ndambona apho umntwanam.
There I saw my child.

Ndalubona uphawu esilevini.
I saw the mark on his chin.

Kodwa ndathi kubo, hayi, asingomntwana wam lo.
But I said to them, this is not my child.

Asingomntwana wam lo.
This is not my child.

Asingomntwana wam lo.
This is not my child.

Act Two: 2

Dim lighting. PA UBU *is wheeled in behind the table. He is drinking. On screen, animation of a radio which keeps on transmogrifying into a cat. The cat-radio taunts* PA UBU. PA UBU *cowers under a large chair. His backside projects out from under the chair.* MA UBU *enters, carrying her handbag, which is also a puppet of a crocodile.*

MA UBU   What's going on here, in the dark? *(She switches on the lights.)*

CAPTION ON SCREEN   **The Light of Truth**

(She places the bag down on the table, places PA UBU*'s bottle and glass in the bag.* MA UBU *notices* PA UBU *under the chair.)*

MA UBU   Pa, I see your rump under the chair. Get out here at once, or I'll brand your beef.

PA UBU   Go away, whoever you are. There's no-one here but us rats.

MA UBU   *(to audience)* It may be a rat, but it has only two legs! *(To* PA UBU*)* Very well, then, but first let me catch my breath. *(Sits on chair above* PA UBU*.)*

PA UBU   Shittabugger, what a stench down here. A man could die of it. MA! Get up or you'll murder your husband.

MA UBU   Could it be – my gracious lord and noble master – his arse like a turnip half underground?

PA UBU   We were checking to determine whether the rotation of the earth's axis had produced an incline of the perpendicular to the horizontal. For the scrutiny of which, we had to prostrate ourselves, as you see.

MA UBU   Did you say, castrate yourself, you

great booby? What is this feeble display of cowardice? Did I give up my life for this? Get up, you fool.

PA UBU *(clambering out, blubbering with fear)* SSSHHHH! Not a word. Don't tell them I'm here. O my poor head. I'll lose my ears. I used to be fearless, but soon I'll be earless!

MA UBU   It's not your ears I'll cut off! Don't flatter yourself, Pa. If some woman's husband is coming to get you, he can have you. (MA UBU *storms out in a fury.* PA UBU *falls on his knees, and prays.*)

PA UBU

O the blood, O the blood,
O the blood of the lamb sets me free,
Send a flood, send a flood,
Send your blood like a flood over me.

(*While* PA UBU *is on his knees,* NILES, *the crocodile puppet, comes to life.*)

NILES   Ah, Captain, you seem to be in something of a lather. What's up? Another fight with Ma?

PA UBU   Oh, Niles, such a vision I had. I saw the Great Truth approaching, a rope in its hand. It demanded I speak of the truth of our land.

NILES   Well, as I understand things, you have a choice. You can take your chances, keep silent, and wait to see if the law comes after you. But once they have unmasked you, you'll have to face the music. My advice would be to pre-empt it all. I hear there is to be a Commission to determine Truths, Distortions and Proportions.

PA UBU   I've heard of Truths, and know Distortions, but what are these Proportions you talk about?

NILES   An inquiry is to be conducted by great and blameless men who measure what is done, and why, and how.

PA UBU   And just what can these brilliant mathemunitions do?

NILES   They can beyond all ambiguity indicate when a vile act had a political purpose.

PA UBU   And if they so resolve?

NILES   Then they can and must absolve. The righteous have to forgive the unrighteous. It's the way of the world. But a full disclosure is what they demand. If they

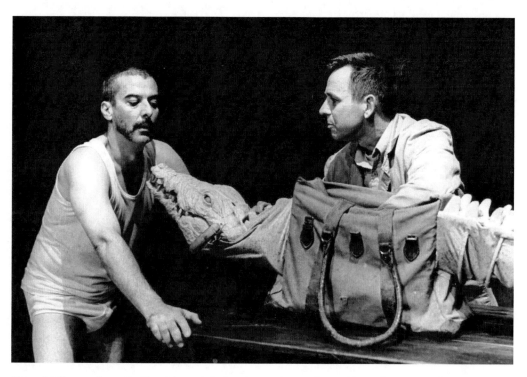

Figure 2 Niles confronts Pa Ubu. *Ubu and the Truth Commission*, directed by William Kentridge, 1997. Photo: Rouphin Coudzer.

should find any dirt under your finger-nails after you have had a complete manicure, they will chop off your hands.

PA UBU So – a full confession?

NILES Quite.

PA UBU Place my own neck in the noose? It is a poor tailor who has to make his own suits. Besides, our Reign of Terror was no Reign of Error. We knew what we did, and still we did it.

NILES All you did was your job. And really, what harm did you do? A little killing here and there never hurt anyone.

PA UBU But if I keep mum, how will they find out? I still have friends in high places.

(*The vulture puppet on a stick squawks, and the following text appears on the screen:* **More killers than saints have dined with princes**.)

NILES I'd advise you, speak before you are spoken to.

PA UBU Never! A man is a man of honour, or a man is not a man.

NILES A man is not a man when his necktie is made of rope.

PA UBU WAAAAH! Save us!

NILES Old Ubu, wait. Let us conduct an experiment after the pattern of the state. (*He picks up two of the oranges.*) These two orbs will measure the man. This, in your right hand, equals your honour, and in your left, it equals your fear. Now weigh your fear and honour in each hand: which has greater weight?

(*Together they mime this weighing.*)

PA UBU It is most sinister. This, here, in my left hand, this fear of mine, it pulls the scale down. The massive and cumbrous burden of our millstone fright makes into airy nothing the counterpose of our valour. Niles, we have thus demonstrated by reason and scientific verification, that WE ARE A COWARD!

(*Partial blackout.* NILES *exits, while* PA UBU *gasps with impotent fear.* MA UBU *enters.*)

Act Two: 3

MA UBU Pa, you great baby! You sound as if you're afraid of your own shadow!

PA UBU Wh – wh – who? wh – wh – what?

MA UBU Father! Pull yourself together.

PA UBU For – for – forgery – forgive me.

MA UBU What is this? Do you truly repent? If you promise, no more women . . .

PA UBU What? Oh, yes, yes. (*Aside*) Our foolish self almost betrayed us. (*To* MA UBU) Forgive me, Ma. I love only you!

CAPTION ON SCREEN **The Consolations of the Flesh**

(*A dance interlude.* MA UBU *comes down from the chair.* PA UBU *seizes her in his arms, and they dance 'langarm'. As they dance in front of the audience during this scene, they each address the audience, holding temporary friezes, while the music volume drops.*)

MA UBU (*to audience*) A woman wants to be wanted. So we take them back. Always, we take them back, but nothing changes.

(*Dancing. Freeze. Music volume drops.*)

PA UBU (*to audience*) I must, above all things, hide my stories from Ma. Who knows how she might react? Thus we must keep our own council. After all, to betray our men is to damn ourself. We can bravely face their exposure, but are a little more circumspect about our own. Therefore a soldier must bite his tongue. Furthermore, we are piously shocked by this confession nonsense. Gallons of blood and then gallons of tears to wash the walls clean.

(PA UBU *dances* MA UBU *off.*)

PA UBU And Ma? She has no idea of what she says, for she has no idea of who I was. We would burn down the world before we would give away our country.

(*An animation sequence on screen, in which a pig's head is blown up by rigged earphones, links this to the next scene.*)

Act Two: 4

The second witness puppet enters, with puppeteer.

WITNESS
Sebakanyana ga tsena mongwe mme a re, ba fisa ngwana wa gago.
Someone came and told me, they are burning your son.

Ka simolola ka matha.
I started to run.

Ke ne ke sa itse kwa ke ne keya teng, ke ne ke matha fela.
I don't know where to, I just ran.

Figure 3 Witness puppet. *Ubu and the Truth Commission*, directed by William Kentridge, 1997. Photo: Rouphin Coudzer.

Ebe e le gore basadi bangwe ba mpiletsa morago.
Then some women called me back.

'Tlaya kwango, ba tsene jaana'.
'Come here, they went this way'.

Ga ke fitlha kwateng ba ne ba motsentse taere mo mmeleng, ba mo tshetse ka petrolo.
When I arrive there they have put a tyre around his body, they've doused him with petrol.

Ba mpha letlhokwana la metshisi le letukang gore ke le lathele kwa go ene.
And they then gave me a burning match to throw onto him.

Ka letlhela letlhokwana kwa morago ga legetla me.
I threw the match over my shoulder.

Ba mpha le lengwe gape mme ba ntse be ntshosa.
They gave me one again and threatened me.

Ka le lathela kwa morago ga legetla la me.
I threw it over my shoulder.

Ke dirile jalo go fitlhela bone ba lathela letlokwana le letukang mo mmeleng wa agwe.
I kept on doing that until they threw a burning match on his body.

A tshwara mollo.
He caught flame.

Ebe e legore ba tshaba.
Then they ran away.

Go ne ga salla nna go lwela bophelo ba gagwe.
And it was left to me to fight for his life.

Ka matha go ya go batla metsi, ga seke ga thusa.
I ran to get water, but it didn't help.

Kelekile go mo gasa ka mmu.
I tried to put soil on him.

35

Mme o ne o semontsi.
But there wasn't enough.

Bofelong ka tima malakabe ka kobo.
Eventually I killed the flames with a blanket.

Ka motshwara.
I hold him.

Mmele othe wa gagwe one o tshele kwa ntle ga nko.
His whole body was burned except his nose.

O ne a nteba.
He looked up at me.

Molomo wa gagwe o bulega – o tswlega.
His mouth opened – and closed.

O bulegwa – o tswalega.
Opened – and closed.

Taaka wa nonyane.
Like a bird's.

Morago matlho a gagwe a fetola mmala.
Then his eyes changed – their colour.

(*Lights out. An animation sequence links this to the following scene.*)

Act Two: 5

The stage is empty, except for the table. A puppet enters. The puppet takes centre-stage, setting up bits and pieces for his Spaza shop in the middle of the table. He has Jik, methylated spirits, as well as various oddments, bottles of lotion. In the background, the sound-track of someone selling street wares sets the mood. The process of setting up shop is slow and deliberate. While this proceeds, MA UBU *and* PA UBU *settle down at the table to eat. They are unaware of the individual presence of the shop-keeper, but become aware of the goods on offer, which they take, gradually and cavalierly, as if all things are available for their own consumption. The shop-keeper throughout is unaware of who steals his belongings, although he is painfully aware of their disappearance. He has a limited arc of vision, so that he never looks at either extreme end of the table, where the* UBUS *sit.* PA UBU *strides in.*

PA UBU FOOD, Madam, FOOOOOOD! Nothing like a bit of fear to fuel a man's appetite. We are so hungry we could eat a nag. What slop have you prepared?

MA UBU (*voice off*) Are your hands clean?

PA UBU (*to audience*) By no means. My carrion acts cling to my digits like gloves. But the feeding of our appetites helps us to forget. (PA UBU *sits down at one end of the table, hammering with his eating utensils.*)

PA UBU (*hammering on table*) MAA – If you keep me hungry, you make me angry. You don't want to see me angry, Mother.

MA UBU (*entering with bowls*) I don't want to see you at all, you ugly rhinoceros.

PA UBU Hippopotamus!

MA UBU Warthog!

PA UBU Jellyfish!

MA UBU Eel!

PA UBU (*tasting food*) Mmmmm, delicious seasoning, <u>our mother</u>.

MA UBU I'm pleased you like it, <u>our father</u>.

(*Pause. During the following dialogue,* MA UBU *and* PA UBU *help themselves to items from the Spaza shop.*)

PA UBU (*eating, muttering aloud*) First thing tomorrow, we'll remove the evidence and blow up his arse.

MA UBU Well, at last! <u>And then you can bury the bones.</u>

PA UBU (*startled, looks up at* MA UBU) What?

MA UBU I said, you can dig over that patch at the back and clear out the stones.

PA UBU Aaaah, of course.

(MA UBU *and* PA UBU *begin to help themselves from the Spaza shop, and eat.* MA UBU *examines the price on one item.*)

MA UBU I see that prices are still rising.

PA UBU What uprising?

MA UBU Today, everything costs an arm and a leg.

PA UBU I had nothing to do with it!

MA UBU Pass me the salt.

PA UBU Who said it was assault?

MA UBU Pa?

(PA UBU *looks up at* MA UBU *as if he doesn't recognize her. She however ignores him, takes some snuff, sneezes.*)

PA UBU It looks like brain.

MA UBU Mmmmm?

PA UBU (*looking absently ahead of him*) It looks like brain.

MA UBU I spend hours, weeks, in the kitchen, and this is all you have to say? It's not fair, Pa! You don't appreciate me.

PA UBU Psshii – shhh, shhh. Now, Ma,

sorry, hey, sorry. Holy sherbert, this is good, really.

MA UBU Thaaank you, Pa. (*She smiles warmly at him.*)

(*Pause.* PA UBU *reaches again for something from the Spaza shop. This time it is a box of poison.*)

PA UBU (*holding up poison*) By my shittabrush! We are beset on every side! Even our wife is trying to poison us. What is this mortal potion doing on our dining table? Let me assure you, madam, you could kill us as easily with your cooking!

MA UBU Pooh, as to that! Who knows how poison finds its way? As they say, the knife finds its own sheath.

PA UBU Silence, baggage! To turn against your husband is treason against the state. Therefore, Ma, we accuse you of treasonous acts, for which the penalty is beheading.

MA UBU Judge not, Pa. And you know why.

PA UBU NOT GUILTY! (PA UBU *collapses, defeated and dejected, after bellowing these words.*)

Act Two: 6

Lights out on stage. We hear PA UBU'*s whistle, over, which is followed by an animation sequence in which* PA UBU, *assisted by his dog, makes up a parcel.* PA UBU *flings the parcel on its way, and the package drifts over a series of map-like details. As we watch, the parcel settles over and over again, now in a house, now in a bar. Each time the parcel comes to rest, it blows up, transforming the original drawing into a blast-site.*

Act Two: 7

Puppeteer enters with witness puppet.

WITNESS

Mapodisa a ne a tla go ntsaya mo ntlong yame.
The police came to fetch me in my house.

Bare ba bone ditopo tsa bana rona, bare ke tsamaye le bone goya go dibona.
They said they had found the bodies of our children, they must take me to see them.

– Ga ke dibona –
When I saw them –

Di ne disena matlho.
They didn't have eyes.

Kajalo ka gopola gore mollo o phantse matlho a bone.
Well, I thought, the fire exploded their eyes out.

Di ne disena golo fa ga tlhogo.
They didn't have this of the head (*indicating the top of the head with her hands, running the hands over the cranium*).

E ne ele fela, ele fela golo fa –
It is just this, this, this part (*She rubs her forehead, above her brows.*)

Fa gone – gone goseyo.
This part (*indicating the top of the head.*) This part wasn't there.

Gape ba ne basena matsogo, ba sena maoto.
And they haven't got hands, they haven't got legs.

(*Puppet exits.*)

Act Two: 8

The scene begins with an animation sequence on the screen and the caption: **The Shadow-Dance**. *The projected shadow is a vast, rotund figure modelled after Jarry's conception of Ubu. The actor playing the role of* PA UBU *responds to the sequence of shadow moves. Finally,* PA UBU *rushes about the stage, retrieving things.*

NILES Grrrreetings, General. Here's a fine commotion. Do I smell the making of a covert operation?

PA UBU Well, Niles, we took your advice under advisement, but have opted for concealing rather than revealing.

NILES Not wise, old man. Some little breadcrumbs always lead the way back home.

PA UBU Then you'll just have to help with cleaning up.

(*As he says this,* PA UBU *grabs* NILES *and begins to stuff documents down his throat. In the intervals, while* PA UBU *retrieves more pieces,* NILES *interjects.*)

NILES What's this I taste?
A bit of skull shattered in pieces,
A pair of hands torn off at the wrists,

Some poisoned scalps shorn of their
     fleeces,
Some half-burned skin injected with cysts.

As they say, *fiat experimentum in corpore
vili*, that is, let experiment be made on a
worthless body. But here are some tougher
bits, not so easily digested.

A piece of tongue that would not be silent,
A beaten back that ignored the ache,
A hand up-raised in gesture defiant,
A blood-red heart that would not break.

Here, Cap'n. These oddments you feed me
are most unsavoury. (*Burps,*) Hello, that bit
tasted familiar.

PA UBU   Eat up, Niles, there's a good boy, or
you'll find yourself attached to a pair of
leather soles. (*Stuffing* NILES *again.*)

NILES   OOOhh – I recognise that. It's given
me quite a lump in my throat. (PA UBU
stuffs NILES.)

NILES   But, I say, I think you've left out one
or two things. What about those meaty bits
in the bottom drawer?

PA UBU   Damn and blast! What do you know
of these matters? (*He dashes over to retrieve
film reels, stuffs them into* NILES.)

NILES   MMMMMmmmm. (*Makes satisfied
noises.*) Delectable! Still, where's the main
course? How about that bag of tricks in
your bedroom?

PA UBU   Shittabugger! (*He dashes off stage,
brings back a bag of crumpled bits and pieces
that he stuffs into* NILES.)

NILES   And the box in the bathroom
cupboard?

PA UBU   Buggerashitt! Information is the
beacon of our enlightenment, but a man is
cursed when his information is turned to
shine on himself. (*He dashes off to retrieve
more, stuffs it into* NILES.)

NILES   Now it's given me heart-burn.
ENOUGH!! Secure the rest 'til later. It's safe
enough for now. OOOoooooh. (*Moaning
with discomfort, he lies down on the floor.
Comments, to the audience, as he lies down.*)
A little knowledge is a dangerous thing. It
is also not wise to know too much. We only
make ourselves safe by knowing all.

(*The vulture puppet on a stick squawks, and
the following text appears on the screen: **It is
enough for the zebra to know about grass**.*
NILES *settles himself to sleep on the table, to
digest his meal. Lights out.*)

Act Three: 1

When the scene opens, MA UBU *is on stage,
alone in her armchair, although* NILES *is lying
asleep on the table.*

MA UBU   Another night alone at home. Is
this a marriage?

(*The vulture puppet on a stick squawks,
and the following text appears on the
screen: **The game warder's wife wears a
fur collar**.*)

MA UBU   Every night out with his dogs.
No-one to dinner, and no invitations. It
isn't normal. Old Ubu, what of the balls and
concerts we used to know? Those were
heroic days, so cosmopolitan. Now I sit in
the silent darkness, and wait for his return.
If I could only find some proof of Pa's
whoring, I'd take him to court and grind 'til
his pockets bled gold. (MA UBU *climbs off
the armchair. She begins to search about the
room.*) Where will I find the charms and
letters? (*She begins to exit. At this point,*
NILES, *who is still sleeping on the bed, whines
in his sleep, moves a bit, whimpers. This
catches* MA UBU'*s attention.*) And what gives
you uneasy dreams and such a full belly?
Here my lovely, come to Mama. (*She draws
NILES toward her, against her breasts.*)

NILES   Here, watch your fingers, old girl.

MA UBU   But Niles, I only want to see what
lies he's been feeding you.

NILES   Well, perhaps in the scheme of things,
you're one of the ones who Needs to Know.

Act Three: 2

MA UBU *opens* NILES' *handles, tipping out
the contents that* PA UBU *had stuffed into him.
A stack of crumpled papers and rags comes out
of him. These are all bits and pieces of evidence,
document of* PA UBU'*s political-criminal
activities. As* MA UBU *spreads these out, piece
by piece, images fill the screen and sounds fill
the auditorium. At two distinct points in this
sequence,* PA UBU *emerges on stage to
participate in the revelation. He speaks in
Afrikaans, while* MA UBU *translates his words
into English.*

PA UBU   (*as perpetrator*) **Ons het dit
'tubing' genoem.**

MA UBU   We called it 'tubing'.

**Ons vat 'n binneband en trek dit oor
die gesig van die gevangene.**

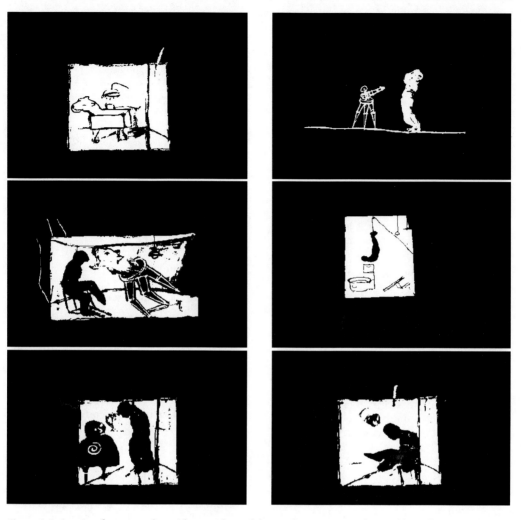

Figure 4 Animation fragment: the evidence. *Ubu and the Truth Commission*, directed by William Kentridge, 1997. Artist: William Kentridge.

We would take an inner tube, and put it over the face of the detainee.

Ons sny 'n spleet in die binneband vir die tong.
We cut a slit in the tube for the tongue.

Dis hoe ons die waarheid kry.
This is how we got the truth.

Ons wurg hom, totdat hy iets het om to vertel.
We would suffocate him, until he had something to tell us.

Aan die lengte van die tong kan ons aflei hoe naby hy aan versmoring is.

From the length of the tongue we could tell how close he was to asphyxiation.

Ook as sy broek nat word, dan weet jy hy staan by die Pearly Gates.
Also, when he wet his pants, you knew he was standing at the Pearly Gates.

As hulle nog steeds weier om te praat
If they still refused to talk

Het ons hulle doodgeslaan met ysterpype wat in die plaasstoor gele het.
We beat them to death with iron pipes which we found in the farmhouse.

Dit het ons in Cradock gedoen.
This we did in Cradock.

(*Finally,* PA UBU *makes the following statement in English.*)

PA UBU   They put the makarov pistol to the top of his head and pulled the trigger. The gun jammed. We got another gun from one of the askaris. That didn't work either, so in the end we beat him to death with a spade. Then we each grabbed a hand and a foot, and put the body on the pyre of tyre and wood, poured petrol on it, and set it alight. Now of course, the burning of a body to ashes takes about seven hours; it is – ah – and – ah – whilst that happened we were drinking and even having a braai next to the fire.

(*At the end of the sequence of evidence, we return to* MA UBU.)

MA UBU   (*weeping*) The sly old jackal. I had no idea Pa was so important! All along, I thought he was betraying me and here he was, hard at work, protecting me from the Swart Gevaar. (*Wipes her eyes sentimentally. Change of mood.*) Still, this is my chance. A girl can't be too careful! Who can she turn to once her charms begin to fade? While the overstuffed dummy is out of the way, I will seize this little stash of daring tales and sell them, to secure my old age, which is of course a long way off.

(*She grabs her handbag by the handles and exits. Lights out.*)

Act Four: 1

PA UBU *enters.*

PA UBU   MAAAAA! We are thirsty. (*Silence.*)
PA UBU   MAAAAA! We are hungry. (*Silence.*)
PA UBU   MAAAAA! We are being ignored!! (*Silence.*)
PA UBU   Now where is the woman? She knows she's not allowed to go out when I might want her. Ma? . . . Mama? . . . Little Mommy? Boo hoo. We are abandoned, orphaned at the tender age of forty-seven. All alone. WE ARE ALONE. Only the empty arms of the night around us. Night night. Mama, come home.

(PA UBU *curls up in a foetal position. He takes out his music box which, as he turns the handle, plays 'Nkosi Sikelel'iAfrika'. As* PA UBU *goes to sleep, he dreams.*)

Act Four: 2

While he sleeps, PA UBU *has tormented dreams. These are suggested through animation on screen. A small tripod figure dances above* PA UBU's *head, stabbing at him with its spiked limbs. The puppet, who had a Spaza shop at the* UBU *dining-table, appears and takes up his position standing behind the body of the sleeping* PA UBU. *He presents the following testimony:*

CAPTION ON SCREEN   A Scholar's Tale
WITNESS
Lomlungu wesikhafu esibomuu, wadubula lomntwana ngompu.
This white man with a red scarf, he shot at the child with his rifle.

Ndambona eruqa umntwana wam u Scholar.
I saw him dragging my child, Scholar.

U Scholar wayeseswekekile.
Scholar was already dead.

Wayemtsala ngemilenze njengenja njengenja ecunyuzwe endleleni.
He was dragging him by the legs, like a dog, like a dog that is crushed in the road.

Ndambona esimba umgodi wokufaka ubuchopo buka Scholar.
I saw him digging a hole – for Scholar's brains –

Ilanga lalithe nka kodwa suke kwabamnyama xa ndimbona elele apho eli linxeba elingasoze liphele.
The sun was bright but it went dark when I saw him lying there. It's an everlasting pain.

Andiqondi ukuba iyakuze iphele entliziyweni yam.
I do not think that it will ever stop in my heart.

Babephethe abantu okwe zilwanyana yiyo lento endenza ndikhale kungoku,
They were treating people like animals . . . that's what makes me cry right now,

nokuba sekuyinja, awuyibulali ngoluhlob,
. . . even a dog . . . you don't kill it like that,

noba yimbovane, inmobane encinci,
even an ant, a small little ant,

uba novelwano ngembovane,
you have feelings for an ant,

kodwa ngoku, abantwana bethu, babengathathwa nanjengembovane.
but now, our children, they were not even taken as ants.

(PA UBU *writhes as he sleeps. Finally, he wakes up, and stares before him.*)

Act Four: 3

PA UBU *wakes from his dream to see* MA UBU's *head, vast and disembodied, in an animation on the screen. She is in mid-interview, as if on a giant TV screen.*

SCREEN MA (*to TV interviewer*) Oh no. He was very polite, and such a good dancer. We called him the Nijinsky of Nylstroom.

PA UBU What the bloody hell's going on here?

SCREEN MA Mind you, he wasn't a homo, if you know what I mean.

PA UBU Who said I was?

SCREEN MA Always over weekends, he'd go fishing with the guys. He was a man's man. Although he was also a bit of a lady's man.

PA UBU What do you think you're saying?

SCREEN MA (*She frowns down at him, irritated.*) He was proud, you know, took care of himself.

PA UBU Old sow, what are you doing?

SCREEN MA (*ignoring him*) He had a creative side, too. Always doing things with his hands.

PA UBU Thula, phela khula! (MA UBU *notices* PA UBU. *He tries to turn her off with the remote control for the TV.*)

SCREEN MA (*to TV interviewer*) He spoke Xhosa before he spoke English. He could always communicate with the garden boys. Oooh, how he loved the weight of a spade in his hand.

PA UBU Wait a bit – where's this going now? Mother, we will debrain you, if you don't stop babbling. And if we can't find your brain, we will cut your head off.

SCREEN MA His favourite meal? (*She hums, trying to recollect.*)

PA UBU Meat, you old cow.

SCREEN MA (*as if recollecting*) It was meat – he always liked his meat. A nice steak, with a monkey-gland sauce. He liked to drink –

PA UBU I'm no bloody alcoholic!

SCREEN MA – but I never saw him drunk.

PA UBU HEY!

SCREEN MA He could hold his liquor.

PA UBU HEY! – Hey, hey, hey!!!!

SCREEN MA (*aside to* PA UBU) Hey! Ndidikwe yilembaxo uyenzayo wena, kunini uphoxana phakathi kwabantu![1] (*To TV interviewer*) If he has a fault, I'd have to say that he is too loyal.

PA UBU What would you know about loyalty, you traitor!

SCREEN MA (*aside, to* PA UBU) Yintoni ozokuyenza olokuqala nje, ufunantoni apha?[2] (*To TV interviewer*) When I discovered what he had been doing all these years, you could have knocked me down with a feather.

PA UBU What are you talking about?

SCREEN MA I have maps, and plans, and names, important names.

PA UBU Madam! Those are official secrets.

SCREEN MA And cheque books, and films, and tapes, and so many things. He knew everyone.

PA UBU If I go down, you do down with me!

SCREEN MA (*screaming at* PA UBU) Kutheni lento uzokuphoxisa ngam phakathi kwabantu abaninzi kangaka? Uyaintoyokuba, mna, njengoba ndilapha nje ndize ngenxa yoba ndizokwenza umabonakude. Ngoku uzokuphoxisa ngam phakathi abazinzi kangaka. Yhu! Uqaqadekile yaz'ba uqaqadekile. Yaz'ba bendingakwazi uba uqatsele kangaka. Yhu! Awusoze undiphoxe mna andiphoxakali kalulu. Ukrwada into oqale ngayo. Ufuzile ufuz'unyoko ngobukrwada obungaka.[3]

PA UBU (*screaming at* MA UBU) Jou dom ding – wat die vok doen jy? Jy het ons al twee vermoor – weet jy nie wat angaan nie? Wie die donner dink jy is ek? Ek gaan jou slaan teen die muur totdat jou tande uitval, jou blerrie stuk biltong. Kom, kom. Ek sal vir jou wys, wat is 'n man! Kom! Jou Ma se gat![4]

SCREEN MA (*back to TV interviewer*) No, we haven't actually signed any contracts yet, but we've got some things in the pipeline.

(*At this point,* PA UBU *mutes* MA UBU *on screen with the TV remote.*)

PA UBU I can't believe it. I know that we should be sceptical of phenomena witnessed in the televisual media – but Ma (*gesturing toward the screen*) – she's turned us in! Sold us out! Buggered us up! Struck us down. There she is, selling our secrets to the highest bidder. You stupid cuttlefish!

Just wait 'til I get you back home!
Remember the sjambok, Ma.

Act Four: 4

*Toyi-toying music is heard in the background.
The large* PA UBU *shadow figure enters.*

PA UBU W – w – who's there?

SHADOW We've met before.
In times of war.

PA UBU Oh, it's you again.

SHADOW I'm here with some advice. Would
it be correct to say, that at present you've
considered only two options: conceal or
reveal?

PA UBU How economically expressed.

SHADOW I have another suggestion: shift
the burden of guilt. Take the initiative; find
a name, and remove yourself from all trace
of blame. Extract yourself from the plot of
your own history.

PA UBU We have nothing to be ashamed of.
We were only doing our job!

(*A puppeteer enters with a witness puppet.*)

WITNESS

**Indlela abambulala ngayo unyana
wam, bemntitha edongeni, saza
samfumana enentloko edumbileyo,**
The way they killed my son, hitting him
against a wall, and we found him with a
swollen head,

**bambulala ngolunya andiqondi ukuba
ndingaze ndixole kwelityala,**
they killed him in a tragic manner and I
don't think I'll ever forgive, in this case,

**ngakumbi lamapolisa enza lento nala
ayekhona.**
especially the police who were involved
and who were there.

**Andiqondi ukuba noba ndingabekwa
ukuba ndibe ngumsebenzi
emakhitshini ukuba ndingadlisa
ityhefu abantwana babelungu.**
I wouldn't think anything, if ever I was to
be brought as a maid, if I were to poison
these white men's children.

PA UBU It wasn't personal. It was war!

(*This puppet exits. Another enters.*)

WITNESS

**Ba ne sa utlwisa bonna jwa me
botlhoko ka motlakase.**
They electrocuted my private parts.

**Mongwe wa bona o ne a gotetsa
motlakatse.**
The one switched on the switch.

**O mongwe o ne a gatelletse go botsa
'A oa batla go re bolella gore Edwin a
kae?'**
The other one kept on asking, 'Do you
want to tell us where Edwin is?'

**Kgapetsa kgapetsa ke ne ke babollela
gore ga ke itse kwa a leng teng.**
I kept on telling them I didn't know where
he was.

**O mongwe o ne a tshwere bontlha
bongwe ba toulo mme o mongwe a
tshwere bo bongwe.**
They also strangled me with a towel.

Bobedi ba bone ba e goga ka thata.
The one was holding one end of the towel,
the other was holding the other end, and
each one was pulling.

**Ke a itse gore ke bo mang banna ba
badirileng se mo gonna.**
I know who these men are who did this to
me.

PA UBU (*shouting at the puppet*)
Communists!!!

SHADOW These voices will be heard. Ignore
me at your peril.

(*The* SHADOW *disappears.* PA UBU *is left
alone. There should be a momentary sense of
his bewilderment. Then he recovers himself.*)

PA UBU Perhaps the old man had a point
after all. I begin to feel the pitchfork
prodding my arse.

Act Four: 5

PA UBU *picks up his lavatory brush, looks into
it as a mirror. He scrutinizes his face; squeezes
pimples. This triggers a sequence of animations
on screen, which coincide with* PA UBU *on stage
decoding his own body, using the toilet-brush as
a kind of Geiger counter.* PA UBU *clears his
throat, straightens an invisible tie, poses,
rehearses as if preparing to make a formal
statement.*

PA UBU There's one thing that I will have to
live with until the day I die – it's the
corpses that I have to drag with me to my
grave, of the people I have killed. Remorse,
I can assure you, a lot, a hell of a lot. (*He
looks up.*) Now that we have seen what we
are made of, it seems that we have very
few options. We will have to get Brutus to

Figure 5 Pa Ubu implicates Brutus. *Ubu and the Truth Commission,* directed by William Kentridge, 1997. Photo: Rouphin Coudzer.

join our submission; then we'll blame all on politics and beguile the Commission.

(*The vulture puppet on a stick squawks, and the following text appears on the screen: **High tide may vary, but low tide finds its mark**.*)

PA UBU   Here Brutus! Here boys. (*He whistles* PA UBU'*s whistle. The dogs come lolloping onto the stage.*)

HEAD ONE   How can we serve?
HEAD TWO   How may we flatter?
HEAD THREE   Who's head is wanted on a platter?
PA UBU   Boys, you'll have to clean up your act – we're going into show business.

(*The dogs begin to snarl.*)

HEAD ONE   Not so fast, old Ubu. It occurs to me that what you have in mind is the 'show-and-tell' business.
HEAD TWO   We hate to disagree with you, boss, but we've discussed this option, and have decided that we're better off biting our tongues.
HEAD THREE   After all, what's there to link us with any of it? Not a paw-print anywhere.

HEAD TWO   They don't have a single bone to pick with us.

(*At this quip, the dogs laugh inanely together.*)

HEAD ONE   We respectfully advise you to follow us, master. A split in our ranks could hasten disaster.
HEAD TWO   We'd deeply regret any signs of dissent.
HEAD THREE   A collusion of silence is our joint intent.
HEAD TWO   That's it! Keep quiet, lie low, and in a year or two we'll all have our old jobs back.
PA UBU   Yes, yes. No doubt you're right. We must all stick together.

(*At this point* PA UBU *and the dogs break into a song routine.*)

PA UBU   Old Brutus here has said it's one for all
CHORUS OF HEADS   It's one for all
PA UBU   He'd persuade me that we stand as one or fall
CHORUS   Until we fall
PA UBU   A pact of silence these three dogs and I now jointly share

CHORUS   The joints we share

PA UBU   Our acts of violence are too awful for us to declare

CHORUS   The awful we declare

PA UBU   We claim extenuation from post-traumatic stress disorder

CHORUS   We stress disorder

PA UBU   We'll avoid the pious call, as we've put Tu and Tu together

CHORUS   Tu Tu Tu Tu

PA UBU   The Archbishop's plans may promise rainbows, but for us it's heavy weather.

CHORUS   Tu Tu Tu Tu.

(*An idea dawns. While the dogs sing a jazz routine,* PA UBU *tiptoes out, returns with documents. As the dogs finish their song, they fall asleep.* PA UBU *gingerly opens* BRUTUS's *suitcase belly, fills the belly with the evidence.*)

PA UBU   (*front of stage*) Good, we've hopefully muzzled our dogs. Now to cover them in dirt before we send them to the cleaners. (PA UBU *goes to a drawer and takes out his old photograph album. He begins to page through it, rearranging images.* PA UBU *sneaks off stage. On the screen, the image of the three dog-bowls with neck-cuffs, sounds of the dogs howling.*)

Act Five: 1

In the following scene, we have the sentencing of BRUTUS.

JUDGE: In the matter of the state versus Brutus, Brutus, and Brutus: it has been determined that there is unequal culpability, and we thus hand down, separately, three distinct sentences.

With regard to the first case: a head of political affairs cannot always foresee how his vision will be implemented. We thus exonerate you, and retire you with full pension.

With regard to the head of the military: there is no evidence to link you directly to these barbarous acts. Nonetheless, an example must be made of you, or who knows where we'll end up. You are thus sentenced to thirty years in the leadership of the new state army.

Finally, to the dog who allowed himself to become the agent of these ghastly deeds: you have been identified by the families of victims; you have left traces of your activities everywhere. We thus sentence you to two hundred and twelve years imprisonment.

(*As the sentences are handed down, the dogs react.*)

HEAD THREE   This judgement is a sham.

HEAD TWO   We're all being tarred with the same brush.

HEAD THREE   Amnesty! We appeal for amnesty! Let us come before the Truth Commission. We have other stories to tell!

HEADS TWO and THREE   Yes, we have stories, oooh, what we could tell you! Let us speak!

(*Lights out. On screen, we see a drawing of prison bars.* BRUTUS *remains on stage, the bars on screen behind him.*)

Act Five: 2

PA UBU *enters. He addresses the audience.*

PA UBU   A good lawyer can be a skeleton key, but it seems that Brutus's judge was a deadbolt who would lock him away forever. We can't say we blame him for looking for amnesty. But the truth is, some of his stories might cast us as lead. Our only solution is to cast him in lead.

(*There is the clanging of metal doors and the sounds of footsteps approaching. It is evident that we are in the prison. As* PA UBU *approaches, the dogs start sniffing.*)

CAPTION ON SCREEN   **The Smell of Blood and Dynamite**

HEAD ONE   I know that smell!

(PA UBU *enters. The dogs whimper and whine at his arrival.* PA UBU *makes hushing gestures. He leads the dogs off.*)

PA UBU   (*to audience*) As my father always said, if you want something done properly, you've got to do it yourself. And clean up afterwards.

(*Lights off on stage. Image of hanged dogs on screen.*)

Act Five: 3

On screen, images of tripod-figures rushing back and forth. MA UBU *enters. She struts into centre stage, waving her hand to invisible crowds. At*

Figure 6 Animation fragment: the hanging of Brutus. *Ubu and the Truth Commission*, directed by William Kentridge, 1997. Artist: William Kentridge.

the same time, PA UBU *strides purposefully onto the stage, a file of papers under his arm. They bump into each other at centre stage.*

MA UBU Oh! ahhh – umm. Good Day, Pa.

PA UBU She greets me! The two-faced sow greets me! (*Murderously, under his breath*) Curse you, Madam, for your betrayal. A wife is such a nuisance that we resolve never to marry. Only now it's too late, because we are already married, and thus you have made a liar of us and we are entitled to bash you.

MA UBU What are you going on about, you great bladder?

PA UBU You've stolen our best defence, which was the record of our offence. We have nothing left to bargain with.

MA UBU But Pa, I did it for us.

PA UBU Do you think we were born yesterday? You did it for yourself. My father always said never trust a woman unless you can fill her purse.

MA UBU He wasn't talking about money, Pa! But what do you know of a woman's needs?

PA UBU We know they need to be beaten and then scrambled.

MA UBU No, stinkpot, not any more. I won't take it. No more threats. I have too much on you.

PA UBU Not as much as you might think, Ma. It's a question of who you know, not just of who we knew. We've washed our hands so clean, they're almost spotless.

VOICE OVER MICROPHONE Will the next witness to testify please come forward. Mister . . . Ubu?

Act Five: 4

CAPTION ON SCREEN **Ubu Tells The Truth**
PA UBU *steps up to the podium. He taps one of the microphones: hollow echoing tapping noise, feedback.* PA UBU *steps forward to speak. A spotlight comes up on him.*

PA UBU I stand before you with neither shame nor arrogance. I am not a monster. I am an honest citizen, and would never break the law. Like all of you, I eat, and sleep, and dream dreams. These vile stories, they sicken me. When I am told of what happened here, I cannot believe it. These things, they were done by those above me; those below me; those beside me. I too have been betrayed! I knew nothing.

(*There is a shift in performance style here, which is marked also by the shift from 'I' back to 'we' in* PA UBU*'s speech. At the same time, the microphones, which are puppets controlled from below the podium, begin to move about, taunting and mocking* PA UBU, *avoiding his grasp.*)

PA UBU I love my family. But their future was being stolen from them. Our destiny used to be in our own hands. Then the international conspiracies against us cut off our arms. Where could we go, we other Africans? Our children became the servants of servants, with their bowing, and vowing, and scraping, and it was left to our corpulent self to do the whipping, and stripping, and raping. Such loyalty is no longer fashionable, except in some smaller countries. But how is an army to survive if it will not reward in public what it knows is done in secret? I tell you, I served in bloody . . . I served in bloody . . . I served in bloody good units. And I'm proud to have served with them. Soldiering is not a selfish profession, as a true soldier is prepared to lay down his life for his fellow citizens and for his country. THIS IS MY COUNTRY. And I won't give it away without a damn good fight.

(PA UBU *finally, in frustration, seizes a microphone in his hand. He now makes a very still and formal statement, the one which we have heard him rehearse earlier.*)

PA UBU   There's only one thing I will have to live with until the day I die – it's the corpses that I will have to drag with me to my grave, of the people I have killed. Remorse, I can assure you, a lot, a hell of a lot.

(PA UBU *sings his hymn. The screen is filled with images of archival film documenting a spontaneous public celebration following the unbanning of the African National Congress.*)

How dark is my day at noon, Oh God,
How unjust the sins that I bear
Despite all the dangerous paths that I trod
To save my own people despair.
CHORUS
O the blood, O the blood,
O the blood of the lamb sets me free
Send a flood, send a flood
Send your blood like a flood over me.
PA UBU
And then I recall another dark day
When you hung on the arms of the cross,
You carried all our vile deeds away
And burned up our past sins as dross.
CHORUS
O the blood, O the blood,
O the blood of the lamb sets me free
Send a flood, send a flood
Send your blood like a flood over me.

(*Throughout the hymn, there are images from the evidence sequence on screen. As his hymn concludes, the full-bodied voice of a massed chorus singing 'Nkosi' swells and fills the auditorium, and crowds are projected on the screen.* PA UBU *finally freezes, unable to compete with the masses projected around him in image and song. He is wheeled off stage on his lectern, as if he is a statue being removed. Lights out.*)

Act Five: 5

MA UBU *and* PA UBU *on a boat. The vulture is with them, as is* MA UBU*'s kitty.*

MA UBU   What a lovely breeze!
PA UBU   We are moving at an almost miraculous speed. I say, our mother, the wind is rather refreshing. I hope we don't capsize!
MA UBU   (*doing nothing*) Hoist the mainsail. Man the jib.
PA UBU   (*doing nothing*) Close haul the mizzen mast.
MA UBU   See, Pa, how well we can manage if we just stick together. How much further is it?
PA UBU   (*looking down a telescope*) By my computations, about half an hour. Not much more, anyway, than two or three days; ten months at the absolute outside.
MA UBU   I say, Pa, what's that bobbing in the water?

(*At this,* NILES *swims into view, following the boat.*)

NILES   Ahoy there, Captain, what a fine day. Looks like there'll be plain sailing ahead. Would there be room for me on board?
PA UBU   Niles! Old friend! How unlikely to see you here, in the Sargasso. Climb in!

(NILES *clambers aboard.*)

PA UBU   Well now, this is more like it. Three's a Company . . .
NILES   As old Brutus always used to say.
PA UBU   Er, yes, well, quite.
MA UBU   I'm going to miss all the old friends. Still, enough of the past. What we need is a fresh start.
NILES   A clean slate.
MA UBU   A new beginning.
PA UBU   A bright future.

(*The vulture puppet on a stick flaps his wings repeatedly and squawks. The following text appears on the screen:* **My slice of old cheese and your loaf of fresh bread will make a tolerable meal**. *This text is replaced by an image of* MA UBU *and* PA UBU*'s boat floating on a sea, towards the giant eye. The eye turns into a setting sun, as the boat floats off toward the horizon. Lights out.*)

Notes

1 Hey, I'm sick and tired of this nonsense. How long have you been degrading me in front of people?

2 What are you doing here in the first place? What do you want hey?

3 Why are you belittling me in front of all these people? Do you know my reason for being here is to be interviewed on television? And now you're mocking me in front of all these people. You are a pest, a bloody pest! I wasn't aware you were such a nuisance. You are never going to make a fool of me. That doesn't happen easily. You're so rude. You have inherited this rudeness from your mother.

4 You stupid thing – what the fuck are you doing? You've killed us – don't you know what is going on? Who the hell do you think I am? I'm going to knock you against the wall so hard your teeth will fall out. You bloody piece of biltong. Come on – I'll show you who's a man! Come on! Your mother's arse . . . !

4 Wole Soyinka _____

The Strong Breed
Nigeria

ᏉᎷᎷᎷ

Introduction

To introduce any play by Wole Soyinka is a
formidable task, necessarily invoking both
the astounding achievements of this 1986
Nobel prize-winner and the extensive critical
debates they have spawned. Undeniably
Africa's most prolific, prominent and
versatile playwright, Soyinka has influenced
at least a generation of dramatists, not only
in Nigeria but also in other parts of Africa as
well as in the African diaspora in the
Caribbean and the United States. He has
gained widespread international recognition
for his work and provoked no small degree of
controversy, whether about his work or his
political activism. In the role of academic and
teacher, having worked variously in Nigeria,
London, the United States, Ghana and other
African nations, Soyinka has also bestowed a
considerable intellectual and pedagogical
legacy on his students and colleagues.

Born to Yoruba parents in Nigeria in 1934,
Soyinka received a largely Western-style
education, before entering the University
College in Ibadan. After two years he
transferred to the University of Leeds in
England where he studied Western literature
and also took a course on world drama. While
in England, he worked for the Royal Court
Theatre as a script reader and participated in
dramatic improvisations. Some of his early
plays were written during this time, notably
The Swamp-Dwellers, staged at the University
of London Drama Festival in 1958, and *The
Lion and the Jewel* (1959). Soyinka returned to
his homeland in 1960, the year Nigeria
achieved independence from Britain, and
rapidly became the driving force of his
country's theatre, as well as holding various
university teaching posts. He established two
theatre companies, the 1960 Masks and the
Orisun Theatre, to promote his own and
other African plays, thereby vitalising

English-language theatre in the region. His
vast dramatic output since the late 1950s has
included such social satires as *The Trials of
Brother Jero* (1960), *Opera Wonyosi* (1977) and
A Play of Giants (1984), though he is better
known for his predominantly tragic ritual
dramas, including *A Dance of the Forests*
(1960), *Kongi's Harvest* (1964), *The Road*
(1965) and *Death and the King's Horseman*
(1975). During this time he has been an
active participant in Nigerian social and
political life, a regular commentator in the
Nigerian media and an outspoken critic of
political tyranny. In 1967, during the
Nigerian–Biafran War, he was imprisoned on
political grounds for 26 months, much of
which was spent in solitary confinement.
From this experience, he produced the play
Madmen and Specialists (1971), the poems of
A Shuttle in the Crypt (1973), the novel *Season
of Anomy* (1973) and the prison notes *The
Man Died* (1972).

This abbreviated résumé can only begin to
suggest the remarkable variety of Soyinka's
work. As well as being Africa's most
successful playwright, he has a considerable
reputation as a poet and novelist, and has
explored other media, such as radio,
television, records and film, for the
dissemination of his ideas. He is also highly
respected for his critical and philosophical
analyses of African culture, having published
two major books of essays in this field, *Myth,
Literature and the African World* (1975) and
Art, Dialogue and Outrage (1988). To add to
this diversity, he has worked as an editor, a
theatre manager, an actor and a translator,
while continually being active in public
affairs.

Soyinka's creative writings in all genres
draw upon both Western and Nigerian
traditions, and his theatre work can be seen
as a synthesis of Yoruba and European
performance idioms and philosophical

concepts. Many of his most compelling tragedies explore the connection between ritual and theatre in a postcolonial context. While *Death and the King's Horseman*, about the intervention of colonial administrators in a mourning ritual, is the only one to deal directly with colonisation, part of Soyinka's theatrical project has been to address the schism that Western theorists have constructed between ritual and theatre. *The Strong Breed*, published in 1963 and first performed in 1964, gives extended play to a theme obsessively reworked in Soyinka's drama: the need of societies to sacrifice one of their own to bring about purgation and rejuvenation of the community. However, the value placed on such sacrifice is characteristically complex and open-ended.

The narrative of *The Strong Breed* begins in an atmosphere of foreboding as Sunma urges Eman, who is a stranger to her village, to leave before evening. Her reason, revealed only gradually to both Eman and the audience, is that the village has an annual New Year purification rite in which the sins and guilt of the villagers are heaped on a 'carrier' or scapegoat – a stranger – so that the community may regain spiritual health for the following year. The dramatic action revolves around Eman's decision to be that scapegoat, even if he is not initially aware that this is his task, or cognisant of its implications. Through a series of flashbacks that gives the play a complex temporal structure with constant shifts between the past and present, he comes to understand his role in relation to this ritual. These glimpses of Eman's past establish that his home village engaged in a similar practice, but always using a member of their own community as scapegoat, unlike Sunma's people. Eman's family, the 'strong breed' of the title, had the task of symbolically bearing the evil of his village in a vessel set adrift each year in the river. Eman had renounced his role as the next carrier, becoming estranged from his father; yet, as the play makes clear, he has a destiny that he must eventually accept.

To complicate the issue of destiny, *The Strong Breed* also addresses questions of free will, since Eman actively decides to stay in the village and take on the role of sacrificial victim, substituting himself for the idiot boy, Ifada. As the ritual proceeds, however, Eman learns that it is easier to choose his destiny than to live it. His attempts to escape escalate the violence, showing how easily the ritual may be compromised, and also extending the play's thematic and philosophical exploration of intersections between will and destiny in the Yoruba world-view. Eman's eventual sacrificial death does not appear to satiate the villagers but rather evokes their horror, dread and guilt. The tone of moral disgust that permeates the play gives it an uncertain and ambiguous feeling, leaving the audience unsure as to whether the community has been purified by the sacrifice or not. In this respect, the cynicism of the manipulative village elders, and their mechanisation of the carrier ritual, seem to undo the potential for healing. However, the tragic events also set up the conditions for remorse; hence, the villagers' disinclination to rejoice over Eman's death presages a degree of spiritual redemption and communal gain. Paradoxically, the ritual may thus be rendered more valuable in its violation than in its adherence.

The play is not based on any existing ritual, and exhibits none of the performance codes of African ritual. There is no singing or dancing and, in the stage directions, Soyinka insists on relentless dialogue-driven action, claiming that scene changes or a break (other than the one indicated) would be 'ruinous'. The ritual of purification, moreover, is never shown, but its brutality is indicated by both Eman's and Ifada's terror. *The Strong Breed* is therefore best seen as a generalised examination of ritual and its role in a community context. As Soyinka has noted,

> The theme of the carrier . . . is common enough to every human community, though the expression itself 'the carrier' may be at first unfamiliar. The carrier is simply a cleansing device – it's the ritual of purification for the community at the turn of the year. The carrier is in its original sense, the scapegoat.
>
> (quoted in Katrak 1986: 111)

While the particular enactment of the ritual in *The Strong Breed* makes its potential for cruelty obvious, Soyinka does not indict the carrier ritual itself as mythopoeic mumbo-jumbo, unlike Femi Osofisan who has found Soyinka's 'unprogressive' and 'sentimental' immersion in Yoruba cosmology problematic. Instead, the play seems to suggest that death is a crucial marker in the struggle between individual will and community wholeness: if the death of the individual initiates community redemption, or prompts the villagers towards heightened self-awareness, the individual has not sacrificed his or her life in vain.

This is the premise that underlies Christianity as well, and it may be no accident that the play evokes connections with this creed since Soyinka was brought up as a Christian after his parents' conversion. The death of Eman and the closing image of the hanging effigy bear a striking resemblance to the crucifixion of Christ, which is, in the New Testament, the principal reflection of Christianity's adherence to the concept of self-sacrifice for the larger good. There are several other parallels. Eman thirsts, as Jesus did; he is a teacher who assists the down-trodden such as Ifada; and he is eventually betrayed, as Jesus was. Prior to his death, Eman arrives at a state of transcendental knowledge and acceptance of his role in the village's cycle of purgation and renewal – not unlike Christ on Calvary. Tellingly, both Eman and Christ are earmarked by their lineage for the task of self-sacrifice, and both eventually embrace their fate as members of the strong breed after displaying initial doubt and intense anxiety. Finally, Eman, like Christ, dies to redeem the faults of others.

The play's emphasis on the tension between individual will and tragic destiny also reflects Soyinka's interest in Greek tragedy, which is manifest in his highly acclaimed 1973 adaptation of Euripides' *The Bacchae*. In this reading, Eman is also an Oedipus figure moving relentlessly towards self-knowledge. By trying to avoid his destiny as a member of the strong breed, he ends up stumbling across it, and living it even more violently than had he stayed in his home village. Similarly, it is only by turning his back on his father's tradition that he fulfils that tradition. Like Oedipus, Eman, who shares the hubris of tragic heroes, finds himself doing exactly that which he sought resolutely to avoid.

At another level, Eman is associated with the Yoruba deity, Ogun, 'patron saint' of craft-workers and god of creation and destruction. In Yoruba mythology, Ogun, distressed by the separation between gods and mortals, throws himself into the dividing abyss to build a bridge toward humanity. Soyinka's theoretical statements on the nature of traditional Yoruba ritual, especially those in honour of Ogun, explore the nature of this abyss (which Soyinka terms 'the fourth stage'), an intermediary realm between the three co-existing realms of the unborn, the living and the dead. The abyss, characterised by chaos and formlessness, is a field of transformation that is both creative and destructive. Eman's transformative power as carrier situates him in the abyss, a position emphasised through the recurring motif of interrupted rituals. In his home village, Eman has broken off his initiation, which means the communal ritual carried by his family will no longer be continued. In his new village, he escapes during the preparatory phase, and is killed, so the ritual cannot be successfully completed. The motif of the interrupted ritual, which occurs in several of Soyinka's dramas, suggests the 'difficult processes of cultural and social transition' being undertaken by postcolonial societies, while the abyss becomes a stunning 'theatrical metaphor for a social and spiritual state where old traditions are no longer completely intact' (Balme 1999: 80).

Many commentators have noted the ambivalent representations of women in *The Strong Breed*. Certainly, the play emphasises the supposed attributes of masculinity and the rejection of womanish behaviour necessary for members of the strong breed. Yet, this portrayal is complicated by the fact that the original sacrifice through which the community's sin is expiated is made by a woman, since 'no woman survives the bearing of the strong ones'. Moreover, the representations of both Sunma and Omae are more complex than they might at first seem. Omae is the traditional, faithful wife who gives her life bearing Eman's child; yet it is her interference that leads him to break off his first initiation when his tutor, like Jaguna and Oroge, is revealed to be a hypocrite. Sunma, although presented as selfish and individualistic at the play's beginning, is simultaneously portrayed as a daughter willing to challenge her father's authority. At the same time, Sunma reveals the process through which the village comes to disavow the stranger within. In this respect, her references to Ifada as useless are ultimately disingenuous, for she is fully aware of the indefensible way that he will be put to use for the community's greater good. As Wright asserts, Sunma 'is going through the ritual motions and mechanics of insult and anathematization, the process of redefinition by dissociation that will rid her of her personal share in the collective guilt and purchase a token, theoretic innocence' (Wright 1993: 59).

Soyinka is one of the most outspoken of African artists in consistently arguing for political commitment among writers, and in his analysis of writing as an *inherently* political act. In his view, any writing which has ceased to engage with external political realities has lost touch with its vital audience, but writing which serves only the propagandist purposes of political regimes has sacrificed all pretence to the status of art. Soyinka's incarceration, and his exile during particular periods of tumult in Nigeria, demonstrate the personal price he has paid in following his artistic vision. Osofisan intriguingly compares Soyinka to Eman in commenting on his inhuman experience of solitary confinement at the hands of the Nigerian junta: 'At that harrowing cost, he has emerged as one of the Strong Breed, those pathetically heroic characters who haunt his plays as self-appointed scapegoats of the relentless ritual of communal purification and rejuvenation' (Osofisan 1978: 153). This backhanded tribute forcefully expresses both the awe and the profound discomfort that has sometimes characterised responses to Soyinka's controversial work.

Production history

The Strong Breed was first performed in 1964 in Ibadan. It has also had productions in London (1966) and New York (1967).

Select bibliography

Balme, C. (1999) *Decolonizing the Stage: Theatrical Syncretism and Post-Colonial Drama*, Oxford: Clarendon Press.

Booth, J. (1992) 'Human sacrifice in literature: the case of Wole Soyinka', *Ariel* 23, 1: 7–24.

Crow, B. and Banfield, C. (1996) *An Introduction to Post-Colonial Theatre*, Cambridge: Cambridge University Press, 78–95.

Gates, H.L. (ed.) (1991) *The Essential Soyinka: A Reader*, New York: Pantheon.

Gibbs, J. (ed.) (1980) *Critical Perspectives on Wole Soyinka*, Washington, DC: Three Continents Press.

Katrak, K.H. (1986) *Wole Soyinka and Modern Tragedy: A Study of Dramatic Theory and Practice*, Westport, CT: Greenwood Press.

Larsen, S. (1983) *A Writer and his Gods: A Study of the Importance of Yoruba Myths and Religious Ideas in the Writing of Wole Soyinka*, Stockholm: University of Stockholm.

Lyonga, L. (1977) 'The theme of sacrifice in Wole Soyinka's *The Strong Breed*', *Ngam* (Université de Yaounde) 1/2: 140–54.

Moody, D. (1992) 'The prodigal father: discursive rupture in the plays of Wole Soyinka', *Ariel* 23, 1: 25–38.

Ndiaye, M. (1993) 'Female stereotypes in Wole Soyinka's *The Strong Breed* and *The Lion and the Jewel*', *Bridges: An African Journal of English Studies* 5: 19–24.

Obiechina, E. (1994) 'The theme of victimization in select African plays and novels', in K. Ogbaa (ed.) *The Gong and the Flute: African Literary Development and Celebration*, Westport, CT: Greenwood Press, 149–83.

Osofisan, F. (1978) 'Tiger on stage: Wole Soyinka and Nigerian theatre', in O. Ogunba and A. Irele (eds) *Theatre in Africa*, Ibadan: Ibadan University Press, 151–75.

Soyinka, W. (1976) *Myth, Literature and the African World*, Cambridge: Cambridge University Press.

Wright, D. (1993) *Wole Soyinka Revisited*, New York: Twayne.

Audiovisual resources

Wole Soyinka: A Voice of Africa (1990) Produced by Colin Napthine, Nobel Prize Series, Los Angeles, CA: Trans World International and IMG Educators.

The Strong Breed

Wole Soyinka

Characters

EMAN a stranger
SUNMA Jaguna's daughter
IFADA an idiot
A GIRL
JAGUNA
OROGE
Attendant stalwarts
The villagers

From EMAN's *past:*
OLD MAN his father
OMAE his betrothed
TUTOR
PRIEST
Attendants
The villagers

The scenes are described briefly, but very often a darkened stage with lit areas will not only suffice but is necessary. Except for the one indicated place, there can be no break in the action. A distracting scene change would be ruinous.

A mud house, with space in front of it. EMAN, *in light buba and trousers stands at the window, looking out. Inside,* SUNMA *is clearing the table of what looks like a modest clinic, putting the things away in a cupboard. Another rough table in the room is piled with exercise books, two or three worn text-books, etc.* SUNMA *appears agitated. Outside, just below the window crouches* IFADA. *He looks up with a shy smile from time to time, waiting for* EMAN *to notice him.*

SUNMA (*hesitant*) You will have to make up your mind soon Eman. The lorry leaves very shortly.

(*As* EMAN *does not answer,* SUNMA *continues her work, more nervously. Two villagers, obvious travellers, pass hurriedly in front of the house. The man has a small raffia sack, the woman a cloth-covered basket. The man enters first, turns and urges the woman who is just emerging to hurry.*)

SUNMA (*seeing them, her tone is more intense*) Eman, are we going or aren't we? You will leave it till too late.

EMAN (*quietly*) There is still time – if you want to go.

SUNMA If I want to go . . . and you?

(EMAN *makes no reply.*)

SUNMA (*bitterly*) You don't really want to leave here. You never want to go away – even for a minute.

(IFADA *continues his antics.* EMAN *eventually pats him on the head and the boy grins happily. Leaps up suddenly and returns with a basket of oranges which he offers to* EMAN.)

EMAN My gift for today's festival enh?

(IFADA *nods, grinning.*)

EMAN They look ripe – that's a change.

SUNMA (*She has gone inside the room. Looks round the door.*) Did you call me?

EMAN No. (*She goes back.*) And what will you do tonight Ifada? Will you take part in the dancing? Or perhaps you will mount your own masquerade?

(IFADA *shakes his head, regretfully.*)

EMAN You won't? So you haven't any? But you would like to own one.

(IFADA *nods eagerly.*)

EMAN Then why don't you make your own?

(IFADA *stares, puzzled by this idea.*)

EMAN Sunma will let you have some cloth you know. And bits of wool . . .

SUNMA (*coming out*) Who are you talking to Eman?

EMAN   Ifada. I am trying to persuade him to join the young maskers.

SUNMA   (*losing control*) What does he want here? Why is he hanging round us?

EMAN   (*amazed*) What . . . ? I said Ifada, Ifada.

SUNMA   Just tell him to go away. Let him go and play somewhere else!

EMAN   What is this? Hasn't he always played here?

SUNMA   I don't want him here. (*Rushes to the window.*) Get away idiot. Don't bring your foolish face here any more, do you hear? Go on, go away from here . . .

EMAN   (*restraining her*) Control yourself Sunma. What on earth has got into you?

(IFADA, *hurt and bewildered, backs slowly away.*)

SUNMA   He comes crawling round here like some horrible insect. I never want to lay my eyes on him again.

EMAN   I don't understand. It *is* Ifada you know. Ifada! The unfortunate one who runs errands for you and doesn't hurt a soul.

SUNMA   I cannot bear the sight of him.

EMAN   You can't do what? It can't be two days since he last fetched water for you.

SUNMA   What else can he do except that? He is useless. Just because we have been kind to him . . . Others would have put him in an asylum.

EMAN   You are not making sense. He is not a madman, he is just a little more unlucky than other children. (*Looks keenly at her.*) But what is the matter?

SUNMA   It's nothing. I only wish we had sent him off to one of those places for creatures like him.

EMAN   He is quite happy here. He doesn't bother anyone and he makes himself useful.

SUNMA   Useful! Is that one of any use to anybody? Boys of his age are already earning a living but all he can do is hang around and drool at the mouth.

EMAN   But he does work. You know he does a lot for you.

SUNMA   Does he? And what about the farm you started for him! Does he ever work on it? Or have you forgotten that it was really for Ifada you cleared that bush. Now you have to go and work it yourself. You spend all your time on it and you have no room for anything else.

EMAN   That wasn't his fault. I should first have asked him if he was fond of farming.

SUNMA   Oh, so he can choose? As if he shouldn't be thankful for being allowed to live.

EMAN   Sunma!

SUNMA   He does not like farming but he knows how to feast his dumb mouth on the fruits.

EMAN   But I want him to. I encourage him.

SUNMA   Well keep him. I don't want to see him any more.

EMAN   (*after some moments*) But why? You cannot be telling all the truth. What has he done?

SUNMA   The sight of him fills me with revulsion.

EMAN   (*Goes to her and holds her.*) What really is it? (SUNMA *avoids his eyes.*) It is almost as if you are forcing yourself to hate him. Why?

SUNMA   That is not true. Why should I?

EMAN   Then what is the secret? You've even played with him before.

SUNMA   I have always merely tolerated him. But I cannot any more. Suddenly my disgust won't take him any more. Perhaps . . . perhaps it is the new year. Yes, yes, it must be the new year.

EMAN   I don't believe that.

SUNMA   It must be. I am a woman, and these things matter. I don't want a mis-shape near me. Surely for one day in the year, I may demand some wholesomeness.

EMAN   I do not understand you. (SUNMA *is silent.*) It was cruel of you. And to Ifada who is so helpless and alone. We are the only friends he has.

SUNMA   No, just you. I have told you, with me it has always been only an act of kindness. And now I haven't any pity left for him.

EMAN   No. He is not a wholesome being. (*He turns back to looking through the window.*)

SUNMA   (*half-pleading*) Ifada can rouse your pity. And yet if anything, I need more kindness from you. Every time my weakness betrays me, you close your mind against me . . . Eman . . . Eman . . .

(A GIRL *comes in view, dragging an effigy by a rope attached to one of its legs. She stands for a while gazing at* EMAN. IFADA, *who has crept back shyly to his accustomed position, becomes somewhat excited when he sees the effigy. The girl is unsmiling. She possesses, in fact, a kind of inscrutability which does not make her hard but is unsettling.)*

GIRL   Is the teacher in?

EMAN   (*smiling*) No.

GIRL   Where is he gone?

EMAN   I don't really know. Shall I ask?

GIRL   Yes, do.

EMAN   (*turning slightly*) Sunma, a girl outside wants to know . . .

(SUNMA *turns away, goes into the inside room.*)

EMAN   Oh. (*He returns to the girl, but his slight gaiety is lost.*) There is no one at home who can tell me.

GIRL   Why are you not in?

EMAN   I don't really know. Maybe I went somewhere.

GIRL   All right. I will wait until you get back. (*She pulls the effigy to her, sits down.*)

EMAN   (*slowly regaining his amusement*) So you are all ready for the new year.

GIRL   (*without turning around*) I am not going to the festival.

EMAN   Then why have you got that?

GIRL   Do you mean my carrier? I am unwell you know. My mother says it will take away my sickness with the old year.

EMAN   Won't you share the carrier with your playmates?

GIRL   Oh, no. Don't you know I play alone? The other children won't come near me. Their mothers would beat them.

EMAN   But I have never seen you here. Why don't you come to the clinic?

GIRL   My mother said No. (*She gets up, and begins to move off.*)

EMAN   You are not going away?

GIRL   I must not stay talking to you. If my mother caught me . . .

EMAN   All right, tell me what you want before you go.

GIRL   (*Stops. For some moments she remains silent.*) I must have some clothes for my carrier.

EMAN   Is that all? You wait a moment.

(SUNMA *comes out as he takes down a buba from the wall. She goes to the window and glares almost with hatred at the girl. The girl retreats hastily, still impassive.*)

By the way Sunma, do you know who that girl is?

SUNMA   I hope you don't really mean to give her that.

EMAN   Why not? I hardly ever use it.

SUNMA   Just the same don't give it to her. She is not a child. She is as evil as the rest of them.

EMAN   What has got into you today?

SUNMA   All right, all right. Do what you wish. (*She withdraws. Baffled,* EMAN *returns to the window.*)

EMAN   Here . . . will this do? Come and look at it.

GIRL   Throw it.

EMAN   What is the matter? I am not going to eat you.

GIRL   No one lets me come near them.

EMAN   But I am not afraid of catching your disease.

GIRL   Throw it.

(EMAN *shrugs and tosses the buba. She takes it without a word and slips it on the effigy, completely absorbed in the task.* EMAN *watches for a while, then joins* SUNMA *in the inner room.*)

GIRL   (*after a long, cool survey of* IFADA) You have a head like a spider's egg, and your mouth dribbles like a roof. But there is no one else. Would you like to play?

(IFADA *nods eagerly, quite excited.*)

GIRL   You will have to get a stick.

(IFADA *rushes around, finds a big stick and whirls it aloft, bearing down on the carrier.*)

GIRL   Wait. I don't want you to spoil it. If it gets torn I shall drive you away. Now, let me see how you are going to beat it.

(IFADA *hits it gently.*)

GIRL   You may hit harder than that. As long as there is something left to hang at the end. (*She appraises him up and down.*) You are not very tall . . . will you be able to hang it from a tree?

(IFADA *nods, grinning happily.*)

GIRL   You will hang it up and I will set fire to it. (*Then, with surprising venom*) But just because you are helping me, don't think it is going to cure you. I am the one who will get well at midnight, do you understand? It is my carrier and it is for me alone. (*She pulls at the rope to make sure that it is well attached to the leg.*) Well don't stand there drooling. Let's go.

(*She begins to walk off, dragging the effigy in the dust.* IFADA *remains where he is for some moments, seemingly puzzled. Then his face breaks into a large grin and he leaps after the procession, belabouring the effigy with all his strength. The stage remains empty for some moments. Then the horn of a lorry is sounded and* SUNMA *rushes out. The hooting continues for some time with a rhythmic pattern.* EMAN *comes out.*)

EMAN   I am going to the village . . . I shan't be back before nightfall.

SUNMA   (*blankly*) Yes.

EMAN   (*hesitates*) Well what do you want me to do?

SUNMA   The lorry was hooting just now.

EMAN   I didn't hear it.

SUNMA   It will leave in a few minutes. And you did promise we could go away.

EMAN   I promised nothing. Will you go home by yourself or shall I come back for you?

SUNMA   You don't even want me here?

EMAN   But you have to go home haven't you?

SUNMA   I had hoped we would watch the new year together – in some other place.

EMAN   Why do you continue to distress yourself?

SUNMA   Because you will not listen to me. Why do you continue to stay where nobody wants you?

EMAN   That is not true.

SUNMA   It is. You are wasting your life on people who really want you out of their way.

EMAN   You don't know what you are saying.

SUNMA   You think they love you? Do you think they care at all for what you – or I – do for them?

EMAN   *Them?* These are your own people. Sometimes you talk as if you were a stranger too.

SUNMA   I wonder if I really sprang from here. I know they are evil and I am not. From the oldest to the smallest child, they are nourished in evil and unwholesomeness in which I have no part.

EMAN   You knew this when you returned?

SUNMA   You reproach me then for trying at all?

EMAN   I reproach you with nothing. But you must leave me out of your plans. I can have no part in them.

SUNMA   (*nearly pleading*) Once I could have run away. I would have gone and never looked back.

EMAN   I cannot listen when you talk like that.

SUNMA   I swear to you, I do not mind what happens afterwards. But you must help me tear myself away from here. I can no longer do it by myself . . . It is only a little thing. And we have worked so hard this past year . . . surely we can go away for a week . . . even a few days would be enough.

EMAN   I have told you Sunma . . .

SUNMA   (*desperately*) Two days Eman. Only two days.

EMAN   (*distressed*) But I tell you I have no wish to go.

SUNMA   (*suddenly angry*) Are you so afraid then?

EMAN   Me? Afraid of what?

SUNMA   You think you will not want to come back.

EMAN   (*pitying*) You cannot dare me that way.

SUNMA   Then why won't you leave here, even for an hour? If you are so sure that your life is settled here, why are you afraid to do this thing for me? What is so wrong that you will not go into the next town for a day or two?

EMAN   I don't want to. I do not have to persuade you, or myself about anything. I simply have no desire to go away.

SUNMA   (*His quiet confidence appears to incense her.*) You are afraid. You accuse me of losing my sense of mission, but you are afraid to put yours to the test.

EMAN   You are wrong Sunma. I have no sense of mission. But I have found peace here and I am content with that.

SUNMA   I haven't. For a while I thought that too, but I found there could be no peace in the midst of so much cruelty. Eman, tonight at least, the last night of the old year . . .

EMAN   No Sunma. I find this too distressing; you should go home now.

SUNMA   It is the time for making changes in one's life Eman. Let's breathe in the new year away from here.

EMAN   You are hurting yourself.

SUNMA   Tonight. Only tonight. We will come back tomorrow, as early as you like. But let us go away for this one night. Don't let another year break on me in this place . . . you don't know how important it is to me, but I will tell you, I will tell you on the way . . . but we must not be here today. Eman, do this one thing for me.

EMAN   (*sadly*) I cannot.

SUNMA (*suddenly calm*) I was a fool to think it would be otherwise. The whole village may use you as they will but for me there is nothing. Sometimes I think you believe that doing anything for me makes you unfaithful to some part of your life. If it was a woman then I pity her for what she must have suffered. (EMAN *winces and hardens slowly.* SUNMA *notices nothing.*) Keeping faith with so much is slowly making you inhuman. (*Sees the change in* EMAN.) Eman. Eman. What is it? (*As she goes towards him,* EMAN *goes into the house.*)

SUNMA (*Apprehensive, follows him.*) What did I say? Eman, forgive . . . forgive me, forgive me please.

(EMAN *remains facing into the slow darkness of the room.* SUNMA, *distressed, cannot decide what to do.*)

I swear I didn't know . . . I would not have said it for all the world.

(*A lorry is heard taking off somewhere nearby. The sound comes up and slowly fades away into the distance.* SUNMA *starts visibly, goes slowly to the window.*)

SUNMA (*as the sound dies off, to herself*) What happens now?

EMAN (*joining her at the window*) What did you say?

SUNMA Nothing.

EMAN Was that not the lorry going off?

SUNMA It was.

EMAN I am sorry I couldn't help you.

(SUNMA, *about to speak, changes her mind.*)

EMAN I think you ought to go home now.

SUNMA No, don't send me away. It's the least you can do for me. Let me stay here until all the noise is over.

EMAN But are you not needed at home? You have a part in the festival.

SUNMA I have renounced it; I am Jaguna's eldest daughter only in name.

EMAN Renouncing one's self is not so easy – surely you know that.

SUNMA I don't want to talk about it. Will you at least let us be together tonight?

EMAN But . . .

SUNMA Unless you are afraid my father will accuse you of harbouring me.

EMAN All right, we will go out together.

SUNMA Go out? I want us to stay here.

EMAN When there is so much going on outside?

SUNMA Some day you will wish that you went away when I tried to make you.

EMAN Are we going back to that?

SUNMA No. I promise you I will not recall it again. But you must know that it was also for your sake that I tried to get us away.

EMAN For me? How?

SUNMA By yourself you can do nothing here. Have you not noticed how tightly we shut out strangers? Even if you lived here for a lifetime, you would remain a stranger.

EMAN Perhaps that is what I like. There is peace in being a stranger.

SUNMA For a while perhaps. But they would reject you in the end. I tell you it is only I who stand between you and contempt. And because of this you have earned their hatred. I don't know why I say this now, except that somehow, I feel that it no longer matters. It is only I who have stood between you and much humiliation.

EMAN Think carefully before you say any more. I am incapable of feeling indebted to you. This will make no difference at all.

SUNMA I ask for nothing. But you must know it all the same. It is true I hadn't the strength to go by myself. And I must confess this now, if you had come with me, I would have done everything to keep you from returning.

EMAN I know that.

SUNMA You see, I bare myself to you. For days I had thought it over, this was to be a new beginning for us. And I placed my fate wholly in your hands. Now the thought will not leave me – I have a feeling which will not be shaken off, that in some way, you have tonight totally destroyed my life.

EMAN You are depressed, you don't know what you are saying.

SUNMA Don't think I am accusing you. I say all this only because I cannot help it.

EMAN We must not remain shut up here. Let us go and be part of the living.

SUNMA No. Leave them alone.

EMAN Surely you don't want to stay indoors when the whole town is alive with rejoicing.

SUNMA Rejoicing! Is that what it seems to you? No, let us remain here. Whatever happens I must not go out until all this is over.

(*There is silence. It has grown much darker.*)

EMAN I shall light the lamp.

SUNMA (*eager to do something*) No, let me do it. (*She goes into the inner room.*)

(EMAN *paces the room, stops by a shelf and toys with the seeds in an 'ayo' board, takes down the whole board and places it on a table, playing by himself. The* GIRL *is now seen coming back, still dragging her 'carrier'.* IFADA *brings up the rear as before. As he comes round the corner of the house two men emerge from the shadows. A sack is thrown over* IFADA's *head; the rope is pulled tight rendering him instantly helpless. The* GIRL *has reached the front of the house before she turns round at the sound of scuffle. She is in time to see* IFADA *thrown over the shoulders and borne away. Her face betraying no emotion at all, the* GIRL *backs slowly away, turns and flees, leaving the 'carrier' behind.* SUNMA *enters, carrying two kerosene lamps. She hangs one up from the wall.*)

EMAN One is enough.

SUNMA I want to leave one outside. (*She goes out, hangs the lamp from a nail just above the door. As she turns she sees the effigy and gasps.* EMAN *rushes out.*)

EMAN What is it? Oh, is that what frightened you?

SUNMA I thought . . . I didn't really see it properly.

(EMAN *goes towards the object, stoops to pick it up.*)

EMAN It must belong to that sick girl.

SUNMA Don't touch it.

EMAN Let's keep it for her.

SUNMA Leave it alone. Don't touch it Eman.

EMAN (*Shrugs and goes back.*) You are very nervous.

SUNMA Let's go in.

EMAN Wait. (*He detains her by the door, under the lamp.*) I know there is something more than you've told me. What are you afraid of tonight?

SUNMA I was only scared by that thing. There is nothing else.

EMAN I am not blind Sunma. It is true I would not run away when you wanted me to, but that doesn't mean I do not feel things. What does tonight really mean that it makes you so helpless?

SUNMA It is only a mood. And your indifference to me . . . let's go in.

(EMAN *moves aside and she enters; he remains there for a moment and then follows.*)

She fiddles with the lamp, looks vaguely round the room, then goes and shuts the door, bolting it. When she turns, it is to meet EMAN's *eyes, questioning.*)

SUNMA There is a cold wind coming in.

(EMAN *keeps his gaze on her.*)

SUNMA It *was* getting cold.

(*She moves guiltily to the table and stands by the 'ayo' board, rearranging the seeds.* EMAN *remains where he is a few moments, then brings a stool and sits opposite her. She sits down also and they begin to play in silence.*)

SUNMA What brought you here at all, Eman? And what makes you stay?

(*There is another silence.*)

SUNMA I am not trying to share your life. I know you too well by now. But at least we have worked together since you came. Is there nothing at all I deserve to know?

EMAN Let me continue a stranger – especially to you. Those who have much to give fulfil themselves only in total loneliness.

SUNMA Then there is no love in what you do.

EMAN There is. Love comes to me more easily with strangers.

SUNMA That is unnatural.

EMAN Not for me. I know I find consummation only when I have spent myself for a total stranger.

SUNMA It seems unnatural to me. But then I am a woman. I have a woman's longings and weaknesses. And the ties of blood are very strong in me.

EMAN (*smiling*) You think I have cut loose from all these – ties of blood.

SUNMA Sometimes you are so inhuman.

EMAN I don't know what that means. But I am very much my father's son.

(*They play in silence. Suddenly* EMAN *pauses, listening.*)

EMAN Did you hear that?

SUNMA (*quickly*) I heard nothing . . . it's your turn.

EMAN Perhaps some of the mummers are coming this way. (EMAN, *about to play, leaps up suddenly.*)

SUNMA What is it? Don't you want to play any more?

(EMAN *moves to the door.*)

SUNMA   No. Don't go out Eman.

EMAN   If it's the dancers I want to ask them to stay. At least we won't have to miss everything.

SUNMA   No, no. Don't open the door. Let us keep out everyone tonight.

(*A terrified and disordered figure bursts suddenly round the corner, past the window and begins hammering at the door. It is* IFADA. *Desperate with terror, he pounds madly at the door, dumb-moaning all the while.*)

EMAN   Isn't that Ifada?

SUNMA   They are only fooling about. Don't pay any attention.

EMAN   (*Looks round the window.*) That is Ifada. (*He begins to unbolt the door.*)

SUNMA   (*pulling at his hands*) It is only a trick they are playing on you. Don't take any notice Eman.

EMAN   What are you saying? The boy is out of his senses with fear.

SUNMA   No, no. Don't interfere Eman. For God's sake don't interfere.

EMAN   Do you know something of this then?

SUNMA   You are a stranger here Eman. Just leave us alone and go your own way. There is nothing you can do.

EMAN   (*He tries to push her out of the way but she clings fiercely to him.*) Have you gone mad? I tell you the boy must come in.

SUNMA   Why won't you listen to me Eman? I tell you it's none of your business. For your own sake do as I say.

(EMAN *pushes her off, unbolts the door.* IFADA *rushes in, clasps* EMAN *round the knees, dumb-moaning against his legs.*)

EMAN   (*Manages to re-bolt the door.*) What is it Ifada? What is the matter?

(*Shouts and voices are heard coming nearer the house.*)

SUNMA   Before it's too late, let him go. For once Eman, believe what I tell you. Don't harbour him or you will regret it all your life.

(EMAN *tries to calm* IFADA *who becomes more and more abject as the outside voices get nearer.*)

EMAN   What have they done to him? At least tell me that. What is going on Sunma?

SUNMA   (*with sudden venom*) Monster! Could you not take yourself somewhere else?

EMAN   Stop talking like that.

SUNMA   He could have run into the bush couldn't he? Toad! Why must he follow us with his own disasters!

VOICES OUTSIDE   It's here . . . Round the back . . . Spread, spread . . . this way . . . no, head him off . . . use the bush path and head him off . . . get some more lights . . .

(EMAN *listens. Lifts* IFADA *bodily and carries him into the inner room. Returns at once, shutting the door behind him.*)

SUNMA   (*Slumps into a chair, resigned.*) You always follow your own way.

JAGUNA   (*Comes round the corner followed by* OROGE *and three men, one bearing a torch.*) I knew he would come here.

OROGE   I hope our friend won't make trouble.

JAGUNA   He had better not. You, recall all the men and tell them to surround the house.

OROGE   But he may not be in the house after all.

JAGUNA   I know he is here . . . (*to the men*) Go on, do as I say. (*He bangs on the door.*) Teacher, open your door . . . you two stay by the door. If I need you I will call you.

(EMAN *opens the door.*)

JAGUNA   (*Speaks as he enters.*) We know he is here.

EMAN   Who?

JAGUNA   Don't let us waste time. We are grown men, teacher. You understand me and I understand you. But we must take back the boy.

EMAN   This is my house.

JAGUNA   Daughter, you'd better tell your friend. I don't think he quite knows our ways. Tell him why he must give up the boy.

SUNMA   Father, I . . .

JAGUNA   Are you going to tell him or aren't you?

SUNMA   Father, I beg you, leave us alone tonight . . .

JAGUNA   I thought you might be a hindrance. Go home then if you will not use your sense.

SUNMA   But there are other ways . . .

JAGUNA   (*turning to the men*) See that she gets home. I no longer trust her. If she gives trouble carry her. And see that the women stay with her until all this is over.

(SUNMA *departs, accompanied by one of the men.*)

JAGUNA   Now teacher . . .

OROGE   (*Restrains him.*) You see, Mister Eman, it is like this. Right now, nobody knows that Ifada has taken refuge here. No one except us and our men – and they know how to keep their mouths shut. We don't want to have to burn down the house you see, but if the word gets around, we would have no choice.

JAGUNA   In fact, it may be too late already. A carrier should end up in the bush, not in a house. Anyone who doesn't guard his door when the carrier goes by has himself to blame. A contaminated house should be burnt down.

OROGE   But we are willing to let it pass. Only, you must bring him out quickly.

EMAN   All right. But at least you will let me ask you something.

JAGUNA   What is there to ask? Don't you understand what we have told you?

EMAN   Yes. But why did you pick on a helpless boy? Obviously he is not willing.

JAGUNA   What is the man talking about? Ifada is a godsend. Does he have to be willing?

EMAN   In my home, we believe that a man should be willing.

OROGE   Mister Eman, I don't think you quite understand. This is not a simple matter at all. I don't know what you do, but here, it is not a cheap task for anybody. No one in his senses would do such a job. Why do you think we give refuge to idiots like him? We don't know where he came from. One morning, he is simply there, just like that. From nowhere at all. You see, there is a purpose in that.

JAGUNA   We only waste time.

OROGE   Jaguna, be patient. After all, the man has been with us for some time now and deserves to know. The evil of the old year is no light thing to load on any man's head.

EMAN   I know something about that.

OROGE   You do? (*Turns to* JAGUNA *who snorts impatiently.*) You see I told you so didn't I? From the moment you came I saw you were one of the knowing ones.

JAGUNA   Then let him behave like a man and give back the boy.

EMAN   It is you who are not behaving like men.

JAGUNA   (*advances aggressively*) That is a quick mouth you have . . .

OROGE   Patience Jaguna . . . if you want the new year to cushion the land there must be no deeds of anger. What did you mean my friend?

EMAN   It is a simple thing. A village which cannot produce its own carrier contains no men.

JAGUNA   Enough. Let there be no more talk or this business will be ruined by some rashness. You . . . come inside. Bring the boy out, he must be in the room there.

EMAN   Wait.

(*The men hesitate.*)

JAGUNA   (*hitting the nearer one and propelling him forward*) Go on. Have you changed masters now that you listen to what he says?

OROGE   (*sadly*) I am sorry you would not understand Mister Eman. But you ought to know that no carrier may return to the village. If he does, the people will stone him to death. It has happened before. Surely it is too much to ask a man to give up his own soil.

EMAN   I know others who have done more.

(IFADA *is brought out, abjectly dumb-moaning.*)

EMAN   You can see him with your own eyes. Does it really have meaning to use one as unwilling as that?

OROGE   (*smiling*) He shall be willing. Not only willing but actually joyous. I am the one who prepares them all, and I have seen worse. This one escaped before I began to prepare him for the event. But you will see him later tonight, the most joyous creature in the festival. Then perhaps you will understand.

EMAN   Then it is only a deceit. Do you believe the spirit of a new year is so easily fooled?

JAGUNA   Take him out. (*The men carry out* IFADA.) You see, it is so easy to talk. You say there are no men in this village because they cannot provide a willing carrier. And yet I heard Oroge tell you we only use strangers. There is only one other stranger in the village, but I have not heard him offer himself. (*Spits.*) It is so easy to talk is it not?

(*He turns his back on him. They go off, taking* IFADA *with them, limp and silent. The only sign of life is that he strains his neck to keep his eyes on* EMAN *till the very moment that he disappears from sight.* EMAN *remains where they left him, staring after the group.*)

(*A blackout lasting no more than a minute. The lights come up slowly and* IFADA *is seen returning to the house. He stops at the window and looks in. Seeing no one, he bangs on the sill. Appears surprised that there is no response. He slithers down on his favourite spot, then sees the effigy still lying where the* GIRL *had dropped it in her flight. After some hesitation, he goes towards it, begins to strip it of the clothing. Just then the* GIRL *comes in.*)

GIRL   Hey, leave that alone. You know it's mine.

(IFADA *pauses, then speeds up his action.*)

GIRL   I said it is mine. Leave it where you found it.

(*She rushes at him and begins to struggle for possession of the carrier.*)

GIRL   Thief! Thief! Let it go, it is mine. Let it go. You animal, just because I let you play with it. Idiot! Idiot!

(*The struggle becomes quite violent. The* GIRL *is hanging on to the effigy and* IFADA *lifts her with it, flinging her all about. The girl hangs on grimly.*)

GIRL   You are spoiling it . . . why don't you get your own? Thief! Let it go you thief!

(SUNMA *comes in walking very fast, throwing apprehensive glances over her shoulder. Seeing the two children, she becomes immediately angry. Advances on them.*)

SUNMA   So you've made this place your playground. Get away you untrained pigs. Get out of here.

(IFADA *flees at once, the* GIRL *retreats also, retaining possession of the 'carrier'.* SUNMA *goes to the door. She has her hand on the door when the significance of* IFADA'*s presence strikes her for the first time. She stands rooted to the spot, then turns slowly round.*)

SUNMA   Ifada! What are you doing here? (IFADA *is bewildered.* SUNMA *turns suddenly and rushes into the house, flying into the inner room and out again.*) Eman! Eman! Eman! (*She rushes outside.*) Where did he go? Where did they take him? (IFADA *distressed, points.* SUNMA *seizes him by the*

arm, drags him off.) Take me there at once. God help you if we are too late. You loathsome thing, if you have let him suffer. (*Her voice fades into other shouts, running footsteps, banged tins, bells, dogs, etc., rising in volume.*)

(*It is a narrow passage-way between two mud-houses. At the far end one man after another is seen running across the entry, the noise dying off gradually. About half-way down the passage,* EMAN *is crouching against the wall, tense with apprehension. As the noise dies off, he seems to relax, but the alert hunted look is still in his eyes which are ringed in a reddish colour. The rest of his body has been whitened with a floury substance. He is naked down to the waist, wears a baggy pair of trousers, calf-length, and around both feet are bangles.*)

EMAN   I will simply stay here till dawn. I have done enough. (*A window is thrown open and a woman empties some slop from a pail. With a startled cry* EMAN *leaps aside to avoid it and the woman puts out her head.*)

WOMAN   Oh, my head. What have I done! Forgive me neighbour. . . Eh, it's the carrier! (*Very rapidly she clears her throat and spits on him, flings the pail at him and runs off, shouting.*) He's here. The carrier is hiding in the passage. Quickly, I have found the carrier!

(*The cry is taken up and* EMAN *flees down the passage. Shortly afterwards his pursuers come pouring down the passage in full cry. After the last of them come* JAGUNA *and* OROGE.)

OROGE   Wait, wait. I cannot go so fast.

JAGUNA   We will rest a little then. We can do nothing anyway.

OROGE   If only he had let me prepare him.

JAGUNA   They are the ones who break first, these fools who think they were born to carry suffering like a hat. What are we to do now?

OROGE   When they catch him I must prepare him.

JAGUNA   He? It will be impossible now. There can be no joy left in that one.

OROGE   Still, it took him by surprise. He was not expecting what he met.

JAGUNA   Why then did he refuse to listen? Did he think he was coming to sit down to a feast? He had not even gone through one compound before he bolted. Did he think he was taken round the people to be blessed? A woman, that is all he is.

OROGE No, no. He took the beating well enough. I think he is the kind who would let himself be beaten from night till dawn and not utter a sound. He would let himself be stoned until he dropped dead.

JAGUNA Then what made him run like a coward?

OROGE I don't know. I don't really know. It is a night of curses Jaguna. It is not many unprepared minds will remain unhinged under the load.

JAGUNA We must find him. It is a poor beginning for a year when our own curses remain hovering over our homes because the carrier refused to take them.

(*They go. The scene changes.* EMAN *is crouching beside some shrubs, torn and bleeding.*)

EMAN They are even guarding my house . . . as if I would go there, but I need water . . . they could at least grant me that . . I can be thirsty too . . . (*he pricks his ears*) . . . there must be a stream nearby . . .

(*As he looks round him, his eyes widen at a scene he encounters: An* OLD MAN, *short and vigorous looking, is seated on a stool. He also is wearing calf-length baggy trousers, white. On his head, a white cap. An* ATTENDANT *is engaged in rubbing his body with oil. Round his eyes, two white rings have already been marked.*)

OLD MAN Have they prepared the boat?

ATTENDANT They are making the last sacrifice.

OLD MAN Good. Did you send for my son?

ATTENDANT He's on his way.

OLD MAN I have never met the carrying of the boat with such a heavy heart. I hope nothing comes of it.

ATTENDANT The gods will not desert us on that account.

OLD MAN A man should be at his strongest when he takes the boat my friend. To be weighed down inside and out is not a wise thing. I hope when the moment comes I shall have found my strength.

(*Enter* EMAN, *a wrapper round his waist and a 'danski' over it.*)[1]

OLD MAN I meant to wait until after my journey to the river, but my mind is so burdened with my own grief and yours I

could not delay it. You know I must have all my strength. But I sit here, feeling it all eaten slowly away by my unspoken grief. It helps to say it out. It even helps to cry sometimes. (*He signals to the* ATTENDANT *to leave them.*) Come nearer . . . we will never meet again son. Not on this side of the flesh. What I do not know is whether you will return to take my place.

EMAN I will never come back.

OLD MAN Do you know what you are saying? Ours is a strong breed my son. It is only a strong breed that can take this boat to the river year after year and wax stronger on it. I have taken down each year's evils for over twenty years. I hoped you would follow me.

EMAN My life here died with Omae.

OLD MAN Omae died giving birth to your child, and you think the world is ended. Eman, my pain did not begin when Omae died. Since you sent her to stay with me son, I lived with the burden of knowing that this child would die bearing your son.

EMAN Father . . .

OLD MAN Don't you know it was the same with you? And me? No woman survives the bearing of the strong ones. Son, it is not the mouth of the boaster that says he belongs to the strong breed. It is the tongue that is red with pain and black with sorrow. Twelve years you were away my son, and for those twelve years I knew the love of an old man for his daughter and the pain of a man helplessly awaiting his loss.

EMAN I wish I had stayed away. I wish I never came back to meet her.

OLD MAN It had to be. But you know now what slowly ate away my strength. I awaited your return with love and fear. Forgive me then if I say that your grief is light. It will pass. This grief may drive you now from home. But you must return.

EMAN You do not understand. It is not grief alone.

OLD MAN What is it then? Tell me, I can still learn.

EMAN I was away twelve years. I changed much in that time.

OLD MAN I am listening.

EMAN I am unfitted for your work father. I wish to say no more. But I am totally unfitted for your call.

OLD MAN It is only time you need son. Stay longer and you will answer the urge of your blood.

EMAN   That I stayed at all was because of Omae. I did not expect to find her waiting. I would have taken her away, but hard as you claim to be, it would have killed you. And I was a tired man. I needed peace. Because Omae was peace, I stayed. Now nothing holds me here.

OLD MAN   Other men would rot and die doing this task year after year. It is strong medicine which only we can take. Our blood is strong like no other. Anything you do in life must be less than this, son.

EMAN   That is not true father.

OLD MAN   I tell you it is true. Your own blood will betray you son, because you cannot hold it back. If you make it do less than this, it will rush to your head and burst it open. I say what I know my son.

EMAN   There are other tasks in life father. This one is not for me. There are even greater things you know nothing of.

OLD MAN   I am very sad. You only go to give to others what rightly belongs to us. You will use your strength among thieves. They are thieves because they take what is ours, they have no claim of blood to it. They will even lack the knowledge to use it wisely. Truth is my companion at this moment my son. I know everything I say will surely bring the sadness of truth.

EMAN   I am going father.

OLD MAN   Call my attendant. And be with me in your strength for this last journey. A-ah, did you hear that? It came out without my knowing it; this is indeed my last journey. But I am not afraid.

(EMAN *goes out. A few moments later, the* ATTENDANT *enters.*)

ATTENDANT   The boat is ready.

OLD MAN   So am I.

(*He sits perfectly still for several moments. Drumming begins somewhere in the distance, and the* OLD MAN *sways his head almost imperceptibly. Two men come in bearing a miniature boat, containing an indefinable mound. They rush it in and set it briskly down near the* OLD MAN, *and stand well back. The* OLD MAN *gets up slowly, the* ATTENDANT *watching him keenly. He signs to the men, who lift the boat quickly onto the* OLD MAN's *head. As soon as it touches his head, he holds it down with both hands and runs off, the men give him a start, then follow at a trot. As the last man disappears* OROGE *limps in and comes face to face with* EMAN, *as carrier, who is now seen still standing beside the shrubs, staring into the scene he has just witnessed.* OROGE, *struck by the look on* EMAN's *face, looks anxiously behind him to see what has engaged* EMAN's *attention.* EMAN *notices him then, and the pair stare at each other.* JAGUNA *enters, sees him and shouts, 'Here he is', rushes at* EMAN *who is whipped back to the immediate and flees,* JAGUNA *in pursuit. Three or four others enter and follow them.* OROGE *remains where he is, thoughtful.*)

JAGUNA   (*re-enters*) They have closed in on him now, we'll get him this time.

OROGE   It is nearly midnight.

JAGUNA   You were standing there looking at him as if he was some strange spirit. Why didn't you shout?

OROGE   You shouted didn't you? Did that catch him?

JAGUNA   Don't worry. We have him now. But things have taken a bad turn. It is no longer enough to drive him past every house. There is too much contamination about already.

OROGE   (*not listening*) He saw something. Why may I not know what it was?

JAGUNA   What are you talking about?

OROGE   Hm. What is it?

JAGUNA   I said there is too much harm done already. The year will demand more from this carrier than we thought.

OROGE   What do you mean?

JAGUNA   Do we have to talk with the full mouth?

OROGE   S-sh . . . look!

(JAGUNA *turns just in time to see* SUNMA *fly at him, clawing at his face like a crazed tigress.*)

SUNMA   Murderer! What are you doing to him. Murderer! Murderer!

(JAGUNA *finds himself struggling really hard to keep off his daughter; he succeeds in pushing her off and striking her so hard on the face that she falls to her knees. He moves on her to hit her again.*)

OROGE   (*comes between them*) Think what you are doing Jaguna, she is your daughter.

JAGUNA   My daughter! Does this one look like my daughter? Let me cripple the harlot for life.

OROGE   That is a wicked thought Jaguna.

JAGUNA Don't come between me and her.

OROGE Nothing in anger – do you forget what tonight is?

JAGUNA Can you blame me for forgetting? (*Draws his hand across his cheek – it is covered with blood.*)

OROGE This is an unhappy night for us all. I fear what is to come of it.

JAGUNA Let's go. I cannot restrain myself in this creature's presence. My own daughter . . . and for a stranger . . .

(*They go off,* IFADA, *who came in with* SUNMA *and had stood apart, horror-stricken, comes shyly forward. He helps* SUNMA *up. They go off, he holding* SUNMA *bent and sobbing.*)

(*Enter* EMAN, *as carrier. He is physically present in the bounds of this next scene, set at the side of a round thatched hut. A young girl, about fourteen, runs in, stops beside the hut. She looks carefully to see that she is not observed, puts her mouth to a little hole in the wall.*)

OMAE Eman . . . Eman . . .

(EMAN, *as carrier, responds, as he does throughout the scene, but they are unaware of him.*)

EMAN (*from inside*) Who is it?

OMAE It is me, Omae.

EMAN How dare you come here!

(*Two hands appear at the hole and pushing outwards, create a much larger hole through which* EMAN *puts out his head. It is* EMAN *as a boy, the same age as the girl.*)

Go away at once. Are you trying to get me into trouble!

OMAE What is the matter?

EMAN You. Go away.

OMAE But I came to see you.

EMAN Are you deaf? I say I don't want to see you. Now go before my tutor catches you.

OMAE All right. Come out.

EMAN Do what!

OMAE Come out.

EMAN You must be mad.

OMAE (*Sits on the ground.*) All right, if you don't come out I shall simply stay here until your tutor arrives.

EMAN (*About to explode, thinks better of it and the head disappears. A moment later he emerges from behind the hut.*) What sort of a devil has got into you?

OMAE None. I just wanted to see you.

EMAN (*His mimicry is nearly hysterical.*) 'None. I just wanted to see you'. Do you think this place is the stream where you can go and molest innocent people?

OMAE (*coyly*) Aren't you glad to see me?

EMAN I am not.

OMAE Why?

EMAN Why? Do you really ask me why? Because you are a woman and a most troublesome woman. Don't you know anything about this at all? We are not meant to see any woman. So go away before more harm is done.

OMAE (*flirtatious*) What is so secret about it anyway? What do they teach you?

EMAN Nothing any woman can understand.

OMAE Ha ha. You think we don't know eh? You've all come to be circumcised.

EMAN Shut up. You don't know anything.

OMAE Just think, all this time you haven't been circumcised, and you dared make eyes at us women.

EMAN Thank you – woman. Now go.

OMAE Do they give you enough to eat?

EMAN (*testily*) No. We are so hungry that when silly girls like you turn up, we eat them.

OMAE (*feigning tears*) Oh, oh, oh, he's abusing me. He's abusing me.

EMAN (*alarmed*) Don't try that here. Go quickly if you are going to cry.

OMAE All right, I won't cry.

EMAN Cry or no cry, go away and leave me alone. What do you think will happen if my tutor turns up now?

OMAE He won't.

EMAN (*mimicking*) 'He won't'. I suppose you are his wife and he tells you where he goes. In fact this is just the time he comes round to our huts. He could be at the next hut this very moment.

OMAE Ha ha. You're lying. I left him by the stream, pinching the girls' bottoms. Is that the sort of thing he teaches you?

EMAN Don't say anything against him or I shall beat you. Isn't it you loose girls who tease him, wiggling your bottoms under his nose?

OMAE (*going tearful again*) A-ah, so I am one of the loose girls eh?

EMAN Now don't start accusing me of things I didn't say.

OMAE But you said it. You said it.

EMAN I didn't. Look Omae, someone will

hear you and I'll be in disgrace. Why don't you go before anything happens.

OMAE   It's all right. My friends have promised to hold your old rascal tutor till I get back.

EMAN   Then you go back right now. (*Going in*) I have work to do.

OMAE   (*Runs after and tries to hold him. EMAN leaps back, genuinely scared.*) What is the matter? I was not going to bite you.

EMAN   Do you know what you nearly did? You almost touched me!

OMAE   Well?

OMAN   Well! Isn't it enough that you let me set my eyes on you? Must you now totally pollute me with your touch? Don't you understand anything?

OMAE   Oh, that.

EMAN   (*nearly screaming*) It is not 'oh that'. Do you think this is only a joke or a little visit like spending the night with your grandmother? This is an important period of my life. Look, these huts, we built them with our own hands. Every boy builds his own. We learn things, do you understand? And we spend much time just thinking. At least, I do. It is the first time I have had nothing to do except think. Don't you see, I am becoming a man. For the first time, I understand that I have a life to fulfil. Has that thought ever worried you?

OMAE   You are frightening me.

EMAN   There. That is all you can say. And what use will that be when a man finds himself alone – like that? (*Points to the hut.*) A man must go on his own, go where no one can help him, and test his strength. Because he may find himself one day sitting alone in a wall as round as that. In there, my mind could hold no other thought. I may never have such moments again to myself. Don't dare to come and steal any more of it.

OMAE   (*this time, genuinely tearful*) Oh, I know you hate me. You only want to drive me away.

EMAN   (*impatiently*) Yes, yes, I know I hate you – but go.

OMAE   (*Going, all tears. Wipes her eyes, suddenly all mischief.*) Eman.

EMAN   What now?

OMAE   I only want to ask one thing . . . do you promise to tell me?

EMAN   Well, what is it?

OMAE   (*gleefully*) Does it hurt? (*She turns instantly and flees, landing straight into the arms of the returning* TUTOR.)

TUTOR   Te-he-he . . . what have we here? What little mouse leaps straight into the beak of the wise old owl eh?

(OMAE *struggles to free herself, flies to the opposite side, grimacing with distaste.*)

TUTOR   I suppose you merely came to pick some fruits eh? You did not sneak here to see any of my children.

OMAE   Yes, I came to steal your fruits.

TUTOR   Te-he-he . . . I thought so. And that dutiful son of mine over there. He saw you and came to chase you off my fruit trees didn't he? Te-he-he . . . I'm sure he did, isn't that so my young Eman?

EMAN   I was talking to her.

TUTOR   Indeed you were. Now be good enough to go into your hut until I decide your punishment. (EMAN *withdraws.*) Te-he-he . . . now now my little daughter, you need not be afraid of me.

OMAE   (*spiritedly*) I am not.

TUTOR   Good. Very good. We ought to be friendly. (*His voice becomes leering*) Now this is nothing to worry you my daughter . . . a very small thing indeed. Although of course if I were to let it slip that your young Eman had broken a strong taboo, it might go hard on him you know. I am sure you would not like that to happen, would you?

OMAE   No.

TUTOR   Good. You are sensible my girl. Can you wash clothes?

OMAE   Yes.

TUTOR   Good. If you will come with me now to my hut, I shall give you some clothes to wash, and then we will forget all about this matter eh? Well, come on.

OMAE   I shall wait here. You go and bring the clothes.

TUTOR   Eh? What is that? Now, now, don't make me angry. You should know better than to talk back at your elders. Come now. (*He takes her by the arm, and tries to drag her off.*)

OMAE   No no, I won't come to your hut. Leave me. Leave me alone you shameless old man.

TUTOR   If you don't come I shall disgrace the whole family of Eman, and yours too.

(EMAN *re-enters with a small bundle.*)

EMAN   Leave her alone. Let us go Omae.

TUTOR   And where do you think you are going?

EMAN   Home.

TUTOR   Te-he-he . . . As easy as that eh? You think you can leave here any time you please? Get right back inside that hut! (EMAN *takes* OMAE *by the arm and begins to walk off.*)

TUTOR   Come back at once. (*He goes after him and raises his stick.* EMAN *catches it, wrenches it from him and throws it away.*)

OMAE   (*hopping delightedly*) Kill him. Beat him to death.

TUTOR   Help! Help! He is killing me! Help!

(*Alarmed,* EMAN *clamps his hand over his mouth.*)

EMAN   Old tutor, I don't mean you any harm, but you mustn't try to harm me either. (*He removes his hand.*)

TUTOR   You think you can get away with your crime. My report shall reach the elders before you ever get into town.

EMAN   You are afraid of what I will say about you? Don't worry. Only if you try to shame me, then I will speak. I am not going back to the village anyway. Just tell them I have gone, no more. If you say one word more than that I shall hear of it the same day and I shall come back.

TUTOR   You are telling me what to do? But don't think to come back next year because I will drive you away. Don't think to come back here even ten years from now. And don't send your children. (*Goes off with threatening gestures.*)

EMAN   I won't come back.

OMAE   Smoked vulture! But Eman, he says you cannot return next year. What will you do?

EMAN   It is a small thing one can do in the big towns.

OMAE   I thought you were going to beat him that time. Why didn't you crack his dirty hide?

EMAN   Listen carefully Omae . . . I am going on a journey.

OMAE   Come on. Tell me about it on the way.

EMAN   No, I go that way. I cannot return to the village.

OMAE   Because of that wretched man? Anyway you will first talk to your father.

EMAN   Go and see him for me. Tell him I have gone away for some time. I think he will know.

OMAE   But Eman . . .

EMAN   I haven't finished. You will go and live with him till I get back. I have spoken to him about you. Look after him!

OMAE   But what is this journey? When will you come back?

EMAN   I don't know. But this is a good moment to go. Nothing ties me down.

OMAE   But Eman, you want to leave me.

EMAN   Don't forget all I said. I don't know how long I will be. Stay in my father's house as long as you remember me. When you become tired of waiting, you must do as you please. You understand? You must do as you please.

OMAE   I cannot understand anything Eman. I don't know where you are going or why. Suppose you never came back! Don't go Eman. Don't leave me by myself.

EMAN   I must go. Now let me see you on your way.

OMAE   I shall come with you.

EMAN   Come with me! And who will look after you? Me? You will only be in my way, you know that! You will hold me back and I shall desert you in a strange place. Go home and do as I say. Take care of my father and let him take care of you. (*He starts going but* OMAE *clings to him.*)

OMAE   But Eman, stay the night at least. You will only lose your way. Your father Eman, what will he say? I won't remember what you said . . . come back to the village . . . I cannot return alone Eman . . . come with me as far as the crossroads.

(*His face set,* EMAN *strides off and* OMAE *loses her balance as he increases his pace. Falling, she quickly wraps her arms around his ankle, but* EMAN *continues unchecked, dragging her along.*)

OMAE   Don't go Eman . . . Eman, don't leave me, don't leave me . . . don't leave your Omae . . . don't go Eman . . . don't leave your Omae . . .

(EMAN, *as carrier, makes a nervous move as if he intends to go after the vanished pair. He stops but continues to stare at the point where he last saw them. There is stillness for a while. Then the* GIRL *enters from the same place and remains looking at* EMAN. *Startled,* EMAN *looks apprehensively round him. The* GIRL *goes nearer but keeps beyond arm's length.*)

GIRL   Are you the carrier?

EMAN   Yes. I am Eman.

GIRL   Why are you hiding?

EMAN   I really came for a drink of water . . . er . . . is there anyone in front of the house?

GIRL   No.

EMAN   But there might be people in the house. Did you hear voices?

GIRL   There is no one here.

EMAN   Good. Thank you. (*He is about to go, stops suddenly.*) Er . . . would you . . . you will find a cup on the table. Could you bring me the water out here? The water-pot is in a corner.

(*The* GIRL *goes. She enters the house, then, watching* EMAN *carefully, slips out and runs off.*)

EMAN   (*sitting*) Perhaps they have all gone home. It will be good to rest. (*He hears voices and listens hard.*) Too late. (*Moves cautiously nearer the house.*) Quickly girl, I can hear people coming. Hurry up. (*Looks through the window.*) Where are you? Where is she? (*The truth dawns on him suddenly and he moves off, sadly.*)

(*Enter* JAGUNA *and* OROGE, *led by the* GIRL.)

GIRL   (*pointing*) He was there.

JAGUNA   Ay, he's gone now. He is a sly one is your friend. But it won't save him for ever.

OROGE   What was he doing when you saw him?

GIRL   He asked me for a drink of water.

JAGUNA   } Ah! (*They look at each other.*)
OROGE

OROGE   We should have thought of that.

JAGUNA   He is surely finished now. If only we had thought of it earlier.

OROGE   It is not too late. There is still an hour before midnight.

JAGUNA   We must call back all the men. Now we need only wait for him – in the right place.

OROGE   Everyone must be told. We don't want anyone heading him off again.

JAGUNA   And it works so well. This is surely the help of the gods themselves Oroge. Don't you know at once what is on the path to the stream?

OROGE   The sacred trees.

JAGUNA   I tell you it is the very hand of the gods. Let us go.

(*An overgrown part of the village.* EMAN *wanders in, aimlessly, seemingly uncaring of discovery. Beyond him, an area lights up, revealing a group of people clustered round a spot, all the heads are bowed. One figure stands away and separate from them. Even as* EMAN *looks, the group breaks up and the people disperse, coming down and past him. Only three people are left, a man –* EMAN– *whose back is turned, the village* PRIEST *and the isolated one. They stand on opposite sides of the grave, the man on the mound of earth. The* PRIEST *walks round to the man's side and lays a hand on his shoulder.*)

PRIEST   Come.

EMAN   I will. Give me a few moments here alone.

PRIEST   Be comforted.

(*They fall silent.*)

EMAN   I was gone twelve years but she waited. She whom I thought had too much of the laughing child in her. Twelve years I was a pilgrim, seeking the vain shrine of secret strength. And all the time, strange knowledge, this silent strength of my child-woman.

PRIEST   We all saw it. It was a lesson to us; we did not know that such goodness could be found among us.

EMAN   Then why? Why the wasted years if she had to perish giving birth to my child? (*They are both silent.*) I do not really know for what great meaning I searched. When I returned, I could not be certain I had found it. Until I reached my home and I found her a full-grown woman, still a child at heart. When I grew to believe it, I thought, this, after all, is what I sought. It was here all the time. And I threw away my new-gained knowledge. I buried the part of me that was formed in strange places. I made a home in my birthplace.

PRIEST   That was as it should be.

EMAN   Any truth of that was killed in the cruelty of her brief happiness.

PRIEST   (*Looks up and sees the figure standing away from them, the child in his arms. He is totally still.*) Your father – he is over there.

EMAN   I knew he would come. Has he my son with him?

PRIEST   Yes.

EMAN   He will let no one take the child. Go and comfort him priest. He loved Omae like a daughter, and you all know how well she looked after him. You see how strong we really are. In his heart of hearts the old man's love really awaited a daughter. Go and comfort him. His grief is more than mine.

(*The priest goes. The* OLD MAN *has stood well away from the burial group. His face is hard and his gaze unswerving from the grave. The* PRIEST *goes to him, pauses, but sees that he can make no dent in the man's grief. Bowed, he goes on his way.*)

(EMAN, *as carrier, walks towards the graveside, the other* EMAN *having gone. His feet sink into the mound and he breaks slowly on to his knees, scooping up the sand in his hands and pouring it on his head. The scene blacks out slowly.*)

(*Enter* JAGUNA *and* OROGE.)

OROGE We have only a little time.

JAGUNA He will come. All the wells are guarded. There is only the stream left him. The animal must come to drink.

OROGE You are sure it will not fail – the trap I mean.

JAGUNA When Jaguna sets the trap, even elephants pay homage – their trunks downwards and one leg up in the sky. When the carrier steps on the fallen twigs, it is up in the sacred trees with him.

OROGE I shall breathe again when this long night is over.

(*They go out. Enter* EMAN, *as carrier, from the same direction as the last two entered. In front of him is a still figure, the* OLD MAN *as he was, carrying the dwarf boat.*)

EMAN (*joyfully*) Father.

(*The figure does not turn round.*)

EMAN It is your son. Eman. (*He moves nearer.*) Don't you want to look at me? It is I, Eman. (*He moves nearer still.*)

OLD MAN You are coming too close. Don't you know what I carry on my head?

EMAN But Father, I am your son.

OLD MAN Then go back. We cannot give the two of us.

EMAN Tell me first where you are going.

OLD MAN Do *you* ask that? Where else but to the river?

EMAN (*visibly relieved*) I only wanted to be sure. My throat is burning. I have been looking for the stream all night.

OLD MAN It is the other way.

EMAN But you said . . .

OLD MAN I take the longer way, you know how I must do this. It is quicker if you take the other way. Go now.

EMAN No, I will only get lost again. I shall go with you.

OLD MAN Go back my son. Go back.

EMAN Why? Won't you even look at me?

OLD MAN Listen to your father. Go back.

EMAN But father! (*He makes to hold him. Instantly the* OLD MAN *breaks into a rapid trot.* EMAN *hesitates, then follows, his strength nearly gone.*) Wait father. I am coming with you . . . wait . . . wait for me father . . .

(*There is a sound of twigs breaking, of a sudden trembling in the branches. Then silence.*)

(*The front of* EMAN's *house. The effigy is hanging from the sheaves. Enter* SUNMA, *still supported by* IFADA. *She stands transfixed as she sees the hanging figure.* IFADA *appears to go mad, rushes at the object and tears it down.* SUNMA, *her last bit of will gone, crumbles against the wall. Some distance away from them, partly hidden, stands the* GIRL, *impassively watching.* IFADA *hugs the effigy to him, stands above* SUNMA. *The* GIRL *remains where she is, observing. Almost at once, the villagers begin to return, subdued and guilty. They walk across the front, skirting the house as widely as they can. No word is exchanged.* JAGUNA *and* OROGE *eventually appear.* JAGUNA, *who is leading, sees* SUNMA *as soon as he comes in view. He stops at once, retreating slightly.*)

OROGE (*almost whispering*) What is it?

JAGUNA The viper.

(OROGE *looks cautiously at the woman.*)

OROGE I don't think she will even see you.

JAGUNA Are you sure? I am in no frame of mind for another meeting with her.

OROGE Let's go home.

JAGUNA I am sick to the heart of the cowardice I have seen tonight.

OROGE That is the nature of men.

JAGUNA Then it is a sorry world to live in. We did it for them. It was all for their own common good. What did it benefit me whether the man lived or died? But did you see them? One and all they looked up at the man and words died in their throats.

OROGE It was no common sight.

JAGUNA   Women could not have behaved so shamefully. One by one they crept off like sick dogs. Not one could raise a curse.

OROGE   It was not only him they fled. Do you see how unattended we are?

JAGUNA   There are those who will pay for this night's work!

OROGE   Ay, let us go home.

(*They go off.* SUNMA, IFADA *and the* GIRL *remain as they are, the light fading slowly on them.*)

Note

1   A danski is a brief Yoruba attire.

5 Femi Osofisan

Once Upon Four Robbers
Nigeria

Introduction

In the programme notes to the first production of *Once Upon Four Robbers* (1978), Femi Osofisan provocatively states that 'the phenomenon of armed robbery seems to be an apt metaphor for our age' (1980: vii). He cites the gross material inequities characteristic of post-independence Nigerian society as the fundamental root of this kind of crime, suggesting that the rich are themselves robbers of the country's oil wealth:

> Take a look at our salary structures, at the minimum wage level, count the sparse number of lucky ones who even earn it . . . and then take a look at the squalid spending habits of our egregious 'contractors', land speculators, middle men of all sorts, importers, exporters, etc. Or take a look at our sprawling slums and ghettos, our congested hospitals and crowded schools, our impossible markets . . . and then take another look at the fast proliferation of motorcars, insurance agencies, supermarkets, chemist shops, boutiques, discotheques etc. The callous contradictions of our oil-doomed fantasies of rapid modernisation. It is obvious that as long as a single, daring nocturnal trip with a gun or machete can yield the equivalent of one man's annual income, we shall continue to manufacture our own potential assassins.
>
> (Osofisan 1980: vii–viii)

This image of modernity highlights the sense of anomie caused by neo-colonial and technological developments that benefit only a select few, leaving the majority condemned to poverty or crime. Osofisan also points indirectly to the widespread corruption engendered by successive political systems in a country where a cycle of failed civilian governments and subsequent military coups has become the norm. His concern with class oppression and social injustice lies at the heart of *Once Upon Four Robbers*, one of the most popular plays in a wide-ranging dramatic corpus which consistently demonstrates his conviction that art may be used as an ideological weapon to start debate.

Osofisan's materialist socialist perspective may be traced in part to his own experience of poverty as a child; however, his caustic portraits of a dystopian culture also reflect deep distress at Nigeria's failure to foster a more democratic society after it had officially cast off the shackles of colonialism. Born in 1946, Osofisan witnessed his country's transition to self-government after a century of British rule ended in 1960; but, as he notes in a recent essay, this was a 'flag independence', doomed to failure because it was built on the same autocratic power structures that had undergirded imperial rule (Osofisan 1998: 12). Osofisan had just begun studies as a French Honours student at the University of Ibadan when simmering political tensions turned into the terrible bloodbath of Nigeria's three-year civil war, which, in turn, was followed by a series of brutal military regimes. This history, the tragic development of what Osofisan calls a 'post-colonial, military state' (1998: 11), forms the context for his prodigious work in the theatre as playwright, director, actor, university teacher and dramatic theorist. He also writes poetry, as well as a weekly column for *The Comet*, one of Nigeria's national newspapers.

Among the forty or more dramas that Osofisan has written, almost all demonstrate an acute historical consciousness, whether that emerges through a reinterpretation of the past, an engagement with traditional Yoruba performance forms or a conscious positioning of current political and social turmoil *in* history. Early plays such as *The Chattering and the Song* (1974) and *Morountodun* (1979) reconsider history from the point of view of the oppressed lower classes, both staging complex interactions between past and present in order to critique the contemporary social order. Osofisan's revisionist historical project has also extended to the realm of key civil and political figures, including Kwame Nkrumah, Amilcar Cabral and Sekou Touré, three early revolutionary African leaders whose particular actions and philosophies are explored in *Nkrumah ni . . . , Afrika ni . . .* (1995). Other Osofisan plays draw their subject matter from theatre history itself – European and African – which he mines for narratives to restyle in ways that speak to local and present contingencies. The key texts in this particular counter-discursive project are *No More the Wasted Breed* (1982), Osofisan's subversive response to Wole Soyinka's *The Strong Breed*, and *Another Raft* (1988), his reworking of J.P. Clark-Bekederemo's national allegory, *The Raft*. With these plays, Osofisan radically interrogates his predecessors' political and aesthetic visions while at the same time extending their cultural work.

Osofisan's engagement with Yoruba history and cosmology has inevitably led his work to be compared with that of Soyinka, whose 'traditionalist' plays often tend to support Western liberal humanism's emphasis on individual moral responsibility. Osofisan, restive with this kind of metaphysical view, conceives of human choice as fundamentally determined by economic and social conditioning. Hence, he reads Yoruba traditions with a specifically ideological slant, arguing that recourse to mythology can merely mystify present social relations unless the narratives and rituals invoked are critically reinterpreted (see Obafemi 1982: 238). As dramatic spokespersons for their culture, Osofisan and Soyinka thus seem to be worlds apart, yet political divergences between the two have been exaggerated, in many instances, by critics relying on over-easy generational divisions. Soyinka's conception of the role of the playwright in modern Africa *is* a firmly political one, and Osofisan has frequently emphasised his great regard for Soyinka's complex handling of Yoruba traditions and beliefs in his dramaturgy.

A continual experimentation with both Western and African performance modes, and their associated narrative structures, marks Osofisan's work. In the early 1970s, he spent two years in France extending his knowledge of European theatre, yet the vivid theatricality of his work owes more to the West African performance traditions on which he wrote his doctoral dissertation. Many of his plays incorporate songs, dance and music drawn from Yoruba folk culture; they also utilise the riddling, storytelling and overt role-playing skills for which the Yoruba are justly famous. Sometimes indigenous deities, for instance Esu, the Yoruba god of contradictions, transformations and the unpredictable, are staged as characters in a dialectical engagement with popular mythology. While Osofisan's primary project is to mobilise the educated classes to lead a revolutionary restructuring of Nigerian society, his harnessing of theatrical traditions that make his work accessible well beyond the precinct of the English-speaking elite also allows him to further his other passionate aim: to create genuinely popular theatre.

Once Upon Four Robbers meshes popular theatre with revolutionary ideology, enacting a form of 'surreptitious insurrection' (Osofisan's term) designed to evade censorship and/or political reprisal. It is the first of Osofisan's 'magic boon' plays – the second is *Esu and the Vagabond Minstrels* (1984) – dramas in which impoverished protagonists are given some kind of tira (charm) capable of altering their circumstances. *Once Upon Four Robbers* was written and first staged against a background of escalating armed robberies and the public execution of 'convicted' offenders, a punishment instituted in the early 1970s as a 'public order' tactic by the military regime of General Gowon. By casting his narrative as a deceptively simple folk entertainment, Osofisan is able to evoke a degree of empathy for the robbers and so encourage the audience to look at the contexts in which their heinous crimes are perpetrated. This shift in perspective is facilitated by the central metaphor of the marketplace, which, in Yoruba lore, is the symbolic site of all social transactions (Irele 1995: xxvi). Hence, the profiteering endemic to the market points to a broader societal characteristic, suggesting that the four felons are themselves logical outcomes of a nation constructed systematically upon robbery: by the Government from the state, by the army from the populace, by citizens from citizens. While the various social strata are not implicated equally in their nation's failures, the play is marked by a 'radical refusal to exonerate any one group from responsibility' (Olaniyan 1999: 179).

At the beginning of *Once Upon Four Robbers*, the Storyteller greets the audience and then initiates a traditional call-and-response song that indicates the subject of the 'ancient and modern' tale about to be performed. As the song progresses, the actors emerge from the audience, eventually making their way to the stage where they choose roles and gradually establish their characters. The opening scene thus implicates the audience in the action to follow and establishes role-playing as an important aspect of the play. This performative motif provides the means through which Osofisan is able to satirise the political system and its attendant social effects without necessarily staging characters drawn from the groups most responsible for Nigeria's problems. The robbers' scornful mimicking of job advertisements, the soldiers' aping of their superior officers, and Alhaja's artful performance as a corn-seller, all function to suggest ways in which a corrupt ruling elite maintains power by setting the masses against each other in a struggle for survival. Each of these metatheatrical moments provides an opportunity for detachment and critical assessment as well as humour. Similarly, the songs are intrinsic to Osofisan's reformist agenda, their lyrics often carrying the most pungent social criticism. The market song, for instance, encapsulates the greed of a commodity culture developed out of the cash nexus introduced by colonialism. Such devices, like the mimed execution that begins (and may end) the Aafa's tale, crystallise important issues in the narrative while simultaneously tapping into local performance traditions.

When the Aafa freezes the action at the folktale's climax to demand that the audience supply a suitable ending after debating the relative merits of executing or freeing the robbers, his abrupt intervention breaches the mythological frameworks shaping the entire play. The fantastic tale just staged is thus reframed as 'a means to a shatteringly

realistic end, a diorama through which to view the morbid harlequinade of a profiteering, cannibalistic rabble' (Osundare 1980: 148). With this radical 'ending', Osofisan casts audience members as active participants in the action rather than mere spectators. By compelling viewers to determine the story's outcome, and to face the consequences of their difficult choice, the play underlines the point that individual political decision-making is as important outside of the theatre as within. Structural experimentation of this kind can be found in other Osofisan plays, notably *The Chattering and the Song*, which, the stage directions tell us, 'does NOT end', and *Esu and the Vagabond Minstrels*, which features an audience debate that no side wins. Such open-ended and ultimately anti-illusionist dramaturgy forwards, in the most literal manner, the Brechtian aim to provoke critical thinking and debate. In this respect, Osofisan has written about audience responses to *Once Upon Four Robbers*, noting that heated discussion continues even after a decision has been made and performed: 'Arguments run as if the audience has just left a real event, not an invented tale' (Osofisan 1988: 30). He sees this as evidence that the play has achieved its immediate purpose, which is to end public apathy about the complex connections between state corruption, armed robbery and public executions.

The particularised treatment of armed robbery and its controversial punishment may seem to bind *Once Upon Four Robbers* to a specific historical moment; yet political developments in Nigeria have, until recently, given the play an uncanny currency. Although the mandatory execution sentence for armed robbery was repealed in 1979 with the coming into office of a civilian government, it was re-enacted in 1983 and remained in force for some time. Continued abuses of political power, and the consequent perpetuation of mass poverty and criminal violence throughout most of the 1980s and 1990s, have provided numerous occasions for the play to be updated and restaged in ways that have intervened in contemporary debates. This achievement in a period during which political dissent of any kind could be perilous attests to the great power of Osofisan's iconoclastic theatre.

Production history

Once Upon Four Robbers was first staged in March 1978 at the University of Ibadan Arts Theatre, with a student cast directed by Femi Osofisan. The play has been widely performed in Nigeria and has also had productions abroad, including in England and the USA.

Select bibliography

Awodiya, M. (ed.) (1993) *Excursions in Drama and Literature: Interviews with Femi Osofisan*, Ibadan: Kraft Books.
—— (1995) *The Drama of Femi Osofisan: A Critical Perspective*, Ibadan: Kraft Books.
Dunton, C. (1992) *Make Man Talk True: Nigerian Drama Since 1970*, London: Hans Zell, 67–94.
Griffiths, G. (1995) 'Radical messages: content, form and agency in the drama of Femi Osofisan', *Essays in Theatre* 14, 1: 15–24.
Irele, A. (1995) 'Introduction', in F. Osofisan, *The Oriki of a Grasshopper and Other Plays*, Washington, DC: Howard University Press, ix–xxxviii.
Jeyifo, B. (1985) *The Truthful Lie: Essays in a Sociology of African Drama*, London: New Beacon Books.
—— (1995) 'Interview with Femi Osofisan', *Yearbook of Comparative and General Literature* 43: 120–32.
Obafemi, O. (1982) 'Political perspectives and popular theatre in Nigeria', *Theatre Research International* 7, 3: 235–44.
Olaniyan, T. (1999) 'Femi Osofisan: provisional notes on the postcolonial incredible', in H. Gilbert (ed.) *(Post)Colonial Stages: Critical and Creative Views on Drama, Theatre and Performance*, Hebden Bridge, UK: Dangaroo, 174–89.
Olaogun, M.O. (1988) 'Parables in the theatre: a brief study of Femi Osofisan's plays', *Okike* 27/28: 43–55.
Onwueme, T. (1988) 'Osofisan's new hero: women as agents of social reconstruction', *Sage* 5, 1: 25–8.
Osofisan, F. (1982) 'Ritual and the revolutionary ethos: the humanistic dilemma in contemporary Nigerian theatre', *Okike* 22: 72–81.
—— (1998) '"The revolution as muse": drama as surreptitious insurrection in a post-colonial, military state', in R. Boon and J. Plastow (eds) *Theatre Matters: Performance and Culture on the World Stage*, Cambridge: Cambridge University Press, 11–35.
Osundare, N. (1980) 'Social message of a Nigerian dramatist', *West Africa* [UK] 28 January: 147–50.
Richards, S. (1996) *Ancient Songs Set Ablaze: The Theatre of Femi Osofisan*, Washington, DC: Howard University Press, 117–52.
Savory, E. (1998) 'Femi Osofisan', in P.N. Parekh and S.F. Jagne (eds), *Postcolonial African Writers: A Bio-Bibliographical Critical Sourcebook*, Westport, CT: Greenwood, 374–81.

Once Upon Four Robbers _____

Femi Osofisan

Characters

Robbers

ANGOLA
MAJOR
HASAN
ALHAJA
AAFA

Soldiers

SERGEANT
CORPORAL
SOLDIER 1
SOLDIER 2
SOLDIER 3
SOLDIER 4
SOLDIER 5

Market women

MAMA ALICE
MAMA TOUN
MAMA UYI
BINTU
YEDUNNI

Traders and customers

Prologue

Lights begin to fall off in the auditorium, gradually leaving behind a pool of light which should be suggestive of moonlight. Commanding this spotlight is the STORY-TELLER, *with a set of castanets or a sekere.[1] He shouts out the traditional introductory formula: ALO O! As usual everybody replies: AAALO! He repeats this, gets the same response, and playing his instrument, starts the 'Song of the Story-teller'. The audience picks up the simple refrain – ALUGBINRIN GBINRIN! – after each line. As the song gathers momentum, the musicians and the actors,*

hitherto lost within the audience, begin to assemble on the stage.

Iton mi dori o dori
O dori o dori
Dori olosa merin o
Danondanon akoni ni won
Ajijofe apanilekun
Awodi jeun epe
Arinko sole dahoro
Ron ni sorun apapandodo!

Iton mi dori o dori
Dori olosa merin o
Lojo ino ijoba jo won
Owo boga gbogbo jaguda
Ijoba wa kehin re sokun
Iku egbere seriya oro
Seriya iku ni won da fun
Seriya ota ibon
Kibon Kibon titibon-n-bon
Ha! eniyan kuku ewure
O wa dorun apapandodo!

Iton mi dori o dori
Dori olosa merin o
Ti won pade mi lojo kan
Ojo kan, olojo nkajo
Won ni: 'Aafa a bewu yetu!
Yetu-yetu!

Eleni, yetu yetu!
Birugbon, yetu yetu!

Ah, jowo gba wa lowo won,
Eniyan araye titun
Owo nini o jewon o kobira
Owo nini o, owo yepere
Owo nini, ika sise,
Ika sise fi kole agbara
Ile kiko, ile yanturu
Gbanilaya, wa faye su ni
Daniloro fagbara ko ni!'

Iton mi dori o dori
Dori olosa merin o
Danondanon akoni ni won

Ajijofe apanilekun
Awodi jeun epe

Awodi jeun epe
Arinko sole dahoro
Ran ni sorun apapandodo
Ran ni sorun apapandodo

Already the actors and musicians have gathered on the stage, evidently all in a light mood, as they recognise one another and exchange warm greetings. Then, discovering the costumes, they begin to pick and choose, and then to dress up, gradually establishing the various roles they will be playing. The STORY-TELLER, *still chanting, joins them, and is promptly offered a long flowing buba in white, a mat and a small kettle.*[2] *He shrugs and accepts, and the song ends in a slow fade out.*

Part One

A market in a small town, with stalls and various items. The time is dawn. Centre-stage is a set of barrels, arranged one upon another behind a tall white stake. Now people begin to gather in various groups in the half light. SOLDIERS *lead in a prisoner and tie him to the stake. Then, at the orders of their officer, they take position. They fire. The prisoner slumps. A doctor steps forward to examine the body. The* SOLDIERS *untie the corpse and carry it out. One by one, the crowd drifts out after the* SOLDIERS *in the direction of town. The entire scene is mute, except for the military march, which starts before the coming of lights and fades out with the departure of the* SOLDIERS. *As lights slowly increase now with the growing day, a cock crows, and we notice that a group of four – a woman and three men – has stayed behind, watching the departing crowd. The woman, who is* ALHAJA, *is sobbing and soon collapses.* MAJOR *turns and goes to her. She begins a slow dirge:*

ALHAJA (*singing*)
   Eni lo sorun kii bo
   Alani o digbere, o darinnoko o
   Eni lo sorun, aremabo o
   Alani o digbere, o doju ala o!
   Ohun won nje lorun ni o bawon je,
   Ma jokun, ma jekolo o,
   Alani o digbere, o darinnoko o . . .

(HASAN *and* ANGOLA *are also standing by her now, the latter still shaking with fury.*)

74

ANGOLA What do you think they'll do with his body?
HASAN Eat it, the cannibals. Share the meat among their wives and children.
ALHAJA (*sobbing*) My husband!
ANGOLA Like a ram. They slaughtered our Leader like a Ramadan lamb.
HASAN Or worse. With that cloth tied over his face, they denied him even the privilege of bleating.
ANGOLA They must pay for this.
HASAN (*rising*) They will pay. They or their children.
ALHAJA My poor husband.
MAJOR Let's go, Alhaja. I told you not to come.
HASAN It was disgusting. Five o'clock in the morning, as cold as in harmattan, yet they all came out to watch, to gloat over his death.
ANGOLA And their faces, did you see that? None of them flinched even once at the crack of the guns. They were so eager to devour him.
HASAN Like vultures.
ANGOLA Like hounds.
HASAN Each one went away with a piece of his flesh. Enough to last a month's feast of gossiping.
ANGOLA I know the sergeant. His wife sells at that stall over there. It won't be difficult to get him.
MAJOR Let's go now Alhaja. I'll see you home.
ANGOLA Leave her alone, abi!
MAJOR The morning's rising.
HASAN Let it rise. We've got a wound to avenge.
MAJOR No. Not any more.
ANGOLA What do you mean? I say what do you mean?
MAJOR Are you all so blind then that you can't see the truth? It's finished, finished. We've come to the end of the road.
ANGOLA What! What's that rubbish from your mouth?
MAJOR The only rubbish I know is you standing there, you bundle of guinea-worm . . .
ANGOLA By Allah, I'll . . .
HASAN (*interposing*) No!
ANGOLA Let me mangle the foul-mouthed coward.
MAJOR Coward! Is your grandfather present then?
ANGOLA You hear him!

HASAN   I say wait. Let him explain.

ANGOLA   What does he have to explain? A chicken, that's what he's always been. Even when the Leader was alive.

MAJOR   Raise your voice now. Other people are here to save you from harm. The dog boasts in town, but everybody knows the tiger's in the bush.

ALHAJA   (*who has been looking at them in horror*) Oh my poor husband. They've taken his body away, and all you can do is fight among yourselves! I'm going away! I'm going after them.

MAJOR   Hold it, Alhaja. Listen to me, if only for the last time. The party's over and it's going to be every man for himself from now on.

ANGOLA   You hear!

MAJOR   Face the truth man! Ever since this new decree on armed robbery,[3] we've been finished! You can only walk that far on the edge of a blade. Sooner or later, the blade cuts in.

ANGOLA   And so you'll run, isn't it? Like a cheap half-kobo pick-pocket in the market pursued by women. You think –

MAJOR   (*taking out his knife*) One more step, Angola and your blood's going to wet this market. You think because you have the brain of an ox, everybody's got to be as dumb? They've got the Leader, what more is left?

HASAN   We are left. We'll fight them.

MAJOR   Till the last man! Well, good luck to you. I am off. I want to live.

ANGOLA   Only if we let you, don't forget. No one deserts and lives.

MAJOR   As in the joke book, eh? (*Laughs.*) There's none of you that can stop me now the Leader's dead. Either singly or all together. You can try. (*They form a ring round him. He waits. No one moves.*) Alhaja, let's go.

HASAN   You've always been a friend, Major. Even if I wanted, I could never raise my knife against you. But what's this you're doing? With an oath, we bound our lives together –

MAJOR   Yes. Our lives, not our corpses.

ANGOLA   Listen to him! It's disgusting! What are you if not a corpse! Tell me. You were born in the slum and you didn't know you were a corpse? Since you burst out from the womb, all covered in slime, you've always been a corpse. You fed on worms and left-overs, your body nude like a

carcass in the government mortuary, elbowing your way among other corpses. And the stink is all over you like a flooded cemetery in Lagos . . .

MAJOR   I'll be a living corpse then! Our Leader swore the whole army could not subdue him. He is dead now.

(ALHAJA *is singing the dirge. They pause and watch her,* HASAN *smoking.*)

ANGOLA   And he died bravely.

MAJOR   Yes, but he died! The decree smashed him.

ANGOLA   Don't go with him, Alhaja. He's on their side, you can see. The Leader always suspected it too. Every time we went on a raid and had to kill, he broke down and sobbed like a silly school pickin.

MAJOR   Life is life, and human life's still valuable.

ANGOLA   Pele o, alufa![4] Only you never failed to collect your share of the loot.

MAJOR   Because I always did my share. And more, whatever the personal cost! On that famous raid on the UAC store at Mapo, who was it that silenced the guards? Three of them, and single-handed! And when the Police drove in with their guns and dogs, was it not me who covered the rear while you escaped with the goods? And the trip to the customs shed at Ikeja, who planned it? Who tore that crazy captain off the locks of the gate in defiance of the electrified wires? Who slipped back afterwards to set the place on fire so as to cover our tracks? And others. And more . . .

HASAN   Yes, go on, Major! Omo jaguda![5] Sleek snake of the underworld!

MAJOR   (*Pleased, starts song. They all join in.*)
Awa ti wa a o ko, a o ko
Sasangbaku wosi wosi
A belemu memu
A belelubo jelubo
Kako won nisu
Samusamu la mu
Gbegede de ge
Sasara lobe
Danfo la duro!

MAJOR   (*exultant*) That Alhaji in Kano with his ten Alsatians and fifty guards! That night, when his lorries of contraband arrived from Maradi! Have you forgotten their faces when I rose up from among the bales of lace cloth, two machine guns under my armpit? (HASAN *is on his knees, pleading desperately for mercy.*)

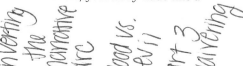

Ha ha ha! The police sing my name in sixteen states!

HASAN (*Singing and stamping his foot.* MAJOR *joins in.*)
Bi e ba gbo giri, e sa o!
Awa la ro giri, kile ya!
Bi a ba de giri, e sa o!
Awa la ro giri, kile ya!
Awa la ro giri, kile ya!

MAJOR (*breaking off*) But alas it's finished. I knew it that day we failed to rescue the Leader from prison. (ALHAJA *starts to dirge softly, he faces her.*) Sing on, Alhaja, sing on, but we shall not mourn! Tears are useless, they screen off the truth of sight. We built a world, and they tore it down. Think, that night! The lives wasted, the blood spilt. How many men did we lose, how many of us left now of a whole army of warriors!

HASAN (*sad*) Just the four of us, but still –

MAJOR Four! The others slaughtered, fine, fine men, the best . . . Sarumi, the leader of the coast, who knew the creeks like the back of his palm –

HASAN He handled boats like cradling a child –

MAJOR His ringing laugh! When he cunningly led officers on his trail to quicksand and watched them flounder like agbegijo[6] . . . Poor fish of the creeks, you had no feet deft enough for land. As he scaled the prison walls that night by my side, the police bullets ripped his flesh. I can still hear his dying scream . . . And Agala –

HASAN The darling of the Lebanese –

MAJOR Yes, of those white-skinned Ogboni of Gbagi.[7] He understood too well their weakness for young rounded black flesh, and had an army of women at his command. Oh! He never failed to know weeks in advance of coming consignments, especially those arriving through the numerous underground channels which the Lebanese control –

ALHAJA He too, they cut him down that night as he ran forward with the explosives. The blast took him and his men.

MAJOR Lamilami, the eternal husband of the women of Jankara[8] –

HASAN Ebiti, his assistant at Oyingbo[9] who tried to branch out to Sapon[10] –

HASAN Till the women found out that his main supply was a unique strain of Gonorrhea –

(*They laugh.*)

ALHAJA The bullets have cured that now. He went with the others –

MAJOR Sir Love, De Niger Nigger –

HASAN The best car thieves of the century, who could drive a car non-stop from Mushin[11] to the Cameroon border, sell it –

MAJOR And steal it back again to sell to young officers ambitious for rapid promotions! Shall I go on? Sago? Bente? Mada? Who could pick the lock of any house with their teeth.

ALHAJA All, all mown down in one single night.

(*The mourning mood returns.* MAJOR *starts singing a funeral tribute in which they all join. He breaks off.*)

MAJOR Listen, Angola, Hasan, Alhaja! Listen to me, this is the end. The guns will get us too in our turn, unless we quit.

HASAN But for what? Where do we go?

ALHAJA Nowhere. They've trapped us with their guns and decrees.

HASAN All we have left is the Bar Beach.[12] And then six feet in the ground.

ALHAJA (*sings a dirge*)
O se kere-e-e-e
O se kere e-e-e
O se kere eye ora
Eye ora ti nfori so
Arugbo n sunkun a fi so fa
A fi sofa a fi ya loge
Aloge yo gongo laya
A se kere-e-e-
O se kere-e-e . . .

MAJOR But perhaps? . . . If we tried . . . somewhere . . . ?

(ALHAJA *is still singing. But suddenly, over her voice, rises another song, from behind one of the stalls. They start, and then instinctively dash for cover,* MAJOR *dragging* ALHAJA *with him. The* STORY-TELLER, *as* AAFA *now, emerges with a mat and a small kettle.*)

AAFA (*singing as he spreads the mat*)
Ataiyatu: lilahi
Azakiyatu: lilahi
Ike Oluwa lilahi
Ige Oluwa lilahi
Ko lo ba Mohamadu: lilahi
Ataiyatu Salamatu: lilahi!

(*He starts to wash his hands and feet preparatory to starting his prayer.* ANGOLA and HASAN *are crawling towards him stealthily, but he feigns not to notice. But as they raise their hands to grab him, he shouts:*) Robi Najini wahaali mimo yahamalum![13] (ANGOLA *and* HASAN *swivel towards each other instead and begin to embrace, grinning sheepishly.*)

AAFA (*without looking at them or interrupting his ablutions*) Haba! Will you lay your filthy hands upon the servant of Allah? Walahu hairu hafizan, wauwa arihamu rohimin![14]

(ANGOLA *and* HASAN *separate and begin to slap each other methodically, bowing politely each time and seeming to enjoy the pain.*)

AAFA (*looking at them*) The bat has no eyes, but it roams with ease in the dark. They think chameleon is a dandy, but if he were to talk what strategies of dissimulation he'd teach our cleverest spies. (*Seems to calm down.*) Bisimilahi ar-rahmani rahim![15] Sit down, it is time for prayers. (ANGOLA *and* HASAN *cease their fighting and take praying postures. They begin to knock their foreheads on the mat in a slowly growing rhythm.* AAFA, *who has shut his eyes, suddenly cries out.*) Come out, you two! Come out! (ALHAJA *and* MAJOR *creep out.*)

ALHAJA (*hesitantly*) Sallu ala nabiyyi karim![16]

AAFA (*grudgingly*) Salla lahu alayhi wasalam![17] I see you have been able to pick up a few things from your lovers.

ALHAJA Whoever you are –

AAFA Join us. It is time for prayers.

MAJOR Aafa, whoever you are, we meant you no harm –

AAFA No, only to rob me.

MAJOR It was a mistake, Allah! We don't steal from men of God –

AAFA You only cut their throat.

ALHAJA I swear to you Aafa! One death is enough for the morning. We supplied the corpse.

AAFA Alihamidu lilai. Your husband, was it? (ALHAJA *and* MAJOR *are startled.* AAFA *chuckles.*) Alhaja! Yes, I recognise you. At the war-front, when you traded across the lines, selling to both sides, it was convenient then, wasn't it, to call yourself Alhaja? But your longest pilgrimage as we all know was to the officers' beds, not to Mecca!

ALHAJA (*furious*) And so what, you disgusting old man! I survived, didn't I?

And what do you think matters beyond that? I survived, but I don't go raking up muck like a municipal waste disposal van. Spill it out then, since you are a refuse depot, let's hear the rest of the rubbish!

MAJOR (*trying to restrain her*) Alhaja . . . Alhaja . . .

ALHAJA No! I am not scared of him! No one trifles with me, even on a day like this, and gets away with it! A pebble sits light in a catapult, but it still squashes the lizard. Let him take care!

AAFA Leave her. Truth is a bitter thing. I suppose you take me for a leather merchant.

ALHAJA Release these men from your diabolical spell!

AAFA Not me, but Allah, whose ways are mysterious. He has chosen to reclaim these lost souls for his service. Who are we to intervene? See, their zeal is an example even to the devout.

MAJOR Old man, we don't know you. We've done you no harm. Or are you from the Police?

AAFA I am not concerned about the Police. Grey hair, they say, is of age.

MAJOR I understand, Aafa. We're sorry.

ALHAJA I am not!

MAJOR Aafa, nobody quarrels so much with his head that he wears his hat on his knees.

AAFA Allah akbar! Grey hair is not sold in the market. When fools mistake a beard for the moustache of impertinence, then they must pay the penalty.

MAJOR Forgive us. It's hunger that drives us.

AAFA As it drives other people. But not into crime.

ALHAJA (*angrily*) You mean, not publicly.

MAJOR We are honest. We only steal from the rich.

AAFA Foolish! (*Gestures.*) Get up you two, Allah is not likely to hear your prayers. Fools, all of you. You steal from the rich, so where will you hide? The rich are powerful.

MAJOR Yes, we know.

AAFA Where will you run? They make the laws.

MAJOR Yes, and they build the law courts.

HASAN Train the lawyers.

ANGOLA They own the firing squads. (*Sings.*) O se kere-e-e . . .

AAFA So why not give up? There's enough employment in the country.

MAJOR   Yes. The rich also own the servants.

AAFA   And you cannot be servants? You? You? (*Looks at them in turn.*) And you self-styled Alhaja? (*The* ROBBERS *laugh heartily.*)

ALHAJA   (*in an 'illiterate' accent*) 'Wanted urgently: Four boy and a one girls. Standard Six an adfantage but not compulsory . . . Position – '

HASAN   (*same game*) 'Service Boys. Waiter. Attractive salary – '

MAJOR   'Five naira per week'.

ALHAJA   (*reading off* AAFA's *bald head*) 'Vacancy. Fast-growing company. Excellent opportunities for ambitious young men willing to work with their hands . . . Position – '

ANGOLA   'Cleaner!'

HASAN   'Cook!'

ALHAJA   'Housemaid, part-time mistress!'

MAJOR   'Washerman!'

ANGOLA   Like dogs. To lap up the excrement.

AAFA   Your pride! Is that it? The eloquent pride of the masses! Will that feed you? Clothe you? Shelter your children? Will it halt the bullets when your backs are tied to the stake?

MAJOR   (*jeering, starts the song:*)
O ja lori obi
O ja lori obi o fiton se
E so faya wo!
Eni ba rohun tafala ti o mu
Eni ba rohun taraka ti o gbe o
Sonitohun yode, sohun mi siwin
Sonitohun dope, sohun mi rago!
Kerikeri! Kerikeri!
Bi we ti mbo kode i pa e loru?
Omugo jaguda lode ma i pa
Jaguda ni won pe wa
Sugbon awa ma mo pe ise la nse!
Eni Esu ba ron lowo, ko deno de wa
Eni ba fe ku, ko ni bo lawa ma gba?
Ifun alayen, ni gbangba ni o ba!
Edo oniyen, ni gbangba ni o ba!

ANGOLA   Right, Aafa, so the journey ends. At the Bar Beach, in some market place, at the outskirts of town. What does it matter? For those not in the privileged position to steal government files, award contracts –

HASAN   Alter accounts –

ANGOLA   Swear affidavits –

ALHAJA   Grant sick leaves –

HASAN   Sell contraband –

MAJOR   Collude with aliens[18] –

ANGOLA   And buy chieftaincy titles as life

insurance! No, let our obituaries litter the public places and one day –

AAFA   What illusions.

(*They assault* AAFA *suddenly, led by* ALHAJA *who deliberately and obscenely violates the startled man. They are singing in chorus, with* HASAN *taking the solo:*)

Eyi lo ye ni
Hen hun hen!
Eyi lo ye ni
Hen hun hen!
Ogun lo nrogun
Hen hun hen!
Epon meje
Hen hun hen!
Okon fota
Hen hun hen!
Meji femu
Hen hun hen!
Merin fato!
Hen hun hen!

(*As* AAFA *retreats in a rather ungainly fashion, the* ROBBERS *collapse in laughter. But gradually* AAFA *himself is infected by their mirth. He smiles. Visibly his mood turns benign as he sits down among them.*)

AAFA   Alright, I'll help you.

ANGOLA   We're no beggars!

AAFA   I said, help. I can make you rich.

HASAN   You?

MAJOR   How?

AAFA   I'll put a power in your hands that will take you out of the gutters. Into the most glittering palaces.

ALHAJA   Don't mock us, Aafa.

AAFA   Alhaja, we know each other, don't we? We can hardly afford children's games.

ALHAJA   Then talk.

AAFA   (*smiling*) You're a cunning one. You put on this cloth of earth and you think no one will recognise you.

ALHAJA   What do you mean?

AAFA   It will come out one day, I assure you. Maybe in violent conflict.

ALHAJA   I have known conflicts, old man. Look in the police records. Violence, I feed on it. Don't think you can frighten me.

MAJOR   But what's the man talking about? I thought you wanted to make us rich?

ANGOLA   He's beginning to dodge.

AAFA   She's deep. Deep. She has such reserves of power. Fortunately the earth has folded her in its skin.

ANGOLA   Let us go.

MAJOR   Old man –

AAFA   Promise!

ANGOLA   (*amidst the general exclamation*) I beg your pardon?

AAFA   If you want to leave your poverty behind, on the dungheap of this day, promise me.

MAJOR   We do not understand.

AAFA   Three promises, and you'll be on the highway to riches.

MAJOR   The first?

AAFA   Never to rob the poor.

ANGOLA   But we've just told you –

AAFA   Promise! (*Holds out his tira.*[19]) I know the poor, they do not love each other.

MAJOR   (*licking the tira*) Promised. (*They do so in turn.*)

ANGOLA   And the second promise?

AAFA   To rob only the public places. Not to choose your victims as you do among solitary women. Not to break into homes.

MAJOR   Alright, promised! (*Again, the ritual of assent.*)

HASAN   Now let's hear the third.

AAFA   The most important. You must promise never again to take a human life.

ANGOLA   No, Aafa, too many objections. First, one Sergeant owes us a debt. Then there are many citizens who must be made to account for their wealth, and the poverty of their workers. Such accounts can be settled only one way.

HASAN   And what of our protection? If one of the victims recognises us in the course of an operation, shall we let him go?

AAFA   It's a risk you must take.

HASAN   And the Sergeant?

AAFA   He also goes free. And as for the others, you will have to allow the country to settle its own accounts. On these conditions alone will I give you my help, if you still want to be rich. Do you promise or shall I go on my way?

MAJOR   Yes, promised! (*They do so again, all but* ANGOLA.)

ANGOLA   Aafa, too many people ride their cars along the sore-ridden backs of the poor. Is there no other way?

AAFA   None, son. Otherwise it'll be an empty force in your hands. I do not control it.

MAJOR   Promise, Angola. Let's first have the power.

AAFA   It's not a power you can cheat, I warn you. It makes its own laws.

ANGOLA   (*after much prodding from others*) Alright, I promise.

AAFA   The last thing I want to tell you is that you can use this power only three times. Three times. After that it dies. But if you use it well, even once is sufficient to make you rich.

HASAN   Don't worry, Aafa. We need just enough to be able to organise ourselves again.

AAFA   Well, it's just that you never can tell about human greed. And because of that, I am going to teach each of you only one part of the formula, so none can cheat the others. No, no, don't protest. I have a knowledge of human beings. The power will work only if all of you combine and each speaks his verse in his own voice. Now, take one for each of you. (*He distributes four seeds.*) Swallow it. (*From the folds of his buba, he brings out an opele.*[20] *The* ROBBERS *are surprised.*) Ah, if only one way led to the stream, how many women would fill their pots? Just say after me now. (*He chants the following verse, the* ROBBERS *repeating antiphonally the lines.*)

> Omo Enire
> Omo Enire
> Omo enikan saka bi agbon
> Ifa ka rele o
> Ewi nle Ado
> Onsa n'Deta
> Erinmi lode Owo
> Ifa ka rele o
> Gbolajokoo, omo okinkin
> Tii meriin fon
> Ifa ka rele o
> Omo opolopo imo
> Tii tu jijia wodo
> Omo asese yo ogomo
> Tii fun nigin nigin
> Omo ejo meji
> Tii sare ganranganran lori irawe
> Omo ina joko mo jeeluju
> Ifa ka rele o

AAFA   That's it! All that remains now is for you to sing –

ALL   Sing!

AAFA   Yes, sing and dance. It's an irresistible power. Once you begin to sing, anyone within hearing distance stops whatever he is doing and joins. He will sing and dance and then head for his home to sleep. And he won't wake till the next morning.

HASAN   (*suspicious*) You're not pulling our leg, Aafa?

AAFA   Haba! You're so hard to please. I've given you so much power for free! No more fear of the Bar Beach if you keep the injunctions. Robbery, but without violence –

MAJOR   Aafa, don't mind us. It's just that it's all so . . . so bewildering . . .

AAFA   I know it is. But if you don't want to try it –

MAJOR   Of course we do! We've nothing else anyway.

AAFA   Right, it's a lot, and I don't want it wasted. If you're sure of using it, I'll teach you the opening formula now . . . but look, I can see the women coming, let's leave this place.

(*They go out hastily. The market women begin to arrive now, in groups or singly. The usual greetings, and then the bustle of opening the stalls, setting out the wares. The goods are the usual items of the West African market: foodstuff, bales of cloth, clothes, utensils, portable electronic equipment, etc., items that should generally be easy to clear from the stage. The discussions focus mainly on the execution of that morning, and the expected relief from* ROBBERS *for some time. Then suddenly, from off stage, the first strains of music approaching. The* ROBBERS *are singing.*)

Ewe a je	Herbs will answer!
Oosa a je	Gods will respond!
Ewe a je	Herbs will answer!
Oosa a je	Gods will respond!
E-e-e!	E-e-e!
Boo gbaso wa oja	If you have come to market with cloth
Maa jo, etc.	Dance!
Boo gbesu wa oja	If with yams, Dance! etc. . . .

(*Other items of the market are mentioned in the song. As the song grows louder, even before the* ROBBERS *appear on stage, the traders and clients, in very abrupt transitions, join the song and begin to dance. The robbers dance in. The scene recalls a carnival. One by one, in small groups, the market people dance out, leaving the robbers who soon fall down laughing.*)

MAJOR   It worked! Ah, it worked!

HASAN   God, what a harvest!

ANGOLA   I can't believe it!

ALHAJA   Get up, you fools. Let's start packing, it's going to take the whole day.

(*They begin to assemble the items into convenient packs, singing and dancing. Lights fade slowly into a blackout.*)

Interlude

As the stage is prepared for the next scene, the AAFA *appears in a spotlight, singing and dancing. As before, the refrain is sung by actors, stage-hands and audience. The* AAFA *sings:*

> Iton mi dori o dori
> Dori olosa merin o
> Mo wa fun won lagbara
> Agbara orin kiko
> Orin kiko ijo jijo
> Ijo jijo fi kun won lorun
> Emi Aafa a bewu yetu!
> Yetu-yetu!
> Eleni, yetu, yetu!
> Birugbon, yetu yetu!
> Ologbon, yetu yetu!
>
> Bee mo setutu fun won
> Nitori araye titun
> Owo nini o jewon o kobira
> Owo nini, ika sise
> Ika sise fi kole agbara
> Ile kiko, ile yanturu
> Gbanilaya, wa faye su ni
> Daniloro fagbara koni
>
> Iton mi dori o dori
> Dori olosa merin o
> Danondanon akoni ni won
> Ajijofe apanilekun
> Awodi jeun epe
> Arinko sole dahori
> Ron ni sorun a sunlo fonfon . . .

(*The lights slowly fade out.*)

Part Two

Same market about a fortnight later. Late afternoon going into evening. The market obviously in its dying moments: stalls are being shut, boxes arranged, accounts added. People are chanting and singing, and there is a general air of satisfaction. Fully visible are some SOLDIERS *on guard. The* SERGEANT, *going around, finally stops by the stall of* MAMA ALICE, *leader of the market women.*

SERGEANT   Well, Mama Alice, good sales today?

MAMA ALICE   Extraordinary, Sergeant. In all my days of trading, I can't recollect another day like this. And I can see, looking round, that it's the same for everybody. It's a pity your wife chose today of all days to be ill. (*Giving him a stool*) Sit?

SERGEANT Yes. I'm thirsty.

MAMA ALICE As always! You don't have to announce it.

SERGEANT You and the others made great profits today, but it's because we've been on our feet all day.

MAMA ALICE Oh I'm grateful, but the day I see you otherwise than thirsty – (*Calls.*) Bintu, any wine left or is it all gone?

BINTU No, one keg left, but it's the only one. Sale's been fantastic today.

MAMA ALICE Bring it, I'll buy the last one.

BINTU (*coming with the keg, seeing the* SERGEANT) If it's for Baby Mayo –

MAMA ALICE Who else do you think?

BINTU I knew it just had to be him!

SERGEANT Listen, you women –

BINTU Sergeant, today's my lucky day, you can have the wine free. You and your men have been wonderful.

MAMA ALICE Yes, Bintu, call the other soldiers to share the wine, I don't think Sergeant will mind. They all deserve our gratitude.

SERGEANT Yes, they can leave their posts now. The sun's falling anyway.

(BINTU *goes to call the* SOLDIERS.)

MAMA ALICE You're right. We're already packing up. Our problem is going to be how to carry our profits home. Some of us will need porters!

SERGEANT I'm glad. I need a promotion.

MAMA ALICE If they ask for a recommendation, come to me. All the market women will sign for you. Ah, the goddess of the market woke with us today. Right from dawn the customers came pouring in.

SERGEANT What do you expect, after two weeks of shutting the market?

MAMA ALICE What we lost in that last raid! I tell you, if the government hadn't given us protection, none of us would have come back.

(*The other* SOLDIERS *join in.* MAMA ALICE *and* BINTU *pour out the wine for them. The* SERGEANT *waves aside the salutes and lights his pipe.*)

SERGEANT Well . . . your friends didn't come today.

MAMA ALICE No, thanks to you. And they are not my friends.

SERGEANT (*laughing*) Alright, no need to take offence. You see, our guns were so

cocked and alert that, had we heard so much as a humming, the market would have been littered with corpses. Ask these brutes!

(*General laughter. More women, prepared for home, join the group from time to time.*)

CORPORAL Ah, you should have seen me, Serg! Once, when I thought I heard a song –

(*He leaps forward suddenly, grabs one of his mates by the neck, forcing him down with a 'gun' to his ribs. They begin to play-act.*)

CORPORAL Caught you, you scoundrel.

SOLDIER 1 (*stammering with fear*) So-so-so . . . ja! Soja!

CORPORAL 'Do-re-mi', is it? I will 'do-re-mi' you with bullets today! Robber!

SOLDIER 1 Bu-u-u-ut, soja . . .

CORPORAL Quiet! You can't even sing a healthy, masculine song! 'Do-re-mi-fa-soh'! Disgusting! Are you one of these wall geckos from England?

SOLDIER 1 I'm telling you –

CORPORAL No! You want to sing, abi? You think that can work on a soldier? There, sing now! I've got my palm across your smelling mouth, and if you – yeah!

(*Sudden scream. He rolls off clutching his fingers.*)

SERGEANT What happened, Corple?

CORPORAL No respect for fair play, Serg. Teeth! He bit me!

SERGEANT Ah-ha, so did you arrest him?

CORPORAL Serg, I couldn't.

SERGEANT He bit you again?

CORPORAL No, Serg. It was my own uncle, Chief Okedoke. Oh the kick he gave me afterwards . . .

(*More laughter. Some of the women retie their visibly bulging wallets.*)

BINTU He should have broken your head, I don't know why he didn't!

MAMA ALICE You see how they mock us.

MAMA TOUN They don't believe we were robbed.

SERGEANT By musicians! Tell us another.

MAMA ALICE You know, I almost wish the robbers had returned today.

WOMEN Ah, no-o! The gods forbid! Especially not today!

MAMA ALICE No, I mean, if only to convince these men.

SOLDIER 2   I am convinced. And I can even make a few guesses. The robbers didn't turn up because, last night, their leader developed a sore throat.

SOLDIER 3   No, no. It was the lead drum. It burst in rehearsal.

SOLDIER 4   They thought of a better method, I tell you. They are waxing the music on a disc, then they can rob the whole nation by playing it on the radio.

SOLDIER 5   The hit parade!

BINTU   You hear them! So the whole market was drunk or dreaming? And the goods lost?

(*The* SERGEANT *starts the song which the others take up and sing with great enthusiasm.*)

Eni maye je
E e ni gungi agbon o
Eni fe kaye re o gun
E e ni gungi agbon se!
Bi ofun yun ni a o ronu iko
Bi ofun yun ni a ronu kele
Eni ba salejo fun Mus'limi
Se ohun logbejo salamulekum o!
Paga! bi gunungun ba lorule
Oro penuda, inowo poosi
Ohun buruku ma semi lalejo o,
Ng o ni reru gagagugu
Arun laa wo,
A ma i woku o!

(*They collapse in laughter. Some women help* MAMA ALICE *to tidy her stall, etc. . . . .*)

SERGEANT   Alright, so there was a robbery. But tell us, in earnest, what really happened?

BINTU   How many times do you want us to repeat it? Suddenly there was this song, from nowhere –

SOLDIER 2   From nowhere –

BINTU   It was so enchanting, so sweet –

SOLDIER 3   So sweet –

SOLDIER 4   Africa 70!

SOLDIER 5   Shut up, I'm beginning to hear it myself!

BINTU   It's the truth! Mama Toun here began to dance.

MAMA TOUN   Ah, it was Mama Uyi!

MAMA UYI   Me? I only followed Yedunni!

YEDUNNI   Liar! You danced first!

MAMA ALICE   We all danced. No one could resist the music.

SERGEANT   Ah, women!

MAMA ALICE   There were men in the market too. And they danced.

BINTU   I tell you no one could resist it. We sang and danced in a kind of dream.

CORPORAL   You sang too?

BINTU   We were all possessed.

CORPORAL   And then you fell asleep.

BINTU   When we woke –

SERGEANT   The next morning –

MAMA ALICE   Yes the next morning, can you believe that!

BINTU   And no one in the town even getting suspicious –

MAMA TOUN   Until the next morning!

BINTU   Too late, everything was gone, all we brought to sell.

SOLDIER 1   To where?

YEDUNNI   Why don't you tell us idiot!
(*General laughter as* SOLDIER 1 *pursues her.*)

MAMA ALICE   Well, my friends, night is falling fast and we must leave. But before we go, please let us show our gratitude to Baba Mayo and his men by singing them our market song.

(*She starts, and they join in, dancing and singing the 'Song of the Market'.*)

The work of profit
Brought us to this world,
This life that is a market.
Some sell with ease and flourish
And some are clients
Who pay their greed in gold!
Edumare Oba toto!

Among the crowd
That's born each day,
Just to sweep the rubbish,
And scour round like dogs,
Count not our kins!
Let's not only stay
Rambling around the market,
To eat discarded bits!

The lure of profit
Has conquered our souls
And changed us into cannibals:
Oh praise the selfless British
Who with the joyous sound
Of minted coins and gold
Brought us civilisation!

We make inflation
And hoard away
As much as we may relish
Essential commodities
Like sugar and salt
Like milk and oil

So we can leave the market
Each day a-rolling in wealth!

The lust of profit
Keeps us in this world
This life that is a market:
Refuse to join and perish,
Rebel and quench!
For those who spit at gold,
Otosi asinniwaye!

Among the few
That's seen each day
Whipping the world with lashes
And strutting round like lords,
Let's count our sons!
Let's also say
As we collect our profit
That life is heaven on earth!

SERGEANT   To be frank with you, I'm just dying to meet your musicians. I'm sure I could do with some exercise.

MAMA ALICE   Apart from drinking, you mean. A dance will certainly do something to your pregnancy!

(*They are still laughing when the first strains of the* ROBBERS' *music float in. The music grows louder, approaching. With an oath, the* SERGEANT *springs up, spilling his drink, and reaches for his gun. But it's too late, his movement ends unexpectedly in a dance posture. The women point at him and laugh, and before they know it, have started to dance and sing. The transition as in the last scene must be very abrupt. Now the robbers come in as before, singing and drumming. They hasten among the traders to untie their wallets, search their bags and all other places they suspect money will be, including inside their bras. The* SOLDIERS *of course are not neglected in the search. Finally, on the last stanza of the song, the* TRADERS *and the* SOLDIERS *dance out.* MAJOR *follows them, but is not immediately noticed by the others.*)

HASAN   (*exultant*) I told you, didn't I? See how it worked!

ALHAJA   You're a genius, Hasan!

ANGOLA   So easy. No more tedious work like last time. Carrying off those heavy baskets and boxes. Finding a place to hide them. Then looking for a market to sell them without being suspected.

HASAN   All that's gone. Now we just wait till they've finished the haggling and hustling

and are ready to go home with the profits. Then we pounce.

ALHAJA   A tune and a song. And we rake a fortune.

ANGOLA   Look at this. Who would believe these women made so much even in one month?

HASAN   What I have here is going to need a basket to carry.

ANGOLA   And did you see the soldiers? They actually brought soldiers to catch us!

HASAN   Fools! Guns to catch a song!

ALHAJA   I particularly liked that Sergeant. It was a delight to watch his dance. (*Dances in imitation. They laugh, except* HASAN.)

HASAN   (*pensive*) Yes, the Sergeant. How time changes fast.

ALHAJA   What?

HASAN   Time changes all of us.

ANGOLA   You knew him?

HASAN   A corpse, that's what we all become in the end. Yes, I knew the Sergeant, intimately. But how he has changed!

ALHAJA   Lucky then that he didn't recognise you.

HASAN   A corpse! (*Laughs suddenly.*) Forget it, the death mark is on all of us, even if we never reach the Bar Beach.

ANGOLA   Hasan, this is no time to be mournful. Look at what you have in your hands.

HASAN   (*listlessly*) Money . . .

ANGOLA   A fortune! The Aafa was right. We didn't make much last time, having to sell through shady channels. But this time we've got enough to last many life-times of poverty.

ALHAJA   Let's go! I'm dying to count.

HASAN   Wait, where's Major?

MAJOR   (*Enters. He has one of the* SOLDIERS' *guns.*) Here.

HASAN   What do you want with a –

MAJOR   Stop! Don't move any of you. (*Kicks out a sack.*) Alhaja, take this sack and collect all the money. You heard me! (*Reluctantly, she does so.*) And I warn you, no one else is to move. I love you all, but I won't hesitate to shoot any of you.

HASAN   (*handing his share over to* ALHAJA) This is treachery.

MAJOR   Treachery?

HASAN   The money belongs to all of us.

MAJOR   Bring it to me, Alhaja. Slowly. (*Takes it from her.*) Thanks. The money belongs to me now.

ALHAJA   (*angrily*) My husband brought you

out of the slum. From the cold, he put clothes on your back. From the rain, he found you shelter. He put your scattered life together, raised you into a man. He put the first gun in your hand, taught you to stand and fight, for justice. He gave your life a purpose. And now . . . (*She is too overpowered to continue.*)

MAJOR   Yes? And now what? Treachery, as Hasan said? (*Laughs.*) You are all little men. Like me. Our Leader, your husband Alhaja, he was a great man. But his death taught you nothing. Nothing! When the man walking in front stumbles into a pit, what should those behind do? Loyalty? Affection? Love? Should they, because of these passions, follow him into the pit? The grass-cutter of the forest, what must he do to claim the elephant's legend? Dress himself in ivory tusks? Listen, we were all brought up in a church and what did you learn there apart from how to break the ten commandments? There was a Messiah, once, and one was enough! For all the centuries. One great monumental mistake and nobody since has been in any hurry to repeat it. They crawl to the cross, they fall on their faces, wail and moan, but no worshipper asks to mount it and leave his life there. No! The nails and blood, the crown of thorns, all is a charade, kept for the tourist value and the ritual of house-cleaning. Afterwards are the buntings and the picnics to affirm the reality of living, of survival. And it's privilege, living. That's what the Leader's death says to us if you will clean your ears! Every man for himself. And all the rest: 'rob the rich, feed the poor'. They're all part of the furniture. You hear! Each man for himself!

HASAN   You're filthy, Major. Your mind has grown rotten.

MAJOR   You can't understand? This is the end. The beginning. I am leaving the filth. I am leaving you.

HASAN   How long? How long will it last?

MAJOR   For ever.

HASAN   It will follow you, the filth.

MAJOR   This is money! Money! A new life. No more scurrying in the smell of back streets. A house the size of a palace! The law, tamed with my bank account! And children! Listen, I am going to be a daddy! I'll own the main streets, six, no, . . . ten Mercedes, the neon lights, the supermarkets . . .

(*They try to rush at him, but he recovers instantly.*)

HASAN   You're doomed, Major! One day, we'll come gunning for you.

MAJOR   I'll be waiting, at the Bar Beach.

ANGOLA   You won't be there to watch it, I swear! Nor will your children.

MAJOR   So you'll never learn? Angola, Hasan, Alhaja? The other side are winners.

ALHAJA   Only for a season.

MAJOR   For ever! We are of the race victims are made of! We dream, we hug the gutters till we're plastered with slime. Then we begin to believe that slime is the only reality. We build it into a cult . . . and others continue to lap the cream of the land.

ANGOLA   (*edging towards him*) You cannot escape. No act of betrayal will alter your kinship.

MAJOR   Stand back or I shoot. There is no kinship. I have crossed to the other side of the street.

HASAN   But do you know the password?

MAJOR   I am going to fly.

HASAN   With what wings? What number of painted spots turn a sheep into a leopard?

MAJOR   There's no way of convincing you. I knew. That's why I am going away. If we meet again –

HASAN   Wait, Major. The Aafa gave us three chances. This is only the second.

MAJOR   I have enough. And only fools wait for a third time when they have all they want. There's no sliding back into slime for me. Only, if you like, I shall teach you my own part of the formula. But tomorrow, after I have hidden the money.

(*He begins to back away from them, still having them covered with the gun. Suddenly, the noise of gunshots from his rear. He wheels round, only to crumple as he is hit.*)

HASAN   The soldiers! The soldiers, they're coming back!

(*He runs, to try and help* MAJOR, *but is driven back by a salvo of shots.*)

ANGOLA   Leave him, he's dead!

HASAN   And the money?

ANGOLA   Are you mad? Come!

(*They run out just as the* SERGEANT *bursts in with his men. One of them is wounded.*)

CORPORAL   They're gone! They've run away!

SERGEANT   Too bad. We got only one of them. Recover that gun.

SOLDIER 1   (*doing so, discovering money*) Look, Serg!

SERGEANT   What?

SOLDIER 1   The money, it's all here!

SERGEANT   (*knocking him down*) Shut up, you fool! Can't you restrain yourself? (*Looks round rapidly.*) Corple, take care of the money. And listen, you dogs who may have been cursed to eternal poverty! As far as we know, the robbers ran away with the money! Is that clear? We found nothing. Okay? Let us meet later tonight, at my brother's house. And if I catch anybody with a running mouth . . .

(*He is still addressing them as lights fade out, fast.*)

Part Three

Same situation, some days later. Dawn again, almost as in Part One. Some SOLDIERS *are seen putting together a platform and a drum for what looks like an execution block, centre-stage among the stalls. The job is nearing completion when the lights come up. One or two of the* SOLDIERS *have their shirts off, but will gradually wear them again in the course of the play. The text below is not rigid, and should encourage free improvisation.*

SOLDIER 1   Ah this country self! If it doesn't reach the very last minute, nobody asks you to do anything: they must wait for the last minute, and then it's 'do this, do that!' And 'I want the work completed before I blink my eye!'

SOLDIER 2   Na religion, you don't know? We have an abounding faith in miracles, ask any of the flourishing apostles on the beach.

SOLDIER 1   Yes, miracles, as long as there are underdogs like me and you to make them happen. Ah, I am tired!

SOLDIER 3   Some of us are born to take orders, you fool, so shut up!

SOLDIER 1   Not me. I am going to be officer, you watch.

SOLDIER 3   And you complain about miracles! Do you think it's the number of craw-craw on your body that they count for promotion?

SOLDIER 1   I pity people like you, you'll always be an underdog.

SOLDIER 3   Go on complaining like that.

Then we'll see who will remain a bloody recruit, till retirement.

SOLDIER 2   Retirement! He's got to be a privileged recruit!

SOLDIER 1   Well, I am tired of these last-minute orders. I can just picture the Sergeant calling his wife one day: 'Darring . . . Answer now'.

SOLDIER 2   'Yessaaah!'

SOLDIER 1   'Darrrring mi!'

SOLDIER 2   'Yes, di'yah! I'm here.'

SOLDIER 1   'How many pickin we get?'

SOLDIER 2   'Pardon?'

SOLDIER 1   'Pickin, we pickin. How many we get now?'

SOLDIER 2   'Hm, which kin' question be that? Why you dey axe me? You know say na two I born'.

SOLDIER 1   'Na this tax form here. E says that if we get three children, we go qualify for rebate'.

SOLDIER 2   'I no tell you before? You see yourself now!'

SOLDIER 1   'Shurrup! By this time tomorrow, you hear?'

SOLDIER 2   'Hen-hen?'

SOLDIER 1   'By this time tomorrow, I order you to born anodder pickin!' (*They laugh.*) Believe me, it's no laughing matter! This platform we are just building for the execution this morning, suffering in the cold, tell me, how many days now since the sentence was passed on the armed robber?

SOLDIER 3   Seven. Eight self!

SOLDIER 1   You see?

SOLDIER 2   It was the contractor who failed to complete the job.

SOLDIER 3   Contractor? To build a platform for execution?

SOLDIER 2   Yes, I heard the Sergeant mention it.

SOLDIER 1   Tchei, this country!

SOLDIER 2   Contractor now, he went and bought Obokun[21] –

SOLDIER 3   For the Baba ke!

SOLDIER 2   And took a new wife.

SOLDIER 1   With government money!

SOLDIER 2   No, he borrowed it from you.

SOLDIER 1   I hope they punish him.

SOLDIER 2   Keep hoping. You think the contractor is a fool? That he spent the money all alone by himself?

SOLDIER 1   I see. So that's why we are suffering in the cold like this.

SOLDIER 3   At least you will have no

complaint. It's still better than the guard-room.

SOLDIER 1   That's where your papa lives?

SOLDIER 3   If not for this job you think they would have let you out so soon? Insulting an officer –

SOLDIER 1   Officer na yeye.[22] I tell you, I am going to be officer too one day.

SOLDIER 3   By the grace of Soponno, god of craw-craw!

SOLDIER 1   Siddown there. I won't tell you what I am going to do first after the promotion.

SOLDIER 2   The worst you can do is to try and overthrow the government. And as for that –

SOLDIER 1   Fool, how can I overthrow government when I'll be part of it? Let me tell you: all the fine fine palaces on Victoria Island and Ikoyi,[23] all the better lands at Ibadan, Kaduna, Pitakwa[24] and so on, I will declare them for government.

SOLDIER 3   Meaning, for yourself.

SOLDIER 1   With immediate effect!

SOLDIER 2   Thief man!

SOLDIER 1   Whetin. You never heard of African Socialism?

SOLDIER 3   They will kill you one day, I assure you.

SOLDIER 1   And if their owners refuse, I enquiry them at once.

SOLDIER 2   And then?

SOLDIER 1   The Nigerians among them, I detain. The Oyinbos and the Koras[25] –

SOLDIER 3   You shoot them.

SOLDIER 1   Haba. Where's your sense of hospitality, or are you not an African?

SOLDIER 3   So what will you do with them?

SOLDIER 1   Bushman. With these Oyinbos and Koras, the only decent thing to do is to form company with them. Import and Export Enterprises. Shipping Lines. Engineering Consultants (Nigeria) Limited, etc. For all contracts above five million naira.

SOLDIER 3   Why that one?

SOLDIER 1   How many times I must tell you our people are too useless? Look around you. Which black man get initiative? No, my friend, anything big you must give to expatriates! Expressway fit for visiting Heads of State. Overhead bridges with shining posters. Docks reclaimed from swamp. Airports for Concordes and discords. Hospitals, mortuaries, what more.

Even self, if we elect Lady President one day, no white man go fit to fuck am . . .

(*Above their laughter comes the call of a woman hawking corn. She enters, a covered basin on her head. It is* ALHAJA *disguised.*)

ALHAJA   (*calling*) Lagbe jino o![26] Hot steaming corn! Eager bride for hungry stomachs! Eat my corn and kick like a thoroughbred! Langbe re o![27]

SOLDIER 1   Woman, you're the answer to an unspoken prayer. We were just beginning to be hungry.

ALHAJA   I'm happy then, officer.

SOLDIER 1   (*delighted by the appellation*) Officer! Serve us, one naira worth! I hope your corn is as fine as you!

ALHAJA   (*Serving with a fork. They take it with their hands.*) Tasty, officer?

SOLDIER 1   (*eating*) Delightful! And are you as . . . as available?

ALHAJA   Depends.

SOLDIER 2   On what, I'm interested.

ALHAJA   On how sharp your tooth is.

SOLDIER 3   Ah, you've lost! She wants me!

SOLDIER 1   She's not talking of wisdom teeth, you old rag. She means strength, like mine.

ALHAJA   Well, may be. (*Looking round*) Who's been building a platform?

SOLDIER 1   Me, of course. They were helping.

SOLDIER 3   You hear that!

ALHAJA   But what's it for? (*They look at her with suspicion. Hastily she adds*) There's more corn.

SOLDIER 1   (*reassured*) It's the execution. We get man to kill this morning.

ALHAJA   Ah, the armed robber!

SOLDIER 1   That's right.

ALHAJA   And you . . . you're the soldiers going to . . . to do it?

SOLDIER 2   Yes. It's our job.

ALHAJA   (*leaping on their necks in turn*) Let me . . . let me hold you! Ah, I'm glad, so happy to meet you! What luck today! Take, eat more corn on my account! I never suspected that! Oh, I'm so glad I don't know how to express it! Such courage! I mean, to stand and shoot a man, a dangerous robber! Not many men can do it!

SOLDIER 3   We are soldiers.

ALHAJA   How many soldiers can do it! I tell you, you are heroes!

SOLDIER 1   Well, well –

ALHAJA   Eat! Please eat more! At my expense. To think that – Ah, I too, I am going to be a hero today! When I tell people that I actually met, actually spoke to, no, no, that I even touched yeah! Touched the soldiers who'll carry out the execution! I can imagine the envy! I'll strut, like this, watch me. I'll be like Emotan. Ah, I am going to become a legend! (*She dances and sings:*)

> Wo mi bi moti nredi – kenke!
> Redi fun ololufe – kenke![28]

(*The* SOLDIERS, *chewing, beat out the rhythm with their boots till, their resistance breaking down before her overt sexual provocation, they join her. Finally, at a calculated moment, she falls backwards, laughing, into their arms. As the move is unexpected, they stumble awkwardly forward and all fall down laughing.*)

ALHAJA   I just love you! You've made my day today! I will offer you something in return.

(*She pulls out an ogogoro[29] bottle from the basin, takes a swig and hands it out. The* SOLDIERS *are undecided.*)

SOLDIER 1   See if no one's coming.

ALHAJA   It's not market day today, don't worry. People'll only be coming for the execution.

SOLDIER 2   You're right. It's safe.

(*They drink. She rises to inspect the platform.*)

ALHAJA   Solid! That's why I love professionals. With the man tied up to this there won't be the slightest risk of mistake.

SOLDIER 1   Straight to the heart.

SOLDIER 2   The head.

SOLDIER 3   The kidney.

SOLDIER 1   We aim well.

ALHAJA   Good for them, these vermins. They pillage our homes, our offices, our markets.

SOLDIER 2   They rape women, pssshioo! (*Hissing.*)

SOLDIER 3   They steal children!

SOLDIER 1   They kill in cold blood.

(*They pass the bottle more frequently now.*)

ALHAJA   So wipe them out completely! Like this boy today! Ah when I used to know him –

SOLDIER 1   You knew him!

ALHAJA   Yes, unfortunately. He was not like this then. Edumare alone knows when he changed. For until quite recently, even until his arrest, every one spoke well of him. He was so gentle, so nice.

SOLDIER 3   True?

ALHAJA   Ask his neighbours. And if you knew his mama.

SOLDIER 2   He has a mother?

ALHAJA   Not any more. She died in the war.

SOLDIER 2   Maybe that's what changed him.

ALHAJA   The mother was a . . . the paragon of virtue herself. It's said frequently that she has gone to paradise.

SOLDIER 3   It happens like that, alas. Good woman dey born bad pickins.

ALHAJA   She was almost a saint! Went to church regularly. Taught Sunday school. She wanted to serve the country so much that when the war started, she – er, did you fight in the war?

SOLDIER 1   Of course! Right at the forefront!

SOLDIER 2   Decorated so many times that it became boring.

ALHAJA   I guessed it! You must have met her then.

SOLDIER 2   Er . . .

ALHAJA   She wrote that all the officers knew her.

SOLDIER 1   Of course, I remember her now! She was dark.

ALHAJA   No, very light-skinned!

SOLDIER 1   You're right! And kind of fat like this . . .

ALHAJA   Slim, so slim they called her Opelenge.[30]

SOLDIER 1   That's the woman! Beautiful, with pele[31] marks on her cheek.

ALHAJA   Well, it's possible she got those cut at the war front. Anyway, to tell you the story, as soon as the war started, this brave woman, she volunteered straight as a nurse, yes! Leaving her own little boy behind in her mother's care and . . . and (*sobbing*) do you know what happened?

SOLDIERS What . . . happened?

ALHAJA   They were evacuating Aba, and there was this soldier, a little boy. Still in his teens, he'd already lost both legs. Moremi – that's her name, the mother of this so-called robber – Moremi ran back to carry the soldier, and ran straight into the line of fire . . . and that was it, her son became an orphan.

SOLDIER 2   What a pity!

ALHAJA Think of it! That boy she was trying to save, perhaps it was one of your friends! Perhaps she had even nursed one of you here in those terrible conditions which finally took her life.

SOLDIER 1 Of course there was that woman at Orlu, we never found out her name.

ALHAJA It was Moremi! And now, her only son! See what they're doing to him.

SOLDIER 2 What they're doing to him?

ALHAJA That's what the whole town is saying! Will you believe that? All because of Moremi, may her soul rest in peace. They say a mother like that cannot bear a son who will steal, that her son is being framed! They say he was in fact trying to arrest the robbers when he was caught, by mistake. That because the trial was so hurried, the jury never really heard his own side of the case.

SOLDIER 3 That's what they're saying?

ALHAJA All over the town, I swear it to you! They say it's because he's poor and is an orphan!

SOLDIER 1 Just listen to that! I could have sworn the boy was innocent!

ALHAJA They say the big guns behind these robbers are trying to shield themselves by framing this boy!

SOLDIER 1 Lailai! Is that what they're trying to do?

ALHAJA You know how they're always using the poor against the poor! This boy now, he's just like you, poor, and an underling. So they get you to shoot him and nobody'll ever suspect them.

SOLDIER 2 Not this time! Ogun is listening. Not this time, they won't get away with this!

ALHAJA You're not drinking. It's yours, go on. I met Kayode yesterday. Kayode Martins – you know, the football star, centre forward for the Cocoa Champion Club. He was in the company of his friends, on their way back from a match, and you know what they were saying? Very funny. That, were they the soldiers guarding the poor boy, they would not hesitate to release him – by mistake of course – allow him to escape accidentally from prison, but well . . . please drink, it's all for you . . .

SOLDIER 3 We're drinking, don't worry.

ALHAJA Well, I said to Kayode, you don't know soldiers. When it comes to such things as upholding justice, they never interfere. Their ready excuse is always that it's politics, beyond their territory. They haven't the guts for that.

SOLDIER 1 What! You said that!

ALHAJA I said – ah, look, here's Kayode himself, with a friend. (*Enter* ANGOLA *and* HASAN.) Kayode, you're not a bastard. We were just talking about you. You know, our conversation of yesterday.

HASAN (*hostile*) Who're these soldiers?

ALHAJA They're the ones going to –

SOLDIER 1 (*coughing*) Ahem, ahem! How're you Kayode?

HASAN You're the ones going to carry out the execution this morning.

SOLDIER 2 Not really. That is . . . er . . .

HASAN If you are, I don't want to meet you. Go and carry out your murder of that poor orphan, simply because he's not got money on his side. His mother, who died because of you, his mother will thank you from her grave!

ALHAJA Kayode, don't be so harsh. You can't expect soldiers to be like football players who are used to acting according to their conscience. They've got to take orders, even if it's against someone they adore.

SOLDIER 1 No! Who tells you that! Who says we have no conscience!

ALHAJA You can't help this boy to escape –

SOLDIER 1 Who says we can't! Who says we won't!

ALHAJA Look, officer, there's no need to brag. I know as soon as you return to the barracks, that'll be the end of it all!

SOLDIER 1 You'll see! Let's go men! The whole town will learn something today! And those big men who think they can frame an innocent boy and use the army to achieve their evil plan. Let's go!

ALHAJA Officer, come back soon. (*Swings her waist suggestively.*) Your tooth, you said it can bite. I can hardly wait!

(*The* SOLDIERS *go out.*)

HASAN (*laughing*) Alhaja! You've not lost your touch!

ALHAJA (*smiling wearily*) I'm glad it's over. I could do with some food myself. (*Takes out corn and eats.*) Help yourselves.

HASAN (*taking corn*) You were marvellous! Just like in the old days.

ALHAJA Thank you, Hasan.

HASAN Like rabbits they scuttled off. They'll

nibble off the prison locks to prove their honour.

ALHAJA   And Major will be free.

HASAN   Luck's always been on his side. He survived the gunshot, survived the hostile crowds at trial, and he'll survive the firing squad.

ALHAJA   Yes, luck's his mistress. The soldiers won't fail us. I know men.

HASAN   All we do now is wait.

ANGOLA   For his corpse.

HASAN   What?

ANGOLA   I said for his corpse. You really believe the soldiers will release him, don't you?

HASAN   They will, but if they don't, we know who to blame. But for you, we could have rescued him before now. We could have used the song Aafa gave us.

ANGOLA   And lose our last chance of getting funds? How shall we pay for those things we planned?

ALHAJA   The life of a companion, Angola, is worth all the riches of this world.

ANGOLA   But the life of a traitor? What's that worth?

HASAN   Are we going over all that again?

ANGOLA   We shall be here, when they bring him trussed up. They'll walk him up that platform and shoot him like a dog. He'll get the death all traitors deserve. In a common market, among the smell of stale meat and rotten vegetables. He won't even make the Bar Beach.

ALHAJA   Tell me, what do you gain from such hatred?

ANGOLA   He foamed at the mouth! You saw it, he was going to shoot us! His eyes burned like embers. He had caught a mirage, but he leaned on it as one leans on something valuable. On this very spot. You heard his cry of exultation, his song of lust! And for material things, cars, houses, neon lights. A companion! He was no longer with us, he had crossed to the other side of the street.

ALHAJA   Yes, Angola. And that's why he's dearer to me.

ANGOLA   The lost sheep, eh? Don't tell me, I know the parable. And I know he'll be the first to scoff at it.

ALHAJA   What does that matter? He's still one of us.

ANGOLA   Delude yourself.

ALHAJA   My husband made him one of his heirs. Like you.

ANGOLA   And our Leader would have been the first to disinherit him! To have him wiped out.

ALHAJA   Then you never understood my husband. Nor why he brought you together.

ANGOLA   Well, tell me – why?

ALHAJA   If I had thought . . . Hasan, you're the one with words. You talk to him, I am weary.

ANGOLA   Major will be shot, like a dog.

HASAN   And afterwards?

ANGOLA   After what?

HASAN   After his death. Yours. Mine. After our death? After the next betrayal, the hammering of boards together for the state-approved slaughter? What will be left?

ANGOLA   I don't understand . . .

HASAN   You trade in death and danger. By government decree your life's the cheapest commodity in the market, and you don't understand! Listen to Alhaja, man! There'll be nothing after us, you hear, nothing but the empty stalls and their solidarity of suffering, the blood stains . . .

ALHAJA   The market waiting for new corpses, for my sons . . .

HASAN   We're doomed, my brother, and only our solidarity saves us. From the cutting of the cord, earth to earth. You know the myths! What else do they recount but the unending tales of the powerless against the strong. And it's a history of repeated defeat, oppression, of nothing changing . . .

ANGOLA   Alhaja . . .

ALHAJA   (slowly, as she enters a trance-like state) Nothing changing . . . Only my story starting anew. Like before, like always, like ever more. The man will come to me, and together we will share Obatala's apple once again. He will lure me with the same deceits, enter me in a soft moment, and in the ninth month my bastards will spill out again like shit. Oduduwa will be at hand to nurse them, beat them into shape. The shit will breathe the air, drink the moisture of rains, and Edumare will teach them how to use their feet. They will rise then, go into the garden arm in arm, their feet in warm dust, to where, at the foot of the tree, Ogun is waiting in a gourd to be discovered. They will drink then, my children, the sun will be in their eyes, the sun and Esu Laaroye,

in all the cells of their brain, and one will
stab the other and wash his hair in the
blood. Then he will raise his head, crowned
with blood and freedom, and he will have
won the right to give command. Plus, alas,
the right also to die. And all who will not
obey him will be scorched with the grass in
the right season. Including me, his mother,
in my withering. I will shout. I will call my
husband. But lost in the stream of being,
Orunmila will not respond. And all alone
I will swell with the terrible burden of
unwanted seed, unwanted because
condemned to die. I will swell, I will
explode, bearing the laughter of new
corpses . . . (*She is sobbing gently, still
possessed.* HASAN *goes to shake her violently,
but in vain.*)

HASAN   Alhaja! Alhaja! We're still here! (*To*
ANGOLA) See what you have done?

ANGOLA   Throw some sand on her.

HASAN   (*doing so*) Wake up! It's still
morning!

ALHAJA   (*starting*) Where . . . where was I?

HASAN   Too far. Too far back. Don't try it
again, it's dangerous.

ALHAJA   It's always good to meet the gods
again, but you're right. I'll pull myself
together. Angola, I know how you feel, but
we must learn to forgive. Those who fight
for justice must first start in love and
generosity.

ANGOLA   (*stubbornly*) No, not for those who
have changed into monsters.

ALHAJA   You'll not relent? You –

HASAN   Alhaja, look! (*Points in the direction of
town. Some sound, but still faint.*)

ALHAJA   (*Looks.*) Sango-o! Is my husband
asleep in the grave?

ANGOLA   I told you, didn't I?

ALHAJA   (*passionately*) Angola, listen to me
before they bring him in. It's his only
chance!

ANGOLA   He doesn't deserve it. I'm sorry,
Alhaja.

ALHAJA   I hate you! Don't ever talk to me
again. I don't ever want to see you!

ANGOLA   Goodbye. (*Exits, sulking.*)

HASAN   Quick, come Alhaja. Let's get out of
the way!

(*They draw quickly aside. The noise of voices
and feet increases discernibly now. Soon the
crowd bursts in, jeering at* MAJOR *and the*
SOLDIERS *we saw at the beginning of the
scene, but now stripped of their uniforms and*

also in chains. They are led forward by the
SERGEANT, *the* CORPORAL *and other*
SOLDIERS. *The procession stops at the
platform.*)

SERGEANT   Corple!

CORPORAL   Sir!

SERGEANT   As there is space for only one
person at a time, you'll take them in this
order: the robber first, then these sabos[32] in
order of height! Clear?

CORPORAL   Clear, Sir! Soldiers get going!

(MAJOR *is led up into position, the crowd still
jeering.*)

SERGEANT   Prisoner! (*Silence everywhere
now.*) Prisoner, this is your last chance. Do
you still refuse the priest?

MAJOR   I've said it, Serg, I want no odours
around me.

(*General reactions.*)

SERGEANT   Is there anything else you'd like
to say?

MAJOR   Yes (*Pause. Deathly silence.*) This day
is beautiful in the sunlight.

SERGEANT   Is that all?

MAJOR   Yes. The day is beautiful. Your
stomach proves it. (*Laughter.*) But man is
so fragile, so easy to kill! Especially if he
robs and lies, if he wantonly breaks the
law. Serg, today that law is on the side of
those who have, and in abundance, who
are fed and bulging, who can afford several
concubines. But tomorrow that law will
change. The poor will seize it and twist its
neck. The starving will smash the gates of
the supermarkets, the homeless will no
longer yield in fear to your bulldozers. And
your children, yes, your dainty little
children will be here where I stand now,
on the firing block . . .

(*Angry reactions.*)

SERGEANT   Enough! You'll not repent, I see.
Company take position.

(*They fall on one knee.*)

SERGEANT   Aim!

ALHAJA   Hasan, they're going to kill him!

MAJOR   Enough, you say?

SERGEANT   (*counting*) Five . . .

MAJOR   Tomorrow don't forget!

SERGEANT   Four . . .

MAJOR   And the day will still be –

SERGEANT   Three . . .

MAJOR   Like this, beautiful in sunlight.

SERGEANT   Two . . .

(*Suddenly* ALHAJA *runs forward and falls at the feet of* MAJOR.)

ALHAJA   No! Don't kill him!

SERGEANT   What the –

SOLDIER 1   That's she, Serg! That's the woman!

HASAN   (*coming forward*) Alhaja!

ALHAJA   I'm sorry, Hasan.

SOLDIER 2   Yes that's the other one! They're all in it together!

BINTU   You mean they're all robbers!

MAMA UYI   I recognise that one. He took my wallet.

MAMA TOUN   Yes, that woman led them.

CROWD   Shoot them! Kill them! Don't let them escape!

HASAN   You hear them, Sergeant? What are you waiting for?

SERGEANT   Hold your fire! They haven't even been tried! (*Comes forward.*) Hasan?

HASAN   Don't touch me!

SERGEANT   Hasan! You in this gang too?

CROWD   Kill them! Shoot them!

SERGEANT   Stand back! Soldiers! (*They form a protective cordon around the* ROBBERS.)

MAMA ALICE   Give them to us, Baba Mayo! Let's settle our score.

SERGEANT   Mama Alice . . . I can't. Hasan . . .

MAMA ALICE   What?

SERGEANT   It's Hasan, my own brother.

BINTU   Hasan! Let me see.

HASAN   Go away!

BINTU   It's me, Bintu!

HASAN   A corpse, like the rest.

SERGEANT   But what happened. Hasan? Tell me.

HASAN   Same as happened to you. Washed up. You run with the hunters, I with the rabbit.

SERGEANT   When . . . how did you change?

HASAN   You tell me. Ahmed, how did you *not* change?

SERGEANT   I don't understand.

HASAN   Damn it, you understand! Of course you do! You're an animal, you're flesh, you're blood and urine, not a bloody uniform! Take it off! Take the damned thing off and reveal yourself, you smelling primate. Let's see if you're not skin like me. If we didn't come from the same womb. You eat and you belch and you sleep with women, you're a bloody human being. So don't answer me like a uniform. I said, you have eyes, you can see, you know what is going on everywhere, what is happening to people like us. So how can you remain unmoved?

SERGEANT   Who said I'm unmoved? I enlisted, didn't I?

HASAN   From one bloody corner to another, the world getting narrower, shrinking around us, just to give a few bastards more room to fart –

ALHAJA   Go on, Hasan! Tell him.

MAJOR   He enlisted. His stomach grows. As they fatten a sacrificial ram.

SERGEANT   Quiet! I signed off my life. I joined the victors.

ALHAJA   So keep running, beast of prey, among the hunting dogs.

SOLDIER 4   Sergeant –

CROWD   Shoot them!

MAMA ALICE   No! Let's hear what they're saying!

SERGEANT   Hasan, you said, when you were leaving –

HASAN   Yes, Ahmed? What excuse do you think I owe you? Every one has his dream. Every one has a point at which the dream dries up. I have sworn never to be a slave in my own father's land. All I wanted was the right to work, but everywhere they only wanted slaves . . .

SERGEANT   You could have come to me.

HASAN   The family circuit, eh? Like a huge female breast eternally swollen with milk. But it's a mere fantasy, isn't it? The family breast can be sucked dry, however succulent, it can shrivel up in a season of want. Listen, Ahmed. Teacher flogged us at the writing desk – remember his Tuesday specials, when he always came dressed in red? Reverend flogged us with divine curses at the pulpit, the light glinting on his mango cheeks like Christmas lanterns – and poor Mama, she laid it into us routinely behind the locked door, her work-hardened palm stinging even sharper than whips. But for what? So that afterwards the grown man can crawl the street from month to month on his belly, begging for work, for a decent pay, for a roof, for a shelter from the pursuit of sirens? Ahmed, hide behind your bayonet, but I want to pay back all those lashes, and the lies of teacher, priest and parent. The world is a market, we come to slaughter one another and sell the parts . . .

SERGEANT It's not true! It can't –

HASAN No? Ask these women. They'll chop each other to bits at the jingle of coins.

MAMA ALICE (*angry*) It's all right for you to talk. You stalk the street drunken, and idle, and strike at night. But we have got to feed our families, haven't we?

BINTU We've got to pay the rent, pay the tax –

MAMA UYI For the tax-man has no friends –

YEDUNNI And the headmaster wants his fees, threatens to send the children into the street.

MAMA ALICE Brothers die and must be buried.

BINTU Sisters have their wedding day.

MAMA ALICE Children fall ill, needing medicine –

MAMA TOUN Needing food.

BINTU And even the simplest clothes wear out and must be replaced.

MAMA ALICE So who will pay the bill, if the market doesn't?

BINTU Where shall we turn, if not to our stalls?

MAMA TOUN How can we live, if profits lower or cease?

MAMA ALICE How shall we survive, if the Price Control Officer refuses to be bribed?

SERGEANT You hear that? You've been robbing from victims!

MAMA ALICE The market is our sanctuary. (*The women sing the last verse of the song of the market.*)

HASAN A slaughterhouse. Each hacking off the other's limbs. Kill quick, or be eaten.

CORPORAL Serg, I know say this na your own brother. But duty is duty . . .

SERGEANT You hear, Hasan? They're not with you.

HASAN Do your duty, Sergeant. Today is pay day.

SERGEANT We had a choice. You and your friends, my soldiers, and these traders. We could have stuck together and rebuilt our lives. But each went his own way and . . .

HASAN I am ready to pay the price. But you?

SERGEANT My mind is clear now. Soldiers, arrest them!

MAMA ALICE Baba Mayo. It's your own –

SERGEANT I did not choose it to be so, Mama Alice. Blood is an accident. It's only our beliefs that bind us together, or rip us apart. Hasan and I are on opposite sides of

the street. All I can do is hope that he has a decent trial. Now to get back to our work –

(*Breaking in suddenly, the voice of* ANGOLA, *chanting the formula.*)

HASAN Listen!

ANGOLA (*as he comes into view*)
Adisuuru-gbeje!
Atewo-ni-yagayaga-fi-gboore!
A kii moruko iku ko pani lomode:
Apanisigbomode la a peku!
Odaramogbo la a pe koto oku:
Apeja-pada-lona-orun-alakeji!

(*Confused with this unexpected phenomenon, the* SERGEANT *has paused, puzzled. Profiting from his apparent bewilderment, the other* ROBBERS *hasten to complete the entire formula.*)

HASAN
Olasunlola loruko a a p'Aje
Olasunloro laa p'Esu Odara
Ojinikutukutu-bomi-oro-boju:
A kii modi f'afefe ko ma lee lo!
A kii gbofin ile de era!

MAJOR
Ire lo niki e ba mi re
Iyo ope lo ni ki e maa yo mo mi
Adunkan-adunkan ni ti kukundunkun!

ALHAJA
Bi iwin bi iwin nii soloya
Bii were bii were nii selesu
Ajotapa ajopooyi nii sonisango!

(*The* SERGEANT *has been turning in complete stupefaction to each speaker in turn. Now, too late, he realises what is happening.*)

SERGEANT Zero! Fi . . .

ROBBERS (*cutting in urgently*) E ma jo-ooo! Dance! Raise your voices in song!

(*The stage vibrates with the clashing orders of* SOLDIERS *and* ROBBERS. *In that confusion, everything suddenly comes to a freeze. The lighting is intense. Then, from the auditorium,* AAFA *speaks into the silence, as he walks in for the Epilogue.*)

Epilogue

AAFA (*walking round the auditorium*) A stalemate? How can I end my story on a stalemate? If we sit on the fence, life is bound to pass us by, on both sides. No, I need your help. One side is bound to win in the end. The robbers, or the soldiers, who are acting on your behalf. So you've got to decide and resolve the issue. Which shall it be? Who wins? Yes, Madam? Your reasons please? And you, gentleman? Should the robbers be shot? Please do not be afraid to voice your opinion, we want this play to end. Okay, I'll take five opinions, and then we'll let the majority carry the day . . . yes?

(*He collects the views, making sure there is a full discussion, not just a gimmick, and then, in case the house decides for the* ROBBERS, *he says:*)

Ladies and gentlemen, the robbers win!

(*The* ROBBERS *come out of their freeze and sing their song.* HASAN *frees* MAJOR. *The* ROBBERS *rob the dancers, stripping them of shirts, bubas, geles, even trousers.* ALHAJA *fondles the* SERGEANT's *stomach. Then the* ROBBERS *start on the audience . . . who hurriedly begin to leave, as lights rise in the auditorium.*

But in case the audience decides against the ROBBERS, *then the end is different. The* ROBBERS *are all seized and tied up, in a scene of pantomime as in the Prologue.* MAJOR, *at the stake, is blindfolded. Meanwhile the lights slowly fade to dawn light, as martial music begins. All the movement must be jerky, like in puppetry. The order is given, and the execution done.* MAJOR *is untied and placed aside. Then* ALHAJA *is led to the platform and tied up. The* SOLDIERS *take position to fire. The martial tune rises to an intolerable pitch, and then abruptly cuts off exactly at the same moment as the lights are blacked out.*)

Notes

1 A gourd loosely covered with a blanket of beads strung together.
2 A buba is the top part of a two-piece top and trouser, buba and sokoto, usually made of the same material.
3 The Federal Military Government of Nigeria under General Gowon passed a decree making armed robbery punishable by public execution. The gruesome practice ended only with the coming of a civilian administration in 1979.
4 Literally, 'Thank you, moralizing priest!'

5 Son of a robber!
6 Traditional Yoruba masquerader/acrobat.
7 A feared, secret cult among the Yoruba.
8 Famous markets.
9 Famous markets.
10 Famous markets.
11 A Lagos suburb, overpopulated and crime-infested.
12 The Bar Beach of Lagos was the most notorious venue at this time for the public execution of robbers.
13 Lord, save me and my family from whatever they do!
14 God is the best Protector and He is the most merciful!
15 In the name of God, the Compassionate, the Merciful!
16 Pray for the Noble Prophet!
17 God grant him blessings and peace!
18 In production, the list should be made to include the most recent public scandals.
19 A charm, made by Muslim Malams, people skilled in the esoteric arts related to Islam.
20 Divination chain used by priests of Ifa.
21 Yoruba name for a Mercedes car.
22 Rubbish, nonsense.
23 High-class residential areas of Lagos.
24 Port Harcourt.
25 Whites and Asians.
26 My corn's hot and ready!
27 Here's corn!
28 See me wiggle my waist for my lover.
29 A home brewed gin.
30 Familiar Yoruba nickname for a very slim woman.
31 Facial beauty marks favoured by young girls and women, consisting of a short vertical line on each cheek.
32 Shortened form of 'saboteurs'.

Translations

For productions for non-Yoruba audiences, the songs and incantations may need to be translated into the language of the new locale. I have provided the following approximate renderings in English to facilitate such a transference. There is nothing rigid in this, however. For forms such as dirges and proverbs, with their own specificities, it may be wiser to find appropriate substitutions rather than translations.

1 'Iton mi dori o dori . . .'

An ancient tale I will tell you
Tale ancient and modern
A tale of four armed robbers
Dangerous highwaymen
Freebooters, source of tears
Like kites, eaters of accursed sacrifice
Visitors who leave the house desolate
Dispatchers of lives to heaven!

An ancient tale and modern
A tale of four armed robbers
The day government fire burnt them
And the gang leader was caught
And his back was turned to the sea

Death of the wretched, penalty of pain
Yes he was condemned to die
To die brutally by bullets
Bullets of the rattling gun
Ha! Man dies the death of goats
And so to heaven by force!

My tale is about four robbers
Who came to meet me one day
One day, as days pass away,
And said: 'Aafa of billowing robes
Billowing billowing robes!
Billowing billowing mat
Billowing billowing beard
Billowing billowing wisdom!

'Ah please save us from them
From these your modern men
Money-making has made them mad
Money, empty money
Money-hunting, evil-doing
Evil-doing to amass property
Buildings upon buildings
Wife-stealers, marriage-wreckers
Who teach by the hard way of pain!'

A modern tale I will tell you
A tale of four armed robbers
Dangerous highwaymen
Freebooters, source of tears
Like kites, eaters of accursed food
Visitors who leave the host in ruin
Dispatchers to unexpected heaven . . .

2 'Eni lo sorun . . .'

The traveller to heaven
never returns,
Alani, goodbye, till we meet over there!
The journey to heaven
is a one-way route,
Alani, goodbye, till we meet in dream

Whatever is food in heaven
You will share
You will not eat worms
or centipedes
Alani, so fondly remembered . . .

3 'Awa ti wa . . .'

We are what we are
and no apologies!
We are what we are, gate crashers
Who, uninvited, bash into parties

Consume the drinks
Devour the food
And loot the store
We're scalpel-sharp, we're pungent
Ah do not provoke
For our gash is deadly
Our knives are long
And needle-tipped
Our wounds are ghastly, ghastly
We have no equals!

4 'Bi e ba gbo giri . . .'

If you hear the earth rumble,
quick, run for it.
We're those who make the earth
   tremble and tear apart!
If you hear the earth quake,
don't wait at all!
We're those who make the earth quake
   and split open!

5 'O se kere-e-e-e . . .'

It is nothing but overdaring
Nothing but overdaring
For the old hag who pines and pines
To be like the 'ora' bird
The bird whose flight is so swift
That before she can turn away
She has knocked her head into an
   obstacle
And been deflected involuntarily
but if the woman insists
Doddering old hag, who envies
youth
And longs to be spritely
To be a coquette like the 'ora' bird
Push her forward, catapult her
Into the circle and ask her
To display her credentials . . .
Not all maidens, we know
Have supple breasts . . . !

It is nothing but ambition
Nothing but overdaring
For an old hag to pine and pine
To be like the swift 'ora' bird . . .

6 'O ja lori obi . . . '

You fall from kolanut tree
You fall from kolanut tree
And fracture your thigh
So you have to crawl on your belly!
Who finds something astray
And does not seize it,
Who finds something lying by
And does not claim it
Must be stupid or insane
Must be dotard or deranged
Kerikeri! Kerikeri!

Where are you from that guards
Dare arrest you at night?
Stupid robbers only
Are killed by guards at night!
Yes, they call us robbers
But we're about our trade
Whoever the devil tempts
Should try to ambush us!
Whoever desires death
Should try to block our way.
He'll see his intestines gush out!
He'll watch his kidneys in open air!

7 'Eyi lo ye ni . . . '

This feat becomes a hero
    Hen hun hen (Yes, yes, yes!)
Ogun is marching to war
    Hen hun hen
Is armed with seven testicles
    Hen hun hen
One is loaded with bullets
    Hen hun hen
Two are filled with wine
    Hen hun hen
And four are brimming with sperm!
    Hen hun hen
Ogun! I pay respects!
    Hen hun hen

8 'Omo Enire . . . '

*This 'incantation' is adapted from Wande
Abimbola's recordings of one of the principal
Odu of Ifa, on pages 63–5 of his* Sixteen Great
Poems of Ifa, *published by UNESCO. The
translation here is different from his partly for
reasons of dramaturgy.*

Son of Enire
Son of Enire
Of those who strike sudden and sharp
Ifa, we invite you home!
Ewi of Ado
Onsa of Deta
Erinmi of Owo
Ifa, we beckon you here!
Gbolajakooo, who seats wealth
On sedate throne,
Offspring of elephant
With ivory trumpets
Ifa, hearken to our call!
Source of graceful palmfronds
Which dance and hum by the river
Ifa, we invite you home!
Shoot of tender palmfronds
So fresh and frail and young,
Offspring of two snakes
Which slide so fast on trees
Offspring of bush fire
Which spares the oorun branches
You offspring of bush fire
Which skirts the heart of forest
Ifa, hearken to our call!

9 Interlude: 'Iton mi dori o dori . . . '

I am still telling my tale
The tale of four armed robbers
Who came to meet me one day
Whom I gave a power to magic
The magical power of song
The mystery of song, force of dance
which will send hearers to sleep
I, Aafa, with billowing robes
Billowing billowing robes
Billowing billowing mat
Billowing billowing beard
Billowing billowing wisdom!

Yes, I gave them the right reply
To this your modern world
Money-grabbing has made you mad
Money, empty money
Money-hunting, evil-doing
Evil-doing to amass property
Buildings upon buildings
Wife-stealing, home-destroying
Teaching by the hard way of pain
A modern tale I will tell you
A tale of four armed robbers
Dangerous highwaymen
Freebooters, source of tears
Like kites, eaters of accursed meals

Visitors who leave the house in wreck
Dispatchers to the heaven of
    slumber . . .

10 'Eni maye je . . . '

The man who relishes life
Will not try to climb a coconut tree
The man who loves to live long
Will surely not climb a coconut tree!
When the throat itches,
Prepare for a cough.
If the throat scratches,
Watch out for phlegm!
And if you host a Moslem,
You'll have to bear how many
    'salaam-ailekum'!
Alas! When a vulture alights on the
    rooftop
Prepare for the costs of a coffin!
No! No evil thing will visit me,
For only illness can be cured,
with death it's too late!

11 'Adisuuru-gbeje . . . '

*The incantations here are adapted from
collections of 'ofo' made by O.O. Olatunji for his
1970 thesis, 'Characteristics of Yoruba Oral
Poetry', for the University of Ibadan. The
translations offered here are different from his
for reasons mainly of dramaturgy.*

ANGOLA
Who lurks in patience
To collect a pledge!
The yagayaga plant collects gifts
With open palm
When you name the name of death
He pledges you long life
Death! Your name is
Apanisigbomogbe, I name you
Death! Your home of corpses
Is called Odaramogbo!
I call it roundly, to win
My ransom from sudden death!

HASAN
Honour sleeps in wealth
Is the name we call Aje
Honour beds in affluence
Is the name of Esu Odara
Mothers wash their face in wealth
As they wake in the morning!
Who can wall in the air
That it does not escape?
Oh, how deep the ditch
That will halt the ant?

MAJOR
Ire plant has ordered our friendship
The male palm flower orders rejoicing
Eternal sweetness is the lot of sweet
    potatoes!
ALHAJA
At the sound of dance, the Oya
    worshipper
Runs amock
The Esu worshipper, at the call of drum
Turns into frantic lunatic
The Sango worshipper swoons in a daze
    of whirling feet . . .

6 Ama Ata Aidoo

Anowa
Ghana

Introduction

Ama Ata Aidoo is one of Africa's most prolific and versatile writers. Not only has she written plays, short stories, novels, poetry, essays, letters and criticism, but also, by drawing upon the Ghanaian oral tradition's fusing of narrative techniques, she is able to synthesise these different forms, which are generally split among different genres in Western literary traditions. Aidoo's considerable creative and academic accomplishments have been matched by a strong political activism that has seen her at the forefront of the development of contemporary African feminism.

Born in 1942 in Abeadzi Kyiakor in south central Ghana, Aidoo grew up in the Fanti Royal Household, but her father, an advocate of Western education, sent her to Wesley Girls' High School in Cape Coast. Afterwards, she studied at the University of Ghana in Legon, where she received a bachelor's degree in English, and worked with playwright Efua Sutherland, the influential founder of Ghana Drama Studio. During that time Aidoo put on her first play, *The Dilemma of a Ghost* (1964), which incorporated many of the issues that would come to characterise her work: the legacy of the slave trade, the position of women in African societies, and the dynamics of African diasporic identity. The play, about tensions between a Ghanaian man who returns home from the United States and the African–American wife he brings with him, derived impetus from Aidoo's research into traditional forms of West African storytelling. This marked the beginning of a career-long process of employing the narrative and dramatic traditions of Ghana to articulate issues of contemporary importance. Since that time, Aidoo's stature has grown internationally with the publication of such highly acclaimed prose works as *No Sweetness Here* (1970) and *Our Sister Killjoy* (1979) as well as a number of verse collections, including *An Angry Letter in January and Other Poems* (1992). She has been Professor of English at the University of Ghana, a consulting professor to the Washington branch of the Phelps Stokes Fund's Ethnic Studies Program, and a Minister of Education in Ghana under the Jerry Rawlings government. Since settling in Harare in 1983, she has become involved in the Curriculum Development Unit of the Ministry of Education, and been active in the Zimbabwe Women Writers' Group.

Aidoo's second play, *Anowa* (1970), is set in an earlier historical period than *Dilemma of a Ghost*, but focuses on similar themes and also draws upon Ghanaian forms of storytelling, which Aidoo reveals as the direct inspirational source for her narrative:

> I come from a people who told stories . . . And my mother 'talks' stories and sings songs. *Anowa*, for instance, grew directly out of a story she told me although as the play has come out, she cannot even recognize the story she told.
>
> (quoted in James 1990: 19)

This statement suggests the complex nature of Aidoo's literary project. Although *Anowa* is based on a traditional Ghanaian folktale – the archetypal story of the disobedient daughter who rejects all suitors proposed by her parents, only to marry an attractive stranger who turns out to be the devil in disguise – Aidoo's version infuses it with new meanings. In *Anowa*, the generality of the folktale and its message is adapted to a specific time in history and given contemporary relevance for a postcolonial African society attempting to contemplate its complicity in an execrable past.

Although written in English, *Anowa* has the structure of a traditional tale. Its narrative is comprised of verse, prose, song and mime and incorporates many storytelling elements, including the use of proverbs, laments, colloquialisms, oral idioms and the rhythms and phraseology of oral recitation. This quality of orature is, in Aidoo's conception, a powerful modality for world literature: 'I still believe that one day, when Africa comes into her own, the dynamism of orality might be something that Africa can give to the world' (quoted in James 1990: 23). The fused choral figure of The-Mouth-That-Eats-Salt-And-Pepper, comprised of an old man and old woman of the village, reflects such dynamism. Their role is integral to the play, introducing the audience to the society of Abura and to the characters and themes to be presented, as well as commenting on the narrative action at crucial points.

Anowa is set on the Gold Coast about thirty years after the Bond Treaty, an agreement granting the British trading priority over the Fanti area of what is now Ghana. The bond of 1844 not only bound Fanti slave-traders to the white imperialists but also positioned them at a historical juncture where the narratives of colonialism and capitalism intersected. From the very beginning of the play, the question of Africans' complicity in the slave trade is suggested in the powerful image of British slave forts 'standing at the door/ Of the great ocean'. The figure of the capitalist is embodied in Anowa's husband, Kofi Ako, the Fanti trader who enslaves his fellow men for the accumulation of wealth. While Kofi Ako embodies the emergence of a class of Africans whose interests are aligned with British imperialism, Anowa resists his desire to live off the labour of others, claiming that the limit of one's wealth should be set by what one's own personal labour can provide. The play suggests that Anowa's eventual disintegration is partly caused by the fact that not working deprives her life of meaning, a void portrayed through the dual figure of Panyin-Na-Kakra, a pair of twins whose job it is to fan an empty chair.

In *Anowa*, capitalist and colonialist exploitation is explicitly linked to patriarchal dominance and gender oppression, and the play draws parallels between wives and slaves. In this way, Aidoo establishes the relationship between the personal and the political so that the public and historical story of slave-trading is mirrored in Kofi Ako's treatment of Anowa, who had given so much of her own labour to establish his enterprises. This parallel revolves around the question of sexual desire, and it is significant that the effects of Kofi Ako's endeavours manifest in his impotence: political power is a compensation for sexual inadequacy and, conversely, sexual inadequacy is an effect of political power. The motif of impotence also points indirectly to imperialism's damaging effects on African social organisation, particularly in terms of gender roles. The first part of the narrative establishes Abura as a matrilineal society, stressing that it is Badua and her family's responsibility to arrange Anowa's future, while Osam, her father, plays a lesser role. As the story progresses, the sequence of events suggests that contact with capitalism disrupts traditional matrilineal societies and alters women's roles, while colonial regimes, by bringing their patriarchal systems to Africa, bring advantages for African men, who are provided with the means of subjugating women. As a result, although Anowa and Kofi's relationship is not traditional, it is nonetheless destroyed by the effects of trade and the repositioning of women under capitalist economics.

Anowa's emphasis on matrilineality reflects Aidoo's idea, prevalent in both her creative and critical work, that African women have a feminist precedent in their own culture and need not look to Western feminism to provide them with remedies to their oppression, especially as women in the West have benefited from colonialist expansionism. The abstracted figure of the African mother, expressed most forcefully in Anowa's monologue recalling her childhood nightmare, provides a cultural anchor for the play's critique of patriarchal systems. In her dream, Anowa becomes a symbol of Africa, 'out of which poured men, women and children' who are seized by giant lobsters from the sea, a reference to her grandmother's earlier description of white men as being like lobsters. This haunting image provides a way of reading Anowa's barrenness as an effect of the slave trade, which has robbed her of her fertility. For Anowa, there is no point in producing children if they will be taken away and turned into slaves. Once again, her personal story is linked to the wider political sphere: she becomes the mother of all her people, and, as mother Africa, is betrayed by the male slave trader. Significantly, this dream is triggered by a conversation in which Anowa asks her grandmother, 'Where did the white men get slaves?' Her grandmother replies, 'You must be a witch, child', closing the conversation with the claim that good men and women have forgotten such things. Yet Anowa cannot forget, nor can she keep silent about the injustices she sees around her; she must ask questions, just as the play itself asks questions, making explicit the connection between questioning, crafting narratives and the necessity of remembering. Through this connection, the relationship between speech and witchcraft becomes evident: Anowa is accused of being a witch precisely because of her capacity to bring the ghosts of the dead back to haunt the living. What both Aidoo and Anowa reveal is the cost of silence.

Anowa's raising of complex and uncomfortable questions as a young girl is essential to the play's structure in so far as it conforms to the oral narrative genre of the dilemma tale, with all its accompanying ambiguity. In the world of the dilemma play, there are no easy answers, but the questions need to be raised anyway. The dilemma tale allows for different interpretations that collectively act as a challenge to the logic of singular truths, which are a hallmark of patriarchy. Fashioned in this traditional genre, *Anowa* also enables the portrayal of untenable oppositions for its eponymous hero, who is caught between individual and community tensions. Although turning her back on the small-mindedness of the traditional community, Anowa cannot accept the injustice and corruption at the heart of the new capitalist economy that is replacing it, and particularly its betrayal of fellow Africans in the form of slavery. In the dilemma tale, a range of viewpoints is given, expressed most clearly in the play through the dialogue of competing opinions delivered by The-Mouth-That-Eats-Salt-And-Pepper. This compound 'character' also avoids simple appeals to female solidarity, for it is the old man, described in the stage directions as serene and orderly, who is the voice of tolerance and understanding, and who, interestingly, speaks predominantly in verse. The old woman, by contrast, is the voice of communal prejudices, and she believes a woman's role as both daughter and wife should be one of obedience.

Aidoo's use of the dilemma tale, which does not provide answers but instead initiates thought and discussion, demands an audience response; demands, in fact, remembering. For Aidoo, part of this remembering lies in structure as well as narrative, hence her use of traditional forms to tell her story: 'Everybody needs a backbone. If we do not refer to the old traditions, it is almost like operating with amnesia' (Aidoo 1976: 124). Traditional material, usually considered a conservative force, thus becomes a mode of questioning that has radical potential for social change. In this sense, the play is also about the nature of tales and how they have a life of their own, independent of the teller. It quite self-consciously points to the complex relationship stories have with reality, simultaneously reflecting and producing it. As the old woman says: 'This is the type of happening out of which we get stories and legends'.

Anowa ends with the suicides of both Kofi Ako and Anowa, foreshadowed by the African funeral march that imbues the final phase with impending doom. In the closing commentary by The-Mouth-That-Eats-Salt-And-Pepper, the old woman lays the blame for the tragedy squarely at the feet of Anowa. By contrast, the old man does not individualise blame; rather he assigns it to the society as a whole. Just as his opening assessment of Kofi Ako implicates the wider community in the action to follow by claiming that this pariah 'was, is and shall always be, one of us', the old man's final lines invite audiences to question their own complicity in the horror that the play has explored: 'It is men who make men mad. Who knows if Anowa would have been a better woman, a better person, if we had not been what we are?'

Production history

Anowa was first published in 1970 and had a successful production in London in 1991.

Select bibliography

Adelugba, D. (1976) 'Language and drama: Ama Ata Aidoo', *African Literature Today* 8: 72–84.

Agyemang, K.O. (1996) 'A crisis of balance:

the (mis)representation of colonial history and the slave experience as themes in modern African literature', in W. Zach and K. Goodwin (eds) *Nationalism and Internationalism: (Inter)National Dimensions of Literature in English*, Tubingen: Stauffenberg, 219–28.

Aidoo, A.A. (1976) 'Roundtable discussion', *Issue: A Quarterly Journal of Africanist Opinion* 6, 1: 124–7.

—— (1995) Interview with A.D. Needham, *Massachusetts Review* 36, 1: 123–33.

—— (1999) 'Unwelcome pals and decorative slaves – or glimpses of women as writers and characters in contemporary African literature', in A.U. Azodo and G. Wilentz (eds), *Emerging Perspectives on Ama Ata Aidoo*, Trenton, NJ: Africa World Press, 11–24.

Azodo, A.U. and Wilentz, G. (eds) (1999) *Emerging Perspectives on Ama Ata Aidoo*, Trenton, NJ: African World Press.

Brown, L.W. (1981) 'Ama Ata Aidoo', *Women Writers in Black Africa*, Westport, CT: Greenwood, 84–121.

Eke, M. (1999) 'Diasporic ruptures and remembering history: Africa as home and exile in *Anowa* and *Dilemma of a Ghost*', in A.U. Azodo and G. Wilentz (eds), *Emerging Perspectives on Ama Ata Aidoo*, Trenton, NJ: Africa World Press, 61–78.

Ekpong, M.O. (1994) 'Feminist tendencies in West African drama: an analysis of Ama Ata Aidoo's *Anowa*', in E.N. Emenyonu and C.E. Nnolim (eds), *Current Trends in Literature and Language Studies in West Africa*, Ibadan: Kraft Books, 20–33.

Elder, A. (1987) 'Ama Ata Aidoo and the oral tradition: a paradox of form and substance', *African Literature Today* 15: 109–18.

Hill-Lubin, M. (1989) 'The storyteller and the audience in the works of Ama Ata Aidoo', *Neohelicon* 16, 2: 221–45.

James, A. (1990) 'Ama Ata Aidoo', in A. James (ed.) *In their Own Voices: African Women Writers Talk*, Portsmouth, NH: Heinemann, 8–27.

Jones, E.D. (1976) Review of *Anowa*, by Ama Ata Aidoo, *African Literature Today* 8: 142–4.

McGregor, M. (1972) 'Ama Ata Aidoo', in C. Pieterse and D. Duerden (eds) *African Writers Talking*, London: Heinemann, 19–27.

Odamtten, V.O. (1994) *The Art of Ama Ata Aidoo*, Gainesville, FL: University Press of Florida.

Anowa

Ama Ata Aidoo

* Go with the family OR Do your own thing (ends up being her downfall)
* possession of bodies by others throughout all three plays
* people searching for autonomy in a society that won't allow it without sacrifice.
Can only get 1 so far

Characters

OLD MAN, OLD WOMAN } Being THE-MOUTH-THAT-EATS-SALT-AND-PEPPER
A MAN and A WOMAN who don't say a word
ANOWA a young woman who grows up
KOFI AKO her man who expands
OSAM her father who smokes his pipe
BADUA her mother who complains at the beginning and cries at the end
BOY a young slave, about twenty years old
GIRL a young slave girl
PANYIN-NA-KAKRA a pair of boy twins whose duty it is to fan an empty chair
HORNBLOWER
OTHER MEN and WOMEN slaves, carriers, hailing women, drummers, messengers, townspeople

Setting

The stage is divided into two parts, each with two exits. The upper area is the main stage; the lower stage could be narrower (smaller) than the first and any space between the audience and the real stage can serve this purpose.

Music

The Ghanaian forms may be replaced by other African or any other folk music. The Atentenben, which is here intended as a symbol for ANOWA, is a single, delicate but wild wind instrument. The horn (bull's) is usually old and turned dark brown by sacrificial blood. It is an appendage of the stool and symbol of state, village or group power. An individual acquired a horn (but never a stool) if he felt he was rich and powerful enough. In fact, the acquisition of such a horn was a declaration of power. The horn sang the praises of its owner(s), its language codes being very similar to those of drums. The Fontonfrom is an essentially dignified, low-rumbling drum in a big man's ensemble.

Prologue

Enter THE-MOUTH-THAT-EATS-SALT-AND-PEPPER. OLD MAN *always enters first from the left side of the auditorium.* OLD WOMAN *from the right. Each leaves in the same direction. She is wizened, leans on a stick and her voice is raspy with asthma and a life-time of putting her mouth into other people's affairs. She begins her speeches when she is half-way in and ends them half-way out. Her entries are announced by the thumping of her stick, and whenever she is the last of the two to leave the stage, her exit is marked by a prolonged coughing. She is never still and very often speaks with agitation, waving her stick and walking up and down the lower stage. He is serene and everything about him is more orderly. He enters quietly and leaves after his last statements have been made. The two should never appear or move onto the upper stage. There is a block of wood lying around on which the* OLD WOMAN *sometimes sits.*

OLD MAN

Here in the state of Abura,
Which must surely be one of the best pieces of land
Odomankoma, our creator, has given to man,
Everything happens in moderation:
The sun comes out each day,
But its heat seldom burns our crops;
Rains are good when they fall
And Asaase Efua the earth-goddess gives of herself
To them that know the seasons;
Streams abound, which like all gods
Must have their angry moments and swell,
But floods are hardly known to living memory.

Behind us to the north, Aburabura
Our beautiful lonely mountain sits with
  her neck to the skies,
Reminding us that all of the earth is not
  flat.
In the south, Nana Bosompo, the ocean
  roars on. Lord of Tuesdays,
His day must be sacred. We know him
  well and even
The most unadventurous can reap his
  fish, just sitting on his pretty sands,
While for the brave who read the
  constellations,
His billows are easier to ride than the
  currents of a ditch.
And you, Mighty God, and your hosts our
  forefathers,
We do not say this in boastfulness . . .
(*He bends in the fingers of his right hand
as though he were holding a cup, raises
it up and acts out the motions of pouring
a libation*) . . . but only in true
  thankfulness,
Praying to you all that things may
  continue to be good
And even get better.
But bring your ears nearer, my friends, so
  I can whisper you a secret.
Our armies, well-organised though they
  be,
Are more skilled in quenching fires than
  in the art of war!
So please,
Let not posterity judge it too bitterly
That in a dangerous moment, the lords of
  our Houses
Sought the protection of those
  that-came-from-beyond-the-horizon
Against our more active kinsmen from
  the north;
We only wanted a little peace
For which our fathers had broken away
From the larger homestead and come to
  these parts,
Led by the embalmed bodies of the Three
  Elders.
And yet, there is a bigger crime
We have inherited from the clans
  incorporate
Of which, lest we forget when the time
  does come,
Those forts standing at the door
Of the great ocean shall remind our
  children
And the sea bear witness.
And now, listen o . . . o listen, listen,

If there be some among us that have
  found a common sauce-bowl
In which they play a game of dipping
  with the stranger,
Who shall complain?
Out of one womb can always come a
  disparate breed;
And men will always go
Where the rumbling hunger in their
  bowels shall be stilled,
And that is where they will stay.
O my beloveds, let it not surprise us
  then
That This-One and That-One
Depend for their well-being on the
  presence of
The pale stranger in our midst:
Kofi was, is, and shall always be
One of us.

(*First sign of* OLD WOMAN.)

But what shall we say of our child,
The unfortunate Anowa? Let us just say
  that
Anowa is not a girl to meet every day.

OLD WOMAN That Anowa is something else!
Like all the beautiful maidens in the tales,
she has refused to marry any of the sturdy
men who have asked for her hand in
marriage. No one knows what is wrong
with her!

OLD MAN
  A child of several incarnations,
  She listens to her own tales,
  Laughs at her own jokes and
  Follows her own advice.

OLD WOMAN Some of us think she has just
allowed her unusual beauty to cloud her
vision of the world.

OLD MAN
  Beautiful as Korado Ahima,
  Someone's-Thin-Thread.
  A dainty little pot
  Well-baked,
  And polished smooth
  To set in a nobleman's corner.

(BADUA *enters from a door at upper right
and moves down but stops a few steps before
the lower stage and stands looking at* OLD
MAN *and* OLD WOMAN.)

OLD WOMAN Others think that her mother
Badua has spoilt her shamefully. But let us
ask: why should Anowa carry herself so
stiffly? Where is she taking her 'I won't, I
won't' to? Badua should tell her daughter

that the sapling breaks with bending that will not grow straight.

BADUA (*bursting out suddenly and pointing her fingers clearly at* OLD MAN *and* OLD WOMAN *but speaking to herself*) Perhaps it was my fault too, but how could she come to any good when her name was always on the lips of every mouth that ate pepper and salt?

(*She turns round angrily and exits where she had come from.* OLD MAN *and* OLD WOMAN *do not show they had been aware of her.*)

OLD MAN
But here is Anowa,
And also Kofi Ako.
It is now a little less than thirty years
When the lords of our Houses
Signed that piece of paper –
The Bond of 1844 they call it –
Binding us to the white men
Who came from beyond the horizon.
(*Exits.*)

OLD WOMAN   And the gods will surely punish Abenda Badua for refusing to let a born priestess dance!

Phase One: In Yebi

Lower stage. Early evening village noises, for example, the pounding of fufu or millet, a goat bleats loudly, a woman calls her child, etc. ANOWA *enters from lower right, carrying an empty water-pot. She walks to the centre of the lower stage, stops and looks behind her. Then she overturns the water-pot and sits on it facing the audience. She is wearing her cloth wrapped around her. The upper part of her breasts are visible, and also all of her legs. She is slim and slight of build. She turns her face momentarily towards lower left. During a moment when she is looking at her feet,* KOFI AKO *enters from the lower right. He is a tall, broad, young man, and very good-looking. The village noises die down.*

He is in work clothes and carrying a fish trap and a bundle of baits. He steals quietly up to her and cries, 'Hei!' She is startled but regains her composure immediately. They smile at each other. Just then, a WOMAN *comes in from the lower left, carrying a wooden tray which is filled with farm produce – cassava, yam, plantain, pepper, tomatoes, etc. Close behind her is a* MAN, *presumably her husband also in work-clothes, with a gun on his shoulder and a machet under his arm. They pass by* ANOWA

and KOFI AKO *and walk on towards lower right. The woman turns round at every step to stare at the boy and girl who continue looking shyly at each other. Finally, the* WOMAN *misses a step or kicks against the block of wood. She falls, her tray crashing down.*

ANOWA *and* KOFI AKO *burst into loud uncontrollable laughter. Assisted by her man, the* WOMAN *begins to collect her things together. Having got her load back on her head, she disappears, followed by her* MAN. *Meanwhile,* ANOWA *and* KOFI AKO *continue laughing and go on doing so a little while after the lights have been removed from them.*

Upper stage. The courtyard of MAAMI BADUA *and* PAPA OSAM's *cottage. Village noises as in previous scene. Standing in the centre is an earthen hearth with tripod cooking pot. There are a couple of small household stools standing around. By the right wall is a lie-in chair which belongs exclusively to* PAPA OSAM. *Whenever he sits down, he sits in this. By the chair is a small table. The lower stage here represents a section of a village side street from which there is an open entrance into the courtyard. In the background, upper left and upper right are doors connecting the courtyard to the inner rooms of the house.*

In the pot something is cooking which throughout the scene MAAMI BADUA *will go and stir. By the hearth is a small vessel into which she puts the ladle after each stirring.*

BADUA *enters from upper right, goes to the hearth, picks up the ladle and stirs the soup. She is talking loudly to herself.*

BADUA   Any mother would be concerned if her daughter refused to get married six years after her puberty. If I do not worry about this, what shall I worry about? (OSAM *enters from upper left smoking his pipe.*) Besides, a woman is not a stone but a human being; she grows.

OSAM   Woman, (BADUA *turns to look at him*) that does not mean you should break my ears with your complaints. (*He looks very composed.*)

BADUA   What did you say, Osam?

OSAM   I say you complain too much. (*He goes to occupy the lie-in chair, and exclaims, 'Ah!' with satisfaction.*)

BADUA   (*seriously*) Are you trying to send me insane?

OSAM   Will that shut you up?

BADUA   Kofi Sam! (*Now she really is angry.*)

OSAM   Yes, my wife.

(BADUA *breathes audibly with exasperation. She begins pacing up and down the courtyard, with the ladle in her hand.*)

BADUA (*moving quickly up to* OSAM) So it is nothing at a-a-l-l (*stretching the utterance of the last word*) to you that your child is not married and goes round wild, making everyone talk about her?

OSAM Which is your headache, that she is not yet married, or that she is wild?

BADUA Hmm!

OSAM You know that I am a man and getting daughters married is not one of my duties. Getting them born, aha! But not finding them husbands.

BADUA Hmm! (*Paces up and down.*)

OSAM And may the ancestral spirits help me, but what man would I order from the heavens to please the difficult eye of my daughter Anowa?

BADUA Hmm! (*She goes and stirs the soup and this time remembers to put the ladle down. She stands musing by the hearth.*)

OSAM As for her wildness, what do you want me to say again about that? I have always asked you to apprentice her to a priestess to quieten her down. But . . .

(*Roused again,* BADUA *moves quickly back to where he is and, meanwhile, corks both her ears with two fingers and shakes her head to make sure he notices what she is doing.*)

OSAM (*chuckles*) Hmm, play children's games with me, my wife. One day you will click your fingers with regret that you did not listen to me.

BADUA (*She removes her fingers from her ears.*) I have said it and I will say it again and again and again! I am not going to turn my only daughter into a dancer priestess.

OSAM What is wrong with priestesses?

BADUA I don't say there is anything wrong with them.

OSAM Did you not consult them over and over again when you could not get a single child from your womb to live beyond one day?

BADUA (*reflectively*) O yes. I respect them, I honour them . . . I fear them. Yes, my husband, I fear them. But my only daughter shall not be a priestess.

OSAM They have so much glory and dignity . . .

BADUA But in the end, they are not people. They become too much like the gods they

interpret. (*As she enumerates the attributes of priesthood, her voice grows hysterical and her face terror-stricken.* OSAM *removes his pipe, and stares at her, his mouth open with amazement.*)

They counsel with spirits;
They read into other men's souls;
They swallow dogs' eyes
Jump fires
Drink goats' blood
Sheep milk
Without flinching
Or vomiting
They do not feel
As you or I,
They have no shame.

(*She relaxes, and* OSAM *does too, the latter sighing audibly.* BADUA *continues, her face slightly turned away from both her husband and the audience.*)

I want my child
To be a human woman
Marry a man,
Tend a farm
And be happy to see her
Peppers and her onions grow.
A woman like her
Should bear children
Many children,
So she can afford to have
One or two die.
Should she not take
Her place at meetings
Among the men and women of the clan?
And sit on my chair when
I am gone? And a captainship in the army,
Should not be beyond her
When the time is ripe!

(OSAM *nods his head and exclaims, 'Oh . . . oh!'*)

BADUA But a priestess lives too much in her own and other people's minds, my husband.

OSAM (*sighing again*) My wife, people with better vision than yours or mine have seen that Anowa is not like you or me. And a prophet with a locked mouth is neither a prophet nor a man. Besides, the yam that will burn, shall burn, boiled or roasted.

BADUA (*She picks up the ladle but does not stir the pot. She throws her arms about.*) Since you want to see Nkomfo and Nsofo, seers and dancers . . .

ANOWA   (*from the distance*) Mother!

BADUA   That is her coming.

ANOWA   Father!

OSAM   O yes. Well let us keep quiet about her affairs then. You know what heart lies in her chest.

ANOWA   Mother, Father . . . Father, Mother . . . Mother . . .

(OSAM *jumps up and, confused, he and* BADUA *keep bumping into each other as each moves without knowing why or where he or she is moving.* BADUA *still has the ladle in her hands.*)

BADUA   Why do you keep hitting at me?

ANOWA   Mother!

OSAM   Sorry, I did not mean to. But you watch your step too.

ANOWA   Father!

OSAM   And where is she?

(ANOWA *runs in, lower right, with her empty water-pot.*)

BADUA   Hei. Why do you frighten me so? And where is the water?

ANOWA   O Mother. (*She stops running and stays on the lower stage.*)

OSAM   What is it?

ANOWA   (*her eyes swerving from the face of one to the other*) O Father!

OSAM   Say whatever you have got to say and stop behaving like a child.

BADUA   Calling us from the street!

OSAM   What have you got to tell us that couldn't wait until you reached here?

ANOWA   O Father.

BADUA   And look at her. See here, it is time you realised you have grown up.

ANOWA   (*moving a step or two forward*) Mother . . .

BADUA   And now what is it! Besides, where is the water? I am sure this household will go to bed to count the beams tonight since there is no water to cook with.

ANOWA   Mother, Father, I have met the man I want to marry.

BADUA   What is she saying?

ANOWA   I say I have found the man I would like to marry.

OSAM and BADUA   Eh?

(*Long pause during which* BADUA *stares at* ANOWA *with her head tilted to one side.*)

ANOWA   Kofi Ako asked me to marry him and I said I will, too.

BADUA   Eh?

OSAM   Eh?

BADUA   Eh?

OSAM   Eh?

BADUA   Eh?

OSAM and BADUA   Eh–eh!

(*Light dies on all three and comes on again almost immediately.* OSAM *is sitting in his chair.* ANOWA *hovers around and she has a chewing-stick in her mouth with which she scrapes her teeth when she is not speaking.* BADUA *is sitting by the hearth doing nothing.*)

ANOWA   Mother, you have been at me for a long time to get married. And now that I have found someone I like very much . . .

BADUA   Anowa, shut up. Shut up! Push your tongue into your mouth and close it. Shut up because I never counted Kofi Ako among my sons-in-law. Anowa, why Kofi Ako? Of all the mothers that are here in Yebi, should I be the one whose daughter would want to marry this fool, this good-for-nothing cassava-man, this watery male of all watery males? This-I-am-the-handsome-one-with-a-stick-between-my-teeth-in-the-market-place . . . This . . . this . . .

ANOWA   O Mother . . .

BADUA   (*quietly*) I say Anowa, why did you not wait for a day when I was cooking banku and your father was drinking palm-wine in the market place with his friends? When you could have snatched the ladle from my hands and hit me with it and taken your father's wine from his hands and thrown it in his face? Anowa, why did you not wait for a day like that, since you want to behave like the girl in the folk tale?

ANOWA   But what are you talking about, Mother?

BADUA   And you Kobina Sam, will you not say anything?

OSAM   Abena Badua, leave me out of this. You know that if I so much as whisper anything to do with Anowa, you and your brothers and uncles will tell me to go and straighten out the lives of my nieces. This is your family drum; beat it, my wife.

BADUA   I did not ask for any riddles.

OSAM   Mm . . . just remember I was smoking my pipe.

BADUA   If you had been any other father, you would have known what to do and what not to do.

OSAM   Perhaps; but that does not mean I

would have *done* anything. The way you used to talk, I thought if Anowa came to tell you she was going to get married to Kweku Ananse, or indeed the devil himself, you would spread rich cloth before her to walk on. And probably sacrifice an elephant.

BADUA   And you do not know what this Kofi Ako is like?

ANOWA   What is he like?

BADUA   My lady, I have not asked you a question. (ANOWA *retires into sullenness. She scrapes her teeth noisily.*)

OSAM   How could I know what he is like? Does he not come from Nsona House? And is not that one of the best houses that is here in Yebi? Has he an ancestor who unclothed himself to nakedness, had the Unmentionable, killed himself or another man?

BADUA   And if all that there is to a young man is that his family has an unspoiled name, then what kind of man is he? Are he and his wife going to feed on stones when he will not put a blow into a thicket or at least learn a trade?

OSAM   Anyway, I said long ago that I was removing my mouth from my daughter Anowa's marriage. Did I not say that? She would not allow herself to be married to any man who came to ask for her hand from us and of whom we approved. Did you not know then that when she chose a man, it might be one of whom we would disapprove?

BADUA   But why should she want to do a thing like that?

OSAM   My wife, do remember I am a man, son of a woman who also had five sisters. It is a long time since I gave up trying to understand the human female. Besides, if you think well of it, I am not the one to decide finally whom Anowa is to marry. Her uncle, your brother is there, is he not? You'd better consult him. Because I know your family: they will say I deliberately married Anowa to a fool to spite them.

ANOWA   Father, Kofi Ako is not a fool.

OSAM   My daughter, please forgive me, I am sure you know him very well. And it is only by way of speaking. Kwame! Kwame! I thought the boy was around somewhere. (*Moves towards lower stage and looks around.*)

BADUA   What are you calling him here for?

OSAM   To go and call us her uncle and your brother.

BADUA   Could we have not waited until evening or dawn tomorrow?

OSAM   For what shall we wait for the dawn?

BADUA   To settle the case.

OSAM   What case? Who says I want to settle cases? If there is a case to settle, that is between you and your people. It is not everything one chooses to forget, Badua. Certainly, I remember what happened in connection with Anowa's dancing. That is, if you don't. Did they not say in the end that it was I who had prevented her from going into apprenticeship with a priestess?

(*Light dies on them and comes on a little later. ANOWA is seen dressed in a two-pieced cloth. She darts in and out of upper right, with very quick movements. She is packing her belongings into a little basket. Every now and then, she pauses, looks at her mother and sucks her teeth. BADUA complains as before, but this time tearfully. OSAM is lying in his chair smoking.*)

BADUA   I am in disgrace so suck your teeth at me. (*Silence.*) Other women certainly have happier tales to tell about motherhood. (*Silence.*) I think I am just an unlucky woman.

ANOWA   Mother, I do not know what is wrong with you.

BADUA   And how would you know what is wrong with me? Look here Anowa, marriage is like a piece of cloth . . .

ANOWA   I like mine and it is none of your business.

BADUA   And like cloth, its beauty passes with wear and tear.

ANOWA   I do not care, Mother. Have I not told you that this is to be my marriage and not yours?

BADUA   My marriage! Why should it be my daughter who would want to marry that good-for-nothing cassava-man?

ANOWA   He is mine and I like him.

BADUA   If you like him, do like him. The men of his house do not make good husbands; ask older women who are married to Nsona men.

OSAM   You know what you are saying is not true. Indeed from the beginning of time Nsona men make the best of husbands. (BADUA *glares at him.*)

ANOWA   This does not even worry me and it should not worry you, Mother.

BADUA   It's up to you, my mistress who knows everything. But remember, my lady

– when I am too old to move, I shall still be sitting by these walls waiting for you to come back with your rags and nakedness.

ANOWA You do not have to wait because we shall not be coming back here to Yebi. Not for a long long time, Mother, not for a long long time.

BADUA Of course, if I were you I wouldn't want to come back with my shame either.

ANOWA You will be surprised to know that I am going to help him do something with his life.

BADUA A–a–h, I wish I could turn into a bird and come and stand on your roof-top watching you make something of that husband of yours. What was he able to make of the plantation of palm-trees his grandfather gave him? And the virgin land his uncles gave him, what did he do with that?

ANOWA Please, Mother, remove your witch's mouth from our marriage.

(OSAM *jumps up and from now on hovers between the two, trying to make peace.*)

OSAM Hei Anowa, what is wrong with you? Are you mad? How can you speak like that to your mother?

ANOWA But Father, Mother does not treat me like her daughter.

BADUA And so you call me a witch? The thing is, I wish I were a witch so that I could protect you from your folly.

ANOWA I do not need you for protection, Mother.

OSAM The spirit of my fathers! Anowa, what daughter talks like this to her mother?

ANOWA But Father, what mother talks to her daughter the way Mother talks to me? And now, Mother, I am going, so take your witchery to eat in the sea.

OSAM Ei Anowa?

BADUA Thank you my daughter. (BADUA *and* ANOWA *try to jump on each other.* BADUA *attempts to hit* ANOWA *but* OSAM *quickly intervenes.*)

OSAM What has come over this household? Tell me what has come over this household? And you too Badua. What has come over you?

BADUA You leave me alone, Osam. Why don't you speak to Anowa? She is your daughter, I am not.

OSAM Well, she is not mature.

BADUA That one makes me laugh. Who is not mature? Has she not been mature enough to divine me out and discover I am a witch? Did she not choose her husband single handed? And isn't she leaving home to make a better success of her marriage?

OSAM Anowa, have you made up your mind to leave?

ANOWA But Father, Mother is driving me away.

BADUA Who is driving you away?

ANOWA You! Who does not know here in Yebi that from the day I came to tell you that Kofi and I were getting married you have been drumming into my ears what a disgrace this marriage is going to be for you? Didn't you say that your friends are laughing at you? And they were saying very soon I would be sharing your clothes because my husband will never buy me any? Father, I am leaving this place.

(*She picks up her basket, puts it on her head and moves down towards the lower left.*)

BADUA Yes, go.

ANOWA I am on my way, Mother.

OSAM And where is your husband?

ANOWA I am going to look for him.

OSAM Anowa, stop! (*But* ANOWA *behaves as if she had not heard him.*) Anowa you must not leave in this manner.

BADUA Let her go, and may she walk well.

ANOWA Mother, I shall walk so well that I will not find my feet back here again.

(*She exits lower left.* OSAM *spits with disdain, then stares at* BADUA *for a long time. She slowly bows her head in the folds of her cloth and begins to weep quietly as the lights die on them. Enter* THE-MOUTH-THAT-EATS-SALT-AND-PEPPER.)

OLD WOMAN Hei, hei, hei! And what do the children of today want? Eh, what would the children of today have us do? Parenthood was always a very expensive affair. But it seems now there is no man or woman created in nature who is endowed with enough powers to be a mother or father. (OLD MAN *enters and walks up to the middle of the lower stage passing* OLD WOMAN *on the way.*) Listen, listen. The days when children obey their elders have run out. If you tell a child to go forward, he will surely step backwards. And if you ask him to move back a pace, he would run ten leagues.

OLD MAN But what makes your heart race itself in anger so? What disturbs you? Some of us feel the best way to sharpen a knife is not to whet one side only. And neither can you solve a riddle by considering only one end of it. We know too well how difficult children of today are. But who begot them? Is a man a father for sleeping with a woman and making her pregnant? And does bearing a child after nine months make her a mother? Or is she the best potter who knows her clay and how it breathes?

OLD WOMAN Are you saying that a good parent would not tell his child what should and should not be done?

OLD MAN How can I say a thing like that?

OLD WOMAN And must we lie down and have our children play jumping games on our bellies if this is what they want? (*She spits.*)

OLD MAN Oh no. No one in his rightful mind would say that babies should be free to do what they please. But Abena Badua should have known that Anowa wanted to be something else which she herself had not been . . . They say from a very small age, she had the hot eyes and nimble feet of one born to dance for the gods.

OLD WOMAN Hmm. Our ears are breaking with that one. Who heard the Creator tell Anowa what she was coming to do with her life here? And is that why, after all her 'I don't like this' and 'I don't like that', she has gone and married Kofi Ako?

OLD MAN Tell me what is wrong in that?

OLD WOMAN Certainly. Some of us thought she had ordered a completely new man from the heavens.

OLD MAN Are people angry because she chose her own husband; or is there something wrong with the boy?

OLD WOMAN As for that Kofi Ako, they say he combs his hair too often and stays too long at the Nteh games.

OLD MAN Who judges a man of name by his humble beginnings?

OLD WOMAN Don't ask me. They say Badua does not want him for a son-in-law.

OLD MAN She should thank her god that Anowa has decided to settle down at all. But then, we all talk too much about those two. And yet this is not the first time since the world began that a man and a woman have decided to be together against the advice of grey-haired crows.

OLD WOMAN What foolish words! Some people babble as though they borrowed their grey hairs and did not grow them on

their own heads! Badua should have told her daughter that the infant which tries its milk teeth on every bone and stone, grows up with nothing to eat dried meat with. (*She exits noisily.*)

OLD MAN I'm certainly a foolish old man. But I think there is no need to behave as though Kofi Ako and Anowa have brought an evil concoction here. Perhaps it is good for them that they have left Yebi to go and try to make their lives somewhere else.

(*As lights go out, a blending of the Atentenben with any ordinary drum.*)

Phase Two: On the highway

The road is represented by the lower stage. A dark night. Wind, thunder and lightning. KOFI AKO *enters from lower left. He is carrying a huge load of monkey skins and other hides. He looks exhausted and he is extremely wet from the rain.*

KOFI AKO (*softly and without turning round*) Anowa (*Silence.*) Anowa, are you coming? (*There is no response from anywhere. Then, frenziedly*) Anowa, ei, Anowa!

ANOWA (*also entering from lower left and carrying basket*) O, and what is wrong with you? Why are you so afraid? (KOFI AKO *turns round to look at her.*)

KOFI AKO (*breathing loudly with relief*) It is a fearful night.

ANOWA But you do not have to fear so much for me. Why Kofi, see how your great chest heaves up and down even through the folds of your cloth! (*Laughs.*)

KOFI AKO You just let it be then. (*She giggles more.*) And I can't see that there is anything to laugh at . . . Look at the lightning! Shall we sit here in this thicket?

ANOWA Yes.

(*They move to upper stage, and stay in the central area.* KOFI AKO *puts his own load down with difficulty. He then helps* ANOWA *to unload hers and sits down immediately.*)

ANOWA Hei, you should not have sat down in the mud just like that.

KOFI AKO As if it matters. Now sit here and move nearer. (*He pulls* ANOWA, *shivering, down by him.*) Anowa, see how you shiver! And yet my tongue cannot match yours. (*Mocking her*) 'I am strong . . . O . . . O . . . It is not heavy. My body is small but I am strong!' Ei, Anowa!

ANOWA   But I am strong.

KOFI AKO   We can see that. You know what? Shivering like this, with all your clothes wet, you look like a chick in a puddle.

ANOWA   And how about you? (*Beginning to rummage through her basket as though looking for something.*)

KOFI AKO   Do you compare yourself to me? See how big I am. (*He bares his chest and spreads out his arms.*)

ANOWA   (*pretending to be shocked*) Ahhh! And this is why we should fear more of you. You are so tall and so broad. You really look like a huge something. There is too much of you. (*Touching different parts of him*) Anything can get any part of you . . . a branch from a falling tree . . . a broken splinter, and ow, my mouth is at the dung heap, even lightning . . . But I am so little, I can escape things.

KOFI AKO   I was not born to die in any of these ways you mention.

ANOWA   O seasoned Priest, and how was I born to die, that you are so afraid of me?

KOFI AKO   I have no idea about that one. What I know is that if you stay out longer in this weather, you are going to be ill. And I cannot afford to lose you.

ANOWA   You will never lose me.

KOFI AKO   I thank your mouth.

(ANOWA *fishes out a miserable looking packet of food from the basket.*)

ANOWA   Are you hungry? Here is what is left of the food. Oh, but it is so wet. (*She giggles but gives it to him.*)

KOFI AKO   (*He clutches hungrily at the bundle.*) They are good. How about you?

ANOWA   No, I am not hungry.

KOFI AKO   Perhaps you are ill already. (*Begins to wolf the stuff down.*) Mm . . . This life is not good for a woman. No, not even a woman like you. It is too difficult. It is over two hundred miles to the coast and I wonder how much we have done . . .

ANOWA   We are near Atandasu. This means we have only about thirty miles or more to do . . .

KOFI AKO   Is that it? Do you know how many days we have been walking?

ANOWA   No, I have not been counting the days. All I know is that we have been on the highway for about two weeks now. (*Fights sleep.*)

KOFI AKO   The ghost of my fathers!

ANOWA   But think of it, if we are not too tired to go a little further, we shall be there tomorrow.

KOFI AKO   Ei, Anowa. You ought to have been born a man.

ANOWA   Kofi.

KOFI AKO   Hmm . . . hmm?

ANOWA   Why don't you marry another woman? (KOFI AKO *registers alarm.*) At least she could help us. I could find a good one too. (*Throws up her head to think.*) Let me see. There is a girl in one of the villages we go to e . . . h . . . what is the name?

KOFI AKO   Anowa, please don't go on. You know you are annoying me.

ANOWA   Ah my master, but I don't understand you. You are the only man in this world who has just one wife and swears to keep only her! (*Silence.*) Perhaps it is your medicine's taboo?

KOFI AKO   What medicine are you talking about? What taboo?

ANOWA   Ah Kofi, why has your voice gone fearfully down and so quickly?

KOFI AKO   But you are saying something about medicines and taboos which I don't understand. Were you not the same person who said we didn't need anything of that kind?

ANOWA   And if I said that, then it means from now on I must not mention medicines and taboos, not even in jest? Kofi (*pause*) . . . what use do you think they will be to us? Who is interested in harming you or me? Two lonely people who are only trying something just because the bowels are not as wise as the mind; but like baby orphans, will shriek for food even while their mother's body is cold with death . . .

KOFI AKO   Anowa, the man who hates you does not care if you wait in the sun for your clothes to dry before you can go and join the dance.

ANOWA   But who hates us?

KOFI AKO   My wife, you speak as if we left Yebi with the town singing and dancing our praises. Was not everyone saying something unkind about us? Led by your mother? Anowa, we did not run away from home to go mushroom-hunting or fish-trapping.

ANOWA   I heard you, my husband. But I do not want us to be caught up in medicines or any of those things.

KOFI AKO   I too have heard you, my wife. Meanwhile, I am eating all the food . . .

ANOWA   Set your mouth free. Mine feels as

though it could not stand the smell of anything.

KOFI AKO (*putting his hand on her forehead*) Anowa, please, don't be ill.

ANOWA My mother has often told me that except for the normal gripes and fevers, my body has never known real illness.

KOFI AKO Ah, but my wife seems to be extraordinary in more things than one. Anowa . . .

ANOWA Yes?

KOFI AKO We do need something to protect us. Even though no one dislikes us enough now to want to destroy us, how about when we begin to do well? Shall we not get hosts of enemies then?

ANOWA (*trying to keep her voice light*) But my husband, why should we begin to take to our sick-beds now with illnesses that may affect us in our old age? Kofi, I just don't like the idea of using medicines.

KOFI AKO But there are many things we do in life which we do not like – which we even hate . . . and we only need a bead or two.

ANOWA But a shrine has to be worshipped however small its size. And a kind god angered is a thousand times more evil than a mean god unknown. To have a little something to eat and a rag on our back is not a matter to approach a god about.

KOFI AKO Maybe you feel confident enough to trust yourself in dealing with all the problems of life. I think I am different, my wife.

(*For some time* ANOWA *quietly looks down while he eats.*)

ANOWA Kofi, that was unkindly said. Because you know that I am already worried about not seeing signs of a baby yet.

KOFI AKO It is quite clear that neither of us knows too much about these things. (*Pause.*) Perhaps it is too early to worry about such a problem. We can consult a more grown-up person, but I know you would not like us to do anything like that.

ANOWA (*very loudly*) Listen to what he is saying! Is it the same thing to ask an older person about a woman's womb as it is to contract medicines in pots and potions which would attract good fortune and ward off evil?

KOFI AKO I swear by everything that it is the same. And Anowa, it is too fearful a night to go screaming into the woods.

ANOWA That is true.

(*More thunder and lightning.* ANOWA *begins to nod sleepily. Having finished eating,* KOFI AKO *throws the food wrappers into the woods behind him. Then he notices* ANOWA *nodding.*)

KOFI AKO Anowa, you are very tired. (*Jumping up*) Let me prepare somewhere for you to sleep. (*He goes off stage by upper right.* ANOWA *goes on nodding. Meanwhile the storm continues convulsively.*)

ANOWA (*startled awake by a peal of thunder*) What I am worried about are these things. (*She gropes towards the baskets and begins to feel the skins.*) See how wet they are. Tomorrow, they will be heavier than sheets of rock. And if it continues like this, they will all rot. Creator, (*she looks up*) do as you like but please, let your sun shine tomorrow so we can dry out these skins. We must stop in the next village to dry them out. Yes, we must stop if the sun comes out.

KOFI AKO (*entering with a couple of plantain or banana leaves which he spreads out to form some kind of mat in the centre of lower stage*) To do what?

ANOWA To dry out the skins. They are so wet.

(KOFI AKO *concentrates on preparing the mat.* ANOWA *starts nodding again.*)

KOFI AKO Eh? (*He turns round and sees her.*)

ANOWA (*mumbling*) The storm has ruined the whole corn field, every stalk is down.

KOFI AKO (*Moving with urgency, he picks her up in his arms.*) Come Anowa, you are dreaming. Come to sleep. (*Carries her to the leafy bed.*) Yes, Anowa, sleep well. Sleep well, and let every corn stalk go down. We shall not return to see the ruin. (*Pacing up and down the length of lower stage.*) Sometimes, I do not understand. Wherever we go, people take you for my sister at first. They say they have never heard of a woman who helped her husband so. 'Your wife is good', they say, 'for your sisters are the only women you can force to toil like this for you'. They say that however good for licking the back of your hand is, it would never be like your palms. (*Pause.*) Perhaps if they knew what I am beginning to know, they would not say so much. And proverbs do not always describe the truth of reality. (*His face acquires new determination.*) Anowa truly has a few strong ideas. But I know she will settle down. (*Addressing the sleeping woman*) Anowa, I shall be the new husband and you the new wife.

(*Now the storm is raging harder, thunder roars and lightning occurs more frequently. He stares at her for some time and then as lights begin to dim, he spreads out his big figure by her. Lights off. Pause. When lights come on again, same scene without the leafy bed. The sun is shining and* ANOWA *is spreading out skins from the baskets while* KOFI AKO *stands looking on. Then* ANOWA *holds her nose elaborately. Both of them burst out laughing. He moves in to help her.*)

KOFI AKO   Our noses are certainly suffering.

ANOWA   And yet what can we do? Without them, where would we stand?

KOFI AKO   Nowhere indeed.

ANOWA   (*looking into one of the baskets and picking it up*) About two of them in here are too rotten to do anything with. (*She makes a movement of wiping sweat off her face, then yawns.*)

KOFI AKO   Come out of the sun. (*He takes the basket from her and places it away from them.*) Come, let's sit down in the shade. (*They go and sit near one end of the lower stage.*)

ANOWA   (*breathing audibly*) Did your friend the doctor tell you what is wrong with me?

KOFI AKO   Yes.

ANOWA   What did he say?

KOFI AKO   I should have asked him whether I'm to let you know or not.

ANOWA   Ho! I think you can tell me, because he would not have forgotten to warn you, if he thought I should not know.

KOFI AKO   (*quietly and with a frown*) He says there is nothing wrong with you.

ANOWA   Then why . . . ?

KOFI AKO   Let me finish. He says there is nothing wrong with your womb. But your soul is too restless. You always seem to be looking for things; and that prevents your blood from settling.

ANOWA   Oh!

KOFI AKO   Anowa, are you unhappy? Do I make you unhappy?

ANOWA   (*with surprise*) No.

KOFI AKO   Perhaps this work is too much for you.

ANOWA   No. I think I have always been like that.

KOFI AKO   (*alarmed*) Like what?

ANOWA   I don't know. I can't describe it.

KOFI AKO   Maybe you should stop coming on the roads.

ANOWA   (*alarmed*) No. Why?

KOFI AKO   Why not?

ANOWA   I like this work. I like being on the roads.

KOFI AKO   My wife, sometimes you talk strangely. I don't see what is so pleasing on these highways. The storms? The wild animals or bad men that we often meet?

ANOWA   There are worse things in villages and towns.

KOFI AKO   Listen to her! Something tells me (*he stands up*) it might be better if you stayed at home. Indeed I have been thinking that maybe I should eh . . . eh . . .

ANOWA   My husband, I am listening to you.

KOFI AKO   You remember, you were telling me to marry another woman to help us?

ANOWA   Yes.

KOFI AKO   Hmm, I don't want to marry again. Not yet. But I think . . . I think . . . that perhaps . . .

ANOWA   Eheh!

KOFI AKO   I think the time has come for us to think of looking for one or two men to help us.

ANOWA   What men?

KOFI AKO   I hear they are not expensive . . . and if . . .

ANOWA   (*getting up so slowly that every movement of her body corresponds to syllables or words in her next speech*) MY hus-band! Am I hear-ing you right? Have we risen so high? (*Corking her ears*) Kofi Ako, do not let me hear these words again.

KOFI AKO   (*mimicking her*) 'Do not let me hear these words again'. Anowa, do you think I am your son?

ANOWA   I do not care. We shall not buy men.

KOFI AKO   Anowa, look here. You are not always going to have it your way. Who are you to tell me what I must do or not do?

ANOWA   Kofi, I am not telling what you must do or not do . . . We were two when we left Yebi. We have been together all this time and at the end of these two years, we may not be able to say yet that we are the

richest people in the world but we
certainly are not starving.

KOFI AKO   And so?

ANOWA   Ah, is there any need then to go
behaving as though we are richer than we
are?

KOFI AKO   What do you want to say? I am
not buying these men to come and carry
me. They are coming to help us in our
work.

ANOWA   We do not need them.

KOFI AKO   If you don't, I do. Besides you are
only talking like a woman.

ANOWA   And please, how does a woman
talk? I had as much a mouth in the idea of
beginning this trade as you had. And as
much head!

KOFI AKO   And I am getting tired now. 'You
shall not consult a priest . . . you shall
marry again . . . we do not need medicines
. . . ' Anowa, listen. Now here is something
I am going to do whether you like it or not.
I do not even understand why you want to
make so much noise about something like
this. What is wrong with buying one or two
people to help us? They are cheap . . .
(*Pause.* ANOWA *walks around in great
agitation.* KOFI AKO *continues in a strangely
loud voice.*) Everyone does it . . . does not
everyone do it? And things would be
easier for us. We shall not be alone . . . Now
you have decided to say nothing, eh?
Anowa, who told you that buying men is
wrong? You know what? I like you and the
way you are different. But Anowa,
sometimes, you are too different. (ANOWA
walks away from him.) I know I could
not have started without you, but after
all, we all know you are a woman and I
am the man.

ANOWA   And tell me, when did I enter into a
discussion with you about that? I shall not
feel happy with slaves around . . . Kofi, no
man made a slave of his friend and came to
much himself. It is wrong. It is evil.

KOFI AKO   (*showing alarm*) Hei, where did
you get these ideas from? Who told you all
this?

ANOWA   Are there never things which one
can think out for oneself?

KOFI AKO   Yes, so now you are saying I am a
fool?

ANOWA   (*collapsing*) O the gods of my fathers!

KOFI AKO   What shall the gods of your
fathers do for you? I know you think you
are the wise one of the two of us.

ANOWA   Kofi, are you saying all this just so I
will take a knife and go cut my throat?

KOFI AKO   Am I lying?

ANOWA   When and where and what did I do
to give you this idea?

KOFI AKO   This is the way you have always
behaved.

ANOWA   (*her voice going falsetto*) Kofi! Kofi!
(*He sits down by her.*) Hmm! Kofi, we
shouldn't quarrel.

KOFI AKO   No, we should not.

(*The lights die on them and come up in a little
while, on the upper stage. It is the courtyard
of* BADUA *and* OSAM's *cottage. It is early
evening. Village noises.* OSAM *and* BADUA
are having their evening meal. OSAM *is
sitting in the lie-in chair, his food before him.
He swallows a morsel.* BADUA's *food is on her
lap. She is not eating. Presently she puts it
down and gets up noisily. She turns right, she
turns left. She begins to move around
aimlessly, speaking at the same time.*)

BADUA   I haven't heard the like of this
before. A human being, and a woman too,
preferring to remain a stranger in other
people's lands?

OSAM   (*looking up from his meal*) Sit down, sit
down. Sit down, and eat your food.
(*Shamefaced,* BADUA *sits down.*) Hmmm,
I was telling you. This child of yours . . .
hm . . . She was never even a child in the
way a child must be a child.

BADUA   (*turning round to face him*) And how
must a child be a child?

OSAM   Ei, are you now asking me? I thought
this is what you too have known all along.
Ah, Nana, I beg you. Maybe that was not
well said. (*Pause.*) But I must say it has
happened before us all. Has it not? Walked
out of that door, she did, how long ago is
that?

BADUA   Hmmm!

OSAM   . . . and has never been back since.
I have always feared her.

BADUA   (*shocked*) You have always feared
her? And is that a good thing to say about
your own bowel-begotten child? If you fear
her, then what do other people do? And if
other people fear her then since a crab
never fathers a bird, in their eyes, who are
you yourself? After all, what has she done?
She only went away with her husband and
has not been back since.

OSAM   And that, you will agree with me, is
very strange.

(Guessing he might want a helping of the soup, BADUA gets up and goes for his bowl.)

BADUA Yes, it is strange, but that does not make me say I fear her. (*She takes the bowl to the hearth, and returns it to him after she has filled it.*)

OSAM But don't other women leave their homes to go and marry? And do they stay away forever? Do they not return with their children to the old homestead to attend funerals, pay death debts, return for the feeding of their family stools? And Badua, listen here, if they did not do that, what would homes-and-homes do? Would not the clans break up for lack of people at home? The children of women like Anowa and their children-after-them never find their ways back. They get lost. For they often do not know the names of the founders of their houses . . . No, they do not know what to tell you if you asked them for just the names of their clans.

BADUA Anowa has not yet had children.

OSAM There you are. And is not that too strange? She has not had children. And barrenness is not such a common affliction in your family, is it?

BADUA No, they have been saying it for a long time around here that she and her husband sold her birth-seeds to acquire their wealth.

OSAM Of course, women have mouths to talk with. And indeed they open them anyhow and much of the time what comes out is nothing any real man can take seriously. Still, something tells me that this time she has given them cause.

BADUA O Kofi Sam! (*She returns to her seat and places her bowl on her knee again.*)

OSAM What have I done? I am not saying that they are right. But it certainly looks as if she and her husband are too busy making money and have no time to find out and cure what is wrong with her womb.

BADUA Perhaps I should go and look for her.

OSAM Go and look for her? How? Where? And anyway, who told you she is lost?

BADUA But she is my child.

OSAM And so what? Do you think Anowa will forgive you anymore for that? Please, leave her to live her life!

BADUA Why are you always against me where Anowa is concerned?

OSAM You have been against me too. Did I not tell you to –

BADUA – make her a priestess . . . make her a priestess . . . Always. Why? Why did everyone want me to put my only child on the dancing ground? Since you want to see possessed women so much, why didn't you ask your sisters to apprentice their daughters to oracles?

OSAM (*very angry*) Don't shout at me, woman! Who comes complaining to me about Anowa? . . . They say that that would have been to the good of us all. But now – there she is, as they said she might be, wandering . . . her soul hovering on the outer fringes of life and always searching for something . . . and I do not know what!

BADUA (*quietly*) I don't know what you mean by all this. Who is not searching in life?

OSAM I know you have just made up your mind never to understand me.

BADUA (*bitterly*) Besides, that daughter of ours is doing well, I hear. Yes, for someone whose soul is wandering, our daughter is prospering. Have you heard from the blowing winds how their trade with the white men is growing? And how they are buying men and women?

OSAM Yes, and also how unhappy she is about those slaves, and how they quarrel from morning till night.

BADUA So! I didn't know she was a fool too. She thought it is enough just to be headstrong. (*Laughing dryly*) Before she walked out that noon-day, she should have waited for me to tell her how to marry a man . . .

OSAM Hmm.

BADUA A good woman does not have a brain or mouth.

OSAM Hmm. (*He coughs.*)

BADUA And if there is something wrong with their slaves, why don't they sell them?

OSAM That is not the problem. They say she just does not like the idea of buying men and women.

BADUA What foolishness. People like her are not content to have life cheap, they always want it cheaper. Which woman in the land would not wish to be in her place?

OSAM Anowa is not every woman.

BADUA Tchiaa! And who does she think she is? A goddess? Let me eat my food. (*She goes to sit down and places the food back on her lap.*)

OSAM   And can I have some soup?

BADUA   Yes. (*As she gets up again, the lights die on the courtyard.*)

(*Eight men in a single file carrying skins enter by lower right, move silently up and across the main stage and away lower left.* KOFI AKO *follows closely behind them but stops in the centre of the lower stage. He is better dressed than before. He is carrying what seems to be a ridiculously light load. From off stage,* ANOWA's *voice is heard calling 'Kofi, Kofi'. He stops, she enters from the same direction, dressed as in the last scene although the lapse in time represents years. She is still barefooted. She is carrying nothing but a small stick which she plays with as she talks.*)

KOFI AKO   What is the matter?

ANOWA   Oh I just want you to wait for me.

KOFI AKO   Anowa, you walked faster when you carried loads which were heavier than mine.

ANOWA   Well, *you* took the load off my head. But don't you complain about my steps. I cannot keep up with you. These days you are always with your men.

KOFI AKO   (*smiles.*) Is that it? You know what? Let us sit down. (*They move to their position of the previous scene. Then as if he has remembered something, he moves some steps up towards the left and calls*) Boy!

BOY   (*running in*) Father!

KOFI AKO   Tell the others that you are to sit down and rest a little.

BOY   Is our Mother coming to give us the food?

KOFI AKO   You can share it among yourselves, can you not?

BOY   We can, Father.

KOFI AKO   Then go and tell Yaako to share it up for you.

BOY   Yes, Father. (*He leaves.*)

KOFI AKO   (*Goes back to sit by* ANOWA.) I think we should not come again with them. Yaako is very good and honest and he can manage everything.

ANOWA   (*quietly*) Is that so?

KOFI AKO   I feel so.

ANOWA   (*quietly*) Yes.

KOFI AKO   Why do you say that so sadly?

ANOWA   Did I say that sadly? Maybe I am sad. And how not? I cannot be happy if I am going to stop working.

KOFI AKO   But why, Anowa?

ANOWA   Men whom Odomankoma creates do not stop working . . . yes, they do but only when they are hit by illness or some misfortune. When their bodies have grown impotent with age.

KOFI AKO   Anowa, the farmer goes home from the farm . . .

ANOWA   (*Gets up and starts walking before* KOFI AKO.) And the fisherman brings his boat and nets to the shore . . .

KOFI AKO   And if you know this already, then why?

ANOWA   They return in the morning.

KOFI AKO   But we have finished doing all that needs to be done by us.

ANOWA   Kofi, one stops wearing a hat only when the head has fallen off.

KOFI AKO   (*irritably*) Anowa, can one not rest a tired neck?

ANOWA   Are we coming back after some time?

KOFI AKO   No.

ANOWA   What shall we be doing?

KOFI AKO   Nothing. We shall be resting.

ANOWA   How can a human being rest all the time? I cannot.

KOFI AKO   I can.

ANOWA   I shall not know what to do with myself as each day breaks.

KOFI AKO   You will look after the house.

ANOWA   No. I am going to marry you to a woman who shall do that.

KOFI AKO   You will not marry me to any woman. I am not sending you on that errand.

ANOWA   See if I don't. One of these plump Oguaa mulatto women. With a skin as smooth as shea-butter and golden like fresh palm-oil on yam . . .

KOFI AKO   (*jumping up and showing undue irritation*) Anowa, stop that!

ANOWA   Stop what?

KOFI AKO   What are you doing!

ANOWA   What am I doing? (*Pause.*) Ei, master, let your heart lie cool in your chest.

KOFI AKO   Haven't I told you several times not to talk to me about marrying other women?

ANOWA   Hmm, I am quiet. (*Pause.*)

KOFI AKO   (*cooling down*) And if I marry again what will become of you?

ANOWA   Nothing that is unheard of. Ask your friends. What becomes of other women whose husbands have one, two, or more other wives besides themselves?

KOFI AKO   So what you want to be is my mother-wife?

ANOWA   Yes, or your friend or your sister. Have we not enough memories to talk about from our working days until we get tired of them and each other, when we shall sit and wait for our skins to fall off our bones?

KOFI AKO   Your mood is on. (*He stretches his left arm forward and looks at it intently.*)

ANOWA   (*giggling*) What mood? You are always funny. My nothing is on. It is just that when I throw my eyes into the future, I do not see myself there.

KOFI AKO   This is because you have no children. Women who have children can always see themselves in the future.

ANOWA   Mm . . . children. It would be good to have them. But it seems I'm not woman enough. And this is another reason why you ought to marry another woman. So she can bear your children. (*Pause.*) Mm, I am only a wayfarer, with no belongings either here or there.

KOFI AKO   What? What are you saying? Wayfarer, you? But are you talking about . . . about slaves . . . and you . . . ? But, a wayfarer belongs to other people!

ANOWA   Oh no, not always. One can belong to oneself without belonging to a place. What is the difference between any of your men and me? Except that they are men and I'm a woman? None of us belongs.

KOFI AKO   You are a strange woman, Anowa. Too strange. You never even show much interest in what the oracles say. But you are not at fault; they all say the same thing. Anowa, what makes you so restless? What occupies you?

ANOWA   Nothing. Nothing at all.

KOFI AKO   (*walking away from her*) Anowa, is it true that you should have been a priestess?

ANOWA   O yes? But how would I know. And where did you hear that from? (*Looks genuinely lost.*)

KOFI AKO   Don't think about that one then. It doesn't matter. Still, there is too much restlessness in you which is frightening. I think maybe you are too lonely with only us men around. (*Pause.*) I have decided to procure one or two women, not many. Just one or two, so that you will have companionship of your kind.

ANOWA   (*almost hysterical*) No, no, no! I don't want them. I don't need them.

KOFI AKO   But why not?

ANOWA   No! I just do not need them. (*Long pause.*) People can be very unkind. A wayfarer is a traveller. Therefore, to call someone a wayfarer is a painless way of saying he does not belong. That he has no home, no family, no village, no stool of his own; has no feast days, no holidays, no state, no territory.

KOFI AKO   (*jumping up, furious*) Shut up, woman, shut up!

ANOWA   Why, what have I done wrong?

KOFI AKO   Do you ask me? Yes, what is wrong with you? If you want to go and get possessed by a god, I beg you, go. So that at least I shall know that a supernatural being speaks with your lips . . . (ANOWA's *eyes widen with surprise.*) I say Anowa, why must you always bring in this . . .

ANOWA   What?

KOFI AKO   About slaves and all such unpleasant affairs?

ANOWA   They are part of our lives now.

KOFI AKO   (*shaking his head*) But is it necessary to eat your insides out because of them? (*Then with extreme intensity*) Why are you like this? What evil lies in having bonded men? Perhaps, yes (*getting expansive*) in other lands. Among other less kindly people. A meaner race of men. Men who by other men are worse treated than dogs. But here, have you looked around? Yes. The wayfarer here belongs where he is. Consorts freely with free-born nephews and nieces. Eats out of the same vessel, and drinks so as well. And those who have the brains are more listened to than are babbling nobility. They fight in armies. Where the valiant and well-proven can become a captain just as quickly as anyone. How many wayfarers do we know who have become patriarchs of houses where they used only to serve?

ANOWA   But in all this, they are of account only when there are no free-born people around. And if they fare well among us, it is not so among all peoples. And even here, who knows what strange happenings go on behind doors?

KOFI AKO   (*Irritated beyond words, he seizes and shakes her.*) Anowa, Anowa, where else have you been but here? Why can't you live by what you know, what you see? What do you gain by dreaming up miseries that do not touch you? Just so you can have nightmares?

ANOWA   (*Still cool, she stares at him.*) It
   seems this is how they created me.
KOFI AKO   (*letting go of her*) Hmm. How sad
   . . . And yet if I gave you two good blows on
   your cheeks which flashed lightning across
   your face, all this foolishness would go out
   of your head. (*To himself*) And what is
   wrong with me? Any man married to her
   would have by now beaten her to a pulp,
   a dough. But I can never lay hands on her
   . . . I cannot even think of marrying
   another woman. O it is difficult to think
   through anything. All these strange words!
   (ANOWA *continues to stare at him.*) Anowa,
   what is the difference? How is it you can't
   feel like everybody else does? What is the
   meaning of this strangeness? Who were
   you in the spirit world? (*Laughing
   mirthlessly*) I used to like you very much.
   I wish I could rid you of what ails you, so I
   could give you peace. And give myself
   some. (ANOWA *still only stares at him.*) It is
   an illness, Anowa. An illness that turns to
   bile all the good things of here-under-the-
   sun. Shamelessly, you rake up the dirt of
   life. You bare our wounds. You are too fond
   of looking for the common pain and the
   general wrong. (ANOWA *manages to look
   sad. She sighs audibly, then hangs down
   her head as if ashamed. He looks down at
   her.*) Anowa, you are among women my
   one and only treasure. Beside you, all
   others look pale and shadowless. I have
   neither the desire nor wish to marry any
   other, though we all know I can afford
   dozens more. But please, bring your mind
   home. Have joy in our overflowing wealth.
   Enhance this beauty nature gave you with
   the best craftmanship in cloth and stone.
   Be happy with that which countless women
   would give their lives to enjoy for a day. Be
   happy in being my wife and maybe we
   shall have our own children. Be my
   glorious wife, Anowa, and the contented
   mother of my children.

(ANOWA's *answer is a hard grating laugh
that goes on and on even after the lights have
gone out on them. The lights reappear after a
little while. Enter* THE-MOUTH-THAT-EATS-
SALT-AND-PEPPER. *First,* OLD MAN. *He
walks up to the centre of the lower stage, and
for a short while, stands still with his head
down. Then he raises his head and speaks.*)

OLD MAN   My fellow townsmen. Have you
   heard what Kofi and Anowa are doing now?

They say he is buying men and women as
though they were only worth each a
handful of the sands on the shore. Ei,
Anowa and Kofi. Were those not the same
who left Yebi like a pair of unwanted
strangers? But peace creates forgetfulness
and money-making is like a god possessing
a priest. He never will leave you, until he
has occupied you, wholly changed the
order of your being, and seared you
through and up and down. Then only
would he eventually leave you, but
nothing of you except an exhausted
wreck, lying prone and wondering who
you are. (*Enter* OLD WOMAN.) Besides,
there must be something unwholesome
about making slaves of other men,
something that is against the natural
state of man and the purity of his worship
of the gods. Those who have observed
have remarked that every house is ruined
where they take in slaves.
   As you sit,
   They grow
   And before you know
   Where you are,
   They are there,
   And you are not.
   One or two homes in Abura already show
      this;
   They are spilling over
   With gold and silver
   And no one knows the uttermost hedges
      of their lands.
   But where are the people
   Who are going to sit on these things?
   Yes,
   It is frightening.
   But all at once,
   Girl-babies die
   And the breasts of women in new
      motherhood
   Run dry.

(OLD WOMAN *tries to get in a word,
thumping her stick and coughing.*)

OLD WOMAN
   She is a witch,
   She is a devil,
   She is everything that is evil.
OLD MAN   (*raising his head and showing
   interest*) Who?
OLD WOMAN   Who else but that child of
   Abena Badua?
OLD MAN   And what has she done now?
OLD WOMAN   Have you not heard? (*She is*

even more excited than ever. And for the rest of the scene makes an exhibition of herself, jumping, raising her stick in the air, coughing etc.) She thinks the world has not seen the likes of her before. (*Now with feigned concern*) I wonder what a woman eats to produce a child like Anowa. I am sure that such children are not begotten by normal natural processes.

OLD MAN (*with amused contempt*) But what?

OLD WOMAN Ah! They issue from cancerous growths, tumours that grow from evil dreams. Yes, and from hard and bony material that the tender organs of ordinary human women are too weak to digest.

OLD MAN Are you not sure that you are seeing too much in too little?

OLD WOMAN What are you saying? Am I wrong? What woman is she who thinks she knows better than her husband in all things?

OLD MAN A good husband would himself want advice from his wife, as the head of a family, a chief, a king, any nobleman has need of an adviser.

OLD WOMAN But Anowa is too much. She is now against the very man who she selected from so many. She would rather he was poor than prospering. They say she raves hourly against our revered ancestors and sanctions their deeds in high tones. She thinks our forefathers should have waited for her to be born so she could have upbraided them for their misdeeds and shown them what actions of men are virtuous.

OLD MAN I do not know if I can believe all this you say of the pitiful child. But certainly, it is not too much to think that the heavens might show something to children of a latter day which was hidden from them of old?

(OLD WOMAN *is so flabbergasted at this she opens her mouth wide and turns in the* OLD MAN's *direction while he walks slowly away.*)

OLD WOMAN (*closing her mouth in a heavy sigh*)
But, people of Yebi, rejoice,
For Kofi Ako has prospered
And he is your son.
Women of Nsona house,
They say Kofi Ako can stand
On his two feet to dress up fifty brides
And without moving a step,

Dress up fifty more.
And where and when did this last happen
But in fables and the days of dim
    antiquity?
They say Kofi sits fat like a bullfrog in a
    swamp,
While *that* Anowa daily grows thin,
Her eyes popping out of her head like
    those of
A hungry toad in a parched grassland.
But she is the one
Who must not be allowed to step on any
    threshold here!
When was this infant born,
That would teach us all what to do?
Who is she to bring us new rules to live
    by?
It is good she said she was not coming
    back to Yebi,
But if she so much as crosses the stream
That lies at the mouth of the road,
We shall show her that
Little babies only cry for food
When hungry,
But do not instruct their elders how to
    tend a farm:
Besides
As the sourest yam
Is better than the sweetest guava,
The dumbest man is
Always better than a woman.
Or *he* thinks he is!
And so Kofi shall teach Anowa
He is a man!

(OLD WOMAN *exits coughing and her throat wheezing.*)

Phase Three: The big house at Oguaa

The upper stage is a big central hall. The furniture here is either consciously foreign or else opulent. There are beautiful skins lying on the richly carpeted floor. Other articles include a giant sideboard on which are standing huge decanters, with or without spirits, and big decorative plates. In the central wall is a fireplace and above it, a picture of Queen Victoria unamused. To the left of the Queen is a picture of KOFI AKO *himself, and to the right, a large painting of the crow, the totem bird of the Nsona clan. In the centre of the room is a gilded chair with rich-looking cushions, and in front of it, a leopard skin. The lower stage represents here a path leading from the house into the town and outside generally.*

The lights blaze on both lower and upper stages to a tumult which at first is distant but draws nearer and nearer to lower right. First a group of women, any number from four, enter from the right dancing to no distinct form and with great abandon. Meanwhile they sing, or rather recite.

He is coming!
Nana is coming
He is coming,
The master of the earth is coming.
Give way,
O – o – give way!
For the Master of all you see around is
    coming
Turn your face, the jealous!
Close your eyes, the envious!
For he is coming,
Nana is coming!

(They pass on and away lower left, and after them, a lone man comes blowing KOFI AKO's *horn to the rhythm of just two lines.)*

Turn your face, the jealous!
Close your eyes, the envious!

(The HORNBLOWER *stops on the stage while multitudes enter from the same direction and move away lower left. They are men and women carrying raw materials, skins, copra, crude rubber and kegs of palm oil. Controlling the exportation of the last product has made* KOFI AKO *the richest man, probably, of the whole Guinea Coast. Other men and women are carrying cheap silks and madras cloth, muskets, hurricane lamps, knives and enamel ware.*

KOFI AKO enters, borne by four brawny men in some kind of a carrier chair, basket or sedan. He is resplendent in brilliant kente or velvet cloth and he is over-flowing with gold jewelry, from the crown on his head to the rings on his toes. He is surrounded by more hailing women and an orchestra of horns and drums. As he passes, he makes the gestures of lordship over the area. The procession goes off, lower left; the HORNBLOWER *is the last man to leave.*

When the tumult has died down, ANOWA *enters from upper left and sits on one side of the chairs in the central hall. She looks aged and forlorn in her old clothes. She is still bare-footed. She sits quietly for a while, as though waiting for somebody, then she stands up and begins to pace around, speaking to herself.)*

ANOWA (*As she speaks, she makes childish gestures, especially with her hands, to express all the ideas behind each sentence.*) I remember once. I think I was very young then. Quite young certainly. Perhaps I was eight, or ten. Perhaps I was twelve. My grandmother told me of her travels. She told of the great places she had been to and the wonderful things she had seen. Of the sea that is bigger than any river and boils without being hot. Of huge houses rising to touch the skies, houses whose foundations are wider than the biggest roads I had ever seen. They contained more rooms than were in all the homes I knew put together. Of these houses, I asked:
  Tell me Nana, who built the houses?
  She said:
  Why do you want to know?
  The pale men.
  Who are the pale men?
  I asked.
  You ask too many questions.
  They are the white men.
  Who are the white men?
  I asked.
  A child like you should not ask questions.
  They come from far away.
  Far away from beyond the horizon.
  Nana, what do they look like?
  I asked.
  Shut up child.
  Not like you or me,
  She said.
  But what do they look like, Nana?
  I asked.
  Shut up child or your mouth will twist up
      one day with questions.
  Not like you or me?
  Yes like you or me,
  But different.
  What do they look like, Nana?
  What devil has entered into you, child?
  As if you or I
  Were peeled of our skins,
  Like a lobster that is boiled or roasted,
  Like . . . like . . . but it is not good
  That a child should ask questions.
  Nana, why did they build the big houses?
  I asked.
  I must escape from you, child.
  They say . . . they say they built the big
      houses to keep the slaves.
  What is a slave, Nana?
  Shut up! It is not good that a child should
      ask big questions.

A slave is one who is bought and sold.
Where did the white men get the slaves?
I asked.
You frighten me, child.
You must be a witch, child.
They got them from the land.
Did the men of the land sell other men
  of the land, and women and children
  to pale men from beyond the horizon
  who looked like you or me peeled, like
  lobsters boiled or roasted?
I do not know, child.
You are frightening me, child.
I was not there!
It is too long ago!
No one talks of these things anymore!
All good men and women try to forget;
They have forgotten!
What happened to those who were taken
  away?
Do people hear from them?
How are they?
Shut up child.
It is too late child.
Sleep well, child.
All good men and women try to forget;
  They have forgotten! (*Pause.*)
That night, I woke up screaming hot; my
body burning and sweating from a horrible
dream. I dreamt that I was a big, big
woman. And from my insides were huge
holes out of which poured men, women
and children. And the sea was boiling hot
and steaming. And as it boiled, it threw
out many, many giant lobsters, boiled
lobsters, each of whom as it fell turned
into a man or woman, but keeping its
lobster head and claws. And they rushed
to where I sat and seized the men and
women as they poured out of me, and they
tore them apart, and dashed them to the
ground and stamped upon them. And
from their huge courtyards, the women
ground my men and women and children
on mountains of stone. But there was
never a cry or a murmur; only a bursting,
as of a ripe tomato or a swollen pod.
And everything went on and on and on.
(*Pause.*)
  I was very ill and did not recover for
weeks. When I told my dream, the women
of the house were very frightened. They
cried and cried and told me not to mention
the dream again. For some time, there was
talk of apprenticing me to a priestess. I
don't know what came of it. But since then,

any time there is mention of a slave, I see a
woman who is me and a bursting of a ripe
tomato or a swollen pod.

(*Now she stares straight and sharply at the
audience for a long time, and then slowly
leaves the stage by upper right. Then
suddenly, the voices of an unseen wearied
multitude begin to sing 'Swing Low, Sweet
Chariot'. The song goes on for a while and
stops. Long pause while lights remain on.
Then the lights go off on the lower stage only.
*GIRL enters from the upper right. She
resembles* ANOWA *of a long time ago. She is
dressed in a one-piece cloth wrapped around
her. She too, looks like a wild one, and she is
carrying a broom and a duster with which
she immediately begins to dust and sweep.
Then suddenly she stops and just stands
dreamily. Meanwhile,* BOY *enters from upper
right and quietly steals behind her and cries
'Hei!' She is startled.*)

GIRL (*turning round to face* BOY) How you
  frightened me.
BOY Have you just started working in here?
  And why were you standing there like
  that?
GIRL That is none of your business.
BOY I don't know what is happening in this
  house. I am sure there are more people
  here than in Oguaa town. Yet nothing gets
  done.
GIRL But you!
BOY I what? Is this the hour you were
  instructed to come and clean the place up?
GIRL Well, that is not my fault.
BOY What is not your fault? Look at
  those arms. I wonder what they could
  do even if you were not so lazy. Listen,
  today is Friday and Father is going to
  come in here. And don't stand there
  staring at me.
GIRL And anyway, are you the new
  overseer? Why don't you leave me alone?
BOY (*playfully pulling her nose*) I won't!
GIRL You! (*She raises her arm to hit him, and
  causes one of the decorative plates to fall. It
  breaks.* BOY *is furious.*)
BOY God, what is wrong with you? Look at
  what you've done!
GIRL Well, it's broken, isn't it? I wouldn't
  fuss so much if I were you.
BOY Doesn't anything bother you?
GIRL Not much. Certainly not this plate.
  (*She bends down to pick up the pieces. Then
  she stands up again.*) This mistress will not

miss it. After all, she has no time these days for things like plates.

BOY You are mad, that's all. I thought she said we should always call her 'Mother' and the master 'Father'.

GIRL (*giggling*) Some Mother and Father, heh!

BOY I don't think I have said anything for you to laugh at.

GIRL You are being very unfair. You know I like both of them very much. (*Earnestly*) I wish I really was their child . . . born to them. (*She pouts.*) As for her too.

BOY What has happened now?

GIRL Nothing. Now she flits about like a ghost, talking to herself. (*They stop and listen. The* BOY *moves up to upper left and peeps.*) Is she coming?

BOY (*not turning round*) No. (*Then he moves back towards* GIRL.)

GIRL Listen, they were saying at the fish-kilns that she went and stared at Takoa's baby so hard that the baby is having convulsions . . .

BOY (*shocked*) Ow!

GIRL Takoa is certainly telling everyone that Mistress, I mean Mother, is swallowing the baby because she is a witch.

BOY Hei! (*The* GIRL *is startled. The* BOY *moves closer to face her and begins hitting her lips with the fourth finger of his right hand.*) Don't let me catch you repeating any of the things those awful women say about Mother.

GIRL Yes, grandfather.

BOY And you, where did you hear all these things from?

GIRL (*petulantly*) I said at the kilns. (*Throwing her mouth at him*) Or are you deaf?

BOY I am not deaf but people in this house talk too much.

GIRL It is because of this new affair. And the truth is, she herself talks more about it than anyone else. Whenever she thinks she is alone anywhere, she begins 'O my husband, what have I done, what have I done?' (*She imitates someone puzzled and asks the questions with her hands. Then she giggles.*)

BOY Don't laugh. Have you seen how you yourself will end? (*He picks her duster up and begins to dust around.*)

GIRL Ei, don't turn wise on me. (*Noticing him working*) Good. You should dust since you're keeping me from doing my work . . .

BOY Huh! . . . And are you not a woman too?

GIRL (*promptly and loudly*) And if I am? (*She looks up for some time without saying anything.*)

BOY I did not say you can now rest.

GIRL (*quietly and to herself*) If I had more money than I knew what to do with, but not a single child, I should be unhappy. If my man refused to talk to me, I should soon start talking to myself; if he would not come to my room or allow me in his, I should pace around in the night. (*She now turns to look at the boy.*) And after killing myself for him, he said to me one day, go away, and would not tell me why, I should then die of surprise!

BOY People do not die of surprise.

GIRL See if I do not.

BOY (*whispering*) What do you think is going to happen now?

GIRL Do I know? All I know is that if she goes away, I shall run away too.

BOY I shall come with you.

GIRL (*coyly*) Not if you would be scolding me all the time . . .

BOY (*drawing near her and trying to touch her breasts*) No, I shall not.

(*The* GIRL *hits his hand away. They stand still for a moment. Then they resume working with vigour. The* BOY *begins to whistle some tune.*)

GIRL And the way she carries on with everyone here . . .

BOY Playing with us as though we were her kinsmen?

GIRL Yes; perhaps that is why the master wants to send her away.

BOY Maybe; and she certainly is more poorly dressed than some of us.

GIRL Yes, that is another thing. Can't she do something about herself?

BOY What, for instance?

GIRL Ho, does she not see her friends, how they go around? All those new and fashionable nkabasroto and bubas? The sleeves blowing out in the wind, the full pointed shoes and the stockings . . .

BOY Of course, that is what you would like . . .

GIRL
Why, if I were her, what would I not do, what would I not have?
As much as my eye will fancy and the best my heart desires?

(*She forgets she should be working and lets fall the broom. Her eyes light up with joyful expectation and she acts out her dream to the amazed fascination of* BOY.)

Nkente to sit in for all my work days.
Velvets for visiting. Silks for Sundays.

(ANOWA *enters unnoticed and stands at the door. She looks as she did in the last scene, but wizened now and shabby. She is wearing her old cloth and is barefooted. Her hair is cropped close.*)

GIRL

O if I were her, and she were me
Jewels on my hair, my finger and my
   knee
In my ears the dangles, on my wrists the
   bangles
My sandals will be jeweled, my hair will
   be dressed;
My perfumes will be milled, my talcums
   of the best.
On my soups I will be keen
No fish-heads to be seen
O for her to be me
So that I could be free!

(ANOWA *glides out unseen. The* BOY *and the* GIRL *stand looking at each other. The* GIRL's *eyes glisten with unshed tears while the* BOY *breathes deeply and loudly a couple of times.*)

BOY   Being a woman, of course, that's all you would think about. Though if I were you and so beautiful, I would not worry. Perhaps Father will take you for wife.

GIRL   Chiaa, aa, that man who is afraid of women?

BOY   Listen, it is dangerous talking to you. How can you say a fearful thing like that?

GIRL   But I am not lying . . . they say . . . they say . . .

BOY   Shut up. (*He hits her on the buttocks, runs down lower right and away with the* GIRL *pursuing him, her broom raised. From upper left,* ANOWA *re-enters the hall.*)

ANOWA   (*to the now disappeared* GIRL *and* BOY) You said it right, my child. But the elders gave the ruling before you and even I came: 'The string of orphan beads might look better on the wrist of the leopard but it is the antelope who has lost his mother'.

(*She wanders round aimlessly humming to herself. Presently,* PANYIN-NA-KAKRA *enter. They are about eight years old. They run in from upper right with ostrich feather fans,* stand on either side of the gilded chair and automatically begin fanning the chair. This goes on for some time without ANOWA noticing it. When she does, she laughs out dryly.)

ANOWA   Poor children, I feel like picking them up and carrying them on my back.

PANYIN-NA-KAKRA   (*still fanning*) Mother please, we did not hear you.

ANOWA   It is all right, my children, I was not speaking to you. (*Aside*) They are fanning that chair now so that by the time their lord enters, the space around it will be cool. I suppose this is one of the nice things Yaako is teaching them to do. Hmm . . . woe the childless woman, they warn. Let someone go and see their mother, who is she? Where is she sitting while they stand here fanning an empty chair? Let someone go and see how she suffered bearing them. The nine months dizziness, when food tasted like dung and water like urine. Nine months of unwholesome desires and evil dreams. Then the hour of the breaking of the amnion, when the space between her life and her death wore thin like a needy woman's hair thread. O the stench of old blood gone hot . . . Did she go through all that and with her rest at the end postponed so they (*pointing at the boys*) will come and fan an empty chair? To fan an empty chair? (*She gets up and listlessly goes to the picture of Queen Victoria and addresses it.*) Hei, sister, I hear you are a queen. Maybe in spite of the strange look of you, you are a human woman, too, eh? How is it with you over there? Do you sometimes feel like I feel, that you should not have been born? Nana . . . won't you answer? If you won't answer (*making gesture of riddance*) take your headache . . . and I say, you don't have to look at me like that because I have seen your likes before. (*To herself*) But I shall not cry. I shall not let him see the tears from my eyes. Someone should have taught me how to grow up to be a woman. I hear in other lands a woman is nothing. And they let her know this from the day of her birth. But here, O my spirit mother, they let a girl grow up as she pleases until she is married. And then she is like any woman anywhere: in order for her man to be a man, she must not think, she must not talk. O – o, why didn't someone teach me how to grow up to be a woman? (*Then she*

121

remembers the children.) Hei, Kakra, Panyin! Stop fanning that chair.

PANYIN-NA-KAKRA   (*startled*) But please, Mother, Yaako said . . .

ANOWA   I say. Stop fanning that chair Panyin, go and tell Yaako that I have asked you to stop fanning the chair. (*They put their fans on one of the stools and* PANYIN *goes out.* ANOWA *puts her arms around* KAKRA *and moves down with him. When she sits down he sits on a rug by her.*) Kakra.

KAKRA   Mother.

ANOWA   Where do you and Panyin come from?

KAKRA   The house in Tantri, Mother.

ANOWA   No, I mean before that.

KAKRA   Mother, I don't know.

ANOWA   Kakra, am I growing old?

KAKRA   (*He turns to look at her and then looks away bewildered.*) Mother, I don't know.

ANOWA   No, you don't know. Go and play with your friends, child.

(KAKRA *rises up and leaves.* ANOWA *bows down her head.* KOFI AKO *enters on the arm of* BOY. *He is bedecked as in the last scene.* ANOWA *stares contemptuously at the two of them.* BOY *leads him to the chair and places him in it. Now and any other time in the rest of the scene, when* KOFI AKO *silently examines his limbs, 'Asem yi se nea mokobo tuo' or any African funeral march or drums should be played.*)

BOY   Father, shall I go and fetch Nana the priest?

KOFI AKO   (*hurriedly*) Not yet. I shall call you and send you with a message for him.

BOY   Yes, Father. (*He retires.*)

(*Awkward silence.*)

ANOWA   I was told that you wanted to speak to me.

KOFI AKO   All I want to say Anowa, is that I do not like seeing you walking around the house like this.

ANOWA   You don't like seeing me walk around the house like what?

KOFI AKO   Please, stop asking me annoying questions.

ANOWA   Don't shout. After all, it is you who are anxious that the slaves should not hear us. What I don't understand, Kofi, is why you want to have so many things your own way.

KOFI AKO   (*very angrily*) And I don't think there is a single woman in the land who speaks to her husband the way you do to me. (*Sighs and relaxes.*) Why are you like this, Anowa? Why? (ANOWA *laughs.*) Can't you be like other normal women? Other normal people? (ANOWA *continues laughing, then stops abruptly.*)

ANOWA   I still don't know what you mean by normal. Is it abnormal to want to continue working?

KOFI AKO   Yes, if there is no need to.

ANOWA   But my husband, is there a time when there is no need for a human being to work? After all, our elders said that one never stops wearing hats on a head which still stands on its shoulders.

KOFI AKO   I do not see the reason why I should go walking through forests, climbing mountains and crossing rivers to buy skins when I have bought slaves to do just that for me.

ANOWA   And so we come back to where we have been for a long time now. My husband, we did not have to put the strength of our bodies into others. We should not have bought the slaves . . .

KOFI AKO   But we needed them to do the work for us.

(ANOWA *begins to pace up and down and from side to side and never stops for too long any time during the rest of the scene.*)

ANOWA   As though other people are horses! And now look at us. We do nothing from the crowing of the cock to the setting of the sun. I wander around like a ghost and you sit, washed and oiled like a . . . bride on show or a god being celebrated. Is this what we left Yebi for? Ah, my husband, where did our young lives go?

KOFI AKO   (*angrily*) Stop it, Anowa, stop it. And what is the meaning of all this strange talk? If you feel old, that is your own affair. I feel perfectly young.

ANOWA   Do you?

KOFI AKO   (*fiercely*) Yes, I do. And you stop creeping around the house the way you do. Like some beggar. Making yourself a laughing stock. Can't you do anything to yourself? After all, you are my wife.

ANOWA   Am I your wife? What is there to prove it?

KOFI AKO   I don't understand you.

ANOWA   Don't you? I am asking you what I do or what there is about me that shows I am your wife. I do not think putting on fine clothes is enough.

KOFI AKO   Are you referring to the fact that we have not had children?

ANOWA   An adopted child is always an adopted child and a slave child, a slave . . . Perhaps I am the barren one. But you deserve a son; so Kofi, I shall get you a wife. One of these plump mulatto women of Oguaa . . .

KOFI AKO   Anowa, Stop that!

ANOWA   Besides, such women are more civilised than I, who only come from Yebi. They, like you, have learned the ways of the white people. And a woman like that may be attractive enough to be allowed into your bed . . .

KOFI AKO   Anowa stop that! Stop it, stop it!

ANOWA   (*laughing*) Stop what? Stop what? (KOFI AKO *sighs again and relaxes. He begins to examine his limbs as the funeral music or drums rise and fall, and* ANOWA *plays at digging her toes into the skins or re-arranging the plates on the sideboard.*) And what did the priest say the last time he was here?

KOFI AKO   What do you mean? What has that to do with you?

ANOWA   Too much. I know all this has something to do with what he has been telling you.

KOFI AKO   You are speaking as if your head is not there.

ANOWA   (*screaming*) What did his divination say about me?

KOFI AKO   I don't know. And anyway, listen. I thought you were just as good at this sort of thing as he is. You should know, should you not? Why don't you go and wash your mouth so you can be a priestess at last. I can't stand any more of your strange ways.

ANOWA   (*voice betraying nervousness*) What are you talking about?

KOFI AKO   (*laughing bitterly*) What am I talking about! (*Another awkward pause.*)

ANOWA   Yes, what are you talking about?

KOFI AKO   (*with an almost feigned fatigue*) Please, just leave me alone. O God, Anowa did you have to destroy me too? What does someone like you want from life? Anowa, did you . . . I mean did you make me just to destroy me?

ANOWA   Kofi, what are you saying?

KOFI AKO   Anowa, Anowa, O, Anowa.

ANOWA   So what did the priest say the last time he was here?

KOFI AKO   That has nothing to do with you.

ANOWA   I think it has. Too much, I feel deep inside me that all this business about me leaving you has something to do with what he told you last week.

KOFI AKO   What mad talk!

ANOWA   (*hysterically*) What did the priest's divination say about me?

KOFI AKO   Please stop walking up and down. It irritates me.

ANOWA   Why are you sending me away from you?

KOFI AKO   Just leave me alone.

ANOWA   What have I done wrong?

KOFI AKO   Nothing.

ANOWA   Is it is because I did not give you children? (*Silence. She moves up to him and changes her attitude to one of supplication.*) Do you want to take a new wife who would not like to see me around?

KOFI AKO   Anowa, why do you want to go on asking foolish questions to which you know I cannot give you answers?

ANOWA   But they are not foolish questions.

KOFI AKO   (*unconcerned*) In fact, I thought you would be glad to get away. I don't know what you want, and even if I knew, I am not sure it would have been in my power to give it. And you can't give me the only thing I want from you, a child. Let us part, Anowa.

ANOWA   But going away is one thing. Being sent away is another.

KOFI AKO   And by that you mean, as always, that you have a right to do what you like and as always I am to sit by and watch?

ANOWA   (*She throws up her hands in despair.*) O the god of our fathers! Is there nothing I can say which cannot be twisted around my own neck to choke me?

(*Music or drums as* KOFI AKO *examines his limbs.* ANOWA *paces up and down. Then she speaks, almost to herself.*)

ANOWA   Did the priest say . . . what is there about me which he thinks will not bring you blessings now? I must have done something wrong. I must have done something. I'm not a child. Kofi, I know they say a man whose wife is constantly sleeping with other men does not prosper. Did the priest say I am doing something like that? Or anything as evil as that?

KOFI AKO   (*a bitter smile on his lips*) Just go away and leave me alone, woman.

ANOWA   (*sadly*) I cannot, my husband. Because I have nowhere to go. I swore I would not go back to Yebi. And I can still

123

live here, can I not? I would not disturb you. I can stay in my part of the house. Just don't send me away, we have not seen each other's beds for far too long for it to matter if we don't any more . . . (*She stares at him and utters her next words as though she has just made a discovery.*) A–h–h or is it a death you are dying? We are dying. Listen, my husband, did the priest say you are dying, I am dying, we are dying?

KOFI AKO   You are mad, I am very alive.

ANOWA   (*She gets up and raises her voice.*) Boy!

KOFI AKO   Why are you calling him?

ANOWA   It has nothing to do with you.

BOY   (*running in*) Mother, I am here.

ANOWA   Boy, I am going to ask you a question. (*She resumes pacing up and down.*) Boy, you know your master says I must go away from here and never come back. (BOY *hangs his head down with embarrassment.*) My feet are on the road already and if it were not that he has not yet told me what he has found wrong with me or what I have done wrong, I would already be gone. Boy, do you know why?

BOY   No, Mother.

ANOWA   Boy, have you heard of a man who seeks to divorce his wife and will not say why?

BOY   Mother, I have never known the customs of this land well.

ANOWA   What about where you came from? Did you hear of such a case before you were taken away?

BOY   I do not remember that I did.

ANOWA   Boy, I thank you. Go call for me as many of the older men and women as are around . . . Bring everybody on whom your eyes fall.

BOY   Yes, Mother. (*He leaves.*)

KOFI AKO   (*furiously*) Anowa, what are you doing? Why must they know about this? You have never behaved like a child before – why are you behaving like one now?

ANOWA   I do not know why we must not bring them in. I need their help and they also came from places where men live, eat and die. Perhaps one is among them who can help me. And I am behaving like a child now because I have gained nothing from behaving like a grown-up all my life.

KOFI AKO   (*surprised*) You are mad Anowa.

ANOWA   Not yet!

BOY   (*from doorway*) Are they to come?

ANOWA   Let them come.

(BOY *re-enters followed by as many men and women as possible. The last pair is the twins. They all shuffle around looking wide-eyed.*)

ALL   Mother, we are here.

ANOWA   I see you. Listen. Has any of you heard of a woman whose husband wanted to divorce her but would not tell her why? (*They look bewildered and answer 'No' as if it were a line in a musical round, sung softly: No, no, no, no, no, no . . . They all whisper aloud to each other.*) Then please you may go . . . (*They all turn round at once.*) No wait . . . Eh – eh . . . I would like to send some of you. I am sending you to the oldest and wisest people on this land; go ask them if they have ever heard of a man who sought to divorce his wife and would not tell her why. (*Points at random to different people.*) You go to the bearded woman of Kwaakrom and you to the old priests of Nanaam Mpow. You over there to Bekoe, he whom dwarfs abducted and taught the mysteries of the woods. Go quickly and come back today and walk as you have never walked before. Come quickly, for already I hear too many noises in my head and you must come back before my mind flies and gets lost. (*The crowd disperses through all available exits. Exhausted but still excited,* ANOWA *paces around* KOFI AKO *who is now very silent.*) I have known this was coming for weeks and I have feared. An old man said, 'Fear "it-is-coming" but not "It-has-come"'. But for me 'It-has-come' has brought me no peace. Perhaps . . . Boy!

BOY   (*running*) Mother, I am here.

ANOWA   I hear Nana Abakframpahene Kokroko is here. He and the other chiefs are meeting with the Governor. Go. Whisper in his ears that he is to come to me. Tell him it is urgent and he is to pardon us for not going to him ourselves. All shall be explained in time. He is to come but without his retinue.

KOFI AKO   (*raising himself up*) Anowa, what are you doing all this for?

ANOWA   The times are past when our individual actions had to be explained to each other.

(BOY *looks away with embarrassment.*)

KOFI AKO   Perhaps you are going out of your senses.

ANOWA   That should not mean anything to you.

KOFI AKO   That is not what concerns me, but you shall not let this out before Nana. (*He stamps his feet.*)

ANOWA   Just sit there and look at me.

KOFI AKO   (*shouts*) You may go away, Boy. Forget what your Mother told you.

BOY   Yes, Father. (*He retires.*)

ANOWA   Who are you to say what you shall allow and what you shall not allow me?

KOFI AKO   (*loud with anger*) Nana is my friend and not yours.

ANOWA   That is why I am asking him to come.

KOFI AKO   Anowa, you shall not disgrace me before him.

ANOWA   Darkness has overtaken us already, and does it matter if we hit each against the other? Are you not disgracing me before the whole world?

KOFI AKO   Your strange speeches will not persuade me . . .

ANOWA   I am not trying to. It is a long time since my most ordinary words ceased to have any meaning for me.

KOFI AKO   I say once more that Nana is the only man in this world I respect and honour.

ANOWA   My good husband, in the old days how well I knew you. That is why I want to consult him too.

KOFI AKO   I should have known that you were always that clever.

ANOWA   And certain things have shown that cleverness is not a bad thing.

KOFI AKO   Everyone said you were a witch. I should have believed them.

ANOWA   (*derisively*) Why, have I choked you with the bone of an infant?

KOFI AKO   Stop all this show and just leave me alone, I say.

ANOWA   Then I shall ask advice of whom I please.

KOFI AKO   Anowa, if you do not leave me quietly, but go consulting anybody about this affair, I shall brand you a witch.

ANOWA   (*shocked*) No!

KOFI AKO   (*brought suddenly to life by her exclamation*) And if I do, you know there is more than one person in the world who would believe me.

ANOWA   (*screams*) No, no, no!

KOFI AKO   And there will be those who would be prepared to furnish proof.

ANOWA   Kofi, I am not hearing you right.

KOFI AKO   And then you know what could happen. But, that should not make much

difference to you. Since you do not care to live or behave like everybody else . . .

ANOWA   But what have I done?

KOFI AKO   I just want you to leave me, that's all.

ANOWA   O the Gods of my fathers, what is it? What is it?

KOFI AKO   I shall have the little house built for you, as I promised, but in Yebi . . .

ANOWA   But I cannot go and live there.

KOFI AKO   I will give you half of the trade and half of the slaves, if you want them.

ANOWA   I don't want anything from you.

KOFI AKO   Take away with you all the jewelry.

ANOWA   I say I want nothing . . .

KOFI AKO   And you must leave immediately. I myself shall come to Yebi, or send people you can respect to come and explain everything to your family . . .

ANOWA   No, no, no!

KOFI AKO   . . . I shall ask a few men and women to go with you now, and carry your personal belongings.

ANOWA   But . . .

KOFI AKO   Boy!

ANOWA   Stop!

KOFI AKO   What? (*Unknown to the two, not only* BOY *but several of the slaves, men and women, appear.*)

ANOWA   You cannot send me away like this. Not to Yebi, or anywhere. Not before you have told me why. I swore to Mother I was not returning. Not ever. (*Not shedding a tear but her eyes shining dangerously*) No, I am not in rags. But . . . but I do not have children from this marriage. Ah! Yes, Kofi, (*she moves to him and whispers hoarsely and audibly*) we do not have children, Kofi, we have not got children! And for years now, I have not seen your bed. And Kofi, (*getting hysterical*) now that I think back on it, you have never been interested in any other woman . . .

KOFI AKO   What are you saying, Anowa?

ANOWA   Kofi, are you dead? (*Pause.*) Kofi, is your manhood gone? I mean, you are like a woman. (*Pause.*) Kofi, there is not hope any more, is there? (*Pause.*) Kofi . . . tell me, is that why I must leave you? That you have exhausted your masculinity acquiring slaves and wealth? (*Silence.*) Why didn't you want me to know? You could have told me. Because we were friends. Like brother and sister. You just did not want me to know? And the priest said it was my fault.

That I ate your manhood up? Why did he say I did it? Out of envy? Did he not tell you that perhaps you had consumed it up yourself acquiring wealth and slaves?

(KOFI AKO *looks around and sees the peeping eyes. He is horrified. He gestures to* ANOWA *who doesn't know what is happening and goes on talking. He makes an attempt to go away and then sits down again. The slaves disappear.*)

ANOWA   Now I know. So that is it. My husband is a woman now. (*She giggles.*) He is a corpse. He is dead wood. But less than dead wood because at least that sometimes grows mushrooms . . . Why didn't you want me to know? (*Long pause while they look at each other strangely. Then he gets up to leave.*) Where are you going? Kofi, don't leave. Let us start from the beginning. (*Long pause.*) No, I shall leave you in peace. (*Pause.*) I am leaving, Kofi. I am leaving. I shall leave you in peace.

(*He exits upper left. She watches his receding back until he disappears. She then shifts her gaze to the gilded chair. She stares at that for some time, after which her eyes just wander in general round the room. Then at some point she begins to address the furniture.*)

ANOWA
    Ah, very soon the messengers will be
        coming back,
    Rugs, pictures, you, chair and you, Queen,
    Should they ask of me from you, tell them
        I am gone,
    Tell them it matters not what the wise
        ones say,
    For now, I am wiser than they.

(*She fixes her eyes on the gilded chair again. Suddenly she jumps a step or two and sits in it and begins to dangle her legs like a child, with a delighted grin on her face. She breaks into a giggle. There is a sudden gun-shot off stage, followed by a stillness. As pandemonium breaks out off stage with women and men shrieking,* ANOWA *begins to giggle again. The light dies slowly on her.*
    Lights come on both parts of the stage. Upper is still the great hall. In the centre is the gilded chair unoccupied. In the background can be heard funeral drums and wailing. A few women, led by BADUA, *who is weeping, troop in from upper right and sit down,* BADUA *in the right hand corner nearest the*

lower stage. The women sit around the gilded chair as though it is the funeral bed. A little later, OSAM enters from upper left to sit in the left-hand corner facing BADUA. All are in deep red mourning. The drum and wailing stops, but only to give way to KOFI AKO's HORNBLOWER *who enters immediately after* OSAM, *stands directly behind the chair, blows a sequence of the exhortation and stops. The lights go dim on the upper stage.*
    THE-MOUTH-THAT-EATS-SALT-AND-PEPPER *enters.* OLD WOMAN *first and almost shrieking.*)

OLD WOMAN   Puei, puei, puei! This is the type of happening out of which we get stories and legends. Yebi, I wish you dué, dué, dué. May all the powers that be condole with you. Kofi Ako shoots himself and Anowa drowns herself! This is too much. Other villages produce great men, men of wealth, men of name. Why should this befall us? What tabooed food have we eaten? What unholy ground have we trodden? (OLD MAN *enters, stands in the centre of the stage with his head down.*) O Kofi Ako! Some say he lost his manhood because he was not born with much to begin with; that he had been a sickly infant and there always was only a hollow in him where a man's strength should be. Others say he had consumed it acquiring wealth, or exchanged it for prosperity. But I say that all should be laid at Anowa's doorstep. What man prospers, married to a woman like Anowa? Eh, would even Amanfi the giant have retained his strength faced with that witch? They say she always worked as though she could eat a thousand cows. Let the gods forgive me for speaking ill of the dead, but Anowa ate Kofi Ako up!

OLD MAN   (*looking at her keenly, he chuckles*) There is surely one thing we know how to do very well. And that is assigning blame when things go wrong.

OLD WOMAN   What do you mean by that! I did not shoot Kofi Ako, did I?

OLD MAN   I never said you did.

OLD WOMAN   Was it not that Anowa who made him shoot himself?

OLD MAN   (*quietly and not looking at* OLD WOMAN) Perhaps, perhaps, perhaps. And yet no one goes mad in emptiness, unless he has the disease already in his head from the womb. No. It is men who make men mad. Who knows if Anowa would have been a better woman, a better person if we had not been what we are? (OLD WOMAN *glares at him, spits and wobbles out coughing harder than ever before.*) They used to say here that Anowa behaved as though she were a heroine in a story. Some of us wish she had been happier and that her life had not had so much of the familiar human scent in it. She is true to herself. She refused to come back here to Yebi, to our gossiping and our judgments. Osam and Badua have gone with the others to bring the two bodies home to Yebi. Ow, if there is life after death, Anowa's spirit will certainly have something to say about that!

(*He begins to walk away, while all the lights begin to die. In the approaching darkness, we hear the single Atentenben wailing in loneliness.*)[1]

Note

1   It is quite possible to end the play with the final exit of ANOWA. Or one could follow the script and permit THE-MOUTH-THAT-EATS-SALT-AND-PEPPER to appear for the last scene. The choice is open.

7 Derek Walcott _____

Pantomime
Trinidad

_____

Introduction

Long before he won the 1992 Nobel Prize for
Literature, Derek Walcott had earned a
reputation as a somewhat controversial
writer whose capacious literary embrace
encompassed both the folk traditions of his
native Caribbean and the high art of the
classical European canon. Unlike some of his
nativist compatriots, such as poet Edward
Brathwaite, Walcott did not spurn his
European colonial legacy in favour of a black
sensibility largely devoid of the echoes of
Western myth. Instead, he fashioned himself
as a 'mulatto of style' (Walcott 1970b: 9),
adept at synthesis and dedicated to 'an
electric fusion of the old and new' (1970b:
17). Over more than fifty years and across an
impressive oeuvre that has included more
than twenty plays and ten major collections
of verse plus a number of lyrical essays,
Walcott has grappled frequently with the
politics and poetics of forging a Caribbean
identity from the historical fragments of
colonialism. A paradoxical sense of renewal
located in the colonial crisis of dividedness
permeates his work, both thematically and
stylistically. Colonialism, despite – and even
because of – its brutalities, thus becomes a
kind of alchemy out of which is rendered a
protean postcolonial subject able to move, if
not always with ease, between different
cultures and traditions.

Walcott and his twin brother Roderick, also
a playwright of note, were born in 1930 in
Castries, a small colonial town on the
windward Caribbean island of St Lucia. A
strong family emphasis on education along
with a mixed European and African ancestry
afforded him a degree of social privilege not
available to most of the island's rural black
populace, whose vibrant folk culture
nonetheless held great appeal for the aspiring
writer. Much of Walcott's early poetry reveals

an acute anxiety over his positioning as 'heir'
to two conflicting cultures, though he was
later to see this background as a necessary
crucible for his art, and, more generally, as
typical of the region's cultural plurality. His
first play to be produced, *Henri Christophe*,
staged in 1950 in St Lucia and two years later
in London, took as its subject the Haitian
Revolution and was hailed as a landmark in
West Indian theatre, which, to that point, had
largely consisted of the predictable European
fare of the colonial classes. While *Henri
Christophe* shows stylistic debts to
Elizabethan and Jacobean drama, its focus on
a local historical event draws attention to
contemporary struggles in the Caribbean to
build post-independence societies in the
wake of colonialism.

As the first black republic in the Americas,
Haiti, with its fraught revolutionary history,
was to provide material for other Walcott
plays, including the pageant, *Drums and
Colours*, commissioned for the inauguration
of the West Indian Federation in 1958. Prior
to this event, Walcott had completed an Arts
degree at the University College of the West
Indies in Jamaica, where he played a leading
role in the literary society, writing poetry as
well as directing theatre. His artistic
endeavours at university culminated in what
critics have seen as his first fully realised St
Lucian play, *The Sea at Dauphin* (1954), a
loose adaptation of J.M. Synge's *Riders to the
Sea*. Here, Walcott foregrounds the local not
only in terms of setting and thematics but
also through extensive use of Patois and
Creole speech registers. This interest in the
language and culture of his native island
finds even fuller expression in Walcott's
deceptively simple parable, *Ti-Jean and his
Brothers* (1957), which dramatises a St Lucian
folktale, using the story of three brothers'
attempts to outwit the devil as an allegory of
colonial relations.

In 1958, Walcott travelled to New York, supported by a Rockefeller Foundation Fellowship to study dramaturgy. On his return to the Caribbean a year later, he settled in Port of Spain, where he set up the Trinidad Theatre Workshop with the explicit purpose of creating a vibrant West Indian performative idiom that would transform the inherently theatrical forms of Caribbean popular culture into disciplined theatre. This venture occupied almost twenty years of Walcott's life, a period during which he wrote and staged many of the major works of his dramatic corpus as well as revising earlier scripts and publishing several highly acclaimed collections of poetry. His best known play from these years, *Dream on Monkey Mountain* (1967), winner of an Obie Award for its New York production, demonstrates an ongoing preoccupation with the legacy of plantation slavery and its impact on the common people. Praised for its complex and poetic exploration of the Caribbean psyche, this ritualistic drama enacts 'the powerful effects of colonial brainwashing, which encourages the complicity of European mimesis in one kind of colonial subject' and an adversarial but 'equally problematic notion of a return to "pure" African ancestral roots in another' (Thieme 1999: 71). Among other works of this period are two musicals devised in collaboration with Galt McDermott: *The Joker of Seville* (1974), a Creolised, carnival version of the seventeenth-century Don Juan play, Tirso de Molina's *El Burlador de Sevilla*; and *Oh Babylon!* (1976), an exploration of Rastafarian culture and reggae.

Walcott left the Trinidad Theatre Workshop in 1976 and has since then spent part of each year in the United States where he currently holds a teaching appointment at Boston University. His present reputation as one of the very finest poets writing in English has eclipsed his achievements in drama over the last few decades, even though he has written a number of significant plays in this period, including *Beef, No Chicken* (1981), a farce about American neo-imperialism in the Caribbean, and a stage adaptation of Homer's *The Odyssey*, commissioned by the Royal Shakespeare Company for their 1992 Stratford season. Since the Trinidad experiment, Walcott's passionate engagement with questions about Caribbean performance aesthetics has continued to shape his work,

albeit in a different way. His frequently performed two-hander, *Pantomime* (1978), exemplifies this concern, building on metatheatrical elements of earlier plays to confront directly problems associated with maintaining an indigenous performance tradition in a society where the historical purchase of British and American art forms threatens to overwhelm the local culture.

Pantomime addresses complex issues about Caribbean identity and its typical forms of theatrical expression via a comic investigation of the stereotypes that animate *Robinson Crusoe*, Daniel Defoe's eighteenth-century colonialist fantasy. Set in the Caribbean region and centrally focused on the master–slave dynamic, Defoe's ur-text represents an ideal starting point for Walcott's inventive riffs and re-imaginings of race relations between the modern-day protagonists, Jackson and Trewe. One of the play's major achievements is that it goes well beyond foreshadowing a simple reversal of roles between the coloniser and the colonised, aiming instead to dismantle the binary oppositions on which imperialism depends. In this context, neither the Friday nor Crusoe role is predetermined but rather remains open to the artistic reworkings of the contemporary characters. The attempt to reappropriate the Crusoe myth for a progressive conception of Caribbean identity was already a recurrent motif in Walcott's work well before the writing of *Pantomime*. In several poems from *The Castaway* (1965) and especially in his essay, 'The Figure of Crusoe' (1965), Walcott indicates the immensely complicated and often contradictory web of meanings which attach to this character. Crusoe is simultaneously Adam, first inhabitant of Paradise with the power to name the animals; Columbus, the discoverer of a new world; God, in control of the earth and its 'natives'; a missionary, instructing Friday in the rudiments of Christian belief; and Defoe himself, who may in Crusoe's journal be penning the narrative of his own spiritual exile and isolation. It is, moreover, Crusoe's survivalist pragmatism and openness to new experiences that attracts Walcott, as it attracts Jackson in *Pantomime*. That the play tacitly approves Jackson's Creolised Crusoe, while satirising Trewe's excessively romanticised British version of this particular 'hero', confirms the playwright's faith in the transformative power of a Caribbean sensibility.

Language – in its various uses and deliberate misuses – is another of *Pantomime*'s central concerns. Walcott's life-long interest in the nuances and contradictions of English and its hybrid variants is enacted here in a number of ways. Both characters shift up and down linguistic registers with immense flexibility and precision, though Jackson is obviously the expert at this survivalist form of code-switching. In a virtuoso performance, he playfully skips between the extremes of linguistic incompetence and linguistic dexterity, at one minute mispronouncing words and at the next devising witty impromptu calypsos or upstaging Trewe in a sparkling repartee. Jackson's razor-sharp language skills afford him the subversive power of mimicry so that his various ascribed roles – as servant, as Friday, as a Caribbean Crusoe – represent less a slavish impersonation than a mockery of regressive imperial tropes.

Some of the play's most important debates about language are crystallised through its best comic device, the parrot, around which coalesce various concepts of postcolonial identity. At the most basic level, the parrot alludes to Crusoe's parrot in Defoe's novel, yet its intertextual resonance operates more widely: it is simultaneously the parrot in Chekhov's *The Seagull* and Strindberg's *Miss Julie*, and perhaps also that in Jean Rhys's *Wide Sargasso Sea*. Trewe's caustic reference to the first two of these texts in his accusation that the Caribbean produces only imitation, nothing original, carries the extra intertextual bite of Walcott rebutting critics who accuse him of endless cultural recycling (Huggan 1994). On a more abstract level, the parrot is emblematic of the colonial experience, particularly in the Caribbean. The 'parroting' of European ways by indigenous populations was a process of being 'educated' out of traditional social patterns and into a valorised and imposed Eurocentric norm. The parrot's semi-comic cry of 'Heinegger!' – surely not really the name of a former German proprietor of Trewe's guesthouse – is thus read by Jackson as a cross-cultural sneer at black West Indians' ways of life and cultural values. More specifically, the parrot embodies the postcolonial paradox in relation to language. The taunting cry that the parrot

has been trained to repeat appears to posit language as an oppressive imperialist tool, but the concept of 'parroting' for which it is a symbol opens up the possibilities of linguistic parody and subversion. Cases in point are Jackson's satire of Trewe's high Romantic prose and his inversion of the Crusoe/Friday hierarchy by giving Trewe an object lesson in African language. Encapsulating all three levels of the parrot's symbolic resonance in a put-down of devastating finality, Jackson declares: 'Language is ideas, Mr Trewe. And I think that this pre-colonial parrot have the wrong idea'.

As its title might suggest, *Pantomime* is as much about the nature of theatricality as it is about Caribbean race relations. Trewe, a failed former repertory actor, and Jackson, retired Calypsonian and former 'very serious steel-band man', are adept at modes of popular theatre, which they use to play out their personal conflicts and competitive masculinities. Trewe reminisces, part-affectionately, part-pathetically, about his company's provincial British tours and the classic cross-dressing frisson of the army 'gang show'. Jackson, for his part, also knows the theatrical ropes: he improvises satirical calypsos at will, apes the cringing 'stage nigger' popularised in minstrel entertainments, and eventually impersonates Trewe's wife in the best of English pantomime traditions, complete with mask (represented by the photograph he holds) and high-pitched squeal. The constant tension in the play – the debate over relative racial status springing from the proposed Crusoe pantomime and its possible variations – posits racial identities as themselves artificial, largely theatrical, constructs. At the same time, the audience is continually reminded of the material effects of racial categorisations, in everyday life as well as in the theatre. Hence, Jackson remains sceptical about the general appeal of a pantomime featuring a black Crusoe. This sentiment is echoed in Walcott's later play, *A Branch of the Blue Nile* (1983), where a Trinidadian actress attempting to play Cleopatra feels that she will never be taken seriously in the part because of the colour of her skin.

Overall, *Pantomime* champions a model of syncretic performance that conscientiously stages both the big issues and the minutiae of lived Caribbean experience. Theatre becomes a kind of cultural laboratory in which identities are tested, remodelled, played out – and played with. Within such a paradigm, Walcott's self-conscious reworking of received cultural symbols and performative modes is a crucial first step towards indigenising the politico-cultural system.

Production history

Pantomime was first produced by All Theatre Productions at the Little Carib Theatre, Port of Spain, Trinidad, on 12 April 1978, directed by Albert LaVeau, with Maurice Brash as Harry Trewe and Wilbert Holder as Jackson Phillip. The play has been performed in a wide range of Caribbean venues as well as in Boston and London.

Select bibliography

Hamner, R.D. (1981) *Derek Walcott*. Boston, MA: Twayne.

Huggan, G. (1994) 'A tale of two parrots: Walcott, Rhys, and the uses of colonial mimicry', *Contemporary Literature* 35, 4: 643–60.

Jeyifo, B. (1989) 'On Eurocentric critical theory: some paradigms for the texts and subtexts of post-colonial writing', in S. Slemon and H. Tiffin (eds) *After Europe: Critical Theory and Post-Colonial Writing*, Mundelstrup, Denmark: Dangaroo, 107–18.

Jones, B. (1996) '"With Crusoe the slave and Friday the boss": Derek Walcott's *Pantomime*', in L. Spaas and B. Stimpson (eds) *Robinson Crusoe: Myths and Metamorphoses*, New York: St Martin's Press, 225–38.

Juneja, R. (1992) 'Derek Walcott', in B. King (ed.) *Post-Colonial English Drama: Commonwealth Drama since 1960*, New York: St Martin's Press, 236–66.

King, B. (1995) *Derek Walcott and West Indian Drama*, Oxford: Clarendon.

Stone, J.J. (1994) *Theatre: Studies in West Indian Literature*, London: Macmillan.

Taylor, P. (1986) 'Myth and reality in Caribbean narrative: Derek Walcott's *Pantomime*', *World Literature Written in English* 26, 1: 169–77.

Thieme, J. (1999) *Derek Walcott*, Manchester: Manchester University Press.

Walcott, D. (1970a) *Dream on Monkey Mountain and Other Plays*, New York: Farrar, Straus & Giroux.

—— (1970b) 'What the twilight says: an overture', in his *Dream on Monkey Mountain and Other Plays*, New York: Farrar, Straus & Giroux, 1–40.

—— (1993) 'The figure of Crusoe', [1965] in R.D. Hamner (ed.) *Critical Perspectives on Derek Walcott*, Washington, DC: Three Continents Press, 33–40.

Pantomime

Derek Walcott

Characters

HARRY TREWE English, mid-forties, owner of the Castaways Guest House, retired actor
JACKSON PHILLIP Trinidadian, 40, his factotum, retired calypsonian

Setting

The action takes place in a gazebo on the edge of a cliff, part of a guest house on the island of Tobago, West Indies.

Act I

A small summerhouse or gazebo, painted white, with a few plants and a table set for breakfast. HARRY TREWE enters – in white, carrying a tape recorder, which he rests on the table. He starts the machine.

HARRY (*sings and dances*)
It's our Christmas panto,
it's called: Robinson Crusoe.
We're awfully glad that you've shown up,
it's for kiddies as well as for grown-ups.
Our purpose is to please:
so now with our magic wand . . .

(*Dissatisfied with the routine, he switches off the machine. Rehearses his dance. Then presses the machine again.*)

Just picture a lonely island
and a beach with its golden sand.
There walks a single man
in the beautiful West Indies!

(*He turns off the machine. Stands, staring out to sea. Then exits with the tape recorder. Stage empty for a few beats, then JACKSON, in an open, white waiter's jacket and black trousers, but barefoot, enters with a breakfast tray. He puts the tray down, looks around.*)

JACKSON Mr. Trewe? (*English accent*) Mr. Trewe, your scramble eggs is here! are here! (*Creole accent*) You hear, Mr. Trewe? I here wid your eggs! (*English accent*) Are you in there? (*To himself*) And when his eggs get cold, is I to catch. (*He fans the eggs with one hand.*) What the hell I doing? That ain't go heat them. It go make them more cold. Well, he must be leap off the ledge. At long last. Well, if he ain't dead, he could call.

(*He exits with tray. Stage bare. HARRY returns, carrying a hat made of goatskin and a goatskin parasol. He puts on the hat, shoulders the parasol, and circles the table. Then he recoils, looking down at the floor.*)

HARRY (*sings and dances*)
Is this the footprint of a naked man,
or is it the naked footprint of a man,
that startles me this morning on this
bright and golden sand.

(*To audience*)

There's no one here but I,
just the sea and lonely sky . . .

(*Pauses.*)

Yes . . . and how the hell did it go on?

(*JACKSON enters, without the tray. Studies HARRY.*)

JACKSON Morning, Mr. Trewe. Your breakfast ready.
HARRY So how're you this morning, Jackson?
JACKSON Oh, fair to fine, with seas moderate, with waves three to four feet in open water, and you, sir?
HARRY Overcast with sunny periods, with the possibility of heavy showers by mid-afternoon, I'd say, Jackson.
JACKSON Heavy showers, Mr. Trewe?

HARRY   Heavy showers. I'm so bloody bored I could burst into tears.

JACKSON   I bringing in breakfast.

HARRY   You do that, Friday.

JACKSON   Friday? It ain't go keep.

HARRY   (*gesturing*) Friday, you, bring Crusoe, me, breakfast now. Crusoe hungry.

JACKSON   Mr. Trewe, you come back with that same rake again? I tell you, I ain't no actor, and I ain't walking in front a set of tourists naked playing cannibal. Carnival, but not canni-bal.

HARRY   What tourists? We're closed for repairs. We're the only ones in the guest house. Apart from the carpenter, if he ever shows up.

JACKSON   Well, you ain't seeing him today, because he was out on a heavy lime last night . . . Saturday, you know? And with the peanuts you does pay him for overtime.

HARRY   All right, then. It's goodbye!

(*He climbs onto the ledge between the uprights, teetering, walking slowly.*)

JACKSON   Get offa that ledge, Mr. Trewe! Is a straight drop to them rocks!

(HARRY *kneels, arms extended, Jolson-style.*)

HARRY   Hold on below there, sonny boooy! Daddy's a-coming. Your papa's a-coming, Sonnnnneee Booooooooy! (*To* JACKSON) You're watching the great Harry Trewe and his high-wire act.

JACKSON   (*turning to leave*) You watching Jackson Phillip and his disappearing act.

HARRY   (*jumping down*) I'm not a suicide, Jackson. It's a good act, but you never read the reviews. It would be too exasperating, anyway.

JACKSON   What, sir?

HARRY   Attempted suicide in a Third World country. You can't leave a note because the pencils break, you can't cut your wrist with the local blades . . .

JACKSON   We trying we best, sir, since all you gone.

HARRY   Doesn't matter if we're a minority group. Suicides are tax-payers, too, you know, Jackson.

JACKSON   Except it ain't going be suicide. They go say I push you. So, now the fun and dance done, sir, breakfast now?

HARRY   I'm rotting from insomnia, Jackson. I've been up since three, hearing imaginary guests arriving in the rooms, and I haven't slept since. I nearly came around the back to have a little talk. I started thinking about the same bloody problem, which is, What entertainment can we give the guests?

JACKSON   They ain't guests, Mr. Trewe. They's casualties.

HARRY   How do you mean?

JACKSON   This hotel like a hospital. The toilet catch asthma, the air-condition got ague, the front-balcony rail missing four teet', and every minute the fridge like it dancing the Shango . . . brrgudup . . . jukjuk . . . brrugudup. Is no wonder that the carpenter collapse. Termites jumping like steel band in the foundations.

HARRY   For fifty dollars a day they want Acapulco?

JACKSON   Try giving them the basics: Food. Water. Shelter. They ain't shipwrecked, they pay in advance for their vacation.

HARRY   Very funny. But the ad says, 'Tours' and 'Nightly Entertainment.' Well, Christ, after they've seen the molting parrot in the lobby and the faded sea fans, they'll be pretty livid if there's no 'nightly entertainment', and so would you, right? So, Mr. Jackson, it's your neck and mine. We open next Friday.

JACKSON   Breakfast, sir. Or else is overtime.

HARRY   I kept thinking about this panto I co-authored, man. *Robinson Crusoe*, and I picked up this old script. I can bring it all down to your level, with just two characters. Crusoe, Man Friday, maybe even the parrot, if that horny old bugger will remember his lines . . .

JACKSON   Since we on the subject, Mr. Trewe, I am compelled to report that parrot again.

HARRY   No, not again, Jackson?

JACKSON   Yes.

HARRY   (*imitating parrot*) Heinegger, Heinegger. (*In his own voice*) Correct?

JACKSON   Wait, wait! I know your explanation: that a old German called Herr Heinegger used to own this place, and that when that maquereau of a macaw keep cracking: 'Heinegger, Heinegger', he remembering the Nazi and not heckling me, but it playing a little havoc with me nerves. This is my fifth report. I am marking them down. Language is ideas, Mr. Trewe. And I think that this pre-colonial parrot have the wrong idea.

HARRY   It's his accent, Jackson. He's a Creole parrot. What can I do?

JACKSON   Well, I am not saying not to give the bird a fair trial, but I see nothing wrong in taking him out the cage at dawn, blindfolding the bitch, giving him a last cigarette if he want it, lining him up against the garden wall, and perforating his arse by firing squad.

HARRY   The war's over, Jackson! And how can a bloody parrot be prejudiced?

JACKSON   The same damn way they corrupt a child. By their upbringing. That parrot survive from a pre-colonial epoch, Mr. Trewe, and if it want to last in Trinidad and Tobago, then it go have to adjust. (*Long pause.*)

HARRY   (*leaping up*) Do you think we could work him into the panto? Give him something to do? Crusoe had a parrot, didn't he? You're right, Jackson, let's drop him from the show.

JACKSON   Mr. Trewe, you are a truly, truly stubborn man. I am *not* putting that old goatskin hat on my head and making an ass of myself for a million dollars, and I have said so already.

HARRY   You got it wrong. I put the hat on, I'm . . . Wait, wait a minute. *Cut! Cut!* You know what would be a heavy twist, heavy with irony?

JACKSON   What, Mr. Trewe?

HARRY   We reverse it. (*Pause.*)

JACKSON   You mean you prepared to walk round naked as your mother make you, in your jockstrap, playing a white cannibal in front of your own people? You're a real actor! And you got balls, too, excuse me, Mr. Trewe, to even consider doing a thing like that! Good. Joke finish. Breakfast now, eh? Because I ha' to fix the sun deck since the carpenter ain't reach.

HARRY   All right, breakfast. Just heat it a little.

JACKSON   Right, sir. The coffee must be warm still. But I best do some brand-new scramble eggs.

HARRY   Never mind the eggs, then. Slip in some toast, butter, and jam.

JACKSON   How long you in this hotel business, sir? No butter. Marge. No sugar. Big strike. Island-wide shortage. We down to half a bag.

HARRY   Don't forget I've heard you sing calypsos, Jackson. Right back there in the kitchen.

JACKSON   Mr. Trewe, every day I keep begging you to stop trying to make a entertainer out of me. I finish with show business. I finish with Trinidad. I come to Tobago for peace and quiet. I quite satisfy. If you ain't want me to resign, best drop the topic. (*Exits.*)

(HARRY *sits at the table, staring out to sea. He is reciting softly to himself, then more audibly.*)

HARRY
'Alone, alone, all, all alone,
Alone on a wide wide sea . . .
I bit my arm, I sucked the blood,
And cried, A sail! A sail!'

(*He removes the hat, then his shirt, rolls up his trousers, removes them, puts them back on, removes them again.*)

Mastah . . . Mastah . . . Friday sorry. Friday never do it again. Master.

(JACKSON *enters with breakfast tray, groans, turns to leave. Returns.*)

JACKSON   Mr. Trewe, what it is going on on this blessed Sunday morning, if I may ask?

HARRY   I was feeling what it was like to be Friday.

JACKSON   Well, Mr. Trewe, you ain't mind putting back on your pants?

HARRY   Why can't I eat breakfast like this?

JACKSON   Because I am here. I happen to be here. I am the one serving you, Mr. Trewe.

HARRY   There's nobody here.

JACKSON   Mr. Harry, you putting on back your pants?

HARRY   You're frightened of something?

JACKSON   You putting on back your pants?

HARRY   What're you afraid of? Think I'm bent? That's such a corny interpretation of the Crusoe–Friday relationship, boy. My son's been dead three years, Jackson, and I'vn't had much interest in women since, but I haven't gone queer, either. And to be a flasher, you need an audience.

JACKSON   Mr. Trewe, I am trying to explain that I myself feel like a ass holding this tray in my hand while you standing up there naked, and that if anybody should happen to pass, my name is immediately mud. So, when you put back on your pants, I will serve your breakfast.

HARRY   Actors do this sort of thing. I'm getting into a part.

JACKSON   Don't bother getting into the part, get into the pants. Please.

HARRY Why? You've got me worried now, Jackson.

JACKSON (*exploding*) *Put on your blasted pants, man! You like a blasted child, you know!*

(*Silence.* HARRY *puts on his pants.*)

HARRY Shirt, too? (JACKSON *sucks his teeth.*) There. (HARRY *puts on his shirt.*) You people are such prudes, you know that? What's it in you, Jackson, that gets so Victorian about a man in his own hotel deciding to have breakfast in his own underwear, on a totally deserted Sunday morning?

JACKSON Manners, sir. Manners. (*He puts down the tray.*)

HARRY Sit.

JACKSON Sit? Sit where? How you mean, sit?

HARRY Sit, and I'll serve breakfast. You can teach me manners. There's more manners in serving than in being served.

JACKSON I ain't know what it is eating you this Sunday morning, you hear, Mr. Trewe, but I don't feel you have any right to mama-guy me, because I is a big man with three children, all outside. Now, being served by a white man ain't no big deal for me. It happen to me every day in New York, so it's not going to be any particularly thrilling experience. I would like to get breakfast finish with, wash up, finish my work, and go for my sea bath. Now I have worked here six months and never lost my temper, but it wouldn't take much more for me to fling this whole fucking tray out in that sea and get somebody more to your sexual taste.

HARRY (*laughs*) Aha!

JACKSON Not aha, oho!

HARRY (*drawing out a chair*) Mr. Phillips . . .

JACKSON Phillip. What?

HARRY Your reservation.

JACKSON You want me play this game, eh? (*He walks around, goes to a corner of the gazebo.*) I'll tell you something, you hear, Mr. Trewe? And listen to me good, good. Once and for all. My sense of humor can stretch so far. Then it does snap. You see that sea out there? You know where I born? I born over there. Trinidad. I was a very serious steel-band man, too. And where I come from is a very serious place. I used to get into some serious trouble. A man keep bugging my arse once. A bad

john called Boysie. Indian fellow, want to play nigger. Every day in that panyard he would come making joke with nigger boy this, and so on, and I used to just laugh and tell him stop, but he keep laughing and I keep laughing and he going on and I begging him to stop and two of us laughing, until . . . (*he turns, goes to the tray, and picks up a fork*) one day, just out of the blue, I pick up a ice pick and walk over to where he and two fellers was playing card, and I nail that ice pick through his hand to the table, and I laugh, and I walk away.

HARRY Your table, Mr. Phillip.

(*Silence.* JACKSON *shrugs, sits at the table.*)

JACKSON Okay, then. Until.

HARRY You know, if you want to exchange war experiences, lad, I could bore you with a couple of mine. Want to hear?

JACKSON My shift is seven-thirty to one. (*He folds his arms.* HARRY *offers him a cigarette.*) I don't smoke on duty.

HARRY We put on a show in the army once. Ground crew. RAF. In what used to be Palestine. A Christmas panto. Another one. And yours truly here was the dame. The dame in a panto is played by a man. Well, I got the part. Wrote the music, the book, everything, whatever original music there was. *Aladdin and His Wonderful Vamp.* Very obscene, of course. I was the Wonderful Vamp. Terrific reaction all around. Thanks to me music-hall background. Went down great. Well, there was a party afterward. Then a big sergeant in charge of maintenance started this very boring business of confusing my genius with my life. Kept pinching my arse and so on. It got kind of boring after a while. Well, he was the size of a truck, mate. And there wasn't much I could do but keep blushing and pretending to be liking it. But the Wonderful Vamp was waiting outside for him, the Wonderful Vamp and a wrench this big, and after that, laddie, it took all of maintenance to put him back again.

JACKSON That is white-man fighting. Anyway, Mr. Trewe, I feel the fun finish; I would like, with your permission, to get up now and fix up the sun deck. 'Cause when rain fall . . .

HARRY Forget the sun deck. I'd say, Jackson, that we've come closer to a mutual respect, and that things need not get that hostile. Sit, and let me explain what I had in mind.

JACKSON I take it that's an order?

HARRY You want it to be an order? Okay, it's an order.

JACKSON It didn't sound like no order.

HARRY Look, I'm a liberal, Jackson. I've done the whole routine. Aldermaston, Suez, Ban the Bomb, Burn the Bra, Pity the Poor Pakis, et cetera. I've even tried jumping up to the steel band at Notting Hill Gate, and I'd no idea I'd wind up in this ironic position of giving orders, but if the new script I've been given says: HARRY TREWE, HOTEL MANAGER, then I'm going to play Harry Trewe, Hotel Manager, to the hilt, damnit. So *sit* down! Please. Oh, goddamnit, *sit . . . down . . .* (JACKSON *sits. Nods.*) Good. Relax. Smoke. Have a cup of tepid coffee. I sat up from about three this morning, working out this whole skit in my head. (*Pause.*) Mind putting that hat on for a second, it will help my point. Come on. It'll make things clearer.

(*He gives* JACKSON *the goatskin hat.* JACKSON, *after a pause, puts it on.*)

JACKSON I'll take that cigarette.

(HARRY *hands over a cigarette.*)

HARRY They've seen that stuff, time after time. Limbo, dancing girls, fire-eating . . .

JACKSON Light.

HARRY Oh, sorry. (*He lights* JACKSON'S *cigarette.*)

JACKSON I listening.

HARRY We could turn this little place right here into a little cabaret, with some very witty acts. Build up the right audience. Get an edge on the others. So, I thought, Suppose I get this material down to two people. Me and . . . well, me and somebody else. Robinson Crusoe and Man Friday. We could work up a good satire, you know, on the master–servant – no offense – relationship. Labor–management, white–black, and so on . . . Making some trenchant points about topical things, you know. Add that show to the special dinner for the price of one ticket . . .

JACKSON You have to have music.

HARRY Pardon?

JACKSON A show like that should have music. Just a lot of talk is very boring.

HARRY Right. But I'd have to have

somebody help me, and that's where I thought . . . Want to take the hat off?

JACKSON It ain't bothering me. When you going make your point?

HARRY We had that little Carnival contest with the staff and you knocked them out improvising, remember that? You had the bloody guests in stitches . . .

JACKSON You ain't start to talk money yet, Mr. Harry.

HARRY Just improvising with the quatro. And not the usual welcome to Port of Spain, I am glad to see you again, but I'll tell you, artist to artist, I recognized a real pro, and this is the point of the hat. I want to make a point about the hotel industry, about manners, conduct, to generally improve relations all around. So, whoever it is, you or whoever, plays Crusoe, and I, or whoever it is, get to play Friday, and imagine first of all the humor and then the impact of that. What you think?

JACKSON You want my honest, professional opinion?

HARRY Fire away.

JACKSON I think is shit.

HARRY I've never been in shit in my life, my boy.

JACKSON It sound like shit to me, but I could be wrong.

HARRY You could say things in fun about this place, about the whole Caribbean, that would hurt while people laughed. You get half the gate.

JACKSON Half?

HARRY What do you want?

JACKSON I want you to come to your senses, let me fix the sun deck and get down to the beach for my sea bath. So, I put on this hat, I pick up this parasol, and I walk like a mama-poule up and down this stage and you have a black man playing Robinson Crusoe and then a half-naked, white, fish-belly man playing Friday, and you want to tell me it ain't shit?

HARRY It could be hilarious!

JACKSON Hilarious, Mr. Trewe? Supposing I wasn't a waiter, and instead of breakfast I was serving you communion, this Sunday morning on this tropical island, and I turn to you, Friday, to teach you my faith, and I tell you, kneel down and eat this man. Well, kneel, nuh! What you think you would say, eh? (*Pause.*) You, this white savage?

HARRY No, that's cannibalism.

JACKSON   Is no more cannibalism than to eat a god. Suppose I make you tell me: For three hundred years I have made you my servant. For three hundred years . . .

HARRY   It's pantomime, Jackson, just keep it light . . . Make them laugh.

JACKSON   Okay. (*Giggling*) For three hundred years I served you. Three hundred years I served you breakfast in . . . in my white jacket on a white veranda, boss, bwana, effendi, bacra, sahib . . . in that sun that never set on your empire I was your shadow, I did what you did, boss, bwana, effendi, bacra, sahib . . . that was my pantomime. Every movement you made, your shadow copied . . . (*stops giggling*) and you smiled at me as a child does smile at his shadow's helpless obedience, boss, bwana, effendi, bacra, sahib, Mr. Crusoe. Now . . .

HARRY   Now?

(JACKSON's *speech is enacted in a trance-like drone, a zombie.*)

JACKSON   But after a while the child does get frighten of the shadow he make. He say to himself, That is too much obedience, I better hads stop. But the shadow don't stop, no matter if the child stop playing that pantomime, and the shadow does follow the child everywhere; when he praying, the shadow pray too, when he turn round frighten, the shadow turn round too, when he hide under the sheet, the shadow hiding too. He cannot get rid of it, no matter what, and that is the power and black magic of the shadow, boss, bwana, effendi, bacra, sahib, until it is the shadow that start dominating the child, it is the servant that start dominating the master . . . (*laughs maniacally, like The Shadow*) and that is the victory of the shadow, boss. (*Normally*) And that is why all them Pakistani and West Indians in England, all them immigrant Fridays driving all you so crazy. And they go keep driving you crazy till you go mad. In that sun that never set, they's your shadow, you can't shake them off.

HARRY   Got really carried away that time, didn't you? It's pantomime, Jackson, keep it light. Improvise!

JACKSON   You mean we making it up as we go along?

HARRY   Right!

JACKSON   Right! I in dat! (*He assumes a stern stance and points stiffly.*) Robinson obey Thursday now. Speak Thursday language. Obey Thursday gods.

HARRY   Jesus Christ!

JACKSON   (*inventing language*) Amaka nobo sakamaka khaki pants kamaluma Jesus Christ! Jesus Christ kamalogo! (*Pause. Then with a violent gesture*) Kamalongo kaba! (*Meaning: Jesus is dead!*)

HARRY   Sure. (*Pause. Peers forward. Then speaks to an imaginary projectionist, while* JACKSON *stands, feet apart, arms folded, frowning, in the usual stance of the Noble Savage.*) Now, could you run it with the subtitles, please? (*He walks over to* JACKSON, *who remains rigid. Like a movie director*) Let's have another take, Big Chief. (*To imaginary camera*) Roll it. Sound!

(JACKSON *shoves* HARRY *aside and strides to the table. He bangs the heel of his palm on the tabletop.*)

JACKSON   Patamba! Patamba! Yes?

HARRY   You want us to strike the prop? The patamba? (*To cameraman*) Cut!

JACKSON   (*to cameraman*) Rogoongo! Rogoongo! (*Meaning: Keep it rolling*)

HARRY   Cut!

JACKSON   Rogoongo, damnit!

(*Defiantly, furiously,* JACKSON *moves around, first signaling the camera to follow him, then pointing out the objects which he rechristens, shaking or hitting them violently. Slams table.*)

Patamba!

(*Rattles beach chair.*)

Backaraka! Backaraka!

(*Holds up cup, points with other hand.*)

Banda!

(*Drops cup.*)

Banda karan!

(*Puts his arm around* HARRY; *points at him.*)

Subu!

(*Faster, pointing*)

Masz!

(*Stamping the floor*)

Zohgooooor!

(*Rests his snoring head on his closed palms.*)

Oma! Onaaaa!

(Kneels, looking skyward. Pauses, eyes closed.)

Booora! Booora!

(Meaning the world. Silence. He rises)

Cut! And dat is what it was like, before you come here with your table this and cup that.

HARRY   All right. Good audition. You get twenty dollars a day without dialogue.

JACKSON   But why?

HARRY   You never called anything by the same name twice. What's a table?

JACKSON   I forget.

HARRY   I remember: patamba!

JACKSON   Patamba?

HARRY   Right. You fake.

JACKSON   That's a breakfast table. Ogushi. That's a dressing table. Amanga ogushi. I remember now.

HARRY   I'll tell you one thing, friend. If you want me to learn your language, you'd better have a gun.

JACKSON   You best play Crusoe, chief. I surrender. All you win. *(Points wearily)* Table. Chair. Cup. Man. Jesus. I accept. I accept. All you win. Long time. *(Smiles.)*

HARRY   All right, then. Improvise, then. Sing us a song. In your new language, mate. In English. Go ahead. I challenge you.

JACKSON   You what? *(Rises, takes up parasol, handling it like a guitar, and strolls around the front row of the audience. Sings)*

I want to tell you 'bout Robinson Crusoe.
He tell Friday, when I do so, do so.
Whatever I do, you must do like me.
He make Friday a Good Friday Bohbolee;[1]
That was the first example of slavery,
'Cause I am still Friday and you ain't me.
Now Crusoe he was this Christian and all,
And Friday, his slave, was a cannibal,
But one day things bound to go in reverse,
With Crusoe the slave and Friday the boss.

HARRY   Then comes this part where Crusoe sings to the goat. Little hint of animal husbandry:

(Kneels, embraces an imaginary goat, to the melody of 'Swanee'. Sings)

Nanny, how I love you,
How I love you,
My dear old nanny . . .

JACKSON   Is a li'l obscene.

HARRY   *(music-hall style)* Me wife thought so. Know what I used to tell her? Obscene? Well, better to be obscene than not heard. How's that? Harry Trewe, I'm telling you again, the music hall's loss is calypso's gain. *(Stops.)*

(JACKSON pauses. Stares upward, muttering to himself. HARRY *turns.* JACKSON *is signaling in the air with a self-congratulatory smile.)*

HARRY   What is it? What've we stopped for?

(JACKSON hisses for silence from HARRY, *then returns to his reverie.)*

HARRY   *(miming)* Are you feeling all right, Jackson?

(JACKSON walks some distance away from HARRY. *An imaginary guitar suddenly appears in his hand.* HARRY *circles him. Lifts one eyelid, listens to his heartbeat.* JACKSON *revolves,* HARRY *revolves with him.* JACKSON's *whole body is now silently rocking in rhythm. He is laughing to himself. We hear, very loud, a calypso rhythm.)*

HARRY   Two can play this game, Jackson.

(He strides around in an imaginary straw hat, twirling a cane. We hear, very loud, music hall. It stops. HARRY *peers at* JACKSON.)

JACKSON   You see what you start? *(Sings)*
Well, a Limey name Trewe came to Tobago.
He was in show business but he had no show,
so in desperation he turn to me
and said: 'Mister Phillip is the two o' we,
one classical actor, and one Creole . . .'

HARRY   Wait! Hold it, hold it, man! Don't waste that. Try and remember it. I'll be right back.

JACKSON   Where you going?

HARRY   Tape. Repeat it, and try and keep it. That's what I meant, you see?

JACKSON   You start to exploit me already?

HARRY   That's right. Memorize it. *(Exits quickly.)*

(JACKSON removes his shirt and jacket, rolls up his pants above the knee, clears the breakfast tray to one side of the floor, overturns the table, and sits in it, as if it were a boat, as HARRY *returns with the machine.)*

What's all this? I'm ready to tape. What're you up to?

(JACKSON *sits in the upturned table, rowing calmly, and from time to time surveying the horizon. He looks up toward the sky, shielding his face from the glare with one hand; then he gestures to* HARRY.)

What?

(JACKSON *flaps his arms around leisurely, like a large sea bird, indicating that* HARRY *should do the same.*)

What? What about the song? You'll forget the bloody song. It was a fluke.

JACKSON   (*Steps out from the table, crosses to* HARRY, *irritated.*) If I suppose to help you with this stupidness, we will have to cool it and collaborate a little bit. Now, I was in that boat, rowing, and I was looking up to the sky to see a storm gathering, and I wanted a big white sea bird beating inland from a storm. So what's the trouble, Mr. Trewe?

HARRY   Sea bird? What sea bird? I'm not going to play a fekking sea bird.

JACKSON   Mr. Trewe, I'm only asking you to play a white sea bird because I am supposed to play a black explorer.

HARRY   Well, I don't want to do it. Anyway, that's the silliest acting I've seen in a long time. And Robinson Crusoe wasn't *rowing* when he got shipwrecked; he was on a huge boat. I didn't come here to play a sea bird, I came to tape the song.

JACKSON   Well, then, is either the sea bird or the song. And I don't see any reason why you have to call my acting silly. We suppose to improvise.

HARRY   All right, Jackson, all right. After I do this part, I hope you can remember the song. Now you just tell me, before we keep stopping, what I am supposed to do, how many animals I'm supposed to play, and . . . you know, and so on, and so on, and then when we get all that part fixed up, we'll tape the song, all right?

JACKSON   That suits me. Now, the way I see it here: whether Robinson Crusoe was on a big boat or not, the idea is that he got . . . (*pause*) shipwrecked. So I . . . if I am supposed to play Robinson Crusoe my way, then I will choose the way in which I will get shipwrecked. Now, as Robinson Crusoe is rowing, he looks up and he sees this huge white sea bird, which is making loud sea-bird noises, because a storm is coming. And Robinson Crusoe looks up toward the sky and sees that there is this storm. Then, there is a large wave, and Robinson Crusoe finds himself on the beach.

HARRY   Am I supposed to play the beach? Because that's white . . .

JACKSON   Hilarious! Mr. Trewe. Now look, you know, I am doing you a favor. On this beach, right? Then he sees a lot of goats. And, because he is naked and he needs clothes, he kills a goat, he takes off the skin, and he makes this parasol here and this hat, so he doesn't go around naked for everybody to see. Now I *know* that there is nobody there, but there is an audience, so the sooner Robinson Crusoe puts on his clothes, then the better and happier we will all be. I am going to go back in the boat. I am going to look up toward the sky. You will, *please*, make the sea-bird noises. I will do the wave, I will crash onto the sand, you will come down like a goat, I will kill you, take off your skin, make a parasol *and* a hat, and after that, then I promise you that I will remember the song. And I will sing it to the best of my ability. (*Pause.*) However shitty that is.

HARRY   I said 'silly'. Now listen . . .

JACKSON   Yes, Mr. Trewe?

HARRY   Okay, if you're a black explorer . . . Wait a minute . . . wait a minute. If you're really a white explorer but you're black, shouldn't I play a black sea bird because I'm white?

JACKSON   Are you . . . going to extend . . . the limits of prejudice to include . . . the flora and fauna of this island? I am entering the boat.

(*He is stepping into the upturned table or boat, as* HARRY *half-heartedly imitates a bird, waving his arms.*)

HARRY   Kekkkk, kekkkk, kekkk, kekkkk! (*Stops.*) What's wrong?

JACKSON   What's wrong? Mr. Trewe, that is not a sea gull . . . that is some kind of . . . well, I don't know what it is . . . some kind of *jumbie* bird or something. (*Pause.*) I am returning to the boat. (*He carefully enters the boat, expecting an interrupting bird cry from* HARRY, *but there is none, so he begins to row.*)

HARRY   Kekk! Kekkk. (*He hangs his arms down. Pause.*) Er, Jackson, wait a minute. Hold it a second. Come here a minute.

(JACKSON *patiently gets out of the boat, elaborately pantomiming lowering his body*

139

into shallow water, releasing his hold on the boat, swimming a little distance toward shore, getting up from the shallows, shaking out his hair and hands, wiping his hands on his trousers, jumping up and down on one foot to unplug water from his clogged ear, seeing HARRY, *then walking wearily, like a man who has swum a tremendous distance, and collapsing at* HARRY'S *feet.*)

HARRY   Er, Jackson. This is too humiliating. Now, let's just forget it and please don't continue, or you're fired.

(JACKSON *leisurely wipes his face with his hands.*)

JACKSON   It don't go so, Mr. Trewe. You know me to be a meticulous man. I didn't want to do this job. I didn't even want to work here. You convinced me to work here. I have worked as meticulously as I can, until I have been promoted. This morning I had no intention of doing what I am doing now; you have always admired the fact that whatever I begin, I finish. Now, I will accept my resignation, if you want me to, *after* we have finished this thing. But I am not leaving in the middle of a job, that has never been my policy. So you can sit down, as usual, and watch me work, but until I have finished this whole business of Robinson Crusoe being in the boat *(he rises and repeats the pantomime)* looking at an imaginary sea bird, being-shipwrecked, killing a goat, making this hat *and* this parasol, walking up the beach and finding a naked footprint, which should take me into about another ten or twelve minutes, at the most, I will pack my things and I will leave, and you can play *Robinson Crusoe* all by yourself. My plans were, after this, to take the table like this . . . (*He goes to the table, puts it upright.*) Let me show you: take the table, turn it all around, go under the table . . . (*he goes under the table*) and this would now have become Robinson Crusoe's hut. (*Emerges from under the table and, without looking at* HARRY, *continues to talk.*) Now, you just tell me if you think I am overdoing it, or if you think it's more or less what we agreed on? (*Pause.*) Okay? But I am not resigning. (*Turns to* HARRY *slowly.*) You see, it's your people who introduced us to this culture: Shakespeare, *Robinson Crusoe*, the classics, and so on, and when we start

getting as good as them, you can't leave halfway. So, I will continue? Please?

HARRY   No, Jackson. You will *not* continue. You will straighten this table, put back the tablecloth, take away the breakfast things, give me back the hat, put your jacket back on, and we will continue as normal and forget the whole matter. Now, I'm very serious, I've had enough of this farce. I would like to stop.

JACKSON   May I say what I think, Mr. Trewe? I think it's a matter of prejudice. I think that you cannot believe: one: that I can act, and two: that any black man should play Robinson Crusoe. A little while aback, I came out here quite calmly and normally with the breakfast things and find you almost stark naked, kneeling down, and you told me you were getting into your part. Here am I getting into *my* part and you object. This is the story . . . this is history. This moment that we are now acting here is the history of imperialism; it's nothing less than that. And I don't think that I can – should – concede my getting into a part halfway and abandoning things, just because you, as my superior, give me orders. People become independent. Now, I could go down to that beach by myself with this hat, and I could play Robinson Crusoe, I could play Columbus, I could play sir Francis Drake, I could play anybody discovering anywhere, but I don't want you to tell me when and where to draw the line! (*Pause.*) Or what to discover and when to discover it. All right?

HARRY   Look, I'm sorry to interrupt you again, Jackson, but as I – you know – was watching you, I realized it's much more profound than that; that it could get offensive. We're trying to do something light, just a little pantomime, a little satire, a little picong. But if you take this thing seriously, we might commit Art, which is a kind of crime in this society . . . I mean, there'd be a lot of things there that people . . . well, it would make them think too much, and well, we don't want that . . . we just want a little . . . entertainment.

JACKSON   How do you mean, Mr. Trewe?

HARRY   Well, I mean if you . . . well, I mean. If you did the whole thing in reverse . . . I mean, okay, well, all right . . . you've got this black man . . . no, no . . . all right. You've got this man who is black, Robinson Crusoe, and he discovers this island on which there is this white cannibal, all right?

JACKSON Yes. That is, after he has killed the goat . . .

HARRY Yes, I know, I know. After he has killed the goat and made a . . . the hat, the parasol, and all of that . . . and, anyway, he comes across this man called Friday.

JACKSON How do you know I mightn't choose to call him Thursday? Do I have to copy every . . . I mean, are we improvising?

HARRY All right, so it's Thursday. He comes across this naked white cannibal called Thursday, you know. And then look at what would happen. He would have to start to . . . well, he'd have to, sorry . . . This cannibal, who is a Christian, would have to start unlearning his Christianity. He would have to be taught . . . I mean . . . he'd have to be taught by this – African . . . that everything was wrong, that what he was doing . . . I mean, for nearly two thousand years . . . was wrong. That his civilization, his culture, his whatever, was . . . *horrible.* Was all . . . wrong. Barbarous, I mean, you know. And Crusoe would then have to teach him things like, you know, about . . . Africa, his gods, patamba, and so on . . . and it would get very, very complicated, and I suppose ultimately it would be very boring, and what we'd have on our hands would be . . . would be a play and not a little pantomime . . .

JACKSON I'm too ambitious?

HARRY No, no, the whole thing would have to be reversed; white would become black, you know. . .

JACKSON (*smiling*) You see, Mr. Trewe, I don't see anything wrong with that, up to now.

HARRY Well, I do. It's not the sort of thing I want, and I think you'd better clean up, and I'm going inside, and when I come back I'd like this whole place just as it was. I mean, just before everything started.

JACKSON You mean you'd like it returned to its primal state? Natural? Before Crusoe finds Thursday? But, you see, that is not history. That is not the world.

HARRY No, no, I don't give an Eskimo's fart about the world, Jackson. I just want this little place here *cleaned up,* and I'd like you to get back to fixing the sun deck. Let's forget the whole matter. Righto. Excuse me.

(*He is leaving.* JACKSON'*s tone will stop him.*)

JACKSON Very well. So I take it you don't want to hear the song, neither?

HARRY No, no, I'm afraid not. I think really it was a silly idea, it's all my fault, and I'd like things to return to where they were.

JACKSON The story of the British Empire, Mr. Trewe. However, it is too late. The history of the British Empire.

HARRY Now, how do you get that?

JACKSON Well, you come to a place, you find that place as God make it; like Robinson Crusoe, you civilize the natives; they try to do something, you turn around and you say to them: 'You are not good enough, let's call the whole thing off, return things to normal, you go back to your position as slave or servant, I will keep mine as master, and we'll forget the whole thing ever happened'. Correct? You would like me to accept this.

HARRY You're really making this very difficult, Jackson. Are you hurt? Have I offended you?

JACKSON Hurt? No, no, no. I didn't expect any less. I am not hurt. (*Pause.*) I am just . . . (*Pause.*)

HARRY You're just what?

JACKSON I am just ashamed . . . of making such a fool of myself. (*Pause.*) I expected . . . a little respect. That is all.

HARRY I respect you . . . I just, I . . .

JACKSON No. It's perfectly all right.

(HARRY *goes to the table, straightens it.*)

I . . . no . . . I'll fix the table myself. (*He doesn't move.*) I am all right, thank you. Sir.

(HARRY *stops fixing the table.*)

JACKSON (*with the hint of a British accent*) Thank you very much.

HARRY (*sighs*) I . . . am sorry . . . er . . .

(JACKSON *moves toward the table.*)

JACKSON It's perfectly all right, sir. It's perfectly all . . . right. (*Almost inaudibly*) Thank you.

(HARRY *begins to straighten the table again.*)

No, thank you very much, don't touch anything.

(JACKSON *is up against the table.* HARRY *continues to straighten the table.*)

141

Don't touch anything . . . Mr. Trewe.
Please.

(JACKSON *rests one arm on the table, fist closed. They watch each other for three beats.*)

Now that . . . is MY order. . .

(*They watch each other for several beats as the lights fade.*)

Act II

Noon. White glare. HARRY, *with shirt unbuttoned, in a deck chair reading a paperback thriller. Sound of intermittent hammering front stage left, where* JACKSON *is repairing the sun-deck slats.* HARRY *rises, decides he should talk to* JACKSON *about the noise, decides against it, and leans back in the deck chair, eyes closed. Hammering has stopped for a long while.* HARRY *opens his eyes, senses* JACKSON'*s presence, turns suddenly, to see him standing quite close, shirtless, holding a hammer.* HARRY *bolts from his chair.*

JACKSON   You know something, sir? While I was up there nailing the sun deck, I just stay so and start giggling all by myself.
HARRY   Oh, yes? Why?
JACKSON   No, I was remembering a feller, you know . . . ahhh, he went for audition once for a play, you know, and the way he, you know, the way he prop . . . present himself to the people, said . . . ahmm, 'You know, I am an actor, you know. I do all kind of acting, classical acting, *Creole* acting'. That's when I laugh, you know? (*Pause.*) I going back and fix the deck, then. (*Moves off. Stops, turns.*) The . . . the hammering not disturbing you?
HARRY   No, no, it's fine. You have to do it, right? I mean, you volunteered, the carpenter didn't come, right?
JACKSON   Yes. Creole acting. I wonder what kind o' acting dat is. (*Spins the hammer in the air and does or does not catch it.*) Yul Brynner. *Magnificent Seven.* Picture, papa! A kind of Western Creole acting. It ain't have no English cowboys, eh, Mr. Harry? Something wrong, boy, something wrong.

(*He exits.* HARRY *lies back in the deck chair, the book on his chest, arms locked behind his head. Silence. Hammering violently resumes.*)

JACKSON   (*off*)

Kekkk, kekkkekk, kekk!
Kekkekk, kekkkekk, ekkek!

(HARRY *rises, moves from the deck chair toward the sun deck.*)

HARRY   *Jackson!* What the hell are you doing? What's that noise?
JACKSON   (*off, loud*) I doing like a black sea gull, suh!
HARRY   Well, it's very distracting.
JACKSON   (*off*) Sorry, sir.

(HARRY *returns. Sits down on the deck chair. Waits for the hammering. Hammering resumes. Then stops. Silence. Then we hear, singing loudly*)

I want to tell you 'bout Robinson Crusoe.
He tell Friday, when I do so, do so.
Whatever I do, you must do like me,
He make Friday a Good Friday Bohbolee

(*Spoken*)

And the chorus:

(*Sings*)

Laide-die
Laidie, lay-day, de-day-de-die,
Laidee-doo-day-dee-day-dee-die
Laidee-day-doh-dee-day-dee-die

Now that was the first example of slavery,
'Cause I am still Friday and you ain't me,
Now Crusoe he was this Christian and all,
Friday, his slave, was a cannibal,
But one day things bound to go in reverse,
With Crusoe the slave and Friday the boss . . .
Caiso, boy! Caiso!

(HARRY *rises, goes toward the sun deck.*)

HARRY   Jackson, man! Jesus! (*He returns to the deck chair, is about to sit.*)
JACKSON   (*off*) Two more lash and the sun deck finish, sir! (HARRY *waits.*) Stand by . . . here they come . . . First lash: (*sound*) Pow! Second lash: (*two sounds*) Pataow! Job complete! Lunch, Mr. Trewe? You want your lunch now? Couple sandwich or what?
HARRY   (*shouts without turning*) Just bring a couple beers from the icebox, Jackson. And the Scotch. (*To himself*) What the hell, let's all get drunk. (*To* JACKSON) Bring some beer for yourself, too, Jackson!
JACKSON   (*off*) Thank you, Mr. Robinson . . .

Thank you, Mr. Trewe, sir! Cru-soe, *Trewe-so! (Faster)* Crusoe-Trusoe, Robinson Trewe-so!

HARRY Jesus, Jackson; cut that out and just bring the bloody beer!

JACKSON *(off)* Right! A beer for you and a beer for me! Now, what else is it going to be? A sandwich for you, but none for me.

(HARRY picks up the paperback and opens it, removing a folded sheet of paper. He opens it and is reading it carefully, sometimes lifting his head, closing his eyes, as if remembering its contents, then reading again. He puts it into a pocket quickly as JACKSON returns, carrying a tray with two beers, a bottle of Scotch, a pitcher of water, and two glasses. JACKSON sets them down on the table.)

I'm here, sir. At your command.

HARRY Sit down. Forget the sandwiches, I don't want to eat. Let's sit down, man to man, and have a drink. That was the most sarcastic hammering I've ever heard, and I know you were trying to get back at me with all those noises and that Uncle Tom crap. So let's have a drink, man to man, and try and work out what happened this morning, all right?

JACKSON I've forgotten about this morning, sir.

HARRY No, no, no, I mean, the rest of the day it's going to bother me, you know?

JACKSON Well, I'm leaving at half-past one.

HARRY No, but still . . . Let's . . . Okay. Scotch?

JACKSON I'll stick to beer, sir, thank you.

(HARRY pours a Scotch and water, JACKSON serves himself a beer. Both are still standing.)

HARRY Sit over there, please, Mr. Phillip. On the deck chair. *(JACKSON sits on the deck chair, facing HARRY.)* Cheers?

JACKSON Cheers. Cheers. Deck chair and all. *(They toast and drink.)*

HARRY All right. Look, I think you misunderstood me this morning.

JACKSON Why don't we forget the whole thing, sir? Let me finish this beer and go for my sea bath, and you can spend the rest of the day all by yourself. *(Pause.)* Well. What's wrong? What happen, sir? I said something wrong just now?

HARRY This place isn't going to drive me crazy, Jackson. Not if I have to go mad preventing it. Not physically crazy; but you just start to think crazy thoughts, you know? At the beginning it's fine; there's the sea, the palm trees, monarch of all I survey and so on, all that postcard stuff. And then it just becomes another back yard. God, is there anything deadlier than Sunday afternoons in the tropics when you can't sleep? The horror and stillness of the heat, the shining, godforsaken sea, the bored and boring clouds? Especially in an empty boarding house. You sit by the stagnant pool counting the dead leaves drifting to the edge. I daresay the terror of emptiness made me want to act. I wasn't trying to humiliate you. I meant nothing by it. Now, I don't usually apologize to people. I don't do things to apologize for. When I do them, I mean them, but, in your case, I'd like to apologize.

JACKSON Well, if you find here boring, go back home. Do something else, nuh?

HARRY It's not that simple. It's a little more complicated than that. I mean, everything I own is sunk here, you see? There's a little matter of a brilliant actress who drank too much, and a car crash at Brighton after a panto . . . Well. That's neither here nor there now. Right? But I'm determined to make this place work. I gave up the theater for it.

JACKSON Why?

HARRY Why? I wanted to be the best. Well, among other things; oh, well, that's neither here nor there. Flopped at too many things, though. Including classical and Creole acting. I just want to make this place work, you know. And a desperate man'll try anything. Even at the cost of his sanity, maybe. I mean, I'd hate to believe that under everything else I was also prejudiced, as well. I wouldn't have any right here, right?

JACKSON 'Tain't prejudice that bothering you, Mr. Trewe; you ain't no parrot to repeat opinion. No, is loneliness that sucking your soul as dry as the sun suck a crab shell. On a Sunday like this, I does watch you. The whole staff does study you. Walking round restless, staring at the sea. You remembering your wife and your son, not right? You ain't get over that yet?

HARRY Jackson . . .

JACKSON Is none of my business. But it really lonely here out of season. Is summer, and your own people gone, but come winter they go flock like sandpipers

143

all down that beach. So you lonely, but I could make you forget all o' that. I could make H. Trewe, Esquire, a brand-new man. You come like a challenge.

HARRY   Think I keep to myself too much?

JACKSON   If! You would get your hair cut by phone. You drive so careful you make your car nervous. If you was in charge of the British Empire, you wouldn'ta lose it, you'da misplace it.

HARRY   I see, Jackson.

JACKSON   But all that could change if you do what I tell you.

HARRY   I don't want a new life, thanks.

JACKSON   Same life. Different man. But that stiff upper lip goin' have to quiver a little.

HARRY   What's all this? Obeah? 'That old black magic'?

JACKSON   Nothing. I could have the next beer?

HARRY   Go ahead. I'm drinking Scotch.

(JACKSON *takes the other beer, swallows deep, smacks his lips, grins at* HARRY.)

JACKSON   Nothing. We will have to continue from where we stop this morning. You will have to be Thursday.

HARRY   Aha, you bastard! It's a thrill giving orders, hey? But I'm not going through all that rubbish again.

JACKSON   All right. Stay as you want. But if you say yes, it go have to be man to man, and none of this boss-and-Jackson business, you see, Trewe . . . I mean, I just call you plain Trewe, for example, and I notice that give you a slight shock. Just a little twitch of the lip, but a shock all the same, eh, Trewe? You see? You twitch again. It would be just me and you, all right? You see, two of we both acting a role here we ain't really really believe in, you know. I ent think you strong enough to give people orders, and I *know* I ain't the kind who like taking *them*. So both of we doesn't have to *improvise* so much as *exaggerate*. We faking, faking all the time. But, man to man, I mean . . . (*pause*) that could be something else. Right, Mr. Trewe?

HARRY   Aren't we man to man now?

JACKSON   No, no. We having one of them 'playing man-to-man' talks, where a feller does look a next feller in the eye and say, 'Le' we settle this thing, man to man', and this time the feller who smiling and saying it, his whole honest intention is to take that feller by the crotch and rip out he stones, and dig out he eye and leave him for corbeaux to pick. (*Silence.*)

HARRY   You know, that thing this morning had an effect on me, man to man now. I didn't think so much about the comedy of *Robinson Crusoe*, I thought what we were getting into was a little sad. So, when I went back to the room, I tried to rest before lunch, before you began all that vindictive hammering . . .

JACKSON   Vindictive?

HARRY   Man to man: that vindictive hammering and singing, and I thought, Well, maybe we could do it straight. Make a real straight thing out of it.

JACKSON   You mean like a tradegy. With one joke?

HARRY   Or a codemy, with none. You mispronounce words on purpose, don't you, Jackson? (JACKSON *smiles.*) Don't think for one second that I'm not up on your game, Jackson. You're playing the stage nigger with me. I'm an actor, you know. It's a smile in front and a dagger behind your back, right? Or the smile itself is the bloody dagger. I'm aware, chum. I'm aware.

JACKSON   The smile kinda rusty, sir, but it goes with the job. Just like the water in this hotel: (*demonstrates*) I turn it on at seven and lock it off at one.

HARRY   Didn't hire you for the smile; I hired you for your voice. We've the same background. Old-time calypso, old-fashioned music hall:

(*Sings.*)

Oh, me wife can't cook and she looks like a horse
And the way she makes coffee is grounds for divorce . . .

(*Does a few steps.*)

But when love is at stake she's my Worcester sauce . . .

(*Stops.*)

Used to wow them with that. All me own work. Ah, the lost glories of the old music hall, the old provincials, grimy brocade, the old stars faded one by one. The brassy pantomimes! Come from an old music-hall family, you know, Jackson. Me mum had this place she ran for broken-down actors. Had tea with the greats as a tot. (*Sings*

softly, hums) Oh, me wife can't cook . . .
(*Silence.*) You married, Jackson?

JACKSON   I not too sure, sir.

HARRY   You're not sure?

JACKSON   That's what I said.

HARRY   I know what you mean. I wasn't
sure I was when I was. My wife's
remarried.

JACKSON   You showed me her photo. And
the little boy own.

HARRY   But I'm not. Married. So there's
absolutely no hearth for Crusoe to go home
to. While you were up there, I rehearsed
this thing. (*Presents a folded piece of paper.*)
Want to read it?

JACKSON   What . . . er . . . what is it . . . a
poetry?

HARRY   No, no, not a poetry. A thing I wrote.
Just a speech in the play . . . that if . . .

JACKSON   Oho, we back in the play again?

HARRY   Almost. You want to read it? (*He
offers the paper.*)

JACKSON   All right.

HARRY   I thought – no offense, now. Man to
man. If you were doing Robinson Crusoe,
this is what you'd read.

JACKSON   You want me to read this, right?

HARRY   Yeah.

JACKSON   (*reads slowly*) 'O silent sea,
O wondrous sunset that I've gazed on ten
thousand times, who will rescue me from
this complete desolation? . . . ' (*Breaking*)
All o' this?

HARRY   If you don't mind. Don't act it. Just
read it. (JACKSON *looks at him.*) No offense.

JACKSON   (*reads*) 'Yes, this is paradise, I
know. For I see around me the splendors of
nature . . . '

HARRY   Don't act it . . .

JACKSON   (*pauses; then continues*) 'How I'd
like to fuflee this desolate rock'. (*Pauses.*)
Fuflee? Pardon, but what is a fuflee,
Mr. Trewe?

HARRY   A fuflee? I've got 'fuflee' written
there?

JACKSON   (*Extends paper, points at word.*)
So, how you does fuflee, Mr. Harry? Is
Anglo-Saxon English?

(HARRY *kneels down and peers at the word.
He rises.*)

HARRY   It's F . . . then F-L-E-E – flee to
express his hesitation. It's my own note as
an actor. He quivers, he hesitates . . .

JACKSON   He quivers, he hesitates, but he
still can't fuflee?

HARRY   Just leave that line out, Jackson.

JACKSON   I like it.

HARRY   *Leave it out!*

JACKSON   No fuflee?

HARRY   I said no.

JACKSON   Just because I read it wrong. I
know the word 'flee', you know. Like to
take off. Flee. Faster than run. Is the extra
F you put in there so close to flee that had
me saying fuflee like a damn ass, but le' we
leave it in, nuh? One fuflee ain't go kill
anybody. Much less bite them. (*Silence.*)
Get it?

HARRY   Don't take this personally . . .

JACKSON   No fuflees on old Crusoe, boy . . .

HARRY   But, if you're going to do
professional theater, Jackson, don't take
this personally, more discipline is required.
All right?

JACKSON   You write it. Why you don't read
it?

HARRY   I wanted to hear it. Okay, give it
back . . .

JACKSON   (*loudly, defiantly*) 'The ferns, the
palms like silent sentinels, the wide and
silent lagoons that briefly hold my passing,
solitary reflection. The volcano . . . '
(*Stops.*) 'The volcano'. What?

HARRY   . . . 'wreathed' . . .

JACKSON   Oho, oho . . . like a wreath? 'The
volcano *wreathed* in mist. But what is
paradise without a woman? Adam in
paradise!'

HARRY   Go ahead.

JACKSON   (*restrained*) 'Adam in paradise
had his woman to share his loneliness, but
I miss the voice of even one consoling
creature, the touch of a hand, the look of
kind eyes. Where is the wife from whom
I vowed never to be sundered? How old is
my little son? If he could see his father like
this, mad with memories of them . . . Even
Job had his family. But I am alone, alone, I
am all alone'. (*Pause.*) Oho. You write this?

HARRY   Yeah.

JACKSON   Is good. Very good.

HARRY   Thank you.

JACKSON   Touching. Very sad. But
something missing.

HARRY   What?

JACKSON   Goats. You leave out the goats.

HARRY   The goats. So what? What've you got
with goats, anyway?

JACKSON   Very funny. Very funny, sir.

HARRY   Try calling me Trewe.

JACKSON   Not yet. That will come. Stick to

145

the point. You ask for my opinion and I *gave* you my opinion. No doubt I don't have the brains. But my point is that this man ain't facing reality. There are *goats* all around him.

HARRY You're full of shit.

JACKSON The man is not facing reality. He is not a practical man *ship-wrecked*.

HARRY I suppose that's the difference between classical and Creole acting? (*He pours a drink and downs it furiously.*)

JACKSON If he is not practical, he is not Robinson Crusoe. And yes, is Creole acting, yes. Because years afterward his little son could look at the parasol and the hat and look at a picture of Daddy and boast: 'My daddy smart, boy. He get shipwreck and first thing he do is he build a hut, then he kill a goat or two and make clothes, a parasol and a hat'. That way Crusoe *achieve* something, and his son could boast . . .

HARRY Only his son is dead.

JACKSON Whose son dead?

HARRY Crusoe's.

JACKSON No, pardner. *Your* son dead. Crusoe wife and child waiting for him, and he is a practical man and he know somebody go come and save him . . .

HARRY (*almost inaudibly*)
'I bit my arm, I sucked the blood,
And cried, "A sail! A sail"!'
How the hell does he know 'somebody go come and save him'? That's shit. That's not in his character at that moment. How the hell can he know? You're a cruel bastard . . .

JACKSON (*enraged*) *Because, you fucking ass, he has faith!*

HARRY (*laughing*) Faith? What faith?

JACKSON He not sitting on his shipwrecked arse bawling out . . . what it is you have here? (*Reads*) 'O . . . ' Where is it? (*Reads*) 'O silent sea, O wondrous sunset', and all that shit. No. He shipwrecked. He desperate, he hungry. He look up and he see this fucking goat with its fucking beard watching him and smiling, this goat with its forked fucking beard and square yellow eye just like the fucking devil, standing up there . . . (*pantomimes the goat and Crusoe in turn*) smiling at him, and putting out its tongue and letting go one fucking *bleeeeh!* And Robbie ent thinking 'bout his wife and son and O silent sea and O wondrous sunset; no, Robbie is the First True Creole, so he watching the goat with his eyes narrow, narrow, and he say: '*Blehhh*, eh? You mutherfucker, I go show you *blehhh* in your goat-ass', and vam, vam, next thing is Robbie and the goat, *mano a mano*, man to man, man to goat, goat to man, wrestling on the sand, and next thing we know we hearing one last faint, feeble *bleeeeeeehhhhhhhhhh*, and Robbie is next seen walking up the beach with a goatskin hat and a goatskin umbrella, feeling like a million dollars because *he have faith*!

HARRY (*applauds*) Bravo! You're the Christian. I am the cannibal. Bravo!

JACKSON If I does hammer sarcastic, you does clap sarcastic. Now I want to pee.

HARRY I think I'll join you.

JACKSON So because I go and pee, you must pee, too?

HARRY Subliminal suggestion.

JACKSON Monkey see, monkey do.

HARRY You're the bloody ape, mate. You people just came down from the trees.

JACKSON Say that again, please.

HARRY I'm going to keep that line.

JACKSON Oho! Rehearse you rehearsing? I thought you was serious.

HARRY You go have your pee. I'll run over my monologue.

JACKSON No, you best do it now, sir. Or it going to be on my mind while we rehearsing that what you really want to do is take a break and pee. We best go together, then.

HARRY We'll call it the pee break. Off we go, then. How long will you be, then? You people take forever.

JACKSON Maybe you should hold up a sign, sir, or give some sort of signal when you serious or when you joking, so I can know not to react. I would say five minutes.

HARRY Five minutes? What is this, my friend, Niagara Falls?

JACKSON It will take me . . . look, you want me to time it? I treat it like a ritual, I don't just pee for peeing's sake. It will take me about forty to fifty seconds to walk to the servants' toilets . . .

HARRY Wait a second . . .

JACKSON No, you wait, please, sir. That's almost one minute, take another fifty seconds to walk back, or even more, because after a good pee a man does be in a mood, both ruminative and grateful that the earth has received his libation, so that makes . . .

HARRY Hold on, please.

JACKSON (*voice rising*) Jesus, sir, give me a break, nuh? That is almost two minutes, and in between those two minutes it have such solemn and ruminative behavior as opening the fly, looking upward or downward, the ease and relief, the tender shaking, the solemn tucking in, like you putting a little baby back to sleep, the reverse zipping or buttoning, depending on the pants, then, with the self-congratulating washing of the hands, looking at yourself for at least half a minute in the mirror, then the drying of hands as if you were a master surgeon just finish a major operation, and the walk back . . .

HARRY You said that. Any way you look at it, it's under five minutes, and I interrupted you because . . .

JACKSON I could go and you could time me, to see if I on a go-slow, or wasting up my employer's precious time, but I know it will take at least five, unless, like most white people, you either don't flush it, a part I forgot, or just wipe your hands fast fast or not at all . . .

HARRY Which white people, Jackson?

JACKSON I was bathroom attendant at the Hilton, and I know men and races from their urinary habits, and most Englishmen . . .

HARRY Most Englishmen . . . Look, I was trying to tell you, instead of going all the way round to the servants' lavatories, pop into my place, have a quick one, and that'll be under five bloody minutes in any circumstances and regardless of the capacity. Go on. I'm all right.

JACKSON Use your bathroom, Mr. Harry?

HARRY Go on, will you?

JACKSON I want to get this. You giving me permission to go through your living room, with all your valuables lying about, with the picture of your wife watching me in case I should leave the bathroom open, and you are granting me the privilege of taking out my thing, doing my thing right there among all those lotions and expensive soaps, and . . . after I finish, wiping my hands on a clean towel?

HARRY Since you make it so vividly horrible, why don't you just walk around to the servants' quarters and take as much time as you like? Five minutes won't kill me.

JACKSON I mean, equality is equality and art is art, Mr. Harry, but to use those clean, rough Cannon towels . . . You mustn't rush things, people have to slide into independence. They give these islands independence so fast that people still ain't recover from the shock, so they pissing and wiping their hands indiscriminately. You don't want that to happen in this guest house, Mr. Harry. Let me take my little five minutes, as usual, and if you have to go, you go to your place, and I'll go to mine, and let's keep things that way until I can feel I can use your towels without a profound sense of gratitude, and you could, if you wanted, a little later maybe, walk round the guest house in the dark, put your foot in the squelch of those who missed the pit by the outhouse, that charming old-fashioned outhouse so many tourists take Polaroids of, without feeling degraded, and we can then respect each other as artists. So, I appreciate the offer, but I'll be back in five. Kindly excuse me. (*He exits.*)

HARRY You've got logorrhea, Jackson. You've been running your mouth like a parrot's arse. But don't get sarcastic with me, boy!

(JACKSON *returns.*)

JACKSON You don't understand, Mr. Harry. My problem is, I really mean what I say.

HARRY You've been pretending indifference to this game, Jackson, but you've manipulated it your way, haven't you? Now you can spew out all that bitterness in fun, can't you? Well, we'd better get things straight around here, friend. You're still on duty. And if you stay out there too long, your job is at stake. It's . . . (*consulting his watch*) five minutes to one now. You've got exactly three minutes to get in there and back, and two minutes left to finish straightening this place. It's a bloody mess. (*Silence.*)

JACKSON Bloody mess, eh?

HARRY That's correct.

JACKSON (*in exaggerated British accent*) I go try and make it back in five, bwana. If I don't, the mess could be bloodier. I saw a sign once in a lavatory in Mobile, Alabama. COLORED. But it didn't have no time limit. Funny, eh?

HARRY Ape! Mimic! Three bloody minutes!

(JACKSON *exits, shaking his head.* HARRY *recovers the sheet of paper from the floor and puts it back in his pants pocket. He pours a large drink, swallows it all in two large gulps, then puts the glass down. He looks around the gazebo, wipes his hands briskly. He removes the drinks tray with Scotch, the two beer bottles, glasses, water pitcher, and sets them in a corner of the gazebo. He lifts up the deck chair and sets it, sideways, in another corner. He turns the table carefully over on its side; then, when it is on its back, he looks at it. He changes his mind and carefully tilts the table back upright. He removes his shirt and folds it and places it in another corner of the gazebo. He rolls up his trouser cuffs almost to the knee. He is now half-naked. He goes over to the drinks tray and pours the bowl of melted ice, now tepid water, over his head. He ruffles his hair, his face dripping; then he sees an ice pick. He picks it up.*)

JACKSON'S VOICE   'One day, just out of the blue, I pick up a ice pick and walk over to where he and two fellers was playing cards, and I nail that ice pick through his hand to the table, and I laugh . . . '

(HARRY *drives the ice pick hard into the tabletop, steps back, looking at it. Then he moves up to it, wrenches it out, and gets under the table, the ice pick at his feet. A few beats, then* JACKSON *enters, pauses.*)

JACKSON   (*Laughs.*) What you doing under the table, Mr. Trewe? (*Silence.* JACKSON *steps nearer the table.*) Trewe? You all right? (*Silence.* JACKSON *crouches close to* HARRY.) Harry, boy, you cool? (JACKSON *rises. Moves away some distance. He takes in the space. An arena. Then he crouches again.*) Ice-pick time, then? Okay.
   'Fee fi fo fum,
   I smell the blood of an Englishman . . . '

(JACKSON *exits quickly.* HARRY *waits a while, then crawls from under the table, straightens up, and places the ice pick gently on the tabletop. He goes to the drinks tray and has a sip from the Scotch; then replaces the bottle and takes up a position behind the table.* JACKSON *returns dressed as Crusoe – goatskin hat, open umbrella, the hammer stuck in the waistband of his rolled-up trousers. He throws something across the room to* HARRY'S *feet. The dead parrot, in a carry-away box.* HARRY *opens it.*)

One parrot, to go! Or you eating it here?

HARRY   You son of a bitch.
JACKSON   Sure.

(HARRY *picks up the parrot and hurls it into the sea.*)

First bath in five years.

(JACKSON *moves toward the table, very calmly.*)

HARRY   You're a bloody savage. Why'd you strangle him?
JACKSON   (*as Friday*) Me na strangle him, bwana. Him choke from prejudice.
HARRY   Prejudice? A bloody parrot. The bloody thing can't reason. (*Pause. They stare at each other.* HARRY *crouches, tilts his head, shifts on his perch, flutters his wings like the parrot, squawks.*) Heinegger. Heinegger.

(JACKSON *stands over the table and folds the umbrella.*)

You people create nothing. You imitate everything. It's all been done before, you see, Jackson. The parrot. Think that's something? It's from *The Seagull*. It's from *Miss Julie*. You can't ever be original, boy. That's the trouble with shadows, right? They can't think for themselves. (JACKSON *shrugs, looking away from him.*) So you take it out on a parrot. Is that one of your African sacrifices, eh?
JACKSON   Run your mouth, Harry, run your mouth.
HARRY   (*squawks*) Heinegger . . . Heinegger . . .

(JACKSON *folds the parasol and moves to enter the upturned table.*)

I wouldn't go under there if I were you, Jackson.

(JACKSON *reaches into the back of his waistband and removes a hammer.*)

JACKSON   The first English cowboy. (*He turns and faces* HARRY.)
HARRY   It's my property. Don't get in there.
JACKSON   The hut. That was my idea.
HARRY   The table's mine.
JACKSON   What else is yours, Harry? (*Gestures*) This whole fucking island? Dem days gone, boy.
HARRY   The costume's mine, too. (*He crosses over, almost nudging* JACKSON, *and picks up the ice pick.*) I'd like them back.
JACKSON   Suit yourself.

(HARRY *crosses to the other side, sits on the edge of the wall or leans against a post.* JACKSON *removes the hat and throws it into the arena, then the parasol.*)

HARRY   The hammer's mine.

JACKSON   I feel I go need it.

HARRY   If you keep it, you're a bloody thief.

(JACKSON *suddenly drops to the floor on his knees, letting go of the hammer, weeping and cringing, and advancing on his knees toward* HARRY.)

JACKSON   Pardon, master, pardon! Friday bad boy! Friday wicked nigger. Sorry. Friday nah t'ief again. Mercy, master. Mercy. (*He rolls around on the floor, laughing.*) Oh, Jesus, I go dead! I go dead. Ay-ay.

(*Silence.* JACKSON *on the floor, gasping, lying on his back.* HARRY *crosses over, picks up the parasol, opens it, after a little difficulty, then puts on the goatskin hat.* JACKSON *lies on the floor, silent.*)

HARRY   I never hit any goddamned maintenance sergeant on the head in the service. I've never hit anybody in my life. Violence makes me sick. I don't believe in ownership. If I'd been more possessive, more authoritative, I don't think she'd have left me. I don't think you ever drove an ice pick through anybody's hand, either. That was just the two of us acting.

JACKSON   Creole acting? (*He is still lying on the floor.*) Don't be too sure about the ice pick.

HARRY   I'm sure. You're a fake. You're a kind man and you think you have to hide it. A lot of other people could have used that to their own advantage. That's the difference between master and servant.

JACKSON   That master-and-servant shit finish. Bring a beer for me. (*He is still on his back.*)

HARRY   There's no more beer. You want a sip of Scotch?

JACKSON   Anything.

(HARRY *goes to the Scotch, brings over the bottle, stands over* JACKSON.)

HARRY   Here. To me bloody wife! (JACKSON *sits up, begins to move off.*) What's wrong, you forget to flush it?

JACKSON   I don't think you should bad-talk her behind her back. (*He exits.*)

HARRY   Behind her back? She's in England. She's a star. Star? She's a bloody planet.

(JACKSON *returns, holding the photograph of* HARRY's *wife.*)

JACKSON   If you going bad-talk, I think she should hear what you going to say, you don't think so, darling? (*Addressing the photograph, which he puts down*) If you have to tell somebody something, tell them to their face. (*Addressing the photograph*) Now, you know all you women, eh? Let the man talk his talk and don't interrupt.

HARRY   You're fucking bonkers, you know that? Before I hired you, I should have asked for a medical report.

JACKSON   Please tell your ex-wife good afternoon or something. The dame in the pantomime is always played by a man, right?

HARRY   Bullshit.

(JACKSON *sits close to the photograph, wiggling as he ventriloquizes.*)

JACKSON   (*in an Englishwoman's voice*) Is not bullshit at all, Harold. Everything I say you always saying bullshit, bullshit. How can we conduct a civilized conversation if you don't give me a chance? What have I done, Harold, oh, Harold, for you to treat me so?

HARRY   Because you're a silly selfish bitch and you *killed our son*!

JACKSON   (*crying*) There, there, you see . . . ? (*He wipes the eyes of the photograph.*) You're calling me names, it wasn't my fault, and you're calling me names. Can't you ever forgive me for that, Harold?

HARRY   Ha! You never told him that, did you? You neglected to mention that little matter, didn't you, love?

JACKSON   (*weeping*) I love you, Harold. I love you, and I loved him, too. Forgive me, O God, please, please forgive me . . . (*As himself*) So how it happen? Murder? A accident?

HARRY   (*to the photograph*) Love me? You loved me so much you get drunk and you . . . ah, ah, what's the use? What's the bloody use? (*Wipes his eyes. Pause.*)

JACKSON   (*as wife*) I'm crying too, Harold. Let bygones be bygones . . .

(HARRY *lunges for the photograph, but* JACKSON *whips it away.*)

JACKSON   (*as himself*) You miss, Harold. (*Pause; as wife*) Harold . . . (*Silence.*) Harold . . . speak to me . . . please. (*Silence.*) What

149

do you plan to do next? (*Sniffs.*) What'll you do now?

HARRY What difference does it make? . . . All right. I'll tell you what I'm going to do next, Ellen: you're such a big star, you're such a luminary, I'm going to leave you to shine by yourself. I'm giving up this bloody rat race and I'm going to take up Mike's offer. I'm leaving 'the theatuh', which destroyed my confidence, screwed up my marriage, and made you a star. I'm going somewhere where I can get pissed every day and watch the sun set, like Robinson bloody Crusoe. That's what I'm going to bloody do. You always said it's the only part I could play.

JACKSON (*as wife*) Take me with you, then. Let's get away together. I always wanted to see the tropics, the palm trees, the lagoons . . .

(HARRY *grabs the photograph from* JACKSON; *he picks up the ice pick and puts the photograph on the table, pressing it down with one palm.*)

HARRY All right, Ellen, I'm going to . . . You can scream all you like, but I'm going to . . . (*He raises the ice pick.*)

JACKSON (*as wife*) My face is my fortune.

(*He sneaks up behind* HARRY, *whips the photograph away while* HARRY *is poised with the ice pick.*)

HARRY Your face is your fortune, eh? I'll kill her, Jackson, I'll maim that smirking bitch . . .

(*He lunges toward* JACKSON, *who leaps away, holding the photograph before his face, and runs around the gazebo, shrieking.*)

JACKSON (*as wife*) Help! Help! British police! My husband trying to kill me! Help, somebody, help!

(HARRY *chases* JACKSON *with the ice pick, but* JACKSON *nimbly avoids him.*)

JACKSON (*as wife*) Harry! Have you gone mad? (*He scrambles onto the ledge of the gazebo. He no longer holds the photograph to his face, but his voice is the wife's.*)

HARRY Get down off there, you melodramatic bitch. You're too bloody conceited to kill yourself. Get down from there, Ellen! Ellen, it's a straight drop to the sea!

JACKSON (*as wife*) Push me, then! Push me, Harry! You hate me so much, why you don't come and push me?

HARRY Push yourself, then. You never needed my help. Jump!

JACKSON (*as wife*) Will you forgive me now, or after I jump?

HARRY Forgive you? . . .

JACKSON (*as wife*) All right, then. Goodbye! (*He turns, teetering, about to jump.*)

HARRY (*shouts*) Ellen! Stop! I forgive you!

(JACKSON *turns on the ledge. Silence.* HARRY *is now sitting on the floor.*)

That's the real reason I wanted to do the panto. To do it better than you ever did. You played Crusoe in the panto, Ellen. I was Friday. Black bloody greasepaint that made you howl. You wiped the stage with me . . . Ellen . . . well. Why not? I was no bloody good.

JACKSON (*as himself*) Come back to the play, Mr. Trewe. Is Jackson. We was playing Robinson Crusoe, remember? (*Silence.*) Master, Friday here . . . (*Silence.*) You finish with the play? The panto? Crusoe must get up, he must make himself get up. He have to face a next day again. (*Shouts*) I tell you: man must live! Then, after many years, he see this naked footprint that is the mark of his salvation . . .

HARRY (*recites*)
  'The self-same moment I could pray;
  and . . . tata tee-tum-tum
  The Albatross fell off and sank
  Like lead into the sea'.
  God, my memory . . .

JACKSON That ain't Crusoe, that is 'The Rime of the Ancient Mariner'. (*He pronounces it 'Marina'.*)

HARRY Mariner.

JACKSON Marina.

HARRY Mariner.

JACKSON 'The Rime of the Ancient Marina'. So I learn it in Fourth Standard.

HARRY It's your country, mate.

JACKSON Is your language, pardner. I stand corrected. Now, you ain't see English crazy? I could sit down right next to you and tell you I *stand* corrected.

HARRY Sorry. Where were we, Mr. Phillip?

JACKSON Tobago. Where are you? It was your cue, Mr. Trewe.

HARRY Where was I, then?

JACKSON   Ahhhm . . . That speech you was reading . . . that speech . . .

HARRY   Speech?

JACKSON   'O silent sea and so on . . . wreathed in mist . . . ' Shall we take it from there, then? The paper.

HARRY   I should know it. After all, I wrote it. But prompt . . .

(HARRY *gives* JACKSON *his copy of the paper, rises, walks around, looks toward the sea.*)

Creole or classical?

JACKSON   Don't make joke. (*Silence. Sea-gull cries.*)

HARRY   Then Crusoe, in his desolation, looks out to the sea, for the ten thousandth time, and remembers England, his wife, his little son, and speaks to himself: (*as Crusoe*) 'O silent sea, O wondrous sunset that I've gazed on ten thousand times, who will rescue me from this complete desolation? Yes, this is paradise, I know. For I see around me the splendors of nature. The ferns, the palms like silent sentinels, the wide and silent lagoons that briefly hold my passing, solitary reflection. The volcano wreathed in mist. But what is paradise without a woman? Adam in paradise had his woman to share his loneliness . . . loneliness . . . '

JACKSON   (*prompts*) . . . but I miss the voice

HARRY   (*remembering*) 'but I miss the voice . . . (*weeping, but speaking clearly*) of even one consoling creature, the touch . . . of a hand . . . the look of kind eyes . . . Where is the wife from whom I vowed . . . never to be sundered? How old is my little son? If he could see his father like this . . . dressed in goatskins and mad with memories of them?' (*He breaks down, quietly sobbing. A long pause.*)

JACKSON   You crying or you acting?

HARRY   Acting.

JACKSON   I think you crying. Nobody could act that good.

HARRY   How would you know? You an actor?

JACKSON   Maybe not. But I cry a'ready.

HARRY   Okay, I was crying.

JACKSON   For what?

HARRY   (*Laughs.*) For what? I got carried away. I'm okay now.

JACKSON   But you laughing now.

HARRY   It's the same sound. You can't tell the difference if I turn my back.

JACKSON   Don't make joke.

HARRY   It's an old actor's trick. I'm going to cry now, all right?

(*He turns, then sobs with laughter, covering and uncovering his face with his hands.* JACKSON *stalks around, peers at him, then begins to giggle. They are now both laughing.*)

JACKSON   (*through laughter*) So . . . so . . . next Friday . . . when the tourists come . . . Crusoe . . . Crusoe go be ready for them . . . Goat race . . .

HARRY   (*laughing*) Goat-roti!

JACKSON   (*laughing*) Gambling.

HARRY   (*baffled*) Gambling?

JACKSON   Goat-to-pack. Every night . . .

HARRY   (*laughing*) Before they goat-to-bed!

JACKSON   (*laughing*) So he striding up the beach with his little goat-ee . . .

HARRY   (*laughing*) E-goat-istical, again. (*Pause.*)

JACKSON   You get the idea. So, you okay, Mr. Trewe?

HARRY   I'm fine, Mr. Phillip. You know . . . (*He wipes his eyes.*) An angel passes through a house and leaves no imprint of his shadow on its wall. A man's life slowly changes and he does not understand the change. Things like this have happened before, and they can happen again. You understand, Jackson? You see what it is I'm saying?

JACKSON   You making a mole hill out of a mountain, sir. But I think I follow you. You know what all this make me decide, pardner?

HARRY   What?

(JACKSON *picks up the umbrella, puts on the goatskin hat.*)

JACKSON   I going back to the gift that's my God-given calling. I benignly resign, you fire me. With inspiration. Caiso is my true work, caiso is my true life.

(*Sings*)

Well, a Limey name Trewe come to Tobago.
He was in show business but he had no show,
so in desperation he turn to me
and said: 'Mr. Phillip is the two o'we,
one classical actor and one Creole,
let we act together with we heart and soul.
It go be man to man, and we go do it fine,

and we go give it the title of pantomime'.
La da dee da da da
dee da da da da da . . .

(*He is singing as if in a spotlight. Music, audience applause.* HARRY *joins in.*)

Wait! Wait! Hold it!

(*Silence. He walks over to* HARRY.)

Starting from Friday, Robinson, we could talk 'bout a raise?

(*Fadeout.*)

Note

1   A Bohbolee is a Judas effigy beaten at Easter in Trinidad and Tobago.

8 Sistren Theatre Collective _____

QPH
Jamaica

Introduction

Known internationally for its maverick
achievements in creating popular plays
about the lives of working-class women,
Jamaica's Sistren Theatre Collective
developed from humble beginnings when a
group of women met in Kingston in 1977.
The majority were part of a government
project designed to help segments of the
populace learn basic skills that would
increase their opportunities for employment.
For a national workers' festival that year, the
women, assisted by Honor Ford-Smith, a
director from the Jamaican School of Drama,
created and staged *Downpression Get a Blow*
(1977), a sketch about employment
conditions in a local women's garment
factory and management opposition to
unionisation. This was the first of many
Sistren plays to be developed from
improvisation based on real-life stories by
and about Jamaican women. Of the founding
members of Sistren – Vivette Lewis, Cerene
Stephenson, Lana Finikin, Pauline Crawford,
Beverley Hanson, Jasmine Smith, Lorna
Burrell Haslam, Beverley Elliot, Jerline Todd,
Lillian Foster, May Thompson, Rebecca
Knowles and Barbara Gayle – almost all were
working class and most were single mothers.
Their primary mission became to examine
the ways in which women in their society are
oppressed, particularly by men, but also by
the broader structures that shape Jamaican
culture. During the 1980s and 1990s, this
mission involved the development and
production of more than a dozen plays, some
of which have won awards and/or toured
within the Caribbean and to the United
States and Europe. Sistren's cultural work
has also included running various workshops
and education outreach programmes, and
publishing a magazine dealing with women's
issues.

'Sistren' means 'sisters' or 'sisterhood' with
the added connotation of something in, of
and for the people. The term is also used in
popular churches and rasta, and can be seen
as a response to the rasta language emphasis
on Brethren. Although the collective's
membership and the particular direction of
its work have changed many times over the
years, the group remains committed to
exploring issues that affect Jamaican
women's lives: unemployment, domestic
violence, alcoholism, harassment and
discrimination in the workplace, class
oppression, poverty, racism, first-world
imperialism, sexism, pregnancy and
child-rearing. In early works such as
Bellywoman Bangarang (1978), about teenage
pregnancy, narrative content was drawn
primarily from the personal histories of
women in the group. Later, Sistren members
incorporated research into their work, often
consulting archival sources and conducting
interviews with representative women who
had first-hand experience of the situations to
be dramatised. Over time, the group
developed a play-making process that has
become a model for community theatre in
the Caribbean region and further afield.
This process generally begins with the
selection of a topic and a community in
which research can be carried out, followed
by collection of material for the project, and a
workshopping period using improvisation,
role-playing and games. When a storyline
begins to emerge, the relevant dramaturgical
material is transcribed into a loose working
script for rehearsals. Performance usually
involves taking the production back to the
community whose lives it dramatises (see
Ford-Smith 1986b: 6–10). As cultural work,
Sistren's theatre attempts to initiate a process
of individual and social empowerment.
According to Honor Ford-Smith, the first
artistic director of the collective, its aim is to

facilitate 'change or consolidation through the revelation and understanding of forms of oppression and exploitation, forms of affirmation and celebration' (Ford-Smith 1989–90: 28–9). This conscientising element distinguishes Sistren plays from agit-prop theatre; the intent is not so much to fire up an audience to immediate action, but to 'make strange' a normative situation in ways that show how it came into effect and how it might be improved. The radical potential of such theatre is suggested by the fact that Sistren's work has sometimes been received with hostility by those who perceive it as a threat to gender and race hierarchies or partisan politics within Jamaican society.

Like much community theatre, Sistren's work is informed structurally and aesthetically by popular and folk forms embedded in the local culture. The collective's initial experiments were influenced by renowned playwright, poet and director Dennis Scott, as well as other Caribbean theatre practitioners who had begun the process of translating popular culture into performance. Songs, children's games and street rituals shape the action of *Bellywoman Bangarang* in ways that raise questions about the process of mothering and the social contexts in which it is carried out. A later play, the reggae musical *Muffet Inna All A We* (1985), draws from the Miss Muffet nursery rhyme, fashioning its spider as Anansi (the trickster of Caribbean/West African folklore) to stage a critique of consumer society and international capitalism as they affect working-class women. Dance, mime and ritual movement are also used extensively throughout Sistren's oeuvre. In *Nana Yah* (1980), a historical fantasy about the life of Jamaica's legendary Maroon heroine, Nanny, the narrative unfolds through twelve movements, some of which communicate solely through visual imagery and music. At one point, actors are choreographed to suggest, symbolically, the moment of contact between European colonisers and a traditional African society; then they move into a limbo dance that conveys the transportation of slaves via the Middle Passage to the Caribbean. The overall play is framed as a wake for Nanny, in which the audience is invited to participate in the manner of a revivalist ceremony. These and other examples show how Sistren, by

constantly invoking the rituals and traditions of everyday Jamaican life, imbues its work with an engaging theatricality while at the same time creating popular art firmly rooted in the cultural imaginary.

QPH (1981), one of Sistren's best known plays and winner of a National Theatre Critics' Award, uses the Etu ritual as the appropriate vehicle through which to celebrate the dead and dramatise their unacknowledged contributions to the society. At its most general level, the play commemorates the lives of 167 women who died in a horrific fire at the Kingston Alms House in 1980. The specific focus on the individual experiences of Queenie, Pearlie and Hopie is designed to demonstrate how such women may have become destitute despite their best efforts to eke out independent existences. Through the performance of the Etu ritual, an African retention practised in western Jamaica, the dead women are 'raised' to relive fragments of their lives for the audience. Staged as part of the play, this ritual functions as a mnemonic device that shows evidence of a cultural history at the same time as it moves the action beyond the sphere of received Western theatrical genres such as realism. In a similar fashion, Dennis Scott uses the Nine Night Ceremony to 'raise' the dead in his kaleidoscopic examination of colonial history, *An Echo in the Bone*, first performed in 1972. The creative reshaping of such traditional ceremonial enactments is not uncommon in Caribbean theatre, which frequently draws from the rich performative archive of various syncretic religions, as well as from rituals associated with carnival, to root its stories in the community.

The practice of 'witnessing' – listening to personal and often intimate testimonies – which has long been a part of the Jamaican rhetorical tradition, meshes with both the ritual framework of *QPH* and the actual methods through which the play was first developed. Moments of direct audience address suggest that the respective stories of Queenie, Pearlie and Hopie are to be witnessed as testimonials, which are imbued with a certain truth value and spiritual resonance by their containment within the Etu ritual. Thus the stories move outwards from personal experiences to their socio-political causes. This process parallels the way in which Sistren worked to create the play, first listening to eye-witness accounts by women who survived the fire, and then transforming their stories into a broader narrative indictment of a society that fails to respect or take care of its aged.

All of Sistren's work is informed by oral storytelling traditions, which in turn achieve their full effects through the use of the people's language, variously termed Patwah or Creole or simply Jamaican. In this arena, the collective goes much further than many other Caribbean dramatists in creating dialogue that captures local rhythms, lexical patterns and grammatical structures. Following such trailblazers as performance poet Mis' Lou (Louise Bennett), Sistren capitalises on the expressivity of the Jamaican language in order to speak to audiences outside the elitist enclaves of middle-class theatre. In various plays, the choice of language also immediately signals class – or class pretensions – as characters adopt different linguistic registers according to their particular situations. Most of QPH's characters speak Patwah, excepting Pearlie whose position as a 'red-skin' girl presumably demanded habituation in the use of standard English, in line with expectations of class mobility. When she eventually joins the Alms House community as an ageing prostitute unable to make a living, her language more closely approximates that of the other residents. The social gap between Hopie's poverty-stricken rural background and the more affluent world of her Auntie Vantie is also expressed in the contrast between Patwah and English. At the end of the play, monologues in Patwah by Begga, Eva and Queenie supply a moving finale to the action while directly invoking audience solidarity with the class of women whose stories have been dramatised. While such linguistic strategies may present difficulties for some readers of this anthology, they are crucial to Sistren's political mission to create popular theatre that is accessible to its constituency. At the same time, the deliberate use of non-standard English speaks to a more general decolonising project in which the received colonial language is displaced from its position of privilege as the 'natural' artistic medium.

Sistren members discuss in their interviews the ways in which black women are positioned at the intersection of racial, sexual and class oppression. No single one of

these interlocking systems is given precedence in their work; the key is to understand their interaction in the material and spiritual lives of Jamaican women. In QPH, Hopie's experiences as an unpaid servant in what is essentially slave labour suggest the appalling employment conditions of 'domestics', a group that still accounts for a large percentage of Caribbean women workers. This particular topic is taken up in another Sistren play, Domestik (1982), which charts the typical patterns of low pay, long hours and family disruption that have historically marked the domestic worker's role in Jamaican society.

As well as dramatising various sorts of social stratification, QPH shows how Pearlie's relatively privileged upbringing nevertheless fails to protect her from being sexually exploited by the family's gardener, and, in more violent ways, by the men to whom she later prostitutes herself for a living. Queenie, for her part, is denied the opportunity to be a religious leader because the flock cannot contemplate having a woman in this role. The play thus depicts a society in which gender oppression has infiltrated all aspects of women's lives. Men are apparently free to objectify women, to get them pregnant without having to take any responsibility, to physically abuse them and to leave them impoverished with no means of support. By including scenes that show how the downtrodden also oppress one another in tacit support of this patriarchal system, QPH urges women to take the initiative in addressing the institutionalised sexism that limits their potential in both the domestic and public spheres.

At the end of QPH, Queenie makes an impassioned speech to the commission investigating the fire, outlining the ways in which the surviving Alms House women might help to rebuild their particular community and thereby contribute to social reform. In her vision of a more humane future, the aged have a special place as repositories of history and tradition: 'Everybody haffi get old but member, di old have the key to di future cause we have di secrets of di past'. Queenie's words are intended to address the audience, and the kind of grass-roots activism she advocates reflects Sistren's own self-help philosophy. The collective's extraordinary survival, despite many difficulties, over more than twenty years testifies to the strength of this kind of artistic and social commitment.

Production history

QPH was first performed in 1981 at the Barn Theatre, Kingston, directed by Hertencer Lindsay, and later that year toured to Carifesta '81 in Barbados and also to Canada. The play featured as part of Sistren's European tour in 1983, travelling to such cities as London, Amsterdam and Berlin. In 1999 Lindsay directed a revised version of QPH in Atlanta, with men playing the male roles, unlike in the original production.

Select bibliography

Allison, H. (1986) *Sistren Song: Popular Theatre in Jamaica*, London: War on Want.

Cobham, R. (1990) '"A wha kind a pen dis?": the function of ritual frameworks in Sistren's *Bellywoman Bangarang*', *Theatre Research International* 15, 3: 233–49.

Di Cenzo, M. and Bennett, S. (1992) 'Women, popular theatre, and social action: interviews with Cynthia Grant and the Sistren Theatre Collective', *Ariel* 23, 1: 73–94.

Fido, E.S. (1990) 'Finding a way to tell it: methodology and commitment in theatre about women in Barbados and Jamaica', in C.B. Davies and E.S. Fido (eds) *Out of the Kumbla: Caribbean Women and Literature*, Trenton, NJ: Africa World Press, 331–43.

—— (1992) 'Freeing up: politics, gender, and theatrical form in the Anglophone Caribbean', in L. Senelick (ed.) *Gender in Performance: The Presentation of Difference in the Performing Arts*, Hanover, NH: University Presses of New England, 281–98.

Ford-Smith, H. (1986a) 'Sistren women's theatre, organizing and conscientization', in P. Ellis (ed.) *Women of the Caribbean*, London: Zed Books, 122–8.

—— (1986b) 'Sistren: exploring women's problems through drama', *Jamaica Journal* 19, 1: 2–12.

—— (1989–90) 'Notes towards a new aesthetic', *Melus* 16, 3: 27–34.

Fuchs, A. (1990) 'Why do women perform?', *Commonwealth: Essays and Studies* 13, 1: 48–54.

Gilbert, H. (1997) 'Woman talawah: an interview with Beverly Hanson and Pauline Matthie of the Sistren Theatre Collective, Jamaica', in J. Holledge and J. Tompkins (eds) *Interviews from the International Women Playwrights' Conference*, Brisbane: ADSA Teaching Texts, 22–8.

Goodman, E. (1993) *Contemporary Feminist Theatres: To Each her Own*, London: Routledge, 163–6.

Sistren, with H. Ford-Smith (ed.) (1986) *Lionheart Gal: Life Stories of Jamaican Women*, London: Women's Press.

Audiovisual resources

Videos of many Sistren performances may be purchased from Sistren Theatre Collective, 20 Kensington Crescent, Kingston 5, Jamaica. Fax: +1 876 9680501.

QPH

Sistren Theatre Collective

QPH was developed from improvisation, and scripted and directed by Hertencer Lindsay.

Characters

QUEENIE
PEARLIE
HOPIE
ETU DRUMMERS
CHORUS OF WOMEN
Other characters are played by various members of the chorus.

Production note

The Etu ritual involves singing, dancing and feasting, with women playing important roles in the ceremony. A table is set with ritual food and rum for the ancestors, and players are anointed with a goat-blood cross to the forehead and bisi (kola nut) to the tip of the tongue. The drummers on the ire drum and the achata (kerosene tin) control the proceedings while the Queen, as lead dancer, controls the dancers. Each soloist represents a family with its own song and dance patterns. Dance movements are centred on the pelvic area, symbol of fertility, birth and rebirth.

Setting

The stage is set with three coffins arranged centre stage in the form of a cross. Above the coffins is a round disc approximately 6 feet in diameter. A bird's eye view of the coffins and the disc gives the universal symbol for woman. The disc also symbolises the moon – the moon signifies the cycle of womanhood. At the beginning three crescent shapes, in red (for PEARLIE), amber (for HOPIE) and blue (for QUEENIE), are outlines on the disc. As each woman's life is enacted, the disc takes on her colour.

Upstage left, is a small table set for the Etu ritual with white rum, cream soda, champagne soda, orange soda, foo-foo and okra stew. Also on the table is a Bible, a tape measure, ruler, pencils, and QUEENIE's waist cord with scissors. A calabash of blood is downstage left, a calabash of bisi is downstage right. A backdrop depicting flames and smoke forms a cyc. The Etu drummers are onstage throughout.

Prologue

At the beginning of the play only the disc is illuminated. PEARLIE *is inside the coffin on stage right,* HOPIE *is in the coffin on stage left,* QUEENIE *is on the centre coffin, bandaged and in a hospital gown. As the opening action progresses, we realise that she is recalling the lives of the women and reliving the nightmare events leading up to a fire. Off stage, the* CHORUS *chants, in a round, to the tune of 'London's Burning'.* QUEENIE *is delirious, in hospital.*

CHORUS   (*off stage*)
　　Queenie's burning (*repeat*)
　　Look yonder (*repeat*)
　　Fire, fire
　　And we have no water.

　　Pearlie's burning (*repeat*)
　　Look yonder (*repeat*)
　　Fire, fire
　　And we have no water.

　　Hopie's burning (*repeat*)
　　Look yonder (*repeat*)
　　Fire, fire
　　And we have no water.

(CHORUS *of old, crippled, shuffling women enters. They form a half moon around coffins, with backs to audience, upstage. In a hoarse whisper they chant:*)

Queenie, Queenie, Queenie
Pearlie, Pearlie, Pearlie
Hopie, Hopie, Hopie
Fire, Fire, Fire
Help, Help, Help!

(*Ambulance and police sirens.* QUEENIE *screams, sits up, looking frightened.* NURSE *enters.*)

NURSE   What's the matter, Miss McQueen? Are you going to wake all the other patients in the hospital?

QUEENIE   Is horrible, the flames, the smoke, the fire, the bawling . . . Pearlie, Hopie . . .

NURSE   It's only a dream, a nightmare. Relax and try and get some sleep.

QUEENIE   Mi cyaan sleep. Beg yuh a lickle water, nuh, Nurse? Mi throat dry.

(NURSE *fetches water.*)

QUEENIE   (*Looks around in panic at the environment and feels her person.*) Is alright, Nurse. Mi nuh thirsty again.

NURSE   Okay. Lie down now and get a good night's rest. (*She exits.*)

(*Etu drums beat and penetrate* QUEENIE's *consciousness. The* CHORUS *of old women is transformed into the celebrants of the Etu ritual. They chant* QUEENIE's *name three times.* QUEENIE *rises and is transformed into the Queen of the ritual. The Etu drums pulsate and crescendo. Two women of the* CHORUS *turn* QUEENIE's *head and arm bandages into a ritual headwrap and an Etu shawl which is draped around her neck. A third takes off the hospital gown; underneath she has on her ritual dress.* QUEENIE *dances to the table, takes the white rum, puts some in her mouth, sprays the coffins with it, and raises* PEARLIE *and* HOPIE *from the dead. They emerge from the closed coffins. The ritual begins by* QUEENIE *marking each woman's forehead with the sign of the cross in blood, beginning with* PEARLIE *and* HOPIE. *Then she gives each woman the bisi on her tongue. During all this,* QUEENIE *is singing her song, 'Kola Kuja', and dancing her steps. Each woman –* QUEENIE, PEARLIE *and* HOPIE *– sings her call-and-response song and dances her Etu steps.*)

QUEENIE   Kola kuja
CHORUS   Iwa, iwa, iwa

(*Song is repeated.*)

QUEENIE   Tell mi wha yuh say.
HOPIE
Onie, chonie, onie
Afa onie.

(*Song is repeated four times.*)

PEARLIE
Ay aré ru
Yep a bey.

(*Song is repeated three times.* QUEENIE *shawls* HOPIE *and* PEARLIE *respectively.*)[1]

Act I Scene 1

Etu drums, QUEENIE *directs the women to change the scene. The three coffins are rearranged to form items of furniture in* SISSY's *room.* QUEENIE's *coffin is placed vertically upstage centre and becomes a closet or wardrobe.* HOPIE's *coffin becomes the dressing table seat downstage left. The mirrored dressing table is mimed.* PEARLIE's *coffin becomes a bed, stage right. It is important that the women in the ritual bear the burden of moving these coffins and that no stage hands come onstage. The placement should indicate a small bedroom, so travelling with the coffins is not too burdensome.*

Hopie's shawling

HOPIE   Onie, chonie, onie
CHORUS   Afa onie. (*Repeat four times.*)

(QUEENIE *directs* HOPIE *to move forward downstage centre; the women, task completed, form a semi-circle and sing and dance with* HOPIE. QUEENIE *directs the chorus woman who is to play* AUNTIE VANTIE *to come forward during* HOPIE's *song and dance.* VANTIE *moves forward with the shawl that is actually* SISSY's *skirt.* VANTIE *shawls and dips* HOPIE. *They freeze as* QUEENIE *directs the lights to change. The moon turns amber, the ritual light changes and we have lighting suggesting the interior of a room in the tropics, late afternoon.* QUEENIE *and the* CHORUS *leave, dancing out stage left to* HOPIE's *rhythm. As they leave* VANTIE *and* HOPIE *unfreeze.* HOPIE *does a quick change to become a young girl as* VANTIE *examines the skirt.*)

Sequence One

(HOPIE *and* VANTIE *in* SISSY's *room.*)

VANTIE   Imagine, look how long mi give yuh di skirt fi sew eeh? What yuh do from morning? A di whole morning yuh tek fi wash out yuh few lickle pieces a small clothes, eeh? Wait, mi talking to yuh. What yuh do since morning?

HOPIE   A whole heap a work, Auntie.

VANTIE   Nuh back answer mi! Oh, tru yuh monthly cycle begin at last yuh tink yuh a woman! Imagine, all yuh had to do was wash di two lickle plate dem and scour di two lickle pot, sweep out di house and clean out di dog kennel, wash and iron yuh cousin dem clothes. Just dem lickle sinting deh yuh couldn't do. Yuh tink yuh napkins more important, eeh? Mi tek yuh from country from yuh lickle bit so, because yuh madda did have a whole heap a oonoo and she never have notten fi give oonoo and mi tek yuh and grow yuh and tek care a yuh . . .

HOPIE   (*grumbles*) A so yuh call tek care.

VANTIE   (*beats* HOPIE *with the skirt*) Yuh ungrateful lickle wretch yuh.

HOPIE   (*cries*) No Auntie, no!

VANTIE   Shut up yuh mouth. Ah don't want any scandal in here. Only my mouth alone must be heard in this house. Yuh getting yuh good food to eat, good clothes to put on, all Miss Sissy clothes that cannot fit her anymore. Mass Alex and Miss Sissy teaching yuh all that dem learning in school, and now yuh don't want to sew the skirt for your cousin Sissy.

HOPIE   (*Grabs skirt, kneels on the floor still crying.* VANTIE *grabs her up.*) Wai! Wai! Mi a go dead!

VANTIE   Wait, is fight yuh fighting mi off inna mi own house? Yuh waan beat mi now? A only one woman in yah.

HOPIE   No, Auntie, is peepee mi waan peepee.

VANTIE   Mine mi expensive rug, yuh know, mine mi expensive rug. If yuh wet it up Ah hang yuh!

HOPIE   After di one Sissy go over di fence go tear her skirt.

VANTIE   Who yuh calling di one Sissy? Yuh fresh and out a order.

HOPIE   Cousin Sissy, maam.

VANTIE   Say Miss Sissy, no Cousin Sissy for you. Look how they have been good to you.

Mi waan di skirt done now! (*Throws the skirt into* HOPIE's *face as she turns to leave.*)

HOPIE   Yes, maam.

VANTIE   By the way, you drink that thing in the kitchen that I leave in there from morning for you?

HOPIE   No, Auntie, it smell bad.

VANTIE   Smell bad, it good for you, it will protect you.

HOPIE   Den yuh expect mi fi drink sinting weh come from mi own body, maam?

VANTIE   How you mean, you don't have to scorn yourself. It will help yuh fi get a good husband fi tek yuh off mi hand. Yuh is a burden. Now yuh start see yuh monthly cycle yuh will go out there mek boy trouble yuh. Furthermore milk in deh. My mother give it to me and it never kill me. (*She exits.*)

(HOPIE *sits on the floor, sewing the skirt and grumbling.*)

SISSY   (*off stage*) OK. I won't be late, see you at the party later. (*Enters, giving* HOPIE *her feet to take off her shoes.*) Hopie, set my bath and get me a cup off coffee. Clean these shoes for me. No, don't bother, get out my blue suede ones and clean Mass Alex cream serge suit. Hopie, where is my leg of mutton blouse and, Hopie, did you wash my bloomers? I need one. Hopie, I can't find my garters and stockings! Oh, Hopie, get my comb and brush. Hopie, help me comb my hair. Hopie, put the curling iron on the stove, I need to curl my hair. Come and help me comb my hair. Hopie, is my bath ready and where's my coffee?

HOPIE   Aunt Vantie out di fire!

SISSY   Well, catch it up again! Wait . . . What is my skirt doing on the floor? If it's dirty you have to wash it again. Hurry up, I want it to wear tonight. (*Pause.*) Hopie, what's wrong with you? Straighten up. You are always slouching. Look at you, years younger than me and already you look like an old woman. You hear me? Straighten up! Hopie, where is my mother? (*Sound of a car horn.* SISSY *rushes to look out a window downstage right.*) Is that Mass Alex and oh my Lord I'm not ready. Hopie where is my nail varnish?

(HOPIE *puts skirt on dressing table chair with needle sticking up.* SISSY *rushes back from window, sits on needle and screams out. Freeze on* HOPIE *grinning and* SISSY *furious.*)

Sequence Two

(*In* SISSY's *room.* SISSY *is weeping delicately.*)

HOPIE (*touching* SISSY) Cousin Sissy . . .

SISSY Don't touch me! And don't call me Cousin Sissy. Since my Mama die you are coming to take liberty.

HOPIE Don't take it so hard. Member say that we have each other, you know!

SISSY What you mean by we have each other?

HOPIE Mi wi stay here and tek care a yuh and di house.

SISSY I have my husband to take care of me.

HOPIE So what yuh gwine do now?

SISSY Brother Alex and I have sold the place. The people are moving in a few days from now and I am going back to England.

HOPIE Sell di place? Dat mean seh yuh sell mi too. What gwine happen to mi now?

SISSY (*annoyed*) I don't know!

HOPIE So a out a street yuh a tell mi seh mi fi go now, eeh? After yuh and Alex gawn a Foreign, say oonoo gawn study and don't come back all dese years. And Aunt Vantie get old, tun back to baby, a mi one haffi do everyting: give her bed-pan, bathe her, put on her clothes, feed her, help her walk. Everyting is mi . . . and now yuh tell mi yuh sell di place!

SISSY Have you forgotten that when Mummy took you out of the bush as a little girl, she gave you a roof over your head, food, clothes to wear and took care of you FREE! What more do you want? You've been living under Mummy's roof over thirty years now, eating, drinking and sleeping free. You have to stop living off us now!

HOPIE Wait, tek care? A so oonoo call tek care? She never send mi a no school. After she say oonoo fi teach mi, oonoo carry mi round a bush, tek yuh dirty bloomers beat mi. Alex bax mi down. A whole heap a time mi tell her seh, mi gwine look a work, she say mi musn't go no way. If mi stay she wi see dat mi won't want. Weh mi bound mi must obey. Man all come yah say him waan married to mi.

SISSY Man? Who'd ever want to marry you?

HOPIE She run him! Anyting mi waan out a street now it pass gone long time so mi nah know weh yuh a tell mi seh. Aunt Vantie wouldn't so wicked, she must lef lickle sinting fi mi, some lickle legacy. She lef a will, and all mi mind tell mi seh yuh, Alex and oonoo lawyer mek up and burn di will!

SISSY Get out of here. You've gone too far. If you don't go I'll get the police to throw you out.

HOPIE Enh enh! We'll see, for di two a we a come out pon di stretcher today.

SISSY (*after a pause*) Hopie, I don't know what's come over you. You used to be such an obedient girl. Now you want to trace and fight me off. I was thinking that when I got back to England I'd send for you, for a friend of mine want someone to look after the children and do a little light housework . . . But I wouldn't dream of doing so now!

HOPIE Do, Cousin Sissy. (SISSY *glares at her.*) Miss Sissy, mi a beg yuh pardon, maam. Mi never mean fi rude but is di shock . . . losing good Auntie Vantie.

SISSY I am shocked too and I am *not* carrying on like you. She was *my mother*, remember that!

HOPIE Den Miss Sissy, yuh really gwine help mi fi true, maam? Carry mi back a Foreign wid yuh? What else yuh waan inna di grip? Dis – see it here, maam? Di grip ready!

SISSY I'll think about it, Hopie. Please remember to clean out the place good for me. The people are coming tomorrow but their maid is not due from the country till next week.

HOPIE Member yuh know, maam. Yuh see, maam. Member do! Alright, maam. (*Cleans* SISSY's *shoes as* SISSY *exits.*)

(*Blackout.*)

Sequence Three

(HOPIE's *monologue, on the street. She uses the audience and exits through the audience begging as she goes.*)

HOPIE Nice lady, Hopie a beg yuh a ten cents. How yuh a treat Hopie so bad today? Work, maam? Hopie cyaan work again. Yuh know if ah did only get lickle good education mi woulda able fi work an help miself today. But dem nevah sen mi a school, dem nuh send mi at all. Mi cyaan even scribble mi own name di one good name mi madda give mi. Hope Sherington. Hi sir beg yuh a fifty cents, nuh. Oh di rice and peas mi show yuh already! How yuh so bodderation? Di bwoy dem come fi trouble di rice and peas and mi tell dem seh mi gwine tell police. Mi a go a station go tell police seh dem waan fi rape Hopie. Hi sah! Hopie begging yuh a dollar. Ah waan one pound rice, quarter pound salt fish, some seasoning, big jill coconut oil, cause a going down a Almshouse go cook lickle season rice. Yuh hear? Ten cent more lady, God bless yuh.

(*Blackout.*)

Act I, Scene 2

Pearlie's shawling

Transition ritual. Etu drums sound QUEENIE's *rhythm. Dancing, she leads on the* CHORUS *of women and directs them to change the scene to* PEARLIE's *bedroom. The upright coffin upstage is moved downstage left to become a dressing table. The mirror is mimed. The bed remains the same. When the scene is set, the women again form a semicircle upstage and dance to* PEARLIE's *steps.* PEARLIE's *song is sung.*

PEARLIE   Ay aré ru
CHORUS   Yep a bey.

(*Song is repeated three times.* QUEENIE *directs the chorus woman who is to play* MUMMY *to come forward with the shawl, which is in reality a chiffon scarf to match* PEARLIE's *engagement dress. The woman dances forward downstage centre and shawls and dips* PEARLIE. PEARLIE *and* MUMMY *freeze.* QUEENIE *directs the lights to change – the moon disc turns red and the ritual lighting changes to interior of* PEARLIE's *bedroom in the tropics, early evening.* QUEENIE *leads the* CHORUS *off stage right.* PEARLIE *and* MUMMY *unfreeze.*)

Sequence One

(PEARLIE *and* MUMMY *in* PEARLIE's *bedroom.*)

MUMMY   (*arranging scarf on* PEARLIE *in several styles*) Now sweetheart, tonight is your engagement party. Oh, my lucky baby! Engaged to the Custos' son. George is such a wonderful young man: handsome, a university graduate. So many mothers were after him but, sweetheart, he chose me . . . I mean you! You must look just right tonight!
PEARLIE   But it's choking me!

MUMMY   Keep still! It matches the dress – just the right colour for you. (*Pause.*) But darling, the dress is looking a bit tight. I hope the dressmaker didn't skimp the material to steal a piece of my imported Liberty print. It's fit only for royalty. Darling, do keep still. You're looking a bit pale. Come put on an insy bit of rouge.
PEARLIE   I don't like it.
MUMMY   (*ignoring* PEARLIE) Oh my! We haven't put on your stocking and shoes. Ivy, Ivy! Fetch Miss Pearl's new stocking from the parcel I left on the sideboard. Hurry!
IVY   (*off stage*) Yes, missis.
MUMMY   Oh my! Look at my pretty little girl.
PEARLIE   This thing on my neck . . . is choking me.

(IVY *enters with stockings.*)

MUMMY   Put it on Miss Pearl's foot.
PEARLIE   I don't like it, don't put it on.
IVY   Yuh madda say mi mus put it on.
PEARLIE   Ivy, leave my foot. Move I say. Leave me alone! (*She kicks down* IVY.)
MUMMY   Pearl, stop this behavior. (PEARLIE *throws herself on the bed.*) Pearl, why are you lying down in your new dress? Ivy, go and put the coal in the iron! (*To* PEARLIE *as* IVY *exits*) What's wrong with you? A big sixteen year old engaged miss and you are carrying on like this? Get up! At once!
PEARLIE   I'm not going!
MUMMY   What? What's wrong with you? You should be feeling so happy.
PEARLIE   I don't feel like going.
MUMMY   Pearlie, don't let me lose my temper. You are an ungrateful girl. Look at all the money we've spent on *you* our only daughter: sending you to private school, grooming you for this moment. George and his family have spent so much money for this party and now you're telling me you don't *feel* like going. You know how many girls would cut off their right arm to marry the Custos' son?
PEARLIE   (*flouncing away*) Let them have him! I don't want him!
MUMMY   Come back here! (*Raises hand to strike* PEARLIE, *realises what she is doing. Changes tone.*) Pearlie, sweetheart, what's wrong? Remember you used to trust Mummy. Confide in me. Poopsie, what's wrong?

PEARLIE I am not feeling well . . . I've got pains.

MUMMY Where?

PEARLIE All over.

MUMMY We'll send for the doctor. There's still time. Ivy! Ivy!

PEARLIE No, Mummy! (IVY *enters.*)

MUMMY Fetch the doctor.

PEARLIE No, Ivy, no! I don't want a doctor. (*Grabs* IVY.)

MUMMY (*to* PEARLIE) Pearlie! (*To* IVY) Ivy, you heard me. I've had quite enough of this.

PEARLIE I'm alright now!

MUMMY So come on! Finish getting ready! (IVY *exits.*)

PEARLIE Mummy, please! I can't! I don't know what to do.

MUMMY What's the matter? You and George have had a little tiff? Have you heard something about him? Men will be men, you know. Or do you love somebody else? Tell Mummy, sweetheart. Sit down, don't worry! Ivy will iron it out!

PEARLIE Mummy! I . . . please forgive me!

MUMMY Tell Mummy everything.

PEARLIE It was James.

MUMMY James? Which family? James who?

PEARLIE The gardener . . . he . . . when I went by the shed . . . he . . . and . . .

MUMMY (*almost a whisper*) James . . . the gardener. (*Shouts*) Ivy, Ivy! Get James! (*To* PEARLIE) When? How? What . . . Oh my God . . .

PEARLIE A few months ago. I was afraid and . . . Mummy, I haven't seen my monthly cycle . . .

MUMMY (*shocked*) A few months ago! You're pregnant and you didn't tell me? Ivy! Ivy! WHERE IS JAMES?

IVY (*off stage*) I don't know, maam.

MUMMY Find him!

IVY (*off stage*) Ah look everywhere, maam. Mi nuh see him from morning.

MUMMY Why didn't you tell me? A few months . . . but . . . but . . . your napkins were bleached as usual and hung on the line.

PEARLIE Ivy . . . Ivy . . . wet them . . . and . . .

MUMMY So you and Ivy and James plan this, enh? Well Ivy, James and the Sambo in yuh belly, leave mi house . . . Get out!! My only daughter . . . Oh God, all the money, my wedding, the plans, the cake . . . the disgrace . . . the shame . . .

You hear me? Get out! Get out of my sight!

(PEARLIE *runs off.* MUMMY *freezes pointing her out. Blackout.*)

Sequence Two

(*Music: 'Cover the Waterfront' by Billie Holiday. Nighttime on a street near Kingston Harbour.* PEARLIE, *now the infamous Pearl Harbour, dressed in a tight red dress, fish net stockings and red high heels, strolls along the waterfront looking for customers.*)

SAILOR Hi, sugar! Got a date?

PEARLIE No.

SAILOR Waiting for someone?

PEARLIE (*coyly*) Maybe . . .

SAILOR What's your name?

PEARLIE Pearlie.

SAILOR Ah! Pearlie, pretty girl, pretty name. Your real name?

PEARLIE Thank you, yeah!

SAILOR What's up, Pearlie?

PEARLIE Nothing much.

SAILOR What's a pretty girl like you doing out here? And ain't got a date?

PEARLIE Just work . . . Ah mean . . . just strolling. Enjoying the harbour breeze, looking around.

SAILOR Looking for somebody . . . special?

PEARLIE Not really.

SAILOR How can I get to know Pearlie better? Is there some place we can go to enjoy ourselves?

PEARLIE You got money?

SAILOR Money? Money – no problem!

PEARLIE Well, there's lots of places: Glass Buckett, Silver Slipper, Bournemouth, Rainbow . . . Let's go to the Myrtle Bank Hotel. It's just around the corner and it's my favourite. It's quiet and . . . romantic.

SAILOR Lead the way, sugar! (*They walk.*) Oh, Jamaica is so pretty and the girls . . . you're all so lovely. Now look at that one . . . but she's not half as pretty as my Pearlie.

PEARLIE Why thanks! What ship did you come in on?

SAILOR Ship? Ah yes . . . ship . . . Oh . . . *Sugar Bird*! Yeah, *Sugar Bird* . . . docked around the corner in your lovely harbour.

PEARLIE I'd like to go on it sometime.

SAILOR Yeah, sure! I'll take you before we sail.

PEARLIE I'm holding you to that promise,

you know! Ah, here we are . . . Myrtle Bank.

SAILOR   Oh it's beautiful. All those palm trees.

(WAITER *enters and escorts them to their seats.*)

WAITER   A table for two, sir? Ready to order, sir?

SAILOR   Just a minute. (*To* PEARLIE) What are you drinking, Pretty Pearlie?

PEARLIE   Rum, Myers rum. And get some cigarettes.

SAILOR   Myers rum! Sounds good! What cigarettes?

PEARLIE   Four Aces.

SAILOR   Got that, waiter? A bottle of Myers rum, a packet of ten Four Aces, a cool coke and some ice. Make it quick! (WAITER *exits.*) Yeah. Pearlie, where are you from? East, West, North or South?

PEARLIE   The North, over by Montego Bay. You know there?

SAILOR   Yeah! All those hotels and beaches and things!

WAITER   (*enters*) Here we are, sir.

SAILOR   (*pours drinks*) Chaser, Pearlie? (WAITER *exits.*)

PEARLIE   No! I like it neat.

SAILOR   What shall we drink to? To sweet Jamaica and Pretty Pearlie. (PEARLIE *drinks in one gulp and pours another.*) Hey! Pearlie, why you drink so fast? Take it easy. Relax, sip your drink.

PEARLIE   Cigarette!

SAILOR   (*Lights* PEARLIE*'s cigarette. Flame of match nearly burns* PEARLIE. *She draws back.*) What do you do for a living, Pearlie? You work?

PEARLIE   Uh . . . yeah, I do secretarial work . . . part-time secretary, you know!

SAILOR   So life for you is okay? Kinda easy!

PEARLIE   Easy? It's damn tough, rough.

SAILOR   (*Keeps pouring drinks in* PEARLIE*'s glass to get her drunk.*) Your family in North don't help you?

PEARLIE   Family? Family! I haven't seen them for years, not since I was sixteen.

SAILOR   How come?

PEARLIE   I got pregnant . . . they threw me out!

SAILOR   What happened to the guy that got you pregnant? He never helped?

PEARLIE   Helped? The gardener! He left town fast!

SAILOR   The gardener! Wow, that's tough.

PEARLIE   Yeah.

SAILOR   So where's the child now?

PEARLIE   I don't even know. I think my brother took her away while I was in hospital. Took her as his own. I didn't even get to give her her name. Ebony, Ebony . . . Anyhow, let's forget about that. Let's only think about tonight and enjoy it.

SAILOR   Yeah! Come on, let's dance.

(*They dance to Glen Miller music.* PEARLIE *is drunk.* SAILOR *pretends to be drunk.*)

SAILOR   Let's go, Pearlie. Time to go home!

PEARLIE   Let's have one more for the road!

SAILOR   Waiter! My bill!

(WAITER *enters with bill.* PEARLIE *sneaks a peep at* SAILOR*'s money in her powder mirror.* SAILOR *also tries to see where* PEARLIE *has her money.*)

WAITER   One pound two and sixpence, please, sir!

SAILOR   Keep the change! Let's go, Pearlie.

(PEARLIE *sings 'One for My Baby and One for the Road' as they leave.*)

SAILOR   Oh, Pearlie! Jamaica is such a beautiful place. What's that over there?

PEARLIE   Enh? Oh! That's the light, man, where we coming from . . . (SAILOR *hits her. She cries out in pain.*) Help! Thief! Police! Murder! Thief! You white nayga trash yuh. Help! Help!

SAILOR   Shut up yuh mout! Yuh red bitch. Yuh a Pearl Harbour. Yuh know how long mi a watch yuh? A pure foreigner yuh want! Yuh no waan no Jamaican nuh. Well I get yuh now! Gimme di money! Gimme! (*Raises his fist to strike her again.*) Take dis!

(*Blackout.*)

Sequence Three

(*On the street.* PEARLIE*'s monologue. Song: 'Nobody Wants You When You're Down and Out'.* PEARLIE *is in gutter with a bottle of white rum from which she drinks continuously. She talks to herself. The conversation is broken up with coughs and hiccups.*)

PEARLIE   Pearlie, yeah! Pearlie McPherson, Esquire. (*Giggles at her own joke.*) Sit up! Sit upright in the carriage and wave to the people! (*Gets up and dances with herself.*) Club Havana, yeah! Hit it, Don, play that sax. (*Sound of Don Drummond tune on a saxophone.* PEARLIE *falls and begins to think of her daughter.*) Ebony! Ebony McPherson! Gentle Jesus meek and mild, is this a monkey or a child! Made something of yourself! That's my girl. Ebony McPherson. Marry well, now, you hear? But don't marry the Custos' son. (*Drinks. Giggles.*) Hey, Corny, pass me a corn, nuh?

CORNY'S VOICE   (*off stage, laughing nastily*) Mi nuh have no corn fi give yuh fi what yuh waan it for.

PEARLIE   You are damned impertinent! *Sell me a corn, I have my money. I not begging you anything.* You think when I was Miss Pearl McPherson I would allow you to address me. Keep you corn, you ole nayga. (*Stumbles away, drinks, wipes mouth, tries to put on lipstick. Waves down a bus.*) Conductor, I would like to ride to Slipe Pen Road.

CONDUCTOR'S VOICE   (*off stage, sneeringly*) Wait! Nah Pearl Harbour? Move yourself! Paying passengers only! Later mi wi come check yuh and give yuh a ride. (*Laughs.*)

PEARLIE   What, you say what, bwoy? Who are you? You know your father? There's no part of me that could be any part of you.

VOICE   (*off stage*) Move out a di way. Pay up or get off.

PEARLIE   Wait, you have shares in J.O.S., the Jamaica Omnibus Service? I am entitled to a free ride! Have already paid my dues to society! (*She is pushed off, lands in the gutter.*) That's right, throw oonoo bombs, drop them, drop oonoo bombs. They can't touch me! (*Drinks from bottle.*) From the gutter you all came and to the gutter you shall return!

(*Blackout.*)

Act I, Scene 3

Queenie's shawling

Transition ritual. Etu drums to QUEENIE'S *rhythm. Ritual lights. The moon disc turns blue. The* CHORUS *of women enter to* QUEENIE'S *movements and set up the scene for her open air church: two coffins become pews and the third will become her pulpit.* QUEENIE *dances downstage centre, followed by the chorus woman who will play* SISTER JAMES. *The rest of the* CHORUS *are in a semi-circle upstage. They sing* QUEENIE'S *song and dance her rhythm.*

QUEENIE   Kola kuja

CHORUS   Iwa, iwa, iwa

(*Song is repeated.*)

QUEENIE   Tell mi wha yuh say.

(SISTER JAMES *joins* QUEENIE *carrying a long white sash, which will become* QUEENIE'S *Pocomania headwrap in her first sequence.*[2] *She shawls and dips* QUEENIE. *They freeze. The* CHORUS *exits stage right. The light changes to a moonlit night at a makeshift outdoor church.*)

Sequence One

(*Transition from shawling ritual to churchyard.* CHORUS *of women, as church flock off stage, softly hums 'Come Down', a popular Pocomania song.* SISTER JAMES *is helping* QUEENIE *to get dressed as a Pocomania mother or preacher. She helps her to do the Pocomania head wrap with the shawl and during the ensuing conversation, makes several trips to the ritual table to get other items such as the sash with the scissors for* QUEENIE'S *waist, the pencils which are stuck in the elaborate headwrap and the tape measure which goes round* QUEENIE'S *neck.*)

QUEENIE   Come on, nuh, Sista James, mek hase. How yuh tek so long fi di lickle piece a tiehead?

SISTER JAMES   Hold still please, Sista Queenie.

QUEENIE   When mi go out deh now, everybody face long and dem mouth heng dung and gawn different way. Look how mi beg yuh last night fi bring yuh red tiehead come lend mi and yuh still lef it.

SISTER JAMES   Den Sista Queenie, mi nuh tell yuh seh mi haffi wear it and mi cyaan find di odder old one? Anyway, since yuh a lead tonight dis wi show yuh leadership and a commemoration night so, di white one wi do!

QUEENIE   Dat nuh say. Yuh know how di people dem tan!

SISTER JAMES   A di people dem yuh a watch? God send yuh yah fi do Him work. A God provide yuh fi Bishop.

QUEENIE   Just carry di Bible come, and di ruler and di scissors. Yuh member di text? Yuh mark it?

SISTER JAMES   Yes, Sista!

QUEENIE   Acts Two. And yuh have di song dem write out and everyting?

SISTER JAMES   Yes, Sista!

QUEENIE   Come on den.

(FLOCK *enters singing and humming the Poco chorus 'Come Down'.* QUEENIE *and* SISTER JAMES *hum half-heartedly checking the order of service. That song hadn't been chosen for the service; the* FLOCK *has changed it to send a message to* QUEENIE. *They hum and dance Poco movements until they reach their seat in the pews.*)

QUEENIE   Praise di Lord! Praise Him!

FLOCK   Praise di Lord! He is so real! Alleluya.

QUEENIE   We'll ask Sista Penny to lead us in the words of the chorus.

FLOCK   (*sings maliciously*)
  Come down, Come down,
  Come down off your pomp and pride.
  For yuh nuh hear the voice of Jesus say
  'Come down, Come down,
  Come down, Come down'.

QUEENIE   (*interrupting*) Amen! Amen! Praise di Lord! On dis special night I call upon Sista James to read tonight's lesson.

SISTER JAMES   Tonight's lesson is taken from the Book of Acts, Chapter Two, reading from Verse One. 'And when the day of the Pentecost was fully come, they were all with one accord in one place and suddenly there came a sound from Heaven as of a rushing mighty wind and it fill all the house where they were sitting. And there appear unto them cloven tongues of fire and it cast upon them and they were all filled with the Holy Ghost and began to speak in tongues. And they were all amazed and marvelled saying one to another, "Behold are not all which speak Galileans? These men are full of wine". But Peter said unto them, "These are not drunks as ye suppose". This is that which was spoken of by the prophet. "And it shall come to pass in the last days", saith God, "I will pour out my Spirit upon all flesh and your sons and your daughters shall prophesy and your young men shall see visions and your old men shall dream dreams. And on my servants and on my handmaidens I will pour out in those days of my Spirit and they shall prophesy and I will show wonders in Heaven above and signs in the earth beneath; blood and fire and vapour of smoke. The sun shall be turned into darkness and the moon into blood before that great and notable day of the Lord come"'.

QUEENIE   (*preaches*) Praise di Lord! Yuh hear what di Good Book say? On di day of Pentecost when God sent down di tongues of fire/ No backbiters was dere/ No warmongers was dere/ No pretenders was dere/ Di tongues of flame/ Come down on di righteous/ And pure in heart/ Dem did clean/ Praise Him!/ Praise di Lord/ Mmmmmm/ Some people don't wants to praise Him/ Mmmmmm/ Dem know why/ Pentecostal beware!/ Be careful/ Dat di Lord/ Don't tek way di gift of di Spirit/ Mek sure yuh sanctified/ Mek sure yuh clean/ Some people/ When dem hear we tongues/ Dem say we drunk/ Or we mad/ But when di cloven tongues get yuh/ Yuh haffi move/ We haffi talk/ Yuh haffi move/ Praise Him/ God send Him only Son fi die fi we/ Praise Him!/ mmmmmm/ Di next time when Him a come/ mmmmmm/ A no water dis time/ Him say Him shall cleanse di earth with brimstone and fire/ Yuh hear me?/ Is di fire next time/ So decide yuh mind/ Whether yuh waan/ Di fire of di Holy Ghost/ Or di fire of God's wrath and everlasting damnation/ Hell. Sista James will lead us to di throne of Grace.

SISTER JAMES   Dear Father, Lord, as we come before Thee this evening we thank Thee that Thou has spared our lives to meet again. But Thou seest we are not *together*. Help us to be of one accord like the Disciples in the upper room. Thou seest our hearts are not pure. I ask You to purify us, oh Lord! Send down upon us the tongues of flame, like on the day of Pentecost when You sent down the fire of the Holy Spirit. Fill us with that fire and let all of us meet that great day. We ask these mercies in Jesus name.

FLOCK   (*Sings 'Holy Ghost Power is Moving Just Like a Magnet' and 'Let the Fire Fall on Me, My Lord'.* QUEENIE *dances around them, cutting the evil out of them with her scissors. The* FLOCK *moves out of the pews.* SISTER FRANCIS *and* SISTER PENNY *go towards* QUEENIE *and* SISTER JAMES.)

QUEENIE   Thank you, Sista James. Good service!

SISTER FRANCIS   (*clearing her throat*) One word, Sista Queenie. The other day we held a meeting, yuh know?

QUEENIE   Meeting? Yuh knew about it, Sista James?

SISTER JAMES No, Sister.

SISTER FRANCIS We did not invite yuh. Di members are very concerned and ask mi to ask yuh a few questions. First we waan know what happen to Bishop?

QUEENIE But you all know that Bishop is on church business. Yuh hear when he announce it every week before he left, dat he was going to a conference at headquarters in America?

SISTER FRANCIS Yes! But him should come back weeks ago and *we* don't hear anything from him.

QUEENIE I don't hear anything either. Any letter I get I would read it out in church.

SISTER FRANCIS Well, di members dem fed up. Dem hate to come a church and hear a woman preach to dem. And I know in di Bible God said, 'Shepherd lead your flock'. And di Shepherd is a man not a woman. We cyaan come to church to listen to a woman. Dat's not right.

SISTER JAMES Anybody can preach; you, Sista, and myself. Anybody can be a leader. You putting down a woman like yourself.

QUEENIE But Sister Francis. Yuh don't haffi be a man or a woman to preach di word of God. God choose yuh whoever yuh might be fi carry out His work.

SISTER PENNY *We* have been working so hard. Anyone of us could be doing what you are doing. Working so hard without even a recompense! And Bishop go all the way to Hanover and come back with this woman.

SISTER FRANCIS We don't even know if she is baptised or saved or even filled with di Holy Ghost.

SISTER PENNY Or Sanctified!

SISTER FRANCIS We have even heard that in Hanover yuh were dealing with Paganism and for all we know yuh still doing it. Worshipping Satan!

SISTER PENNY The Devil, Lucifer, Beelzebub. Help us Lord, Amen, Alleluia!

SISTER FRANCIS And Bishop pick yuh up wid two children nobody know bout and while yuh here preaching one of dem is roaming di street like a leggo beast. No discipline. She has no example.

SISTER PENNY No, because you and Bishop are living a sinful, sweetheart and concubine life in here.

SISTER FRANCIS Yes. Di life Bishop waan fi live with yuh. Bishop know none of *us* would put up with it. It can't work in here!

SISTER PENNY The church is unclean.

QUEENIE Judge not lest ye be judged! Remember di Pharisees and di Sadducees who felt they were better than the Lord! As for my child I am showing her to live right and if she won't do what I tell her, I cyaan buss her head and put it in! Bishop choose mi to cook, wash and clean and do whatsoever thing is needed in di church. Di Lord led Bishop to choose me!

SISTER FRANCIS So, Sista Queenie, yuh telling us dat the Lord tell yuh and Bishop to FORNICATE!

SISTER PENNY Amen. If the head of the stream is dirty the rest of it can't be clean.

SISTER FRANCIS Only di odder day I went to the prayer room in di house and who did I see but Sister Queenie and Bishop hugging and kissing, excuse me Sista Penny!

QUEENIE So you come a church fi watch and peep.

SISTER PENNY Bishop do worse. Only the other day after service Brother Brown put his arm around me, you know, running a joke and Bishop made one scandal. He even preached it in church. I was so embarrassed.

SISTER FRANCIS Another ting! Di members want fi know what happen to our money. For years di Lord give us health and strength fi work and we throw our tithes and offering and extra fi mek di house and build di church. Every night we haffi be out here in di night dew. When it raining only a trapalin over we head. What happen to we money?

QUEENIE Mi nuh know anyting bout money. Yuh haffi ask Bishop dat.

SISTER FRANCIS Well, if and when Bishop come back we will tell him what we telling yuh now. You haffi leave and we mean immediately.

SISTER PENNY NOW!

SISTER FRANCIS And when yuh going leave everyting dat belongs to the church including yuh clothes, for is we money buy dem.

QUEENIE So mi must leave, just so?

SISTER PENNY Just so.

SISTER FRANCIS And by di way, if Bishop was here, you would never dare wear dat white tie head tonight. You would haffi wear di red one. Dat's all I haffi say.

QUEENIE Alright, mi a go. But member dis weh Queenie tell yuh. Apart from God's obeah, di biggest obeah mi know is time. Mi wi let dat tek care of yuh!

SISTER FRANCIS Cleanse her Lord!

SISTER PENNY Forgive her Lord!

SISTER FRANCIS Amen, Alleluia.

SISTER PENNY Amen. Praise the Lord.

(SISTER PENNY *and* SISTER FRANCIS *run* SISTER JAMES, *who exits left. The* FLOCK *trumps Poco as* SISTER FRANCIS *and* SISTER PENNY *disrobe* QUEENIE.[3] *They leave with all her preaching paraphernalia, singing* 'Come Down', *but changing the words to* 'She come down'. QUEENIE *freezes.*)

(*Blackout.*)

Sequence Two

(*On the street.* QUEENIE *selling her wares.*)

QUEENIE (*speaking to herself*) Lord, mi only hope mi get fi sell lickle sinting today. Di two and sixpence mi have mi tek it buy di goods fi mek di tings dem. Di tram car cost mi sixpence fi come back after mi walk go down. Mi hope mi sell sinting today fi give di lickle gal Faithy a good dinner fi eat fi go to her bed. Eating dem sweet tings yah all di time a mek her belly big. She must be have all worm. A same ting mek Government haffi tek way Ruby when she go a road go fight and tief. A only hope it nuh rain! Dem pickney dem should be coming out a school. (*She calls out wares.*) Sham shuggie, Flan, Flan, Stretch mi, Chowbow! Mi have everyting! (*Voices off stage criticise goods.*) Just gwan yuh ways, yuh hear, lickle boy. A yesterday mi mek dem, how dem must stale?

(SISTER JAMES *enters with a letter.*)

Praise di Lord, Sista James, Praise di Lord. Mi still a praise di Lord, even though mi have di whole heap a trouble. And mi head, di pressure yuh know and di sugar.

SISTER JAMES Den yuh nah must have it if all you a eat is dem sweet-sweet things dat yuh mek.

QUEENIE Anyway, di sugar nuh so bad now. Mi use to buy di sulphur bitters a drug store but mi cyaan afford it now. Anyway, mi have a lickle friend a market who bring bush fi mi, so mi drink di rice bitters morning and night, di cerassee like tea, yuh know, and di single bible when mi thirsty and waan water. But di head, Lawd!

SISTER JAMES Mind a Bishop yuh a fret pon mek yuh pressure gawn up! A time fi yuh forget bout him after all dese years.

QUEENIE No sah! Sometimes di head so bad is like a clock in dere ticking away. Den business so bad mi cyaan even visit mi big dawta Ruby, di bad one Government tek way. Mi shame cause mi have nothing fi carry give her.

SISTER JAMES But yuh must still go look fi her, let her know dat yuh still care fi her. Yuh nuh haffi carry nothing but yuhself.

QUEENIE Yes, yuh right. Den a what breeze blow yuh here now?

SISTER JAMES Well, mi bring dis letter dat mi get fi yuh.

QUEENIE A wonder who writing mi?

SISTER JAMES Hmmm . . . a must be from Bishop.

QUEENIE Yes . . . But no foreign stamp nuh deh pon it!

SISTER JAMES Yuh right . . . it inna brown envelope. It look like it from di Government. Yuh lucky Government know yuh.

QUEENIE Sista James, read it fi mi, nuh? Di eyes get bad, and di head!

SISTER JAMES (*reads silently then translates*) Government serve yuh notice. Dem a evict yuh. Dem say yuh fi move because dem gwine bulldoze di place.

QUEENIE What? Move? Move go where? Lord!

SISTER JAMES And dem give yuh thirty days. It write from di first and is di twentieth today so yuh only have ten days left.

QUEENIE Den a what mi a go do? Sista James . . . uh . . .

SISTER JAMES No! No! Sista Queenie, mi cyaan help yuh. Mi have one miserable husband deh. Him nuh want a Jesus Christ soul fi come dere. Him nuh even want mi church sista dem fi come wait pon mi a Sunday day! No, Sista Queenie.

QUEENIE A nuh fi mi. Is mi youngest gal, Faithy, mi just asking yuh fi keep her till mi find somewhere.

SISTER JAMES Di ickle gal? Mi nuh know. Lickle from dis she might go turn mi out too. Anyway, mi wi talk to mi husband tonight. Yuh know when we go to bed mi can talk to him good and ask him.

QUEENIE Thank you, Sista James! And first ting tomorrow morning mi a go start walk and look see if mi cyaan find anodder lickle place fi capture and build back di lickle shack.

SISTER JAMES Den yuh nuh see Government a bulldoze everywhere and a put up new building now?

QUEENIE Den what mi a go do?

SISTER JAMES Mi nuh know, Sista. Den yuh nuh have nothing save so yuh can rent a place?

QUEENIE No, Sista.

SISTER JAMES Den when Bishop was here, nuh yuh use to go a market and buy groceries? Yuh couldn't save ickle something?

QUEENIE Sista, yuh nuh know Bishop. Him use to write out list with di price beside and if farthing change leave yuh haffi bring it back.

SISTER JAMES But mi still say yuh coulda find cheaper tings and save sinting. If a man give yuh quatty save farthing. Den yuh nuh find anodder little man fi help yuh?

QUEENIE No, Sista James. Mi nuh want depend pon no man again.

SISTER JAMES Den why yuh don't go back a country?

QUEENIE Go do what? Di distant relative dem, every minute dem send to mi fi sinting! Di lickle piece a dry lease land not bearing nothing! And di lickle board shack a tumble down. Since mi deh a town, a mi dem a depend on fi send tings fi dem. Mi did all try fi start anodder church one time, yuh know, but di church sista dem walk and spread mi name all over. Even after all dese years dem still a carry grievance. Dem talk so till dat even di lickle school pickney dem nuh want buy from mi.

SISTER JAMES Mi nuh know what fi say.

QUEENIE Give mi di letter, Sista. Well, if mi nuh find nowhere else mi can capture, mi a go dung to di people who send mi dis letter. Dem wi haffi find shelter fi mi, for a little while, till mi can get on mi feet again! For a long time poor people a suffer and a time dem fi help we properly.

SISTER JAMES You right, Sista! A no ickle work yuh work and no try yuh nuh try, and now yuh a ickle older and a try something to be independent, dem a bulldoze yuh out fi mek up office building. Go to dem yes, Sista.

QUEENIE So Sista, mi must send up my lickle gal Faithy wid her bundle of clothes tonight?

SISTER JAMES Yes, Sista.

QUEENIE Mi have a lickle iron bed. Mi can carry dat up fi her fi sleep pon.

SISTER JAMES No, Sista, she can sleep pon floor. Di place chuck-up already. And besides, it might all have chink in dere.

(SISTER JAMES *exits left.* QUEENIE *holds her head in agony and spins round and round as the Etu drums begin. The* CHORUS *of women enters and changes the scenery back to the Prologue setting. The* NURSE *enters, dresses* QUEENIE *in the hospital gown and bandages and leads her back to the hospital bed – that is, on top of the centre coffin.*)

Sequence Three

QUEENIE (*delirious in hospital as in opening prologue*) Ruby, Ruby! Look how mi try, mi try everyting. All weh mi do, a tru oonoo, just fi see oonoo grow up properly! Look how mi tek up wi Bishop and mi work and help him. And what him do? Throw dirty water in mi face. A who yuh tink mi do it for? Mi send yuh a school, yuh go fight, yuh go tief and Government haffi tek yuh and bring disgrace pon mi. What else mi coulda do? Mi do everyting a madda could do. Yuh is di bigger one and before yuh hold up yuh head fi set example to Faithy, look what yuh do. Mi end up a street a walk a beg so mi wouldn't be a burden to oonoo. Sista James so kind fi tek Faithy from she lickle and even offer fi tek yuh when yuh come out a Formitory School. But no. Yuh go live careless life by yuhself and now yuh end up even a sell yuh body. Yuh is a disgrace to mi, but mi cyaan disown yuh cause yuh come offa mi navel string. Look where mi end up, Almshouse! And yuh wouldn't even spare lickle time fi walk come look fi mi. Not even a line yuh would write. All mi know bout yuh is from di remarks weh people haffi mek bout yuh. Only Faithy one come see mi. If anybody did ever tell mi seh mi woulda end up yah so. Oh Ruby, Ruby, Faithy, Faithy, Pearlie, Pearlie, Hopie, Hopie.

CHORUS (*off stage*) Queenie, Pearlie, Hopie. (*Repeat each name like an echo.*) FIRE! HELP!

(*Sound of sirens.* QUEENIE *screams. Blackout.*)

Act II, Scene 1

Scene is set as for Prologue, but the three women are on top of their coffins. QUEENIE *is still bandaged in hospital and delirious. Kumina drumming. Two chorus women who will play* EVA *and* BEGGA *in Act II lead* CHORUS *on from stage left and right dancing Kumina to a frenzy.* QUEENIE *gets increasingly agitated at the Kumina. She screams out, 'NO', and signals the drums to change to her Etu rhythm.*[4] *There is a reprise of* QUEENIE's, PEARLIE's *and* HOPIE's *Etu songs and dances but this time slower and with less energy. The ageing process has begun. Each member of the* CHORUS *whispers women's names at random.* HOPIE, PEARLIE *and* QUEENIE *rise in that order. Each sings and dances her song twice.* QUEENIE *fights the ageing process with an energetic dance, 'Dinki Mini', and the call-and-response song, 'Butler fi di Yard, Fiyah under Yuh'.*[5] *As* QUEENIE, PEARLIE *and* HOPIE *play this game, the* CHORUS *changes the scene to the fenced yard of the Almshouse. The coffins become pieces of log that the women sit on. The* CHORUS, QUEENIE, PEARLIE *and* HOPIE, *become old people in the yard engaged in various activities. Along the length of the yard extends a fence.* HOPIE *is cooking,* QUEENIE *is brewing and drinking coffee,* PEARLIE *is making up her face, and* EVA *leans against the fence smoking a cigarette, lit side inside her mouth, after furtively hiding something in a hole dug under a tree.* ROCKA, *a crippled deaf mute, sits in a corner rocking incessantly, oblivious to the people around her.* BEGGA *moves from one person to the next. She speaks in a nasal, whining tone.*

BEGGA   Hey Eva, Eva what yuh a do! Beg yuh di cigarette butt, nuh? Cho man, gimme.

EVA   Gweh! Cho! All yuh do is come a Almshouse fi beg and pester people, eenh. See't deh, gwan! (*She throws the cigarette butt on the ground.*) Get pon mi nerves now, beg too much.

BEGGA   That is dat why di pickney dem won't help yuh. When yuh get di money from di man all yuh do is buy cigarette and now yuh nah even waan leggo di butt.

EVA   Gweh! Dat's all yuh do inna Almshouse, fass inna people business.

BEGGA   Po!

PEARLIE   You better mind who you taking butts from. You might end up at 'Black Fence'.

BEGGA   A mi yuh a talk to? Every day yuh a powder pon yuh dutty face.

PEARLIE   Go and bathe yourself and get some deodorant for under your arm.

BEGGA   When yuh go a road fi ketch di man dem yuh tell dem fi bathe demselves first?

PEARLIE   I don't take any low type nayga man that you would tek. Only high class men I go with. Not even a Samba would want you.

BEGGA   Yuh tan deh! A di high class man dem have di disease cover up under dem! Hello Queenie, beg yuh lickle a di coffee, nuh man?

QUEENIE   Mi nuh have nothing a give way today. Tomorrow. Mi tired a yuh now. Good God! Cho!

BEGGA   Ssh, tek time talk, nuh. (*Gesturing towards* PEARLIE) She can powder, eenh? Every night she lef yah go a road.

QUEENIE   Move from over mi coffee tea!

BEGGA   Yuh not giving mi di lickle coffee?

QUEENIE   Move! Yuh beg too much. Dem soon poison yuh.

BEGGA   Yuh galang! A poison dem poison yuh, mek yuh ben up so.

EVA   (*to* HOPIE) Hey! A what kind a food yuh have deh?

HOPIE   Lickle season rice.

EVA   Season rice! Gimme a plate, nuh? Lord . . . di arthritis. (*Sits.*)

BEGGA   Hopie, pass lickle food give mi, nuh? Listen, don't leggo di food till yuh get di money!

HOPIE   Wait, Begga. (*She serves* EVA *then* BEGGA.)

BEGGA   Oh, a wha kind a oil in yah?

HOPIE   Coconut oil, di good ole coconut oil.

BEGGA   Weh yuh get coconut oil and yuh nuh have no money?

HOPIE   Eva, Eva one and six yuh fi give mi. One and six.

EVA   A mi yuh a talk to . . . wha happen now?

HOPIE   Yes. One shilling and sixpence fi di season rice.

EVA   One and six! Yuh ever go a restaurant go nyam yet? Yuh nyam a restaurant yet? For when yuh go a restaurant yuh siddung and nyam in peace and when yuh done nyam yuh pay fi di food. And now oonoo hitch up inna Almshouse and want mi fi pay fi food before mi done nyam.

HOPIE   Mi never have no casion fi eat a restaurant. Mi was in mi good Auntie house. Come offa good table. Had no casion fi eat a restaurant. One shilling and sixpence.

BEGGA   Weh di drinks? Pass di drinks!

HOPIE   Only lickle cerassee tea mi have.

BEGGA   Pass it. Yuh have anything fi rub mi knee? Arthritis in deh a kill mi. (*She belches.*)

HOPIE   Ask Eva, she have some winter green.

EVA   (*Grumbles as she takes out kerchief with money out of her bosom. She hides and counts the money.*) After all di damn facetyness. See yuh money yah, eenh.

HOPIE   Eva, is what dis? Dis a old time sixpence. It have no use. It mark 1953, and it no have no use.

EVA   Wha dat? Mek mi see what yuh a talk bout yah!

HOPIE   Ole time sixpence, naw nuh use.

EVA   But mi God, mi give yuh too much. That value ten cents now, shilling. Good God, mi all give yuh tip and yuh a complain. Yuh lucky!

HOPIE   But mi cyaan go spend it out a road fi go buy mi goods.

EVA   Go a bank wid it!

HOPIE   Den mi fi lef yah go chuck a bank fi go change sixpence?

EVA   Den save it! Bury it! Damn renk. Mi cyaan even find di saltfish inna di season rice and give di gal tip too and she a complain . . . Yuh know what . . .

PEARLIE   Disgusting, quarrelling over food cooked in these insanitary condition. Government provide four meals a day and you still not satisfied.

EVA   Yuh nuh know seh di nice nurse dem a tek out di food and linen and carry home a dem yard?

QUEENIE   No sah, not all di nurse dem. Some of the nurse dem are very good people and Supe too, good people.

PEARLIE   Don't tell lies on the nursing staff. Is you same ones must be break the store and take out the food to cook here. Where you can get money to buy goods? I am going to report it to the Superintendent.

HOPIE   Yuh could always tell dem because dem cyaan put mi out, yah. Mi people dem a pay fi mi stay yah. A must be some yuh want.

PEARLIE   I could never eat from you. By the way you have a food handler's permit?

BEGGA   Gweh, Pearl Harbour. When di man dem a dock inna a yuh, yuh ask dem if dem have permit fi dock in deh?

PEARLIE   Just go away, nayga gal.

(BEGGA *moves towards* EVA *who covers her food.*)

EVA   As di gal pass near mi, mi stomach sick. Cyaan nyam no more. (*Puts down food, gets up to move towards* QUEENIE.)

BEGGA   (*Eats* EVA's *left overs.*) Hey, Eva, beg yuh some a yuh wintergreen, nuh?

EVA   Cho! Mi tell oonoo di damn gal can beg! Gimme a chance let mi get lickle coffee tea from Queenie fi belch off di rancid rice off mi stomach. Lawd, yuh nuh hear joke Queenie gal? Di gal Pearlie come and condemn Hopie food fi one and sixpence. Lawd, what a joke on mi old bone! (*Sits.*)

QUEENIE   Yuh waan some a di coffee? Mi have fresh grotto too!

EVA   Yes, gal. Gimme some nuh!

QUEENIE   A sixpence for it.

BEGGA   Get it and gimme some mek mi belch off di gas.

EVA   Mi Lawd! Di beg-beg gal jus a walk an follow up people. She come in like any jeng-jeng fly. Queenie gal, yuh know what gwine happen to her? She is one a dem dat gwine end up bury inna di breadfruit coffin, bury a pauper. But mi nah end up so. Mi save fi-mi money and give di nice nurse fi put up fi mi bury inna di nice coffin wid satin and dem tings and inna mi nice long white frock. (*To* BEGGA) Yuh a live offa taxpayers' money!

BEGGA   Yuh gwan talk. If mi did have money like oonoo, yuh tink mi woulda in yah? Once oonoo inna Almshouse, a Almshouse.

QUEENIE   Eva, Hopie, mi worried. Mi nuh hear from my lickle gal. She always come visit every Sunday or write a letter.

PEARLIE   Your daughter is not a bad looking girl, Queenie!

HOPIE   Nuh fret! It must be sickness. Can be sickness, yuh know. Fi-mi cousin Sissy still a send di four dollar a year to Government fi tek care a me. She neva miss di date!

QUEENIE   Mi a consider dat anybody can end up in yah. Yuh member dat very famous entertainer? A did two a dem, usually sing and act together, and when one dead out a street di odder one end up in yah. Till people start say is a disgrace and Government and dem other people tek him out and tek care a him!

PEARLIE   Yuh mean that little short man, name Bam? Yes, very nice man!

HOPIE   Yes, Bam of Bim and Bam. Very nice. Him could dance, yuh see! And act and use to tell we nice joke. Him did always know di ole time tings dem.

QUEENIE   And him coulda sing! Ah trying to member one him teach mi. Yes! One dat have di mento beat. 'Gal a Who Wash yuh Rice'.

EVA   Yes, but is 'Gal a Who a Trash yuh Rice, Is di Same Ole Yankee Man'.

(*They get up singing and dancing.* ROCKA's *movements increase their intensity. She makes grunting sounds of approval. But suddenly a conflicting beat intrudes.* DREAD 1 *and 2 enter with taped reggae music blasting out of a huge boom box. They stand on the other side of the fence.*)

DREAD 1   (*watching* QUEENIE *dance*) Woah! Hey, fat gal! I man waan deal wid yuh!

(QUEENIE *stops dancing, then the others follow suit.* ROCKA *cowers behind* QUEENIE *and* HOPIE *alternatively as the* DREADS *shift their attention from one to the other.*)

DREAD 2   A dat ben-up gal deh yuh a chat to?

DREAD 1   If I ketch dat, yuh wi see I straighten her up on di odder side.

DREAD 2   Yuh waan check something good? See a professional cross deh! Pearlie! Just go check her. Pearlie, weh yuh a say, sexy? Wha happen? Yuh no waan two rum?

DREAD 1   Whoah, Iya! Red nayga gal! I man no deal wid pork, Iya. A strickly beef I a deal wid!

BEGGA   Gweh! Gweh wid oonoo noise from di tape oonoo tief! Move from di fence. Careless boy, oonoo.

DREAD 2   A who yuh a run from fence? Come move mi! If I ketch yuh tonight yuh see, I wi move yuh! (*Laughs disgustingly.*)

DREAD 1   Bruck it up, star!

BEGGA   Gweh! Di dutty boy dem smell like dawg. Oonoo go tek off crablouse off oonoo mumma back.

DREAD 2   A fi yuh back mi waan get on! (*Laughs.*)

HOPIE   Gwey, all oonoo do is come over di fence a night and bruck di place and tek out di sinting dem and waan rape we off.

DREAD 2   A yuh I waan rape.

DREAD 1   Tief? Tief it yes! Government a waste money pon oonoo, fi feed and tek care a oonoo, when man out yah nuh have roof and nuh even have no water fi drink.

Look pon oonoo! Oonoo have any use to society? Yuh see oonoo, right now oonoo fi sweep off dis land.

HOPIE   Gweh! We pay we taxes and we people dem out deh pay taxes. Inna fi-we days dem would a cat a nine oonoo and heng oonoo up.

BEGGA   Gweh! Inna fi-mi days when mi did young, you tink mi woulda even look pon scavenger like oonoo?

QUEENIE   Wait deh lickle. Oonoo cyaan quarrel wid di young people dem. Yuh must respect oonoo age. If oonoo no respect oonoo age, how di bwoy dem must respect oonoo? Nuh pay dem no mind.

BEGGA   Mek di bwoy dem go way! Dem a tief.

QUEENIE   Member it tek two fi mek a war.

DREAD 2   Eh, bend up gal! I man can deal wid dem!

QUEENIE   And oonoo, yuh cyaan talk to yuh elders so. Oonoo gwan yah! Member seh oonoo have madda and granmadda. Dem could in yah yuh know!

DREAD 2   Who? My madda couldn't end up in there!

DREAD 1   Wha?

QUEENIE   One day oonoo go old too, yuh know, and can end up right yah. Man in yah too, yuh know.

DREAD 2   Who? I man would rather end up dead with mi bucky in mi hand dan come yah!

DREAD 1   Cho! Wha!

QUEENIE   Never mind! Di whole a we a one colour people. We must live good. No bodder wid di war. Walk good.

DREAD 2   Is alright, madda. Yuh alright. But wha! Yuh see dem two deh? We gwine come back fi dem. Blood and fiyah fi oonoo!

DREAD 1   Fiyah!

(*Orange Lane* FIRE VICTIM *enters, carrying grip. She is followed by her* DAUGHTER *who carries a bundle. They try to move past* DREAD 1 *and* DREAD 2 *who block their way.*)

DREAD 1   Hi Auntie! Yuh a go in fi go jine dem too? Gwan and leave di young dawta wid we, nuh?

DREAD 2   Hi, princess. I waan check yuh tonight.

FIRE VICTIM   Move oonoo criminal self! Is mi one daughter oonoo waan come mash up.

(DREAD 1 *and* DREAD 2 *let them past, then exit, flinging curses at the women as they go and turning up the volume on their music.*)

FIRE VICTIM (*to* DAUGHTER *who looks longingly at the young men*) Come on, come on. If anybody did ever tell mi dat yuh father would dead leave mi, I . . . come on!

DAUGHTER Den a weh we a go, Mama?

FIRE VICTIM Over Almshouse.

DAUGHTER Almshouse, Mama? No, mi nah go deh.

FIRE VICTIM Is not in deh exactly, is on di odder side, but it might as well be in deh. If anybody ever tell mi dat after all di years mi woulda come to dis, Lord!

(*They enter the Almshouse yard.*)

DAUGHTER Den we a go live wid dem yah people, Mama? (*Points to* ROCKA) Look pon dat one, how she nasty-nasty wid food paste all over her face.

FIRE VICTIM Come on! Since dem burn we out in Orange Lane and di Government mek up di lickle shack dem in yah, mi haffi go. Come on! If anybody did ever tell mi seh mi woulda ever come to dis after mi wuk so hard . . .

DAUGHTER (*Recoils at the sound of* BEGGA *belching.*) No, Mama, no! Mi nuh want to go. Listen to dat one!

FIRE VICTIM Is alright. Is gas she have. She old, she cyaan help it. Come on!

QUEENIE Hey, Lady! Yuh is one a dem people dem burn out in di fire inna Orange Lane downtown?

FIRE VICTIM Yes, maam.

QUEENIE And is yuh daughter dat? Nice lickle gal. Yuh waan some coffee tea and grotto?

DAUGHTER No Mama. Nah tek nothing fi eat from dem. Look pon all di fly round dem. Come, Mama.

FIRE VICTIM Come. Hold di lickle bundle good. Dem desperate. Dem wi tief it weh.

DAUGHTER (*bumps into* PEARLIE) Mama, look pon she! She live in here too?

PEARLIE Are you blind? Look where you're going. Move yourself, girl!

FIRE VICTIM You see, all colour end up in yah, even mulatto. But nuh scorn dem. Yuh madda will get old and might end up in here. Especially if yuh poor, is either yuh dead young or get old and end up like dem.

DAUGHTER Mama, mi nah end up so! And I promise that when I grow up, I will get education and a good job and mind you. You can't end up in here.

FIRE VICTIM Yes, mi chile, yes. Come!

DAUGHTER Den Mama, mi cyaan let mi friend dem know mi live in yah.

FIRE VICTIM Most of dem get burn out too and in yah already. So come on!

(*They exit,* DAUGHTER *looking fearfully over her shoulder.*)

QUEENIE Bwoy, Hopie! Di people dem nowadays wicked. Dem a burn out man, woman and even pickney!

HOPIE Pressure, Queenie, pressure.

QUEENIE Is another Middle Passage and now all a we a travel again inna di same boat![6]

(*Lights cross fade as women softly sing 'Gal a Who a Thrash yuh Rice' and change the set. Coffins now become three beds belonging to* QUEENIE, PEARLIE *and* HOPIE, *inside the dormitory style bedroom of the Almshouse.* EVA, BEGGA *and* ROCKA *share the room, their beds are on the floor beside the three coffins which are lined up diagonally upstage left to downstage right.*)

Act II, Scene 2

In the dormitory. QUEENIE *sits on her bed and plaits* HOPIE's *hair.* HOPIE *starts to cry.*

QUEENIE Hopie, wha do yuh? A cry yuh a cry?

HOPIE Lawd, Queenie! Mi just a consider mi young days when mi up at Auntie Vantie house and di young man deh use to come look fi mi, yuh know. Mi did love him but mi couldn't let him know. Mi coulda married him, yuh know. And now di odder day when mi see di young boy dem a di gate, it just put mi in mind a mi young days and it just mek mi feel so downhearted cause mi shouldn't be in dis yah place at all. Yuh see when yuh depend pon man dem just let yuh down. Mi coulda mek life inna Foreign by now, but Sissy never keep her promise.

BEGGA (*Enters and climbs into her bed.*) Hopie, what time? Got di time? Hey, Hopie! Queenie!

HOPIE Yuh nuh hear fi shut up yuh mout when big people a talk?

QUEENIE But Hopie, dat pass and gawn long

time. Yuh cyaan tink pon it too much. Just mek it gwan. Just tink about now and di future. Yuh haffi help yuhself now. Mi know yuh a do lickle bit fi help yuhself but yuh a give way too much. Look how yuh give way yuh life and labour to yuh Auntie and her family and end up in yah now. Yuh a try help yuhself wid di lickle season rice but yuh waan give it way to even nurse and Supe who nah need it.

HOPIE Yuh right, yuh know.

EVA (*enters*) Wha happen deh, Queenie gal? And Hopie? A wha oonoo a chat so late inna night yah?

HOPIE Yuh know we always haffi exchange lickle thoughts before we go sleep. (*As the conversation continues she finishes preparing for bed and crawls under the covers.*)

EVA Always a chat chat chat. And di gal Hopie, him can chat bout fi-him ole time days, yuh see!

BEGGA Mi friend, yuh come.

EVA Cho! Friend? A who and yuh friend, gal?

BEGGA Cyaan sleep, man. Di chink dem a bite mi.

EVA But yuh right fi cyaan sleep. Yuh go a bathroom go bathe from night yet? Look how yuh dutty and tan!

BEGGA When dem go out a nighttime and ketch dem man and carry in all kind a louse and insect come bathe it off inna di bathroom, yuh expect mi fi bathe in deh? Dats why mi sleep same way.

EVA Dats why di chink dem a bite yuh. Mi mek sure mi carry mi Jays and Dettol and clean the bathroom before I bathe.

BEGGA Every day yuh a cream and powder up. What happen? By now yuh should have a nice man fi tek care a yuh out a road and tek yuh out yah.

EVA How yuh know mi nuh did have one and didn't waan him? Mi work and save mi money and buy good things fi look after mi body. (*Gets into bed.*)

BEGGA Den weh yuh a do wid it?

EVA Yuh too damn fass. Das why yuh end up in yah a suffer.

BEGGA Yuh have any bambi? Mi hungry.

EVA Yuh nyam and beg too much das why . . .

BEGGA (*Rummages through bags and behind beds.*) Den weh yuh waan mi do? Mi nuh have nothing, mi haffi walk and beg? Yuh waan mi go tief? (*Gets into bed.*)

(NURSE *guides in* ROCKA *in clean nightshirt.* ROCKA *takes up her usual position, rocking back and forth.*)

BEGGA Rocka, yuh alright?

EVA What happen, Rocka gal? My God! Even Rocka cleaner dan yuh cause nurse bathe her and fix her up so she can sleep comfortable and yuh dutty and nasty. Down to cow foot cleaner than fi-yuh. No wonder when yuh go dung a man ward, dem run yuh. Mi nuh know why dem put mi next to yuh. Mi cyaan even sleep in peace.

BEGGA (*looking at her feet*) Dem prettier than fi-yuh. Mi nuh inna no argument cause a Almshouse yuh deh, like mi.

(ROCKA *finds a paper bag discarded by* BEGGA *containing leftover food and starts to eat with her hands, smearing the food on her face and clothing.*)

QUEENIE Alright, mek we have lickle peace. We mustn't put down one another. We all in dis together. (*Noticing* ROCKA) Rocka, wha yuh a do? Look how yuh do yuh face. Di milo and banana all inna yuh nose! (*Fusses around, trying to clean up* ROCKA.)

EVA Queenie gal, yuh betta ask di beggy-beggy gal fi come lick it off Rocka's face. Yuh lucky she never nyam it off before!

QUEENIE Hopie, Hopie, yuh a sleep?

HOPIE Mmmm.

QUEENIE Mi have sinting fi tell yuh. Mi get a letta toady from mi dawta, at last. Di one Faithy. She say she a come fi mi. She get one good work and soon married.

HOPIE Den a how Hopie a go manage when yuh gawn?

QUEENIE Mi nuh decide mi mind yet because she young and mi no waan be any burden to her, and later mi nuh waan no son-in-law come tek liberty wid mi. But if mi go, mi promise fi come back regular come look fi yuh.

HOPIE No, Queenie. When yuh go live inna big house chack inna di hills, dem nuh gwine waan yuh fi down come look fi we.

QUEENIE Mi mek yuh a promise, and a promise is a promise.

(PEARLIE *enters, drinking. Stumbles into furniture.*)

PEARLIE (*hiccupping*) Ssh! Ssh!

HOPIE What dat a gwan deh, Queenie?

QUEENIE   A Pearlie dis a come in! Pearlie, Ah waan talk to yuh. Come tek yuh time and sit down. Pearlie, why yuh so wicked, wicked to yuhself? Yuh is a sick woman. A weh yuh a come from dis hours a di morning wid di rum flask inna yuh hand and di smell a di man dem pon yuh? Yuh sick. Yuh just a come out a hospital. And yuh still a roam di streets inna di night cold.

PEARLIE   Dis keep mi warm. Is mi medicine.

QUEENIE   White rum cyaan betta di consumption. It wi just bun out yuh liver. Gimme!

PEARLIE   No man! It give mi di strength to go on. Medicine.

QUEENIE   Gimme.

PEARLIE   Go to yuh bed and leave mi alone. Mi better off than yuh cause I get what I want. Yuh get what yuh want? I go and wet my thirst.

QUEENIE   (Takes rum from PEARLIE.) Give mi di rum. Tomorrow I will beat ginger and pimento and put in it, den yuh have medicine. Yuh just tek it rub yuh chest. Yuh no haffi drink it.

PEARLIE   No, give mi! (Starts sobbing.)

QUEENIE   Pearlie, listen! Why yuh do dis to yuhself? Respect yuhself, yuh is woman. Tek care of yuh body. Don't mek di man dem batta yuh out. Come to yuh sense. Yuh not getting any younger, yuh nuh no spring chicken. Tink of yuh daughter, as much as yuh nuh know her. How you would feel if she see yuh like dis? She must be big shot out deh. She might all even pass yuh a street and see yuh so and yuh nuh know!

PEARLIE   (hitting her bed in anger) God, stop it man! I don't want to hear anymore!

QUEENIE   Face di truth. Mi is yuh friend. If mi cyaan say it a who can? Respect yuh age. Gwan lickle better.

PEARLIE   (weeping) Queenie, yuh nuh understand. Yuh nuh know what mi go through. Mi a fi do dese tings fi blot out what in mi mind. Sometime when mi sit down and consider how fi-mi life turn out because of one little mistake. Yuh nuh understand at all.

QUEENIE   Mi understand.

PEARLIE   And mi so tired. Mi tired, yuh know.

QUEENIE   Yes, yes, mi know! Try get some rest. Lie down.

PEARLIE   (Coughs loudly.) Oh, mi stomach, mi throat. It's choking me. One lickle rum and it wi ease.

BEGGA   Dem come wid dem bad disease. Run her out! Gimme some a di rum.

HOPIE   Go back to sleep. Pearlie tired . . . we all tired!

PEARLIE   Queenie, one lickle drop. Mi stomach . . . one lickle drink.

QUEENIE   Is alright, Pearlie. Go to sleep, get some rest.

PEARLIE   Mi stomach. (Coughing) Nurse!

QUEENIE   Sleep. Pearlie, sleep. No nurse nuh deh yah now!

(As PEARLIE coughs, EVA asleep with cigarette, splutters. Cigarette drops out of her mouth. BEGGA takes up butt. Fade out. Fade up on ROCKA who smells smoke and tries to wake BEGGA, EVA and HOPIE. QUEENIE wakes, smells fire, sounds alarm and gets out ROCKA. EVA and BEGGA stumble out but faint at door. QUEENIE returns and gets them out, but on coming back can't get into the ward. HOPIE and PEARLIE wake.)

HOPIE   Queenie, Queenie! Yes, Cousin Sissy, yuh come at last. Ah coming. Yes, Auntie Vantie, Ah coming. (Curls up in corner as she dies.)

QUEENIE   (being held back by others) Hopie, Pearlie . . . Dem still in deh! Pearlie, see mi hand yah. Hold on!

PEARLIE   No, leave mi. Gwan. Dis solve all my problem. (Dies, screaming.)

(Drums. Haitian Death March – three times or as long as it takes for CHORUS to change quickly. CHORUS enters, singing. They carry on burial clothes for PEARLIE and HOPIE. As they sing they lay out the dead women, and anoint and dress them. Other CHORUS members rearrange the coffins into a cross, like in the prologue. When this is done, CHORUS members lift PEARLIE and HOPIE above their heads and do a slow death march as they take them and lay them on top of their coffins.)

CHORUS
    Sleep on Pearlie, sleep on and take your rest
    Lay down your head upon your dear friend's breasts
    We love you but your time has come to rest
    Good night, Goodnight, Goodbye.

(*Repeat for* HOPIE. *The* CHORUS *of women take a last loving look at* PEARLIE *and* HOPIE *and exit singing and swaying. Lights, drumming and singing slowly fade to blackout.*)

Act II, Scene 3

Office of the Investigative Commission. Haitian Death March drums in the background. QUEENIE's *centre coffin becomes the witness chair. A follow spot or baby spot lights the seat.*

VOICE (*off stage from the audience*) Next.

BEGGA (*enters*) Eveling, suh. Not quite so bad, tenk God suh! Mi name Adassa Wright, suh. Tenk God mi never bun up inna di fire! Haffi tenk Queenie most. A she save we, carry we, mi and mi friend Eva, under di cotton tree. Good people, Queenie, always a help. Neva had time fi save her two friend. Mi sick wid arthritis inna mi knee, can hardly walk. Ketch up cold in deh from when mi use to scrub floor for dis woman for years. She let mi go when mi couldn't move so fast. Mi get lickle factory work but dem fire mi. Couldn't pay di rent so di land missis throw mi out. Mi three pickney left long time fi look life fi demself. Mi couldn't help dem. Nuh know where dem puppa deh. Dem have pickney fi demselves and cyaan look after dem much less look bout mi. But mi use to pay insurance and tax fi di short time at di factory, so mi suppose to come yah and get care. Better mi come yah dan walk up and down pon di streets and give worries. We use to lef out yah but Queenie encourage we fi start lickle sinting fi weself. But di place run dung . . . Sometime di ole dutty bwoy dem bruck in. Di place under no rule. Coulda all dem bwoy start di fire, but nuh bodder say mi say, yuh hear, suh. Finish already suh. Beg yuh a fifty cent, nuh suh, and a cigarette. God bless yuh, suh. Yuh must come back and visit we, yuh hear, suh.

VOICE (*off stage*) Next.

EVA (*enters*) Mi name Eva Hamilton. Say wha? Di fire? Tell yuh di truth mi is a women when mi put down fi-mi head at night mi nuh hear one damn ting till morning. Dem have one gal call Begga beside mi. A she wake mi up inna night. Say wha? If mi did a sleep so sound, how mi must know how fire start? Mek mi tell yuh sinting, suh, a one set a people mi know ketch fire inna di yard. Hopie a one. Every minute she a cook and no out di fire properly, yuh know. And di big gal Queenie. A mi friend but every day she a boil coffee tea. And di one Begga, she beg di cigarette butt. And so fass as she see yuh light anodder one, she dash way di ole one careless. So di place coulda burn all way. Mi, mek me tell yuh sinting. Mi nuh have no chance fi dash way butt careless, cause Begga is always dere to ketch dem. So wha yuh waan say? A mi dat cause di fire? Mi work hard, up pon a hill dat name after di rock rock dem . . . yes same place, Stony Hill. For years, from mi was a lickle gal from country . . . look after di whole family . . . grow up all di pickney and di pickney dem pickney. Mi neva even get a chance fi see man, much less fi have pickney fi miself. Say wha? Yes, dem pay mi lickle sinting. Mi save every penny. Mi dear suh, yuh haffi save sinting fi death. Yuh cyaan just dead and lef everything pon people so. Mi must bury good. Mi no waan bury like Pearlie and Hopie in di raw pauper coffin like a dawg. Say wha, suh? Dat's all? . . . Yes, mi did waan go long time . . .

(*Grumbles as she exits.*)

VOICE (*off stage*) Next.

QUEENIE (*enters*) Howdie do, suh? A mi name Elizabeth McQueen. Dem call mi Queenie. Was a terrible sight, suh. Di fire, di smoke, di flame, di bawling. I did almost tun fool, suh, but mi never panic too much. Only when mi couldn't reach mi two friend. Dem building shoulda condemn long time, so-so old board. Is a lucky ting di fire never down weh di deformed pickney dem deh. Some a dem cyaan even open dem mouth, much less fi bawl fi help. Special Hospital School should build fi dem. Dem parents dash dem way when dem born wrong-shape. But dem is human being and we have a duty fi tek care a dem. Yes suh, as mi was saying, if yuh ever see how we chuck-up, chuck-up. About seven hundred and odd a we inna di whole Almshouse, yuh know, and two hundred and whole heap did inna di ward dat ketch fire. All now dem nuh know how much a we get way. Some a di nurse dem try but what dem can do? Dem only have two hand. And Supe, too, good people. Him come look fi mi when mi did inna hospital. Him tek lickle time and bring milo and

175

milk fi mi. Mi hear seh dem a go build a new Almshouse fi we, inna di hill or bush. We nuh waan dat. We waan it fi build back right yah so, near to where we people can get vehicle fi come visit we, if is only once a year. Dem must build it properly, with good gates and guard to check who a come and go. And *ask we* what we want. We old but we no fool-fool. Build decent bathroom and toilet like what oonoo have inna oonoo house. Make Public Service wire di place properly and come check it regular. Could even have we own electrician. Whole heap a bad wire in yah dat can cause fire. Mek space fi we plant and do lickle cultivating. We old but we active and waan occupation. Give we materials and we wi mek tings and sell fi help tek care a we, instead a just having we siddung so. Some a we have di time and patience fi teach di deformed pickney dem in yah dat dem give up on, say dem a imbecile. We teach dem fi talk and do tings fi demselves. And organise lickle cultural tings fi we. Sometimes we organise we self and sing and dance. Dem must arrange trips and tek we on outings sometimes. No carry we go a no bush or hill where yuh cyaan see we, so oonoo can have a free conscience. We waan live! Everybody haffi get old but member, di old have the key to di future cause we have di secrets of di past.

(QUEENIE *freezes. Etu drumming.* CHORUS *enters. A member brings white rum to* QUEENIE. *She sprinkles coffins and sprays people as they circle around her.* PEARLIE *and* HOPIE *rise and join* QUEENIE *on her coffin. They dance to the table and acknowledge the ancestors in dance.* CHORUS *dances round and acknowledges drummers,* HOPIE, PEARLIE *and* QUEENIE *last. All celebrate life as they reprise Etu sequences. Drummers take centre stage. Lights slowly fade to black.*)

Notes

1   The shawling in the original ritual occurs when the representative of each family is invited into the circle by the Queen; she acknowledges the person by placing the shawl around their neck, holds them with one hand on their chest and the other supporting their back, and bends them backwards as when an adult is being baptized in the river.

2   Pocomania is a religious practice mixing Christian fundamentalism with some African religious customs. The leader is usually a male, called 'Bishop' or 'Shepherd'. The 'Mother' of the Shepherd's 'flock' is usually a respected woman and, since women cannot be Shepherds, she is the Shepherd's assistant. The word 'Pocomania' has Spanish roots and, literally translated, means 'little madness'.

3   Trumping is a particular sound and movement that indicates getting into the spirit; it is part of the singing and dancing and sometimes indicates the beginning of possession by the spirits.

4   Kumina is a religious ceremony found among people of Congo origin, and especially associated with eastern Jamaica. Rites are held to celebrate birth, death or any other significant occasion. They are accompanied by drumming, possession, dancing, animal sacrifice and speech in 'country', a ritual language containing many Congo-based words. Kumina invites dead ancestors to possess the participants, whereas Etu invites ancestors to come and watch and then carry the spirits of the newly departed over, so that is why this apparent dream is disturbing to Queenie.

5   'Dinki Mini' is a very energetic dance done with the knees bent together, and one foot pivoting back and forth or swinging the dancer around in circles. It is a social, as opposed to a ritual or religious dance, and each dancer tries to outdo the others. The song, 'Butler in di Yard', is a call-and-response song. There is an underlying sexuality to the dance and words.

6   'Middle Passage' is a reference to the slave trade and the sea journey between West Africa and the West Indies.

Glossary

This glossary contains Jamaican words and English words with non-standard usages as they appear in the text. For further information, see F.G. Cassidy and R.B. Le Page (eds) (1967) *Dictionary of Jamaican English*, London: Cambridge University Press.

a   is, be, am, are, it is, there are, to, of, in, at

again   anymore, any longer

ah   I

anyting anything
anyweh anywhere
beg yuh please, please give
ben been
bisi the Kola nut and the tree bearing it
bodder bother
bodderation a vexation or annoyance, a person or thing that annoys
bruck break
bun burn
business bother, take interest in, usually used with negative 'me no business'
buss burst
bwoy boy
calabash the shell of a gourd used as a vessel
carry give take along and give
cerassee tea bush
chack separately
check pass by, contact, indicate sexual interest in another
chile child
chink bed bug
cho interjection of anger, impatience, disappointment
chuck-up full up
cyaan can't
dah that, that one, at, in, on to; dah + verb is equivalent to 'to be' + present participle (e.g. me dah go – I am going)
dan than
das that is, that's
dat that
dawg dog
dawta daughter, woman
deh there
deh pon to be about
dem them, also used to indicate plural (e.g. di key dem – the keys)
den then
dere there
dese these
di the
dis this
Dreads members of a religious group which takes Ras Tafari, Haile Selassie, the former Emperor of Ethiopia, as a deity; Rastas or Dreads avow a desire to return to Africa physically or spiritually by establishing an African society where they live
dung down
dutty dirty
facety rude, impertinent
fass interfering, meddlesome, quick to intrude in others' business

fi for, to
fi-her hers
fi-him his or hers
fi-we ours
fi-yah yours
foo-foo (or fufu) starch food boiled and pounded; it may be eaten so, or further prepared and cooked
foreign abroad
galang go along
gawn gone
grow yuh bring you up
gweh go away
gwine going to
haffi have to
hase haste
heng hung
him his, her, he, she
jeng-jeng ragged, in tatters
ketch catch
lef leave, left
leggo let go
lickle little
madda mother
mash-up beat, break, smash, destroy
mass mister, master
mek make
member remember
mento a dance; a two-step
mi I, me, my
mine mind
mout mouth
nah (or nuh) not
nayga negro, derogatory term implying stupidity
no not, an, is, are not, please, won't you
notten nothing, anything
nyam eat
odder other
offa off of
oonoo you (plural)
out a out of
pickney child
pon at, upon, on
quatty a penny ha'penny
renk having an offensive smell
run chase; to chase out
sah sir
seh say, that
sen send
siddung sit down
sinting something
so thus, emphasises adverb of places, e.g. deh-so, yah-so
tan stand, to be in a specified state
tek take

tenk thank
tief thief
tink think
trace curse, quarrel
tru because, because of, since
tun turn
waan want
wah (or wha) what

way away
weh which, what, whatever, where
wi will
wid with
wuk work
yah here
yah so here
yuh you, yours

9 Girish Karnad

Hayavadana
India

Introduction

My generation was the first to come of age after India became independent of British rule. It therefore had to face a situation in which tensions implicit until then had come out in the open and demanded to be resolved without apologia or self-justification: tensions between the cultural past of the country and its colonial past, between the attractions of Western modes of thought and our own traditions, and finally between the various visions of the future that opened up once the common cause of political freedom was achieved. This is the historical context that gives rise to my plays and those of my contemporaries.

(Karnad 1995a: 3)

This observation by Girish Karnad, born in 1938 and considered to be one of India's foremost playwrights, needs to be understood in the context of modern Indian drama as it emerged in the nineteenth century. From this period until well into the twentieth century, most plays staged in Indian cities were largely European in inspiration, both structurally and thematically. India's colonial past had masked its indigenous performance traditions to the extent that Karnad, who had been a Rhodes Scholar at Oxford University in the early 1960s, had overlooked his cultural roots. When looking for a dramatic tradition that he could call his own, he found that 'there was nothing to refer to: the natak companies and yakshagana seemed to belong to another world altogether' (Karnad 1989: 334). Yet, as his reference to these forms indicates, India has its own rich and highly theorised theatrical tradition, which dates back some two thousand years. Although the pan-Indian classical period of Sanskrit drama declined around AD 700, its influence lived

on in the various regional folk theatre traditions that replaced it across the subcontinent. It was to this shared heritage of rural folk theatre, which 'reveals a startling unity of conception' in spite of its many regional and linguistic differences (Juneja 1980: 38), that theatre practitioners returned in post-independent India. If, as Karnad has claimed, the basic concern of his country's theatre 'has been to try to define its "Indianness"' (Karnad 1995a: 17), then folk theatre came to be seen as the vehicle through which a distinctively Indian performance idiom might be developed.

Karnad's early dramatic works *Yayati* (1961), from a tale from the *Mahabharata*, and *Tughlaq* (1964), based on the life of the fourteenth-century Sultan of Delhi, explore Indian history and mythology, refashioning their source material in ways that pose complex political and philosophical questions for a modern audience. *Hayavadana* (1972) follows folk theatre conventions more closely than these earlier plays by adopting, as its specific performative model, Yakshagana, the rural theatre form associated with southern Karnataka, Karnad's birthplace. Yakshagana's open-air performances combine music, dance and improvised dialogue, and take place under the patronage of temple authorities. Karnad's use of this dynamic theatrical form in *Hayavadana*, which won the Natya Sangh Award in 1971, was widely seen by critics as a seminal development that marked the beginning of contemporary Indian theatre's 'encounter with tradition' (Awasthi 1989: 49).

Karnad has continued his engagement with indigenous traditions in plays such as *Nāga-Mandala: Play with a Cobra* (1988), which combines two Kannada folktales in an examination of marital disharmony, and *Agni Mattu Male* (*The Fire and the Rain*) (1995), based on another *Mahabharata* legend. He was the winner of the Jnanapith Award in 1998 for an outstanding contribution to Indian literature, and has had a multifaceted career including work in the United States and England, where he is currently director of the Nehru Centre, the cultural wing of the Indian High Commission in London. Karnad is also known for his significant achievements in film, as an actor, director and screenwriter, which have won him several national awards; nevertheless, he thinks of himself as essentially a playwright. This may be related to his youthful fascination for the Natak companies, strolling groups of performers who would pass through his small town: 'I loved going to see them and the magic has stayed with me' (Karnad 1995b: 360).

Hayavadana combines traditional Indian and contemporary Western influences, at the level of both form and content, around a philosophical question that has dominated both Western and Indian philosophy: whether the essence/identity of an individual is derived from the head or the body. Although the play is based on a story from a collection of Sanskrit tales, the *Kathasaritsagara*, Karnad explicitly draws on Thomas Mann's 1957 version, 'The Transposed Heads'. *Hayavadana* opens with the Ganesha Puja, invocatory rituals to Ganesha, the god who ensures completion of any endeavour. According to mythology, Ganesha, who has the body of a human being and the head of an elephant, was accidentally beheaded by his father, Shiva. Since his original head could not be found, an elephant's head was substituted in its place. The Ganesha Puja, which are found in both classical and folk drama, not only establish a link with traditional theatre but also anticipate and complicate the play's thematic exploration of the human search for wholeness.

The Bhagavata, who undertakes the opening ritual, is also integral to Yakshagana performances. In *Hayavadana*, he fulfils the multifunctional role of stage manager, musical director and narrator, as he would in both classical theatre and Yakshagana. He introduces the characters and comments on the action, while mediating between the audience and the fictional characters. He also points to the paradox of Ganesha, 'the Lord and Master of Success and Perfection', 'who seems the embodiment of imperfection, of

incompleteness', reminding us that the nature of completeness is a mystery that 'no mere mortal can comprehend'. The entrance of the character of Hayavadana, a word that simply means 'the one with a horse's head', introduces the sub-plot, which frames and intensifies the main plot. Karnad reveals that he invented the story of Hayavadana, who wants to lose his horse's head and become fully human, because he had 'always felt tremendous fascination for Shakespeare's sub-plots – how he tells us the same story twice, from two different points of view' (quoted in Dhanavel 1993: 118). *Hayavadana*'s thematic concerns are thus dramatised on a broad spectrum from the animal, through the human, to the divine.

During Hayavadana's search for completion, the story of Devadatta, the man of the intellect, and Kapila, the man of the body, is played out. These close friends both fall in love with Padmini, who becomes Devadatta's wife though she is also attracted to the handsome Kapila. Jealousy and suspicion between the men soon lead to their double suicide by chopping off their own heads in a scene that is more comic than tragic. At the end of Act I, the pregnant Padmini, who is assisted in bringing the two back to life by the goddess Kali, puts the wrong head on each body, thus raising the dilemma of who is her husband and the father of her child. The Bhagavata invites his audience to consider this dilemma during the interval. At the beginning of Act II, we discover that the three had gone to visit a rishi, or holy man, who resolved the issue, deciding that the person with Devadatta's head is Padmini's husband. Mann's version of the tale ridicules this artificial divide between head and body, found in Indian and Western philosophy alike, by taking such a solution to its logical conclusion: each of the bodies gradually transforms to match the head to which it is attached. The rishi's pronouncement is revealed as a self-enclosed circle of logic that serves to re-establish the separation between mind and body, and Padmini, who thought she had the best of both worlds, is disappointed. The synthesis she desired is made impossible by the very logic that enabled it.

Just as *Hayavadana* provides an ironic commentary on the philosophical model that the story draws upon, it also ironises the theatrical devices used to tell such stories. The 'half-curtain', for instance, is a standard Yakshagana device for prolonging the entrance of new characters who will be revealed in all their glory. This contrasts with European theatre, where the curtain typically acts as a screen between the world of illusion and that of the audience. Karnad both utilises and simultaneously subverts the conventions he invokes, producing almost the opposite theatrical effect. At the start of the play, instead of revealing Hayavadana in all his splendour, the half-curtain becomes a prop for him to duck behind to hide his humiliating situation. Similarly, the terrifying revelation of the goddess Kali with her mouth opened wide is anti-climactic once the audience realises she was merely yawning.

Notwithstanding this strong folk influence, Karnad asserts that the idea for *Hayavadana* 'started crystallizing in [his] head right in the middle of an argument with B.V. Karanth . . . about the meaning of masks in Indian theatre and theatre's relationship to music' (Karnad 1995a: 12). Masks, not traditionally used in Yakshagana, which usually relies on elaborate make-up, enable a more complex exploration of the play's themes about the nature of selfhood. The masks help to dramatise and problematise the logic of the narrative and the primacy it gives the head over the body. Although they are devices that enable the required head-swap, the masks become meaningful only in relation to specific bodies. The play relies on bodies, and all they signify, to make its point, revealing the impossibility of disassociating heads from bodies; the masks, and the heads they represent, cannot encompass on their own what it means to be human.

The two doll characters represent *Hayavadana*'s most marked deviation from traditional Indian theatre. Karnad explains their specific purpose:

In the first half, the Devadatta–Kapila– Padmini story goes on without interruptions . . . In the second half the story is continually interrupted by the dolls [and] the songs and the Bhagavata interferes in the action, talks to the characters, comments on their mental state. This is done merely to bring out the disintegrated state of the three people's lives. In the first half everything is neat and clear, but in the second I wanted to

create the impression of a reflection in a broken mirror – all fragmented, repetitious, out-of-focus, all bits and pieces.

(quoted in Banfield 1996: 149)

The dolls, with their ability to see Padmini's subconscious longings and dreams, describe things that cannot be represented visually. Their commentary provides psychological depth as well as extending the play's inquiry into the paradoxical nature of humanity. Such anti-naturalist techniques work against any attempt to uphold the theatrical illusion so common in modern European theatre. This links Karnad's work to that of Brecht, whose rejection of psychological realism and emotional identification sensitised Karnad and his contemporaries 'to the potentialities of nonnaturalistic techniques available in [their] own theatre' (Karnad 1995a: 15).

Given that *Hayavadana* revolves around the question of synthesis, it is fitting that the two plots merge at the end of the play. The boy who cannot speak or laugh turns out to be Padmini's child. His inability to interact with humans and his refusal to be separated from his dolls suggest that he lacks the human wholeness Padmini desired for him. Hayavadana returns, but following the premise of the main plot, he is a complete horse, not a complete human being. Yet, his transformation also subtly subverts the play's logic because it is the animal in him that ultimately triumphs over the human. Significantly, Hayavadana is trying to shed his last vestige of humanity, the ability to speak, by singing the national anthem which he believes is guaranteed to ruin a voice. The spectacle of a singing horse provokes the boy to drop the dolls, clap his hands and laugh, which in turn enables Hayavadana to lose his voice. It seems as if Hayavadana, who was neither horse nor man, and the child, who was neither Kapila's nor Devadatta's, are able to perceive in each other their own incompleteness, a mutual recognition that paradoxically completes them. The play as a whole suggests that it is through this ability to acknowledge human insufficiency that Indian societies might forge a sense of nationhood, founded not in philosophical models that dissect human identity, nor in empty gestures of unity such as the singing of national anthems, but in the recognition and integration of differences.

181

Performance history

Hayavadana was written in Girish Karnad's native tongue, Kannada, and published in 1971. In the following year, its Kannada premiere in Bangalore, directed by B.V. Karanth, was followed by a Bombay production in Hindi and a Madras production in English. The play was performed under the name *Divided Together* for a New York season in 1993, directed by Erin B. Mee. It has also played in London as well as at the Deutsches Nationaltheater, Weimar.

Select bibliography

Awasthi, S. (1989) '"Theatre of roots": encounter with tradition', *Drama Review* 33, 4: 48–69.

Babu, M.S. (1997) *Indian Drama Today: A Study in the Theme of Cultural Deformity*, New Delhi: Prestige, 82–99.

Balme, C. (1999) 'Indian drama in English: transcreation and the indigenous performance tradition', in H. Gilbert (ed.) *(Post)Colonial Stages: Critical and Creative Views on Drama, Theatre and Performance*, Hebden Bridge, UK: Dangaroo, 146–60.

Banfield, C. (1996) 'Girish Karnad and an Indian theatre of roots', in B. Crow and C. Banfield, *An Introduction to Post-colonial Theatre*, New York: Cambridge University Press, 136–60.

Chari, A.J. (1995–6) 'Girish Karnad's *Hayavadana* and *Nāgamandala*: a study in postcolonial dialectics', *Commonwealth Review* 7, 2: 148–53.

Dhanavel, P. (1993) 'The romance of influence: a Bloomian perspective on Girish Karnad's *Hayavadana*', *Indian Journal of American Studies* 23, 1: 118–20.

Juneja, R. (1980) 'Two modern Indian dramatists in search of tradition', *South Asian Review* 4, 1: 37–45.

Karnad, G. (1989) 'Theatre in India', *Daedalus* 118, 4: 331–52.

—— (1995a) *Three Plays: Nāga-Mandala, Hayavadana, Tughlaq*, Delhi: Oxford University Press.

—— (1995b) 'Performance, meaning, and the materials of modern Indian theatre', interview by A. Dharwadker, *New Theatre Quarterly* 11, 44: 355–70.

Raykar, S.S. (1990) 'The development of Girish Karnad as a dramatist: *Hayavadana*', in S. Pandey and F. Taraporewala (eds) *Contemporary Indian Drama*, Delhi: Prestige, 46–63.

Shrotri, S. and Majan, M.M. (1975–6) 'Karnad's *Hayavadana* and Mann's "Transposed Heads": a comparison', *Journal of the School of Languages* 3, 2: 78–84.

Sinhá, A.K. (1994) 'Girish Karnad: thematic concerns and technical features', in S. Pandey and F. Barua (eds) *New Directions in Indian Drama*, Delhi: Prestige, 104–23.

Hayavadana

Girish Karnad

Characters

BHAGAVATA
ACTOR 1
HAYAVADANA
DEVADATTA
KAPILA
PADMINI
DOLL 1
DOLL 2
KALI
CHILD
ACTOR 2
(Actors 1 and 2 may also play Kapila and Devadatta.)

Production note

In translating this play, I have not tried to be consistent while rendering the songs into English. Some have been put in a loose verse form while, for others, only a straightforward prose version has been given.

Setting

The stage is empty except for a chair, kept centre-stage, and a table on stage right – or at the back – on which the BHAGAVATA and the musicians sit.

Act I

At the beginning of the performance, a mask of Ganesha is brought on stage and kept on the chair. Pooja is done. The BHAGAVATA *sings verses in praise of Ganesha, accompanied by his musicians. Then the mask is taken away.*

O Elephant-headed Herambha
Whose flag is victory
And who shines like a thousand suns,
O husband of Riddhi and Siddhi,
Seated on a mouse and decorated with a
 snake,

O single-tusked destroyer of
 incompleteness,
We pay homage to you and start our play.

BHAGAVATA May Vighneshwara, the destroyer of obstacles, who removes all hurdles and crowns all endeavours with success, bless our performance now. How indeed can one hope to describe his glory in our poor, disabled words? An elephant's head on a human body, a broken tusk and a cracked belly – whichever way you look at him he seems the embodiment of imperfection, of incompleteness. How indeed can one fathom the mystery that this very Vakratunda-Mahakaya, with his crooked face and distorted body, is the Lord and Master of Success and Perfection? Could it be that this Image of Purity and Holiness, this Mangalamoorty, intends to signify by his very appearance that the completeness of God is something no poor mortal can comprehend? Be that as it may. It is not for us to understand this Mystery or try to unravel it. Nor is it within our powers to do so. Our duty is merely to pay homage to the Elephant-headed god and get on with our play.

This is the city of Dharmapura, ruled by King Dharmasheela whose fame and empire have already reached the ends of the eight directions. Two youths who dwell in this city are our heroes. One is Devadatta. Comely in appearance, fair in colour, unrivalled in intelligence, Devadatta is the only son of the Revered Brahmin, Vidyasagara. Having felled the mightiest pundits of the kingdom in debates on logic and love, having blinded the greatest poets of the world with his poetry and wit, Devadatta is as it were the apple of every eye in Dharmapura.

The other youth is Kapila. He is the only son of the iron-smith, Lohita, who is to the

183

King's armoury as an axle to the chariotwheel. He is dark and plain to look at, yet in deeds which require drive and daring, in dancing, in strength and in physical skills, he has no equal. (*A scream of terror is heard off stage. The* BHAGAVATA *frowns, quickly looks in the direction of the scream, then carries on.*) The world wonders at their friendship. The world sees these two young men wandering down the streets of Dharmapura, hand in hand, and remembers Lava and Kusha, Rama and Lakshmana, Krishna and Balarama.

(*Sings*) Two friends there were
– one mind, one heart –
(*The scream is heard again. The* BHAGAVATA *cannot ignore it any more.*) Who could that be – creating a disturbance at the very outset of our performance? (*Looks.*) Oh! It's Nata, our Actor. And he is running. What could have happened, I wonder?

(*The* ACTOR *comes running in, trembling with fear. He rushes on to the stage, runs round the stage once, then sees the* BHAGAVATA *and grabs him.*)

ACTOR Sir, Bhagavata Sir –

BHAGAVATA (*trying to free himself*) Tut! Tut! What's this? What's this?

ACTOR Sir . . . oh my God! – God!

BHAGAVATA Let me go! I tell you, let go of me! (*Freeing himself.*) Now what's this? What . . .

ACTOR I – I – I – oh God!

(*Grabs him again.*)

BHAGAVATA Let me go! (*The* ACTOR *moves back.*) What nonsense is this? What do you mean by all this shouting and screaming? In front of our audience too! How dare you disturb . . .

ACTOR Please, please, I'm – sorry . . . But – but . . .

BHAGAVATA (*more calmly*) Now, now, calm down! There's nothing to be afraid of here. I am here. The musicians are here. And there is our large-hearted audience. It may be that they fall asleep during a play sometimes. But they are ever alert when someone is in trouble. Now, tell us, what's the matter?

ACTOR (*panting*) Oh – Oh – My heart . . . It's going to burst . . .

BHAGAVATA Sit down! Sit. Right! Now tell me everything quietly, slowly.

ACTOR I was on my way here . . . I was already late . . . didn't want to annoy you . . . So I was hurrying down when . . . Ohh! (*Covers his face with his hands.*)

BHAGAVATA Yes, yes. You were hurrying down. Then?

ACTOR I'm shivering! On the way . . . you see . . . I had drunk a lot of water this morning . . . my stomach was full . . . so to relieve myself . . .

BHAGAVATA Watch what you are saying! Remember you are on stage . . .

ACTOR I didn't do anything! I only wanted to . . . so I sat by the side of the road – and was about to pull up my choti when . . .

BHAGAVATA Yes?

ACTOR A voice – a deep, thick voice . . . it said 'Hey, you there – don't you know you are not supposed to commit nuisance on the main road?'

BHAGAVATA Quite right too. You should have known that much.

ACTOR I half got up and looked around. Not a man in sight – no one! So I was about to sit down again when the same voice said . . .

BHAGAVATA Yes?

ACTOR 'You irresponsible fellow, can't you understand you are not to commit nuisance on the main road?' I looked up. And there – right in front of me – across the fence . . .

BHAGAVATA Who was there?

ACTOR A horse!

BHAGAVATA What?

ACTOR A horse! And it was talking.

BHAGAVATA What did you have to drink this morning?

ACTOR Nothing, I swear. Bhagavata Sir, I haven't been near a toddy-shop for a whole week. I didn't even have milk today.

BHAGAVATA Perhaps your liver is sensitive to water.

ACTOR (*desperate*) Please believe me. I saw it clearly – it was a horse – and it was talking.

BHAGAVATA (*resigned*) It's no use continuing this nonsense. So you saw a talking horse? Good. Now go and get made up . . .

ACTOR Made up? I fall to your feet, Sir, I can't . . .

BHAGAVATA Now look here . . .

ACTOR Please, Sir . . . (*He holds up his hand. It's trembling.*) You see, Sir? How can I hold up a sword with this? How can I fight?

BHAGAVATA (*thinks*) Well then. There's only one solution left. You go back . . .

ACTOR Back?

BHAGAVATA . . . back to that fence, have another look and make sure for yourself that whoever was talking, it couldn't have been that horse.

ACTOR No!

BHAGAVATA Nata . . .

ACTOR I can't!

BHAGAVATA It's an order.

ACTOR (*pleading*) Must I?

BHAGAVATA Yes, you must.

ACTOR Sir . . .

(*The* BHAGAVATA *turns to the audience and starts singing.*)

BHAGAVATA
   Two friends there were
   – one mind, one heart –
   Are you still here? (*The* ACTOR *goes out looking at the* BHAGAVATA, *hoping for a last minute reprieve. It doesn't come.*) Poor boy! God alone knows what he saw – and what he took it to be! There's Truth for you . . . Pure Illusion.
   (*Sings*) Two friends there were
   – one mind, one heart –
(*A scream in the wings. The* ACTOR *comes rushing in.*) Now look here . . .

ACTOR It's coming. Coming . . .

BHAGAVATA What's coming?

ACTOR Him! He's coming . . . (*Rushes out.*)

BHAGAVATA Him! It! What's coming? Whatever or whoever it is, the Actor has obviously been frightened by its sight. If even a hardened actor like him gets frightened, it's more than likely that our gentle audience may get frightened too. It's not proper to let such a sight walk on stage unchallenged. (*To the wings*) Hold up the entry-curtain!

(*Two stage-hands enter and hold up a half-curtain, about six feet in height – the sort of curtain used in Yakshagana or Kathakali. The curtain masks the entry of* HAYAVADANA, *who comes and stands behind it.*)

Who's that? (*No reply. Only the sound of someone sobbing behind the curtain.*) How strange! Someone's sobbing behind the curtain. It looks as though the Terror which frightened our Actor is itself now crying! (*To the stage-hand*) Lower the curtain!

(*The curtain is lowered by about a foot. One sees* HAYAVADANA's *head, which is covered by a veil. At a sign from the* BHAGAVATA, *one of the stage-hands removes the veil, revealing a horse's head. For a while the horse-head doesn't realize that it is exposed to the gaze of the audience. The moment the realization dawns, the head ducks behind the curtain.*)

A horse! No, it can't be!

(*He makes a sign. The curtain is lowered a little more – just enough to show the head again. Again it ducks. Again the curtain is lowered. This goes on till the curtain is lowered right down to the floor.* HAYAVADANA, *who has a man's body but a horse's head, is sitting on the floor hiding his head between his knees.*)

Incredible! Unbelievable!

(*At a sign from the* BHAGAVATA, *the stage-hands withdraw. The* BHAGAVATA *goes and stands near* HAYAVADANA. *Then he grunts to himself as though he has seen through the trick.*)

Who are you?

(HAYAVADANA *lifts his head, and wipes the tears away. The* BHAGAVATA *beckons to him to come centre-stage.*)

Come here!

(HAYAVADANA *hesitates, then comes forward.*)

First you go around scaring people with this stupid mask. And then you have the cheek to disturb our show with your clowning! Have you no sense of proportion? . . . Enough of this nonsense now. Take it off – I say, take off that stupid mask! (HAYAVADANA *doesn't move.*) You won't? – Then I'll have to do it myself! (*Holds* HAYAVADANA's *head with both his hands and tries to pull it off.* HAYAVADANA *doesn't resist.*) It is tight. Nata – My dear Actor . . .

(*The* ACTOR *comes in, warily, and stands open-mouthed at the sight he sees.*)

Why are you standing there? Don't you see you were taken in by a silly mask! Come and help me take it off now.

(*The* ACTOR *comes and holds* HAYAVADANA *by his waist while the* BHAGAVATA *pulls at the head.* HAYAVADANA *offers no resistance, but can't help moaning when the pain becomes unbearable. The tug-of-war continues for a while. Slowly, the truth dawns on the* BHAGAVATA.)

Nata, this isn't a mask! It's his real head!

(*The* ACTOR *drops* HAYAVADANA *with a thud.* HAYAVADANA *gets up and sits as before, head between knees.*)

Truly, surprises will never cease! If someone had told me only five minutes ago that there was a man with a horse's head, I would have laughed out in his face. (*To* HAYAVADANA) Who are you?

(HAYAVADANA *gets up and starts to go out. The* ACTOR *hurriedly moves out of his way.*)

Wait! Wait! That's our green room there. It's bad enough that you scared this actor. We have a play to perform today, you know.

(HAYAVADANA *stands, dejected.*)

(*Softly*) Who are you? (*No reply.*) What brought you to this? Was it a curse of some rishi? Or was it some holy place of pilgrimage, a punyasthana, which you desecrated? Or could it be that you insulted a pativrata, dedicated to the service of her husband? Or did you . . .

HAYAVADANA Hey . . .

BHAGAVATA (*taken aback*) Eh?

HAYAVADANA What do you mean, Sir? Do you think just because you know the puranas you can go about showering your Sanskrit on everyone in sight? What temple did I desecrate? What woman did I insult? What . . .

BHAGAVATA Don't get annoyed . . .

HAYAVADANA What else? What rishi? What sage? What? Who have I wronged? What have I done to anyone? Let anyone come forward and say that I've done him any wrong. I haven't – I know I haven't yet . . . (*He is on the point of beginning to sob again.*)

BHAGAVATA Don't take it to heart so much. What happened? What's your grief? You are not alone here. I am here. The musicians are here. And there is our large-hearted audience. It may be that they fall asleep during a play sometimes . . .

HAYAVADANA What can anyone do? It's my fate.

BHAGAVATA What's your name?

HAYAVADANA Hayavadana.

BHAGAVATA How did you get this horse's head?

HAYAVADANA I was born with it.

BHAGAVATA Then why didn't you stop us when we tried to take it off? Why did you put up with our torture?

HAYAVADANA All my life I've been trying to get rid of this head. I thought – you with all your goodness and punya . . . if at least you managed to pull it off . . .

BHAGAVATA Oho! Poor man! But, Hayavadana, what can anyone do about a head one's born with? Who knows what error committed in the last birth is responsi . . .

HAYAVADANA (*annoyed*) It has nothing to do with my last birth. It's this birth which I can't shake off.

BHAGAVATA Tell us what happened. Don't feel ashamed.

HAYAVADANA (*enraged*) Ashamed? Me? Why should I . . .

BHAGAVATA Sorry. I beg your pardon. I should have said 'shy'.

HAYAVADANA (*gloomy*) It's a long story.

BHAGAVATA Carry on.

HAYAVADANA My mother was the Princess of Karnataka. She was a very beautiful girl. When she came of age, her father decided that she should choose her own husband. So princes of every kingdom in the world were invited – and they all came. From China, from Persia, from Africa. But she didn't like any of them. The last one to come was the Prince of Araby. My mother took one look at that handsome prince sitting on his great white stallion – and she fainted.

ACTOR Ah!

HAYAVADANA Her father at once decided that this was the man. All arrangements for the wedding were made. My mother woke up – and do you know what she said?

ACTOR and BHAGAVATA What?

HAYAVADANA She said she would only marry that horse!

ACTOR What!

HAYAVADANA Yes. She wouldn't listen to anyone. The Prince of Araby burst a blood-vessel.

ACTOR Naturally.

HAYAVADANA No one could dissuade her. So ultimately she was married off to the white stallion. She lived with him for fifteen years. One morning she wakes up –

and no horse! In its place stood a beautiful Celestial Being, a gandharva. Apparently this Celestial Being had been cursed by the god Kuvera to be born a horse for some act of misbehaviour. After fifteen years of human love he had become his original self again.

BHAGAVATA   I must admit several such cases are on record.

HAYAVADANA   Released from his curse, he asked my mother to accompany him to his Heavenly Abode. But she wouldn't. She said she would come only if he became a horse again. So he cursed her . . .

ACTOR   No!

HAYAVADANA   He cursed her to become a horse herself. So my mother became a horse and ran away happily. My father went back to his Heavenly Abode. Only I – the child of their marriage – was left behind.

BHAGAVATA   It's a sad story.

ACTOR   Very sad.

HAYAVADANA   What should I do now, Bhagavata Sir? What can I do to get rid of this head?

BHAGAVATA   Hayavadana, what's written on our foreheads cannot be altered.

HAYAVADANA   (*slapping himself on the forehead*) But what a forehead! What a forehead! If it was a forehead like yours, I would have accepted anything. But this! . . . I have tried to accept my fate. My personal life has naturally been blameless. So I took interest in the social life of the Nation – Civics, Politics, Patriotism, Nationalism, Indianization, the Socialist Pattern of Society . . . I have tried everything. But where's my society? Where? You must help me to become a complete man, Bhagavata Sir. But how? What can I do? (*Long silence. They think.*)

BHAGAVATA   Banaras?

HAYAVADANA   What?

BHAGAVATA   If you go to Banaras and make a vow in front of the god there . . .

HAYAVADANA   I've tried that. Didn't work.

ACTOR   Rameshwar.

HAYAVADANA   Banaras, Rameshwar, Gokarn, Haridwar, Gaya, Kedarnath – not only those but the Dargah of Khwaja Yusuf Baba, the Grotto of Our Virgin Mary – I've tried them all. Magicians, mendicants, maharshis, fakirs, saints and sadhus – sadhus with short hair, sadhus with beards – sadhus in saffron, sadhus in the

altogether – hanging, singing, rotating, gyrating – on the spikes, in the air, under water, under the ground . . . I've covered them all. And what did I get out of all this? Everywhere I went I had to cover my head with a veil – and I started going bald. (*Pause. Shyly*) You know, I hate this head – but I just can't help being fond of this lovely, long mane. (*Pause.*) So – I had to give the miss to Tirupati. (*Long silence.*)

BHAGAVATA   Come to think of it, Hayavadana, why don't you try the Kali of Mount Chitrakoot?

HAYAVADANA   Anything you say.

BHAGAVATA   It's a temple at the top of Mount Chitrakoot. The goddess there is famous for being ever-awake to the call of devotees. Thousands used to flock to her temple once. No one goes now, though.

HAYAVADANA   Why not?

BHAGAVATA   She used to give anything anyone asked for. As the people became aware of this they stopped going.

HAYAVADANA   Fools!

BHAGAVATA   Why don't you try her?

HAYAVADANA   (*Jumps up.*) Why not? I'll start at once . . .

BHAGAVATA   Good. But I don't think you should go alone. It's a wild road . . . You'll have to ask a lot of people, which won't be easy for you. So . . . (*To the* ACTOR) You'd better go with him.

ACTOR   Me?

BHAGAVATA   Yes, that way you can make up for having insulted him.

HAYAVADANA   But, Bhagavata Sir, may I point out that his roadside manners . . .

ACTOR   There! He's insulting me now! Let him find his own way. What do I care?

BHAGAVATA   Come, come, don't let's start fighting now. (*To* HAYAVADANA) Don't worry. There's no highway there. Only a cart-track at best. (*To the* ACTOR) You've no reason to feel insulted – actually you should admire him. Even in his dire need, he doesn't lose his civic sense. Be off now.

HAYAVADANA   (*to the* ACTOR) Please, don't get upset. I won't bother you, I promise. (*To the* BHAGAVATA) I am most grateful . . .

BHAGAVATA   (*blessing him*) May you become successful in your search for completeness. (*The two go.*) Each one to his own fate. Each one to his own desire. Each one to his own luck. Let's now turn to our story. (*He starts singing. The following is a prose rendering of the song.*)

BHAGAVATA (*sings*) Two friends there were – one mind, one heart. They saw a girl and forgot themselves. But they could not understand the song she sang.

FEMALE CHORUS (*sings*) Why should love stick to the sap of a single body? When the stem is drunk with the thick yearning of the many-petalled, many-flowered lantana, why should it be tied down to the relation of a single flower?

BHAGAVATA (*sings*) They forgot themselves and took off their bodies. And she took the laughing heads, and held them high so the pouring blood bathed her, coloured her red. Then she danced around and sang.

FEMALE CHORUS (*sings*) A head for each breast. A pupil for each eye. A side for each arm. I have neither regret nor shame. The blood pours into the earth and a song branches out in the sky.

(DEVADATTA *enters and sits on the chair. He is a slender, delicate-looking person and is wearing a pale-coloured mask. He is lost in thought.* KAPILA *enters. He is powerfully built and wears a dark mask.*)

KAPILA (*even as he is entering*) Devadatta, why didn't you come to the gymnasium last evening? I'd asked you to. It was such fun . . .

DEVADATTA (*preoccupied*) Some work . . .

KAPILA Really, you should have come. The wrestler from Gandhara – he's one of India's greatest, you know – he came. Nanda and I were wrestling when he arrived. He watched us. When I caught Nanda in a crocodile-hold, he first burst into applause and said . . . (*notices that* DEVADATTA *isn't listening and stops. Pause.*)

DEVADATTA (*waking up*) Then?

KAPILA Then what?

DEVADATTA (*flustered*) I mean . . . what did Nanda do?

KAPILA He played the flute.

DEVADATTA (*more confused*) No . . . I mean . . . you were saying something about the wrestler from Gandhara, weren't you?

KAPILA He wrestled with me for a few minutes, patted me on the back and said, 'You'll go far'.

DEVADATTA That's nice.

KAPILA Yes, it is . . . Who's it this time?

DEVADATTA What do you mean?

KAPILA I mean – who – is – it – this – time?

DEVADATTA What do you mean who?

KAPILA I mean – who is the girl?

DEVADATTA No one. (*Pause.*) How did you guess?

KAPILA My dear friend, I have seen you fall in love fifteen times in the last two years. How could I not guess?

DEVADATTA Kapila, if you've come to make fun of me . . .

KAPILA I am not making fun of you. Every time, you have been the first to tell me about it. Why so shy this time?

DEVADATTA How can you even talk of them in the same breath as her? Before her, they're as . . .

KAPILA . . . as stars before the moon, as the glow-worms before a torch. Yes, yes, that's been so fifteen times too.

DEVADATTA (*exploding*) Why don't you go home? You are becoming a bore.

KAPILA Don't get annoyed.

DEVADATTA You call yourself my friend. But you haven't understood me at all.

KAPILA And have you understood me? No, you haven't. Or you wouldn't get angry like this. Don't you know I would do anything for you? Jump into a well – or walk into fire? Even my parents aren't as close to me as you are. I would leave them this minute if you asked me to.

DEVADATTA (*irritated*) Don't start on that now. You've said it fifty times already.

KAPILA . . . And I'll say it again. If it wasn't for you I would have been no better than the ox in our yard. You showed me that there were such things as poetry and literature. You taught me . . .

DEVADATTA Why don't you go home? All I wanted was to be by myself for a day. Alone. And you had to come and start your chatter. What do you know of poetry and literature? Go back to your smithy – that's where you belong.

KAPILA (*hurt*) Do you really want me to go?

DEVADATTA Yes.

KAPILA All right. If that's what you want. (*He starts to go.*)

DEVADATTA Sit down. (*This is of course exactly what* KAPILA *wants. He sits down on the floor.*) And don't speak . . . (DEVADATTA *gets down on the floor to sit beside* KAPILA. KAPILA *at once leaps up and gestures to* DEVADATTA *to sit on the chair.* DEVADATTA *shakes his head but* KAPILA *insists, pulls him up by his arm.* DEVADATTA *gets up.*) You are a pest. (*Sits on the chair.* KAPILA *sits down on the ground happily. A long pause.*)

DEVADATTA (*slowly*) How can I describe her, Kapila? Her forelocks rival the bees, her face is . . . (*All this is familiar to* KAPILA *and he joins in, with great enjoyment.*)

BOTH . . . is a white lotus. Her beauty is as the magic lake. Her arms the lotus creepers. Her breasts are golden urns and her waist . . .

DEVADATTA No. No!

KAPILA Eh?

DEVADATTA I was blind all these days. I deceived myself that I understood poetry. I didn't. I understood nothing. *Tanvee shyama* –

BOTH . . . shikharidashana pakvabimbadharoshti – Madhye kshama chakitaharineeprekshana nimnanabhih.

DEVADATTA The Shyama Nayika – born of Kalidasa's magic description – as Vatsyayana had dreamt her. Kapila, in one appearance, she became my guru in the poetry of love. Do you think she would ever assent to becoming my disciple in love itself?

KAPILA (*aside*) This is new!

DEVADATTA (*his eyes shining*) If only she would consent to be my Muse, I could outshine Kalidasa. I'd always wanted to do that – but I thought it was impossible . . . But now I see it is within my reach.

KAPILA Then go ahead. Write . . .

DEVADATTA But how can I without her in front of me? How can I concentrate when my whole being is only thinking of her, craving for her?

KAPILA What's her name? Will you at least tell me that?

DEVADATTA Her name? She has no name.

KAPILA But what do her parents call her?

DEVADATTA (*anguished*) What's the use? She isn't meant for the likes of me . . .

KAPILA You don't really believe that, do you? With all your qualities – achievements – looks – family – grace . . .

DEVADATTA Don't try to console me with praise.

KAPILA I'm not praising you. You know very well that every parent of every girl in the city is only waiting to catch you . . .

DEVADATTA Don't! Please. I know this girl is beyond my wildest dreams. But still – I can't help wanting her – I can't help it. I swear, Kapila, with you as my witness I swear, if I ever get her as my wife, I'll sacrifice my two arms to the goddess Kali, I'll sacrifice my head to Lord Rudra . . .

KAPILA Ts! Ts! (*Aside*) This is a serious situation. It does look as though this sixteenth girl has really caught our Devadatta in her net. Otherwise, he isn't the type to talk with such violence.

DEVADATTA I mean it! What's the use of these hands and this head if I'm not to have her? My poetry won't live without her. The *Shakuntalam* will never be excelled. But how can I explain this to her? I have no cloud for a messenger. No bee to show the way. Now the only future I have is to stand and do penance in Pavana Veethi . . .

KAPILA Pavana Veethi? Why there?

DEVADATTA She lives in that street.

KAPILA How do you know?

DEVADATTA I saw her in the market yesterday evening. I couldn't remove my eyes from her and followed her home.

KAPILA Tut! Tut! What must people have thought . . . ?

DEVADATTA She went into a house in Pavana Veethi. I waited outside all evening. She didn't come out.

KAPILA Now tell me. What sort of a house was it?

DEVADATTA I can't remember.

KAPILA What colour?

DEVADATTA Don't know.

KAPILA How many storeys?

DEVADATTA I didn't notice.

KAPILA You mean you didn't notice anything about the house?

DEVADATTA The door-frame of the house had an engraving of a two-headed bird at the top. I only saw that. She lifted her hand to knock and it touched the bird. For a minute, the bird came alive.

KAPILA (*jumps up*) Then why didn't you tell me before? You've been wasting all this precious time . . .

DEVADATTA I don't understand . . .

KAPILA My dear Devadatta, your cloud-messenger, your bee, your pigeon is sitting right in front of you and you don't even know it? You wait here, I'll go, find out her name . . .

DEVADATTA (*incredulous*) Kapila – Kapila . . .

KAPILA I'll be back in a few minutes . . .

DEVADATTA I won't ever forget this, Kapila . . .

KAPILA Shut up! . . . And forget all about your arms and head. This job doesn't need

189

either Rudra or Kali. I'm quite enough. (*Goes out.*)

DEVADATTA Kapila – Kapila . . . He's gone. How fortunate I am to have a friend like him. Pure gold. (*Pause.*) But should I have trusted this to him? He means well – and he is a wizard in his smithy, in his farm, in his field. But here? No. He is too rough, too indelicate. He was the wrong man to send. He's bound to ruin the whole thing. (*Anguished*) Lord Rudra, I meant what I said. If I get her my head will be a gift to you. Mother Kali, I'll sacrifice my arms to you. I swear . . . (*Goes out. The* BHAGAVATA *removes the chair.* KAPILA *enters.*)

KAPILA This is Pavana Veethi – the street of merchants. Well, well, well. What enormous houses! Each one a palace in itself. It's a wonder people don't get lost in these houses. (*Examines the doors one by one.*) Now. This is not a double-headed bird. It's an eagle – This? A lotus. This is – er – a lion. Tiger. A wheel. And this? God alone knows what this is. And the next? (*In disgust*) A horse! – a rhinoceros – another lion. Another lotus! – Where the hell is that stupid two-headed bird? (*Stops.*) What was the design? I couldn't make out? (*Goes back and stares at it. Shouts in triumph.*) That's it! Almost gave me the slip! A proper two-headed bird. But it's so tiny you can't see it at all unless you are willing to tear your eyes staring at it. Well now. Whose house could this be? (*Looks around.*) No one in sight. Naturally. Why should anyone come here in this hot sun? Better ask the people in the house. (*Mimes knocking. Listens.* PADMINI *enters humming a tune.*)

PADMINI . . . Here comes the rider – from which land does he come?

KAPILA (*Gapes at her. Aside*) I give up, Devadatta. I surrender to your judgment. I hadn't thought anyone could be more beautiful than the wench Ragini who acts Rambha in our village troupe. But this one! You're right – she is Yakshini, Shakuntala, Urvashi, Indumati – all rolled into one.

PADMINI You knocked, didn't you?

KAPILA Er – yes . . .

PADMINI Then why are you gaping at me? What do you want?

KAPILA I – I just wanted to know whose house this was.

PADMINI Whose house do you want?

KAPILA This one.

PADMINI I see. Then who do you want here?

KAPILA The master . . .

PADMINI Do you know his name?

KAPILA No.

PADMINI Have you met him?

KAPILA No.

PADMINI Have you seen him?

KAPILA No.

PADMINI So. You haven't met him, seen him or known him. What do you want with him?

KAPILA (*aside*) She is quite right. What have I to do with him? I only want to find out his name . . .

PADMINI Are you sure you want this house? Or were you . . .

KAPILA No. I'm sure this is the one.

PADMINI (*pointing to her head*) Are you all right here?

KAPILA (*taken aback*) Yes – I think so.

PADMINI How about your eyes? Do they work properly?

KAPILA Yes.

PADMINI (*showing him four fingers*) How many?

KAPILA Four.

PADMINI Correct. So there's nothing wrong with your eyes. As for the other thing, I'll have to take you on trust. Well then. If you're sure you wanted this house, why were you peering at all those doors? And what were you mumbling under your breath?

KAPILA (*startled*) How did you know?

PADMINI I am quite sane . . . and I've got good eyes.

KAPILA (*Looks up and chuckles.*) Oh, I suppose you were watching from the terrace . . .

PADMINI (*in a low voice, mysteriously*) Listen, you'd better be careful. We have any number of thefts in this street and people are suspicious. Last night there was a man standing out there for nearly two hours without moving. And today you have turned up. It's just as well I saw you. Anyone else would have taken you to the police – Beware! (*Aloud*) Now tell me. What are you doing here?

KAPILA I – I can't tell you.

PADMINI Really! Who will you tell it to?

KAPILA Your father . . .

PADMINI Do you want my father or do you want the master of this house?

KAPILA Aren't they the same?

PADMINI (*as though explaining to a child*) Listen, my father could be a servant in this house. Or the master of this house could be my father's servant. My father could be the master's father, brother, son-in-law, cousin, grandfather or uncle. Do you agree?

KAPILA Er – Yes.

PADMINI Right. Then we'll start again. Whom should I call?

KAPILA Your father.

PADMINI And if he's not in?

KAPILA (*lost*) Anyone else.

PADMINI Which anyone?

KAPILA Perhaps – your brother.

PADMINI Do you know him?

KAPILA No.

PADMINI Have you met him?

KAPILA No.

PADMINI Do you know his name?

KAPILA (*desperate*) Please, please – call your father or the master or both, or if they are the same, anyone . . . please call someone!

PADMINI No. No. That won't do.

KAPILA (*looking around; aside*) No one here. Still I have to find out her name. Devadatta must be in pain and . . . He will never forgive me if I go back now. (*Aloud*) Madam, please. I have some very important work. I'll touch your feet . . .

PADMINI (*eager*) You will? Really? Do you know, I've touched everyone's feet in this house some time or the other, but no one's ever touched mine? You will?

KAPILA (*slapping his forehead as he sinks to the ground*) I'm finished – decimated – powdered to dust – powdered into tiny specks of flour. (*To* PADMINI) My mother, can I at least talk to a servant?

PADMINI I knew it. I knew you wouldn't touch my feet. One can't even trust strangers any more. All right, my dear son! I opened the door. So consider me the door-keeper. What do you want?

KAPILA (*determined*) All right! (*Gets up.*) You have no doubt heard of the Revered Brahmin Vidyasagara.

PADMINI It's possible.

KAPILA In which case you'll also know of Devadatta, his only son. A poet. A pundit. Knows the Vedas backwards. Writes the grandest poetry ever. Long, dark hair. Delicate, fair face. Age twenty. Height five feet seven inches. Weight . . .

PADMINI Wait a minute! What's he to you?

KAPILA Friend. Greatest in the world! But the main question now; What's he going to be to you? (*Sudden silence.*)

PADMINI (*blushing as the import of the remark dawns on her*) Mother! (*Runs in.* KAPILA *stands, staring after her.*)

KAPILA Devadatta, my friend, I confess to you I'm feeling uneasy. You are a gentle soul. You can't bear a bitter word or an evil thought. But this one is fast as lightning – and as sharp. She is not for the likes of you. What she needs is a man of steel. But what can one do? You'll never listen to me. And I can't withdraw now. I'll have to talk to her family . . . (*Follows her in.*)

BHAGAVATA Need one explain to our wise and knowing audience what followed next? Padmini is the daughter of the leading merchant in Dharmapura. In her house, the very floor is swept by the Goddess of Wealth. In Devadatta's house, they've the Goddess of Learning for a maid. What could then possibly stand in the way of bringing the families together? (*Marriage music.*) Padmini became the better half of Devadatta and settled in his house. Nor did Devadatta forget his debt to Kapila. The old friendship flourished as before. Devadatta – Padmini – Kapila! To the admiring citizens of Dharmapura, Rama – Sita – Lakshmana.

(*Enter* DEVADATTA *and* PADMINI.)

PADMINI Why is he so late? He should have been here more than an hour ago . . . (*Looks out of a window.*)

DEVADATTA Have you packed your clothes properly?

PADMINI The first thing in the morning.

DEVADATTA And the mattresses? We may have to sleep out in the open. It's quite chilly . . . we'll need at least two rugs.

PADMINI Don't worry. The servant's done all that.

DEVADATTA And your shawl? Also some warm clothes . . .

PADMINI What's happened to you today? At other times you are so full of your books, you even forget to wash your hands after a meal. But today you've been going on and on and on all morning.

DEVADATTA Padmini, I've told you ten times already . . . I don't like the idea of this trip. You should rest – not face such hazards. The cart will probably shake like an earthquake. It's dangerous in your condition. But you won't listen . . .

PADMINI   My condition! What's happened to me? To listen to you, one would think I was the first woman in this world to become pregnant. I only have to stumble and you act as though it's all finished and gone . . .

DEVADATTA   For God's sake . . . will you stop it?

PADMINI   (*laughs*) Sorry! (*Bites her tongue in repentance.*) I won't say such things again.

DEVADATTA   You've no sense of what not to say. So long as you can chatter and run around like a child . . .

PADMINI   (*back at the window*) Where is Kapila?

DEVADATTA   . . . and drool over Kapila all day.

PADMINI   (*taken aback*) What do you mean?

DEVADATTA   What else should I say? The other day I wanted to read out a play of Bhasa's to you and sure enough Kapila drops in.

PADMINI   Oh! That's biting you still, is it? . . . But why are you blaming me? He was your friend even before you married me, wasn't he? He used to drop in every day then . . .

DEVADATTA   But shouldn't he realize I'm married now? He just can't go on as before . . .

PADMINI   Don't blame him. It's my fault. He learnt a bit about poetry from you and I thought he might enjoy Bhasa. So I asked him to come . . . He didn't want to – but I insisted.

DEVADATTA   I know that.

PADMINI   Had I realized you would get so upset, I wouldn't have.

DEVADATTA   I'm not upset, Padmini. Kapila isn't merely a friend – he's like my brother. One has to collect merit in seven lives to get a friend like him. But is it wrong for me to want to read to you alone – or to spend a couple of days with you without anyone else around? (*Pause.*) Of course, once he came, there wasn't the slightest chance of my reading any poetry. You had to hop around him twittering 'Kapila! Kapila!' every minute.

PADMINI   You aren't jealous of him, are you?

DEVADATTA   Me? Jealous of Kapila? Why do you have to twist everything I say . . .

PADMINI   (*Laughs. Affectionately*) Don't sulk now. I was just trying to be funny. Really you have no sense of humour.

DEVADATTA   It's humour for you. But it burns my insides . . .

PADMINI   Aw, shut up. Don't I know how liberal and largehearted you are? You aren't the sort to get jealous. If I fall into a well tomorrow, you won't even miss me until my bloated corpse floats up . . .

DEVADATTA   (*irritated*) Padmini!

PADMINI   Sorry, I forgot. I apologize – I slap myself on the cheeks. (*Slaps herself on both cheeks with her right hand several times in punishment.*) Is that all right? The trouble is I grew up saying these awful things and it's become a habit now. But you are so fragile! I don't know how you're going to go through life wrapped in silk like this! You are still a baby . . .

DEVADATTA   I see.

PADMINI   Look now. You got annoyed about Kapila. But why? You are my saffron, my marriage-thread, my deity. Why should you feel upset? I like making fun of Kapila – he is such an innocent. Looks a proper devil, but the way he blushes and giggles and turns red, he might have been a bride.

DEVADATTA   (*smiles*) Well, this bride didn't blush.

PADMINI   No one taught this bride to blush. But now I'm learning from that yokel. (*They both laugh. She casually goes back to the window and looks out.*)

DEVADATTA   (*aside*) Does she really not see? Or is she deliberately playing this game with him? Kapila was never the sort to blush. But now, he only has to see her and he begins to wag his tail. Sits up on his hind legs as though he were afraid to let her words fall to the ground. And that pleading in his eyes – can't she really see that? (*Aloud*) Padmini, Kapila isn't used to women. The only woman he has known in his life is his mother . . .

PADMINI   You mean it's dangerous to be with him? The way you talk one would never imagine he was your best friend.

DEVADATTA   (*incensed*) Why do you have to paint everything I say . . .

PADMINI   (*conciliatory*) What did I say? Listen, if you really don't want to go to Ujjain today, let's not. When Kapila comes, tell him I'm ill.

DEVADATTA   But . . . you will be disappointed.

PADMINI   Me? Of course not. We'll do as you feel. You remember what the priest said – I'm your 'half' now. The better half! We can go to Ujjain some other time . . . In another couple of months, there's the big Ujjain fair. We'll go then – just the two of us. All right? We'll cancel today's trip.

DEVADATTA (*trying to control his excitement*) Now – if you aren't going to be disappointed – then – truly – that's what I would like most. Not because I'm jealous of Kapila – No, I'm not, I know that. He has a heart of gold. But this is your first baby . . .

PADMINI What do you mean first? How many babies can one have in six months?

DEVADATTA You aren't going to start again . . .

PADMINI No, no, no I won't say a word.

DEVADATTA (*pinching her cheek*) Bad upbringing – that's what it is. I don't like the idea of your going so far in a cart in your present condition, that's all.

PADMINI Ordinarily I would have replied I had a womb of steel, but I won't – in the present condition. (*Both laugh.*) All right. If you are happy, so am I.

DEVADATTA (*happy*) Yes, we'll spend the whole day by ourselves. The servants are going home anyway. They can come back tomorrow. But for today – only you and me. It's been such a long time since we've been on our own.

KAPILA (*off stage*) Devadatta . . .

PADMINI There's Kapila now. You tell him. (*She pretends to go in, but goes and stands in the corner of the stage, listening.* KAPILA *enters excited.*)

KAPILA I'm late, ain't I? What could I do? That cartman had kept the cart ready but the moment I looked at it, I knew one of the oxen was no good. I asked him to change it. 'We won't reach Ujjain for another fortnight in this one', I said. He started . . .

DEVADATTA Kapila . . .

KAPILA . . . making a scene, but I stood my ground. So he had to fetch a new one. These cart-hirers are a menace. If ours hadn't gone to Chitrapur that day . . .

DEVADATTA Kapila, we have to call off today's trip.

KAPILA (*suddenly silenced*) Oh!

DEVADATTA (*embarrassed*) You see, Padmini isn't well . . .

KAPILA Well, then of course . . . (*Silence.*) I'll return the cart then . . .

DEVADATTA Yes.

KAPILA Or else he may charge us for the day.

DEVADATTA Uhm.

KAPILA (*aside*) So it's off. What am I to do for the rest of the day? What am I to do for the rest of the week? Why should it feel as though the whole world has been wiped out for a whole week? Why this emptiness . . . Kapila, Kapila, get a tight hold on yourself. You are slipping, boy, control yourself. Don't lose that hold. Go now – don't come here again for a week – Devadatta's bound to get angry with you for not coming. Sister-in-law will be annoyed. But don't come back. Go, Go! (*Aloud*) Well then – I'll start.

DEVADATTA Why don't you sit for a while?

KAPILA No, no – we might upset sister-in-law more then with our prattle.

DEVADATTA That's true. So – come again.

KAPILA Yes, I will. (*Starts to go.* PADMINI *comes out.*)

PADMINI Why are you sitting here? When are we going to start? We are already late . . . (*They look at her, surprised.*)

KAPILA But if you aren't well, we won't . . .

PADMINI What's wrong with me? I'm perfect. I had a headache this morning. But a layer of ginger-paste took care of that. Why should we cancel our trip for a little thing like that?

(DEVADATTA *opens his mouth to say something but stays quiet.*)

(*To* KAPILA) Why are you standing there like a statue?

KAPILA No, really, if you have a headache . . .

PADMINI I don't have a headache now!

DEVADATTA But, Padmini . . .

PADMINI Kapila, put those bundles out there in the cart. The servant will bring the rest. (KAPILA *stands totally baffled. He looks at* DEVADATTA *for guidance. There's none.*) Be quick. Otherwise I'll put them in myself. (KAPILA *goes out.* PADMINI *goes to* DEVADATTA, *pleading*) Please don't get angry. Poor boy, he looked so lost and disappointed, I couldn't bear to see it. He has been running around for us this whole week.

DEVADATTA (*turning his head away*) Where's the box in which I put the books? I'll take it . . .

PADMINI You are an angel. I knew you wouldn't mind . . . I'll bring it. It's quite light. (*Goes out.*)

DEVADATTA (*to himself*) And my disappointment? Does that mean nothing to you? (*Aloud*) Don't. I'll take it. You don't lift anything. (*Goes in after her.*)

BHAGAVATA Why do you tremble, heart? Why do you cringe like a touch-me-not bush through which a snake has passed? The sun rests his head on the Fortunate Lady's flower. And the head is bidding good-bye to the heart.

(KAPILA, *followed by* PADMINI *and* DEVADATTA, *enter, miming a cart-ride.* KAPILA *is driving the cart.*)

PADMINI How beautifully you drive the cart, Kapila! Your hands don't even move, but the oxen seem to know exactly where to go. (KAPILA *laughs happily.*) Shall we stop here for a while? We've been in this cart all day and my legs feel like bits of wood.

KAPILA Right! Ho – Ho . . . (*Pulls the cart to a halt. They get down. She slips but* DEVADATTA *supports her.*)

PADMINI What a terrible road. Nothing but stones and rocks – but one didn't feel a thing in the cart! You drove so gently – almost made it float. I remember when Devadatta took me in a cart – that was soon after our marriage – I insisted on being shown the lake outside the city. So we started – only the two of us and Devadatta driving – against my advice, I must say. And we didn't even cross the city-gates. The oxen took everything except the road. He only had to pull to the right, and off they would rush to the left! I've never laughed so much in my life. But of course he got very angry, so we had to go back home straight! (*Laughs. But* KAPILA *and* DEVADATTA *don't join in.*) Kapila, what's that glorious tree there? That one – covered in flowers?

KAPILA Oh that! That's called the Fortunate Lady's flower – that means a married woman . . .

PADMINI I know! But why do they call it that?

KAPILA Wait. I'll bring a flower. Then you'll see. (*Goes out.*)

PADMINI (*watching him, to herself*) How he climbs – like an ape. Before I could even say 'yes', he had taken off his shirt, pulled his dhoti up and swung up the branch. And what an ethereal shape! Such a broad back – like an ocean with muscles rippling across it – and then that small, feminine waist which looks so helpless.

DEVADATTA (*aside*) She had so much to talk about all day, she couldn't wait for breath. Now – not a word.

PADMINI (*aside*) He is like a Celestial Being reborn as a hunter. . . How his body sways, his limbs curve – it's a dance almost.

DEVADATTA (*aside*) And why should I blame her? It's his strong body – his manly muscles. And to think I had never *ever* noticed them all these years . . . I was an innocent – an absolute baby.

PADMINI (*aside*) No woman could resist him.

DEVADATTA (*aside*) No woman could resist him – and what does it matter that she's married? What a fool I've been. All these days I only saw that pleading in his eyes stretching out its arms, begging for a favour. But never looked in her eyes. And when I did – took the whites of her eyes for their real depth. Only now – I see the depths – now I see these flames leaping up from those depths. Now! So late! Don't turn away now, Devadatta, look at her. Look at those yellow, purple flames. Look how she's pouring her soul in his mould. Look! Let your guts burn out – let your lungs turn to ash – but don't turn away. Look – and don't scream. Strangle your agony. But look deep into these eyes – look until those peacock flames burn out the blindness in you. Don't be a coward now.

PADMINI (*aside*) How long can one go on like this? How long? How long? If Devadatta notices . . . (*Looks at* DEVADATTA. *He is looking at her already and their eyes meet. Both look away.*)

PADMINI (*aloud*) There he comes. All I wanted was one flower and he's brought a heap.

(KAPILA *comes in, miming a whole load of flowers in his arms and hands. He pours them out in front of her.*)

KAPILA Here you are. The Fortunate Lady's flowers.

PADMINI And why a 'Fortunate Lady', pray?

KAPILA Because it has all the marks of marriage a woman puts on. The yellow on the petals – then that red round patch at the bottom of the petals – like on your foreheads – then – here that thin saffron line – like the parting of your hair – Then – uhm . . . oh yes – here near the stem a row of black dots – like a necklace of black heads –

PADMINI What imagination! (*To* DEVADATTA) You should put it in your poetry. It's good for a simile.

DEVADATTA Shall we go? It's quite late.

PADMINI Let's stay. I have been sitting in that cart for I don't know how long. I didn't know the road to Ujjain was so enchanting . . .

KAPILA The others take a longer route. This is a more wooded area – so very few come this way. But I like this better. Besides, it's fifteen miles shorter.

PADMINI I wouldn't have minded even if it were fifteen miles longer. It's like a garden . . .

KAPILA Isn't it? Look there, do you see it? That's the river Bhargavi. The poet Vyasa had a hermitage on its banks. There's a temple of Rudra there now.

DEVADATTA (*suddenly awake*) A temple of Rudra?

KAPILA Yes, it's beautiful. And – there – beyond that hill is a temple of Kali. (*Two stage-hands come and hold up a half-curtain in the corner to which he points. The curtain has a picture of Goddess Kali on it. The* BHAGAVATA *puts a sword in front of it.*) It was very prosperous once. But now it's quite dilapidated.

DEVADATTA (*as though in a trance*) The temple of Rudra!

KAPILA Yes, that's old too. But not half as ruined as the Kali temple. We can have a look if you like.

PADMINI Yes, let's.

DEVADATTA Why don't you go and see the Kali temple first?

KAPILA No, that's quite terrible . . . I saw it once – bats, snakes, all sorts of poisonous insects – and no proper road. We can go to the Rudra temple, though. It's nearer.

PADMINI Come on. Let's go.

DEVADATTA You two go. I won't come.

PADMINI (*pause*) And you?

DEVADATTA I'll stay here and watch the cart.

KAPILA But there's no fear of thieves here . . . (*sensing the tension*) Or else, I'll stay here . . .

DEVADATTA No, no. You two go. I'm also a little tired.

PADMINI (*aside*) He has started it again. Another tantrum. Let him. What do I care? (*Aloud*) Come, Kapila, we'll go.

KAPILA But – perhaps in your condition . . .

PADMINI (*exploding*) Why are you two hounding me with this condition? If you don't want to come, say so. Don't make excuses . . .

KAPILA Devadatta, it's not very far. You come too . . .

DEVADATTA I told you to go. Don't force me . . .

PADMINI Let's not go. I don't want the two of you to suffer for my sake.

DEVADATTA (*to* KAPILA) Go.

KAPILA (*He has no choice.*) Come. We'll be back soon. (KAPILA *and* PADMINI *go out.*)

DEVADATTA Good-bye, Kapila. Good-bye, Padmini. May Lord Rudra bless you. You are two pieces of my heart – live happily together. I shall find my happiness in that. (*Agonized*) Give me strength, Lord Rudra. My father, give me courage. I'm already trembling, I'd never thought I would be so afraid. Give me courage, Father, strengthen me. (*He walks to the temple of Kali. It's a steep and difficult climb. He is exhausted by the time he reaches the temple. He prostrates himself before the goddess.*) Bhavani, Bhairavi, Kali, Durga, Mahamaya, Mother of all Nature – I had forgotten my promise to you. Forgive me, Mother. You fulfilled the deepest craving of my life – you gave me Padmini – and I forgot my word. Forgive me, for I'm here now to carry out my promise. (*Picks up the sword.*) Great indeed is your mercy. Even in this lonely place some devotee of yours – a hunter perhaps or a tribesman – has left this weapon. Who knows how many lives this weapon has sacrificed to you . . . (*Screaming*) Here, Mother Kali, here's another. My head. Take it, Mother, accept this little offering of my head. (*Cuts off his head. Not an easy thing to do – he struggles, groans, writhes. Ultimately succeeds in killing himself. The head – that is, the mask – rolls off and blood flows. A long silence.* PADMINI *and* KAPILA *return to the cart.*)

PADMINI (*enters talking*) . . . he should have come. How thrilling it was! Heavenly! But of course he has no enthusiasm for these things. After all . . . (*Notices* DEVADATTA *isn't there.*) Where's Devadatta? (*They look around.*) He said he'd stay here!

KAPILA (*calls*) Devadatta – Devadatta . . .

PADMINI   He's probably somewhere around. Where will he go? He has the tenderest feet on earth. They manage to get blisters, corns, cuts, boils and wounds without any effort. So . . .

KAPILA   (calls) Devadatta . . .

PADMINI   Why are you shouting? Sit down. He'll come. (KAPILA inspects the surrounding area. Gives a gasp of surprise.) What's it?

KAPILA   His footprints. He has obviously gone in that direction. (Pause.) But – that's where the Kali temple is!

PADMINI   You don't mean he's gone there! How absurd!

KAPILA   You stay here. I'll bring him back.

PADMINI   But why do you have to go? There's nothing to fear in this broad daylight!

KAPILA   (hurrying off) It's very thick wood there. If he gets lost, he'll have to spend the whole night in the jungle. You stay here. I'll come back soon. (Runs out.)

PADMINI   (exasperated) He's gone! Really, he seems more worried about Devadatta than me.

(She sits down. KAPILA goes to the Kali temple – but naturally faster than DEVADATTA did. He sees the body and his mouth half opens in a scream. He runs to DEVADATTA and kneels beside him. Lifts his truncated head and moans.)

KAPILA   You've cut off your head! You've cut off your head! Oh my dear friend, my brother, what have you done? Were you so angry with me? Did you feel such contempt for me – such abhorrence? And in your anger you forgot that I was ready to die for you? If you had asked me to jump into fire, I would have done it. If you had asked me to leave the country, I would have done it. If you had asked me to go and drown in a river, I would have accepted. Did you despise me so much that you couldn't even ask me that? I did wrong. But you should know I don't have the intelligence to know what else I should have done. I couldn't think – and so you've pushed me away? No, Devadatta, I can't live without you. I can't breathe without you. Devadatta, my brother, my father, my friend . . . (Picks up the sword.) You spurned me in this world. Accept me as your brother at least in the next. Here, friend, here I come. As always, I follow in your path. (Cuts off his head. It's an easier death this time. PADMINI, who has been still till now, moves.)

PADMINI   Where are they? Now this Kapila's disappeared too. He couldn't still be searching for him. That's not possible. Devadatta's too weak to have gone far. They must have met. Perhaps they're sitting now, chatting as in the old days. For once no bother of a wife around . . . No, more likely Devadatta's sulking. He's probably tearing poor Kapila to shreds by just being silent and grumpy. Yes, that would be more like him. (Pause.) It's almost dark. And they aren't back. Shameless men – to leave me alone like this here! No, it's no use sitting here any longer. I had better go and look for them. If I die of a snake-bite on the way, so much the better for them. (Walks to the temple, slowly. Rubs her eyes when she reaches there.) How dark it is? Can't see a thing. (Calls) Kapila – Kapila – Devadatta isn't here either. What shall I do here? At this time of night! Alone! (Listens.) What's that? Some wild beast. A wolf! It's right outside – what shall I do if it comes in? . . . Ah! It's gone. Mother Kali, only you can protect me now. (Stumbles over the bodies.) What's this? What's this? (Stares at the bodies and then lets out a terrified scream.) Oh God! What's this? Both! Both gone! And didn't even think of me before they went? What shall I do? What shall I do? Oh, Devadatta, what did I do that you left me alone in this state? Was that how much you loved me? And you, Kapila, who looked at me with dog's eyes – you too? How selfish you are – how unkind! What shall I do now – where shall I go? How can I go home? (Pause.) Home? And what shall I say when I get there? What shall I say happened? And who'll believe me? They'll all say the two fought and died for this whore. They're bound to say it. Then what'll happen to me? No, Mother Kali, no – it's too horrible to think of. No! Kapila's gone – Devadatta's gone. Let me go with them. (Picks up the sword.) I don't have the strength to hack off my head. But what does it matter how I die, Mother? You don't care. It's the same to you – another offering! All right. Have it then – here's another offering for you. (Lifts the sword and puts its point on her breast when, from behind the curtain, the goddess's voice is heard.)

VOICE   Hey . . . (PADMINI *freezes.*) Put it down! Put down that sword! (PADMINI *jumps up in fright and, throwing the sword aside, tries to run out of the temple. Then stops.*)

PADMINI   Who's that? (*No reply.*) Who's that?

(*A tremendous noise of drums.* PADMINI *shuts her eyes in terror. Behind the curtain one sees the uplifted blood-red palms of the goddess. The curtain is lowered and taken away and one sees a terrifying figure, her arms stretched out, her mouth wide open with the tongue lolling out. The drums stop and as the goddess drops her arms and shuts her mouth, it becomes clear she has been yawning.*)

KALI   (*Completes the yawn.*) All right. Open your eyes and be quick. Don't waste time.

(PADMINI *opens her eyes and sees the goddess. She runs and falls at her feet.*)

PADMINI   Mother – Kali . . .

KALI   (*sleepy*) Yes, it's me. There was a time – many many years ago – when at this hour they would have the mangalarati. The devotees used to make a deafening racket with drums and conch-shells and cymbals. So I used to be wide awake around now. I've lost the habit. (*Yawns.*) Right. What do you want? Tell me. I'm pleased with you.

PADMINI   Save me, Mother . . .

KALI   I know. I've done that already.

PADMINI   Do you call this saving, Mother of all Nature? I can't show my face to anyone in the world. I can't . . .

KALI   (*a little testily*) Yes, yes, you've said that once. No need to repeat yourself. Now do as I tell you. Put these heads back properly. Attach them to their bodies and then press that sword on their necks. They'll come up alive. Is that enough?

PADMINI   Mother, you are our breath, you are our bread – and – water . . .

KALI   Skip it! Do as I told you. And quickly. I'm collapsing with sleep.

PADMINI   (*hesitating*) May I ask a question?

KALI   If it's not too long.

PADMINI   Can there ever be anything you already don't know, Mother? The past and the future are mere specks in your palm. Then why didn't you stop Devadatta when he came here? Why didn't you stop Kapila? If you'd saved either of them, I would have

been spared all this terror, this agony. Why did you wait so long?

KALI   (*surprised*) Is that all you can think of now?

PADMINI   Mother . . .

KALI   I've never seen anyone like you.

PADMINI   How could one possibly hide anything from you, Mother?

KALI   That's true enough.

PADMINI   Then why didn't you stop them?

KALI   Actually if it hadn't been that I was so sleepy, I would have thrown them out by the scruff of their necks . . .

PADMINI   But why?

KALI   The rascals! They were lying to their last breaths. That fellow Devadatta – he had once promised his head to Rudra and his arms to me! Think of it – head to him and arms to me! Then because you insisted on going to the Rudra temple, he comes here and offers his head. Nobly too – wants to keep his word, he says – no other reason! Then this Kapila, died right in front of me – but 'for his friend'. Mind you! Didn't even have the courtesy to refer to me. And what lies! Says he is dying for friendship. He must have known perfectly well he would be accused of killing Devadatta for you. Do you think he wouldn't have grabbed you if it hadn't been for that fear? But till his last breath – 'Oh my friend! My dear brother!' Only you spoke the truth.

PADMINI   It's all your grace, Mother . . .

KALI   Don't drag me into it. I had nothing to do with it. You spoke the truth because you're selfish – that's all. Now don't go on talking. Do what I told you and shut your eyes.

PADMINI   Yes, Mother . . . (*Eagerly,* PADMINI *puts the heads – that is, the masks – back. But in her excitement she mixes them up so that* DEVADATTA's *mask goes to* KAPILA's *body and vice versa. Then presses the sword on their necks, does namaskara to the goddess, walks downstage and stands with her back to the goddess, her eyes shut tight.*) I'm ready, Mother.

KALI   (*in a resigned tone*) My dear daughter, there should be a limit even to honesty. Anyway – So be it!

(*Again the drums. The curtain is held up again and the goddess disappears behind it. During the following scene the stage-hands, the curtain, as well as the goddess, leave the stage.* PADMINI *stands immobile with her eyes shut. The drums stop. A long silence follows. The dead bodies move. Their breathing becomes loud and laboured. They sit up, slowly, stiffly. Their movement is mechanical, as though blood-circulation has not started properly yet. They feel their own arms, heads and bodies, and look around, bewildered. Henceforth the person wearing the mask of* DEVADATTA *will be called* DEVADATTA. *Similarly with* KAPILA. *They stand up. It's not easy and they reel around a bit.* PADMINI *is still.*)

DEVADATTA   What – happened?
KAPILA   . . . What happened?

(PADMINI *opens her eyes, but she still doesn't dare to look at them.*)

PADMINI   Devadatta's voice! Kapila's voice! (*Screaming with joy*) Kapila! Devadatta! (*Turns and runs to them. Then suddenly stops and stands paralysed.*)
KAPILA   Who . . . ?
DEVADATTA   Padmini?
KAPILA   What – happened? My head – Ooh! It feels so heavy!
DEVADATTA   My body – seems to weigh – a ton.
PADMINI   (*running around in confusion*) What have I done? What have I done? What have I done? Mother Kali, only you can save me now – only you can help me – What have I done? What have I done? What should I do? Mother – Mother . . .
DEVADATTA   (*a little more alive*) Why are you – crying?
KAPILA   What's – wrong?
PADMINI   What shall I tell you, Devadatta? How can I explain it, Kapila? You cut off your heads – but the goddess gave you life – but – I – I – in the dark . . . Mother, only you can protect me now – Mother! I – mixed up your heads – I mixed them up! Forgive me – I don't deserve to live – forgive me . . .
KAPILA   (*looking at* DEVADATTA) You mixed up . . .
DEVADATTA   . . . the heads? (*They stare at each other. Then burst in to laughter. She doesn't know how to react. Watches them. Then starts laughing.*)
DEVADATTA   Mixed-up heads!
KAPILA   Heads mixed-up!
DEVADATTA   Exchanged heads!
KAPILA   Heads exchanged!

DEVADATTA   How fantastic! All these years we were only friends . . .
KAPILA   Now we are blood-relations! Body-relations! (*Laughing*) What a gift!
DEVADATTA   Forgive you? We must thank you . . .
KAPILA   We'll never be able to thank you – enough . . .
DEVADATTA   Exchanged heads! (*They roar with laughter. Then all three hold hands and run round in a circle, singing.*)
ALL THREE   (*together*)
  What a good mix!
  No more tricks!
  Is this one that
  Or that one this?
  Ho! Ho!
(*They sing this over and over again until they collapse on the floor.*)
KAPILA   Oooh – I'm finished!
PADMINI   . . . dead!
DEVADATTA   Nothing like this could have ever happened before.
PADMINI   You know, seeing you two with your heads off was bad enough. But when you got up it was terrible! I almost died of fright . . . (*They laugh.*)
KAPILA   No one will believe us if we tell them.
PADMINI   (*suddenly*) We won't tell anyone.
DEVADATTA   We'll keep our secrets inside us.
PADMINI   'Inside us' is right. (*Laughter.*)
KAPILA   But how can we not tell? They'll know soon . . .
DEVADATTA   No one'll know.
KAPILA   I'm sure they'll . . .
DEVADATTA   I'll take any bet.
KAPILA   But how's that possible?
DEVADATTA   You'll see. Why worry now?
PADMINI   Come. Let's go . . .
KAPILA   It's late.
DEVADATTA   No Ujjain now. We go back home!
KAPILA   Absolutely.
PADMINI   This Ujjain will last us a lifetime. Come. (*They get up. Every now and then someone laughs and then all burst out together.*) Devadatta, I really don't know how we're going to keep this from your parents. They'll guess as soon as they see you bare-bodied.
DEVADATTA   They won't, I tell you. They take us too much for granted . . .
KAPILA   What do you mean?

DEVADATTA   Who ever looks hard at a person he sees every day?

KAPILA   I don't mean that . . .

PADMINI   I'm not so sure. I'm afraid I'll get the blame for it ultimately . . .

DEVADATTA   Stop worrying! I tell you it . . .

KAPILA   But what has she got to do with you now?

DEVADATTA   (stops) What do you mean?

KAPILA   I mean Padmini must come home with me, shouldn't she? She's my wife, so she must . . .

(Exclamations from DEVADATTA and PADMINI.)

PADMINI   What are you talking of, Kapila?

KAPILA   (explaining) I mean, you are Devadatta's wife. I have Devadatta's body now. So you have to be my wife . . .

PADMINI   Shut up . . .

DEVADATTA   Don't blather like an idiot! I am Devadatta . . .

PADMINI   Aren't you ashamed of yourself?

KAPILA   But why, Padmini? I have Devadatta's body now . . .

DEVADATTA   We know that. You don't have to repeat yourself like a parrot. According to the Shastras, the head is the sign of a man . . .

KAPILA   (angry now) That may be. But the question now is simply this: Whose wife is she? (Raising his right hand) This is the hand that accepted her at the wedding. This the body she's lived with all these months. And the child she's carrying is the seed of this body.

PADMINI   (frightened by the logic) No, no, no. It's not possible. It's not. (Running to DEVADATTA) It's not, Devadatta.

DEVADATTA   Of course, it isn't, my dear. He is ignorant . . . (To KAPILA) When one accepts a partner in marriage, with the holy fire as one's witness, one accepts a person, not a body. She didn't marry Devadatta's body, she married Devadatta – the person.

KAPILA   If that's your argument, I have Devadatta's body, so I am Devadatta – the person.

DEVADATTA   Listen to me. Of all the human limbs the topmost – in position as well as in importance – is the head. I have Devadatta's head and it follows that I am Devadatta. According to the Sacred Texts . . .

KAPILA   Don't tell me about your Sacred Texts. You can always twist them to suit

your needs. She married Devadatta's body with the holy fire as her witness and that's enough for me.

DEVADATTA   (laughs) Did you hear that, Padmini? He claims to be Devadatta and yet he condemns the Texts. You think Devadatta would ever do that?

KAPILA   You can quote as many Texts as you like, I don't give a nail. Come on, Padmini . . . (Takes a step towards her. But DEVADATTA steps in between.)

DEVADATTA   Take care!

PADMINI   Come, Devadatta. It's no use arguing with this rascal. Let's go.

DEVADATTA   Come on . . .

KAPILA   (stepping between them) Where are you taking my wife, friend?

DEVADATTA   Will you get out of our way or should . . .

KAPILA   It was you who got in my way.

DEVADATTA   (pushing KAPILA aside) Get away, you pig.

KAPILA   (triumphant) He's using force! And what language! Padmini, think! Would Devadatta ever have acted like this? This is Kapila's violence . . .

DEVADATTA   Come. Padmini.

KAPILA   Go. But do you think I'll stay put while you run away with my wife? Where will you go? How far can you go? Only to the city, after all. I'll follow you there. I'll kick up a row in the streets. Let's see what happens then. (DEVADATTA stops.)

PADMINI   Let him scream away. Don't pay him any attention.

DEVADATTA   No. He's right. This has to be solved here. It'll create a scandal in the city . . .

PADMINI   But who'll listen to him? Everyone will take you for Devadatta by your face.

KAPILA   Ha! You think the people in Dharmapura don't know my body, do you? They've seen me a thousand times in the wrestling pit. I've got I don't know how many awards for body-building. Let's see whom they believe.

PADMINI   (pleading) Why are you torturing us like this? For so many years you have been our friend, accepted our hospitality . . .

KAPILA   I know what you want, Padmini. Devadatta's clever head and Kapila's strong body . . .

PADMINI   Shut up, you brute.

DEVADATTA   Suppose she did. There's nothing wrong in it. It's natural for a woman to feel attracted to a fine figure of a man . . .

KAPILA I know it is. But that doesn't mean she can just go and live with a man who's not her husband. That's not right.

PADMINI (*crying out*) How can we get rid of this scoundrel? Let's go – let's go anywhere – to the woods – to the desert – anywhere you like.

KAPILA You'll have to kill me before you really escape me. You could. I don't have the strength to resist Kapila.

PADMINI (*using a new argument*) But I gave you life –

KAPILA That was no favour. If you hadn't, you would have been a widow now. Actually he should be grateful to me because my wife saved his life. Instead, he's trying to snatch you away.

(PADMINI *moans in agony*.)

DEVADATTA This way we won't get anywhere, Kapila . . .

KAPILA Call me Devadatta . . .

DEVADATTA Whatever you are, this is no way to solve the problem.

KAPILA Of course not. If marriage were a contract it would be. But how can Padmini's fancy be taken as the solution?

DEVADATTA Then what is the solution to this problem? (*They all freeze.*)

BHAGAVATA What? What indeed is the solution to this problem, which holds the entire future of these three unfortunate beings in a balance? Must their fate remain a mystery? And if so shall we not be insulting our audience by tying a question-mark round its neck and bidding it good-bye? We have to face the problem. But it's a deep one and the answer must be sought with the greatest caution. Haste would be disastrous. So there's a break of ten minutes now. Please have some tea, ponder over this situation and come back with your own solutions. We shall then continue with our enquiry.

(*The stage-hands hold a white curtain in front of the frozen threesome, while the* BHAGAVATA *and others relax and sip tea.*)

Act II

The white curtain is removed.

BHAGAVATA What? What indeed is the solution to this problem, which holds the entire future of these three unfortunate beings in a balance? Way back in the ages, when King Vikrama was ruling the world, shining in glory like the earth's challenge to the sun, he was asked the same question by the demon Vetala. And the king offered a solution even without, as it were, batting an eyelid. But will his rational, logical answer backed by the Sacred Texts appeal to our audience?

(*Sings*)

The future pointed out by the tongue safe inside the skull is not acceptable to us.
We must read the forehead which Brahma has disconnected from the entrails.
We must unravel the net on the palm disclaimed by the brain.
We must plumb the hidden depths of the rivers running under our veins.

Yes, that would be the right thing to do. So our three unfortunate friends went to a great rishi in search of a solution to their problem. And the rishi – remembering perhaps what King Vikrama had said – gave the solution: (*in a loud, sonorous voice*) As the heavenly Kalpa Vriksha is supreme among trees, so is the head among human limbs. Therefore the man with Devadatta's head is indeed Devadatta and he is the rightful husband of Padmini. (*The three spring to life.* DEVADATTA *and* PADMINI *scream with joy and move to one corner of the stage laughing and dancing.* KAPILA, *brokenhearted, drags his feet to the other corner.*)

DEVADATTA (*embracing* PADMINI) My Padmini . . . my lovely Padmini . . .

PADMINI My King – My Master . . .

DEVADATTA My little lightning . . .

PADMINI The light of my joy . . .

DEVADATTA The flower of my palm . . .

PADMINI My celestial-bodied Gandharva . . . My sun-faced Indra . . .

DEVADATTA My Queen of Indra's Court . . .

PADMINI (*caressing his shoulders*) Come. Let's go. Let's go quickly. Where the earth is soft and the green grass plays the swing.

DEVADATTA Let us. Where the banyan spreads a canopy and curtains off the skies . . .

PADMINI What a wide chest. What other canopy do I need?

DEVADATTA My soft, swaying Padmini. What other swing do I want?

PADMINI   My Devadatta comes like a bridegroom with the ornament of a new body . . .

DEVADATTA   (*a manly laugh*) And who should wear the ornaments but the eager bride . . .

PADMINI   Let's go. (*Pause.*) Wait. (*She runs to* KAPILA.) Don't be sad, Kapila. We shall meet again, shan't we? (*In a low voice, so* DEVADATTA *can't hear*) It's my duty to go with Devadatta. But remember I'm going with your body. Let that cheer you up. (*Goes back to* DEVADATTA.) Good-bye, Kapila.

DEVADATTA   Good-bye. (*They go out, laughing, rubbing against each other.* KAPILA *stands mute for a while. Then moves.*)

BHAGAVATA   Kapila – Kapila . . . (*No reply.*) Don't grieve. It's fate, Kapila, and . . .

KAPILA   Kapila? What? Me? Why am I Kapila? (*Exit.*)

BHAGAVATA   So the roads diverged. Kapila went into the forest and disappeared. He never saw Dharmapura again. In fact he never felt the wind of any city again. As for Devadatta and Padmini, they returned to Dharmapura and plunged into the joys of married life.

(PADMINI *enters and sits. She is stitching clothes.* DEVADATTA *enters. He is carrying in his hands two large dolls – which could be played by two children. The dolls are dressed in a way which makes it impossible to decide their sex.* DEVADATTA *comes in quietly and stands behind* PADMINI.)

DEVADATTA   Hey!

PADMINI   (*startled*) Oh! Really, Devadatta. You frightened me. The needle pricked me! Look, my finger's bleeding.

DEVADATTA   Tut-Tut! Is it really? Put it in my mouth – I'll suck it.

PADMINI   No, thanks. I'll suck it myself. (*Sees the dolls.*) How pretty! Whose are these?

DEVADATTA   Whose? Ours, of course! The guest is arriving soon – he must have playmates.

PADMINI   But the guest won't be coming for months yet, silly, and . . .

DEVADATTA   I know he isn't, but you can't get dolls like these any time you like! These are special dolls from the Ujjain fair . . .

PADMINI   They are lovely! (*Hugs the dolls.*) They look almost alive – such shining eyes – such delicate cheeks . . . (*Kisses them.*) Now sit down and tell me everything that happened at the fair. You wouldn't take me with you . . .

DEVADATTA   How could I – in your condition? I went only because you insisted you wanted to keep your word. But I'm glad I went. A very funny thing happened – there was a wrestling pit and a wrestler from Gandhara was challenging people to fight him. I don't know what got into me – Before I'd even realized it, I had stripped, put on the pants given by his assistant and jumped into the pit.

PADMINI   (*fondling the dolls*) You didn't! You've never wrestled before . . .

DEVADATTA   Didn't think of anything. I felt – 'inspired'! Within a couple of minutes, I had pinned him to the ground.

PADMINI   (*laughs*) What would your father say if he heard of this?

DEVADATTA   My few acquaintances there were quite amazed.

PADMINI   (*caressing his arm*) That day in the gymnasium you defeated the champion in a sword-fight. Now this! Don't overdo it – people may start suspecting.

DEVADATTA   Of course they won't. I was standing there bare-bodied and not a soul suspected. A friend even asked me if I'd learnt it from Kapila.

PADMINI   You have, after all! (*They laugh.*)

DEVADATTA   You know, I'd always thought one had to use one's brains while wrestling or fencing or swimming. But this body just doesn't wait for thoughts – it acts!

PADMINI   Fabulous body – fabulous brain – fabulous Devadatta.

DEVADATTA   I have been running around all these days without even proper sleep – and yet I don't feel a bit tired. (*Jumps up.*) Come on, we'll have a picnic by the lake. I feel like a good, long swim.

PADMINI   (*mocking*) In my condition?

DEVADATTA   I didn't ask you to swim. You sit there and enjoy the scenery. Once our son's born, I'll teach you to swim too . . .

PADMINI   You go on about it being a son. What if it's a daughter?

DEVADATTA   If she's a daughter like you, I'll teach the two of you together.

PADMINI   Ready! (*He pulls her to him.*) Now – now – what about the picnic?

DEVADATTA   Quite right. First things first.

PADMINI   (*pause*) Devadatta . . .

DEVADATTA   Yes?

PADMINI   Why do you – have to apply that sandal oil on your body?

DEVADATTA   I like it.

PADMINI   I know, but . . .

DEVADATTA   What?

PADMINI   (*hesitating*) Your body had that strong, male smell before – I liked it . . .

DEVADATTA   But I've been using sandal oil since I was a child!

PADMINI   I don't mean that. But – when we came back from the temple of Kali – you used to smell so manly . . .

DEVADATTA   You mean that unwashed, sweaty smell Kapila had? (*Incredulous*) You liked that?

PADMINI   (*Pause. Then lightly*) It was just a suggestion. Come on, let's start. We'll be late.

(*They go out. A long silence.*)

DOLL 1   Not a bad house, I would say.

DOLL 2   Could have been worse. I was a little worried.

DOLL 1   This is the least we deserved. Actually we should have got a palace. A real palace!

DOLL 2   And a prince to play with. A real prince!

DOLL 1   How the children looked at us at the fair! How their eyes glowed!

DOLL 2   How their mothers stared at us! How their mouths watered!

DOLL 1   Only those beastly men turned up their noses! 'Expensive! Too expensive!'

DOLL 2   Presuming to judge us! Who do they think they are!

DOLL 1   Only a prince would be worthy of us.

DOLL 2   We should be dusted every day . . .

DOLL 1   . . . dressed in silk . . .

DOLL 2   . . . seated on a cushioned shelf . . .

DOLL 1   . . . given new clothes every week.

DOLL 2   If the doll-maker had any sense, he'd never have sold us.

DOLL 1   If he had any brains, he should never have . . . given us to this man . . .

DOLL 2   . . . with his rough labourer's hands.

DOLL 1   Palms like wood . . .

DOLL 2   A grip like a vice . . .

DOLL 1   My arms are still aching . . .

DOLL 2   He doesn't deserve us, the peasant.

(DEVADATTA *comes running in, tosses the dolls in the air, catches them and kisses them.*)

DEVADATTA   My dolls, your prince has arrived! The prince has come!

DOLL 1   (*in agony*) Brute! An absolute brute!

DOLL 2   (*in agony*) Beast! A complete beast!

DEVADATTA   (*Runs to the* BHAGAVATA.) Here, Bhagavata Sir, take these sweets. You must come to the feast tomorrow at our house.

BHAGAVATA   What's it for?

DEVADATTA   Haven't you heard? I've got a son like a gem – a son like a rose – Yippeee . . . (*He goes out dancing some Lezim steps. A long silence.*)

DOLL 1   Is that little satan asleep yet?

DOLL 2   Think so. God! It's killing me . . .

DOLL 1   . . . crying, all day . . .

DOLL 2   . . . making a mess every fifteen minutes.

DOLL 1   What have we come to! One should never trust God . . .

DOLL 2   It's our fault. We should have been wary from the moment we saw that child in her dreams . . .

DOLL 1   We should have noticed she was bloating day by day.

DOLL 2   We should have suspected foul play then.

DOLL 1   It wasn't our fault. How could we know she was hiding this thing inside her?

DOLL 2   How she was swelling! Day by day! Week by week! As though someone were blowing air into her . . .

DOLL 1   How ugly she looked . . .

DOLL 2   . . . not to her husband, though!

DOLL 1   When they were alone, he would place his hand on her belly and say, 'Is he kicking now?'

DOLL 2   (*seriously*) We should have been on our guard.

DOLL 1   (*dispirited*) We should.

DOLL 2   And then comes this son of a satan . . .

DOLL 1   . . . this lump of flesh . . .

DOLL 2   He doesn't even have proper eyes or ears . . .

DOLL 1   . . . but he gets all the attention.

DOLL 2   (*in disgust*) Ugh . . .

DOLL 1   (*sick*) Awk . . .

(DEVADATTA *and* PADMINI *enter with the child – for which a wooden doll may be used. They walk across the stage, engrossed in talking to and about the child, and go out.*)

DOLL 1   A spider's built its web on my shoulders.

DOLL 2   Yesterday a mouse nibbled at my toe.

DOLL 1   The other day a cockroach ate my left eye.

DOLL 2   Six months – and not a soul has come near us.

DOLL 1   Six months – and not a hand has touched us.

DOLL 2   Six months and we reach this state. What'll happen in a year's time?

(PADMINI *and* DEVADATTA *enter.*)

PADMINI   Listen . . .

DEVADATTA   Yes.

PADMINI   You mustn't say 'no' – at least this time.

DEVADATTA   To what?

PADMINI   We'll take him to the lake.

DEVADATTA   In this cold?

PADMINI   What if it's cold? He's older now. There's no need to mollycoddle him. I grew up running around in heat and cold and rain – and nothing happened to me. I'm all right . . .

DEVADATTA   No, it's unnecessary trouble for everyone.

PADMINI   What do you mean trouble? What's happened to you these days? You sit at home all day. Never go out. You've forgotten all your swimming and sports . . .

DEVADATTA   I'm a Brahmin, Padmini. My duty . . .

PADMINI   I've heard all that!

DEVADATTA   It was fun the first few days because it was new. All that muscle and strength. But how long can one go on like that? I have the family tradition to maintain – the daily reading, writing and studies . . .

PADMINI   I don't know.

DEVADATTA   (*affectionate*) Now look here, Padmini . . . (*Puts his hand round her shoulder. She suddenly shudders.*) Why? What happened?

PADMINI   Nothing – I don't know why – I suddenly had goose flesh. (*Pause.*)

DEVADATTA   (*withdrawing his hand*) Do you know where I've kept the copy of *Dharma Sindhu*? I've been looking for it.

PADMINI   I think I saw it on the shelf. Must be there . . . (DEVADATTA *goes to* DOLL 1, *moves it aside and picks up the book.* DOLL 1 *shudders.*)

DOLL 2   Why? What happened?

DOLL 1   He touched me, and . . .

DOLL 2   Yes?

DOLL 1   His palms! They were so rough, when he first brought us here. Like a labourer's. But now they are soft – sickly soft – like a young girl's.

DOLL 2   I know. I've noticed something too.

DOLL 1   What?

DOLL 2   His stomach. It was so tight and muscular. Now . . .

DOLL 1   I know. It's loose . . .

DOLL 2   Do you think it'll swell up too? (*They laugh.*)

DOLL 1   (*holding its hands in front of its stomach to suggest a swollen belly*) It'll swell a little . . .

DOLL 2   (*holding its hands a little further in front*) – then more . . .

DOLL 1   (*even more*) – more and . . .

DOLL 2   (*even further*) – and more until . . .

DOLL 1   . . . if it's a woman . . .

DOLL 2   . . . there'll be a child . . .

DOLL 1   . . . and if it's a man . . .

DOLL 2   BANG! (*They roll with laughter.* PADMINI *comes in with the child. She sings a lullaby.*)

PADMINI

Here comes a rider!
From what land does he come?
On his head a turban
with a long pearly tail.
Round his neck a garland
of virgin-white jasmines.
In his fist a sword
with a diamond-studded hilt.
The white-clad rider
rides a white charger
which spreads its tossing mane
against the western sky,
spreads its mane like breakers
against the western sky.
Sleep now my baby
and see smiling dreams.
There he comes – here he is!
From which land does he come?
But why are the jasmines on his chest
Red O so red?
What shine in his open eyes?
Pebbles O pebbles.
Why is his young body
cold O so cold?
The white horse gallops
across hills, streams and fields.
To what land does he gallop?
Nowhere O nowhere.

(*Half-way through the lullaby,* DEVADATTA *comes in and sits by* PADMINI's *side, reading. They don't look at each other. At the end of the lullaby, they fall asleep.*)

DOLL 1 (*in a hushed voice*) Hey . . .

DOLL 2 Yes . . .

DOLL 1 Look . . .

DOLL 2 Where . . .

DOLL 1 Behind her eyelids. She is dreaming.

DOLL 2 I don't see anything.

DOLL 1 It's still hazy – hasn't started yet . . . Do you see it now?

DOLL 2 (*eagerly*) Yes, yes. (*They stare at her.*)

DOLL 1 A man . . .

DOLL 2 but not her husband.

DOLL 1 No, someone else.

DOLL 2 Is this the one who came last night?

DOLL 1 Yes – the same. But I couldn't see his face then.

DOLL 2 You can now. Not very nice – rough. Like a labourer's. But he's got a nice body – looks soft.

DOLL 1 Who do you think it is?

DOLL 2 I – it's fading. (*Urgently*) Remember the face!

DOLL 1 It's fading – Oh! It's gone!

DOLL 2 And she won't even remember it tomorrow.

(PADMINI *and* DEVADATTA *sit up.*)

PADMINI Are you ill?

DEVADATTA Why?

PADMINI You were moaning in your sleep last night.

DEVADATTA Was I?

PADMINI Aren't you feeling well?

DEVADATTA Who? Me? I'm fine . . . (*Gets up energetically to show how well he feels. Suddenly grabs his shoulder with a groan.*)

PADMINI What's wrong? Tell me . . .

DEVADATTA (*avoiding her eyes*) Nothing. I went to the gymnasium yesterday morning. Then went swimming . . .

PADMINI To the gymnasium? After all these years? But why?

DEVADATTA I just felt like it. That's all. Don't go on about it.

PADMINI (*without irony*) Are you going again today?

DEVADATTA (*flares up*) No, I'm not. And there's no need to laugh. I know I've made a fool of myself by going there. I won't again. (*Goes out. Long pause.*)

PADMINI What are you afraid of, Devadatta? What does it matter that you are going soft again, that you are losing your muscles? I'm not going to be stupid again. Kapila's gone out of my life – forever. I won't let him come back again. (*Pause.*) Kapila?

What could he be doing now? Where could he be? Could his body be fair still, and his face dark? (*Long pause*) Devadatta changes. Kapila changes. And me? (*Closes her eyes.*)

DOLL 1 There he is again.

DOLL 2 In the middle of the day?

DOLL 1 (*doubtful*) I'm not sure this is the usual visitor. This one looks rougher and darker.

DOLL 2 It's him all right. Look at his face.

DOLL 1 He goes to her . . .

DOLL 2 . . . very near her . . .

DOLL 1 (*in a whisper*) What's he going to do now?

DOLL 2 (*even more anxious*) What? (*They watch.*)

DOLL 1 (*baffled*) But he's climbing a tree!

DOLL 2 (*almost a wail of disappointment*) He's dived into a river!

DOLL 1 Is that all he came for?

DOLL 2 It's going . . .

DOLL 1 . . . going . . .

DOLL 2 Gone! Wretched dreams – They just trickle and fade away.

(PADMINI *wakes up and mimes putting the crying child to sleep.*)

PADMINI (*suddenly vicious*) Change! Change! Change! Change! Change! The sand trickles. The water fills the pot. And the moon goes on swinging, swinging, swinging, from light to darkness to light.

(DEVADATTA *comes in. He is now completely changed to his original self – that is, the slender actor who came as* DEVADATTA *at the beginning of the play comes back again with the* DEVADATTA *mask on.*)

DEVADATTA A pundit's coming to see me. He wants me to explain some verses to him. Can you keep some sweets and lime-juice ready?

PADMINI Yes. (*Pause.*) Did you hear . . . ? The maid was telling me . . .

DEVADATTA What?

PADMINI Kapila's mother died this morning. (*Pause.*) Poor thing! She'd been bed-ridden all these years, ever since . . .

DEVADATTA (*snapping at her*) What did you expect me to do about it? (*Then embarrassed*) Get the lime-juice ready soon. (*They go out.*)

DOLL 1 Each one to his fate!

DOLL 2 Each one to her problems!

DOLL 1   As the doll-maker used to say, 'What are things coming to!'

DOLL 2   Especially last night – I mean – that dream . . .

DOLL 1   Tut-tut – One shouldn't talk about such things!

DOLL 2   It was so shameless . . .

DOLL 1   I said be quiet . . .

DOLL 2   Honestly! The way they . . .

DOLL 1   Look, if we must talk about it, let me.

DOLL 2   You didn't want to talk about it. So . . .

DOLL 1   You don't understand a thing. They . . .

DOLL 2   What do you know? Last night . . .

DOLL 1   Let me! In dream . . .

DOLL 2   I'm . . .

DOLL 1   Shut up!

DOLL 2   You shut up!

(*They start arguing, then fighting. They roll on the ground, on top of each other, biting, scratching, hitting each other. They shout, scream and giggle. As they fight, the giggles become louder and more frantic. Their clothes get torn. At last they lie side by side panting, bursting with little giggles. They sit up.* PADMINI *enters, looks at them.*)

PADMINI   Just look at the dolls! The baby's really torn them to pieces – how long can we go on with them! (*Calls*) Listen . . .

DEVADATTA   (*entering*) Yes.

PADMINI   We must get new dolls for our baby. These are in tatters.

DEVADATTA   You're right. I hadn't noticed.

PADMINI   The Ujjain fair is to be held in another four days. Why don't you go and get new dolls there? If you start today you'll be there in time for it. It's unlucky to keep torn dolls at home . . .

DOLL 1   (*to* DOLL 2) Did you hear that? She wants to throw us out . . .

DOLL 2   She wants new dolls.

DOLL 1   The whore.

DOLL 2   The bitch.

DOLL 1   May her house burn down.

DOLL 2   May her teeth fall out.

DEVADATTA   (*to* PADMINI) All right. (*He picks them up by their collars.*)

DOLL 1   See how he picks us up. Like stray puppies.

DOLL 2   That ball of flesh will remain here. But it's the dung-heap for us . . .

DEVADATTA   (*to* PADMINI) It'll take me more than a week to go to Ujjain and come

back. Shall I ask one of the neighbours to get them for us?

DOLL 1   (*to* DEVADATTA) You wretch – before you throw us out watch out for yourself.

DOLL 2   Cover your wife before you start worrying about our rags.

PADMINI   (*to* DEVADATTA) Who knows what sort of dolls they'll get for us? We must bring things ourselves for our baby . . .

DEVADATTA   But . . .

PADMINI   If you don't want to go, say so. Don't . . .

DEVADATTA   Shall I ask one of the servants to come and sleep here at night?

PADMINI   No need. We are not in the middle of a forest.

DOLL 1   (*to* DEVADATTA) Watch out, you fool . . .

DOLL 2   Refuse, you idiot . . .

DEVADATTA   All right. I'll start at once. Take care of yourself. (*He drags the dolls out.*)

DOLL 1   Villain . . .

DOLL 2   Rascal . . .

DOLL 1   Swine . . .

DOLL 2   Bastard . . .

(*One can hear them screaming curses as he takes them out.* PADMINI *stands watching him go. Then to the child in her arms.*)

PADMINI   My poor child, you haven't yet seen the witching fair of the dark forest, have you? Let's go and see it. How can I describe it to you? There's so much. Long before the sun rises, the shadows of twigs draw alpanas on the floor. The stars raise arati and go. Then the day dawns and the fun begins. The circus in the tree-tops and the cock-fights in a shower of feathers. And the dances! The tiger-dance, and the peacock-dance, and the dance of the sun's little feet with silver anklets on the river. In the heart of the forest stands the stately chariot of the shield-bearer. It's made of pure gold – rows of birds pull it down the street, and rows of flames of the forest salute it with torches. Then the night comes, and our poor baby is tired – so we blow gently and out goes the moon. But before we leave there's one more thing to do. Right outside the fair, watching it from a distance, stands the tree of the Fortunate Lady. It's an old tree, a close friend of ours. We have to say 'hello' to it. All right? (*She goes out with the child. A long silence.*

KAPILA *enters. He too is as he was at the beginning of the play – tough and muscular.*)

BHAGAVATA   Who? Kapila?

KAPILA   Yes.

BHAGAVATA   It's such a long time since we met.

KAPILA   Yes.

BHAGAVATA   Where are you now?

KAPILA   Here.

BHAGAVATA   Here? In this jungle? It's difficult to believe any man could live here.

KAPILA   Beasts do. Why not men?

BHAGAVATA   What do you do?

KAPILA   Live.

BHAGAVATA   Have you had any news from the city?

KAPILA   Long ago. Father sent word asking me to come back. I said, 'I won't come. No need for you to come here either!' That's all.

BHAGAVATA   You mean – you don't know your father died last year? – Also your mother . . .

KAPILA   (*expressionless*) No.

BHAGAVATA   And Padmini has a son.

KAPILA   I see.

BHAGAVATA   Why this anger, Kapila?

KAPILA   What anger?

BHAGAVATA   It shows in the way you stand, you move.

KAPILA   All that is your poetry. (*Moves on.*)

BHAGAVATA   Kapila! Kapila!

(KAPILA *goes round the stage once. He mimes picking up an axe and felling a tree. A long silence. Only the soundless image of* KAPILA *cutting the tree.* PADMINI *enters, child in arms. She is scared and walks in rapidly. She sees* KAPILA *and stands transfixed.* KAPILA *doesn't see her for a while and when he does stands paralysed. A long silence.*)

KAPILA   (*slowly*) You?

PADMINI   Yes.

KAPILA   Here?

PADMINI   My son had never laughed with the river or shivered in the wind or felt the thorn cut his feet. So I brought him out. I lost my way in the woods.

KAPILA   You shouldn't have lost it this far.

PADMINI   The wrong road stuck to my feet – wouldn't let go.

KAPILA   You shouldn't have lost it this far. Wild beasts – robbers – pathless paths – all sorts of dangers.

PADMINI   I asked the villagers . . . And the pilgrims. And the hunters. And the tribesmen. When there wasn't anyone any more, I asked myself. Everyone saw to it that I didn't lose the wrong road. (*Pause.*)

KAPILA   Is that your son?

PADMINI   Yes. And yours.

KAPILA   Mine?

PADMINI   Your body gave him to me.

KAPILA   Mine? (*Erupting*) Not mine. I'm Kapila, Padmini. I didn't accept it that day. But I accept it now, I'm Kapila.

PADMINI   (*softly*) And how's Kapila? (*The* BHAGAVATA *sings. The following is a prose rendering of the song.*)

BHAGAVATA   I spread my wings, and kicked away the earth and flew up. I covered the seven continents, the ten shores and measured the sky. Now because you have a child at your breast, a husband on your thighs, the red of rust on the lips of your late-opening mouth, I pick a picture here, and there a card of fate, and live for the grace of a grain – an astrologer's bird.

KAPILA   Can I look at him?

PADMINI   That's why I brought him. (KAPILA *looks at the child.*)

KAPILA   What's wrong with me? You've come so far and I haven't even asked you to sit down. Why don't you go in and take a little rest?

(*She goes in with the child. He stands as in a daze. She comes out without the child.*)

KAPILA   Why . . .

PADMINI   I don't need any rest. (*Long silence.*)

KAPILA   How are you?

PADMINI   I'm well. No illness, problems or difficulties.

KAPILA   Your son looks exactly like you.

PADMINI   (*a slight pause*) And you. (KAPILA *doesn't reply.*) He has the same mole on his shoulder.

KAPILA   What mole? (*She comes to him and points out the mole on his shoulder.*)

PADMINI   This one. Which other could it be? That's the only one you have on your shoulder.

KAPILA   Oh! I hadn't seen it. I don't much look at this body.

PADMINI   (*quietly*) Do you despise it that much? (*No reply.*) Why have you tortured it so? (*Takes his hand in hers.*) When this went to you, it was so soft, like a prince's. These arms were so slender and fair. Look at them now. Why have you done this to yourself?

KAPILA When this body came to me, it was like a corpse hanging by my head. It was a Brahmin's body after all – not made for the woods. I couldn't lift an axe without my elbows moaning. Couldn't run a length without my knees howling. I had no use for it. The moment it came to me, a war started between us.

PADMINI And who won?

KAPILA I did.

PADMINI The head always wins, doesn't it?

KAPILA Fortunately, yes. Now I can run ten miles and not stop for breath. I can swim through the monsoon floods and fell a banyan. The stomach used to rebel once – now it digests what I give. If I don't, it doesn't complain.

PADMINI Must the head always win?

KAPILA That's why I am Kapila now. Kapila! Kapila with a face which fits his body.

PADMINI
    What a good mix –
    No more tricks –
    Is this one that
    Or that one this?
    Do you remember the song we sang in the Kali temple?

KAPILA So?

PADMINI Nothing. I often remember it. It's almost my autobiography now, Kapila! Devadatta! Kapila with Devadatta's body! Devadatta with Kapila's body! Four men in one lifetime.

KAPILA (suddenly) Why have you come away from him?

PADMINI What do you want me to say? (They freeze.)

BHAGAVATA How could I make you understand? If Devadatta had changed overnight and had gone back to his original form, I would have forgotten you completely. But that's not how it happened. He changed day by day. Inch by inch. Hair by hair. Like the trickling sand. Like the water filling the pot. And as I saw him change – I couldn't get rid of you. That's what Padmini must tell Kapila. She should say more, without concealing anything, 'Kapila, if that rishi had given me to you, would I have gone back to Devadatta some day exactly like this?' But she doesn't say anything. She remains quiet.

KAPILA (to PADMINI) Why have you come here?

PADMINI I had to see you.

KAPILA Why? (No reply.) Why? Why did you have to come just when I thought I'd won this long and weary battle? Why did you have to pursue me just when I had succeeded in uprooting these memories? I am Kapila now. The rough and violent Kapila. Kapila without a crack between his head and his shoulders. What do you want now? Another head? Another suicide? – Listen to me. Do me a favour. Go back. Back to Devadatta. He is your husband – the father of this child. Devadatta and Padmini! Devadatta and Padmini! A pair coupled with the holy fire as the witness. I have no place there, no peace, no salvation – So go. I beg of you. Go. (A long silence.)

PADMINI I will. If you want me to.

KAPILA (almost a moan) Oh God!

PADMINI Why?

KAPILA Nothing. Another memory – when I too was asked to go – Yes, go back. Now.

PADMINI I will. But can I ask a little favour? My son's tired. He's asleep. He has been in my arms for several days now. Let him rest a while. As soon as he gets up I'll go. (Laughs.) Yes, you won, Kapila. Devadatta won too. But I – the better half of two bodies – I neither win nor lose. No, don't say anything. I know what you'll say and I've told myself that a thousand times. It's my fault. I mixed the heads up. I must suffer for it. I will. I'm sorry I came – I didn't think before I started – Couldn't. But at least until my child wakes up, may I sit here and look at you? Have my fill for the rest of my life? I won't speak a word. (Long pause.)

KAPILA What does it matter now whether you stay or go? You've done the damage. I had buried all those faceless memories in my skin. Now you've dug them up with your claws.

PADMINI Why should one bury anything?

KAPILA Why shouldn't one? Why should one tolerate this mad dance of incompleteness?

PADMINI Whose incompleteness? Yours?

KAPILA Yes, mine. One beats the body into shape, but one can't beat away the memories in it. Isn't that surprising? That the body should have its own ghosts – its own memories? Memories of touch – memories of a touch – memories of a body swaying in these arms, of a warm skin against this palm – memories which one cannot recognize, cannot understand, cannot even name because this head wasn't there when they happened . . .

PADMINI Kapila . . .

KAPILA (*without anger*) Why did you come? You came. You touched me. You held my hand – and my body recognized your touch. I have never touched you, but this body, this appendage, laughed and flowered out in a festival of memories to which I'm an outcaste . . .

PADMINI Poor Kapila!

KAPILA Don't pity me.

PADMINI Be quiet, stupid. Your body bathed in a river, swam and danced in it. Shouldn't your head know what river it was, what swim? Your head too must submerge in that river – the flow must rumple your hair, run its tongue in your ears and press your head to its bosom. Until that's done, you'll continue to be incomplete. (KAPILA *raises his head and looks at her. She caresses his face, like a blind person trying to imprint it on her finger-tips. Then she rests her head on his chest.*) My Kapila! My poor, poor Kapila! How needlessly you've tortured yourself. (KAPILA *lifts her up and takes her in.*)

BHAGAVATA
You cannot engrave on water
nor wound it with a knife,
which is why
the river
has no fear
of memories.

FEMALE CHORUS
The river only feels the
pull of the waterfall.
She giggles, and tickles the rushes
on the banks, then turns
a top of dry leaves
in the navel of the whirlpool, weaves
a water-snake in the net of silver
    strands
in the green depths, frightens the frog
on the rug of moss, sticks and bamboo
    leaves,
sings, tosses, leaps and
sweeps on in a rush –

BHAGAVATA
While the scarecrow on the bank
has a face fading
on its mudpot head
and a body torn
with memories.

(DEVADATTA *enters. He is holding a sword in one hand, and in the other, two dolls, made of cloth.*)

BHAGAVATA Who! Devadatta?

DEVADATTA Where does Kapila live here?

BHAGAVATA Uhm – well – Anyway, how are . . . you . . .

DEVADATTA If you don't want to tell me, don't. I can find out for myself.

BHAGAVATA There. Behind those trees.

DEVADATTA How long has Padmini been here?

BHAGAVATA About four or five days.

DEVADATTA Amazing! Even a man like me found the road hard. But how quickly she covered it – and with a child in her arms.

BHAGAVATA Devadatta . . . (DEVADATTA *moves on.*) Devadatta moves on. There are only two words which make sense to him now – Kapila and Padmini! Kapila and Padmini! The words carry him along like a flood to the doorstep of Kapila's hut. But suddenly he stops. Until this moment he has been yearning to taste the blood of Kapila. But now he is still and calm.

(KAPILA *comes out.*)

KAPILA Come Devadatta. I was waiting for you. I've been expecting you since yesterday. I have been coming out every half an hour to see if you'd arrived. Not from fear. Only eager. (PADMINI *comes out and stands watching them.*) You look exactly the same.

DEVADATTA (*laughs*) You too.

KAPILA (*points to the sword*) What's that?

DEVADATTA (*extending the hand which holds the dolls*) Dolls. For the child. I came home from the fair. There was no one there. So I came here.

(PADMINI *steps forward and takes the dolls. But neither speaks.* PADMINI *goes back to her place and stands clutching the dolls to her bosom.*)

KAPILA Come in and rest a while. There'll always be time to talk later. (DEVADATTA *shakes his head.*) Why? Are you angry?

DEVADATTA Not any more. (*Pause.*) Did my body bother you too much?

KAPILA It wasn't made for this life. It resisted. It also had its revenge.

DEVADATTA Did it?

KAPILA Do you remember how I once used to envy you your poetry, your ability to imagine things? For me the sky was sky, and the tree only a tree. Your body gave me new feelings, new words – I felt awake as I'd never before – even started – writing poems. Very bad ones, I'm afraid. (*They laugh.*) There were times when I hated it for what it gave me.

DEVADATTA   I wanted your power but not your wildness. You lived in hate – I in fear.

KAPILA   No, I was the one who was afraid.

DEVADATTA   What a good mix – no more tricks. (*They laugh.*) Tell me one thing. Do you really love Padmini?

KAPILA   Yes.

DEVADATTA   So do I.

KAPILA   I know. (*Silence.*) Devadatta, couldn't we all three live together – like the Pandavas and Draupadi?

DEVADATTA   What do you think?

(*Silence.* PADMINI *looks at them but doesn't say anything.*)

KAPILA   (*laughs*) No, it can't be done.

DEVADATTA   That's why I brought this. (*Shows the sword.*) What won't end has to be cut.

KAPILA   I got your body – but not your wisdom.

DEVADATTA   Where's your sword then?

KAPILA   A moment. (*Goes in.* PADMINI *stands looking at* DEVADATTA. *But he looks somewhere far away.*)

BHAGAVATA
    After sharing with Indra
    his wine
    his food
    his jokes
    I returned to the earth
    and saw from far –
    a crack had appeared
    in the earth's face –
    exactly
    like Indra's smile.

(KAPILA *returns with his sword. They take up positions.*)

KAPILA   Are you still in practice?

DEVADATTA   Of course not. But you'd learned well. And you?

KAPILA   I learnt again. But one's older now – slower at learning.

DEVADATTA   (*pause*) You realize it's immaterial who's better with a sword now, don't you?

KAPILA   Yes, I do.

DEVADATTA   There's only one solution to this.

KAPILA   We must both die.

DEVADATTA   We must both die.

KAPILA   With what confidence we chopped off our heads in that temple! Now whose head – whose body – suicide or murder – nothing's clear.

DEVADATTA   No grounds for friendship now. No question of mercy. We must fight like lions and kill like cobras.

KAPILA   Let our heads roll to the very hands which cut them in the temple of Kali!

(*Music starts. The fight is stylized like a dance. Their swords don't touch. Even* PADMINI's *reaction is like a dance.*)

BHAGAVATA   (*sings*)
    Like cocks in a pit
    we dance – he and I . . .
    foot woven with foot
    eye soldered to eye.
    He knows and I know
    all there's to be known
    the witch's burning thirst
    burns for blood alone.
    Hence this frozen smile,
    which cracks and drips to earth,
    and claw-knives, digging flesh
    for piecemeal death.
    The rishi who said 'Knowledge gives rise to
    Forgiveness' had no knowledge of death.

(KAPILA *wounds* DEVADATTA *who falls to his knees and fights. He stabs* KAPILA. *Both fight on their knees, fall and die. A long silence.* PADMINI *slowly comes and sits between the bodies.*)

PADMINI   They burned, lived, fought, embraced and died. I stood silent. If I'd said, 'Yes, I'll live with you both', perhaps they would have been alive yet. But I couldn't say it. I couldn't say, 'Yes'. No, Kapila, no, Devadatta – I know it in my blood you couldn't have lived together. You would've had to share not only me but your bodies as well. Because you knew death you died in each other's arms. You could only have lived ripping each other to pieces. I had to drive you to death. You forgave each other, but again – left me out.

BHAGAVATA   (*without leaving his seat*) What is this? It's a sight to freeze the blood in one's veins. What happened, child? Can we help you?

PADMINI (*without looking at him*) Yes, please. My son is sleeping in the hut. Take him under your care. Give him to the hunters who live in this forest and tell them it's Kapila's son. They loved Kapila and will bring the child up. Let the child grow up in the forest and the rivers and trees. When he's five take him to the Revered Brahmin Vidyasagara of Dharmapura. Tell him it's Devadatta's son.

BHAGAVATA And you?

PADMINI Make me a large funeral pyre. We are three.

BHAGAVATA You mean you are performing sati? But why, child?

PADMINI (*Puts the dolls on the ground.*) Give these dolls to my son. I won't see him . . . He may tempt me away from my path. (*At a sign from the* BHAGAVATA, *two stage-hands come and place a curtain in front of* PADMINI.) Kali, Mother of all Nature, you must have your joke even now. Other women can die praying that they should get the same husband in all the lives to come. You haven't left me even that little consolation. (*Does namaskara.*)

(*The stage-hands lift the curtain, slowly, very slowly, very slowly, as the song goes on. The curtain has a blazing fire painted on it. And as it is lifted, the flames seem to leap up. The female musicians sing a song. The following is a prose rendering of it.*)

FEMALE CHORUS Our sister is leaving in a palanquin of sandalwood. Her mattress is studded with rubies which burn and glow. She is decked in flowers which blossom on tinder-wood and whose petals are made of molten gold. How the garlands leap and cover her, aflame with love. The Fortunate Lady's procession goes up the street of laburnums, while the makarandas tie the pennants and the jacarandas hold the lights. Good-bye, dear Sister. Go you without fear. The Lord of Death will be pleased with the offering of three coconuts.

BHAGAVATA (*Picks up the dolls and comes downstage.*) Thus Padmini became a sati. India is known for its pativratas – wives who dedicated their whole existence to the service of their husbands – but it would not be an exaggeration to say that no pativrata went in the way Padmini did. And yet no one knows the spot where she went sati. If you ask the hunting tribes who dwell in these forests, they only point to a full-blossomed tree of the Fortunate Lady. They say that even now on full moon and on new moon nights a song rises from the roots of the tree and fills the whole forest like a fragrance.

FEMALE CHORUS (*sings*) Why should love stick to the sap of a single body? When the stem is drunk with the thick yearning of the many-petaled, many-flowered lantana, why should it be tied down to the relation of a single flower? A head for each breast. A pupil for each eye. A side for each arm. I have neither regret nor shame. The blood pours into the earth and a song branches out in the sky.

(*When the song ends, the* BHAGAVATA *does a namaskara to the audience. The audience should get a definite feeling that the play has ended when a scream is heard in the wings.*)

BHAGAVATA What's that? No! Nata, our Actor!

(ACTOR 2 *comes rushing out. He doesn't even see the* BHAGAVATA *in his desperate hurry.*)

Why is he running? Where's the National Anthem?

(ACTOR 2 *suddenly stops in his tracks.*)

ACTOR 2 The National Anthem!

BHAGAVATA What?

ACTOR 2 How did you know?

BHAGAVATA Know what?

ACTOR 2 Please, Bhagavata Sir, how did you know . . .

BHAGAVATA Know what?

ACTOR 2 About the National Anthem.

BHAGAVATA What do you mean?

ACTOR 2 Please, Sir, I beg of you. I implore you. Don't make fun of me. How did you know it was the National Anthem . . . ?

BHAGAVATA Why? Haven't you seen an audience . . . ?

ACTOR 2 (*relieved*) Phew! *That*! Ram Ram!

BHAGAVATA Why? What happened?

ACTOR 2 What happened? Sree Hari! Look . . . (*lifts his hand. It's trembling.*)

BHAGAVATA Why? What . . .

ACTOR 2 I almost died of fright . . .

BHAGAVATA Really?

ACTOR 2 I was coming down the road – when I heard someone singing at a distance – at the top of his voice. He was singing, 'Jhanda Ooncha Rahe Hamara' (May our flag fly high!) He started on 'Sare Jahan se Acchha Hindostan Hamara' (Our

India is better than the whole world.) Then 'Rise, Rise my Kannada Land'. Then 'Vande Mataram' . . .

BHAGAVATA   Then?

ACTOR 2   I was baffled . . . A true patriot at this time of night? I had to find out who it was. A house – a big, thick fence around with not a gap in it – But I managed to find a hole to crawl through. I was just half-way in when I saw . . .

BHAGAVATA   What? (*The* ACTOR *wipes his brow.*) Come on . . . what did you see?

ACTOR 2   A horse!

BHAGAVATA   A horse?

ACTOR 2   Yes. It turned to me and in a deep, sonorous voice said, 'Friend, I'm now going to sing the National Anthem. So please to stand up to attention!'

BHAGAVATA   Listen, Nata, are you sure . . .

ACTOR 2   I swear . . .

BHAGAVATA   No, no, what I mean is . . . (*Commotion in the wings.*) What's that now?

(ACTOR 1 *enters with a boy of about five. The boy is very serious – even sulky. There's not a trace of laughter on his face. He is holding the two cloth dolls which we have already seen – but the dolls are dirtier now. The commotion comes from* ACTOR 1, *who is so busy trying to make the child laugh – making faces at him, clowning, capering and shouting – he doesn't notice the* BHAGAVATA.)

BHAGAVATA   (*delighted*) Oh! Nata! You again!

ACTOR 1   (*turns round and sees the* BHAGAVATA.) Oh, sir, it's you!

BHAGAVATA   Well well, you'll live to be a hundred.

ACTOR 1   Why? What have I done?

BHAGAVATA   I was just thinking of you and you turned up. Just now this Nata (*pointing to* ACTOR 2) was saying he saw a horse-headed man and I wondered if it was Hayavadana. So I remembered you.

ACTOR 2   Bhagavata Sir . . .

ACTOR 1   (*ignoring* ACTOR 2) There's an actor's fate in a nutshell for you. Always remembered for someone else . . .

BHAGAVATA   Where's Hayavadana now? Has he come back?

ACTOR 1   I don't know, sir. He chased me away the moment we reached the Kali temple. Wouldn't let me stay there a minute longer . . .

BHAGAVATA   Oh! I very much hope the goddess granted him what he wanted. (*Sees the child.*) Who's this child?

ACTOR 1   Him? Well? (*To the child*) Go on, tell him. (*The child remains silent, doesn't answer any questions.*)

BHAGAVATA   Who are you, child? – What's your name? – Where are you parents?

ACTOR 1   You see? Not a word. Children of his age should be out talking a dictionary, but this one doesn't speak a word. Doesn't laugh, doesn't cry, doesn't even smile. The same long face all twenty-four hours. There's obviously something wrong with him . . . (*Bends before the child and clowns a bit.*) See? No response – no reactions. When he grows up he should make a good theatre critic.

ACTOR 2   (*restless*) Bhagavata Sir . . .

BHAGAVATA   (*to* ACTOR 1) Where did you find him?

ACTOR 1   In a tribal village of hunters. On my way back I had to stay a night there and a tribal woman brought him to me. Said 'This is not our child. It's from the city. Take it back'.

BHAGAVATA   A child of this city? (ACTOR 1 *nods.*) How strange! (*Notices the dolls.*) But – but – these dolls . . . (*Tries to touch the dolls. The child reacts violently and moves away angry, terrified.*)

ACTOR 1   I was about to warn you! Whatever you do don't touch his dolls! At other times he'll starve and freeze to death rather than say a word. But touch the dolls and he'll bare his fangs. He almost bit off my finger once . . .

ACTOR 2   Bhagavata Sir . . .

BHAGAVATA   (*to* ACTOR 1) But Nata – (*Pause.*) Child, let me see your shoulder . . . (*The child moves back.*) No, no, I won't touch the dolls. I promise you. Just your shoulder . . . (*Inspects his shoulder. Then with a cry of triumph*) Nata . . .

ACTOR 2   Bhagavata Sir . . .

ACTOR 1   Yes . . .

BHAGAVATA   Look, the mole. It's Padmini's son . . . there's no doubt about it . . .

ACTOR 1   Padmini? Which . . .

ACTOR 2   (*shouting at the top of his voice*) Bhagavata Sir! (ACTOR 1 *and the* BHAGAVATA *react.*)

BHAGAVATA   Yes? Why are you shouting?

ACTOR 2   I have been calling you for the last half-an-hour . . .

BHAGAVATA   Yes, yes. What's it?

ACTOR 2   You said I'd seen a horse-headed

man. I didn't. What I saw was a complete, perfect, proper . . . (*a voice is heard off stage singing the third stanza of 'Jana Gana Mana'.*) There it is!

(*All stare in the direction of the song. A* HORSE *enters the stage singing.*)

HORSE
    Tava Karunaruna Rage
    Nidrita Bharata Jage
    Tava Charane Nata Matha
    Jaya Jaya Jaya He Jaya Rajeshwara . . .

(*Comes and stands in front of them.*)

Hohoo! What's this? Mr Bhagavata Sir! My Actor Friend! Well, well, well! What a pleasant surprise! Delightful! How are you, Sir, how are you?

BHAGAVATA It's not – not Hayavadana, is it?

HAYAVADANA Your most obedient servant, Sir . . .

BHAGAVATA But what . . .

ACTOR 2 You mean you know this horse?

BHAGAVATA (*bursts into a guffaw*) We're old friends.

ACTOR 1 (*laughing*) Fellow-pilgrims!

HAYAVADANA But not fellow-travellers. What? (*They roar with laughter. Suddenly the boy too starts laughing. Doubles up with laughter. The* DOLLS *fall out of his hand as he claps his hands.*)

THE BOY (*clapping his hands*) The horse is laughing! The horse is laughing!

ACTOR 1 (*jumping with delight*) The boy is laughing!

HAYAVADANA (*goes to the boy*) Why, my little friend, you may laugh – but I may not?

(*The* BOY *is in hysterics.*)

BHAGAVATA That's Padmini's son, Hayavadana . . .

HAYAVADANA Padmini? I am not aware of . . .

BHAGAVATA You don't know her. But this poor child – he hadn't laughed, or cried, or talked in all these years. Now you have made him laugh . . .

HAYAVADANA Delighted. Delighted.

BHAGAVATA But tell me – you went to the goddess to become a complete man, didn't you? What happened?

HAYAVADANA Ah! That's a long story. I went there, picked up a sword which was lying around – very unsafe, I tell you – put it on my neck and said 'Mother of all Nature, if you don't help me I'll chop off my head!'

ACTOR 1 Then?

HAYAVADANA The goddess appeared. Very prompt. But looked rather put out. She said – rather peevishly, I thought – 'Why don't you people go somewhere else if you want to chop off your stupid heads? Why do you have to come to me?' I fell at her feet and said, 'Mother, make me complete'. She said 'So be it' and disappeared – even before I could say 'Make me a complete man!' I became a horse.

ACTOR 1 I am sorry to hear that . . .

HAYAVADANA Sorry? Whatever for? The goddess knew what she was doing. I can tell you that. Ha Ha! Being a horse has its points . . . (*Pause.*) I only have one sorrow . . .

BHAGAVATA Yes?

HAYAVADANA I have become a complete horse – but not a complete being! This human voice – this cursed human voice – it's still there! How can I call myself complete? If I only could. What should I do, Bhagavata Sir? How can I get rid of this human voice?

BHAGAVATA I don't know what to tell you, Hayavadana.

HAYAVADANA That's why I sing all these patriotic songs – and the National Anthem! That particularly! I have noticed that the people singing the National Anthem always seem to have ruined their voices – so I try. But – but – it – it doesn't seem to work . . . What should I do? (*He starts to sob.*)

BOY Don't cry, horse. Don't cry. Stop it now . . .

HAYAVADANA No, I won't cry. The boy's right. What's the point of shedding tears?

BOY Don't cry – you look nice when you laugh . . .

HAYAVADANA No, I won't cry. I won't give up trying either. Come, little friend, let's sing the National Anthem together.

BOY What is that?

BHAGAVATA How could he? He has been brought up in a forest . . .

HAYAVADANA Then sing some other song. Look, if you sing a song, I'll take you round on my back.

BOY (*excited*) Yes – please . . .

HAYAVADANA Well, then, what are we waiting for? Get on my back. Quick.

(*The* BHAGAVATA *seats the child on the* HORSE'*s back.*)

BOY   Hiya – Hiya –

HAYAVADANA   No, no. You sing first. Then we start.

BHAGAVATA   Sing, son.

(*The* BOY *sings and the* HORSE *goes around in a slow trot.*)

> Here comes a rider.
> From what land O what land?
> On his head a turban.
> Sleep now, sleep now.
> Why his chest
> Red O red?
> Why his eyes
> Pebbles O pebbles?
> Why his body
> Cold O cold?
> Where goes the horse?
> Nowhere O nowhere.

(*As the song ends, the* HORSE *comes and stands in front of the* BHAGAVATA.)

HAYAVADANA   Mr Bhagavata Sir . . .

BHAGAVATA   Yes.

HAYAVADANA   It seems to me the rider described in the song is dead. I am right?

BHAGAVATA   Er – I think so – yes.

HAYAVADANA   Who could have taught this child such a tragic song?

BOY   Mother . . .

BHAGAVATA   What's there in a song, Hayavadana? The real beauty lies in the child's laughter – in the innocent joy of that laughter. No tragedy can touch it.

HAYAVADANA   Is that so?

BHAGAVATA   Indeed. What can match a child's laughter in its purity?

HAYAVADANA   To be honest, Mr Bhagavata Sir, I have my doubts about this theory. I believe – in fact I may go so far as to say I firmly believe – that it's this sort of sentimentality which has been the bane of our literature and national life. It has kept us from accepting Reality and encouraged escapism. Still, if you say so, I won't argue. Come, child, let's have another song.

BOY   I don't know . . .

HAYAVADANA   Then sing the same song again.

BOY   You laugh first.

HAYAVADANA   Laugh again? – Let me try. (*Tries to laugh.*) Ha Ha Ha! No, it's not easy to laugh – just like that . . .

BOY   (*mimes whipping*) Laugh – laugh . . .

HAYAVADANA   All right. All right. I'll try again. Ha! Ha! Ha! Ha! – Huhhuh . . . Heahhh . . . (*His laughter ends up as a proper neigh.*)

ALL   What's that?

BHAGAVATA   Hayavadana – Hayavadana . . .

HAYAVADANA   Heahhh . . . (*his human voice is gone now. He can only neigh and leaps round with great joy.*)

BHAGAVATA   Careful – careful. Don't drop the child . . . (*But the* HORSE *is too happy to listen. It prances around, neighing gleefully. The* BOY *is also enjoying himself, singing bits of the song and urging the* HORSE *on.*) So at long last Hayavadana has become complete. (*To the* ACTORS) You two go and tell the Revered Brahmin Vidyasagar that his grandson is returning home in triumph, riding a big, white charger . . .

ACTOR 2   And the dolls?

BHAGAVATA   Throw them away. There's no further need for them . . . (*The* ACTORS *go out with the dolls.*) Unfathomable indeed is the mercy of the elephant-headed Ganesha. He fulfils the desires of all – a grandson to a grandfather, a smile to a child, a neigh to a horse. How indeed can one describe his glory in our poor, disabled words? Come, Hayavadana, come. Enough of this dancing. Our play is over and it's time we all prayed and thanked the Lord for having ensured the completion and success of our play.

(HAYAVADANA *comes and stands by the* BHAGAVATA. *The* BHAGAVATA *helps the child down. At this point the curtain, with the fire painted on it – which has been there all the time – is dropped and* PADMINI, KAPILA *and* DEVADATTA *step forward and join the* BHAGAVATA *in prayer.*)

> Grant us, O Lord, good rains, good crop,
> Prosperity in poetry, science, industry
>   and other affairs.
> Give the rulers of our country success in
>   all endeavours,
> And along with it, a little bit of sense.

10 Manjula Padmanabhan

Harvest
India

[handwritten notes:]
SU
* Monday, February 19th - success day
 - Contextualization for Unit Response, come
   with questions
* Wednesday, February 21st - Unit Response
 - about Harvest, The strong Breed, and
   Anowa

"cartoonist (suki)

Until 1997, when her play, *Harvest*, won the inaugural Onassis Prize for Theatre (the world's richest playscript award), Manjula Padmanabhan was better known as a cartoonist, and for a while had a daily comic strip in *The Pioneer*, a Delhi-based newspaper. However, she had previously written several plays that address complex moral and social issues while evincing flashes of the penetrating wit that is honed to a fine art in *Harvest*. Of these earlier works, *Lights Out!* (1984) examines communal apathy in relation to a pack rape, *The Artist's Model* (1995) deals with metaphysical questions relating to art and exploitation, and *Sextet* (1996) comprises a series of six short skits about aspects of sexuality. These dramatic experiments notwithstanding, it is perhaps Padmanabhan's book of short stories, *Hot Death, Cold Soup* (1995), that best anticipates both the matter and the mode of her award-winning play. Using surrealist and Gothic forms, several stories in this collection focus on issues such as sati, dowry murder, and suicide, while others satirise government bureaucracy in India and the culture of acquiescence that leads the public to accept the status quo. In one Kafka-esque tale, 'A Government of India undertaking . . . ' (Padmanabhan 1993), the image of the common citizen worn down and mystified by an endless process of queuing and form-filling suggests the kind of dehumanisation taken to the extreme in *Harvest*. The story's metaphysical exploration of its protagonist's efforts to exchange her body with that of someone rich, famous and indolent more specifically anticipates the global trade in body organs that is the play's central focus.

Padmanabhan explains that her storytelling tends to 'veer off into science-fiction or the surreal' because these modes allow her to 'cut loose from the annoying constraints of realistic detail' (Sethi 1997: 101). Her refractive vision of contemporary Indian society reveals little about her personal life, unlike some of the more autobiographical works in this anthology. Born in Delhi in 1953, Padmanabhan, whose father was a diplomat, had a fairly itinerant childhood, followed by several years in boarding school as a teenager. After attending college, her determination to make her own way in life led to various kinds of work in publishing and media-related fields. As well as creating comic strips and writing newspaper columns, she has worked as an artist, illustrated children's books and devised scripts for television. Her early knowledge of theatre was shaped by exposure to Shakespeare's works and Broadway musicals but, after returning to India in her teens, she became aware of such notable dramatists as Vijay Tendulkar and Girish Karnad, whose *Tughlaq* was the first modern Indian play she had ever seen performed. Padmanabhan's dramatic endeavours have been frustrated, however, by the generally weak infrastructure of India's English-language theatre, which is poorly resourced and inclined to stage well-known foreign plays catering to a Westernised elite. With these constraints in mind, she says that she wrote *Harvest* knowing it would surely languish in a filing cabinet unless it won something in the Onassis competition. Fortunately, the prestigious award has ensured a very different fate for the play: it was given a much-lauded production in Greece as part of the prize benefit, and has since been broadcast by BBC Radio, as well as being translated into German, and adapted for a film version in Hindi that is soon to be released under the title of *Deham*.

Sunil Sethi has described *Harvest* as 'a modern morality play' in which Padmanabhan questions the limits of poverty, material ambition and individual dignity (Sethi 1997: 98). Om Prakash's Faustian pact with InterPlanta organ transplant services brings into focus the spiritual emptiness of a society so seduced by the promise of wealth that its members will sell their body parts for material profit. As the narrative progresses, the full horrors of this kind of trade are suggested not only by the gradual disintegration of the donor body but also by the complete breakdown of the Prakash family as a social unit. Ma's bizarre retreat into the media-controlled oblivion of her SuperDeluxe VideoCouch with 750 channels represents only a slightly more palatable future than Om's grovelling capitulation to the InterPlanta world-view, or his brother Jeetu's eventual disappearance into the abyss of the organ bazaar. In their hollow quest for affluence, all have betrayed family members and/or lovers, and, perhaps more critically, they have compromised their humanity. Only Jaya refuses to be taken in by the glittering illusions of Western-style capitalism, her lone stand against exploitation suggesting a glimmer of hope in an otherwise bleak vision of human society at the beginning of the twenty-first century.

The science-fiction elements in *Harvest*, while crucial to the play's tightly plotted narrative, are held largely within the bounds of late-twentieth-century life, so that the future presented remains on this side of plausibility. Most of the hi-tech devices that fascinate, and fool, the Prakash family derive from technologies currently available in many parts of the world: the contact module, for instance, suggests a video-conferencing unit with added virtual reality features, while Jeetu's artificial replacement eyes operate on the same principle as the bionic ear, sending external stimuli direct to the brain rather than through a damaged sensory organ. Even Ma's elaborate VideoCouch sarcophagus has recognisable elements, being something of a cross between a dialysis machine and an entertainment unit, though its features are comically exaggerated to enhance the text's critique of rampant materialism. Such gadgetry aside, the portrayal of InterPlanta as the sinister face of corporate business in the twenty-first century also draws from current models of large, transnational corporations staffed by human automatons with little sense of individuality.

Padmanabhan's visceral satire is not without some sympathy for the Prakash family. Like many parables, *Harvest* is just as concerned with social structures as it is with the individual's moral choices. In particular, the play highlights the ways in which poverty can limit moral options and degrade human lives, and it also demonstrates that a modern trade in body parts can be understood only within the context of gross material inequities between first and third worlds. The selection of the global organ trade as a compelling metaphor through which to dramatise the West's exploitation of its cultural Others suits the futuristic bent of the play because it draws on the familiar science-fiction motif of body-snatching; yet this trope is also based in historical fact. A number of media reports, some more factual than others, claim that, along with Cairo, Indian cities such as Calcutta and Bombay are major locations for a multimillion dollar trade in human organs, especially kidneys and corneas. Such reports frequently employ the image of the oriental bazaar to suggest the development of a rapacious 'commerce' that seems to be premised on the general assumption that the bodies of the poor are worth more as spare parts than as living persons.

While examples of organ trade between rich and poor nations *within* Asia and the Middle East show that this kind of commerce sometimes operates along unexpected routes of capital dependence (Frow 1998: 51), Padmanabhan's particular take on the issue suggests the ease with which Western nations position themselves as the 'natural' recipients of other cultures' human and material resources. In this respect, the macabre trade dramatised in *Harvest* readily evokes its imperial precursor, the trans-Atlantic slave trade, which saw millions of racialised bodies bought, sold and exchanged for the benefit of European mercantile expansionism. By presenting images of the colonised body plundered for its specific parts, the play also recalls such imperial practices as 'souveniring' native heads, bones and skin in the names of science and anthropology. These resonances between past and present forms of traffic in human bodies and/or body parts situate the contemporary trade in organs within a continuum of exploitative cross-cultural relationships. That InterPlanta also administers a transnational sexual economy of sorts, encompassing a trade in exotic babies, strengthens the suggestiveness of the historical parallels. Hence, *Harvest* can be read not only as a cautionary tale about the possible (mis)uses of modern medical and reproductive science, but also as a reflection on the economic and social legacies of Western imperialism, particularly as they converge with new technologies.

With skilful irony, Padmanabhan employs the always loaded motif of cannibalism to distil some of the moral issues raised by the organ trade. Om's taunt that Jeetu has been sent to a human game sanctuary where the rich hunt socially disadvantaged types neatly refigures the connotative reach of cannibalism so that it points to characteristics of developed rather than 'primitive' societies. The Western cannibalising of third-world bodies in *Harvest* also has a ritualistic element in so far as it is driven by a myth of resurrection – the restoration of youth and wholeness. When Jeetu's organs are transplanted to Ginni/Virgil, the transaction is not merely a medical one; symbolic 'capital' also flows from the young, the poor and the beautiful to the old, the rich and the ugly. On another level, the cannibalism motif intensifies the play's critique of a dehumanised Indian society, which is depicted in microcosm through the savage conflicts within the Prakash family.

Harvest's narrative also harnesses the figurative power of disease to convey the moral ills of a world driven by greed and self-interest to the extent that a lucrative trade in body parts has become the norm. However, the disease metaphor operates in complex ways, suggesting that the 'contaminated' realm outside the sanitised Prakash housing unit may be preferable to the sterile environment in which Om, Ma and Jaya are forced to live after their 'contract' with InterPlanta comes into effect. When Jeetu enters the unit covered with muck and grime and weeping sores, his presence precipitates a crisis in the fragile relationship between Donors and Receivers: because he embodies the threat of contamination, he disrupts the power and authority of the carefully regulated Receiver world. At this point, Jaya's rebellion against her bullying family and the demands of the system in which they have become enmeshed provides one of the few tender moments of the play, as she gently dresses Jeetu's wounds.

At the end of her chilling tale, Padmanabhan explores the nexus between sexuality and cultural difference to address the myth of the exotic, sexually available, and yet potentially dangerous Other that still circulates in Western discourse. Virgil's desire to impregnate Jaya, and his simultaneous fear that she would pollute him if their coupling were to happen anywhere but in the virtual realm, could be read as a modern instance of the ambivalence that infused imperial sexuality. Jaya refuses point blank to be party to a transaction that effectively puts Virgil in control of her sexuality, just as she has previously refused to suppress her sexual desires by playing the demure wife to Om. Her demand that Virgil meet her in the flesh before she will consider his proposition functions as a more general challenge to Western societies to put aside damaging stereotypes and obsessive fears about contamination in order to interact with other cultures on a more equal, and respectful, footing. In this sense, like much science-fiction, *Harvest*'s bitter narrative is driven by a utopian impulse to suggest the impossible possibility of a world in which there are no winners or losers, only partners.

Production history

Harvest had its formal premiere in Greek on 20 January 1999 at Karolous Koun Theatre, Athens, directed by Mimis Kouyiouintzis. The play has also had amateur stagings in India, including a Delhi production by Yatrik at the Sriram Centre in July 1999, directed by Joy Michaels.

Select bibliography

Frow, J. (1998) 'Bodies in pieces', in L. Dale and S. Ryan (eds) *The Body in the Library*, Amsterdam: Rodopi, 35–53.
Padmanabhan, M. (1993) 'A Government of India undertaking . . . ', *Critical Quarterly* 35: 66–79.
—— (1995) *Hot Death, Cold Soup*, Delhi: Kali for Women.
Roy, P. (1998) *Indian Traffic: Identities in Question in Colonial and Post-colonial India*, Berkeley, CA: University of California Press.
Sethi, S. (1997) 'Of a future Mephistopheles', *Outlook* 15 December: 97–101.

Harvest

Manjula Padmanabhan

[Handwritten annotations at top:]
Satire - overexaggeration of an idea in society used to make fun of power structures
Om chooses autonomy - gives up his body
↳ Is anything a choice?
Jeetu chooses to be a prostitute with his body

Characters

[Handwritten annotation: *Jaya can carry a baby*]

Donors

OM   Twenty years old, he has been laid off from his job as a clerk and is the breadwinner of his small family. He is of medium height, nervy and thin. He would be reasonably good-looking if not for his anxious expression.

JAYA   Om's wife. Thin and haggard, she looks older than her nineteen years. Her bright cotton sari has faded with repeated washing, to a meek pink. Like the others, she is barefoot at the outset. She wears glass bangles, a tiny nose-ring, ear-studs, a slender chain around her neck. No make-up aside from the kohl around her eyes and the red bindi on her forehead (the colour indicates that she is married).

MA   Om's mother. She is sixty years old, stooped, scrawny and crabby, wears a widow's threadbare white on white sari. Her hair is a straggly white.

JEETU   Om's younger brother, seventeen and handsome. The same height as Om, he [handwritten: *loses his sight*] is wiry and conscious of his body. He works as a male prostitute and has a dashing, easy-going, likeable personality.

BIDYUT-BAI   An elderly neighbour, very similar in appearance to Ma, but timid and self-effacing.

Also urchins and the crowd outside the door. The crowd is audible rather than visible.

Guards and Agents

The GUARDS are a group of three commando-like characters who bear the same relationship to each other whenever they appear. GUARD 1 is the leader of the team, a man in his mid-forties, of military bearing. GUARD 2 is a young and attractive woman, unsmiling and efficient. GUARD 3 is a male clone of GUARD 2. Only GUARD 1 interacts with the DONORS.

The AGENTS are space-age delivery-persons and their uniforms are fantastical verging on ludicrous, like the costumes of waiters in exotic restaurants. Their roles are interchangeable with the GUARDS, though it must be clear that they do not belong to the same agency.

Receivers

GINNI   We see only her face and hear her voice. She is the blonde and white-skinned epitome of an American-style youth goddess. Her voice is sweet and sexy.

VIRGIL   He is never seen. He has an American cigarette-commercial accent – rich and smoky, attractive and rugged.

Setting

For the sake of coherence, this play is set in Bombay, the DONORS are Indian and the RECEIVERS, North American. Ideally, however, the DONORS and RECEIVERS should take on the racial identities, names, costumes and accents most suited to the location of the production. It matters only that there be a highly recognisable distinction between the two groups, reflected in speech, clothing and appearance. The GUARDS and AGENTS are intermediate between the extremes, but resemble DONORS more than RECEIVERS.

The year is 2010. There are significant technical advances, but the clothes and habits of ordinary people in the 'Donor' World are no different to those of Third World citizens today. Except for the obviously exotic gadgets described in the action, household objects look reasonably familiar.

Act I, Scene 1

The sound of inner-city traffic: grimy, despairing, poison-fumed. It wells up before the curtains open, then cuts out to a background rumble as . . . the lights reveal a single-room accommodation in a tenement building. It is bare but neat. In the foreground, stage left, is a board-bed across the tops of three steel trunks. MA *sits on the bed. Near her is the front door.* JAYA *stands by the window stage right. To the rear is the kitchen area.*

MA Ho – you! Come here –

JAYA What is it?

MA It's no use staring out the window!

JAYA I'll stare if I wish.

MA Wasting time! Why – you could be pressing my legs instead.

JAYA He said he'd be back in time for lunch –

MA And you think your staring will bring him home faster?

JAYA No, but –

MA Or help him get a job?

JAYA I don't want him to get it!

MA Eh?

JAYA I said I'm hoping he *doesn't* get the job –

MA Oh – I forgot! Missie Madam *doesn't* want her husband to earn a living wage – like she should! Like any reasonable, respectable wife would –

JAYA You don't understand –

MA My son's wife doesn't appreciate him, that's what I understand –

JAYA Like every husband's mother before you.

MA And how would you know what a mother knows?

JAYA I have your example don't I? Oh, there! I think I see him –

MA Well – job or not, he's not got wings, *that* I can tell you. He'll *still* have to climb four floors getting up here. But – what does he look like? Is his face shining? Are his footsteps sweet?

JAYA It's a bit far to see such details –

MA Pah! As if you can see them when he's right in front of you. Now I can see them even without looking at him. Just the sound of his feet. His little feet! Like flowers they were!

JAYA Oh – please! The way you go on!

MA Jealous!

JAYA You'd like to think that –

MA And rude too. Why, you're hardly human! You must have grown up in a jungle!

JAYA Leave me alone –

MA Alone, alone! Have you seen your neighbours? Ten in that room, twenty in the other! And harmonious, my dear! Harmonious as a TV show! But you? An empty room would be too crowded for you!

JAYA That's because I live with two people who pretend the other two don't exist –

MA Meaning what?

JAYA Meaning that you and Om behave as if I and Jeetu don't exist.

MA Don't talk to me about Jeetu –

JAYA See what I mean? You pretend he's not here – so I'm the one who cooks for him, I'm the one who worries about him –

MA You worry far too much about that one, if you ask me –

JAYA Your younger son!

MA Nah. The gods left a jackal in my belly by mistake when they made him – maybe that's why you like him – he's just like you, rude, insolent, ungrateful –

JAYA I? *Like* him!

MA Think I don't see the way you wet yourself when he walks in the door. Yes! Your brother-in-law – ohhh, the shame of it! You'll suffer in your next life. See if you don't! You'll be made into a cockroach and I'll have to smash you – (*lifts her bare foot and stamps hard*) just like this one. (*Shows* JAYA *the underside of the foot.*) See? Do you see your fate?

JAYA (*paying no attention, her ear cocked to the door*) There! That's Om. (*Goes quickly to the door, steps out.*)

MA (*Makes a face behind her back.*) Yah, yah! Go on – running out to meet him, like some idiot schoolgirl! Think I'm taken in by it? Because I'm not! I see everything! Even inside your head!

(*The door opens –* OM *walks in.*)

MA Ah, my son! My own boy! What news?

(OM, *carrying a bulky parcel, looks dazed.* JAYA *comes in behind him and shuts the door.*)

MA No hope? Nothing at all?

(JAYA *stares at* OM.)

MA They are fools, that's all! Don't recognise a diamond when they see one! It's their loss. Still . . . it would have been nice. A change. A god-send. How'll we manage now?

JAYA   What is it? What happened?

OM   I got it. (*Puts the package down.*)

(JAYA *stifles a sob.*)

MA   What? Say that again?

OM   I got it. I got the job.

MA   Oh! Say it again! Say the blessed words again! Never stop saying it! 'I – have – got – the – job!' Ah my soul, my heartbeat! Come, kiss me! Let me hold you, fondle your ears! Why am I surprised? You deserve every success.

OM   Yes. It was quite easy, in the end.

MA   (*to* JAYA) Bring him a glass of milk! Bring him two glasses! Come here, my darling boy! My only delight! Let your old mother hug you to her belly!

OM   There were six thousand men –

MA   Six thousand! Waiting in the sun!

OM   No. Inside a building like a big machine. They had – like iron bars – snaking around and around. And everywhere there were guards –

MA   Police, you mean?

OM   You'll see them for yourself any minute – they're coming –

JAYA   Right now?

OM   They have to check. To set it all up.

MA   Set what all up?

JAYA   You mean it's not certain yet?

OM   They're just checking the building.

MA   For what –

JAYA   Better train your mother to tie her tongue down!

MA   Hear that? How your wife speaks of your mother?

OM   Ma – when the men come, you *must keep quiet.*

MA   As if I ever get a chance to speak!

JAYA   She can pretend she doesn't understand!

OM   Yes, Ma. It's the best way. Behave as if you don't understand, when they ask.

MA   But why? Have you done something wrong?

OM   There's no time to explain! You'll know for yourself any minute now –

JAYA   For how long is the job?

OM   They didn't say –

MA   And what will they pay you?

OM   A lot.

MA   Huh! That's how paupers talk – 'a lot'. Listen to the rich. They're on first name terms with all the leading numbers – hundreds, thousands, hundred-thousand –

OM   We'll have more money than you and I have names for! Who'd believe there's so much money in the world?

MA   Ho!

JAYA   Can we be sure?

MA   You met with the top men? They spoke to you themselves?

OM   No . . .

MA   Pooh! Then you've got nothing!

OM   We were standing all together in that line. And the line went on and on – not just on one floor, but slanting up, forever. All in iron bars and grills. It was like being in a cage shaped like a tunnel. All around, up, down, sideways, there were men –

JAYA   Doing what?

OM   Slowly moving. All the time. I couldn't understand it . . . Somewhere there must be a place to stop, to write a form? Answer questions? But no. Just – forward, forward, forward. One person fainted but the others pushed him along. And at the corners, a sort of pipe was kept . . .

MA   For what?

JAYA   To make water, what else!

MA   Even while moving?

OM   You had to be quick. Other men would squeeze past behind the fellow who was doing his business. Sometimes there was no place and he'd have to move on before he finished. Still dripping.

MA   Shee!

OM   What could we do? Foo! The stench! It was terrible!

JAYA   And then?

OM   The stench! The heat!

MA   But what happened?

OM   I don't know for how long we moved. Then there was a door. Inside it was dark, like being in heaven! So cool, so fresh! I too fainted then, with pleasure, I don't know. (*Reliving his movements*) I wake up to find now the ground is moving under me –

MA   What? How's that?

OM   I don't know. But the floor is moving. Then there's a sign: 'REMOVE CLOTHING' –

MA   Naked!

OM   So we do that. Still moving. Then each man gets a bag. To put the clothes inside.

JAYA   But why?

OM   Then – a sort of – rain burst. I wonder if I am dreaming! The water is hot, scented. Then cold. Then hot air. Then again the

219

water. It stings a little, this second water. Smells like some medicine. Then air again. Then we pass through another place . . . I don't know what is happening. Ahead of me a man screams and cries, but we are in separate little cages now, can't move. At one place, something comes to cover the eyes. There's no time to think, just do. Put your arm here, get one prick, put your arm there, get another prick – *pissshhh! – pissshhh!* Sit here, stand here, take your head this side, look at a light that side. On and on. Finally at the end there's another tunnel, with pretty pictures and some music. And the sign comes: 'RESUME CLOTHING'. I just do what I have to do. All the time, the ground keeps moving. Then at the end, the ground stops, we are back on our feet, there are steps. It must be the other side of the building. And as we come down, guards are standing there, waiting for us. And to me they say, 'You, come – ' And that was it!

MA I can't believe this –

JAYA Are they mad?

OM Some other men were also with me, all looking like me, I suppose. Blank. They told us we had been selected. They wrote down our names, addresses . . . and . . . this-that. All details. Then they gave us these packets, told us not to open them and said we must go home, the guards would come with us for final instructions.

MA But what is the work? The pay-packet? The hours?

OM I'll be in the house . . .

MA What?! All the time?

JAYA You don't really know what it's going to be like, do you?

MA What kind of job pays a man to sit at home?

OM Oh – there was some pamphlet they gave us to read, right in the beginning. Just to tell us to be relaxed and to do whatever we were told. In that it said that once we were selected, each man would get special instructions. That we would be monitored carefully. Not just us but our . . . lives. To remain employed, we have to keep ourselves exactly as they tell us.

JAYA But *who* will tell us – how'll we afford it?

(*There is an excited tapping on the door. A* CHILD *bursts in.*)

CHILD Auntie! Auntie! They're coming to your house! Police!

(*From the corridor, approaching footsteps.* JAYA *shoos the* CHILD *from the door as she stands by it. The footsteps come to a halt.*)

OM Let them in –

GUARD 1 InterPlanta Services wishes to confirm that this is the residence of Om Prakash?

OM Yes –

(*Enter* GUARD 2 *and* GUARD 3. *They are both carrying equipment which they set down and immediately begin to ready for installation.* GUARD 3 *produces collapsible cartons that he begins to set up.* GUARD 2 *starts to install a power generating device after which she will set up the* CONTACT MODULE.)

MA Who are these people? What are they doing?

GUARD 1 (*to* OM) We can start.

OM What do I have to do?

GUARD 1 Just listen. Congratulations! InterPlanta Services is proud and honoured to welcome Mr Om Prakash to its program! (*To* OM) Sir, you have received the Starter Kit? Yes. There it is. Sir: you are directed to open the kit and make it operational after our departure. Instructions are provided within. Any questions? (OM *shakes his head.* GUARD 1 *nods and ticks.*) All right.

(*In the background,* GUARD 3 *has got two cartons set up. He wears large plastic mitts over his existing skin-tight gloves and starts dumping all the items on the kitchen counter into the cartons.*)

JAYA (*to* GUARD 3) Hey! What're you doing? (*Turns to* OM.) See – see what's happening! (*Back to* GUARD 3, *who goes ahead.*) Who said you can touch my things? (*Tugs at his arm.*) Stop that!

GUARD 1 (*to* OM) Sir: we will set up the Contact Module. It will start functioning in approximately two hours.

OM I – I'm sorry, but I must –

GUARD 1 Sir: *pay no attention!* About the Contact Module, all details will be found in the Starter Kit –

(*Meanwhile, downstage, the* GUARDS *dismantle the kitchen.*)

JAYA Who told you to do that! You can't! It's my house! No! Oh! Stop it, you monster, you beast! Don't you understand what I'm saying? Are you a machine? Answer me! Oh! (*Abruptly she turns away, realising it is useless.*)

(GUARD 3 *continues with his job unperturbed in the course of the other events at stage front. After removing everything but the counter top and shelf, he cleans and swabs the entire area, then sprays it with attention to corners. After that he reaches into his kit and brings out a cooking device and bottles full of multi-coloured pellets.* GUARD 2 *continues her installation without interruption.*)

GUARD 1   (*regardless of the commotion behind him*) At the time of first contact, you and your Receiver will exchange personal information. Your physical data has been sent for matching and we are confident that you will both be well satisfied. Any questions?

OM   Uhh – uhh – but what about . . . I mean, when will I actually have to –

GUARD 1   Sir: any questions to the information received so far?

OM   No . . . I mean –

GUARD 1   Right. When we have confirmed that the Contact Module is functioning, you will not be responsible for anything but the maintenance of your personal resources. Any questions?

OM   But what about –

GUARD 1   Sir! Any questions?

OM   No.

GUARD 1   Right. All implements of personal fuel preparation will be supplied exclusively by InterPlanta Services. Henceforward, you and your domestic unit will consume only those fuels which will be made available to you by InterPlanta. We will provide more than enough for the unit described in your data sheet, but will forbid you from sharing, selling or by any means whatsoever, commercially exploiting this facility. Any questions?

OM   No.

GUARD 1   Good. Now if I can just interview the members of your domestic unit –

JAYA   I have a question!

GUARD 1   (*doesn't acknowledge her*) – beginning with the oldest member –

JAYA   Your – your man has thrown my stove into his bag and broken it! Who is going to replace that?

OM   Not now, Jaya! Just be patient –

JAYA   Be patient! While my house is broken up!

GUARD 1   (*approaching* MA *and addressing her*) Madam: full name?

OM   (*interceding*) She doesn't understand your speech. Her name's Indumati. Missiz.

GUARD 1   (*continuing to address* MA) Missiz Indumati . . . Relationship with Donor?

OM   Mother.

GUARD 1   Have you understand all that has been said so far?

OM   Yes.

GUARD 1   (*His hand wavers. He looks up at* OM. *A flicker of normal communication.*) You will explain to her?

OM   Yes –

GUARD 1   Right. Good. Now – (*he turns*) next relative? (*He sees* JAYA) Missiz – (*he consults the sheet*) Kumar – come this way, please.

JAYA   Yes –

GUARD 1   Full name?

JAYA   Jaya. Mrs Jaya . . . J. Kumar.

(MA *stares at* JAYA.)

GUARD 1   Missiz . . . Jaya J. Kumar. Relationship with Donor?

JAYA   (*in a barely audible voice*) Sister.

(MA *registers a shock.*)

GUARD 1   Madam: please repeat response.

JAYA   Sister. He's my – I mean, I'm his – sister.

GUARD 1   Right. Husband?

JAYA   At work.

GUARD 1   Full name?

JAYA   Jeetu – Jeeten. Jeeten Kumar.

GUARD 1   Right. InterPlanta recommends that those members absent at this briefing make themselves available at the nearest registration centre not later than twenty-four hours from the time of our departure, failing which such member will lose all rights to the facilities provided by us. Any questions? (*He does not wait for confirmation.*) Good. (*Turns to the other two* GUARDS.) Briefing complete, initiate departure procedure.

(*Behind him,* GUARD 2 *and* GUARD 3 *have both completed their tasks and are awaiting orders. Hanging from the ceiling is a white, faceted globe.*)

GUARD 1   Officer Contact Module Installation, activity report: installation complete?

GUARD 2   Yessir.

GUARD 1   Contact Module in operational mode?

GUARD 2   Yessir.

(GUARD 2 *moves swiftly over to the* CONTACT MODULE *and points a remote at it. There are musical notes and clicks. A screen-saver pattern appears. The* CONTACT MODULE *moves, is raised and lowered a couple of times, then switched off again.* GUARD 2 *steps back.*)

GUARD 1   Officer Fuel Supplies and Installation, activity report: delivery of six months' fuel supplies for family of four complete?

GUARD 3   Yessir.

GUARD 1   Good. Proceed with departure.

(GUARD 2 *and* GUARD 3 *station themselves by the door.*)

GUARD 1   (*approaching* OM) Mr Om Prakash, thank you for your cooperation. I and my colleagues deeply appreciate the contribution you are about to make towards creating a healthier, happier and longer lived world!

(GUARD 1 *exits and the other two follow suit.* JAYA *shuts the door once the* GUARDS *have left.*)

MA   What sort of job makes a wife into a sister?

OM   Don't get confused, Ma. What they write in their reports doesn't change our lives.

MA   But what *is* she, really?

JAYA   How shall I cook now? They've taken all our things! Every last grain!

MA   Who is Jeetu, now? Is he a son? Or a son-in-law?

OM   Nothing's changed! The words are different, that's all.

MA   But these aren't words! They're people!

JAYA   Are you listening to me, brother? What are we to do for food?

MA   How can my daughter be married to my son? What will people think?

JAYA   Tell me, brother!

OM   It's in this package. Whatever we need to know.

JAYA   Even about food?

OM   Even about food.

(*Lights snap out.*)

Act I, Scene 2

The same room. OM *and* MA *are sitting upstage centre. A mat is spread on the floor and they are eating the coloured pellets of their new food.* JAYA *is leaning her head and shoulders against the side of the bed. The package is opened. Its contents are strewn about. There are brightly coloured instruction leaflets, elaborately devised containers for pills and powders and a number of small gadgets similar in size and shape to a slide-viewing device but of obscure purpose.*

MA   Tell me again: all you have to do is sit at home and stay healthy?

OM   Not *sit* necessarily –

MA   And they'll pay you?

OM   Yes.

MA   Even if you do nothing but pick your nose all day?

OM   They'll pay me.

MA   And what about off-days?

OM   Well. *Every* day is off, in one sense –

JAYA   Why don't you tell her the truth?

MA   Isn't this the truth?

OM   Jaya –

JAYA   Tell her. Tell your mother what you've really done –

MA   Shoo! Don't speak to your husband in that voice.

OM   The walls are thin. Everyone can hear. When you talk like this –

JAYA   Everyone knows already! D'you think you're the only one with this *job*? D'you think everyone doesn't know what it means . . . when the guards come from the agency? All that remains to be known is which part of you's been given away!

MA   What's this, what's this? Who's giving away parts of whom?

OM   She's just trying to make trouble –

JAYA   Huh!

MA   Who cares about her? Wife or sister, Mother comes first! So tell me – these people, your employers, who exactly are they?

OM   It's – it's well, actually it's just one person.

MA   Just one person! With so much money to give away!

JAYA   It's a foreigner. That's why it's so much –

MA   What?

OM   The money comes from abroad –

MA   Really! But . . . doesn't that mean you'll have to go there? Abroad?

OM   Ma – no-one goes abroad these days . . .

JAYA   Not whole people, anyway!

OM   I'm warning you now, Jaya –

MA   What's that? What d'you mean?

JAYA   Not his whole body. Just parts of it –

MA   What's your wife saying?

OM   (*to* JAYA) Why're you doing this? Why're you making trouble?

JAYA   You said it wouldn't affect us – but see what it's done already!

OM   So *tell* me – what? In exchange for your old kitchen you have a new modern one –

JAYA   You call this food? This goat-shit? (*She indicates the pellets they have been eating.*)

MA   It's better than what you make –

JAYA   And calling me your sister – what's that? If I'm your sister, what does that make you? Sister, huh! My forehead burns, when I say that word, 'sister'!

MA   Shoo! Are you a street woman? To speak in such a voice?

OM   You think I did it lightly. But at the cost of calling you my sister . . . we'll be *rich*! Very rich! Insanely rich! But you'd rather live in this one small room, I suppose! Think it's such a fine thing – living day in, day out, like monkeys in a hot-case – lulled to sleep by our neighbours' rhythmic farting! Dancing to the tune of the melodious traffic! And starving. Yes, you'd prefer this to being called my sister on a stupid slip of paper no-one we know will ever see!

MA   Why fight over what is finished? Tell me about this rich foreigner, your employer! Who is he? Why does he love you so much? That's what I don't understand – where did he meet you?

JAYA   Ohh – just tell her, tell her!

OM   We've never met, Ma . . .

MA   What!

OM   He's rich – and old. That's all I know about him. Probably suffering from some illness –

MA   Then why's he paying you so much!

JAYA   Oh *Ma*! Don't you see it? Isn't it obvious?

MA   (*to* JAYA) You're so smart that you can hear God himself thinking but I, I need to hear with my ears. (*Turns to* OM.) Tell me, my son –

OM   Oh, you won't understand, Ma –

JAYA   I'll tell you! He's sold the rights to his organs! His skin. His eyes. His arse. Sold them! Oh God, oh God! What's the meaning of this nightmare! (*To* OM) How can I hold

your hand, touch your face, knowing that at any moment it might be snatched away from me and flung across the globe! If you were dead I could shave my head and break my bangles – but this? To be a widow by slow degrees? To mourn you piece by piece? Should I shave half my head? Break my bangles one at a time?

MA   (*turns to* OM.) How is it possible?

OM   (*to* JAYA) If you weren't so busy feeling sorry for yourself, you'd have read what they say about respecting the donor –

JAYA   Of course! They bathe him in praise while gutting him like a chicken!

MA   But why must they come to us?

OM   See? (*Holds up a pamphlet.*) Look? In this paper it says that one third of all donors are left absolutely intact!

MA   Don't they have enough of their own people?

JAYA   And where does that leave you? Two thirds a man? Half a wit?

OM   (*to* MA) They don't have people to spare.

JAYA   And we do, of course. We grow on trees, in the bushes!

MA   Well. So long as they don't hurt you . . .

(*At this moment, a loud tone sounds. All three react, looking immediately at the globe.*)

MA   Hhh! What's that sound? I must wash my hands! (*She gets up.*)

(*The* CONTACT MODULE *comes to life. It displays a young woman's face, beautiful in a youthful, glamorous First World manner.*)

MA   (*She sees the globe head-on.*) Ahhh! Who is this angel?

(*There is the sound of an international phone call about to commence.*)

GINNI   . . . Hello? Hello?

OM   Yes!

GINNI   I see you! Oh, my Gad! I see you! Is that really you? Auwm? Praycash?

OM   Yes, it's me, Om!

GINNI   Well – hi! That's really great! This is Virginia – Ginni – speaking! Can you see me? How's your reception?

OM   Quite good – quite perfect, I should say! Fantastic!

GINNI   Wow! Yeah . . . well it's pretty wonderful for me too, you know! I mean, I can't *tell* you . . . how much this means to me –

MA (*to* JAYA) What's it saying? I can't understand when they speak so fast –

OM No, Madam! It's our pleasure! Our duty, I mean! Anything we can do to help –

JAYA (*to* MA) She's saying that she's happy –

GINNI It's the most wonderful day of my life! I feel I've got hope, at last! And all because of you –

OM Oh, so kind of you Madam –

GINNI Is it – I mean, can you see me clearly, Auwm?

OM Perfectly clear.

GINNI Okay – I'm just switching screens here – there we go – I can see . . . oh my gad, it's magical, it's wonderful! I'm really talking to India – this is really happening! And that lady in the pink sarong – is that your mother?

JAYA No! *I'm* his sister!

OM My wife –

GINNI Excuse me?

JAYA (*to* OM) Sister. I'm your sister.

GINNI You said just now –

OM I mean, she is my sister, you see –

GINNI Auwm – it says here on your form, you're not married.

OM I'm not. She's my sister.

GINNI You're sure you're not kidding me or anything?

OM Sure, sure, of course I'm sure!

GINNI Because it's important for us to trust one another. I mean, one little slip like that one – and I dunno. I mean, it's hard for me to tell, from so far away –

OM No, no! I'm telling the truth! I swear on my God!

GINNI Okay. I mean, 'coz I've gotta know, you know. If you're married –

JAYA Why?

GINNI What's that?

JAYA Why does it matter?

GINNI Uhh – I'll get back to you on that, okay? Just now . . . lemme see . . . there's two more people in your household, am I right, Auwm? There's (*as if checking a list*) . . . your mother and your brother-in-law. Right?

JAYA That is right.

GINNI Just a moment – uhh – Zhaya? (*The* CONTACT MODULE *swivels towards* JAYA, *who nods.*) Is that your name? Yeah – okay, now honey: I can't handle two people at a time, okay? I mean, it's just this dumb camera, you know, can't look at two people at a time, okay? So – I'm talking to Auwm,

well I can't talk to you as well, okay? I mean, no offence –

JAYA Okay.

OM My mother is also here –

GINNI Yes. Okay. I'm turning the scanner around (*the* CONTACT MODULE *turns*) . . . I'm panning across the room . . . Jeeezus! It's not very much, is it? I mean – oh! Okay! I see her. Hi! Mrs Praycash? Hi! This is Ginni! Can you hear me?

MA (*shielding her eyes against the light*) What?

GINNI I said, this is Virginia! I'm – uh, well just look up, if you can –

OM Ma – just take your hand down –

GINNI Look towards the Contact Module! You know the thing hanging in the room?

MA (*to* JAYA) What's happening?

JAYA Ma – just look at that light –

OM The light! The light!

MA (*straightens up to snap at* OM.) Stop shouting!

GINNI Ahhright! I see you! Mrs Praycash, glad to meet you!

MA I can't understand a word of what that thing is saying! Is it a man or a woman?

GINNI What do I look like to you, Mrs Praycash?

MA Ehh?

JAYA Ma – she wants to know, what she looks like –

OM She can't understand, you see –

JAYA (*to* MA) Ma – look up at that light and say what you see –

MA (*looks up.*) I see an angel.

GINNI (*laughing*) Ha! I look good to you?

MA Good, bad, I don't know. All I know is I've got to go to the toilet. (*She turns around.*)

GINNI (*embarrassed laugh*) Heh! Mm. But – wait! I'm not through yet!

OM (*as* MA *begins to move away*) Don't go yet, Ma – she's not finished –

MA Since when did I need anyone's permission to go to the toilet?

GINNI I'm sorry, Mrs Praycash, this won't take a minute –

MA Nothing doing. I'll piss myself if I don't go right away. (*She reaches the door.*)

GINNI Hey! I didn't let you go!

OM She has some problem, you see –

MA Wait till you're my age! (*Opens the door.*) Why they can't keep a bathroom on each floor I don't know. (*Exit* MA.)

OM The toilet is two floors down, you see –

GINNI Hmmm. Your mother's some character, Auwm. I don't know if I can handle it. I mean – walking out on me like that!

OM   She takes a long time to get there. Old people, you know!

GINNI   Wait a minute – did you say two floors down? What about in your house? There's no toilet in your house?

JAYA   (*bitter laugh*) Huh!

OM   No-one has a toilet in the house. Forty families share one. And my mother walks so slowly –

GINNI   Forty families! My Gad. Well I'm sorry, Auwm. But that's shocking. Shocking! I can't accept that!

OM   (*embarrassed laugh*) Well – I –

GINNI   No! It's wrong! It's disgusting! And I – well, I'm going to change that. I can't accept that. I mean, it's unsanitary!

OM   Of course, of course!

GINNI   We'll just have to install one in your house.

JAYA   What? In this room?

GINNI   Is that you again, Zhaya?

OM   (*to* JAYA) Shh!

JAYA   I'm sorry – but we *can't*! There's no place for a toilet!

GINNI   Excuse me, but you'll have to find the space. It's inexcusable not to have your own toilet! Forty families! It's a wonder you're all not dead of the plague years ago!

JAYA   There's only this one room!

GINNI   Look – there's enough place for a married couple and two others – you! You're married, right, Zhaya?

JAYA   Yes, but –

GINNI   Then there's place for a toilet. I'm sorry, Zhaya, but there's no way around this one. What d'you do for baths?

JAYA   I – we –

GINNI   You – you *do* bathe, don't you? I mean, at least once a day?

(JAYA, *overcome by the humiliation, bends her head and sobs.*)

GINNI   Hey – wait! No, please! Don't cry! I didn't mean to upset you – oh Jeez – stop, please! Look – it's not your fault, okay?

OM   It's all right, she'll be all right. (*He goes over to* JAYA *and thumps her on the back.*) She's fine!

GINNI   Look, Zhaya – I'll make it up to you, okay? I'll send you something, okay? Just tell me what you like and it's yours, okay? Jewellery, perfume, you name it –

OM   (*to* JAYA) Come on, now, come on! It'll be all right – that's enough now –

GINNI   I tell you what, I'll send you some chocolate, okay? I'll send you my favourite candy and – tell you what? I'll sign off now. Okay? It's been a big day for all of us, we're all tired, aren't we? Auwm? Could you look here for a moment?

OM   (*straightening up*) Me?

GINNI   Okay – look, I'll get back to you, okay? And I'm sorry about Zhaya. Really.

OM   No, no –

GINNI   Yeah. Well – the first contact is always a little . . . ah, intense, you know? And I meant that about . . . the toilet, okay? It'll be with you in about an hour.

OM   An hour!

GINNI   Oops! Time's up – Byeeee.

(*The tone sounds again. The light fades from the* CONTACT MODULE. OM *sits down, suddenly, next to* JAYA *who is wiping her eyes.*)

OM   My god! That was something! (*Puts his arm around* JAYA.) A lady!

JAYA   Not old, not sick, nothing –

OM   Oh, she must be sick – or else why spend all this money?

JAYA   It's too late to ask questions now!

OM   But what can be her problem?

JAYA   Maybe there's no problem. Maybe she just likes to suck the life out of young men, like a vampire!

OM   Sometimes you talk rubbish –

JAYA   At least I only talk.

OM   (*holds her a little tighter.*) I did it, all of it, for us –

JAYA   (*moving to loosen his hold*) Careful. I'm your sister, remember?

OM   (*jerks his arm away.*) Oh! Sorry.

JAYA   Me too.

(*Lights fade out.*)

Act I, Scene 3

Moonlit night, on the roof of the tenement building. City skyline in the backdrop. Clotheslines, watertanks, TV antennas and water pipes snaking in all directions. There is a sense of shadowy figures, movements in the background, murmured conversations. JAYA *appears, holding a small torch to her face.*

JAYA   Jeetu? Are you there? Jeetu – it's me, Jaya!

(*Two shadows move away. One shadow materialises in front of* JAYA.)

JEETU   Who told you to come? This is not the right time –

JAYA   I had to. Jeetu – you don't know what's happened –

JEETU   Huh! I know everything –

JAYA   So – so you've heard?

JEETU   Which part? That my brother's sold himself to the foreigners? Or that you're my wife? The second one is hardly . . . news!

JAYA   But you must come – they're asking for you!

JEETU   They? Who –

JAYA   The guards. They came again in the evening. To install the toilet –

JEETU   In the room?!

JAYA   And a bath-shower as well, imagine! We have our own water supply now, as much as we want – and there's no place to sneeze any more.

JEETU   Or . . . to do anything else, no doubt?

JAYA   That . . . there never was.

JEETU   Didn't bother us, though, did it?

JAYA   And now there won't be any reason for Ma to go downstairs! We'll never be alone in the room again, never!

JEETU   So what? If we can shit in public, we can just as well screw in public too – especially since you're now officially my wife!

JAYA   Don't joke about it –

JEETU   Why not? I joke about everything else –

JAYA   My throat bulges with the lies trapped within it.

JEETU   Here – let me kiss it –

JAYA   Get away! That's all finished now!

JEETU   As you wish.

JAYA   So easy! Won't you protest a little at least?

JEETU   Make up your mind!

JAYA   You are all I have, now that my husband has become my brother . . .

JEETU   According to you he was never much else.

JAYA   Still. He would come to me now and then –

JEETU   Maybe incest is more his style.

JAYA   No! He's too afraid! Before it was his mother. Now it's this . . . *job.*

JEETU   Ahh – forget him! You waste your time thinking of my brother.

JAYA   But what about me?

JEETU   Why? Now that you have a new . . . (*mockingly*) husband! (*Reaches for her shoulder.*)

JAYA   (*slipping out of reach*) Oh you! You're a free-lancer –

JEETU   (*laughing*) No! My lance costs money! (*Squats down on a low ledge and starts to roll himself a joint.*) Had you forgotten?

JAYA   And anyway – I'm looking for a plough, not a lance –

JEETU   Oops – sorry! Wrong number! I can't afford any . . . crops!

JAYA   As if I don't know that! And in any case . . . I feel guilty. I feel soiled –

JEETU   My, my! Such delicacy! Don't worry – I'll tell the world that I forced my attentions on you – routinely, in phase with my mother's bowel movements.

JAYA   Oh stop! You always make such a joke of everything.

JEETU   That's all that life is, one long joke. The only trick is in learning when to laugh.

JAYA   Easy for you to laugh! What do you care of my needs, my desires?

JEETU   I thought I was the *only* one who cared about your desires.

JAYA   You care – you care – but not enough! A woman wants more than just . . . satisfaction.

JEETU   Ah – get off my case! You women are gluttons for satisfaction – that's the bare fact of it! You cry when you don't get it – and when you do, you cry that it's not often enough!

JAYA   I cry because – because you satisfy one hunger while awakening the other!

JEETU   That other hunger is insatiable. A man has to protect himself against that hunger or he will find himself sucked dry by new little mouths, screaming 'Papa! Papa!' Little mouths with big, big appetites – oh no! I'm afraid of that other hunger! Mortally afraid!

JAYA   I suppose that's why so many of your 'clients' are men!

JEETU   Not really. It's just that there are more men with money to spare on services such as mine –

JAYA   You should be ashamed of yourself! A man – behaving like a vagrant bull!

JEETU   Why? I'm not fussy – cows, pigs, horses, I'll service all – for a price.

JAYA   You don't need to sell yourself anymore. There'll be enough money in the house now!

JEETU   But not for me –

JAYA   Yes – for all of us. For the whole building –

JEETU   No. I don't mind being bought – but I won't be *owned*!

(*There is a space of silence.*)

JAYA   (*fidgeting*) Well – I suppose I should go –

JEETU   Yes – run home before the agency comes to fetch you!

JAYA   Jeetu –

JEETU   (*looking lazily up at her*) . . . unless you had something else in mind.

JAYA   No . . . no . . . (*She can't face him.*) I mean . . . I – didn't bring any food.

JEETU   Ah . . . so we're asking for credit, are we?

JAYA   There's no food in the house any more! Only those goat-shit pills and some strange powders. And – and – it's all measured out, you see! I couldn't take a portion without having to explain –

JEETU   Never mind. As a long-time client, you are permitted certain liberties. Come here. (*He is seated on a step, leaning back. She doesn't move.*) I said, come here –

JAYA   Jeetu – there are other people around!

JEETU   Turn the other way. (*She turns her back to him.*) Your left foot up on this step. (*He pats the narrow ledge on which he sits. She rests the heel of her left foot there. He puts his arm up her sari unobtrusively, barely shifting his position, looking steadily up at her. She looks straight ahead.*) Now tell me about this food. I'm told that it's quite tasty?

JAYA   (*her voice is thick and strangled*) Yes! It looks like plastic beads but . . . it's *quite tasty*!

JEETU   And filling too, they say –

JAYA   (*gasping slightly*) Filling, yes. It . . . is. But it's not . . . natural – it's not real food. (*She holds the loose end of her sari around her mouth.*)

JEETU   But it must be, don't you think? And healthy? I mean, isn't that the point? To keep us . . . healthy?

JAYA   Yes . . . yes, of course . . . but (*she's finding it difficult to concentrate on what she says*) . . . but . . . who knows if it's . . . *good* for us! . . . (*Gasps.*)

JEETU   Everything's good that tastes good and feels right –

JAYA   (*she breathes in gasps.*) No . . . no . . . that's not true . . . it's *false* food – uhh! – like it's a *false* marriage – Uhh! – *false* – *false*. (*Her voice wobbles.*) False. (*Breathes out, shudderingly.*) False . . . life. (*A pause.*)

JEETU   (*wiping his fingers on the hem of her sari*) False for my brother, yes. But not you –

JAYA   No! All of us. If we get sick, he might get sick too. So we all have to eat this excuse for food and live like virgin brides –

JEETU   Good! Now there's no reason at all for me to come home!

JAYA   No! You have to, Jeetu –

JEETU   Are you mad? When they find out what I do for a living they won't be pleased!

JAYA   They've asked for you twice now – they'll cancel your permit if they can't confirm your presence –

JEETU   Too bad! My brother will have to find some dummy to take my place –

JAYA   Please, Jeetu! Please . . . think of me –

JEETU   I can't afford to think of you. Thinking of you causes too many problems. I'll have to go away –

JAYA   What'll I do? You can't leave me –

JEETU   I can if I must. Don't worry – your guards will probably have a cure for the disease of dissatisfaction as well – just ask them.

JAYA   But why? When there's enough money for all of us?

JEETU   Because no employer pays his staff to do as they please. At least when I sell my body, I decide which part of me goes into where and whom! But it's the money in the end, isn't it? My poor brother. Thought he was so pure. But he's like everyone else after all! Only as pure as the price of his rice.

(*Lights dim out.*)

Act II, Scene 1

Two months later. The same room, but transformed into a sleek residence with gleaming surfaces, chrome, steel and glass. The furniture is largely of the convertible kind (bed-cum-sofa, etc), in keeping with the restricted space. In addition, there are the gadgets – TV set, computer terminal, mini-gym, an air-conditioner, the works. To the rear and right, there are two cubicles containing the bathroom and toilet. The changes are functional rather than cosmetic. In the middle of the space is a low, Japanese-style dining table.

JAYA is sitting by herself, lost in thought, a glossy magazine lies open on her lap. She looks better dressed than before, but not significantly

altered by the change in her circumstances. MA
*is wearing a quilted dressing gown and is
watching TV, upstage right.* OM *is wearing a
fluorescent Harlequin track-suit and sits at the
computer terminal. All sport new footwear.*
JAYA *in Hawaiian sandals,* MA *in cuddly-toy
bedroom slippers,* OM *in inflatable track shoes
with blinking rear lights.*
Suddenly OM *leaps up.*

OM   Look at the time! Ma!

MA   Don't call me – it's your wife's turn to do
the food.

JAYA   It's your turn remember? I did it the
last time because your program was on.

MA   Just hush! It's about to end –

OM   (*Rushing over to dining area, he starts to
set it up.*) Come on, come on! Ginni will be
with us –

MA   Better get Bidyut-bai out first –

OM   Out? Out of where?

MA   Out of the toilet. Didn't you see her
going in? She's been there all morning.

OM   Why! Who let her use it –

MA   She can't stay away from it, she says.
Gets cramps, poor thing, from waiting for
the one downstairs –

OM   I don't care about her cramps! I want to
know how she got into the habit of using
our toilet at all!

MA   Who knows what happens when my
back is turned?

JAYA   Huh! The Empress of the Bath-house
herself! (*To* OM) If your mother had her
way, half this building would be bathing up
here. But how would you know? You never
bother to talk to us any more!

MA   We have so much! Can't we share a little
at least? As it is, my former friends tell me
I've put on airs –

OM   Ma, I've told you. When we have our
own place, that'll be another thing – but
now, when we're still struggling –

(*At this moment there is the sound of the
flush.* BIDYUT-BAI *comes out of the cubicle,
trying to look inconspicuous.*)

BIDYUT-BAI Oh . . . I hope I'm not intruding –

OM   I'm sorry, Auntie – but who invited you
to use our toilet?

BIDYUT-BAI   No, no! Please! I was just
passing this way –

OM   But you used our toilet, didn't you?

BIDYUT-BAI   Toilet? What toilet? Is there a
toilet in this room? My! That must be a
wonder! May I see it?

OM   Oh just go on, go on!

MA   How can she go on when the door's
been barricaded?

OM   She's your friend, you can let her out
yourself.

MA   But I'm watching my program –

JAYA   Your eyes'll be stuck to that screen
from staring at it twenty-four hours of the
day!

MA   But why can't our busy body open it?
Worn out from the tension of doing
nothing, I suppose?

BIDYUT-BAI   Is anyone going to let me out?

JAYA   Oh! For god's sake! (*Gets up.*) I might
as well apply for a job as a doorkeeper!

MA   And you'd make a bad one –

(*The warning tone sounds.*)

OM   Oh my God – Ginni's call-sound!

JAYA   (*struggling to open the door*) Tell her it's
because your mother can't control her
generosity –

MA   See how your sister insults me! Her own
mother!

OM   Hurry up! Hurry up!

JAYA   (*Throws the door open –* BIDYUT-BAI
wriggles past her and out.) All right, all right.
(*Slams the door shut.* OM *is almost done
setting the table up.*) Anyway it only takes a
few minutes –

OM   (*sitting down, as* JAYA *brings a few things
from the 'kitchen' area*) You know how she
hates it when we're late to eat!

JAYA   Tell your mother to come along –

MA   Shh! Shh!

JAYA   (*sitting down*) One of these days, when
this dream comes to an end, it'll be because
you were too busy watching your damned
TV –

OM   It isn't going to end –

(*The warning tone sounds a third time and
the* CONTACT MODULE *lights up.*)

OM   Ahh –

(MA *scrambles to her feet and scurries over.*)

GINNI   Hello-oo! Guess who-oo!

OM   (*affecting a nasal twang*) Hello, Ginni!
Hi! Howdy!

GINNI   Hey – whatcha doing – eating again?

OM   No! We're just having lunch – why don't
you join us?

GINNI   Lunch! Hey, that's too late – for
lunch!

MA   No, no, Ginni! (*To* OM) Tell her it is only
ten minutes –

GINNI I'm sorry Auwm – but I insist: you *must eat at regular hours* – okay? We've had this problem before!

OM Yes – yes – you see we just had some visitor – heh-heh – these people, you know! Don't understand what it means to keep to a strict schedule –

GINNI Ah-ah! No excuses, now! That's another bad habit you have, Auwm. You don't confront your booboos. Now – you've gotta learn to control it, okay? You can't help it, I know, it's a part of your culture – it's what your people do when they want to Avoid Conflict and it's even got a name: it's called 'face saving'. But we can't go through the whole of our lives Avoiding Conflict, now can we, Auwm? You do see that?

OM Yes – yes – of course, Ginni! It is perfectly clear –

GINNI Good! That's what I like about you, Auwm! You learn real fast.

OM Thank you, Ginni.

GINNI And now – let's look at how your family's doing – Mrs Praycash? I can see the food's suiting you, huh? You're putting on weight!

MA What's that? What's that?

GINNI And Zhaya – how're you doin'? I don't see a smile on your face!

JAYA (*instantly pasting a smile on*) Oh – no, no! I'm fine!

GINNI It's a scientific fact that people who smile longer live longer –

JAYA I'm smiling!

GINNI But not enough, Zhaya. You see, it's important to smile all through the day. After all, if you're not smiling, it means you're not happy. And if you're not happy, you might affect your brother's mood – and then where would we be?

JAYA I understand, Ginni.

GINNI If I've said it once, I've said it a hundred times: The Most Important Thing is to keep *Auwm* smiling. Coz if Auwm's smiling, it means his body's smiling and if his body's smiling, it means his organs are smiling. And that's the kind of organs that'll survive a transplant best, smiling organs – I mean, God forbid that it should ever come to that, right? But after all, we can't let ourselves forget what this program is about! I mean, if I'm going to need a transplant – then by Gad, let's make it the best damn transplant that we can manage! Are you with me?

JAYA Yes, Ginni, of course, Ginni.

(*From the door, there is now a knocking sound.* JAYA *looks around.*)

GINNI (*Reacting at once, the* CONTACT MODULE *swivels.*) What's that? What're you looking at?

OM Oh nothing – just – it's nothing!

GINNI Now – Zhaya – I saw you look –

JAYA Really, Ginni – it's . . . it's . . . the wind –

(*The knocking sounds again.*)

MA (*loud whisper*) There's someone at the door –

GINNI What's that you said, Mrs Praycash? Someone at the door?

JAYA Oh – for God's sake! She treats us like children –

GINNI What? Zhaya – Look! All of you – I've told you once, I've told you a zillion times! I hate it when y'all speak at once!

JAYA (*now faking a sneeze*) Chhoo! Sorry, Ginni, sorry –

GINNI That was a sneeze! Don't deny it – you have a cold, Zhaya, don't you? Come on, confess!

JAYA No, Ginni!

GINNI Don't lie to me, Zhaya – I know a sneeze when I hear one –

JAYA It was the – the *pepper* –

GINNI I'll have to ask Auwm – tell me the truth, Auwm – does your sister have a cold? Does she?

OM Cold? Oh – no, no, no! No cold, Ginni – it was only the –

JAYA Pepper. It's this foreign pepper. I'm not really used to it.

GINNI Then – why haven't you reacted before this?

(*The knocking sounds again, more like a thump.*)

MA (*looking around*) That Bidyut-bai is really shameless –

GINNI What? What was that?

JAYA Nothing. She was just –

GINNI You're keeping something from me! I just know it – you're all keeping something from me!

JAYA Oh god, Ginni – we are not! Really!

GINNI Yes you *are*, Zhaya! I can see it in your lying scheming little face! You think you're such an cutie-pie, Zhaya – but you don't fool me! Not for one instant! Now *tell me* –

OM (*raising his voice and leaning into the viewing field of the* CONTACT MODULE) No

– Ginni – please! You trust me – see, look at me – are you looking? Would I tell you a lie?

GINNI   We-e-e-ell. I don't know! What was all that about? Why did Zhaya sneeze? You know how terrified I am of colds, Auwm! Ever since we eradicated colds from here, where I live, it's like – like having the plague!

OM   Ginni – it's not a cold. I promise you that.

GINNI   If you get a cold, Auwm, I can't take your transplant! You'll be quarantined! This whole program will go to waste!

OM   Ginni – believe me. I will never risk your health.

GINNI   Though – I guess – they screen everything that comes in. Even if you did have a cold, they'd never let your organs through –

OM   I live only for your benefit. You know that –

GINNI   All right, I believe you. I'll make myself believe you. I mean it's been hard to read your faces, you know? You people don't use facial expressions, not like us, anyhow. But what *was* that your mother said just now? It sounded like . . . like . . .

JAYA   She was praying, taking the name of God –

GINNI   Oh. Yeah. Well, I don't know – sometimes I just get the feeling –

OM   Please, Ginni – trust me. I would not do anything to harm our – our relationship. We have known each other only for two months, but from the first day itself, I have felt that you are just like my sister! Yes! I would not keep anything from you –

GINNI   Is that right? You wouldn't keep anything from your sister – is that right, Zhaya? You're his sister, so you should know – does he keep anything from you?

OM   I mean –

JAYA   No, he doesn't. He would never tell a lie. He is pure like fresh cotton.

GINNI   Pure like fresh cotton! Haha! That's quaint! That's really quaint! You know what? Even if I didn't need transplants and if I wasn't so sick and all – I'd get the kick of my life from these conversations! It's like – I dunno. Human goldfish bowls, you know? I mean, I just look in on you folks every now and then and it just like – blows my mind. Better than TV. Better than CyberNet. Coz this is Real Life – and don't think I don't appreciate it! You get to be my

age and you really appreciate human companionship –

JAYA   You look very young –

GINNI   What I meant, people in my country, at my age, they just don't have any worthwhile friends, you know? Nothing to hold on to – nothing precious. Nothing like . . . this. I get to give you things you'd never get in your lifetime and you get to give me, well . . . maybe my life. You know? That's a special bond. Don't think I don't appreciate it.

OM   We know you do, Ginni –

GINNI   And now I'm feeling tired, real tired. You just don't know how tired I get sometimes –

JAYA   Is it your illness?

GINNI   I guess you could say so, Zhaya, in a manner of speaking, yes. It's my illness. But now I've gotta go. Okay? (*The tone sounds.*) Byeeee –

OM   Good-bye, Ginni –

(*Knocking sounds again.*)

OM   (*ignoring the knocking*) See you soo-oon –

(*The* CONTACT MODULE *goes dead.* JAYA *leaps up to go to the door.*)

JAYA   We've got to do something about the door! We can't have people knocking whenever they like!

MA   Oh? Now you're going to have special times for knocking as well?

(JAYA *gets to the door and opens it.*)

JAYA   Ohhh – no!

(MA *and* OM *look up in alarm, as* JEETU *staggers in through the door. His condition is terrible, his clothes in tatters, his hair wild, covered in solid muck and grime.*)

JAYA   My God – he's come back. (*She bolts the door.*)

MA   Who is it?

JEETU   Only . . . your beloved son, Jeetu. Yes, I can see how delighted you are to see me. Oh – wait! Sorry! I'm your son-in-law, now, right?

OM   It's not possible –

JEETU   Don't bother breaking coconuts at my feet! Yes – your arms are wide open with welcome! Thank you for inviting me to share the comforts of your modest home with me, your younger brother! (*Sits down.*) And yes, I'd love to sit in this comfortable sofa – Ahhh!

JAYA   What's the matter – are you in pain?

JEETU   Is it possible to know such ease? It feels so good that it hurts! You know – it's a strange thing with the pavements: no matter how long you sleep on them, they never grow soft.

JAYA   You've been on the pavements!

JEETU   Come, come sit by me, my darling wife! Or have you reverted to being my sister-in-law again? Come –

(JAYA *moves downstage.*)

JEETU   Well! No words to express your delight? Strange . . . at one time, she used to fight for my attention –

OM   Jeetu – you owe us an explanation –

JEETU   I owe no-one anything –

OM   Where have you been?

JEETU   Careful – you might go deaf to hear the things I'd tell you –

OM   But . . . are you here to stay?

JAYA   What else? You can't turn him out!

MA   Maybe we don't have a choice.

JEETU   Ah my loving mother speaks at last! And what does she say? What music does she pour into my parched ears?

OM   Stop it! Things have changed around here –

JEETU   Really? I'd never have noticed –

OM   And the fact is – your permit to live with us was surrendered!

(*There is a silence as* JEETU *processes this idea.*)

OM   Yes. I'm sorry – you had your chance. You chose to leave. We had to make our excuses to the guards. To explain why the fourth member of the family wasn't here. Now it's too late to take you back in – and in any case, you're undoubtedly a health hazard –

JEETU   A 'health hazard' did you say? Heh! That's rich! Me – a health 'hazard'! My brother – I'm not a health hazard, I'm a walking, talking, health CATASTROPHE! Oh, yes! I'm so unhealthy that even my germs have germs . . . yes. My lice are dying on my skull – see? (*He offers his head for examination.*) They're just lying in little black heaps –

JAYA   Stop! Stop it! Why make things worse for yourself?

JEETU   Ah those honeyed words of love! How they soothe my running sores!

JAYA   What do you expect? You're the one who left. And now you come back looking like Death's first cousin – is that our fault?

OM   We'll have no choice –

JEETU   (*turning towards* MA) And you, my mother? I hear your love for me has been bought for the price of a flush toilet?

MA   When you reach my age you'll know that a peaceful shit is more precious than money in the bank!

JEETU   Thank goodness I won't live long enough to be rich –

JAYA   What d'you mean –

JEETU   I'm ill. I'm going to die soon –

OM   Oh God –

JAYA   Don't be foolish –

OM   This is serious, very serious –

MA   Of what?

JEETU   An overdose –

JAYA   Some drug?

JEETU   Called freedom. (*He sinks to the floor.*) I've spent my hoard of years – splurged them all, for a few weeks of freedom on the streets. (*Lies flat.*) Freedom to lie in the filth of the open road and to drink from the open sewer! Yes. Freedom to eat the choicest servings from the garbage dump – shared only with crows, flies and pigs! Ah, such freedom as you newly-rich people never know! (*He is slightly delirious.*) But expensive. For all that it looks so cheap, each mouthful of garbage costs a handful of years off your life. And I gorged myself! So I'm . . . gone. Flat broke. Burnt out . . . (*He turns weakly on his side and starts to throw up.*)

OM   Quick – stop him –

JAYA   A towel – cloth, anything! (*She uses the loose end of her sari to wipe his face.* OM *fetches disposable towels.*)

OM   What a mess! You'll have to incinerate your sari –

MA   And the carpet?

(JAYA *places* JEETU's *head on her lap.*)

OM   We have to disinfect the whole room –

MA   But the lice – the lice can get into everything – then we're finished –

OM   Oh! It would have been better if –

JAYA   (*stroking* JEETU's *dishevelled hair*) Don't say it.

MA   What?

OM   How can we keep him! What will we tell the guards –

JAYA   We're not going to turn him out.

MA   There's no place for him now!

JAYA   We've managed before –

OM   Ginni won't like it – she'll forbid it –

JEETU   Who?

MA   She'll chuck him out!

OM   She'll be so angry, so angry –

JAYA   (to JEETU) Shhhh, don't talk –

OM   Just think of the risk! We've gone so far – given up so much and to lose it! All because of –

JAYA   Your brother. Whatever's written on paper, that's what he really is –

OM   But –

MA   What'll we do for food? There won't be enough for him –

JEETU   Uhhhh . . . if I could just have a little water –

(JAYA *wets one of the disposable towels, soaks it in water and dribbles water into his mouth.*)

JAYA   Don't sit up yet.

OM   It's starting to stink! Ginni'll be furious, *furious* –

JAYA   Look, we'll wrap him up in a sheet and keep him to one side till he's better. Then when he can sit up and talk, we'll just tell Ginni that he's come back. My husband's come back from his – his business trip –

JEETU   Who's this . . . Ginni . . .

JAYA   Shhh . . . shhh – don't talk –

MA   See how she treats him – her brother-in-law!

OM   How long can we keep him wrapped up? And what if Ginni finds out?

JAYA   There's no point getting frantic –

OM   And who'll believe that this . . . this . . . *wreck* was away on business?

MA   Look how she holds him – her darling!

JAYA   We'll have to fix him up, of course. Shave his hair, give him some clothes –

OM   But the diseases – the diseases –

JAYA   Clean water and strong food will cure him of whatever he has.

(*Lights dim.*)

Act II, Scene 2

The same scene, a couple of hours later. JEETU's *wasted and scab-scarred body lies in the centre. He has been shaved and grows cleaner, as* JAYA *washes him and attends to the wounds puckering his skin. He groans occasionally.* MA *is sitting to one side.* OM *is pacing. He and* JAYA *have both changed their clothes.* OM *is trying to master the emotions tearing at his face.*

OM   Any minute now – any minute – she's going to call!

JAYA   Just try and relax –

MA   I don't understand how we plan to hide him –

JAYA   Look at these sores!

OM   How can you touch him with your bare hands? He must be oozing with disease –

MA   And he! Her brother-in-law!

JAYA   How can I leave him to rot?

OM   Wear rubber gloves, for pity's sake!

JAYA   We abandoned him to the streets. The least we can do is to risk our own skin when we touch him –

OM   It's like Ginni says – the curse of the Donor World is sentimentality –

MA   Ginni will throw him out – just you see!

OM   Here I am, willing to give my whole body to improve our lives – and what're you doing? Endangering the whole project by feeling up your brother-in-law –

JAYA   Who switched roles with his brother? Who turned this family inside out?

OM   All I'm saying is – leave him till we can disinfect him at least! Show him to the guards – they'll know what to do.

JAYA   What faith you have in them! They don't care about any of us, not as people, not as human beings –

OM   What're you saying? You don't talk enough to Ginni. If you did, you wouldn't feel this way –

MA   Oh she's jealous of our Ginni-angel! Look at her face. Pinched with envy!

OM   She really cares for us –

JAYA   Oh yes, she *cares* – just as much as she cares about the chicken she eats for dinner.

OM   (*contemptuously*) How little you understand of Westerners! They are not small, petty people.

MA   Oh she's just jealous, jealous! Can't bear to think of you being inside that foreign angel. After all, who wouldn't want to be inside such a divine being? Why – it would be indecent to object –

OM   Now, now, Ma –

MA   Who knows? Maybe she'll even want you for a husband some day – why not? If my son's kidneys are good enough for her why not his –

OM   Ma!

MA   Why not his children, I was going to say! Now that's what I want to know! What a miracle – grandchildren! And with an angel for a daughter-in-law!

JAYA Huh! An angel who shares her bed with her dinner – now that *would* be a miracle!

OM Would she spend so much money on me, then? If I am just – a – a chicken to her? Answer me that! Do you know how much she's spent on us?

JAYA Never mind chicken – have you seen how their beef cattle live? Air-conditioned! Individual potties! Music from loudspeakers – why, they even have their own psychiatrists! All to ensure that their meat, when it finally gets to Ginni's table, will be the freshest, purest, sanest, *happiest* –

OM I'll slap you if you're not careful!

JAYA Mind that you wear your rubber gloves –

(*There's knocking at the door.*)

MA Hear that?

OM Who is it – who?

MA The right-hand neighbours. Wanting to borrow a bucket of water.

OM Well, they're not getting it –

MA Yesterday they offered me money –

OM Tell them to ask the municipality to increase their supply.

MA I told them –

OM Then why don't they shut up?

MA They told me I'd forgotten what it was like before we got this external connection – they started to scream and cry –

OM Ahh! These people! No wonder foreigners think so little of us! We have no pride, no shame!

(*Knocking increases in volume.*)

JAYA (*to* MA) How can you be sure that it's the neighbours?

OM Who else can it be?

MA Listen carefully. There's a code, you see –

JAYA Supposing it's the guards?

OM Why should they come?

(*Sustained knocking.*)

JAYA What kind of code –

MA Three knocks means it's the next-door-right-side. Two knocks means it's the next-door-left-side –

OM There's no reason for the guards to come!

JAYA What does loud thumping with no pattern mean?

(*Thumping on the door.*)

OM (*looking suddenly grey*) You're right – it could be the guards!

MA No, no! It's the neighbours I tell you!

(*Violent thumping.*)

JAYA It's been two months, you know! Time to collect their fattened broiler!

MA Shouldn't you just open the door and find out?

OM I – I – What about – what about Jeetu? What'll we do about hiding him?

JAYA If they've come for you, they won't have eyes for anyone else –

(*Knocking, knocking, knocking.*)

OM But – Ginni looked fine at lunch-time – she looked perfectly normal –

JAYA She told us it could happen suddenly, a breakdown –

OM But she would tell us herself! Not just send the guards –

(*Rhythmic thumping.*)

JAYA Maybe she doesn't have the strength?

OM My god, you're right! It's not happened so far, this knocking!

JAYA Why not just open the door and find out?

OM I always hoped, you see, that it would never actually come to this –

JAYA A vain hope. Answer the door –

OM A dutiful wife would open it for me.

JAYA You forget – I'm your sister –

MA That knocking's getting on my nerves now!

(*Knocking, knocking, knocking.*)

OM My legs! My legs refuse to move!

JAYA Such a hero, my man.

(*Hammering, thumping, knocking.*)

OM At least she could have let us enjoy the illusion for a little longer –

JAYA It's in God's will, when your time is up –

MA What'll they think – this delay?

OM Another month – another week, another day, even –

JAYA But in the end it would always come to this – the bill collector at the door –

OM Do it for me – please! I order you – you're still my wife!

(*Knock, thump, knock, thump. A pleasing rhythm.*)

MA   I'll be driven mad!

OM   Would you prefer to see your son dead?

JAYA   Maybe they just want one of your finger-nails – your hair – something unimportant –

OM   How could I have done this to myself? What sort of fool am I?

(*Knocknocknock.*)

MA   If you don't open the door, I will –

OM   And if you move even one muscle, I'll kill you with my bare hands –

JAYA   Your mother!

OM   Whoever opens that door is my murderer, my assassin –

JAYA   I'm sorry, I cannot live with this –

(*Thumpthumpthump. JEETU gingerly rolls over onto his belly and lies still, as if ready to sleep.*)

OM   No!! I beg of you – please! Please! Leave that cursed door alone!

(*Knockthumpknockthump.*)

JAYA   (*exasperated*) They'll break the door down in a moment!

OM   (*sinks to the floor*) I'll hide in the fridge. I'll just crawl along here, all the way to the fridge and I'll sit there, yes –

MA   (*to OM*) Why are you on the floor?

OM   I'm hiding.

(*JAYA opens the door.*)

JAYA   (*off stage*) Yes? What d'you want?

(*There is an indistinct mumble.*)

JAYA   (*re-enters*) Ma – it's for you –

MA   (*getting to her feet*) What? Already?

JAYA   There must be some mistake –

MA   (*going to the door*) It's very prompt, I must say.

JAYA   You ordered something?

MA   Yes. (*Moves out of sight, off stage.*) Yes? Yes! That's right! But where is it? You haven't brought it? It hasn't come? You'll bring it tomorrow? When? Ah . . . Okay. No – no, I'll be at home – and – sign here? No . . . payment? Oh. Okay. Right. I'll be waiting. (*She re-enters and shuts the door behind her.*)

JAYA   Ma? What was all that?

MA   Oh . . . Just something I've ordered –

JAYA   Ordered!

MA   Something I saw on TV –

JAYA   But . . . how did you place the order?

MA   That thing, the remote – you press some buttons and you can buy things, do things – and they bring it right to the door! But Madam wouldn't know, would she! Too high and mighty to watch TV!

JAYA   (*as she locks the door again*) But what have you ordered? How much will it cost?

MA   You'll see, when it comes!

(*Lights dim.*)

Act II, Scene 3

OM *is lying in a foetal position on the floor, stage front.* JEETU *is sitting at the table. His head is shaved and he is wearing* OM*'s track suit.* JAYA *and* MA *are sitting beside* OM.

JAYA   He doesn't seem to hear anything I say.

MA   He's a good boy.

JAYA   But what'll we do! Ginni notices everything.

MA   She'll understand.

JAYA   Huh!

MA   You're just jealous of her. You don't see what a good, kind, generous, loving person she really is. It's a reflection on you, but of course, you're too fancy to care –

JAYA   Please! This is no time to be criticising me!

MA   Who's criticising? I'm just pointing out some simple truths.

JAYA   Come on, Om – get up! This'll never do –

MA   Want to watch TV? There's something good on in twenty minutes –

JAYA   It's so typical. He can't face things. He never could.

MA   You should watch more TV. You could learn so much –

JAYA   It's amazing that he got this job at all.

MA   On *Happy Families* you can see it, the exact same situation. The mother has one son and one daughter – and the son gets an expensive job –

JAYA   Ma – you have two sons!

MA   But the daughter is jealous! She can't bear to see her brother succeeding, getting all the praise from the mother! The poor mother was widowed in early life and has to struggle – but then one day the father comes back.

JAYA   I thought you just said he was dead?

MA   No, I never! I said the mother was widowed – meaning, she just thought the husband was dead –

JAYA   Oh – it's all so pointless! Any moment now, you won't have a TV to watch!

MA   What!

JAYA   This whole dream will come crashing down around us! The guards will come and take everything back!

MA   No!

JAYA   What d'you think – it's your birthright? To have all this water, these gadgets? The moment Ginni finds out what's happened to her little pet, she'll have the place emptied –

MA   Shoo! Such dirty lies!

JAYA   (*quieter*) And then how'll I cook without a stove?

MA   I'll slap you if you talk like that! Why, my son said so himself – we'll be rich for ever and ever –

JAYA   Look at your son, Ma! Look! He's been reduced to a cabbage!

MA   At least a cabbage doesn't talk back!

JAYA   Oh! At least before there was nothing to lose.

JEETU   Why? You used to have a smile before. You've certainly lost that –

JAYA   Oh shut up, shut up! Who are you to talk! You're just a waster! Drifting about the streets, not caring what happened to yourself, not caring about any of us, but when you're ready to die, where d'you come? To us of course!

MA   Don't speak to your husband like that –

JAYA   He's *not my husband*! He's my brother-in-law!

JEETU   And your lover –

MA   What's this?

JAYA   Ohh! Not now! Not this!

JEETU   How strange it is, to be here. Talking to all of you . . .

MA   Not that I'm surprised. Nothing from this slut surprises me.

JAYA   Doesn't it matter to you that you're trampling on my life? Doesn't it matter what harm you cause to others?

JEETU   When you've lost everything, when you're so weak you can't even eat the cockroaches who walk into your mouth, that's when your life's desire breathes in your ear –

JAYA   And? It tells you to torment your family?

MA   She always was shameless –

JEETU   That I should see you again. You, Jaya. Lying there, covered in shit and dirt, ready to die – *dying* to die! – hearing the engine, roaring in my ears, ready to take me away – I thought of you.

MA   I should have thrown her out from the moment she started making eyes at him – her brother-in-law!

JAYA   And then? Some goddess picked you up?

JEETU   Huh! Yes. Some goddess! A dog . . .

JAYA   What? A dog?

JEETU   Came and peed on me. Straight into my mouth, cheeky bastard! But he revived me all right. Lucky for him he ran off – or I would have sucked him dry! Life is a strange thing. When your pockets are full with it, you throw it away like rich whores buying silk bedsheets. But the moment you've emptied your purse, your throat begins to scream of its own accord, like a beggar in the streets. (*He imitates a beggar's cry.*) Help me, oh God! Please! Just another five minutes – that's all I ask – just another five minutes to drink a last cup of tea – just two minutes! Just one minute, one! One . . . *please* God, help this dying shithead one more time. (*Looks at her, reverts to his normal voice.*) That's when I thought of you. I knew you would revive me. (*Shuts his eyes.*) Just the smell of your hair – just the touch of your finger-nails –

JAYA   Hush! These are not things to be said!

MA   And it's too late, anyway. She's already married. To your elder brother –

OM   Who's a cabbage.

JAYA   Om . . .

JEETU   We don't need anyone. We don't need this fancy prison. We managed before. We'll manage again –

MA   What's the time? Look at the time! It's late – Ginni'll be angry at us –

(*From the corridor, the sound of booted steps.*)

MA   Listen! What's that sound?

(OM *hears and reacts immediately, by attempting to crawl towards the toilet cubicle.*)

JAYA   What's the worst they can do? Take away what was never ours to begin with –

(*From the door, a couple of sharp loud raps.*)

GUARD 1   InterPlanta Services! Open this door, please!

MA   It's the guards!

JAYA   (*looking blankly*) So they *have* come for him, after all.

JEETU   (*holding out his hand*) Come. Let me kiss your hand. Then you can go and open the door. Tell them to bugger off and take all their goodies with them.

GUARD 1 *(from outside)* InterPlanta Services – we know you're in there! Open up!

JAYA *(raising her voice)* Coming! *(She gets up.)* I might as well get it over with. *(To the door)* Wait! It takes a while to unlock the door. *(Works at the bolts.)*

GUARD 1 *(from outside)* Resistance is useless! We are authorised to break down this barrier if you do not comply with our request in ten seconds exactly. *(Starts a count down)* Ten! Nine! Eight! –

(JAYA gets the door open.)

GUARD 1 Sev– ah! *(Enters, pushing JAYA aside as GUARD 2 and GUARD 3 take up defensive positions at the door, holding a fold-up stretcher between them.)* Right – where is the Donor? Come on, quickly now. *(He plunges straight for JEETU.)* The penalty for resistance is –

JAYA But that's not –

(JEETU, who has got to his feet, starts to back away.)

MA *(suddenly, pointing to JEETU)* Go on! Take him – before he runs!

(JEETU panics and runs. GUARD 1 chases him around the room, while the other two GUARDS stand like goal-keepers at the door.)

GUARD 1 Ah! He's running, is he? I'll show him – I'll show the cowardly little shit –

JAYA But he's not the one you want!

JEETU *(as he runs)* You fools! Can't you see I'm not your man?

GUARD 1 *(dodging around the others)* Always the same story – no-one wants to pay their dues – come on! It's hopeless to run away. *(GUARD 1 catches him. JAYA screams.)*

GUARD 1 There – there. *(As JEETU struggles)* I've got you now –

JAYA Don't hurt him – don't hurt him – oh he's sick! Please!

GUARD 1 Resistance is useless. *(Starts to drag JEETU kicking and struggling.)* We'll have you knocked out in a second –

JEETU Jaya! Uhh – tell them –

JAYA You fools! You maniacs –

MA *(Reaches out, grabs JAYA's ankle.)* Let him go – slut!

JAYA He's not the one you want! My husband is there – *(She points to where OM was.)* There! *(But he is not there anymore,*

having reached the toilet cubicle and hidden himself inside it.)

GUARD 1 Ohh! That's what they all say when we come to take them! *(In a falsetto, as he subdues JEETU)* 'Not me! Not me! It's my brother you want! My uncle! My son'. Huh! Lying scum –

GUARD 1 *(to the other two GUARDS who are now holding JEETU down)* Officer, administer hypo –

(JEETU struggles wildly.)

JAYA They're hurting him! They'll kill him – oh! I can't bear to watch – I can't!

GUARD 1 Officer – I said, administer hypo –

GUARD 2 I'm trying sir – I – *(GUARD 2 holds down JEETU's shoulder with her knee and delivers a punch with the muzzle of the hypo.)*

JEETU AHHHHHHHHHHHHH! AHHHHHHH!

(JEETU's body arcs up in a convulsion – JAYA screams – then all is still. JEETU is limp and inert on the stretcher. The three guards get to their feet, returning as quickly as possible to their professional composure.)

GUARD 1 Officers – initiate departure.

(GUARD 2 and GUARD 3 quickly spread an opaque shield over the stretcher so that JEETU is completely hidden from sight.)

JAYA *(in a dull voice, knowing that she won't be answered)* He's dead, isn't he? They've killed him. I feel it in my bones.

GUARD 2 Donor secured for departure.

GUARD 1 Proceed with departure –

(GUARD 2 and GUARD 3 hoist the stretcher up and exit.)

GUARD 1 *(turning to JAYA)* InterPlanta Services thank you for your co-operation. Your family member is about to fulfil the solemn and noble contract into which he entered. We, on our part, offer you our sincerest assurance that we will do everything in our power to ensure that he will come to no avoidable harm and will suffer no discomforts other than what is deemed normal under the circumstances. *(He pauses.)* Any questions?

JAYA Yes! What part of him is going to be removed?

GUARD 1 I'm sorry, Madam, I am not free to discuss such details.

JAYA You're going to cut him up and you're not even going to tell us what you're going to do with him?

GUARD 1 Madam: full details will be furnished once the formalities have been completed –

JAYA And can I see him? In the hospital, the clinic, wherever?

GUARD 1 Security and health regulations prohibit any contact between Donors and their families –

JAYA Why ask if we have questions when you don't want to answer any of them?

GUARD 1 Right. (*Handing her the clipboard*) And now, if you would be so kind as to sign the despatch voucher –

JAYA (*grabs the pen*) There – there – your stupid forms, your – papers – your – questions . . .

GUARD 1 Thank you, Madam. We are grateful for your kind co-operation and assure you –

JAYA Just get out! Take your lying face away from my door! (*She makes as if to push him.*)

GUARD 1 (*moving out of her range, as he continues his spiel*) – assure you that we will do everything in our power to return your beloved one to you in as short a time as possible. (*He leans on the door handle.*) On behalf of our clients –

JAYA GET OUT! (*She pushes the door shut in his face.*)

GUARD 1 (*completing his parting message through the door*) – we at InterPlanta Services extend our heartfelt gratitude for your family's support and compassion!

(*Sound of boots marching away.*)

JAYA (*leaning against the door*) He's gone! They've taken him – and I could do nothing to prevent it!

MA Can I switch on my TV?

JAYA (*yelling at her*) Your son goes off to the slaughter house and you're just worried about your TV!

MA If you watched more TV you wouldn't dare talk to your mother-in-law that way –

JAYA (*coming back towards her*) Oh! So I've gone back to being your daughter-in-law, have I? (*She stands threateningly in front of MA, who is facing the TV with the remote raised in readiness in her hand.*)

MA I'm your mother-in-law, that's your brother-in-law on the floor there, your husband's gone to work at the spare parts

factory. And you? You're just a slut who happens to be standing between me and my TV!

(*Lights dim.*)

Act II, Scene 4

Night. The only difference between daytime and night-time is the spotlight illumination. MA is snoring in her corner downstage and left. JAYA is standing near the gym equipment. OM lies in his corner, on a sleeping pallet near the TV, apparently asleep. JAYA goes to OM.

JAYA (*shaking him*) Om! Om – wake up! (*He does not respond.*) Om – come on – I know you're not asleep – wake up!

OM Why? What's the point?

JAYA We've got to talk. To decide what to do –

OM About what?

JAYA When they bring Jeetu back – when they realise they've got the wrong man –

OM They've not realised that. They've used him instead of me.

JAYA No! No – they *can't* – they can't be that stupid!

OM You yourself said they don't give a damn about us – why should they care about him? (*He raises himself slowly.*) No. They've used him, take my word for it. Or else they'd have brought him back by now –

JAYA Maybe the part they've taken from him doesn't need to be so special – maybe they've just taken something small, something insignificant –

OM Then they would have come back by now.

JAYA You're right. It must be something bigger. More crucial. What d'you think it is? His stomach? His intestines?

OM Maybe they've found out he's not me and they've just done away with him!

JAYA But they can't just *murder* someone –

OM Why not? There are no laws to protect strays like him. He's not officially on their records – they can do whatever they like –

JAYA No! I don't want to think of it –

OM – give him drugs and sell him to those game sanctuaries –

JAYA Don't! Oh – please –

OM – where the rich have licenses to hunt

socially disadvantaged types. Yes! That's
what they've done with my idiot brother.
Turned him loose to run with his tongue
between his teeth, the dogs snapping at his
heels –

JAYA   It's just your jealousy speaking, isn't
it? Tell me – isn't it?

OM   What's it to you?

JAYA   I'm still your wife.

OM   On paper, you're my sister. In reality,
you're worse than nothing to me. If not for
Ginni I'd throw you out onto the streets. To
be hunted. What do I care? You betrayed
me. Slept with my brother.

JAYA   You never . . . wanted me –

OM   Wanting – not wanting – what meaning
do these words have? Was it my choice that
I signed up for this program?

JAYA   Who forced you? You went of your
own accord!

OM   I went because I lost my job in the
company. And why did I lose it? Because
I am a clerk and nobody needs clerks any
more! There are no new jobs now – there's
nothing *left* for people like us! Don't you
know that? There's us – and the street
gangs – and the rich.

JAYA   You're wrong, there are choices –
there must be choices –

OM   Huh! I didn't choose. I stood in queue
and was chosen! And if not this queue,
there would've been other queues – it's all
just a matter of fate, in the end –

JAYA   Then why didn't you go with the
guards when they came? Why did you lie
down like a corpse?

OM   It was my fate to lie down in a trance.
And my brother's fate to face the knife –

JAYA   And me? What is my fate?

OM   Of no interest to me.

JAYA   How easy for you to say that! As if I'm
nothing but a dried-up coconut shell for
you to scrape out and kick aside.

(*There's a sound, indistinct.*)

JAYA   Listen – What's that?

(*The sound of boots on the corridor,
accompanied by a shuffling.*)

JAYA   Maybe they've come from the agency
– with news of Jeetu.

(*She runs to the door.*)

OM   Whatever they've done to him, it doesn't
matter. He didn't care about his life
anyway –

(JAYA *flings the door open. The footsteps
come to a halt. The shuffling continues.* OM
looks straight ahead, affecting unconcern.
JAYA *stands back, her hand to her mouth.*
JEETU *enters the room, his arms half-raised
in front of him, being steered by* GUARD 2,
impassively. GUARD 1 *enters as well.* JEETU
*is wearing silk pyjamas white on white.
Across his eyes, and wrapped around his
head, heavy bandages.* JAYA *remains where
she is, staring. In the background,* MA *stirs in
her sleep.*)

GUARD 1   Donor Prakash, we have no words
with which to express our deep and sincere
appreciation of your generosity towards
your Receiver. You will be glad to hear that
the transplant has been a tremendous
success and that henceforward you will
receive every benefit and consideration
due to you under the terms of your
contract . . .

(*Lights fade out as he drones on.*)

Act III, Scene 1

Little has changed in the room. JEETU *sits on
the floor with his head between his knees,
facing stage front.* MA *is watching TV, wearing
head-phones.* JAYA *and* OM *are sitting on either
side of* JEETU.

JAYA   Jeetu speak to me –

JEETU   Don't touch me!

OM   What does he care what happens to us?
He's only thinking of himself –

JAYA   Jeetu, you've already paid the price –
now why not live with the reward?

JEETU   (*He lifts his head. In the place of his
eyes are enormous goggles, created to look like
a pair of imitation eyes.*) This . . . is my
reward?

JAYA   Jeetu – if you would only listen a
moment –

JEETU   I won't listen! Because listening
brings acceptance. (*He moves warily.*)
And I will never accept. I will never live
with this –

OM   Selfish, that's what he is –

JAYA   Jeetu, no!

JEETU   I don't need your permission to step
off the bus! I make my own decisions –

OM   Only thinks of himself. Look at me.

JEETU   Yes, my brother! Look at you? Look
at you with these eyes that were meant for
you? These blind eyes – (*He hits his eyes
with his fists.*)

JAYA   But Jeetu – if they think you're Om, then we need you! Without you, they won't maintain us –

JEETU   I don't care! I'm not the one who got this job – and I'm not going to be the one to suffer the consequences.

OM   He was always selfish. Always lived just for himself –

JAYA   Jeetu – just wait till we can ask Ginni – she'll listen at least, maybe even help –

JEETU   Ginni, huh! Ginni only helps herself –

JAYA   No, Jeetu –

JEETU   A rich woman who plucks a poor man's eyes out of his body – huh! That's not a woman, it's a demon!

JAYA   But Jeetu, without you . . .

OM   Just wait till Ginni finds out whose eyes are in her head! Just wait!

JAYA   (*to* OM) Why tell her? If she goes on thinking Jeetu is you then maybe –

OM   Fat chance! It's the guards who made the mistake! The moment she sees me here she'll know what happened – and she'll be mad! She'll be furious! She'll probably have the guards court-martialled –

JAYA   You heard what they said – the transplant was a success. So maybe . . . maybe *it is* all right. Maybe Jeetu's eyes are good enough.

OM   It's not so easy as you think – remember all those injections I had in the beginning? They were to prepare my body, to change it so that it could match Ginni's body perfectly. But now they've taken the wrong pair of eyes – who knows what it'll do to Ginni? And what about Jeetu's infections, all the poisons and germs he's had circulating inside him – what about them? Ginni's scared about catching your cold! What'll she catch from Jeetu?

JAYA   But they *said* –

OM   It takes time to know that a transplant has been a success!

JAYA   How long?

OM   I don't know. I'm not a doctor.

JEETU   I'm not going to live long enough, either way.

JAYA   Please, you can't kill yourself! I don't care what she says – I'm not going to lose you again –

JEETU   You don't know what you're asking of me.

JAYA   Jeetu –

OM   (*to* JAYA) Why waste your breath?

Neither will he listen, nor will it make the slightest difference to the outcome. What will be, will be, regardless of what we try to do about it –

JAYA   But *why* – when it doesn't *have* to be! Why – when all he has to do is to pretend – just for a couple of hours in a day –

JEETU   Why? Because I am in a place beyond death. I am in a place worse than death.

JAYA   There's no place worse than death.

JEETU   Yet I know such a place, now. A bleached and pitted place. Scars and slashes against infinite blackness. No stillness, no dimensions. No here, no there –

JAYA   But can you see me, Jeetu?

JEETU   Yes. I see you. And through you. And through the floor. And through all the gadgets, and through my brother standing there, a blaze of fried nerves, his eyes like ping-pong balls. I see Ma looking like a red bundle hunched in front of the blue glare of her TV. And you, Jaya? You're just a bunch of bright white lines, no nose, no eyes, no skin. When you open your mouth to speak I see a gaping black hole, like the pit of hell yawning open, ready to swallow me up. Everywhere else, it's just a shaping, sparking madness. And I can't turn any of it off. I can't blink, I can't sleep, I can't dream, I can't even cry. This is what you want for me?

(*There is a silence.*)

JEETU   Well? You're not saying anything.

JAYA   I –

JEETU   Is it selfish to want to end this?

OM   I was willing to accept anything for my family –

JEETU   Oh yes! And what happened when the guards came?

OM   That was different. It was the shock, the lack of warning –

JEETU   It was cowardice!

JAYA   Jeetu – we've not asked anything of you so far –

JEETU   This is no time to start!

JAYA   Maybe you'll get used to it in time – maybe they'll be able to improve it –

JEETU   Let me die before I'm too maddened by visions to make the effort!

OM   Just wait, just wait – when Ginni comes, she'll make all the effort for all of us.

JAYA   You think she'll take your side?

OM   Of course she will. And she'll throw the two of you out, for fooling around. For fooling her –

(*The warning tone sounds.*)

JAYA   Oh my God –

OM   Ah! Just let me do the talking – I'll explain everything.

JEETU   What's that? I – I – I *saw* something –

(*The second tone sounds.*)

JAYA   What's the matter Jeetu?

OM   You shut up, both of you! I'll explain it – and don't worry, I won't leave you two out of the picture. But if she asks me, I'll tell her –

JEETU   Something's happening. The blackness is lifting . . . I can see some sort of pattern –

(*The third tone sounds.*)

GINNI   Well – hellooo-oo! Guess whoo-ooo!

JEETU   Ahh! Ahhh . . .

OM   Hello! Howdy! Hi, Ginni –

GINNI   Hello-ooo? Is anybody home? (*The* CONTACT MODULE *swivels.*) Auwm? Isn't that you, Auwm?

OM   (*running around to get in front of the* CONTACT MODULE) No! No – *this* is me! I'm here! Here!

(*The* CONTACT MODULE *flips up and out of* OM's *reach.*)

GINNI   Come in, Auwm! Can you see me? Auwm?

JEETU   My God! My God – I can see!

GINNI   Sure you can see Auwm! That's what we gave you eyes for!

OM   (*screaming*) NO!! It's a mistake! There's been a terrible mistake!

(*But* JAYA *intercepts him.*)

JAYA   Wait – don't disturb them –

JEETU   (*gesturing directly in front of him*) And that . . . and you must be . . .

OM   She's wrong! She's wrong! It's –

JAYA   (*holds* OM *back.*) Shhhhh!

GINNI   Ginni! That's right, Auwm – it's me you're seeing 'coz I'm beaming my video image straight into your mind! So you can see me right in front of you, all of me, for once, not just my face . . . well? What do you think?

(JEETU *moves slowly around, looking at something that no-one else in the room with him can see.*)

JEETU   It's – you're – beautiful. Like . . . magic.

GINNI   You like me, Auwm? You like what you see?

JEETU   Yes. And – and the room! What is this place?

GINNI   Oh . . . it's just where I live, Auwm, it's one of the rooms in my little house –

JEETU   It's a palace –

GINNI   I'm glad you like it Auwm –

JEETU   I can't help but like it! Who wouldn't? (*He points around him.*) Those . . . plants! That . . . light! What are those things there? It's . . . beautiful. Beautiful. I've never seen anything like this. Never.

OM   But it's mine, what he's seeing – MINE!

JAYA   Can't you hush?

OM   It's all a mistake! She'll find out and then what'll happen? What'll happen to us?

JAYA   Shhh!

JEETU   And you . . . is that really . . . you?

GINNI   Yup! It's me, Ginni! You look like you're seeing me for the first time, Auwm!

JEETU   I am! I mean – uh . . . we could only see your face before –

GINNI   Well – now. I'm glad you like me so well, 'coz you know what? Now that the transplants have started, it's time that we talked about the next phase –

JEETU   'Next phase'?

OM   But he's the wrong man!

(JAYA *holds* OM *back.* JEETU *is facing the* CONTACT MODULE, *which now rises above him and glows white as the rest of the stage lights dim.*)

GINNI   The next phase of the transplants. You see, we have to progress rapidly now and I need all your support. Until we reached this platform of contact, we couldn't be sure. But now that we're sure, we've got to move really fast. Are you with me?

JEETU   Yes . . .

GINNI   Because you have to be willing, for what we want to do now. You have to be really willing, Auwm –

JEETU   Tell me, Ginni, tell me what you want. (*He moves towards the illusion he sees.*)

GINNI   Ah-ah – can't touch me Auwm! (*He reacts by jerking his hand away.*) Well . . .

you'll have to go back to the clinic and they'll prepare you –

JEETU (*behaving as if he is standing very close to someone, following her around as she moves out of his reach*) You need some more parts of me?

GINNI Well, yes – I mean, that's one way of looking at it but I – I think you should understand that time is kind of short, Auwm, and we really have to get a move on –

JEETU (*He moves his body seductively.*) Just tell me what you want of me Ginni.

GINNI The guards will come for you and they'll request you to follow them away –

JEETU Anything, Ginni, anything.

GINNI The sooner you can go the better it'll be for you –

JEETU Whatever you say, Ginni.

GINNI I mean, really, Auwm, if it's okay with you, I can tell the guards to come for you right now –

JAYA No!

JEETU That's fine with me, Ginni.

OM Ask her what she wants from you.

JEETU Anything you want is fine, Ginni.

GINNI Okay, Auwm, I'm turning this video session off for the moment and I'm going to ask you to wait for the guards.

JEETU You're – you're going?

GINNI But I'll be back, Auwm, closer than you'd ever believe . . . (*The* CONTACT MODULE *moves high, as its light dims.*)

JEETU (*stretching his arms up*) Don't – don't! Ahh! (*Strikes his eyes.*) AHHHH!

GINNI The guards will come, Auwm, you don't have long to wait – we'll talk again when you're in the clinic, okay?

JEETU NO!! Don't leave me in this blindness –

GINNI Remember to keep smiling Auwm –

JEETU No!

GINNI Byeeee!

(*The* CONTACT MODULE *snaps off.*)

JEETU Ah – no! She's gone – she's gone!

(JAYA *and* OM *come forward around him.*)

JAYA Jeetu – do you know what you've said?

JEETU All I know is that I'm going to her – I'm going –

OM You didn't even find out what they're going to take from you this time –

JEETU You don't understand! I was blind! And now I have the chance to see again –

JAYA But . . . it's not *real*, what you see – I – I mean, we could watch you moving like a madman, waving your arms about, pointing to things that weren't there.

(OM *begins to move away, towards the door.*)

JEETU But they're *somewhere*. And that's all that matters to me.

JAYA Yes – but – she's taken your eyes!

JEETU And left me something even better! I can't tell you what things I saw –

JAYA Really? So much?

JEETU Yes – oh, yes! Of course, I can't see what's directly around me. But maybe they'll find a way to change that.

JAYA You should have asked her –

JEETU I'd not seen her, till just now! I thought she was an old woman! You never told me she was so – so *young*! And beautiful. Why didn't you tell me, Jaya?

JAYA You didn't seem interested – we hardly discussed Ginni at all.

JEETU Well. It would have made all the difference if I had known. I saw all of her, you know! Standing there wearing almost *nothing*! And she kept moving, like this, like that . . . wah! I could have had her, right there and then!

JAYA But she wasn't real!

JEETU She exists. That's enough for me. She's a goddess and she exists. I would do anything for her – anything!

JAYA Yes. I can see that.

JEETU Don't hold it against me, Jaya – think of her as just another client – you were always good at that.

JAYA Your other clients were only interested in short-term contracts. Not permanent ownership!

JEETU You should be happy for me – and anyway, you've got your wish, now. I'll stay alive, and they'll go on looking after all of us.

(*There is a knocking at the door.*)

GUARD 1 (*from outside*) InterPlanta Services!

(*Before he can say 'open up', OM has thrown the door open.*)

OM Yes! Take me! Take me! I'm ready to go!

(*Several things happen at once.* JEETU *and* JAYA *turn towards the door, as* GUARD 1 *and* GUARD 2 *roughly shove* OM *aside, entering the room.*)

JEETU Yes –

GUARD 1   Mr Om Prakash – we have been intimated of your willingness to participate in the second phase of our transplant service.

OM   (*screaming*) No! Not him – take ME!! I'm Om Prakash! Check your records.

(GUARD 3 *entering behind the other two, quickly grabs* OM *and holds him pinned to the wall, struggling.*)

JEETU   Yes – I am Om Prakash –

OM   (*from his pinned position*) NOOO!!! He's lying! A lying, scheming swine!!! He's my brother, I tell you – my younger brother!

GUARD 1   All right sir, if you would just follow us – we're ready to leave.

JEETU   Let's go –

(GUARD 1 *stands aside and* JEETU *moves towards the door.*)

JAYA   Jeetu –

JEETU   Don't call me that!

JAYA   Don't go – just yet! Please! It's too soon, they've not explained anything – I – we – you'll never be the same again –

JEETU   (*He grabs her quickly, gives her a brief hug and pushes her towards* GUARD 2.) You have your husband to look after – he needs you more than I. (*He turns and exits.*)

JAYA   Jeetu! JEETU!! (GUARD 2 *lets go of her and exits.*) What happened to your ideals, your freedoms? Your pride? All gone! So easily gone –

(GUARD 3 *has a brief struggle disengaging himself from* OM, *but he too slips out, slamming the door behind him – then bolting it from the outside.*)

OM   AHHHHHHHHHHH! You've locked us in, you bastards! You've locked us in! (*He roars and pounds on the door.*) You can't do this to us! We've not signed any consent forms! You've not taken any permissions! AHHHHHHHHH! You've locked us in here! AAAAAHHHHHHHH! And you've taken the wrong man – you'll regret it –AAAAAAHHHHHHHH!

(*He subsides onto the floor.* JAYA *looks at the door, too shocked and defeated even to cry. She looks across at* MA, *who is totally absorbed by the TV program she's watching.*)

JAYA   Ma? Ma – (*goes to where* MA *sits*) listen to me! (*But* MA *is wearing headphones and can't hear.* JAYA *shakes* MA *by the shoulder.*) Ma! Listen to me!

MA   (*holding one of her ear-phones up from her ear*) What *is* it?

JAYA   Ma – do you realise they've taken Jeetu?

MA   What?

JAYA   Jeetu – they've taken him away!

MA   So? (*Starts to replace the ear-phones.*) He was never here to begin with –

JAYA   No! You *can't* be so indifferent –

MA   Tch! Let me be! Why should I care what happens to Jeetu? I'm through caring about anybody. (*She replaces the ear-phones and turns back to her set.*)

JAYA   (*for a second she is nonplussed.*) That's – too much! You hear me, Ma? (*She screams*) It's just TOO MUCH! (*She snatches the TV remote from* MA's *hand.*) You can't do this – (*smashes it on the floor*) you've got to be involved with what's going on around you –

MA   GIVE THAT BACK TO ME!

(*They do not notice that* OM *is sitting up alertly, by the door. He is listening to something.*)

JAYA   (*stamping on the remote*) I won't – I won't!

MA   Pig-faced buffalo! Give it back or I'll – I'll shit in the water-supply!

JAYA   You wouldn't dare –

MA   I'll microwave your entrails! (*She pushes* JAYA *away and snatches up the remote.*)

JAYA   (*trying to get the remote back*) I'm sick of being the only one to make decisions around here! There's nothing wrong with you – you're not sick – or busy.

(*The sounds that* OM *has heard are now audible: boots in the corridor.* OM *flattens himself alongside the door as the footsteps come to a halt. A pause and the bolt is opened from outside.*)

MA   Let me go, you barren dog – mmmh! Mmmmh! LET ME GO!

(*At this moment the door is flung open.* JAYA *and* MA *fall apart.* OM *almost manages to wriggle out but is pushed aside as* AGENT 1 *enters. Behind him are* AGENTS 2 *and* 3, *blocking the door with something big, on wheels.*)

AGENT 1   Madam Indumati? Who is Madam Indumati?

JAYA   Om – Om what do you think you're doing?

MA   Me! I'm Madam Indumati!

(OM *struggles to get past the wheeled object.*)

JAYA (*to* AGENT 1) What is this? Who are you?

AGENT 1 VideoCouch Enterprises, Ma'm – please –

MA (*to the* AGENT) Have you brought it?

AGENT 1 Yes, Ma'm.

(AGENT 2 *and* AGENT 3 *push a long gleaming case into the room.* OM *tries to go out of the door, but* JAYA *gets there before him. She closes the door and stands in front of it, daring* OM *to push her aside. He considers the possibility, but ultimately withdraws. Meanwhile* AGENT 2 *and* AGENT 3 *set up the VideoCouch. It is reminiscent of Tutankhamen's sarcophagus, encrusted with electronic dials and circuitry in the place of jewels. The* AGENTS *manoeuvre it into the centre of the room, move the dining platform aside, and install the device in its place.*)

AGENT 1 (*to* MA) Please, Ma'm, sign here –

JAYA Ma – who are these people? What's going on?

MA (*to the* AGENT) How about this insti – instig – ?

AGENT 1 Installation. Just sign this form, Ma'm, to confirm receipt of the unit.

MA (*taking the form and the pen*) How do I know you won't just run away after I've signed this?

AGENT 1 As you wish, Ma'm. (*To the other two* AGENTS) Proceed with installation.

(*The other two* AGENTS *open the case, revealing an equally ornate interior, filled with tubes, switches, circuitry. Inside are a number of containers.* AGENTS 2 *and* 3 *set about attaching the containers to various parts of the case while* AGENT 1 *explains to* MA.)

AGENT 1 This is the SuperDeluxe VideoCouch model XL 5000! We are certain it will provide you, our valued customer, with every satisfaction! This is the nourishment panel – the hydration filter –

JAYA (*goes to* AGENT 1) Stop this at once! Explain to me what's going on!

AGENT 1 Ma'm –

MA (*to* JAYA) Can't you shut up? It's my VideoCouch! It's what I ordered the other day!

JAYA But –

AGENT 1 Ma'm –

MA (*to the* AGENT) Proceed!

AGENT 1 Uhh – This is the SuperDeluxe VideoCouch model XL 5000! We are certain it will provide you, our valued customer, with every satisfaction! This is the organic-input interface – the hydration filter – the pangrometer! Here you see the Lexus Phantasticon which is programmed to receive seven hundred and fifty video channels from all over the world! There are ten modes, seventeen frequencies, three sub-strate couplers, extra-sensory feedback impulses and cross-net capturing facilities! All media access – satellite, bio-tenna, visitelly and radiogonad. Manual control panel, neuro-stimulator and full-body processing capacities – all other queries will be answered on-line from within the VideoCouch self-training program. (*He ends abruptly.*) Any questions, Ma'm?

MA Hanh?

AGENT 1 Ma'm – if you sign the delivery voucher we can complete installation –

MA But I haven't understood a word you've said.

JAYA Ma – You MUST explain what this is about.

MA (*to the* AGENT) If I sign this . . . no-one can take it from me, can they?

AGENT 1 No, Ma'm.

MA And your people won't go till I've got into it? (*She signs the voucher and hands it back, not glancing at the many pages of forms.*)

AGENT 1 No, Ma'm – thank you, Ma'm – If you'll just come this way, Ma'm –

(*The other two* AGENTS *have attached a power-line to the unit and at this moment activate the system. It twinkles with small LCDs. It looks like a tiny space-module.* AGENT 2 *delinks the power connection and the lights continue to twinkle. She detaches the cable from the couch.*)

COUCH (*A fruity voice issues from within the VideoCouch.*) Welcome to Video Paradiso! You will not regret your choice! Please ask our authorised representative to settle you into your customised, contour-gel, fully automated video-chamber! (*Appropriate music plays.*)

(*As the* COUCH *begins speaking,* MA *is helped into it by the* AGENTS. *She lies down and the* AGENTS *huddle around her, connecting her up to various pouches and tubes. They do this very quickly and she gasps and grunts once or twice. There is a breathing mask on her face. Soon they are ready to close the lid.*)

COUCH   Thank you for being co-operative! Your fully automatic Video Paradiso unit is now ready for operation! Just relax and let your guide show you the way to an experience of ultimate bliss.

(*The* AGENTS *shut the lid, seal the edges and lock them. They work extremely fast. The muted sound of the* COUCH's *voice continues but becomes a constant unintelligible background hum.*)

JAYA   But – how will she breathe?

AGENT 1   Ma'm – it's a total-comfort unit Ma'm –

JAYA   Won't she have to – to –

AGENT 1   We have a full recycling and bio-feed-in processor! Your relative will have no further need of the outside world from now 'til – (*he coughs*) 'til she chooses to delink.

JAYA   Does she – how will she –

AGENT 1   (*smoothly*) Everything is now in the customer's operation, Ma'm – the unit is fully self-sufficient.

JAYA   Won't I have to switch it on or off? No food? No water?

AGENT 1   Total self-sufficiency, Ma'm! There is nothing to be done!

(*The other two* AGENTS *are ready to leave.*)

AGENT 1   Ma'm – installation is complete.

JAYA   No – wait – who's paying for this thing?

AGENT 1   Debited from the customer's InterPlanta account Ma'm – (*he brings out his card*) but in case you have any queries Ma'm, please get in touch with our local representative. (*He hands her the card, turns and leaves the room.*)

JAYA   No – you've not explained anything – what happens if there's a malfunction?

(*But there is no-one to answer her.* JAYA *looks around for* OM. *She sees that he has just about finished tying a bundle together. She goes to him.*)

JAYA   Om?

OM   I'm going. Back to InterPlanta. Don't try and stop me.

JAYA   Ohh . . . let it be now. They've taken Jeetu and there's nothing we can do about it.

OM   No! They'll see their mistake if I go there myself. It's my only chance. What's left for me here? (*He picks up the bundle.*) I'll go to them. They took me once, they'll take me again. (*Dusts off his clothes, smartens up.*) I'm sure they will.

JAYA   You . . . you're leaving me?

OM   Not alone. Ma's still there. (*He gestures in the direction of the couch.*) And you've got the house to look after –

JAYA   But what'll I do – what'll I tell the guards?

OM   Lock the door from the inside and don't open it 'til I get back.

JAYA   Om . . . (*She reaches towards him.*)

OM   Please! Just let me go –

(OM *exits.* JAYA *doesn't try to stop him. Lights fade as she slowly does up all the bolts, then comes back to the centre of the room, finally folding herself down beside the couch, looking dazed and lost.*)

Act III, Scene 2

Five days later. The room is unchanged. It is night. JAYA *has fallen asleep at the table-cum-sarcophagus. She is looking worn out. There are occasional hums of sound from the VideoCouch. With jarring suddenness the warning tone sounds.* JAYA *startles awake. The* CONTACT MODULE *is ablaze. It no longer has any images. It hovers over* JAYA.

VOICE   (*a rich, gravelly male voice*) Zhaya . . .

JAYA   Ahhh!

VOICE   Don't be frightened, Zhaya –

JAYA   Who are you! What d'you want?

VOICE   Calm down, honey, be easy – shh, shhh.

JAYA   Go away! Leave me alone!

VOICE   (*Abruptly the* CONTACT MODULE *moves up and away from her.*) Okay, Zhaya – if that's what you really want –

(*The* CONTACT MODULE *moves a comfortable distance away from her. It dims down till it looks like a Japanese paper-lantern. The rest of the stage is in darkness.* JAYA *raises her head. She looks around warily. There is a pregnant silence.*)

JAYA   Have you gone?

VOICE   No.

JAYA   (*Waits to hear more before speaking.*) Hello?

VOICE   I'm here, Zhaya, if you're ready to speak to me –

JAYA   Who are you?

VOICE   Let's just say . . . I'm a friend.

JAYA   But I don't know you!

VOICE   Still – I'm a friend.

JAYA   How can you be – if we've never met?

VOICE   I've seen you. Heard your voice –

JAYA   You mean, you're a friend of Ginni's?

VOICE   A friend? Yeah. Sort of.

JAYA   Huh! This is madness. Talking to a lighted ball.

VOICE   Why don't I tell you my name?

JAYA   It's not natural, any of it –

VOICE   Virgil. That's my name, Zhaya and I can show you myself too, if you want –

JAYA   I don't want to see you. I don't want to start thinking of you as a real person, when all the time you're just a voice in the air!

VIRGIL   Not just my face. All of me.

JAYA   You'll come *here*? In *person*?

VIRGIL   Sort of. A version of me –

JAYA   No! I'm not interested in *versions*. I'm not like Jeetu.

VIRGIL   Tell you what. I'll show you what I look like. Then you decide –

JAYA   No! I'll never pluck my eyes out or get into a box –

VIRGIL   Nothing like that. You'll see me here, with your own eyes –

JAYA   How? You'll send a statue with the guards?

VIRGIL   Just come to the Module.

(*The* CONTACT MODULE *moves until it's within her reach. She flinches back.*)

JAYA   This? You'll come from this?

VIRGIL   Don't worry! It can't harm you.

JAYA   No, but –

VIRGIL   It's very simple. Just do as I say. Reach under the Module.

JAYA   I'm not touching that thing!

VIRGIL   Zhaya, honey, when you see what I look like, I guarantee, you're gonna be very happy!

JAYA   (*Turns away from the* MODULE.) No!

VIRGIL   Come on, Zhaya, be a good girl now. I promise you'll feel better once you see what I look like . . . (*When she refuses to turn*) Aaahhh, all right, then! I guess I'll just have to do it myself.

(*Behind* JAYA'*s back, the* CONTACT MODULE *grows bright, sinks to floor level, making clicking, whirring sounds. When it rises again, a projection appears underneath. A figure is revealed, first its feet, then its bare legs . . . it is* JEETU. *There is no longer any*

visor across his eyes, he looks completely healed. But his expression is unfamiliar and his haircut, the skimpy clothes he wears, the way he holds himself – all of these suggest a transformation that goes beyond mere well-being. He stands still, saying nothing, waiting for* JAYA *to turn. His skin glows slightly.* JAYA *is bathed in the unearthly radiance emanating from him. She fidgets, knowing that she must avoid turning around. Behind her the figure crouches down, so that his head is level with hers. She can no longer bear the suspense. She turns.*)

JAYA   Hhhhhh – Jeetu!

VIRGIL   (*The voice comes from the* CONTACT MODULE *though* JEETU'*s mouth moves.*) Well? What d'ya say now?

JAYA   But . . . you're not – where's that thing across his eyes – he can't be – no! It can't be – it can't be him. (*To the* CONTACT MODULE) What have you done? It can't be him!

VIRGIL   Oh! You're not happy? Don't you like the way I look?

JAYA   What is this *thing* in front of me! What have you done with JEETU! JEETUUUUUU! What have they done to you! Where have you gone?

VIRGIL   This *is* me, Zhaya – don't you recognise me? I'm your Jittoo now –

JAYA   Oh!

VIRGIL   I thought you'd be happy to see me!

JAYA   How can I be happy with a ghost?

VIRGIL   I'm not a ghost –

JAYA   You *can't* be who you look like!

VIRGIL   But I am, in one sense.

JAYA   You can't be. It's all just another madness –

VIRGIL   Why, Zhaya? Trust your eyes –

JAYA   But *you're* not here! And *he's* dead . . . isn't he? The one to whom this . . . *body* belonged?

VIRGIL   Depends. On how you define death.

JAYA   There's only one way to define death!

VIRGIL   Not where I live. The body you knew is still alive. He was willing to sell, I was willing to buy –

JAYA   And you paid him in – in – (*She stops, realising her mistake.*) But . . . it *wasn't* you! It was . . . Ginni?

VIRGIL   What do you think, Zhaya?

JAYA   Ginni . . . was –

VIRGIL   Nothing. Nobody. A

*autonomy - self-governing, independent

computer-animated wet-dream – I'll show you, just a minute. (*A faint buzz, then the voice that issues from the* MODULE *is in* GINNI's *cloying tones.*) Hello, Zhaya! Recognise me now? This is what I sound like when my voice is a few decibels higher.

JAYA (*leaps to her feet*) But then Jeetu was paid in dreams!

VIRGIL (*standing as well*) He sees what he wants to see. He lives what he wants to live.

JAYA And he has no body!

VIRGIL He has a casing.

JAYA But no body!

VIRGIL He is happy, Zhaya. He made his choice –

JAYA I saw his choosing! With his mind bandaged in madness!

VIRGIL Was it any worse than his life? When he was lying on the streets – was that better?

JAYA When he was lying in the streets at least he knew what he was! He was – (*She stops.*) But we never told Ginni any of this –

VIRGIL You did. I listened in to you, Zhaya. I heard every word said in the room – even when the Module was off, it recorded –

JAYA HHhhh!

VIRGIL I know that Jittoo's not Auwm and that Auwm's your husband.

JAYA And about Jeetu being –

VIRGIL Diseased. Yes, but he was more available than his brother. So we took him.

JAYA And it doesn't matter? It makes no difference?

VIRGIL Do I look unwell?

JAYA And you heard every, every thing?

VIRGIL Saw, too.

JAYA Why should I believe you?

VIRGIL Zhaya, *you've* lied to me – but *I've* told you only the truth.

JAYA They said you'd be old! And sick!

VIRGIL I am old and I was sick until I got into this young body –

JAYA They said you were a man –

VIRGIL And I am! Always have been –

JAYA But then you *looked* like a woman! You *spoke* like a woman –

VIRGIL Without being one. Without ever saying I was one –

JAYA You said you wanted Om!

VIRGIL I didn't ask for Auwm. He came to us.

JAYA You said you wanted a healthy body –

VIRGIL Yes, Zhaya – yours!

JAYA *Mine!* But it was Om who got the job!

VIRGIL We're interested in women where I live, Zhaya. Childbearing women.

JAYA But . . .

VIRGIL Om was part of the job, but not all of it. We look for young couples, without children –

JAYA Om said he wasn't married!

VIRGIL His polygraph showed he lied. All donors lie. They think we need singles, they think we need men and only the very desperate apply. That suits us just fine, 'coz unless they're desperate, they won't do as we say. We search for skin and blood matches. Auwm matched mine.

JAYA Yet you've taken *Jeetu's* body!

VIRGIL Jittoo is Auwm's brother. He was an even better match –

JAYA I don't know what to believe.

VIRGIL We look for young men's bodies to live in and young women's bodies in which to sow their children –

JAYA What about your own?

VIRGIL We lost the art of having children.

JAYA How can that be?

VIRGIL We began to live longer and longer. And healthier each generation. And more demanding – soon there was competition between one generation and the next – old against young, parent against child. We older ones had the advantage of experience. We prevailed. But our victory was bitter. We secured Paradise – at the cost of birds and flowers, bees and snakes! So we designed this programme. We support poorer sections of the world, while gaining fresh bodies for ourselves.

JAYA And it works? You live forever?

VIRGIL Not everyone can take it. We fixed the car, but not the driver! I'm one of the stubborn ones! This is my fourth body in fifty years.

JAYA Fourth!

VIRGIL Two were not successful. It hasn't been easy, Zhaya. I won't hide that from you. But so long as I can afford to keep trying – I will.

JAYA (*She is trying to find arguments for resisting.*) But I've never been with child –

VIRGIL I know I can fill your belly.

JAYA (*drops her gaze*) No . . .

VIRGIL You have longed for a child. Your arms cry out for that sweet burden. To hold it in your arms, to cuddle and crush it with kisses –

JAYA   No . . . it was never meant to be! Years ago a seer told me – my stars denied it –

VIRGIL   Yet I sanction it, now, I do. With Jittoo's body –

JAYA   Jeetu's dead and you're a – a phantom –

VIRGIL   Honey, I am real and warm and willing. This body which once belonged to Jittoo now contains a red-blooded all-American man! This body is hot with life and heavy with desire! This body aches for you and to give you what you yearn for –

JAYA   A married woman must not hear such words from a stranger's mouth –

VIRGIL   But this mouth is no stranger to you, Zhaya – my voice is but the latest tenant in a house that you have known –

JAYA   No!

VIRGIL   Can you deny the truth that is throbbing in my newly commissioned veins?

JAYA   Please – ohh, it's madness you're offering me.

VIRGIL   Is it madness to offer you your heart's desire?

JAYA   I had stopped hoping –

VIRGIL   You can start again. I am here to make it possible.

JAYA   But whose child would it be? Jeetu's? Or . . . yours?

VIRGIL   This is Jittoo's body!

JAYA   Yes but –

VIRGIL   It would belong to this body – Jittoo's body.

JAYA   But would it be Jeetu's *child*? Would it look like him? Have his voice?

VIRGIL   No-one can say for certain which parent a child will take after. It could look like you, after all, have your voice.

JAYA   Yes – but . . . (*She extends a hand towards the apparition – there is a crackle as her hand passes through it. She recoils.*) Ohhh!

VIRGIL   Ah-ah! Can't touch!

JAYA   Then – how –

(*There is a knocking at the door.*)

GUARD 1   InterPlanta Services! Request permission to make contact!

VIRGIL   Don't be frightened! It's just the agency. I can tell them to wait, if you want –

JAYA   Wait for what!

VIRGIL   The guards will make the child possible Zhaya. It's just a formality, a device –

JAYA   Device?

VIRGIL   You know, an implant. Something I sent, which they're ready to deliver. And you can take your time. About three days are still within your fertile cycle –

JAYA   What are you talking about?

VIRGIL   Zhaya, I'd love to travel to be with you, but I can't –

JAYA   You who are so powerful – you who can travel from body to body –

VIRGIL   The environment you live in is too polluted for me, Zhaya –

JAYA   Then you are a phantom after all! An illusion come to mock me – again! (*She tries to strike the* CONTACT MODULE, *but it flicks out of her reach.*)

VIRGIL   I'll take you through the procedure, step by step. It's simple and it's painless –

JAYA   (*still trying to hit the globe*) No! The pain tells me I'm alive! I want the pain!

VIRGIL   Then you can have all the pain you want, Zhaya – just as you want. It can take the usual nine months if you want, with diet and exercise and medical personnel to monitor you –

JAYA   (*She starts throwing things at the* MODULE, *roaring in frustration.*) Aarrrrhhhhhhhhh!

VIRGIL   I'll be with you, all the way –

JAYA   You're not here! Jeetu's dead and I'm alone –

VIRGIL   I can set it up so that we can be together, go places, anywhere you want – right inside your room –

JAYA   I don't want your make-believe travels!

VIRGIL   Zhaya we can even be . . . intimate! Really. But I thought you'd like to get to know me first –

JAYA   I want real hands touching me! I want to feel a real weight upon me! (*Looks around for things to throw.*)

VIRGIL   And it's all possible –

JAYA   No! Not without risking your skin! Never! Do you hear me, whoever you are, wherever you are? Never! Never! NEVER! There is no closeness without risk!

(*With this, she manages to get a direct hit. There is a shower of sparks and a crack of electric light. The* CONTACT MODULE *abruptly switches off, the whole room flickers in purple and blue light. When the light stabilises again, the figure of* JEETU *is gone.*)

JAYA   (*looking up, towards the darkened globe*) You! Can you hear me?

(*From the door, a knocking.*)

GUARD 1 (*through the door*) InterPlanta Services! Request permission to enter!

JAYA (*to the* CONTACT MODULE) Look: I've understood you now. I know you're stronger than me, you're richer than me. But if you want me, you must risk your skin for me. Even though it's really Jeetu's skin – I want you to risk it.

GUARD 1 (*hammering at the door*) Madam! Madam! We have an urgent message for you from your Receiver!

JAYA Either that or –

GUARD 1 (*Sounds of mechanical activity at the door.*) Attaching external speaker. (*There is a scraping sound, a crackle.*)

JAYA (*she grabs up a piece of broken glass*) – you won't have me at all!

GUARD 1 Speaker installed. Begin transmission . . .

VIRGIL (*his voice crackles through the door*) Zhaya – listen to me – you can't hope to win against me!

JAYA I've discovered a new definition for winning. Winning by losing. I win if you lose.

VIRGIL Zhaya, this is childish!

JAYA It's your fault. You took everything I have away from me. So I *can't* lose any more! I've got nothing left to lose –

VIRGIL But your life, Zhaya! That's still ahead of you!

JAYA Huh, my life. It's not really mine any more. You've shown me that. The only thing I have which is still my own is my death. My death and my pride –

VIRGIL Pride is nothing. Pride is a poor man's fancy dress –

JAYA And if I let you take it from me, I will be naked as well as poor! You'll never let me have what you have, you're only willing to share your electronic shadows with me, your 'virtual' touch, your plastic shadows – no! If the only clothes I can afford are these rags of pride then I'll wear them with my head held high –

VIRGIL Zhaya – don't make me tell the guards to force the door – if you want respect, then open the door yourself –

JAYA You can't see me, can you? I'm holding a piece of glass against my throat. If you force the door, you will push this glass into my throat.

VIRGIL Zhaya – please! We've got this far – I love your spirit – I really do. In these months and weeks, I have come to admire you and care for you. Don't let me down now!

JAYA Then risk your skin.

VIRGIL You're being unreasonable –

JAYA Is it unreasonable to ask one who has cheated death, to cross the oceans?

VIRGIL Zhaya –

JAYA I'm bored of this argument! Don't you understand? This game is over! Either you have to erase me and start again or . . . you must accept a new set of rules.

VIRGIL You're not stupid, Zhaya – you know it is not possible to win against me –

JAYA Stupid or not, if I lose my life, I win this game.

VIRGIL You won't be alive to savour that victory –

JAYA But I'll die knowing that you, who live only to win, will have lost to a poor, weak and helpless woman. And I'll get more pleasure out of that first moment of death than I've had in my entire life so far!

VIRGIL Zhaya –

JAYA You still can't see me, can you?

VIRGIL No – but –

JAYA That's all right. I'll tell you what I'm doing. (*Matches her actions to her words.*) I'm collecting all the pills and medicines I can find. I'm going to take the ones for staying awake, until I run out of them. And if I don't hear the sound of your own hand on my door before that time, I'll take my life. If the guards cause me any discomfort whatsoever – I'll take my life. If you do anything other than come here in person, I'll take my life!

VIRGIL Zhaya – this is wrong, this is ridiculous –

JAYA (*unperturbed*) And in the meantime, I want you to practise saying my name correctly: It's Jaya – 'j' as in 'justice', 'j' as in 'jam' –

VIRGIL Zhaya –

JAYA I won't talk to you unless you say it right!

VIRGIL (*pause*) Zh . . . Jaya. Jaya. Jaya – listen to me –

JAYA No! You listen to me! I want to be left alone – truly alone. I don't want to hear any sounds, I don't want any disturbances. I'm going to take my pills, watch TV, have a dozen baths a day, eat for three instead of one. For the first time in my life and maybe the last time of my life, I'm going to enjoy myself, all by myself. I suggest you take some rest. You have a long journey ahead of you and it's sure to be a hard one.

(*Lights dim out as* JAYA *settles down comfortably in front of the television, bolstered by cushions. She looks happy and relaxed. She points the remote and turns the sound up loud. Rich, joyous music fills the room. Final curtain.*)

11 Kee Thuan Chye

1984 Here and Now
Malaysia

Introduction

The 1985 production of Kee Thuan Chye's *1984 Here and Now*, which played in Kuala Lumpur over five nights to packed houses under the scrutiny of Special Branch police, was seen as a 'rare event' in Malaysian theatre because it dared to criticise governmental policies openly. Reviewers regarded the play, the first English-language agit-prop drama to be staged in the country, as both courageous and foolhardy in its criticism of the systematic privileging of the Malay community against Chinese, Indian and other minority populations, particularly since the race riots of 1969. In the wake of these riots, following a 1972 amendment prohibiting the public discussion of racial inequities, such 'sensitive' material was, and still is, generally expunged from Malaysian theatre, either by the licensing authority or, pre-emptively, by playwrights themselves. As one reviewer noted, 'Thuan Chye has presented a play that would normally have transformed itself into something else by severe self-censorship. It is rare here to come across a matter we discuss every day expressed in art. This play calls a spade a spade' (Ten 1987: 93). Why *1984 Here and Now* was granted a licence despite its explicit political content remains something of a mystery though there is little doubt that its controversial tenor contributed to its box-office success.

Born in 1954 in Penang, Kee has been writing plays since the early 1970s. His initial works were styled in the absurdist mould, influenced by the drama of Beckett, Ionesco and Pinter. Since moving to Kuala Lumpur in 1979, he has been an active member of the Malaysian arts scene as an actor, director and poet, and also literary editor of the country's main English-language newspaper, *New Straits Times*. Kee is well known for his outspoken views about the policies and administrative practices of the Malaysian government, and political dissent has been the consistent project of his various writings. After *1984 Here and Now*, his next dramatic venture was *The Big Purge* (1988), a savage political satire prompted by the anti-democratic Operation Lallang of 1987. Because it was unlikely to obtain a licence for performance in Malaysia, this play was produced in Essex, England, and dedicated to the Malaysians arrested under the Internal Security Act. Kee's more recent stage works, *We Could **** You, Mr Birch* (1994) and *The Fall of Singapura* (not yet premiered), express their call for political reform in a more elliptical manner by focusing overtly on colonial history and myth while suggesting provocative contemporary parallels.

As its title suggests, *1984 Here and Now* is broadly based on George Orwell's classic novel *1984*. The play appropriates Orwell's images of a ruthless oligarchy to expose the means by which existing hegemonic power structures perpetuate gross inequalities in Malaysian society while containing resistance to the oppressive political regime. Kee's storyline is similar to Orwell's although the emphasis is on racial as opposed to class conflict. While Orwell focuses on the rights of the individual, Kee is concerned with broader social relations and, specifically, with communal groups disadvantaged by race-based policies enshrined in the Malaysian constitution. His play appropriates the terms 'Party members' and 'Proles' to suggest the Malay–non-Malay divide and uses the 'Big Brother' figure to suggest the pervasive surveillance of all levels of social interaction. The Kloots provide the entire political culture depicted in *1984 Here and Now* with a figure of collective Otherness. They represent the threat of communism – one of the historical enemies of the state used by successive governments (beginning with the British) to consolidate political authority. However, the fact that the communists have long been identified with the Chinese in Malaya/Malaysia complicates the issue of insider/outsider in the construction of the national subject.

The initial moments of *1984 Here and Now* resemble the Orwellian Two Minute Hate. Kee's nominal 'hero', Wiran – modelled after both Orwell's Winston Smith character and the traditional Malay hero, or wirawan – watches Party members of all rank and profession whip themselves into a moral frenzy at the disco dancing and soap-opera love scenes that are projected onto the video screen. This opening scene critiques extremist responses to the influence of Western culture in Malaysia as well as setting up the socio-political framework for the rest of the play. Kee demonstrates a keen satirical eye throughout the narrative, especially in his treatment of religious fundamentalism. A subsequent scene comments on the increasing Islamicisation of civil society by depicting Party members spying on a courting couple who have apparently broken the khalwat laws that forbid members of the opposite sex to be in close proximity unless they are married or related. Later, an imam (religious official) is shown in a bar ranting against Wiran and his colleague Jumon for consuming alcohol; however, his rebuke is met with Jumon's taunt that Party leaders are known to drink in private. Through such vignettes, the play suggests the hypocrisy of those responsible for imposing religious norms. This is a common observation among Malaysians but one rarely articulated in public for fear of offending Islamic/Malay sensibilities.

As well as facilitating a kaleidoscopic portrait of Malaysian society, the episodic structure of *1984 Here and Now* allows various performance traditions to be staged in ways that comment on the instatement and maintenance of an official Malay-based or Bumiputera National Culture. Bumiputera, which literally means 'prince/son of the soil', explicitly positions Malays as indigenous (and therefore rightful) inhabitants of Malaysia while casting all other cultural groups as immigrants (Lo 1993: 55). Within this context, the play's tiger dance is a parodic response to intense debate in the early 1980s

about the appropriateness of the Chinese lion dance as a contribution to the National Culture. The then Home Minister incensed Chinese communities by arguing that they should develop, instead, a tiger dance since there were no lions in Malaysia. In the premiere production of Kee's play, the tiger dance was performed by the multiracial ensemble, fusing Chinese, Indian and Malay elements, particularly in the musical accompaniment. The dance appeared to speak to criticisms that 'immigrant' cultures were unable and/or unwilling to develop an organic relationship with the local environment. However, such symbolic offers of reconciliation are rejected by the authorities, who break up the dancers and quell their demands for a 'truly united nation'. This highlights the degree of scepticism and latent anger held by marginalised cultures towards the state which continues to promise (and defer) a place for them within the National Culture.

Whereas the tiger dance in *1984 Here and Now* is accompanied by an intercultural blend of musical forms, sequences depicting Big Brother and the Inner Party use specific music/performance traditions associated with Malay culture in order to foreground Malay hegemony in state administration. Big Brother's appearances on the large screen are heralded by gamelan music and an Inner Party meeting is styled as a wayang kulit sequence. The Inner Party members are played by actors behind a shadow screen, which serves to magnify their physical dimensions while also introducing a disjunctive element since traditional wayang characters are not humans but rather mythical beings such as gods and demons. By appropriating the form to portray the workings of the Inner Party, the text suggests ways in which tradition functions to perpetuate the cultural and political power of the Malay community. The use of human figures rather than traditional puppets manipulated by a dalang or master puppeteer also makes the important point that there is no singular villain in the play or, correspondingly, in the wider political context. Big Brother appears to be omnipotent because he is paradoxically everywhere and nowhere; his remote image transmitted through the wonders of capitalist technology signals the realisation of a police state in which disciplinary practices are internalised by the citizens.

Kee demonstrates a sound ear for capturing the colourful spectrum of Malaysian English – which has much in common with its Singaporean equivalent, 'Singlish' – and using it for political commentary. Marked variations in accent, syntax, rhythm and word choice signal differences in class and race among the characters. The language of Party members approximates Standard English but works metaphorically to represent the designated national language, Bahasa Malaysia. (English, Tamil, Mandarin and so forth are now considered sectarian languages in Malaysia.) The Proles, by comparison, speak a variety of English dominated by Chinese inflections and idioms. At one level, these linguistic patterns have the effect of confirming the racial and political dichotomy, yet the irony of Standard English being used to represent Bahasa Malaysia is unmistakable to a local audience since both languages signify discourses of domination based on myths of racial essentialism and cultural authenticity. The proles' 'pidgin' English thus subverts and displaces the official language by means of abrogation and appropriation (Lo 1995: 234). During the mahjong scene, for instance, the dramatic use of 'pidgin' in a discussion resonant with political overtones heightens the critique of the Malaysian social system.

In one of the most moving scenes in the play, Wiran's Prole lover, Yone, describes how she first became involved with the resistance movement. The flashback scenes highlight the extent to which prejudice permeates the society, from the public sphere through to the smallest social unit, the family. Yone is abused by both her father and brother for socialising with Party members. Her father's demand to know the race of her 'frien' is a typical question in a society that operates along communal lines. The violent sexism within the family parallels the racial chauvinism initiated by the Inner Party against the Proles. Thus, the intersections of gender and racial discourses and the juxtapositions of private and public domains stress that political oppression works on multiple and often contradictory levels. This point is consolidated in the Wiran–Yone relationship when Yone is expected to account (and atone) for her past sexual

liaisons while Wiran's sexual history is never held up to scrutiny. His assumed position of privilege is problematised by the fact that he fails to see the contradictions between his political commitment to social justice and his relationship with women.

Whereas Orwell's novel is concerned with the destruction of human(e) relations in an authoritarian state, *1984 Here and Now* retropes the Winston–Julia relationship into one of hope and perseverance. Wiran and Yone are social exiles who occupy a liminal space within the Party–Prole dichotomy. While Kee does not hide the potential dangers and personal pain that come from inhabiting this space, he also highlights the positive effects of dislocation as a potentially radical experience that disrupts the fixity of racial categories. The play refuses to reveal whether Yone is a plant working for the Inner Party or a mere pawn in the struggle for power between Wiran and his torturer, Shadrin. Wiran's determination to believe in Yone in spite of the apparent evidence of her betrayal not only proves his love but also suggests that within the context of an unjust system everybody is tainted to a certain extent. This also applies to the audience, which is called upon to provide a resolution to the play after Wiran escapes from Room 101 into the auditorium, seeking sanction from the guards. At this point, the deliberate refusal of textual closure moves the action from the fictional realm to the 'here and now' of the society dramatised.

Kee's play has been criticised for its failure to examine class as a category that in contemporary Malaysia cuts across racial barriers, further complicating societal analyses. As Jacqueline Lo argues, however, this omission should not override the positive gains in social practice the play attempts to elicit (1993: 60). The ending calls on the audience to follow the playwright's example in speaking out for democracy, racial equality, humanity and justice. There is often a price to be paid for such courage, as Kee's (temporary) demotion from his editorial position in the wake of *1984 Here and Now*'s outspokenness testifies. Notwithstanding such harassment, he has remained committed to his art and to the belief that change is necessary. As he argues,

> For too long, we have only dared to say what we think is safe to say. We have

languished in the hope that some-day, things will be different and we will finally be allowed to speak up. That day may never come without our working towards it.

(Kee 1985: ii)

Production history

1984 Here and Now was first presented by the Five Arts Centre at the Universiti Malaya Experimental Theatre 12–16 July 1985, directed by Krishen Jit with Kee Thuan Chye playing the roles of Yone's father and all three interrogators. The play was originally scheduled for production in 1984 but was delayed due to the ill-health of both Kee and his director and also because of concerns about obtaining a permit.

Select bibliography

Das, K. (1985) 'No wild cheers just yet, but a quiet yes to *1984*', *Far Eastern Economic Review* 22 August: 93.

Kee Tuan Chye (1985) *1984 Here and Now*, Selangor: K. Das Ink.

Lee, K. (1987) 'Big Brother lives: introduction', in Kee Thuan Chye, *1984 Here and Now*, Selangor: K. Das Ink, iii–xxi.

Lim, S.G.L. (1998) 'Abstracting the nation in Kee Thuan Chye's *1984 Here and Now* and *The Big Purge*: national allegory or modernist theatre', *Tamkang Review* 29, 2: 119–42.

Lo, J. (1993) 'Political theatre in Malaysia: *1984 Here and Now*', *Australasian Drama Studies* 22: 54–61.

—— (1994) 'Kee Thuan Chye', in E. Benson and L.W. Connolly (eds) *Encyclopedia of Post-colonial Literatures, Volume 1*, London: Routledge, 760–1.

—— (1995) 'The politics and practice of opposition and resistance in Singaporean and Malaysian drama in English', PhD dissertation, University of Western Australia.

Nagara, B. (1985) 'When courage is not enough to stir up public concern', in Kee Thuan Chye, *1984 Here and Now*, Selangor: K. Das Ink, 136–40.

Ten, M. (1987) 'Just when we thought it was safe to go to the theatre again', in Kee Thuan Chye, *1984 Here and Now*, Selangor: K. Das Ink, 93–6.

Yeo, R. (1995) Introduction to Kee Thuan Chye, *We Could **** You, Mr Birch*, Kuala Lumpur: Kee Thuan Chye, 7–21.

Yong, M. (1983) 'Malaysian drama in English: is there a case for a post-mortem?', *Theatre Research International* 8: 234–46.

1984 Here and Now

Kee Thuan Chye

Characters

WIRAN
YONE
JUMON
SHADRIN
BAROUK
CHIEF SUB-EDITOR
YONE's FATHER
YONE's MOTHER
INTERROGATORS 1, 2 and 3
ENSEMBLE

Scene 1

Upstage right, 10 to 12 feet above, hangs a wooden frame suggesting a television set. Upstage left is a huge picture of BIG BROTHER. *Both the TV set and the portrait remain as permanent features of the set. As the lights come on, disco-rock music plays and human dancers move in rhythm to it behind the frame as if they are part of the programme that is being aired on the set. Downstage left, at ground level, a group of people are watching – they are all dressed in uniform but their social backgrounds are distinguished by characteristic embellishments. They are all party members (as opposed to the proles) – one is a high-ranking official, a member of the Inner Party; one ostensibly a religious devotee with a long robe draped over his uniform; assorted politicians, teachers, students, policemen and* WIRAN, *a journalist. Some of the women are covered entirely except for their faces.*

Suddenly, all except WIRAN *break into a frenzy. Hysterically, they throw a string of adjectives at what is being seen on the screen –* 'Obscene', 'Immoral', 'It is against our religion', 'Trash', 'Ban the Western programmes', 'Throw the TV into the river', 'Corrupting influence', 'Bad influence on our young', 'A sin to watch', 'We can't allow this', 'God preserve our culture, down with the West', 'The work of the Devil'.

Someone shouts, 'Switch it off!' Blackout on TV screen. The pandemonium continues. The TV comes on again, this time with two human actors, one male, one female, simulating a scene from a Western soap opera. Silence from the viewers. After a brief dialogue filled with passionate innuendo, the two 'actors' embrace in a torrid kiss and physical groping. The tirade starts again. The 'picture' freezes in the embrace. The viewers appear as if in a trance by now. 'God have mercy on our children's morals', 'Obscene, obscene', 'The party must prevail, put a stop to all this', 'Save our souls from this immoral display'.

Someone incites WIRAN *to join in the fray. He resists. They try to drag him in but he breaks away and runs off stage. The frenzy builds. Someone grabs a chair and throws it at the screen. Some women are on their knees, arms pointing upwards in supplication, presumably to God.*

Blackout on TV screen. Moments later, a new image emerges, that of a soldier in jungle green, carrying a rifle, marching to anthem. The frenzy picks up. 'Enemy', 'Threat to our society', 'Kloot', 'Death to the Kloots', 'Kill them, kill them all', 'Crush the Kloot threat', 'Destroy them'.

Blackout again. And almost instantly, the screen comes on again, this time in the form of a genial-looking man in the same uniform as the rest with a name tag above his left breast. Gamelan music in the background. Hatred turns to reverence. A collective sigh of relief emanates from the crowd. 'Long live Big Brother!' *shouts one.* 'Long live! Long live!' *echo the others. Throughout* BIG BROTHER's *following speech, the crowd cheers intermittently.*

BB Peace be with us. I bring you good news, comrades. Today, our military forces attacked a Kloot base on the northeast of our border and killed thirty Kloots. Yesterday, twenty were killed in the southwest. Our war against this threat to our nation is gaining success. We are breaking their morale. But don't let this be construed that we are rid of them. We have still to fight on. We must unite against them. Many more will die, our own soldiers too, but we will continue to battle our common enemy. Our war is for the cause of peace. We must be strong. And to be strong, comrades, you must put your faith in the party. You must put your faith in God, observe the principles of our religion. You must uphold our culture. Do not let it be shaken by foreign influences. The Party is supreme. It will strive for the rights of the Party members, for their place of ascendancy in the nation. Party members must unite, one and all with no exception. As for the Proles who have made their homes in this nation, we welcome them to stay. But they must understand that, above all else, the Party members must be kept happy. The Party members must not feel threatened or deprived in this land that is rightfully theirs. When these conditions are fulfilled, and there is unity among the Party members, there will be stability. Peace be with us, comrades.

(Blackout on TV screen. All the viewers shout, 'Long live Big Brother! Long live!' The chanting goes on as the lights on stage fade out.)

Scene 2

Newspaper office. WIRAN *and some colleagues, among them* JUMON, *are working on video display terminals as the lights come on.* CHIEF SUB-EDITOR *enters.*

CHIEF SUB Jumon, have we got a front-page lead yet?

JUMON There's one story here about Leek accusing Kala of making a seditious statement.

CHIEF SUB You mean Kala's call for Party members to control 45 percent of the economy?

JUMON Yes. Going by the Constitution, it is a seditious statement.

CHIEF SUB But you must understand, Jumon, that Leek is a Prole.

JUMON And Proles don't count, right?

CHIEF SUB No, it's not that. You still don't want to understand that our paper has a policy to follow. Kala is a Party member.

JUMON And, therefore, he can get away with making seditious statements. I'm sure if a Prole had made a similar statement, he would have been arrested.

CHIEF SUB I don't want to argue with you, Jumon. That's the reality of the situation and you should be aware of it.

JUMON But we are a newspaper. Our job is to tell it like it is. Call a spade a spade.

CHIEF SUB You are too much of an idealist.

JUMON I'm only doing my job.

CHIEF SUB Yes, just stick to that. In any case, I hear that Big Brother will be moving for an amendment to the Constitution regarding sedition.

JUMON What? Just like that?

CHIEF SUB Just like that.

JUMON To save Kala's skin?

CHIEF SUB For now, we will use another story for the front page lead – the Inner Party's decision to stop the setting up of a Prole university.

JUMON But according to the Constitution, the Proles have a right to set up a university.

CHIEF SUB You want to tell that to the Inner Party?

JUMON We can tell it to the people.

CHIEF SUB Let me tell you this, Jumon. The Inner Party runs the country, not the people.

JUMON That should not be the case in a democracy.

CHIEF SUB You are an idealist. I'm not going to waste time arguing with you. I'll have to check with the Chief Editor about running the university story as front-page lead. Did you know that yesterday, we ran a public reaction story to the Inner Party's implementation of the Education Policy and one point was considered too critical? Big Brother gave the Chief Editor a shelling, and the Chief Editor took it out on me. The word is, we can't hurt the Inner Party's image. You and I, we just do our jobs.

*(*CHIEF SUB *exits.* WIRAN *comes over to* JUMON.*)*

WIRAN You should have known better.

JUMON Bread-and-butter journalist. You know the latest joke, Wiran? All it takes is for Big Brother or his deputy to fart and he'll get twenty paragraphs on the front page. This morning, the Opposition Party Leader made a reasonable statement about ways of integrating the Proles and the Party members, and I think it should at least be second lead on page two. But the Chief Sub said cut it down to four paras and use it as a cut-off, 24-point heading two lines across two columns.

WIRAN   I know how you feel.

(*Suddenly, there is a commotion.* POLICE OFFICERS *bring in the* CHIEF EDITOR *and a* CARTOONIST. *The* CHIEF SUB-EDITOR, *distraught, follows behind.*)

WIRAN   What's happening?

CHIEF EDITOR   I want to know what the charges are against me.

POLICE OFFICER   You'll know soon enough.

CHIEF EDITOR   I want to call my lawyer.

POLICE OFFICER   You won't need one.

CHIEF EDITOR   There must be a mistake. You can't take me in like this.

POLICE OFFICER   I have my orders.

CHIEF EDITOR   And why are you taking our cartoonist? He hasn't done anything wrong.

(CHIEF EDITOR *and* CARTOONIST *are hustled out. All in the office begin to whisper to each other, wondering what has been happening. They crowd around the* CHIEF SUB, *asking for an explanation.*)

WORKER 2   I heard a rumour that the Inner Party is not happy with some of the things the Chief Editor has allowed to be published. Somewhat critical of the Administration.

CHIEF SUB   We must be extra careful from now on.

WORKER 3   But what about our cartoonist?

WORKER 2   He's been too outspoken with his political cartoons lately. Rumour has it he's sympathetic towards the Kloots.

WORKER 1   That's hard to believe. I know him well, he's not like that.

WORKER 2   Nowadays, you don't know what to believe anymore.

JUMON   We are not getting enough of the truth, that's why.

WORKER 1   What's going to happen to them?

CHIEF SUB   If they don't confess to their crimes, they could remain inside for an indefinite period of time.

WORKER 1   Years?

CHIEF SUB   Yes.

WORKER 1   I hope it will turn out all right. Perhaps they will confess immediately.

CHIEF SUB   But things will not be the same anymore. They will be marked for life.

JUMON   Perhaps they are innocent. Haven't you all thought of that?

WORKER 3   Are you suggesting that they have been framed? Why would the Inner Party do a thing like that?

JUMON   They have their reasons.

WORKER 3   Yes, the peace and stability of the nation. They won't arrest people who are not a threat to our safety.

JUMON   They would arrest people who tell the truth.

CHIEF SUB   It's already six, Big Brother is making an important announcement. Switch on the TV.

(*Light comes on TV screen. Gamelan music plays as* BIG BROTHER *makes his appearance.*)

BB   Peace be with us, I wish to announce, comrades, a new amendment to the Constitution that has been passed in Parliament today. The Opposition Party has accused the Second Minister of Economy of having invoked racist sentiments in calling for Party members to own 45 percent share of the economy. In leveling such an accusation, the Opposition Party itself is committing an irresponsible act. The Opposition Party itself is pandering to racist sentiments. It is making political capital of the issue to whip up sympathy for itself and instigate adverse reaction to the workings of the Inner Party. It is manipulating the issue into a sensitive one. To prevent this and to assure the races of this nation that there has not been an encroachment on their rights, Parliament has today amended the Constitution to waive the ruling on sedition on all matters pertaining to the economy provided they do not question the rights and privileges of Party members, as has been guaranteed by the Constitution. The stability of the nation depends on strict observance of the Constitution. The Inner Party will not hesitate to take stringent action against those who attempt to undermine it. Peace be with us.

(*Total blackout.*)

Scene 3

Out in the streets. Night time. WIRAN *is going home after the day's work. He appears deep in thought. A couple of women covered from head to toe pass him by. One of them has a pair of spectacles peeking out, with a little bit of forehead shown.* WIRAN *looks at them for a while. Music starts in the background: 'Somebody's Watching Me' by Rockwell.*

WIRAN *comes across three Party members crouching stealthily behind a hedge. He stops at a distance to watch. Suddenly, they lurch forward, the man with the torchlight switches it on, and all three drag a courting couple out from the other side of the hedge. The woman is also one of those covered from head to toe except that her shawl has come down, exposing her face. The couple break free and run off. The three men pursue, shouting, 'Sinners! Sinners! Catch them!'*

WIRAN *walks on. He comes across newspaper posters screaming headlines: 'Newsmen detained for threat to peace', 'Students abroad recalled for violating Party policies', 'Party members nabbed for desecrating Prole place of worship', 'Infighting among top leaders of Prole party'. A little distance on,* WIRAN *sees a Prole mother dragging her young son.*

MOTHER   You doan play widem, hnarh. I doan like. You play wit our kind.

SON   I wan, I wan.

MOTHER   You hear wat I say or I beat you.

SON   Wy I carn play widem?

MOTHER   Dey all Party member.

SON   But dey got nice toy.

MOTHER   I doan care. Dey all Party member. You come back.

(WIRAN *watches them go off. 'Somebody's Watching Me' fades off. Approaching sound of drums and festivity. A short while later, a group of Proles enter, watching a tiger dance being performed. Then a* POLICEMAN *comes by, blowing his whistle. The Proles ignore him at first.*)

POLICEMAN   Stop! Stop!

(*The dance comes to a stop.*)

POLICEMAN   Do you have a permit for doing this?

(*The* PERFORMERS *look at each other, then one speaks up.*)

PERFORMER   No.

POLICEMAN   You know you can't do this without a permit, don't you?

PERFORMER   Wy you all wan to make it hard for us? Wy mus take permit one?

POLICEMAN   Don't argue. Stop this at once and go home.

PERFORMER   You tink we scared aah?

POLICEMAN   I'll have you arrested if you don't stop.

(*Reluctantly the group disbands, shouting abuse as they leave.*)

POLICEMAN   These Proles. Sometimes they are too much. They act as if they own this nation. (*Goes off.*)

(WIRAN *walks on. He comes across a group of Proles playing mahjong. The setting can suggest that of a coffeeshop.*)

PLAYER 1   Dam bad luck laa. Never get der card I wan. Mus chane place la.

PLAYER 2   Wy you worry? Nex game, der wind will blow your way laa.

PLAYER 1   Wind from your backside la, like der Party.

PLAYER 3   Haiya, doan tok about der Party now la.

PLAYER 4   Ya, bring more bad luck only. I orso cannot game. Look at my card, all split.

PLAYER 2   Like our Prole party lah. Weak like anyting. Everything Big Broder say, OK. Like balls shaking in der pants, man. And now, quarrelling some more, der leaders. Wan more power, wan top post. Firs, dey should be more strong to bring our problem to Big Broder. Instead, every time big Prole party meeting, big quarrel. Trow chair some more. No shame la, dese people. Meanwile, our people suffer. Our chiren carn get place in university. Every year, only so many people can go in. Not fair la. Ay, ay, wait, wait! I wan der card. Doan lah play so fas!

PLAYER 3   Ay, doan tok so much la. Chuck your card. Wafor you tok so much? Wa can you do?

PLAYER 4   Cannot do anyting lah. Wat to do?

PLAYER 1   Every day, jus come gamble, pass der time, enough lah.

PLAYER 4   Ya, man. Wy boder? We can still do a bit of business, can have mistress, can jolly. Aiya, life is short la, wy worry so much, man?

PLAYER 2   You doan care aah if your son cannot get job in Gahmen office?

PLAYER 4   Cannot get, find oder job lah. Not say cannot get. You got brain, you got arm, you got leg, cannot die one la. Haisay, beautiful card la. Bes in der world!

257

(WIRAN *walks off. His next stop is a pub.* JUMON *is waiting there. Piped-in music plays in the background.*)

JUMON I thought you were not going to come. What took you so long?

WIRAN I took a walk, saw a lot of things.

JUMON Like what?

WIRAN You know, I think the Proles themselves are to blame. They don't care enough. They won't do anything to change their situation.

JUMON The Movement For A New Brotherhood can.

WIRAN What's that?

JUMON It's an organisation that believes in the idea of a truly integrated nation, and it's making a start. It will be slow, it may take generations to achieve that goal. But it's still a start. I'm a member.

WIRAN Who's behind this movement?

JUMON Nobody knows. We have to be careful, you see. But the membership is made up of Party members as well as Proles. Dedicated people. What are you having to drink?

WIRAN Beer.

JUMON Two beers, please. So, do you think you would like to join the Movement?

WIRAN I don't know. I've become very disillusioned with a lot of things. The job at the paper means nothing anymore. Just pushing buttons. Earning my daily bread. I don't have any goals left. Sometimes, I wish I could break away from everything. Just go away somewhere. I don't feel a sense of belonging to anything.

JUMON Then why don't you join the Movement For A New Brotherhood? It could give you a new goal, a new faith. There's much you could contribute. Let me just –

(*They are interrupted by a* PARTY MEMBER *who has just come into the bar and is looking the place over.*)

PARTY MEMBER Hey, you! Don't you know you are not supposed to be in a place like this?

JUMON Then what are you doing here?

PARTY MEMBER Watching out for people like you.

JUMON Mind your own business.

PARTY MEMBER Have you no respect for your religion?

JUMON What I do is between me and God. You have no right to interfere.

PARTY MEMBER You are both sinners! Drinking beer!

JUMON I know Ministers who drink liquor. In private.

PARTY MEMBER You will both roast in Hell!

JUMON That's our problem. Now, get out and leave us alone.

PARTY MEMBER Sinners! Sinners! You will pay for your sins! May you die painful deaths.

JUMON (*as* PARTY MEMBER *leaves*) Ya, same to you. Something ought to be done about these extremists. The situation's getting out of hand, and the Administration is to blame. It started out making religion into a political issue, and now that the extremists have caught on to it, the Administration can't back off. Meanwhile, people like you and I have to put up with these fanatics.

(*The TV screen lights up to reveal* BIG BROTHER *giving a speech.*)

BB The Administration will not entertain any view that questions the policy on national culture. The policy clearly states that the national culture will be based on Party member culture. The people must help speed up the implementation of the national culture with dedication, responsibility, and sincerity. The Administration cannot guarantee the tiger dance a place in the national culture. It is not a question of all races being represented but whether the traditions of each race can enrich and contribute greatly to the national culture . . .

WIRAN I've had a long day. Let's go.

JUMON All right. I'll walk with you and tell you more about the Movement.

(*They leave. Total blackout.*)

Scene 4

Repetitive beat in the background suggests mounting tension. The scene is of an office. BAROUK, *a member of the Movement For A New Brotherhood, enters with* WIRAN. BAROUK *is middle-aged, brusque in manner, almost condescending.*

BAROUK So, Jumon sent you. He must have familiarised you with the kind of work we do.

WIRAN Yes.

BAROUK I'm glad you've decided to join the Movement.

WIRAN   I'm not joining yet.

BAROUK   What do you mean?

WIRAN   I want to see what it's like first.

BAROUK   All right. We have a few projects going on now. You can sit in and observe while you are deciding to join. Next month, we are organising a seminar on democracy. After that, we'll organise a forum on national culture, followed by education, the issue of detention without trial and so on. You follow? At the same time, these issues will be discussed in a magazine we intend to bring out monthly, as soon as we get the publishing permit from the Administration. You might be useful in that area. Any questions?

WIRAN   Not at the moment.

BAROUK   We have to work very carefully, you understand. One slip and the Administration could clamp down on us. Right. That's all for now. We'll get in touch with you.

(*Blackout.*)

Scene 5

The following scene carries no dialogue. The repetitive, ominous beat of the last scene segues into the song 'Every Breath You Take' by The Police. The whole sequence could be choreographed and played to mood lighting. Coming out from somewhere, possibly the office in Scene 4, WIRAN *notices a* PROLE WOMAN *standing a short distance away. She is in a dress and looks very attractive. As he moves on, she disappears around the corner.*

WIRAN *enters a coffee shop for a drink. After he is served and he is bringing the cup to his lips, he stops short. At the other end of the shop sits the* PROLE WOMAN *sipping a cold drink. He reflects for a while, then downs the cup and walks out.* PROLE WOMAN *disappears.*

WIRAN *goes to his newspaper office, sits down and starts to work. A short while later,* PROLE WOMAN *enters. This catches* WIRAN'S *attention. He looks hard at her as she walks off. The song trails off as lights fade.*

Scene 6

BAROUK'S *office. Repetitive ominous beat in background. Lights come on to reveal* BAROUK *and* JUMON *in discussion.*

BAROUK   Wiran knows the First Minister of Truth and Information fairly well.

JUMON   He interviewed him several times when Shadrin was under a different portfolio.

BAROUK   The Movement understands he is sympathetic to our cause and has communicated this to some of our people through subtle means.

JUMON   Can he be trusted?

BAROUK   I know his conviction for corruption has made people wary of him. I also know the eventual pardon he received from Big Brother was a face-saving measure. But you know how things operate in this nation. We need someone on the inside, at the top, to manipulate changes. We are capitalising on the psychology of Party members – their unquestioning loyalty to the people who govern them. In short, we need a man of his position to help our cause. You follow?

JUMON   We also have to be careful.

BAROUK   And practical, you understand. This doesn't mean we are going about it blindly. We have a strategy. Next week, we organise a small-scale demonstration protesting against detention without trial and calling for the release of all political detainees. The Administration will have the demonstrators in for illegal assembly but the Minister of Truth and Information has hinted that he will intervene. If nothing goes wrong, it will be proof that he is sincere in helping us.

JUMON   He could play the double agent and double-cross us. Play at gaining our confidence while actually working closely with the Administration.

BAROUK   We have ways of finding out if that is the case. I'm quite confident that nothing will go wrong. Meanwhile, work some more on Wiran. He ought to be useful in this area.

JUMON   How useful?

(*Blackout. Repetitive beat mounts.*)

Scene 7

As in Scene 5, repetitive beat segues into 'Every Breath You Take'. Again, as WIRAN *comes out of somewhere, he sees* PROLE WOMAN *standing nearby. As he continues walking, she disappears. He goes to a newsstand to buy a paper. As he opens it to read as he walks, he nearly collides with* PROLE WOMAN *standing and reading a magazine. Their eyes meet. They stare at each other for a while. She turns and walks off.* WIRAN *walks into an eating shop and joins the queue lining up for food. A short while later,* PROLE WOMAN *is queuing up behind.* WIRAN *leaves the queue and heads for a flat marked 'GENTS'. He disappears behind it.* PROLE WOMAN *goes in that direction and waits outside.* WIRAN *reappears and walks up behind her. Music stops.*

WIRAN   Why are you following me? (PROLE WOMAN *is startled.*) Who are you?
PROLE WOMAN   I'm a member of der Movemen.
WIRAN   They told you to follow me?
PROLE WOMAN   No.
WIRAN   Then?
PROLE WOMAN   I . . .
WIRAN   What?
PROLE WOMAN   I like you.
WIRAN   What?
PROLE WOMAN   I've watched you for some time.
WIRAN   You like me. So you follow me everywhere?
PROLE WOMAN   I wanted to get to know you.
WIRAN   You don't even know me. How can you like me?
PROLE WOMAN   People tok. And I like wat I see.
WIRAN   For a Prole, you speak the language very well. Except for your accent.
PROLE WOMAN   Lots of Proles can speak it well now. (*Awkward silence.*) I wan to work more wit you in der Movemen.
WIRAN   I haven't joined the Movement yet – not officially.
PROLE WOMAN   Why doan you?
WIRAN   What is your involvement in the Movement?
PROLE WOMAN   To try and get more people to know about wat we are doing.
WIRAN   I don't even know your name. I'm Wiran.
PROLE WOMAN   I know. I'm Yone.
WIRAN   Well, now that we know each other's names, why don't we get something to eat?
YONE   Alright.

(*Blackout.*)

Scene 8

In the dark, the insistent beating of drums. Sound of a huge crowd. Chanting builds up. 'Down with detention!' Sirens. Chaos. Sound of

people running. Police whistles. Pandemonium builds, then fades. When lights come on, setting is of BAROUK's *office.* WIRAN *is there.*

BAROUK   I told you all nothing could go wrong.
WIRAN   People were injured.
BAROUK   It's part and parcel of demonstrations.
WIRAN   It was supposed to be a peaceful demonstration.
BAROUK   The Minister kept his bargain.
WIRAN   People were arrested.
BAROUK   But they got off.
WIRAN   They were fined.
BAROUK   They could have been detained.
WIRAN   I don't want to be a part of this.
BAROUK   Then get out!

(*Silence.* BAROUK *switches on the TV to reveal* BIG BROTHER *giving a speech.*)

BB   Remember Woeful Wednesday![1] We have learned from the lesson of the Woeful Wednesday riots of 37 years ago. Woeful Wednesday demonstrated the folly of allowing narrow racialism to take over. We have since learned that no single race can have all that it wants for itself. Our progress will be . . .
WIRAN   Switch that damn thing off!
BB   . . . The Administration believes in a liberal and open approach . . .
WIRAN   I want to give it another try.

(BAROUK *switches off the TV.*)

BAROUK   All right. There is something you can do for us. Meet with the Minister.
WIRAN   Why me?
BAROUK   He trusts you.
WIRAN   I don't trust him.
BAROUK   See him tomorrow. You will be the first person to make direct contact with him. Let him know what we want. Get his assurance. You understand?

Scene 9

The Ministry of Truth and Information. SHADRIN, *the First Minister, is at work as* WIRAN *enters.*

SHADRIN   Ah, come in, come in, Wiran. It's been a long time. Good to see you again. Please sit down. There's much work to be done here. I'm trying to re-organise the Ministry towards a more open approach.

Big Brother thinks ignorance is strength as far as the Ministry is concerned but I told him that should not be the case. We must tell the people what's going on. That's what my Ministry is for. We provide the truth and the information. How have you been?

WIRAN   All right.

SHADRIN   Good, good. Yes, I want to talk to you about the Movement. I don't want to deal with someone I'm not familiar with. As you know, this is a very delicate matter and I have to be very, very careful about what I do. I like what you people are doing. In fact, I have been thinking along the same lines for some time. It's good that some people have taken the initiative. And since I'm with the Inner Party and have . . . what you would call . . . power, if you like, to institute changes, I think I can at least make some contributions.

WIRAN   For a start, Minister, the Movement thinks you could introduce a programme on television to let people discuss issues that are relevant and –

SHADRIN   Can, can, no problem. I already have this concept of a weekly panel comprising Proles and Party members. Of course, we'll also allow people to sit in on the sessions and discuss, bring up anything they want. I'm not worried about my position, you see. If they think I'm too controversial, they'll give me the boot, but I'm willing to give up my position. That's why, you see, I'm not afraid. I think what's best for the people is best for the Party and the nation. Don't you agree?

WIRAN   Yes.

SHADRIN   Of course you do, of course you do. You know me, Wiran, I don't hold back. I talk straight from the shoulder. If I don't like anything, I'll say it. That's what we should encourage people of this nation to do. They must speak up. For their rights, for their beliefs. That's what democracy is about. I tell you, in the next few months, there are going to be changes in the Ministry, I can promise you that.

WIRAN   You believe in equal opportunities for everybody?

SHADRIN   Oh, of course, of course, no doubt about it. I think it's wrong to deny a good man a job in the civil service, for example. Standards will drop if we only promote Party members even if they are not right for it. What will happen to the spirit of meritocracy? No, we shouldn't allow standards to drop. We must always take in the best. Then the nation will be best. I have also said to Big Brother we must do away with communal political parties. Disband all those existing now and start forming parties with membership for Proles and Party members. We must also have television programmes involving equal numbers of Proles and Party members. No more tokenism.

WIRAN   No more propaganda?

SHADRIN   I'll be frank with you, Wiran. We must still continue to have programmes that educate people, keep them informed about Party policies, about the Kloot threat. If that's propaganda, I don't know what to say.

WIRAN   Is the Kloot threat as dangerous as the Party says it is?

SHADRIN   Between you and me, no. You see, to unite the people, we need a common enemy. It provides the emotional basis for a hierarchical society. It's the same with Woeful Wednesday. The Party keeps bringing it up to remind the people to stay in line. That makes it easier for Party rule. But I don't have to elaborate, Wiran, you already know the answers to the questions.

WIRAN   Did you do anything to stop the police from arresting the demonstrators the other day?

SHADRIN   I didn't say I would do that, Wiran. I only said I would help prevent the situation from getting worse for the Movement. And I did. I persuaded the Administration to let those arrested get off lightly. That much I could do. I can't play my hand too openly at the moment.

WIRAN   What about future demonstrations?

SHADRIN   I give you my word I will be with the Movement every step of the way. You believe me?

(*Blackout.*)

Scene 10

WIRAN's *room. Lights come on and reveal* WIRAN *and* YONE *looking through a pile of papers.*

YONE   Dis article should be good for der magazine.

WIRAN   Let me have a look at it.

YONE   Der media and freedom of speech, it's about.

WIRAN   (*after reading through it quickly*)

Makes quite a good argument. I think we should have enough for the first issue now.

YONE You look tired.

WIRAN Ya, but after this, I have to compile the seminar papers on democracy for publication.

YONE Dis isn't making it hard for you, having also to work at der newspaper?

WIRAN I'm getting jaded working there. Today, I was told to rewrite a report to make the Administration look good. Then there was a directive from the Inner Party saying we should not use the term 'economic recession'. There is no economic recession, they say. Call it 'economic slowdown'.

YONE Someone in der Statistics Department told me dey all have to change der latest population figures. Waa, havoc la. Dey found out dere are more Proles than Party members so der Administration tole dem to make it look like as dough dere are more Party members.

WIRAN I don't know what to believe anymore. I don't know who to trust.

YONE Wat did der Minister of Truth and Information say? Is he siding wit us?

WIRAN He says he is. But I don't know.

YONE You know wat? Someone might come in now and catch us for immoral proximity. Yesterday, a religious head was caught wit a 14-year-old girl (*She laughs.*) Funny aah? He said he was giving her advice . . . but he diden have his pants on! (*Laughs.*) But I don't care. Catch, catch lah. Hnarh, Wiran? Oh, come on, Wiran, why you look so serious?

WIRAN I feel helpless. No direction.

YONE But your work wit der Movemen, it means something?

WIRAN Sometimes, I think I'm not the right person for the Movement. I have felt alienated for so long, I can't really relate with people. It's as if my feelings are dead. How can I communicate with the grassroots? Will they listen to me? There's another demonstration coming up soon. I wonder what's going to happen.

YONE You worry too much.

WIRAN What got you interested in the Movement?

YONE It's a long story la. I dono if you wan to hear it.

WIRAN I do.

YONE You know, I really hate all dis discrimination. I carn stand people who always tink deir race is der bes. Even my family tink like dat, you know. My fader aah, he real terror la. He aah used to tell us all der bad tings about Party members wen we were chiren. Bad la dey all, he orways said. Doan trus dem.

(*Lights dim on area where* WIRAN *and* YONE *are. Lights come on in another area to discover* YONE'S FATHER. YONE *moves to that area. The actress playing* YONE *transforms into a young girl of seventeen.*)

YONE But, Pa, dere are Proles who are bad orso.

FATHER You doan say bad about Proles, hnarh! You are a Prole, you know. You know who is bad? Hnarh? I tole you so many times orready. Dey are bad, dey – Party members! And I doewan you to mix wit dem. You hear me? Hnarh? You hear me or not? Ay, I said you hear me or not?

YONE Yes.

FATHER Unh, you doan say yes and den forget about it, you know.

(YONE'S MOTHER *enters.*)

MOTHER Enough laa, enough laa. Yone is a good girl, wair she got disobey you one?

FATHER Not yet lah but one daaay . . . Yone, you are my only dotter, you know. I doewan you to mix wit der wrong people, you understand? Not say I wan to scold you or anyting, but you mus take care. You know waat, I usually doan scold you. Right or not?

YONE Ya, pa.

MOTHER Haiya, you two ah, one got temper, one so stubborn. Same blood laa, cannot escape.

FATHER As if you got no temper.

MOTHER Aiyo, if I got temper means finish lah. Whole house like pig and dog, man. One dotter stubborn, some more one son orso stubborn. Yone orso growing up so fas. Waa, tomorrow Yone seventeen orready. Big girl now. Dono wat presen your fader give you. Ask lah wat he wan to give you.

FATHER Tomorrow ah?

MOTHER Aiyo, you doan even remember ah your dotter's birday?

FATHER Remember. I know it mus be sometime aroun dis time. Wat do you wan unh, Yone?

MOTHER Tell him lah, doan be shy.

YONE Anyting la, Pa.

(*Lights off on Area B. When they come on,* YONE'S MOTHER *is seated.* YONE'S FATHER *is pacing up and down.*)

FATHER   Wat time orready, she still not home. Hnarh? Wair she wen?

MOTHER   I dono.

FATHER   She diden tell you ah? Wat kind of moder you are? Hnarh? Your dotter go out, she never tell you. (YONE *comes in.*) Wair you go? Hnarh? Wair you go so late?

YONE   Party.

FATHER   Wat party? Wy you never tell me you go party? Doan stand dere dumb. You got no mout ah? Who you wen wit?

YONE   Frien.

FATHER   Wat frien?

YONE   Frien lah.

FATHER   Who?

YONE   You dono dem laa.

FATHER   Wat race? . . . Hnarh? . . . Wat race?

YONE   Party members.

FATHER   Wat? You wen party wit Party members? Hnarh? You dare go party wit dem? I told you not to mix wit dose people.

YONE   Dey are not bad, Pa.

FATHER   Who said dey are not bad? You . . . (*He rushes at her to hit her.* MOTHER *interferes.*) Get away! Come here, you! You doewan to obey me, hnarh? Come here!

MOTHER   Please doan. She woan do it again.

FATHER   I doan care! She did it orready!

MOTHER   No! No! Doan la, doan hit her!

FATHER   I wan to teach her a lesson.

MOTHER   No! No!

FATHER   Get away! You cannot hear ah? Get away! I'm going to teach her good and proper! You jus wait! Jus wait! (*He goes off in a huff.*)

MOTHER   Yone, Yone, wy you make him angry?

YONE   I scared la, Ma.

(*Her* FATHER *comes back, wielding a chopper.*)

MOTHER   Go to your room. Go.

FATHER   Wair is she? Wair is dat stupid girl? I'm going to cut her up!

MOTHER   Go, Yone! Faster!

FATHER   Come back here! Come back! (YONE *runs into her room, separated from the sitting room by a flat.*) Open der door! Open it!

MOTHER   Doan! Doan hurt her! Please . . .

FATHER   (*slaps* MOTHER) You doan disturb!

MOTHER   She's your dotter!

FATHER   Den she obey me. Open der door! Open it or I break it down!

MOTHER   Still young laa, she. Give her a chan.

FATHER   (*Beats* MOTHER *even more.*) You keep quiet! Open der door! Open der door! You listen to me? (*Screaming, he hacks at the flat, as* MOTHER *tries to restrain him. He pushes her away.*) I kill you if you doan stay away!

(MOTHER *recoils. He hacks again and again until he has no more energy.* MOTHER *leads him to the chair and sits him down. He relents as she takes the chopper away from him. Then she goes into* YONE'S *room.*)

YONE   Ma! (*They are both in tears as they hold each other tightly.*) Ma, I wan to move out. Now.

MOTHER   No, doan. Doan go. Tomorrow, he will forget. Your fader like dat one. Bad temper he got, but after dat, he forget.

YONE   I carn stand it la, Ma.

MOTHER   Doan leave us. You know I love you more dan anyone else. If you go, I dono wat to do.

(*They hug. Blackout. Lights come on in* WIRAN'S *room.* YONE *continues telling* WIRAN *her story.*)

YONE   My broder ah – he like my fader, very bad laa his temper. He also doan like me going out wit Party members. One day, he caught me walking wit a Party member. He punch the man and kick him, den he drag me home, calling me all sorts of names . . . One day, I got fed up. After finish schooling lah. I coulden get a place in university because places for Proles limited. So I wen out to work. Wen I got enough money, I move out of der house. My fader woulden let me go. He said I had no shame. My moder was very sad but she understood me. She argued for me. My fader beat her, call her moder of a prostitute. She diden know what to do. She run to her cousin's house, my auntie lah. When my auntie ask wy der blue black, my moder said mosquito bite. After dat, my fader cut her housekeeping money. Gave only harf, you know. But he still expected her to buy der same tings as before. My moder, when she run out of money near end of der mun, she borrow from people, scared my fader complain if he's not satisfied wit der food and oder tings. Den

263

she'll pay back next mun wen he give der money. I help her wen I got der money. Wen I carn, I feel all torn up inside . . .

(WIRAN *is in tears. He reaches out to her and holds her. She responds. They embrace tightly.*)

WIRAN   I'm sorry I asked. Yone . . . Yone . . .

(YONE's *sobs fade. She looks up at* WIRAN. *They look at each other. They kiss. Blackout.*)

Scene 11

The big portrait of BIG BROTHER *takes centre stage. Sound of drums. Down the aisles of the auditorium come prole and party member demonstrators, carrying banners: 'Equal opportunities for everyone', 'We want a truly united nation', 'Let's hear it for freedom of expression', 'Give us our human rights'.* WIRAN, JUMON *and* YONE *are among them. All chant as they move towards the stage: 'Liberty, equality, democracy'. A tiger dance accompanies the proceedings. Another group enters from the opposite direction. They are all Party members. They approach the demonstrators. Their* SPOKESMAN *calls out to the demonstrators.*

SPOKESMAN   Hey! What are you all trying to do! Cause trouble? (*The demonstrators ignore him and go on chanting.*) I am talking to you!

(JUMON *signals to the demonstrators to quieten down.*)

JUMON   We are not trying to cause trouble. We come in the name of peace and humanity.

(*The members of the opposing group laugh.*)

SPOKESMAN   You are a traitor to your own race. You deny your own skin. You allow your culture to be polluted. Look at the people you have with you. Most of them don't belong in this nation. They should leave if they have any pride. We don't want them!

(*The opposing group cheer in support.*)

JUMON   It's people like you who have no place in this nation. You extremists will bring this nation down. You think you are the only race living here, other people don't matter! You are wrong!

(*The opposing group laugh.* WIRAN *tries to hold* JUMON *back.*)

SPOKESMAN   You want peace? You want racial equality? Kick all the Proles out. Then we will only have one race and everyone will be equal.

JUMON   You are sickening!

SPOKESMAN   And you are thick-skinned. Like the Proles! (JUMON *signals to the demonstrators to resume their chanting.*) Go home, all of you! Go to hell! . . . Do you hear me? . . . I am going to count to three. If you don't go away, there will be trouble! . . . One . . . two . . . three!

(*He signals to opposing group. They start throwing stones at the demonstrators. The demonstrators continue to chant. Then the opposing group makes a charge, with parangs. Commotion. Some demonstrators flee, others use the sticks holding the banners to defend themselves. Police whistles are heard. From behind the poster of* BIG BROTHER, *policemen emerge to break up the fight.* WIRAN *and* YONE *flee, dragging* JUMON *along. The opposing group flee, leaving the police to beat the demonstrators and arrest them. Blackout.*)

Intermission

Actors mingle with the audience, passing out leaflets which read:

'There is no resolution to this play. You, the audience, will have to provide it. If there is any hope, it lies with you. You can make things happen. You can make the end of this play the beginning. So, if you are moved to participate, please do not hesitate, do not hold yourself back. If you are moved to contribute to an event, stand up – express yourself, leave your seat, shout if you will, the platform is yours. This will no longer be theatre, it will become real. Your act of participation will matter. It may only be a symbolic gesture of commitment, but it is a first step. In you lies the seed of positive change'.

Scene 12

WIRAN's *room. Low spot on* WIRAN *sitting by himself. The light is behind him so we see only his silhouette. The rest of the room is in darkness.*

YONE's VOICE   Wiran . . . Wiran . . . (*No answer.*) Wat's der matter? Wy are you sitting by yourself? (YONE *switches on a bedside lamp. She sits up in bed and looks anxiously at* WIRAN.) Wat is it? Is it der demonstration? (*She gets out of bed and goes to him.*) Come to bed, Wiran. (*She touches him.*)

WIRAN (*Shakes her off violently.*) Don't touch me!

YONE Wy? (*He moves away, she follows.*) Wat's bodering you? Please tell me, Wiran . . . Please, please talk to me. Doan keep it inside.

WIRAN You're the one who's keeping things from me.

YONE Wat do you mean?

WIRAN Those men you went out with.

YONE Please doan ask me about dat. It's all in der pas.

WIRAN They bother me!

YONE Doan, Wiran, please . . .

WIRAN You slept with them, didn't you? . . . Well, did you? . . . Did you?

YONE Y . . . y . . . yes.

WIRAN How many? . . . I said how many?

YONE Wy do you wan to know?

WIRAN I want to know.

YONE Please doan torture yourself.

WIRAN How many?

YONE I . . . I . . . carn remember.

WIRAN That many? You slut!

YONE Wiran, doan.

WIRAN How could you, you slut?

YONE Wiran, it was before I knew you.

WIRAN I don't care. It shows what kind of a woman you are.

YONE Please doan say tings like dat.

WIRAN I want to know how many. And who they were.

YONE Please doan make me do dis.

WIRAN All right, you won't tell me? Then get out . . . Get out of my life! Get out now!

YONE No.

WIRAN Then tell me!

YONE I'm afraid . . . I'm afraid you woan have anyting to do wit me anymore.

WIRAN For us to continue this relationship, I have to know. I want to start on a clean slate. I don't want to keep on wondering whether it was this man or that man you've slept with before. It hurts me every time we meet some man you know.

YONE All right, I'll tell you.

WIRAN Who was the first?

YONE He was a Party member.

WIRAN I know. You gave yourself to every Party member that came along.

YONE Dat's not true.

WIRAN Isn't it?

YONE No.

WIRAN How many did you give yourself to?

YONE Seven . . . eight . . . I'm not sure.

WIRAN So who was the first?

YONE Somebody I met and fell in love wit.

WIRAN What's his name?

YONE Kasan.

WIRAN And you went to bed with him just like that?

YONE You make it sound so dirty.

WIRAN Well, how did it happen?

YONE I loved him. He was very gentle and kind. We were bot very young den. We dated for a wile. He said he loved me too.

WIRAN And then?

YONE Den he wen away to study. After a year, he wrote to me and said he coulden stan der separation and he found somebody else.

WIRAN Who was the second?

YONE He was . . . a political secretary . . . to . . . an Inner Party member.

WIRAN What's his name?

YONE Please . . .

WIRAN What's his name?

YONE Ru . . . Rumin.

WIRAN That lecher? He's so much older than you. And he's married. Why did you let him do it?

YONE I . . . I . . . I liked him.

WIRAN How did you meet him?

YONE I was introduced to him. Den he took me to a party at a friend's house. It was a New Year's Eve party and I was feeling very depressed. Der friend mixed everybody's drink . . .

WIRAN And then?

YONE Please doan let me go on.

WIRAN What happened?

YONE I got sick. I trew up. Den I wen upstairs to lie down.

WIRAN And you invited him up.

YONE No. I was hardly conscious. He came into der room . . .

WIRAN And you let him make love to you.

YONE I diden know wat was happening. I was so sick. I was still sick der nex morning.

WIRAN You saw each other after that?

YONE A few times. But he became very nasty. He liked to drink a lot. And wen he was drunk, he was very unpleasan. I refused to see him after dat. He called me and I refused to tok to him.

WIRAN   Was it good? . . . Did you have a great time with him in bed? . . . Hnarh? Did you? . . . You bitch! And who was the third?

(*Blackout. The scene reopens a little later.* YONE *is about to finish talking about her past.*)

YONE   . . . He was der las. He told me he would marry me but he diden. I had an abortion. I regretted de affair. I still do.

WIRAN   What else?

YONE   Dere's nutting more to tell.

WIRAN   You know what your sordid love life is like? Do you? Like a porno book. You have no shame.

YONE   I doan tink you will still love me, Wiran. You'll never be able to forget all dis.

WIRAN   You're right, I won't.

YONE   Do you wan me to leave? (*Silence.*) Do you still love me? (*Silence.*) Please tell me . . . do you still love me?

WIRAN   I don't know.

(*Blackout.*)

Scene 13

WIRAN *and a group are peddling books to passers-by. They are approached by two policemen.*

POLICEMAN   What are you doing?

WIRAN   Passing out books.

POLICEMAN   Are they for sale?

WIRAN   Yes.

POLICEMAN   Let me look at them.
   Democracy and the People . . . National Unity . . . Books like these are not allowed.

WIRAN   Why not?

POLICEMAN   They could be subversive. I'm taking the whole lot of you in.

WIRAN   You can't do that.

WIRAN's COLLEAGUE   Run, Wiran, don't argue. Run!

(*A chase ensues. Then when* WIRAN *seems to have escaped the police, he backs into one of them. At that moment,* SHADRIN *enters.*)

SHADRIN   What's the problem, Officer?

POLICEMAN   Oh, Honourable Minister, I caught this man selling books that are questionable. Then he tried to escape.

SHADRIN   It's all right. I know him. He's my friend, Wiran. He's a loyal citizen.

He won't do anything to hurt the nation. Isn't that so, Wiran? I would vouch for it with my own life. Wiran, how are you? You may go now, Officer.

POLICEMAN   Thank you, Honourable Minister.

SHADRIN   How is the Movement after that demonstration fiasco? Everyone back together and rearing to go again with spirits intact? I hope so, Wiran. We've got to keep pushing our ideals on, that's the only way we'll achieve anything.

WIRAN   Thanks for getting me out of that tight spot.

SHADRIN   Yes, it's a good thing I came along at the right time. I seem to have a knack for doing that. But you know me. I'm always there when there's trouble. How's Barouk? Still goading you all on with his shifty eyes? Does he ever trust anyone, that fellow? And how's Yone?

WIRAN   She's all right, I suppose.

SHADRIN   Oh, I'm sorry. I heard you were not together anymore. I'm truly sorry, Wiran.

WIRAN   Who told you about that?

SHADRIN   Don't forget, Wiran, I'm the First Minister of Truth and Information.

WIRAN   What's the latest information about the Inner Party?

SHADRIN   I hear there's going to be some drastic action, stricter rules. It's not the right thing to do, of course, just because of the demonstration. I'm going to see Big Brother and tell him not to be so severe. He'll listen to me. Meanwhile, just watch your step. Be a little extra careful, Wiran. I don't want to see you inside.

(*Blackout.*)

Scene 14

This scene is played wayang-kulit style with human characters behind a large screen. Their dialogue is delivered in heightened manner, their physical mannerisms broad, puppet-like. Altogether, the atmosphere is one of foreboding. Wayang-kulit instruments, particularly the percussive ones, can be used to punctuate key moments. The serunai is played to herald the opening of the scene. Then the characters enter. First, two INNER PARTY MEMBERS, *one from each side of the screen.*

IPM 1   The air is filled with cries of action, the wounds of an angered race have been reopened. We of the Inner Party must be stirred to action.

IPM 2   Big Brother is watching, and he is waiting.

IPM 1   Memo after memo has poured in. With a single voice, all the divisions of the Party have spoken. We cannot disappoint them.

IPM 2   What will happen to the disturbers of peace?

IPM 1   Under the hanging tree, I sold you and you sold me . . .

IPM 2   I foresee rebel betraying rebel, the stain of dishonour spreading wide.

IPM 1   There is no honour among thieves of peace. They are bold of front but weak of spirit. Ideals have no place in the will to survive.

(*Enter* THIRD INNER PARTY MEMBER.)

IPM 3
   Big Brother is coming.
   He has decided.

IPM 1
   It was only a hopeless fancy.
   It passed like a Mad May Day.
   Their dreams, their illusions,
   Will be suddenly swept away!

IPM 3
   They say that time heals all things,
   They say you can always forget;
   Tomorrow, nothing will be remembered,
   The Party will make sure of that.

(*Enter* BIG BROTHER, *his shadow looming larger than the rest, towering over all.*)

BB   We are agreed then.
   There must be a cure for the epidemic.
   We have been too soft, too liberal.
   We shall continue to be liberal,
   But the nation must survive!

IPM 3   Freedom is slavery!

BB   There must be responsibility with freedom. The people must be made to understand that.

IPM 3   Discipline is strength!

BB   We will not compromise the peace of this nation or allow another Woeful Wednesday to happen. The people must always be on guard against the threat posed by the Kloots. It is the responsibility of every citizen to contribute to the continuation of peace and security and to ensure that the nation is free of trouble so that the enemy cannot exploit the situation. No-one is exempted from this responsibility; no-one at all. The nation must survive!

IPM 1   The nation must survive!

IPM 2   The nation must survive!

IPM 3   The nation must survive!

BB   Where is the First Minister of Truth and Information?

(*Blackout.*)

Scene 15

WIRAN*'s room.* YONE *is there, waiting. A short while later,* WIRAN *comes in. He stops as he sees her, surprised.*

WIRAN   What are you doing here?

YONE   I had to see you. (*Silence.*) I carn stay away from you, Wiran . . . Please doan ask me to leave.

WIRAN   What do you want?

YONE   To be wit you . . . I'm so afraid . . . Please doan be so cold to me. Say something.

WIRAN   I can't find Barouk. He seems to have disappeared. And Jumon didn't show up for work the last two days. He's not at home, either. Where is everybody?

YONE   I'm here. (WIRAN *looks hard at* YONE *for a long time. Then he moves towards her and they embrace.*) Oh, Wiran, don't leave me.

WIRAN   You think something has happened to Barouk and Jumon?

YONE   I doewan to tink about dat.

WIRAN   There's bad news everywhere. The Administration is going to do something to the Movement, I can feel it.

YONE   Doan say anymore.

WIRAN   Maybe the best thing for us to do is to get out of here before it's too late, and never see each other again.

YONE   No, I doewan dat.

WIRAN   If they get hold of us, there will be nothing that either of us can do for each other. Neither of us will know what the other is going through.

YONE   Stop!

WIRAN   The one thing that matters is that we shouldn't betray each other. What you say or do doesn't matter. Only feelings matter. If they could make me betray you, that would be the end.

YONE   Dey carn do dat. It's der one ting dey carn do. Dey can make you say anyting but dey carn make you believe it. Dey carn get inside you.

WIRAN   That's true. They can't get inside you. If you can feel that staying human is

267

worthwhile, even when it's futile, you've beaten them. They cannot alter your feelings. They can lay bare everything you have done or said, but they cannot change your heart. (WIRAN *laughs an assured, triumphant laugh.*) They cannot change your heart!

YONE   Oh, I like der way you laugh, it's so healty. (*She tickles him.*)

WIRAN   Stop it! Stop it! (*More laughter.*) Stop or I'll attack!

(YONE *laughs boisterously.*)

YONE   OK, OK . . . peace, peace.

WIRAN   I love you, Yone.

YONE   Hold me . . . Wiran, whatever happens, I wan you to know dat I really love you.

(*Suddenly, there is an urgent knock on the door. They freeze. The knock becomes louder, more urgent. They look at each other.*)

WIRAN   I'll answer it.

YONE   No . . . doan.

(WIRAN *goes off. There is a sound of people rushing in. When* WIRAN *gets back onstage, he is followed by four policemen.*)

POLICEMAN   Come with us . . . both of you.

(YONE *is speechless. Then she turns away and buries her face in her hands.* WIRAN *stands looking at her. Blackout.*)

Scene 16

Lights come on to reveal WIRAN *curled up on the floor. He is in some kind of a cell. Illumination is not very bright. There is a bench near him. He gets up, walks around the space, then sits on the bench. Off stage, the sound of marching feet, ominous, followed by the sound of a heavy metal door being opened, someone being pushed in, and the door closed.* JUMON *enters, haggard, dishevelled. He staggers to the bench. It takes a while before* WIRAN *recognises him.*

WIRAN   Jumon!

JUMON   Wiran! So they got you too.

WIRAN   How long have you been in here?

JUMON   I don't know.

WIRAN   What have they done to you?

JUMON   They are trying to break me, and they are succeeding.

WIRAN   You mustn't give up, Jumon.

JUMON   I can't stand it! . . . I'm going to confess. Maybe then they'll let me go.

WIRAN   You can't give up, Jumon.

JUMON   I damn well can!

WIRAN   What about all those things we stand for?

JUMON   Who cares about that? You think anybody cares?

WIRAN   We do.

JUMON   I don't! . . . not anymore. I just want to get out of here. And nobody is helping me to get out. I was betrayed! Some bastard betrayed me! Some bastard told them about me!

WIRAN   Who?

JUMON   I don't know! . . . They have been watching us closely. The secret police have files on us. Even now, they can hear us. That's why they brought me to see you . . . There's nothing left anymore. No hope. No future.

WIRAN   Jumon, they can make you say anything but they can't make you believe it. They can't get inside you. They can't change the way you feel.

JUMON   Bullshit!

WIRAN   You feel strongly about human rights, about equality for everyone and racial integration, you feel strongly about freedom . . .

JUMON   There's no such thing as freedom. (*Silence.*) Save yourself, Wiran. Confess.

(*Sound of marching feet. Door opening. Two men come in and pick* JUMON *up.*)

WIRAN   Where are you taking him?

MAN   Room 101.

JUMON   No, please, not Room 101, please don't take me there! I will confess everything. Then you won't have to take me there. I will say I'm a Kloot, I will sign a confession and read it on television. Anything, anything, please.

WIRAN   What's Room 101?

MAN   You'll find out soon.

JUMON   Please . . . I'll give you a list of other traitors. I'll do anything. I'll eat shit, I'll go out and kill the Proles, I'll . . .

MAN   Come along.

JUMON   (*indicating* WIRAN) That's the one you should be taking, not me! He's the one that's against the Party. He was one of the rebel leaders. He influenced me to go against the Party. He's the one you want! Take him, not me! He's the one you want! Take him, not me! Not me!

(They drag the struggling JUMON *out. Door clangs shut.* WIRAN *stares in their direction. Blackout.)*

Scene 17

Spot on WIRAN *seated in a chair. He is extremely tired. His* INTERROGATOR *is seated on a table in front of him, his foot resting on* WIRAN'S *lap.*

INTER 1   Let's go over it again. You belong to a subversive organisation.

WIRAN   No, that's not true.

INTER 1   You have been spreading lies about the Administration.

WIRAN   No.

INTER 1   You are a threat to the nation's security.

WIRAN   No.

INTER 1   You have links with the Kloots.

WIRAN   I don't have any sympathy for them.

INTER 1   Liar! You have been spreading Kloot propaganda among the people.

WIRAN   Where is your evidence?

INTER 1   You are the editor of a magazine that publishes subversive statements.

WIRAN   They are not subversive.

INTER 1   They spread ideas that will destroy the nation.

WIRAN   You are overreacting and I am tired of your questioning.

INTER 1   How dare you talk to me like that! You want to get into deeper trouble! I can arrange that.

WIRAN   I'm tired. You haven't allowed me to eat for days. I need to sleep. I haven't slept for so long.

INTER 1   Then make your confession! You will get all the sleep you want if you confess. All the sleep you want. You don't realise what a mess you're in. You don't realise you are powerless. You are at our mercy. We can break you. You hear me! I said, 'Do you hear me?' Come on, wake up! *(He slaps* WIRAN'S *face.)* Wake up!

WIRAN   What do you want?

INTER 1   A confession. You will go on television and admit that you have been wrong. If you repent, you will be released, and you can go back to a normal life.

WIRAN   I have done no wrong.

INTER 1   You have disgraced your own race.

WIRAN   I have only asked my race to be fair to other races.

INTER 1   You don't believe in helping your own race. You don't believe that the culture of your race should prevail over the cultures of other races. You want your race to give up what is rightfully theirs so that other races can take it from them.

WIRAN   You are a racist.

INTER 1   But I'm better off than you!

(Blackout. When the scene reopens a short while later, WIRAN *is faced with a different* INTERROGATOR.)*

INTER 2   So, you think you are tough. But let me tell you this. You are only bringing more suffering on yourself. And for what? You are alone, one man against the nation. Do you think you will win? We are willing to give you a chance but will you take it? No! You prefer to be stubborn. We have tried to reason with you but you insist on lying to us, to yourself, to the whole nation.

WIRAN   You have only tried to frighten me.

INTER 2   Is this how you repay our kindness? We have not even touched your body. We believe in making you see your mistakes. We have been patient in talking to you, and talking to you, and talking to you. We want to give you a chance to repent. But you are too arrogant.

WIRAN   I need to go to the toilet.

INTER 2   You will go when I tell you to.

WIRAN   I have a right to go to the toilet.

INTER 2   You gave up your rights when you chose to deprive others of their rights. Their right to enjoy life in a peaceful nation. Their right to progress and prosperity. Their right to freedom – freedom from fear. You want to cause trouble, stir up racial riots, bring about chaos and suffering.

WIRAN   You are right! You are right! Can I go to the toilet now?

INTER 2   Think about it. Have you thought about the danger your actions could have caused? Have you been acting with responsibility? You are a responsible man, you can think for yourself. What would happen if the Administration told the Party members that they no longer occupy a special position in this nation? There would be blood in the streets. Do you want this on your conscience? Is this the future you want for all of us?

WIRAN   I . . . want . . . to go . . . to . . . the . . . toilet.

INTER 2   You have nowhere to go. In fact, you can stay in here for a long, long time. Do you want that? You won't have any friends, only us. You won't be able to do the things you've always enjoyed doing. You won't have any freedom. What will happen to you? Do you want to throw away all the good things you had? You could have become somebody. You had a respectable job, you were free to do a lot of things. You could express your feelings for other people. You had someone you loved.

WIRAN   Where is she now?

INTER 2   Not with you. But she is going through what you are going through now. You have been responsible for her suffering. Have you thought about that? Do you care? Do you care that she is suffering because she doesn't know what's happening to you now? Can you imagine how afraid she is? How helpless she is, alone at the mercy of her interrogators? How will she stand up to the punishment? How long will she be held in detention? Do you really care? Do you have any real feelings of love inside you?

(WIRAN *breaks down and cries pathetically. The* INTERROGATOR *places a hand on his shoulder.* WIRAN *recoils from it. Blackout. When the scene reopens a short while later, there is yet a different* INTERROGATOR *present.*)

INTER 3   How are you today, my friend? Have you been sleeping well? You look tired. All right, just relax and talk to me, okay? Are you ready to make a confession?

WIRAN   I'm a spy for Papua New Guinea.

INTER 3   You still have a sense of humour. Tell me, do you know or not that you have carried out seditious activities?

WIRAN   I'm a sexual pervert.

INTER 3   Oh, congratulations. Now listen. How big a role did the woman Yone play in the organisation?

WIRAN   I sell drugs to police inspectors.

INTER 3   Oh, no wonder our police force is so inefficient. Come now, no more games. We want you to make a public statement saying Yone is a Kloot.

WIRAN   I suffer from herpes.

INTER 3   That must be painful. OK, let's get serious now. Will you go on television and ask Big Brother to forgive you?

WIRAN   Two plus two make four.

INTER 3   You are a genius in arithmetic, I see. But that's not going to get you out of here, you know. You have to confess.

WIRAN   I think you have a beautiful body.

INTER 3   You are quite impossible. Guard! (GUARD *enters.*) Take him to Room 101.

(*Blackout.*)

Scene 18

WIRAN *is pushed into Room 101. There he sees* SHADRIN, *the First Minister of Truth and Information, seated on a chair. On a table beside him is a TV screen and a video recorder.*

WIRAN   You!

SHADRIN   Don't pretend to be surprised, Wiran.

WIRAN   I knew you couldn't be trusted. (WIRAN *is strapped to a chair.*) What are you doing to me? You have no right to . . . (*He cries in pain as* SHADRIN *pushes a button on the chair.*)

SHADRIN   For a long time, I have watched over you. Now the turning point has come. I shall save you. I am taking trouble with you because you are worth trouble. You can be cured of your false ideas.

WIRAN   Don't lecture me. (*Another bolt of pain.*)

SHADRIN   You realise, Wiran, that I have the power to inflict pain on you at any moment. If you tell me any lies, I will make you cry out with pain. You understand? You have failed in self-discipline, that's why you are here. You would not make the act of submission which is the price of sanity. You prefer to be in the minority. Big Brother once said that the people of this nation are generally docile so it is very easy to control them. He's right, you know. To be frank with you, the Party has succeeded in imposing its views and its policies because the people can be made to accept the most flagrant violations of reality. That is because they are not sufficiently interested in public events to notice what is happening. By lack of understanding, they remain safe. They simply swallow everything, and what they swallow does them no actual harm.

WIRAN   You think the people are fools?

SHADRIN   You don't believe me? Let me tell you a few home truths. The Proles are not political enough. The middle-class Proles are satisfied as long as they have their distractions. Those who are not satisfied simply migrate to other countries. The so-called intellectuals are apathetic. The Party members generally are accustomed to unquestioning loyalty. They entrust practically everything to the leadership. So, you see, if there is going to be any radical change in any policy, it must come from the Administration. It won't come from you or any so-called social reform movement. You are merely a dog barking at a hill. When you delude yourself into thinking that you see something, you assume that everyone else sees the same thing as you. But reality exists in the human mind. Not in the individual mind, which can make mistakes, but only in the mind of the Party, which is collective and immortal. Whatever the Party holds to be truth is truth. The Administration, which controls the Party, controls reality.

WIRAN   Then the Administration is totalitarian. Democracy is just a front.

SHADRIN   That is how you see it. The Party is the guardian of democracy. It does not seek power for its own ends but for the good of the majority. The choice for the people lies between freedom and happiness. For the majority, happiness is better. It is the Party's responsibility to ensure the continuation of that happiness. What is your definition of freedom? The freedom to say that two plus two make four? It is not as clear-cut as that. You talk about freedom of the press. Do you realise that if the Administration allowed everything to be told as it is, the people's sensitivities will be hurt and there will be chaos?

WIRAN   Sensitivity will beget sensitivity. Soon no-one will be able to tolerate anything. They won't dare to face up to reality.

SHADRIN   Reality indeed. How many fingers am I holding up, Wiran?

WIRAN   Four.

SHADRIN   And if the Party says that it is not four but five – then how many?

WIRAN   Four. (*A bolt of pain.*)

SHADRIN   How many fingers Wiran?

WIRAN   Four! Four! (*More pain.*)

SHADRIN   How many fingers, Wiran?

WIRAN   Four. (*More pain.*)

SHADRIN   How many?

WIRAN   Stop it! Stop the pain!

SHADRIN   You are a stubborn man, Wiran. If we set you free, you'll be a danger to society.

WIRAN   How can I be? You just said I was powerless to change anything.

SHADRIN   Yes, but you are a diehard dissident, and we can't allow that. You must become part of the collective mind. Why do you hate the Party and Big Brother?

WIRAN   It's not that I hate the Party or Big Brother, I love the nation more.

SHADRIN   You are a clever doublethinker. (WIRAN *screams with agony.*) But we'll make you submit. Can you not understand that the individual is only a cell? The individual only has power in so far as he ceases to be an individual. Those who have chosen to toe the Party line enjoy freedom – the freedom to be sane and happy. Slavery, if you choose to call it that, is freedom. But you, with all your notions of freedom, are alone. And alone, you will be defeated.

WIRAN   It is you who will be defeated. Your programme of fear and suppression will be defeated.

SHADRIN   How?

WIRAN   Life will defeat you. As long as there are others like me out there, there is a chance you will be defeated. The human spirit will defeat you. Love will defeat you. Love for life, for humanity.

SHADRIN   Love and humanity? How noble. Yet even love is not constant. It can change. It can even be falsified. The one you love, Yone, she betrayed you. She is an agent for the Administration.

WIRAN   You are lying!

SHADRIN   She was planted to trap subversive elements like you. Like Barouk, whom you dealt with in the Movement for a New Brotherhood. He was also planted. But I can see Yone is more relevant here. You were deceived. You thought she loved you, but she was only doing her job. She is a promiscuous woman.

WIRAN   That's not true!

SHADRIN   Oh, didn't you know that? You are probably thinking how could you have loved a slut, aren't you?

WIRAN   No! No! You are only saying that to make me betray her.

SHADRIN   I don't need to do that. She's one of us. She has also slept with many men, most of the time in the line of duty.

WIRAN   Stop that, you bastard! (*A bolt of pain.*)

SHADRIN   You refuse to believe me. All right. Then I'll show you concrete evidence. I have here a videotape that will convince you of the truth. It shows your beloved Yone making love to a man she never told you about. You remember, of course, that she told you of her past and she said she had only gone to bed with Party members. The man in this tape happens to be a Prole.

WIRAN   You forced her to do this, you bastard!

SHADRIN   See for yourself how freely she enjoys the act. (*He plays the videotape.* WIRAN *watches, writhing in his seat.*)

WIRAN   No! No! Turn it off! Turn the damn thing off!

SHADRIN   You feel like getting up and denouncing her for the bitch she is, don't you? You feel like smashing the screen and tearing the tape to shreds? Go ahead.

(*He releases* WIRAN. *In that instant,* WIRAN *gets up and pushes* SHADRIN *down. He pounces on the latter, fingers reaching for the throat.*)

WIRAN   You monster! You think you can make me betray her this way? Never! I love her! And you – you will never understand that! You are inhuman! Not fit to live! (*Then, realising what he is doing,* WIRAN *releases* SHADRIN *and dashes for the door.*) Yone! Yone! I've got to find Yone!

SHADRIN   (*struggling up, hoarsely*) Guards!

(*Blackout.*)

Scene 19

Sirens. Whistles. Sound of running feet. A search spot surveys the auditorium. Another comes on for the same purpose. Then one of them picks up WIRAN *in the auditorium, moving along the aisle. He addresses the audience urgently, moving among them as he speaks.*

WIRAN   Are you all going to sit here and do nothing? The hope of this nation lies with you! Are you going to sit here and let it go to the dogs? Stand up! Stand up and unite! Party members, Proles, whoever you are, wherever you are. Speak up for your rights! This is a democracy. Stand up for your freedom, for racial equality and integration, for humanity and justice, for truth, for a nation capable of greatness! We all have a stake in this nation! If you believe in all these, say yes! If you love this nation and feel a sense of belonging say yes! You have the power to bring about changes. Unite! Stand up and say yes! Yes, the future lies with you! Yes, you will rise above fear and complacency! Yes! Yes! Yes! Yes!

(*The police come after* WIRAN. *It is up to the audience to react as they wish – whether to betray him or protect him. Blackout.*)

Note

1   Woeful Wednesday refers to 13 May 1969, when an opposition uprising led by Kit-siang Li, in protest against the ethnic hierarchies encoded in government policy, failed and Li was imprisoned. Widespread race rioting in Kuala Lumpur resulted in the imposition of martial law.

12 Chin Woon Ping

↳ influenced by Carolee Schneeman (handwritten)

Details Cannot Body Wants

Singapore *– colonized by the British* (handwritten)

Introduction

As the writer and performer of *Details Cannot Body Wants*, which holds the distinction of being the first R-rated play ever to be produced in Singapore, Chin Woon Ping has made an unusual mark on the contemporary theatre history of this island-state. While Chin's work would not have raised many eyebrows among audiences familiar with feminist performance art, Singapore's Public Entertainment Licensing Unit considered aspects of the script offensive, most notably the use of 'adult language' and 'taboo gestures' such as crotch-grabbing and breast examination. The premiere production in 1992 was therefore promoted with a disclaimer noting its adult content, which was deemed suitable only for viewers over the age of twenty. Not surprisingly, this publicity ensured a sell-out season.

Having lived and worked in several countries/regions during her multifaceted career as poet, playwright, performer and academic, Chin incorporates many of the features of a postcolonial diasporic subject. She was born into a Straits Chinese or 'Peranakan' family in Malacca during the British occupation of Malaya. (Peranakan, meaning born of the soil/local-born, refers to a distinct, culturally syncretic group resulting from intermarriages between early Chinese settlers and Malays.) By the time Chin entered undergraduate studies at the University of Malaya, Malaysia was an independent nation, having achieved political autonomy in 1957. Chin later completed her doctoral studies in the United States and has made that country her permanent base, though she continues to maintain strong links with Malaysia and Singapore. Over the last few decades, she has held academic positions at the National University of

Singapore and the Nanyang Technological University, as well as in Malaysia, China and Indonesia. Her other performance works include *From San Jose to San Jose* (1996), a stirring account of the hardships faced by exploited Filipina domestic workers in Singapore, and *Diary of a Madwoman* (1998), an exploration of social constructions of madness.

Chin's diasporic background problematises the national location of *Details Cannot Body Wants*: is it Malaysian? Singaporean? Asian-American? Like its writer, the text defies any attempt to be fixed within absolute terms or categories, even though it occupies a particular place in the Singaporean (counter)canon. As Ien Ang points out, diasporas, and by implication diasporic productions,

> are fundamentally and inevitably transnational in their scope; always linking the local and the global, the here and the there, past and present, they have the potential to unsettle essentialist and totalising conceptions of 'national culture' or 'national identity' and to disrupt their presumption of static roots in geography and history.
>
> (Ang 1994: 16)

The freedom and flexibility accorded to diasporic subjects in claiming a hybrid position between real or imaginary homelands and hostlands enables them to articulate new identities and to use new forms of expression without being subjugated to a myth of cultural authenticity, or assimilated into the dominant culture of the hostland(s). In this respect, the political and cultural references in Chin's play speak to a feminist postcolonial sensibility that traverses Asia, America and Asian-America. The text's fluidity in form and the ways in which it positions its subject are a reflection of the new-found cultural agency associated with diasporic identity formations.

Details Cannot Body Wants is not so much a play as a choreopoem – a poetic text enacted as a dance/movement sequence – that shows the influence of contemporary feminist performance art movements in the United States. Such influence is evident in the conscious foregrounding of the body and its physical functions, the explicit treatment of sexuality, the direct audience address, the satire of patriarchal power, the rapid shifts between dialogue and song, and the intentional instability of the performer's stage persona. Each part of Chin's text corresponds to a section of the title and is aimed at exploring constructions of feminine identity. The focus shifts from the socialisation of a Chinese girl within an Asian context to her gradual exposure to Western culture and critique of its particular regimes of gender and racial inscription. Anti-realist in structure and style, the text's four sections function more in the manner of a musical score or movement than a conventional linear plot. There is no single story to unfold or character to be revealed. The Woman in the text has no unified stable core but is, instead, a postcolonial (and postmodern) fragmented subject occupying multiple subject positions. Similarly, there is no 'self' to be expressed – the Woman is constituted by her performativity in relation to the four elements signalled by the title.

The 'Details' section dramatises the minutiae of the Woman's daily life, the objects, events, actions, sounds, encounters and taboos that she must process and manipulate in order to give some shape to her existence. In the 'Cannot' phase, the performer enacts, and subverts, the disciplinary measures of feminine ascription that she faces as an 'oriental' woman, both within her own culture and in Western contexts. 'Body' shows how the female body becomes the locus of male desire and power, which, in turn, marks women's bodies in quite specific, and sometimes damaging, ways. The final section stages the suppressed desires of the Woman, suggesting 'her socialisation into becoming an inveterate consumer with myriad "wants", in hankering after which she often compromises or effaces herself' (Seet 1997: 516). Overall, the text demonstrates the ways in which the performer is both constituted by and resistant

to the competing demands of 'details', 'cannot', 'body' and 'wants', which together represent the major burdens of women's lives. The title thus becomes a ludic trope for a transformative female subjectivity which insists that the Woman's sum is greater than her parts.

Deliberately syncretic, Chin's text uses a range of languages and a montage of performance styles, which together defy cultural essentialism. The inclusion of the seated chorus whose hand gestures, claps and sound-effects punctuate the action, sometimes ironically, draws from the Malaysian Dikir Barat performance tradition. Peking Opera conventions are also discernible, for instance in the cymbal, pipa and bamboo-clacker accompaniment of the chorus and, notably, in the elaborate stage make-up/mask applied by the performer at the close of the 'Details' section. Here, the Woman takes on the persona of the cross-dressed Peking Opera heroine, complete with a fan and well schooled in the art of the 'show-your-dimples-but-not-your-teeth' smile. In the text's 'Body' section, the solemn cries used for 'adagio' effect are reminiscent of Noh theatre. Elsewhere, African-American culture provides a model for feminine agency in the wise-girl rap of the 'Cannot' section, as well as in the Blues music of a gardenia-wearing Billie Holiday figure who nicely pastiches the more self-assertive of the singer's famous lyrics.

Details Cannot Body Wants plays with – and up to – Western stereotypes of passive, submissive, hyper-feminine Asian womanhood in much the same way that Guillermo Verdecchia's *Fronteras Americanas* enacts a larger-than-life aggregation of the 'Latino', as represented in American popular culture. To expose the power relations masked by orientalist images, Chin investigates, in particular, the myths surrounding Chinese foot-binding, the Madame Butterfly syndrome, Canto pop pin-up girls and *Miss Saigon*-style fiery, though impeccably repressed, sexuality. Chin's deconstructive project is especially visible in the 'Cannot' section when, to highlight the arbitrary composition of such racial stereotypes, the Woman transforms from a Peking Opera performer to a Western man to a *Miss Saigon* sex-doll, before adopting the straight-talking sass of an urban black American. If the actor playing the Woman is of Asian descent, this moment, in performance, is purposely incongruous and destabilising, suggesting that adherence to a female 'type' may be as much an act of rebellious self-determination as a cultural given.

In its head-on engagement with the social and cultural codifications of Asian women in a range of partriarchal contexts, including those of contemporary Singaporean theatre, Chin's project meshes closely with that of other local 'feminist' playwrights such Eleanor Wong, Dana Lam and Ovidia Yu. While these dramatists have all challenged the specific gender assumptions which have shaped their lives as both women and artists, Chin often goes one step further to stage the performing female body as a spectacle that resists consumption even while it incites desire. Hence, the lurid costumes, suggestive movements and 'tarty' impersonations central to *Details Cannot Body Wants* constitute part of a conscious exhibitionism that, in K.K. Seet's terms, 'foils the habit of voyeurism by being the polar opposite of peekaboo' (1997: 517). With this unabashed travesty of glamour and sexiness, Chin hopes to foster the audience's constructive *dis*engagement from the well-worn fantasies that have marked the 'Asian woman' as a highly textualised figure.

Production history

Details Cannot Body Wants was first presented by Chin Woon Ping at the Substation in Singapore on 12 September 1992, directed by K.K. Seet. The play was broadcast in Australia in 1996 and performed by Chin in New York in 1997, with Allen Kuharski as director.

Select bibliography

Ang, I. (1994) 'On not speaking Chinese: postmodern ethnicity and the politics of diaspora', *New Formations* 24, 1: 1–18.

Chin, W.P. (1993) *The Naturalisation of Camellia Song and Details Cannot Body Wants*, Singapore: Times Books International.

—— (ed.) (1996) *Playful Phoenix: Women Write for the Singapore Stage*, Singapore: TheatreWorks/Singapore Press Holdings.

—— (1999) *From San Jose to San Jose*, in H. Gilbert (ed.) *(Post)Colonial Stages: Critical and Creative Views on Drama, Theatre and Performance*, Hebden Bridge, UK: Dangaroo, 253–9.

Gilbert, H. and Lo, J. (1997) 'Performing hybridity in post-colonial monodrama', *Journal of Commonwealth Literature* 32, 1: 5–19.

Le Blond, M. (1998) 'Singapore', in D. Rubin (ed.) *The World Encyclopedia of Contemporary Theatre, Volume 5*, London: Routledge, 397–405.

Lo, J. (1993) Review of Chin Woon Ping's *The Naturalization of Camellia Song*, *Westerly* 38, 3: 87–9.

Peterson, W. (2001) *Theatre and the Politics of Culture in Contemporary Singapore*, Middleton, CT: Wesleyan University Press.

Seet, K.K. (1997) 'Reclaiming the suprasternal notch and other manoeuvres: feminist devices in recent Singapore plays by women', in *Proceedings of the International Conference on Women in the Asia-Pacific Region: Persons, Powers and Politics, 11–13 August 1997*, Singapore: Regional English Language Centre, 510–26.

Details Cannot Body Wants _____

A Four-Part Performance Piece

Chin Woon Ping

Part I

Details

The stage is bare, except for a backdrop of abstract art of red streaks on white. Seated cross-legged, stage-left, is the CHORUS of four, two men and two women, dressed in black. They make background noises with their voices – in a chorus – and also play percussion instruments, their expressions always serious.

Blackness. The spotlight falls on the figure of a woman sprawled on the floor. (Background noises made by the CHORUS of birdsong and other morning sounds – distinct, melodious, rising to a crescendo.)

Slowly, very slowly, the figure starts to move, as if coming alive rather painfully. She stretches her arms, her legs, from the crumpled position she was in. Slowly, she starts to crawl across the center of the stage.

She is wearing skin-colored leotards, so she looks naked. Her expression is of concentration and exertion. It becomes clear, gradually, that she is hauling a load of things behind her – attached to her by long, nearly invisible strings. These objects emerge one by one and sometimes in a group as she keeps moving to the center of the stage. She makes a tremendous effort to get there.

At last she stops to rest. She pants, wipes brows, pulls the things towards her with a tinkling, clattering, rattling sound.

The CHORUS makes giggling and laughing noises, then subsides, before breaking into a chant that grows louder and more insistent: MOGOK, MOGOK, MOGOK, MOGOK, MOGOK, MOGOK . . . The chant then switches to: TAK, TAK, TAK, TAK, TAK, TAK, TAK . . .

The woman gathers the things around her in a heap. One sees: kitchen implements (meat cleaver, blender, large wooden spoons, etc.), groceries, cereal boxes, items of clothing, shoes of all kinds, credit cards in a long, fold-out plastic roll, potted plants, make-up kits in huge vanity cases, stuffed animals . . . They emerge as they are dragged in from off stage . . . the more outrageous the better . . . A motorcycle helmet? A baby swing? A roast turkey in a large roasting pan? A TV set?

WOMAN   Details, details. I weep for details. Without details, I am annihilated. A lipstick smear appears on the wrong side of a lip, on the wrong side of a cheek. A touch on the hand is just a little too hot, a little too long . . . Does that mean I am desired? Please let it mean I am desired. Yesterday I weighed one hundred and twenty pounds. I stopped eating rice altogether. There is no tyranny like the tyranny of the sag. What do we have here?

(She pulls one of the items of clothing near her . . . finds a pair of undies. It is the mama of undies, adorned with bows, lace, plastic fruit such as cherries, strawberries, trinkets. Another spotlight is added on to the figure. She is now suffused in a lurid glow. She starts to hum a tune and then sings it, as she puts on the undies over her leotards, and takes her time getting them to fit nicely. Perhaps the tune is Indonesian: 'O begitu rasanya, hatiku sengsara'. Or, it may be 'Whatever Lola wants, Lola Gets'. Or, it may be another old tune such as 'I Get No Kick From Champagne' . . . She sings with growing relish.)

So many details to remember. When I was three, was it four . . . I got one of my first, important lessons. I had to learn to sit properly. Not like this. (*She spreads her legs wide apart.*)

No, no! Not like this! (*Mimicking someone's shocked response*) Shame, shame, no shame! Why you no shame?

(*She mimes the teasing gesture of shaming someone by flicking forefinger against the cheek. At this point, the* CHORUS *chants in the background as she continues her own chant below:* MALU TAK MALU TAK MALU TAK MALU TAK MALU TAK MALU TAK MALU . . .)

My shame is your shame is her shame is his shame is everyone's shame. (*Repeated once or twice.*) My shame is somewhere here. (*She grabs her crotch.*) It's too shameful to show, too shameful to touch, too shameful to talk about. Sometimes the shame shows on my face, so I must learn to hide it. Like this.

(*She reaches for a paper fan, a very large one, from among her objects and spreads it open with a flick of the wrist, with the calculated aplomb of a Chinese opera virtuoso. Now she takes the fan and, fanning it with little fluttering motions, brings it up to hide half of her face.*)

I had to learn to laugh like this . . . hee . . . hee . . . hee . . . It had to be a demure, dainty, pearly, scintillating, bewitching laugh . . . hee . . . hee . . . hee . . .

(*The* CHORUS *joins in with the same kind of laugh, but keeping their serious expressions.*)

A show-your-dimples-but-not-your-teeth smile. Very hard to do if your teeth were crooked. I learned to hide shame, know shame, place shame, blame shame, shame shame . . . I learned to sit like this. (*She sits up straight, knees pressed straight together.*)

Would you like another piece of cake?
(*Primly, demurely*) No, thank you.

Do you want to go for a ride?
No, thank you.

Does it hurt?
No, thank you.

Can I show you my hurt?
No, thank you.

Can I show you my shame?
No, thank you.

Would you like to go?
No, thank you.

Would you like to come?
No, thank you.

I learned to sing in the voice that fitted my shame, not raucous and loud like I really wanted to or felt like.

(*She bellows 'I Love To Go A-Wandering' or Elvis's 'I Wanna Be Free'. The* CHORUS *makes bass and guitar noises in rhythmic accompaniment.*)

No, I had to have a voice like a meowing cat, like the greatest, most beloved meowing cat in the history of Chinese pop music, the adorable, inimitable, eternal Miss Zhou Xuan!

(*Sings 'Hao hua bu chang kai' with the* CHORUS *making accompanying meowing sounds.*)

I learned to make my shame beautiful.

Reaches for her make-up kit. She starts to apply make-up expertly, deliberately, in full view of the audience. First the base, then the rouge and colors and lipstick. When she's finished, the audience will see that she's done half her face in the traditional colors of the Chinese opera heroine, with the pink cheeks and black curls and ringlets; and the other half in the black colors of the male warrior, rather like the legendary Zhong Mou Yin, whose face was traditionally done in half-black and half-white colors. (To save time, she could don a mask; or, two make-up artists dressed in black can run out to apply the make-up as she has her back to the audience.) Now she looks at herself in a mirror (another object she's pulled out). She primps, she grins, she makes faces of all kinds.

The CHORUS *mimics the cymbal, pipa and bamboo-clacker noises of traditional Chinese opera; or they accompany her with these instruments as she starts to sing an aria from 'Madam White Snake'.*

Part II

Cannot

Now she has risen, and begins to move around the stage with the pained, mincing steps of someone with bound feet. She uses one hand to support herself in the traditional way, i.e., with thumb and pinkie against a wall. Each step is slow and laborious. The CHORUS *can either play background Chinese music of er-hu and flute, or make rhythmic sounds of sobbing and suffering.*

WOMAN (*as she continues walking*) Grandmother had beautiful feet. They were as dainty as lotus buds, encased in embroidery and satin, though they might have smelt a little. When she was four, or was it five, she begged to have her toes broken and smashed, and to be bandaged so tightly until a few finally fell off. When she walked, it was like a willow tree swaying, poetry in motion . . .

(*Recites, as if intoxicated*)

> jin re he qian zi
> xin gwan dwei jyou gwan
> xiao ti ju bu gan
> fang xin zwo ren nan

By the time I was five, I couldn't do what Grandmother did. I simply had to learn the Rules: Mama, Baba, can I go for a walk?

(CHORUS *joining in each refrain*)

> CANNOT
> (*with growing agitation*) Why not? I really want to.
> CANNOT
> But it's such a beautiful night, I really need to commune with nature, I want to smell the
>   night air, I want to stretch my muscles, I want to smell the night . . .
> CANNOT
> Why is it Brother can? Why can't I?
> CANNOT
> What horrible monsters? Who would want to hurt me?
> CANNOT
> I want to go where Brother goes.
> CANNOT.

(*In a petulant tone*) Every time I want to do something interesting, cannot one, so tow yen! Cannot do this, cannot do that, so frustrating one! Everything I want to do for boys only. Cannot go here, cannot go there, cannot even know why cannot!

(*Chants, as she mimes the following gestures, repeating each verse as many times as she likes. She is accompanied by the sound of bamboo-clacker and the* CHORUS' *voice.*)

> Cannot tend (*bending forward, backwards*)
> Cannot bend
>
> Cannot jump (*jumping*)
> Cannot hump (*making motions of copulation*)
>
> Cannot cut
> Cannot strut (*doing a flamboyant Black strut*)

Cannot watch
Cannot scratch (*scratching groin*)

Cannot flub (*falling down*)
Cannot rubba dub

Cannot start
Cannot fart (*squatting as if to make a fart*)

Cannot whinge
Cannot cringe

Cannot fly (*making aeroplane motions, arms out*)
Cannot cry

(*She gets more and more excited as she keeps chanting, all the while doing a warlike whooping dance around the stage, ending with*)

CANNOT CANNOT CANNOT CANNOT
TAK TAK TAK TAK TAK TAK TAK TAK

(*Catching her breath, sighing*) I simply had to learn to WORK. I had to learn to WASH. Rice, for instance. To wash the rice I had to winnow the rice. To winnow the rice I had to pound the rice. To pound the rice I had to harvest the rice. To harvest the rice I had to transplant the rice. To transplant the rice I had to plant the rice.

(*Miming the motions of planting rice, in a plaintive village voice*)

Planting rice is never fun
Bend from morning till set of sun
Cannot stand and cannot sit
Cannot rest a little bit.

(*She is joined by the* CHORUS *in loud refrain, perhaps accompanied by such traditional instruments as the kecapi suling, bells and cymbals. This refrain is repeated several times.*)

Planting rice is never fun
Bend from morning till set of sun
Cannot stand and cannot sit
Cannot rest a little bit.

(*Sitting down on the floor to rest. In a more collected, teacherly voice*)

Lesson Number Two: Opposites. To get what you want you must appear the opposite of what you are, or do the opposite of what you want to do. Weak is the opposite of strong. Quiet is the opposite of brave. Shy is the opposite of loud. Pain is the opposite of pleasure. Yoni is the opposite of Linggam. My first dance.

(*She puts on a circular skirt, the kind worn during the 1950s, with rock and roll motifs all over it. Either she or the* CHORUS *hums and sings a romantic dance tune from the 50s, say, the Platters' 'Only You'. Miming gestures of dancing, necking and resisting as she talks*)

Yes, I like the foxtrot very much. Please, not so close like that. Please your hand is too high. Now it's too low. Yes, my sister sewed this dress. Please don't. (*Averting face*) No, I don't want to be kissed. No petting, please. No necking, please. No, no, no. I mean NO! (*She yells.*)

(*Pausing, in a more conciliatory, thoughtful tone*)

Don't get me wrong. I don't dislike men. I'm not afraid of men. As a matter of fact, I just love men. (*In her best Mae West voice*) A HARD MAN IS GOOD TO FIND. (*In hearty parody of Mae West, she starts to sing 'Can't Help Lovin' That Man of Mine'.*) It's just the kooks that get to me. The kind who without invitation think they're a godsend and it's their godgiven right to ogle you or feel you or save you from yourself.

(*The following lines are delivered in profile, alternating from one side of her face to the other. In a deep, husky voice, with black profile to audience*)

279

Hello Doll. Where you from? I'll bet you're lonesome, aren't you? I bet I know what you want. I know *all* about you. How about some hunky chunky company? How about it, lovey dove?

And you're supposed to reply,

(*In docile, 'Oriental' voice and posture, with white profile to audience*)

Hai. Watashi karimatsu. Arigato gozaimas. Me China Doll, me Inscrutable Doll, me sexy Miss Saigon, me so horny/so so horny/me so horny/me love you long time (*etc. from 2-Live Crew rap song*).

(*The* CHORUS *can pick up the beat and song.*)

BUT WHAT YOU REALLY WANT TO SAY IS,

(*Using loud, sassy black mannerisms and tone, with black profile to audience*)

Hey Muthafukka. Quit messin' round with me and mah sistahs you hear? We don't want yo jive talk an yo bullshittin. You know what's yo problem? You ain't got no RESPECT, that's yo problem. Pick up after yoself! Go wash yo *own* goddam underwear! Clean that toilet seat after you take a leak! Take yo goddam inflated inflatable prick and shove it up yo skinny ass!

We AIN'T gonna be
AIN'T gonna be
AIN'T gonna be
MULES of the WORLD no mo!

(*Vigorously, gleefully, grabbing from the pile of things around her, as if doing a jubilant dance, she waves and then throws off stage: plates, brooms, dusters, plastic chickens, cookie pans, bread pans, empty coffee cans, whatever feels good to throw at that time and whatever makes delicious NOISE. Of course she has taken off her skirt and thrown it away too. As she's doing all this, a drumbeat begins the rhythm of rap. The* CHORUS *chants, in rhythm: MOGOK MOGOK MOGOK MOGOK MOGOK MOGOK MOGOK. In the rhythm and movements of rap – ending with Chinese, Malay, Tamil versions of the same, she chants*)

we yo sistahs and yo muthas and yo lovahs one and all
you see us in the kitchen and you see us in the hall

you think you got us figured out maybe you think you do
want a taste of woman power or a taste of our voodoo

we teach you how to clean yo butt
we teach you how to sing

you never pay attention
cause you think you are the king

we're all alike and different
all doin equal time

what's mine is yours is mine is yours
is mine is yours is mine

so haul yo skinny ass down here and get to work you all
we yo sistahs and yo mothas and yo lovahs one and all

(*Repeats the last three verses as many times as she likes. The* CHORUS *can accompany with musical instruments, drums, whatever.*)

Part III

Body

Blue spotlight on the WOMAN *standing in front of mirror, placed at an angle so the audience sees both the woman and her reflection. She wears the underpants she put on over her leotards in Part I. With one arm raised above her head, she is giving herself a breast examination using the other free arm and hand. She rotates her fingers over each breast in a slow, methodical, attentive fashion.*

The mood is solemn and meditative. This part is played in adagio. You might hear snatches of shakahachi music. Or, the CHORUS *makes the solemn sounds of Noh voices – Eeyo-oh! etc.*

WOMAN (*dreamily, seriously*) Over and over I return to Body. It is a precious jar, vessel of life, receiver of goodness. Whole, it bursts into fullness. Over and over man writes on it his imagination, his bewilderment, his inadequacy, his potency. Over and over, he writes on it his punishment, his wrath, his magnanimity, his fickleness. In darkness and health, he clutches at me and wreaks his jealousy and his longing.

(*Drapes a long, silky veil over her shoulders, pulling it over and around her and luxuriating in its soft folds. Breathlessly, intimately, with growing excitement, as if narrating a special secret*)

I know a place where the water convolvulus grows in dense clutches and jackfruit heavier than worry sit low on the branch. The banana leaf is smooth to touch, dollops of dew roll down its downy parts until you touch innermost recesses of flowering center. There the spirit of banana tree lives, curled in crimson, pert as a virgin's nipple, a promise of golden form, great clump of sweetnesses. The spirit is snowy, silent. He sidles into bed, he is sleek upon first caress, oh lighter than silk, muscularly made.

When he enters, you sigh several times with bliss, he hisses his wants into your ear, he loves to lick. The touch grows heavier as he strokes, he has many ways of lavishing attentions, now cool, now fiery, lapping at your sorest points, he is too cruel, too tender, oh keep the rough handlings right there!

When ghost birds call and the flying fox swoops, he is still cool, still pointed. Aroused to a pitch, you are turned into his purple blossom flaring at edges. He knows the tenderest places and will find them, no moaning will keep him at bay, he is not full, he's working at the mouth.

(*With growing sadness, as the* CHORUS *makes correspondingly sad sounds*)

The breeze will not die down, he swells larger, all color is draining from you, oh he will snort your life away! When dawn clicks on, a slant of light behind the bamboo blind, he is too soon, too sadly gone.

(*Removes the veil. Shoulders drooping, moves to another part of the stage. Finds a patch of cloth and sticks it on her right breast. The patch is an irregular red piece that looks like a puddle or a big ugly scar. She clutches it as if it hurts, or she's been badly hurt.*)

But what if your body is no longer beautiful, will not be beautiful, never was beautiful? What if it is not desirable, not gorgeous, not a piece of cheesecake? What if it is not a piece, not a whole, not a one, NOT, NOT, NOT? How do you live with flatness? How do you live with plainness? How do you live with ugliness? How do you live with emptiness?

(*In different voices of ordinary women*)

'Every time I looked in the mirror and saw this chicken-breasted figure or walking down the street thinking about it, I felt deformed'.
'I'm five-foot-nine, I wear a size 12 and I wore a size A bra. You know, it means so much for a woman because God didn't make her enormous'.

(*She finds and puts on a bra. It is more a falsie, decorated with lace, ribbons and bows. Taking a bicycle pump, she inserts its nozzle into an opening in the bra. She pumps vigorously, so the bra inflates her chest. The* CHORUS *chants solemnly: SILICONE IS SEXY, SILICONE IS SEXY,*

SILICONE IS SEXY . . . She puts the pump away, pleased. Now she straightens herself and puts on a doctor's white gown. She picks up a pointer and points to the mirror as if it is a blackboard.)

Lesson Number Five: Hand. A hand is for holding and for plucking and for massaging. Hand over what you have when asked. Never handle more than you can keep. Keep your hand soft, shapely and attractive. I recommend Nail Polish Number 42, Watermelon Excess, or Nail Polish Number 4, Brazilian Brassiness, or Handcream Number 99, Mushy Magic.

(Reading the following translation from Sutardji Calzoum Bachri as if from an imaginary blackboard, with deadpan seriousness.)

it must be that a hand is not only a hand but a hand that is a hand not merely a hand but a hand that's a hand positively a hand absolutely a hand that can beckon that can wave hello

it must be that a hand is not a clump of fingers writing in vain just a mere thorn writing wounds rubbing eyes yet still the drizzle has not stopped

even a complete hand feels maimed although nearly a hand it feels amputated although one hand it is lopped off although half a hand it's amputated the dismembered hand feels cut off the chopped hand is amputated hand amputated

(She mimes with hands stretched out as if they are amputated.)

all amputated all not hands
only clocks are complete their hands pointing
who knows where

(Removes the white gown. Runs to the other side of the stage, puts on a diaphanous kimono.)

Lesson Number Four. Do you like your mouth? For a mere princely sum you can have your mouth enlarged, thickened, lengthened, voluptuized, desensitized, defamiliarized. Would you like to look like Kim Basinger, or Jean Paul Belmondo, or a Bez Denage? Come to Fanciful Flesh Farms. Leave your mouth to us. Never leave home without your instant, chewable Mouth.

(Finds a huge, Raggedy-Ann doll upon which she inflicts various acts of anger and violence as she chants the following, with the CHORUS making accompanying sounds.)

When he cuts into me when he slices into me when he stabs me
When he stalks me when he hits me when he slaps me
When he throttles me when he poisons me when he maims me
When he chains me when he traps me when he sells me
When he brands me when he ropes me when he tattoos me
When he cripples me when he dumps me when he burns me
When he hangs me when he shoots me when he snuffs me

(Now she cradles the doll like a child, showering upon it gestures of affection and tenderness.)

Is he saying he has forgotten
How to comfort me how to look at me how to tame me
How to work with me how to walk with me
How to lighten me how to learn from me
How to live with me how to cherish me
How to comfort self how to tame self
How to lighten self how to learn from self
How to look at self how to love self
How to heal self how to cherish self

(Removing the kimono, removing the bra and the underpants, standing straight and facing the audience, in an even voice, repeating the chant as many times as she likes, with growing conviction)

I am not my breasts I am not my chin I am not my arms I am not my neck I am not my womb I am not my lips I am not my breasts

(*Moves to another part of the stage. Puts on a pretty gown and a gardenia in her hair. Sings, in Billie Holiday fashion*)

> I'm not much to look at, nothin to see
> just glad I'm livin and lucky it's me
> I've got a man crazy for me
> He's funny that way

Part IV

Wants

The lights come on to show the woman seated on the floor, center-stage in cross-legged position. She is wearing a pyjama-outfit, Chinese samfoo or a Vietnamese peasant costume, preferably in batik or in Sumba print. She recites in a child-like, singsong voice, with the index finger of one hand in the palm of her other hand. At the last word of the rhyme, she playfully takes the index finger out just as she is about to shut her palm. The CHORUS *accompanies with instrumentals, e.g. bamboo clacker.*

WOMAN
> Dam dam giong
> Yeh ji gip sun giong
> Gai dan lou mai sap mm liong
> Hong mou for toi gip min bau
> Jow dou san bar lor yeh jiong
> Dit lok lei
> Bei gai DIONG!

(*Talking in a broad, friendly fashion to the audience*) When I was nine years old I wanted more than anything to please. I wanted to please Grandmother. (*In Cantonese*) Ah Por, ngor tong lei dam guat leh.

(*Miming the motions of pounding someone's neck and giving a backrub, with a goody-goody expression*)

I wanted to please Auntie. (*With Cantonese accent*) *Auntie.* Let me pull your white hairs for you. One cent for each hair I pull? Oh goody, goody. Ahh. Let me pick your lice for you – such beautiful hair. So many shiny, beautiful lice.

(*Miming motions of searching for lice and nits in someone's hair, resembling more and more a monkey looking through another monkey's fur. Once in a while, she takes an imaginary louse to her mouth and bites on it, scratches her armpits, her back, her legs . . . The* CHORUS *makes rhythmic sounds of monkey cries.*)

(*In Cantonese accent*) I wanted to please *Da-ddy.*

(*Picking up an imaginary book, with the look of someone studying very hard, walks up and down as if deeply engrossed. The* CHORUS *chants 'Shou pe shou/pe chiu', etc. Or 'See Jane run', etc.*)

Then, the older I got, the more I wanted. I wanted toys.

(*She drags in a bicycle from off stage. Climbs on and pedals around the stage – if she's adept enough, she can do a few tricks, e.g. without hands, one foot stretched out, etc. – she can have a good time on the bicycle. Dismounts, gives the bicycle a big hug and a kiss.*)

I wanted shoes.

(*Pulling towards her many boxes of shoes. Puts on one pair after another, trying out a different posture, expression and walk with each new pair. After she's put on one of the most outrageous pairs, she sings this song from Impossible Theater.*)

> 'Whenever I get depressed, I buy shoes
> I buy shoes'

(The pace picks up as she finds each object. Perhaps she moves around the stage to find them. She can mime the use of each thing. She lavishes upon each much fuss and attention. The CHORUS *hums 'Jingle Bells' and other cheery Christmas carols.)*

I wanted a telephone. I wanted a TV.

(She can have a lot of fun when she gets to the TV, which should be the frame of a box into which she can put her head. Would she like to do a few lines of Gilda Radner doing Wawa Walters? . . . Richard Nixon . . . Eddie Murphy doing Alfafa . . . Julia Child? . . . Yes, definitely Julia Child . . . The CHORUS *beats a rhythm on instruments.)*

I wanted a ball. I wanted a Swiss army knife. I wanted a purple alligator. I wanted a toy truck. I wanted a flyeater. I wanted a pet turtle. I wanted a Halloween costume. I wanted a tent. I wanted a neon sign. I wanted a set of encyclopaedias. I wanted an antique commode. I wanted a Dutch oven. I wanted a brass toilet seat. I wanted chocolates.

(Gobbling the chocolates, cramming them into her mouth as she continues to talk.)

I wanted a rare vintage wine. I wanted a new pair of glasses. I wanted a stone necklace. I wanted an electric toothbrush. I wanted a titanium watch. I wanted a model airplane . . .

(She has piled all these objects around her, so they begin to crowd her more and more . . . She has to fight her way out of this heap of things. Panting, gasping, she makes her way to another part of the stage. The music/rhythmic beating stops. She puts on a monk's costume, and adopts a different tone altogether.)

What I really wanted was to fly. What I really wanted was to soar, to lift up, out, away. More than anything, I wanted to forget about the big clock ticking, the big box waiting . . .

(Recites, in priestly, solemn fashion another translation from Sutardji Calzoum Bachri)

Will you will you not live your life?
You wait you will want you will want

Who stabbed the curse of time?
My cursetime my cursetime my cursetime

Can you make the quiet stone fly?
Poisonstone poisonstone stonestone

That's sky that's grasping that's sorrowful
My throb my throb my throb

So I learned to trade my wants. Fame. Fortune. Favor. I exchanged one for the other. *Then* I wanted a baby. Oh God did I want a baby – a little, kicking, tickling, pickling, prickling baby.

(Removing the priest's robe. Puts on a maternity dress. With growing fervor, alternating between a lugubrious and hysterical voice)

I wanted my body to become more of me, more of nature, more of myself. I wanted to be overtaken by a seed, by an idea I did not plant. Was that too much to ask? Other women had it, why couldn't I? I wanted to be diminished by fecundity, to be engrossed with fertility. I wanted to join the ranks of those who knew secret pain and secret pleasure, Oh God did I want it!

(Sings in a wistful voice the song from the Chinese movie, 'Jin Feng'. The CHORUS *joins in with sounds of goats bleating and babies bawling.)*

Mei Mei Mama
Mei Mei Mama
Yang you ma
Ren you ma
Jiu shi Jen Feng mei you ma *(etc.)*

(Breaks down and weeps like a lost child)

Oh hell I'm ruining my make-up. I look a sight. Look here, it's eleven o'clock and it's time to go. The goose is in the oven. My goose is cooked. It's time for the goats to come home.

(*Removes the maternity dress. Puts on a long white nightgown. The* CHORUS *makes sounds of wolves, coyotes, or owls. She lights a candle, goes around the stage in a slow, graceful Javanese, Malay or Japanese dance . . . The lights dim, leaving a spotlight that goes out when she exits.*)

Ashes to ashes, dust to dust . . . I say there's no better way to travel than to travel light . . .

(*Sings whimsically, but spiritedly Piaf's 'Non, je ne regrette rien . . .'*)

Good night, ladies, good night. Sweet ladies, good night, good night.

(CHORUS *ends with sound of birdsongs, as at the beginning.*)

13 Louis Nowra

Inside the Island
Australia

Introduction

The mixed critical response to the premiere production of Louis Nowra's 1980 play, *Inside the Island*, could hardly have foreshadowed its author's subsequent rise to become one of only a handful of contemporary Australian playwrights known and respected internationally. Since the mid-1970s, Nowra has penned more than thirty original stage dramas as well as translating a number of European texts for performance. His astonishingly rich oeuvre also includes various radio plays and opera libretti, several film and television scripts, three novels and sundry other works. How Nowra, born in 1950 to working-class parents living in an outer-Melbourne housing-commission estate, has progressed to the forefront of Australian theatre is a story best conveyed by his memoir, *The Twelfth of Never* (1999), a revealing account of his unconventional and sometimes painful upbringing. Suffice it to say here that his imagistic theatre, while only occasionally autobiographical, nevertheless bears the stamp of his turbulent background in oblique and complex ways, especially through its fascination with the emotional power of a physical landscape and the indelible pain of human suffering.

One of Nowra's main themes is history, which he treats in a cavalier fashion in order to reveal the biases and omissions of a mythologised past. Veronica Kelly describes Nowra's vision of national history as 'a distinctively postcolonial one, where tragedy, romance and farce can collide in magic realist mode; where the inarticulate and marginalised possess strengths inaccessible to their oppressors; and where the traumas of the past erupt into the present to be rehearsed, replayed and refigured' (Kelly 1998: xi). Early Nowra plays such as *Inner Voices* (1977), set in tsarist Russia, and *Visions*

(1978), about Paraguay during the genocidal 1870s War of the Triple Alliance, play out their anti-imperial themes by dramatising historical events in countries distant from Australia. The tendency to avoid explicitly Australian subjects during a period which saw an unprecedented growth in nationalist theatre initially prompted critics to label Nowra, along with friend and fellow playwright Stephen Sewell, as 'internationalist' writers who were not particularly interested in local issues. This designation can be misleading, however, because it misses the full resonances of each playwright's early dramatic parables and fails to acknowledge the passionate engagement with Australian culture, history and politics that has consistently informed their respective careers in the theatre.

Nowra explains that his interest in the past derives from an irritation that white Australians lack a sense of their own history, as exiled convicts and/or opportunistic settlers of a foreign land, and, more crucially, as colonisers of Aboriginal peoples. Commenting on the wilful forgetfulness and false nostalgia associated with Australia's official Bicentenary in 1988, he remarks:

> We European Australians have a perfect opportunity to come to terms with what actually happened to the Aboriginal people over the past two hundred years. It means we'll have to confront our history. None of the Bicentennial celebrations will operate on this level. It's a typically Australian form of amnesia.
>
> (Nowra 1987a: 56)

In such plays as *Inside the Island* and *The Golden Age* (1985), both set in Australia in the first part of the twentieth century, Nowra's allusive and highly concentrated visions of the past are designed to confront audiences with their nation's shameful history of colonisation. While neither work includes Aboriginal characters, each is metaphorically 'haunted' by a sense of their presence, evoking images of Aboriginal land and culture as palimpsests written over by wave after wave of Euro-Australian settlers. It is this catastrophic dispossession of indigenous peoples, and white Australians' refusal to fully acknowledge, much less atone for, their ancestral sins, that underwrites each play's savage portrait of a settler society in crisis.

Commenting on the genesis of *Inside the Island*, Nowra cites several very different sources of inspiration (Nowra 1981: 11–13). His starting point was a long-held image of the power of the Australian landscape, conjured through youthful memories of desolate and mysterious rust-brown wheatfields in north-western Victoria. To this setting he transposed a vision of stress-induced madness as detailed in an Australian soldier's diary about the battle of Pozières in 1916. Ergotism, a grain fungal infection causing delirium and hallucinations, became the mechanism through which to dramatise such madness. Nowra not only bases his physical depiction of ergot poisoning on an outbreak in southern France in 1951, but also invests his drama with a ritual undertone that draws from medieval understandings of ergotism as 'The Holy Fire' inducing visions that could be terrifying or ecstatically beautiful.

That some reviewers saw the critical tenor of *Inside the Island* as grossly affronting and even 'un-Australian' suggests the longevity of the nationalist myths that Nowra aims to dismantle. One of the most potent of these myths, the notion of Australia as an egalitarian country, free of the class conflicts, bloody histories and generalised decay of the 'Old World', is radically destabilised throughout the course of the play. To this purpose, Nowra begins his narrative as a razor-sharp satire of a colonial society reluctant to abandon Anglophile attitudes and unable to develop any real affinity with the Australian landscape or climate. The 'island' of the play's title is not only the continent itself, but also the isolated wheat property on which the action takes place, a semi-feudal agrarian settlement that Lillian Dawson rules autocratically, but with the philanthropic posturing of a Victorian 'Lady Bountiful'. One of Nowra's many strong but troubling female protagonists, Lillian is wilful, manipulative

and snobbish. Early scenes focus on her affectations and her husband George's weaknesses, drawing stylistically from the British comedy of manners, but with a much darker subtext. Underneath their comic surface, these scenes reveal the casual violence, both physical and emotional, that seems to penetrate all levels of a society poisoned by the legacies of imperialism. Nowra thus subtly prepares his audience for a tonal shift to the apocalyptic second act in which the visiting soldiers' latent brutality manifests in an orgy of violence that overrides all semblance of civility and leads to the spectacular collapse of Lillian's carefully controlled world.

The landscape itself is one of the most powerful 'characters' in *Inside the Island*'s unforgettable account of the colonising process. It is not a metaphor for social attitudes or psychological states but rather a vast mysterious force that shapes human existence, whether imperceptibly or through violent cataclysms of fire and flood. This is shown most graphically at the end of the play when the hallucinating soldiers who have initiated the mayhem envision roots and flowers growing from their own bodies. At another level, the land is a site of historical memory: it renders visible the traces of prior indigenous occupation as well as current settlers' attempts to inscribe an alien space with their own assertive presence. Thus, the cricket pitch overlaid on the ancient Aboriginal campsite becomes a composite physical 'text' that records the genocidal past revealed narratively in Lillian's casual references to the ways in which her pioneer father 'cleared' tribal blacks from the land. Above all, the landscape is a potential agent of purgation and renewal. Hence, the bushfires that ravage the Dawsons' wheatfields and garrison-style homestead also cauterise the colonial wound, opening up possibilities of different and more enabling relationships between settlers, the landscape and its original inhabitants. Unfortunately, none of the remaining characters seem aware of this potential, a form of blindness conveyed by Lillian's devastatingly ironic final line: 'The strong forget, the weak remember'.

As well as dismantling the deceptively innocuous pastoral myth of settlement in Australia, the human carnage portrayed by *Inside the Island* specifically 'remembers' the nation's participation in the First World War. Although the action is set in 1912 and occurs chronologically before the war's outbreak, its portrayal of crazed and mutilated soldiers wandering, spirit-like, over a blazing landscape is designed to suggest the futility of an enterprise that sacrificed thousands of colonial troops in support of a distant empire. Nowra's demythologising project thus targets events such as the abortive battle at Gallipoli, which most Australians still celebrate as the formative context for their heroic ideal of masculinity. This ideal encompasses the myth of mateship, revealed in the play to be riven with hostilities, rivalries, class tensions and petty one-upmanship. Nowra chooses such an elliptical take on the Gallipoli myth as his preferred form of dramaturgy, one that works 'by metaphor and resonance rather than a direct political attack on events that have become dangerously sacrosanct legends' (Nowra 1987b: 139). The significance of the ergot-infected flour that causes the soldiers' madness is also figured in the metaphorical sweep of *Inside the Island*'s inferno imagery, since a common method of massacring Aborigines in colonial times was by giving them poisoned flour. In this respect, the soldiers signify paradoxically as both victims and perpetrators of Australia's first (unacknowledged) war: the battle for the land itself.

Several of Nowra's plays stage the imported rituals of colonial society only to suggest their inadequacy as a model for a genuinely adaptive settler culture. The carnivalesque tea or dinner party featured in such works as *Visions* and *The Golden Age* is a favoured device by which to subvert the manners and mores of the gentrified classes. *Inside the Island* foregrounds a picnic outing to a game of cricket as a more elaborate example of this trope. This is not incidental, since cricket, the structural fulcrum on which the play's action pivots, has functioned for centuries in far-flung reaches of the British Empire to inculcate 'civilised' values in colonised societies via rituals related to gentlemanly demeanour, particular (white) attire, good sportsmanship, and even specific spectator behaviours. The institutional authority of such a ritual, its illusion of 'fair play', and its historical exclusivity as a sport for the upper classes, are thoroughly dismantled when this most British of games devolves into murderous anarchy. In complex ways,

cricket is connected to the dominant motif of blindness, which is figured literally by Private Miller's self-blinding with a cricket stump, and metaphorically by Lillian's refusal to see the inappropriateness of her cultural project. The play's use of blindness as a central metaphor recalls Shakespeare's *King Lear*, a textual echo that is particularly strong in the final image of George with his murdered and raped daughter in his arms, berating the world for its cruelty and lamenting his own former obliviousness to her needs.

Like almost all of Nowra's work, *Inside the Island* is deliberately anti-naturalistic, its effect emerging from the juxtaposition of a series of highly evocative individual scenes and snapshot images. Because he shares Brecht's view that naturalism is invested with the hegemonic views of the middle classes, Nowra tends to prefer epic structures that accommodate a broad range of theatrical devices, including song, music and dance. However, he delineates his work from Brechtian theatre by stressing its attempt 'to resonate rather than pontificate' (Nowra 1987b: 135). Stylistically, Nowra draws from various high and popular culture genres, his inspirational sources ranging from the live vaudeville he saw as a child in his grandfather's hotel to the work of German expressionists such as Wedekind, and the Gothic horror movies of Canadian director David Cronenberg. These heterogeneous influences ensure that even the semi-autobiographical plays, *Summer of the Aliens* (1989) and *Così* (1992), have touches of the idiosyncratic and the bizzare.

Whereas Nowra's early treatments of Australian history focused most often on the colonising culture's anxious attempts to authenticate its power, his concern with the injustices meted out to indigenous peoples as a routine part of the nation-building process later translated into several plays that positioned Aboriginal characters firmly on centre stage. Notable among these works are *Capricornia* (1988), his stage adaptation of Xavier Herbert's epic saga about early-twentieth-century race relations in Australia's north, *Radiance* (1993), an intense psychological drama written for three Aboriginal women, and *Crow* (1994), a surreal comedy in which the titular heroine struggles to have her claim to her family's land legally recognised. Nowra worked closely with various Aboriginal actors and theatre professionals on these projects, earning a reputation as one of the few non-Aboriginal playwrights to write convincing roles for indigenous Australians. His continued interest in public history has also led to work about recent events such as the Bosnian crisis, and, more locally, instances of political and corporate corruption among high-profile Australians. In *The Temple* (1993), loosely based on the career of disgraced businessman Alan Bond, and *The Incorruptible* (1995), inspired in part by the life of controversial state premier Joh Bjelke-Peterson, Nowra's satire is aimed squarely at contemporary Australian society. These plays continue the political work of his early colonial parables by presenting transgressive visions of a dystopian society still in need of moral and social reform.

Production history

Inside the Island was first performed at the Nimrod Theatre, Sydney, on 13 August 1980, directed by Neil Armfield.

Select bibliography

Gilbert, H. (1994) 'Ghosts in a landscape: Louis Nowra's *Inside the Island* and Janis Balodis's *Too Young for Ghosts'*, *Southern Review* 27: 432–47.

—— (1998) *Sightlines: Race, Gender, and Nation in Contemporary Australian Theatre*, Ann Arbor, MI: Michigan University Press, 97–144.

Griffiths, G. (1984) 'Australian subjects and Australian style: the plays of Louis Nowra', *Commonwealth* 6, 2: 42–8.

Kelly, V. (1985) '"Lest we forget": Louis Nowra's *Inside the Island'*, *Island Magazine* 23: 19–23.

—— (ed.) (1987) *Louis Nowra*. Amsterdam: Rodopi.

—— (1992) 'Louis Nowra', in B. King (ed.) *Post-Colonial English Drama: Commonwealth Drama since 1960*, London: Macmillan, 50–66.

—— (1998) *The Theatre of Louis Nowra*. Sydney: Currency Press.

McCallum, J. (1984) 'The world outside: cosmopolitanism in the plays of Nowra and Sewell', *Meanjin* 43, 2: 286–96.

Makeham, P. (1999) 'Hysterical landscape: Louis Nowra's *Inside the Island'*, in H. Gilbert (ed.) *Post-Colonial Stages: Critical and Creative Views on Drama, Theatre and Performance*, Hebden Bridge, UK: Dangaroo, 201–11.

Nowra, L. (1981) Author's preface, *Inside the Island*, Sydney: Currency, 11–14.

—— (1987a) 'Perfecting the monologue of silence', interview with G. Turcotte, *Kunapipi* 9, 3: 51–67.

—— (1987b) Edited transcript of video interview, in V. Kelly (ed.) *Louis Nowra*, Amsterdam: Rodopi, 134–43.

—— (1993) 'The black hole of our history', interview with P. Makeham, *Canadian Theatre Review* 74: 27–31.

—— (1999) *The Twelfth of Never: A Memoir*, London: Picador.

Inside the Island

Louis Nowra

Characters

GEORGE DAWSON
LILLIAN DAWSON
PETER BLACKWOOD
SUSAN DAWSON
CAPTAIN HENRY
SERGEANT COLLINS
MRS HARRISON
ANDY
TOM
PRIVATE O'NEILL
THE RECTOR
JULIE
ARTHUR
BERT
PRIVATE HIGGS
CORPORAL BURKE
PRIVATE MACDONALD
PRIVATE MILLER
PRIVATE WATSON
SOLDIERS
(Many parts can be doubled)

Setting

North-western New South Wales, Australia.
The time is Summer 1912.

Act I

Scene 1

Night. The sound of bullfrogs. A creek.
GEORGE *enters, drunk. He carries an*
unopened bottle of whiskey wrapped in a
newspaper. He stops and wonders where he
should go now.

GEORGE   Let's see. The creek's there, the . . .
　　another mile! It's taking a long time tonight
　　. . . perhaps I passed out. She'll be furious.
　　(*He sets off again.*)
PETER   (*off, singing*)

Oh, while I was shearing, I used to dream
That the old rouseabout was a girl,
The prettiest girl in the whole wide
　　world.
GEORGE   (*startled*) Who's there?
PETER   (*off*)
Her slippers were made of crystal,
Her combs made from the finest gold.
GEORGE   Who's there? Answer me. (*He turns*
　　in the direction of the singing, trips over a tree
　　trunk and sprawls on the ground.) Shit!
PETER   (*off*)
And though she didn't look more than
　　sixteen,
I knew she was over a hundred years old.
GEORGE   Who's there? (*He jumps up,*
　　frightened.) Who's there? Answer me.
PETER   (*off*)
Oh, her teeth were capped with silver . . .
GEORGE   Who's that singing? *Answer me!* (*He*
　　falls into the creek with a splash.)
PETER   (*off*)
And shone by the light of the moon
As we danced a waltz to this tune.
GEORGE   Help! Help! I can't swim.
PETER   (*off*) Who's there? Hullo!
GEORGE   Here. In the creek. Help me.
　　(PETER *enters with a kerosene lamp and goes*
　　upstage.) Here. Help me. No, over this way.
　　Over here, I'm stuck.

　　(PETER *searches the ground for a stick and*
　　finds one.)

PETER   Grab hold of this.
GEORGE   My foot's caught in a snag.
PETER   Grab the stick.
GEORGE   I can't get free.
PETER   Grab the stick! (*He pulls* GEORGE
　　onto the bank.)
GEORGE   (*gasping and coughing*) Went in,
　　head first. My foot was caught. (*Silence.*
　　PETER *waits for* GEORGE *to recover.*
　　GEORGE *sits up. He shakes his head.*)
　　Fancy nearly drowning in a creek. Thanks,

I – Where's my bottle of whisky? (*He stands up and prepares to go back into the creek.*) I must have dropped it in the creek.

PETER Hold on, I've just pulled you out.

GEORGE No, I remember. I fell over a log. Over there. (*He goes downstage with* PETER.) Ah, there it is. (*He unscrews it and takes a drink.*) Nearly drowned in a bloody creek. Christ. You want some?

PETER No, thanks.

GEORGE Go on. You saved me. Go on, it'll cool you down. (PETER *takes a sip.*) Not bad, is it?

PETER Pretty good.

GEORGE God, it's hot tonight. Nice and cool in the creek. (*Remembering*) Someone was singing.

PETER Uh?

GEORGE Before I fell in . . . someone was singing.

PETER It was me.

GEORGE Gave me a bit of a shock.

PETER I was singing with my squeeze box.

GEORGE What are you doing here?

PETER I live here.

GEORGE Here?

PETER Just over there in that bunch of trees.

GEORGE But this is my land.

PETER The creek too?

GEORGE Everything. I own as far as you can see. Nearly up to those hills. All the flat land around here and the wheat fields are mine. So's the mill. Everything. (GEORGE *takes another drink. Silence.*)

PETER You want me to shift?

GEORGE Shift?

PETER I've got a hut here.

GEORGE (*incredulously*) A hut? How long have you lived here?

PETER A couple of weeks.

GEORGE But this is my land. No wonder I was surprised. No one comes here. (*Taking another drink.*) No one. (*Handing the bottle to* PETER.) I've been down at the pub. I'm on my way home. See that light over there? That's my home.

PETER I see it during the day. I wondered who owned such a big house.

GEORGE Well now you know.

PETER You want me to leave here?

GEORGE Well, I got a surprise . . . that's why . . . you're the first person that ever lived here. That's why I fell in the creek.

PETER I'm not doing any harm. I just live in my hut and play music. I'll be moving soon. (*Pause.*)

GEORGE I haven't thanked you for saving me. What's your name?

PETER Pete. Peter Blackwood.

GEORGE Mine's George.

PETER Do you want to see my hut – seeing it's on your land? (*They go upstage,* PETER *holding his lantern.*)

GEORGE But why are you living in a hut?

PETER The only place I've got.

GEORGE You got any money?

PETER No.

GEORGE You can have a job as one of my workers. You want a job?

PETER I don't care.

GEORGE But you need the money. I'd like to think I can always help people.

PETER Well . . .

GEORGE The hut will have to be torn down.

PETER (*shrugging*) It's your land.

GEORGE You can live with one of my workers.

(*Pause.* PETER *picks up his squeeze box.*)

PETER I sing with this.

GEORGE A concertina.

PETER No, it's a squeeze box. Can you play it?

GEORGE I love music, but can't play a thing.

PETER (*singing*)
Oh, while I was shearing, I used to dream
That the old rouseabout was a girl.
Pretty good, eh?

GEORGE You know any others?

PETER Hundreds. (*He wipes his brow and slaps a mosquito on his arm.*) It's hot tonight.

GEORGE You should jump in the creek, that'll cool you down. (*Pause.*) Play a song.

PETER You want to hear some?

GEORGE (*mimicking* PETER) Hundreds.

PETER (*taking a sip of the whisky*) Helps me sing.

GEORGE (*taking the bottle from* PETER *and drinking*) Helps me listen. All right, let's have it.

PETER This one is called 'Big Black Jack'. Ever hear of it? (GEORGE *shakes his head.*) First one I learnt on my squeeze box. 'Big Black Jack'.
Big Black Jack
Was always fighting
So they threw him out of the pub.
So angry was he
That he lit a big fart

And blew the pub apart.
Oh, Big Black Jack –

(*Sudden blackout.*)

Scene 2

Darkness. Someone plays Elgar's 'Imperial March' on the piano. Lights slowly up on SUSAN DAWSON *at the piano in the living room. Two* SOLDIERS *enter,* CAPTAIN HENRY *and* SERGEANT COLLINS, *followed by* LILLIAN DAWSON. *The* SOLDIERS *stand uneasily as the music is played. At the end of the piece, both men, not knowing what to do on such occasions, applaud.*

LILLIAN   Susan, this is Captain Henry and Sergeant Collins.

SUSAN   How do you do?

CAPTAIN   I'm very well, thank you.

SERGEANT   That was pretty good playing.

SUSAN   I wasn't playing.

CAPTAIN   Excuse me, I . . .

LILLIAN   It's a pianola.

CAPTAIN   Oh, I see.

LILLIAN   Unfortunately, there are no piano teachers here. We hope she will be able to take lessons later on this year. You look uncomfortable, gentlemen; please sit. Sit down. My husband will be home soon. Would you like some refreshments? We have alcohol and lemonade. I don't drink alcohol.

CAPTAIN   I'm a teetotaller, too.

LILLIAN   In the Army and not a drinker! You must be unique.

CAPTAIN   Just about. My father was a non-drinker.

LILLIAN   Well, that explains it. (*To the* SERGEANT) I suspect you're not a teetotaller.

SERGEANT   I enjoy a glass now and then.

LILLIAN   And it's then, now? Susan, a decanter of sherry for the Sergeant and a jug of lemonade for us. (LILLIAN *sits.*)

CAPTAIN   Lovely house.

LILLIAN   Why, thank you. My father built it forty years ago. He was a great man. When he first came here it was just bush – a huge plain of Aboriginals and gum trees. He got rid of the blacks, except for those whom he converted; removed the gum trees. His picture is on the wall. Painted by a very talented Aboriginal youth who died soon after. Ah, refreshment. (SUSAN *enters with the tray.*) Our cook is away at the moment.

Sherry for the Sergeant. (SUSAN *pours the sherry from a decanter.*) Lemonade for three. (*Giving glass of lemonade to* CAPTAIN HENRY) One lemonade.

CAPTAIN   Thank you.

SERGEANT   (*to* SUSAN) Thank you, miss.

LILLIAN   Ah, nice and cold. (*Sipping lemonade*) So refreshing on a night like this.

CAPTAIN   It's excellent.

LILLIAN   Home-made. (*She is stunned by the sight of the* SERGEANT *downing his sherry in one gulp.*) Nice, Sergeant?

SERGEANT   Lovely. Generally I don't like sherry. It gives me a pain in the guts –

CAPTAIN   Sergeant!

SERGEANT   Uh? (*Understanding*) Sorry, missus. It gives me a pain in the . . . tummy. But this is lovely.

LILLIAN   Help yourself, Sergeant. I'm sure you'll need no prompting. (*The* SERGEANT *does so.*) My husband should not be too long.

CAPTAIN   That's all right, we're in no hurry.

LILLIAN   It seems strange to me that the Army should suddenly start sending men up here.

CAPTAIN   They don't know if it'll be a regular thing yet. We're quite a small outfit. Fifty men.

LILLIAN   And only you two are officers?

CAPTAIN   Sergeant Collins is not quite an officer, yet. My Lieutenant left by rail this morning to go back to Sydney to fix up our supplies.

LILLIAN   So how long will you be staying here?

CAPTAIN   A month all told.

LILLIAN   In tents?

CAPTAIN   That's half the exercise. Roughing it. I don't know if you know the area where we're camped . . .

LILLIAN   Oh yes. When I was a girl I'd ride out there on my school holidays. My father gave it to the Government just before he died.

CAPTAIN   As a gift?

LILLIAN   Just a straight-out gift. He had a good sense of the magnanimous gesture. More lemonade?

CAPTAIN   No, thank you.

LILLIAN   (*looking with distaste at the* SERGEANT'*s heavy drinking*) Are you on fire, Sergeant?

SERGEANT   Uh?

LILLIAN   Your intake would seem to suggest you were.

SERGEANT   I was thirsty.

LILLIAN   Do you want some water?

SERGEANT   No, thank you.

(*The* SERGEANT *pours his third glass of sherry. Realising he has been ill-mannered, he pours the sherry back into the decanter. He then returns to his chair with an empty glass.*)

LILLIAN   It's so comforting to know that the Army is here. Oh, I don't mean protection for me personally, but the knowledge that the Army is doing something. We're so isolated, Australia is like a giant sloth; it doesn't seem to realise that there are eight hundred million Asiatics eyeing us with envy.

CAPTAIN   If needed, I think you'll find us awake.

LILLIAN   I hope so. What am I saying? Of course, you will be. Your men will be. I worry, perhaps unnecessarily, but everything seems exaggerated out here: the loneliness, the isolation. When I was young, a Chinaman came to our front door and begged for some money. My father gave him a few coins and when the Chinaman smiled his thanks, I saw his teeth were gold – all of them. They caught the sun and it looked as if his whole face were ablaze. Imagine that! Walking around begging when he held a fortune in his mouth. That's their mentality, their duplicity. (*Pause.*)

   I wonder where my husband could be. I told him to be home at seven. It's a long walk from the mill. Oh, it slipped my mind – biscuits? (*She opens a musical box; it plays a tune.*) I bought it when a young girl in England. (*She offers it to the* CAPTAIN, *who takes one biscuit.*)

CAPTAIN   Thank you.

SERGEANT   (*taking three biscuits*) Ta.

LILLIAN   Have you been in the Army all your life, Sergeant?

SERGEANT   (*missing the mockery*) No. I used to work as a miner, but the mine ran out of coal, so I joined the Army. At least with the Army you get regular food and pay.

LILLIAN   I don't know what that says about our Army . . . (*spotting his confusion*) but I'm sure it's something good.

SERGEANT   It was near the sea.

LILLIAN   Excuse me?

SERGEANT   The mine was near the sea. On the coast. I like the sea.

LILLIAN   Perhaps you should have joined the Navy.

SERGEANT   I get sea-sick. Still, it's a job.

LILLIAN   It's more than a job, isn't it? You have to fight.

SERGEANT   Fight? I guess so.

LILLIAN   Have you ever been in a battle?

SERGEANT   A real one? No, missus. I did see a man run over by one of those new mechanical ploughs last year. He was chewed up something bad. I guess a battlefield is a bit like that.

LILLIAN   What a morbid imagination you have.

CAPTAIN   Perhaps we should go. It's getting late.

LILLIAN   I can't understand where Mr Dawson could be. Perhaps a few more minutes. While we're waiting I'll show you my indoor garden, Captain. It's in the conservatory. Susan, entertain the Sergeant while we're gone. This way, Captain. (*As they exit*) My fuschias are famous throughout the whole district. (*Silence.*)

SUSAN   Do you want a biscuit?

SERGEANT   Yes, please.

SUSAN   (*with distaste*) Help yourself.

SERGEANT   Ta. (*He opens music box roughly.*)

SUSAN   Careful!

SERGEANT   Sorry. (*Examining it as it plays 'Silent Night'*) I think I . . . hello, it's just a little spring here. All it needs is just a push – ah! Right as rain. (*Taking out three biscuits, he gives the music box to* SUSAN, *who has held out her hand for it. She inspects it glumly even though it still works.*) Nice biscuits. You make them?

SUSAN   The cook did. I can't cook.

SERGEANT   It's easy, you'll get the hang of it. My mum was a great cook. Cooked for six boys. (*An awkward silence.*)

SUSAN   Do you like the country around here?

SERGEANT   A bit flat. I like mountains.

SUSAN   I thought you liked the sea.

SERGEANT   I like the mountains and the sea. (*Pause.*)

SUSAN   Some lemonade?

SERGEANT   No thanks. Not too keen on it. None of me family were. We called it sugar syrup.

SUSAN   (*sarcastically*) I'm sorry we have nothing better.

SERGEANT   (*missing the sarcasm*) That's all right.

(*Silence. The* SERGEANT *is restless. Finally he takes out a dirty sock from his pocket and makes it into a hand puppet.*)

SERGEANT (*with a squeaky voice*) Hello, Suzy. (SUSAN *turns and notices the hand puppet. She is astonished.*) It's a nice day, isn't it? My, my, what a big girl you are. I see you're surprised. My friend, Sergeant Collins, keeps me in his pocket, all nice and cosy, and when I'm awake, I come out to play . . . Oh, I forgot to introduce myself. My name is Johnno. Hello, Suzy. Aren't you going to say hello to me?

SUSAN Sergeant, I'm seventeen years old, not ten.

SERGEANT Sorry. (*To the sock*) Goodnight, Johnno. (*In a squeaky voice*) Goodnight, Clarence. (*Putting away the sock*) The kids down at the mill like him.

SUSAN I'm sure they do. Goodnight, Sergeant.

SERGEANT Goodnight, Miss Dawson. (SUSAN *leaves in a huff.* SERGEANT *adopts a squeaky voice*) Nighty night, Suzy.

(*The* SERGEANT *doesn't know what to do. He looks around the room. Making sure he is not being watched, he opens the music box and steals a handful of biscuits, then he picks up the decanter of sherry and drinks greedily from it. He looks at the level of the liquid, and, seeing that he may have drunk too much, pours lemonade into the decanter up to the previous level. Listening to the music box tune, he carries the box over to the piano. After placing the box on the piano top, he begins to pedal the piano. While he is playing and eating at the same time,* LILLIAN *and* CAPTAIN HENRY *enter.*)

LILLIAN Susan not here?

SERGEANT (*startled, almost choking on his biscuit*) No, missus. She went to bed. She told me to make myself at home before she went. Always wanted to play the piano.

LILLIAN More sherry, Sergeant?

SERGEANT No thanks. I only drink it in moderate amounts.

LILLIAN Susan was probably tired. She's been a rather busy girl lately: she leaves for England very soon. I can well imagine how excited she is. When my father sent me to England I could hardly sleep on the voyage over. And when I saw England! Everywhere I looked . . . I could hardly believe my eyes: green, green, green.

Everything so green, it hurt my eyes. (*Pause.*)

I wonder where my husband is. Maybe he's still at the mill. Some problem or other. (*Gesturing*) All this is his in name only. He got it all by marrying me. He knows nothing about flour or wheat. To be honest he's a bit lost out here. It gives him something to do to go and talk with the workers at the mill. My father wanted a son, naturally, but got a daughter, and when a woman marries she signs over everything to her husband automatically. Don't you think that odd? In reality, if not in theory, I own all the land, the flour mill, the village. Except for the hired hands, everyone of working age works in my mill. I am, I suppose you could say, a Mandarin. Is that the right word? What is a female Mandarin called? (*She looks at* CAPTAIN HENRY *and then at the* SERGEANT.)

SERGEANT An orange.

LILLIAN (*to the* CAPTAIN) Is your Sergeant's stupidity feigned?

SERGEANT It was a joke.

LILLIAN Oh, then it wasn't feigned . . . (*Spotting a large, leather-bound book*) Ah, just the thing. I was looking at it just before you arrived. (*Picking it up*) My visitor's book. I generally have it in the hallway. Not very impressive in the latter section, but earlier on there are some wonderful names. I've kept it since I was a girl. My father was very famous and a lot of famous people used to visit here. So many wonderful names. (*She places the book on the table next to the writing equipment.*) I would be pleased if you would both sign it.

CAPTAIN We'd be delighted.

LILLIAN I'll get the blotting paper. (*She exits. The* SERGEANT *and the* CAPTAIN *sign the book.* LILLIAN *hurries back into the living room.*) It looks like my husband won't be back in time, so I'll tell him when he gets home that you've come and also about the picnic cricket match. (*She goes to blot the book.*) What's this?

CAPTAIN Our signatures.

LILLIAN This!

SERGEANT My signature.

LILLIAN It's an X! (*The* SERGEANT *looks embarrassed.*)

CAPTAIN I'm afraid Sergeant Collins has never been to school, Mrs Dawson.

LILLIAN But an X! Someone will think it's a joke. There are no other Xs in my book.

SERGEANT I'm sorry, missus.

LILLIAN The page will have to be torn out. Perhaps I can use some sort of erasure. (*Heavy footsteps are heard entering the house and stumbling.*) Is that you, George?

(*No answer. Suddenly* GEORGE *appears in the doorway, dirty, wet and swaying with drunkenness.*)

GEORGE I fell in the creek. (*He collapses onto the floor. Blackout.*)

Scene 3

The living room. The next day. SUSAN *is standing in the middle of the room wearing a half-completed dress. Sunlight shines in bands through the unseen slats of venetian blinds.* GEORGE *enters.*

GEORGE Where's your mother?

SUSAN Getting some pins.

GEORGE Have you seen my bike?

SUSAN No. (*Pause.*)

GEORGE Do you want me to close the blinds?

SUSAN Too gloomy.

GEORGE Mum making you a new dress, is she?

SUSAN For the picnic.

GEORGE What picnic?

SUSAN With the soldiers.

GEORGE Why?

LILLIAN (*entering*) Because I thought it would be good manners.

GEORGE How many soldiers are there?

SUSAN Fifty.

GEORGE What? Fifty soldiers here?

LILLIAN At the cricket ground. Captain Henry wanted to know if he could use the ground for a cricket match for his soldiers and I said yes. I also suggested making it into a picnic. (*Placing a wide-brimmed hat on* SUSAN) There, that looks excellent.

SUSAN It's too wide.

LILLIAN It will protect your complexion. You don't want to look like a factory girl, do you? Besides, a wide-brimmed hat – oh, the pins. I forgot the pins. (*She exits.*)

GEORGE (*spotting a beautiful evening dress on a chair*) Your mother made this for you?

SUSAN It arrived this morning from Sydney.

GEORGE You can't use it for a picnic, it's far too good for that.

SUSAN It's not for picnics – it's an evening dress.

GEORGE You won't get much use for it here.

SUSAN I know, it's coming with me to England.

GEORGE Eh?

SUSAN With my other clothes.

GEORGE What's this about England?

SUSAN On my trip.

GEORGE It's definite?

SUSAN Mum made the booking last week.

GEORGE She didn't tell me.

SUSAN You agreed.

GEORGE No, I didn't. You and your mum are always talking about such things. A new house. Trips to England. Living in Sydney . . .

SUSAN I want to see England. To travel.

GEORGE You can travel here.

SUSAN Here? This place? I want to see beautiful cities, learn refinement and be educated in nice things. I want to see and do those things. I can't get them here.

GEORGE It's not my fault. Look, I know it must be hard for a girl as pretty as you to be here –

SUSAN It's not only being here.

GEORGE It's me?

SUSAN Mum told me what happened last night.

GEORGE I fell in the creek. (*Realising* SUSAN *is annoyed with his lie*) And I had a little bit too much.

SUSAN Do you know why I never brought any of my school friends back here to stay in the holidays?

GEORGE You can't say that –

SUSAN It's true. It's true.

GEORGE Don't say that. I . . . I try very hard. I'll try very hard, but please, don't say things like that! (*He hugs her. She goes rigid.*) I love you. You're the most important thing in my life. I've never hurt you. Surely you must realise that. (*Pause.*) When are you going?

SUSAN (*nervously, yelling*) Mum, look in the right drawer.

GEORGE You listen to your mother too much. When are you going?

SUSAN In a month. (*Yelling*) Mum, look in the right drawer.

GEORGE I don't want you to go. You're all I have. I know you think me weak . . . you must believe that I'll do anything for you.

SUSAN You can do Mum and me a favour.

GEORGE I'll do *you* a favour.

SUSAN Don't come and see me off on the ship. (GEORGE *looks stunned.*) You'll be drunk as usual and embarrass everybody. A lot of my friends are coming to see me off.

GEORGE I won't embarrass you.

SUSAN You will. I can't trust you, Dad. You said you'd do me a favour. (*Yelling*) Mum, the right drawer.

LILLIAN (*as she enters*) No need to shout. They were in the left drawer. (*To* GEORGE) I thought you were going to the mill?

GEORGE Uh? The . . . I was looking for my bike.

LILLIAN It's on the front verandah.

(LILLIAN *starts pinning* SUSAN's *dress.*)

GEORGE You're sending her to England.

LILLIAN She'll be staying with Aunt Annie.

SUSAN I want to go.

GEORGE Can't it wait?

LILLIAN She's going. We've discussed this before. She's going to be a great lady. She can't spend the rest of her life in this backwater with riff-raff. She has to learn, and experience what the world has to offer. Hold still, Susan.

GEORGE She'll come back from England like you.

LILLIAN More to her advantage, isn't it?

CAPTAIN (*off*) Mrs Dawson . . . (CAPTAIN HENRY *suddenly arrives at the doorway.*) Mrs Daw – Oh, I'm sorry. I didn't know. Your cook said just to go down the corridor. (*Spotting* GEORGE) Good morning, Mr Dawson. (GEORGE *nods perfunctorily.*)

LILLIAN The cook?

CAPTAIN I knocked on the front door, she answered it.

LILLIAN She should never be allowed out of the kitchen. Never mind, what was it you wanted?

CAPTAIN I'm afraid our cook under-ordered before we left Sydney. New supplies should be coming next week, but we need some flour for the cricket match. Can we buy some from you? Just some for the match. Not much. Cook wants to make bread and cakes. He fancies himself as a bit of a pastry-cook.

LILLIAN It doesn't sound like much. It's a privilege to have you in the district. You can have the flour as a gift. Is that all right, George?

GEORGE Sure.

LILLIAN (*to the* CAPTAIN) Send one of your men over to the mill and ask the foreman, his name is Arthur, to give you what you want from Bin Five.

CAPTAIN That's very kind.

GEORGE Bin Five? You can't use the stuff from Bin Five.

LILLIAN Why not?

GEORGE There's something wrong with it.

LILLIAN Nonsense, I saw it yesterday morning. (*Turning to the* CAPTAIN) Sorry, Captain Henry, I must, in all due honesty, point out that the wheat isn't first class.

CAPTAIN That's all right. It's only for the non-coms. They won't know the difference.

LILLIAN Exactly. Mr Dawson will get the foreman to arrange for the bags to be picked up by your men.

CAPTAIN I'm very grateful, Mrs Dawson. And to you, Mr Dawson. Not many people would be as kind as you to give us such a gift.

LILLIAN Our pleasure. The least we can do. It's a gift like the land my father gave the Government. (*Pause.*)

CAPTAIN I'm sorry for the intrusion.

LILLIAN No apologies necessary, Captain. We were glad to be of help.

CAPTAIN Good morning, Mr Dawson, Mrs Dawson, Miss Dawson, and thank you again. (*He exits.*)

LILLIAN (*to* GEORGE) Why do you make such a fuss?

GEORGE Fuss? How could I compete with your theatrical gestures?

LILLIAN You wouldn't know a magnanimous gesture if it bit you.

GEORGE There's something wrong with the flour in Bin Five.

LILLIAN It's all right. I saw it yesterday.

GEORGE I don't know; it's very grey.

LILLIAN We won't be using it.

GEORGE (*angrily*) Look, I'm telling you there's something wrong with it.

LILLIAN You wouldn't know. Soldiers have the appetites of horses. You could feed them chaff and they wouldn't know the difference. Fix it up with Arthur before lunch. Bin Five. Two bags should be enough. No, better make it four. (GEORGE *begins to go.*) You'll be back for lunch?

GEORGE *No.*

(*He exits. Mother and daughter work on the dress.*)

LILLIAN Don't slouch.

SUSAN I'm tired.

LILLIAN Posture affects beauty. You're not that attractive yet. Beauty flows from within.

SUSAN   I shall be the only female at this picnic, won't I?

LILLIAN   I'm not female?

SUSAN   I mean, unattached.

LILLIAN   I'm sure the Captain will tell his boys to be on their best behaviour.

SUSAN   I guess I'll be extremely popular.

LILLIAN   A seventy-two-year-old spinster with rickets would be popular at such a gathering if she were the only female.

SUSAN   Well that's a comfort.

LILLIAN   You need to be cut down a peg or two occasionally. (*Pause.*) Don't forget, tomorrow evening you have Mrs Harrison and her son. (*As* SUSAN *looks annoyed*) I did my duty when I was your age. We must help those who are less fortunate than ourselves. It is our duty, our good works. (*She sticks in another pin.*) Last night I heard you moaning.

SUSAN   Me?

LILLIAN   Perhaps you were dreaming? I came and stood at your door.

SUSAN   I don't remember.

LILLIAN   When you're in England you'll learn more restraint; cultivation will follow. Look at your father, no restraint. The good thing about Australians is that they have learnt not to indulge in soul-searching. Your father, as usual, is the exception to this rule, hence his drinking. Sometimes I believe he's going around the bend.

SUSAN   Why did you marry him?

LILLIAN   (*smiling*) Momentary insanity. In his own way he is kind, but he's so weak he can afford to be kind. (LILLIAN *steps back and looks at the dress.*) Hmmmm, not too bad. (*She goes to the small table and pours herself a glass of sherry from the decanter.*) Men. When you're in England, my dear, you'll think the men are different. Better. More civilised. Be warned, only their techniques are different. (*She takes a sip of sherry and is disgusted by the taste. She holds the glass up to the light.*) Strange . . . (*Blackout.*)

Scene 4

Evening. The verandah. Cicadas. SUSAN *is sitting in a cane chair.* MRS HARRISON *and her son,* ANDY, *are sitting on a bench facing her.* SUSAN, *bored, listens to* MRS HARRISON *laboriously reading from a children's book.* MRS HARRISON *is barely literate. Her son,* ANDY, *is a half-wit.*

MRS HARRISON   The boy sits . . . on . . . on . . . the chair. The girl says . . . (*She says 'says' to rhyme with 'daze'.*)

SUSAN   Says.

MRS HARRISON   Sorry. Says. The girl . . . says . . . I . . . I . . .

SUSAN   (*knowing the book off by heart*) Look.

MRS HARRISON   Sorry. Look. I look at the boy. The boy e . . . e . . .

SUSAN   Eats.

MRS HARRISON   Sorry. Eats. Eats too much. He will b . . . b . . . bust.

SUSAN   Break.

MRS HARRISON   Break the chair.

SUSAN   (*unenthusiastically*) Very good. Next page.

MRS HARRISON   Oh, good. The one with the picture of the beautiful girl. (*To* ANDY *who is squirming with boredom*) Be still.

(LILLIAN *comes out of the house onto the verandah.*)

LILLIAN   Good evening, Mrs Harrison.

MRS HARRISON   (*standing*) Good evening, Mrs Dawson.

LILLIAN   Sit down, Mrs Harrison. Good evening, Andy. (ANDY *appears not to have heard.*)

MRS HARRISON   (*grabbing her son's hand to gain his attention*) Say hello to Mrs Dawson, Andy.

ANDY   Hello, Mrs Dawson.

LILLIAN   (*to* MRS HARRISON) Susan keeping you busy?

MRS HARRISON   We're on to the third story.

LILLIAN   Soon there will be no stopping you.

MRS HARRISON   I hope so. (LILLIAN *looks at* ANDY *who is scratching his knee with intense concentration.* MRS HARRISON *spots her.*) I'm afraid Andy will never learn how to read. I think he likes the stories. As long as he likes something.

LILLIAN   I'm sure he does.

MRS HARRISON   I told meself when me husband ran off after he saw how Andy was turning out. I said, no, Andy's not going to end up in a looneybin. (SUSAN *giggles.* LILLIAN *and* MRS HARRISON *look at her sternly.*) He's got to end up living proper in *this* world. That's why I bring him here, Mrs Dawson. He'll never learn to read or write, I know that now, but he'll learn good manners, the right things, the *proper things.* It's not too late, is it?

LILLIAN   Certainly not. I'm sure he appreciates what you're doing. Learning to read at your age – he knows your sacrifices. Would you like a cup of tea? I'm about to have one. Susan? (SUSAN *nods.*) I'll bring them out. And a glass of lemonade for Andy. (*She returns inside.*)

SUSAN All right, let's go on.

ANDY No, no, no.

MRS HARRISON Andy! (*He squirms on the bench.*)

ANDY Mummy.

MRS HARRISON What do you want?

ANDY The tiger and the butter.

SUSAN Oh, no, Andy. You must be bored by that.

MRS HARRISON Tell it quickly, Susan, then he'll calm down. He loves the way you tell it.

SUSAN If I tell the story will you be a good boy?

ANDY Yes.

SUSAN (*from memory*) One day, while out walking, Little Black Sambo saw three tigers creeping after him. He was so scared that he began to run and the three ferocious tigers chased after him, snarling and growling. He ran fast as he could to the nearest tree and climbed up it. The tigers couldn't climb after him so they started to chew the tree. To stop them Little Black Sambo took off his clothes and threw them down to the tigers who loved them so much that they fought for them. One of the tigers grabbed all the clothes and the others chased him around the tree faster and faster, while Little Black Sambo yelled for help, crying out, 'The tigers are going to eat me up'.

(GEORGE *enters wheeling his bicycle.*)

ANDY 'The tigers are coming to chew me up . . . the tigers are coming to chew me up'.

MRS HARRISON Evening, Mr Dawson.

GEORGE Hello, Mrs Harrison. Andy.

MRS HARRISON Susan's telling him a story.

GEORGE Not 'The Tigers and the Butter' again?

ANDY (*suddenly spotting something off stage and pointing*) Look, look, in the tree.

GEORGE (*laughing*) There's nothing there, Andy.

(ANDY *suddenly jumps up and runs off stage.*)

MRS HARRISON Andy! (*They watch him clamber up the tree.*) Up the tree again. What a boy!

GEORGE It's the only pepper tree in the district. I think he likes it.

MRS HARRISON Honestly, sometimes I don't know what I'm going to do with him, Mr Dawson.

GEORGE He'll be all right.

MRS HARRISON I don't know. You've always been kind to him, but not everyone is like you. People can be cruel to people like Andy. A few weeks ago I took him to Annimogie to me sister's and he disappeared, just like that. Quick as a flash. I searched for him all afternoon and found him huddled outside the slaughter-yard covered in blood. I said, 'What's the matter, Andy?' He didn't make sense. Babbled. You know. Later on I found out he had wandered into the slaughter-yard. The men thought he was funny. You know Andy, Mr Dawson. Do anything. So they shoved him inside a bullock carcass. For a lark. A lark! He was hollering to be let out, but they held him there. Thought it a great joke. He has nightmares about it. Wouldn't you?

ANDY (*yelling, laughing*) Ohhhhh! Yeeeeehhhhh!

MRS HARRISON Come down, Andy. Oh, I am sorry, Mr Dawson.

(LILLIAN *comes out with the tea.*)

LILLIAN What's happening?

SUSAN Andy's up the tree again.

LILLIAN Andy, come down and have a glass of lemonade.

ANDY (*gleefully*) No, no, no.

LILLIAN Don't worry, he'll come down when he sees us having our tea. (*They prepare to sit down for tea.*)

MRS HARRISON (*watching* ANDY) Andy! Stop that! (*The others look back at the tree.*) Andy, I want you to stop that.

LILLIAN (*standing*) Susan, go inside.

SUSAN What's the matter?

MRS HARRISON Put them back on. Andy, put them back on. (ANDY'S *trousers are flung down at their feet.*) Andy! Naughty boy!

(GEORGE *laughs.* SUSAN *is fascinated.* LILLIAN *is annoyed.*)

ANDY (*triumphantly*) Yeeeeehhhhhhhhh! (*Blackout.*)

Scene 5

A church bell rings. Lights slowly up. In the penumbra we see two men cutting wheat with sickles. Nearby, lying in the grass, smoking a cigarette and staring at the sky, is a SOLDIER, O'NEILL. *As the two men cut the wheat, they sing.*

TOM and PETER
    Old Johnny's up at the crack of dawn
    Then he kisses his wife goodbye.
    He goes out into his fields
    Where the wheat is four foot high.

    The soil is red, the wheat is brown
    And the sky is as blue as the sea.
    Old Johnny wipes sweat from his brow
    And leaves a trail of wheat on the ground.

(TOM stops and wipes his forehead.)

TOM   *(to* O'NEILL*)* You lot never do any work.
O'NEILL   You're jealous.
TOM   *(returning to work, to* PETER*)* We'll stop in half a mo' and have a drink.
PETER   That's all right by me. *(Silence as they cut the wheat.)*
TOM   Oh, here she comes.
PETER   Who is it?
TOM   You know that fellow who got you the job?
PETER   George.
TOM   His wife, Mrs Dawson.

(MRS DAWSON and SUSAN enter in their Sunday best. PRIVATE O'NEILL *stands up, looking uncomfortable.)*

LILLIAN   Hello, Tom. No church today?
TOM   I think me missus is going.
LILLIAN   She hasn't been in fifteen years.
TOM   She keeps promising to go.
LILLIAN   A poor excuse. And who are you?
O'NEILL   Private O'Neill. I'm waiting for help to arrive from camp. My wagon is broken down. Broken axle.
LILLIAN   Shouldn't you go and tell them you need help?
O'NEILL   Private Johnson has gone to get help.
LILLIAN   *(looking at* PETER*)* Suddenly strangers everywhere. And who are you?
PETER   Peter Blackwood, missus.
TOM   Mr Dawson gave him a job.
LILLIAN   I do wish he'd tell me these things. I – incidentally, Tom, what are you doing harvesting on Sunday?

TOM   You said last week that I could have the wheat growing along the track as long as I cut it in my spare time.
LILLIAN   So I did. I wonder why I never remember my generosities. Perhaps I'm growing forgetful. Paddling up the River Lethe on my bark canoe. What about along there, are you going to cut that for yourself? Perhaps we should establish a boundary; for both our sakes.

(TOM and LILLIAN go upstage. While they talk about the boundary, PETER continues working. SUSAN and O'NEILL suddenly become aware that they are near each other.)

SUSAN   How long will your friends be?
O'NEILL   *(shyly)* Excuse me?
SUSAN   To bring the new axle.
O'NEILL   Don't know. Shouldn't be long now. *(Silence.)*
SUSAN   You . . . are you with the other soldiers over at the camp?
O'NEILL   Yes. *(Uncomfortable silence.)*
SUSAN   Did you – }
O'NEILL   I saw – } *(together)*

(They laugh as they both speak at once.)

SUSAN   What's in the wagon?
O'NEILL   Wood. For firewood.
SUSAN   We don't see many men in uniforms.
O'NEILL   I've never seen so much wheat. *(They both laugh.)*
SUSAN   You're from the city?
O'NEILL   Sydney.
SUSAN   Why did you join the army then?
O'NEILL   Something to do. Beats working in a factory.
LILLIAN   *(calling, irritated at seeing her daughter with a* SOLDIER*)* Susan, come along or we'll be late for church.
SUSAN   Sorry. I must be off. Goodbye.
O'NEILL   Bye.
LILLIAN   Private, I think your friends are coming down the track.
O'NEILL   Thank you, Mrs Dawson. *(He walks off left; they walk off right.)*
LILLIAN   *(just before exiting)* Tom, at least take the afternoon off.
TOM   Yes, missus. *(To* PETER, *after* LILLIAN *and* SUSAN *have gone)* That's easy for her to say.

(The two men sing as they cut wheat.)

TOM and PETER
    Old Johnny's back is bent for hours
    From morning until dusk;

But he has to harvest the wheat
Before the rain brings rust.

At twilight he returns home,
He has a beer and eats his meat.
Later on he makes love to his wife
And when he's asleep he dreams of
wheat.

(GEORGE *enters, walking his bicycle.*)

TOM   Morning, Mr Dawson.

GEORGE   Morning, Tom, Peter. (PETER *nods.*) What are you doing working this morning?

TOM   Mrs Dawson said me and me missus could have the wheat along the track. Pete's boarding with us and he's helping me.

GEORGE   (*to* PETER) I was hoping I'd find you.

PETER   You torn down my hut yet?

GEORGE   No, why?

PETER   I still got a few things in there.

GEORGE   What about your squeeze box? (TOM *moves away and cuts wheat upstage.*)

PETER   I got it.

GEORGE   There's a cricket match picnic thing next Saturday, would you sing a few songs for us? You know, just a few. (PETER *shrugs.*) I was hoping you'd say yes.

PETER   I'm leaving Tuesday.

GEORGE   Leaving?

PETER   Made enough money.

GEORGE   But that's hardly anything.

PETER   I don't need much.

GEORGE   Tuesday? I got you the job. I found you.

PETER   I wasn't that desperate . . .

GEORGE   Look, Wednesday, Thursday, Friday, that's only three more days – then you can sing for us on Saturday.

PETER   I'd sooner . . . you know –

GEORGE   (*almost threatening*) I never pay anyone on a Tuesday. (*Pause.*)

PETER   (*realising* GEORGE *is blackmailing him*) Saturday?

GEORGE   After the picnic.

PETER   All right.

GEORGE   Just a few tunes. (*Watching* PETER *return to work*) How come you're not going to use the harvester?

PETER   Can't work it along the track.

GEORGE   You've used a sickle before?

PETER   Used to.

GEORGE   So you used to work on a farm?

PETER   Hundreds. I'm a jack of all trades, master of none.

GEORGE   Can I have a look?

PETER   (*handing him the sickle*) Careful, it's sharp.

GEORGE   Looks it.

PETER   You ever worked in the fields?

GEORGE   Me? No. (*Swishing it back and forth*) Not bad.

PETER   It's pretty good.

GEORGE   Let's see. I hold it like this? (PETER *nods.*) All right . . . let's see how it cuts. (GEORGE *starts to cut the wheat. He looks inexperienced.*) Certainly gives you a bad back. Bloody sharp.

PETER   Careful. No, hold the handle further back, you'll . . . here, let me show you. (PETER *goes to grab the sickle.* GEORGE *does not notice.*)

GEORGE   Like this? (*Suddenly one of* GEORGE'*s swishes of the sickle catches* PETER *on the arm. He cries out in alarm.* GEORGE *drops the sickle.*) I'm sorry.

PETER   It's all right . . . just caught it.

GEORGE   It's bleeding.

TOM   What happened?

GEORGE   I accidentally cut him.

TOM   Here. (TOM *wraps his handkerchief around the wound.*)

PETER   It's all right. Only a nick. I'll be right.

GEORGE   You sure?

PETER   Yes.

GEORGE   I'm terribly sorry.

PETER   It's nothing. (TOM *finishes wrapping* PETER'*s arm.*)

TOM   That should do the job. Go home to me wife, she'll put some disinfectant on it.

PETER   No, I'll stay here. If we leave it until next week, the wheat will be rotten. Let's get on with it.

TOM   You sure?

PETER   (*irritated*) Yes. (*Picking up the sickle*) Let's get moving.

GEORGE   (*quietly*) Sorry, Peter. Tom?

TOM   Yes, Mr Dawson.

GEORGE   Did you see my wife this morning?

TOM   Went that way. To church.

GEORGE   Right. Sunday.

(*He turns his bicycle around in the opposite direction. The church bell sounds in the distance. He watches* TOM *and* PETER *work for a few moments, then walks off with his bike. Blackout.*)

Scene 6

The rear of the church. The RECTOR *is in a small dilapidated shed upstage.* LILLIAN *arrives.*

LILLIAN   Rector?

RECTOR   Here, Mrs Dawson. (*He appears from inside the shed, dragging a long box.*)

LILLIAN   You wanted to see me?

RECTOR   (*fiddling with the box, trying to open it*) Yes, before you went home.

LILLIAN   Do you want some help?

RECTOR   No, no. Ah, there. (*He opens the box.*) Well . . . (*He inspects the contents of the box quickly and then turns his attention back to* LILLIAN.) A very small congregation today.

LILLIAN   As the years pass we seem to be dwindling.

RECTOR   Dwindling at an alarming rate.

LILLIAN   I don't know why. Years ago, before you came, it was packed. Oh, I don't mean it's your fault. Your sermons are excellent. Times change, I guess. My workers don't seem to be as interested in religion as they used to.

RECTOR   It would appear so. (*Looking at the box again*) Ah! (*He takes out two croquet mallets.*) Years since I've seen these. Remember, this back lawn saw many a titanic struggle. You were very good at it, Mrs Dawson. I – funny (*spotting paintings on the two mallet heads*), someone has painted on these mallet heads. Look . . . a woman with a smile and a man with a smile. Who could have done a thing like that?

LILLIAN   Surely you haven't forgotten? That itinerant painter you got to paint those scenes from the life of Jesus on the church walls.

RECTOR   Those disgusting scenes.

LILLIAN   Obscene. You and Mr Norman had to paint over them. Revolting paintings. How anyone could even imagine such things is beyond me; but he did have a marvellous technique.

RECTOR   That weekend we spent painting over his obscenities, we found other paintings, little, delicate ones on the backs of prayer books, behind the altar and now here. (*Looking at the mallet head closely*) Do you think that one looks like you?

LILLIAN   No.

RECTOR   Wonder who it is? It does look like you. (*He takes a croquet ball from the box and puts it on the ground.*) Pity the cows have been let loose here. Impossible to play now. (*Hitting the ball*) Impossible. Oops, I think I've chipped off your nose. (*He examines the painting on the mallet head.*) Oh, well, the back garden of Annimogie Church will be perfect. I'll take them with me.

LILLIAN   I'm sorry to rush you, Rector, but I must be home by one for lunch.

RECTOR   Of course, of course. This has been difficult for me. I tried to mention it in today's sermon, but . . . how can I explain this? (*Pause.*) As from the end of next month, I will not be coming here.

LILLIAN   Not coming? You're sending a replacement, of course?

RECTOR   I'm sorry, no. I've talked to the Church Board and they see no sense in me having to do early services in Annimogie just to come here to preach to eight or nine people. I don't agree with them, but they think this congregation should travel to Annimogie every Sunday. I know this must upset you, and how much this little church means to you, but, as you said before, attendances have fallen off. I can't argue with the Board.

LILLIAN   My father's workers built this. Dozens of them.

RECTOR   It's one of the most beautiful churches in the state. A lovely church. But I must have a flock to preach to. (*Silence.*)

LILLIAN   I understand. I'm sorry, Rector, to seem annoyed. There's so much space out here that it's very easy to lose a sense of proportion. I'm guilty of it myself, sometimes. I've tried to get the workers interested. Perhaps once they see you go they'll realise how foolish they've been. Strange, I have the same number of workers as my father had, but everything seems smaller.

RECTOR   You'll come to Annimogie of a Sunday?

LILLIAN   Of course. You'll be preaching here for a few more Sundays yet?

RECTOR   Two. (*Pause.*)

LILLIAN   I feel as though I have let you down.

RECTOR   It's the times, Mrs Dawson. Religion means very little to the younger generation.

LILLIAN   I'm afraid you may be right, Rector. But Australians have never had a sense of the religious, no sense of occasion

301

either; if the Apocalypse came they wouldn't know it; they'd think it was a public holiday. Next week, seeing it's your penultimate visit, could we have a special memorial service for Mrs Burge's husband?

RECTOR What happened?

LILLIAN He fell into a wheat bin a few days ago. Drowned in the wheat. The other workers saw him fall in, but couldn't get to him in time. They even heard him crying for help as the wheat smothered him. When they pulled him out his mouth was filled with wheat. If he hadn't cried for help he would have stayed alive much longer, perhaps even been saved.

RECTOR I never knew him.

LILLIAN He wasn't religious; neither is his wife. But I feel it's only good manners to have a memorial service.

RECTOR Of course. If only people were as well-mannered as you, Mrs Dawson. Will you excuse me for a moment?

LILLIAN Certainly.

(*The* RECTOR *exits.* LILLIAN *kicks the mallet angrily. As she stoops to pick it up she spots someone off stage.*)

LILLIAN Julie? Julie, is that you? Come here. (JULIE *enters, pregnant.*) What are you doing slinking around the side of the church?

JULIE I wanted to see the Rector.

LILLIAN (*regarding her appearance*) What has happened?

JULIE I . . .

LILLIAN Did I miss your marriage?

JULIE No. I'm . . . I'm not married, Mrs Dawson. I wanted to talk to the Rector about it.

LILLIAN What a silly thing to do.

JULIE I know. I didn't know.

LILLIAN I wondered why I hadn't seen you in church lately. Your mother said you were ill – a peculiar illness. What about the father? (JULIE *shrugs.*) You don't know who he is?

JULIE Oh, yes. Only he won't marry me. Can't.

LILLIAN Did he promise to marry you?

JULIE Yes, but there were problems.

LILLIAN Problems can be solved.

JULIE I don't think we would be a suitable couple.

LILLIAN My dear, marriage has nothing to do with suitability. If it did, no one would be married. Take Mrs Bentley. Married three times. Widowed three times. She hasn't given up. I hear she's marrying some fellow in Annimogie. She respected the institution of marriage and her deceased husbands. Why, she has their ashes in an urn in the living room; their ashes are separated by doilies, of course. See? Marriage should be a part of you as life and death. You must marry your fellow, even if it means a lifetime of misery. Your child must have a name. Do you see that?

JULIE Yes, Mrs Dawson.

LILLIAN Is the fellow from the mill? (JULIE *nods.*) Ask him to marry you, if he doesn't want to, I'll go and talk to him. I hear that the visits of Mrs Lillian Dawson have surprising results! Do it soon, Julie. Don't dawdle over it. It would be nice if the Rector conducted the marriage ceremony before he leaves.

JULIE He's leaving?

LILLIAN Only two more Sundays here. So you must hurry. He's going to Annimogie. Goodness, what's all this about Annimogie? The town is over-rated as the next best cultural centre to Broken Hill – why, I once invited the ladies of the Annimogie Music and Dramatic Arts Appreciation Society out here to hear my new piano rolls. They swooned over the Mozart thinking it was Beethoven, then attacked the savories with a violence not seen since Attila the Hun. Oh, dear, it must be nearing one. I'd better be going. Can you tell the Rector I will see him next Sunday? (JULIE *nods distractedly.*) And you take my advice.

(LILLIAN *exits. After a silence the* RECTOR *enters with a book in his hand.*)

RECTOR Mrs Dawson . . . (*Spotting* JULIE *and jolting*) Julie!

JULIE You didn't tell me you're only here two more Sundays.

RECTOR Now listen –

JULIE You'll have to marry me.

RECTOR You know the problems.

JULIE Leave your wife. You said you would. If you don't, I'll tell everybody. (*Silence.*)

RECTOR All right.

(*Lights fade on the couple. They remain as silhouettes, separate from each other, as downstage, in the penumbra,* TOM *and* PETER *cut the wheat at twilight. They sing, moving slowly off stage as night falls.*)

TOM and PETER
>   When old Johnny dreams, he dreams of
>   wheat,
>   He dreams of nothing else.
>   Year in, year out,
>   Through the flood, through the drought.

Scene 7

Outside the mill. Day. ARTHUR *and two*
WORKMEN *are sitting down drinking beer from*
mugs. ANDY *is wandering around near the*
wheat bags.

ARTHUR   (*to* TERRY) Haven't we got a glass?
TERRY   (*referring to their mugs*) Best we can
do. (*Pause.*)
BERT   Shit it's hot. (*Silence.*)
TERRY   Church yesterday, Arthur?
ARTHUR   Yeah, I'll be all right when I knock
on the Gates.
TERRY   (*to* BERT) Get him, will you? Your
nose is pretty brown, Arthur.
ARTHUR   It's how you get to be foreman; rise
above the shit, so to speak.

(*The three laugh.*)

BERT   I'd hate to be married to that bitch.
ARTHUR   Mrs Dawson?
BERT   Who do yer think? Hullo, Mafeking
'bout to be rescued.

(HIGGS, *a rather frail-looking* SOLDIER,
enters.)

HIGGS   I'm supposed to pick up some flour,
do any of you know anything about it?
BERT   The foreman.

(HIGGS *looks at* ANDY *who has suddenly*
come into view. Realising he is not the
foreman, he looks at ARTHUR.)

HIGGS   Do you know anything –
ARTHUR   (*pointing to four bags*) We were
expecting you earlier.
HIGGS   The wagon broke down.
TERRY   God, I'd hate to see you lot in a war.

(HIGGS *points to the bags.*)

HIGGS   These?

(ARTHUR *nods.* HIGGS *goes to the bags. He*
tries to lift one but it's so heavy he can barely
do so. The three men are considerably
amused.)

ARTHUR   Heavy, mate?
HIGGS   I thought they'd be smaller. Can you
give us a hand?

BERT   Sorry, mate, lunch break. Besides,
they're light as a feather. (HIGGS *tries*
again, but fails.) Jesus! (BERT *goes over and*
lifts up the sack easily.) See? What are yer, a
weakling or something? Light as a feather.
Easy. Look, turn around. Once it's on your
back, it's easy. (HIGGS *staggers when the*
sack is thrown on his back. The three men
laugh.) See? Come on, keep yer eyes on the
wagon and think about sex. Here, I'll give
yer a push.

(HIGGS *staggers out, much to the amusement*
of the three men.)

ARTHUR   Christ – you seen 'em all? They're
all like that galah . . . I saw 'em Saturday
morning marching down Watson's track,
tripping and falling. (*They laugh.* GEORGE
enters. ARTHUR *stands.*) Mr Dawson.
GEORGE   Lunch?
ARTHUR   Just started.
GEORGE   A bit late.
ARTHUR   Too busy to take it before. You
know, Mr Dawson: harvest time.
GEORGE   Christ it's hot – must be over a
hundred already.
ARTHUR   Want a drink? Homebrew.
TERRY   Don't worry, Mr Dawson, my wife
made it. (*They laugh.*)
ARTHUR   (*to* TERRY) Go inside and get Mr
Dawson a mug.

(TERRY *exits and* HIGGS *returns.*)

GEORGE   Bloody soldiers everywhere. What's
he doing here?
ARTHUR   Picking up the bags of flour. You
know, Mrs Dawson's gift.

(BERT *goes over to* HIGGS.)

GEORGE   (*to* ARTHUR) Forgot to pick up the
delivery book on Friday. Mrs Dawson
wants to see it.
BERT   (*to* HIGGS) Even though it's my lunch
hour I'll give yer a hand. (*He throws another*
bag of flour on HIGGS' *back. The* SOLDIER
staggers and nearly falls.) Upsadaisy. What's
yer name?
HIGGS   Private Higgs.

(TERRY *returns with a mug and pours a beer*
for GEORGE.)

BERT   All right, Higgs. Eyes on yer wagon,
thoughts on sex. Righto. (BERT *pushes him*
off. HIGGS *exits with the bag.*)
ARTHUR   Lousy stuff, Mr Dawson. (TERRY
gives the mug of beer to GEORGE.)

GEORGE (*to* TERRY) Thanks. (*To* ARTHUR) Eh?

ARTHUR The flour, it's shit stuff, wouldn't give it to a dog.

GEORGE Mrs Dawson's decision, not mine. Tell her if you like. (*Sarcastically*) I'm sure you will, Arthur. (*Pause.*) Oh, by the way . . . on the way over here I saw the harvester stopped in the middle of the field near the creek. The bloody thing is always breaking down.

ARTHUR Everything's under control. That new fellow you got – he and Tom are repairing it.

GEORGE Pete?

ARTHUR Yes. He's supposed to be pretty good with machines. We need someone like that. He's pretty handy.

GEORGE Well, I guess I can choose as good as my wife, eh? He's staying until Saturday. I'll try and change his mind about going. You heard his squeeze box?

ARTHUR It's a bit hard with his hand – don't go swinging that sickle again.

GEORGE Don't go trying to add figures again, Arthur. (HIGGS *returns.*)

TERRY Better watch out Bert, he'll faint.

BERT (*ready to load* HIGGS *up again*) Not my Higgsy. Will yer Higgsy? (*He loads another sack on* HIGGS.)

HIGGS (*irritated by the ribbing, but pretending not to hear them*) Thanks. (*He staggers off slowly.*)

TERRY There goes a prime specimen of Australian manhood.

ARTHUR Saw Miss Dawson riding her horse this morning. First time I've seen her since she returned for her holidays. Certainly grown this past year.

GEORGE Too much. She wants to go to England and become a lady or something. Bloody British.

ARTHUR Careful, Mr Dawson. Bert'll get offended. (*They all laugh.*) Bert, give us the plum in your voice. Go on, like the other day.

BERT (*imitating an English upper-class accent*) I went to the Queen's garden-party where we ate tarts which made us all break wind – it was a tarty farty party. (*They all laugh.*)

TERRY Hello, old Higgs can't put it into the wagon.

BERT Give 'er the old 'eave 'oe, Higgsy.

GEORGE Is that Andy?

ARTHUR Been hanging around all morning.

GEORGE He's likely to fall into one of the bins or on one of the machines. I told you before, Arthur. (*Calling*) Andy, come over here. Why doesn't his mother control him?

ARTHUR Control Andy? Bloody impossible controlling that moron. (ANDY *enters slowly, aware he's been doing something wrong.*)

GEORGE Didn't I tell you, Andy. You're not to play around here. Didn't I tell you about Mr Burge? Where's your mum?

ANDY Home. (HIGGS *enters.*)

BERT Come on Higgsy. One more and we'll give yer a beer.

GEORGE She know you're gone? (ANDY *doesn't answer.*)

BERT (*throwing the bag on* HIGGS' *shoulder*) Last one, this'll be easy. (HIGGS *starts to walk off, but stops and, like a man with rubber legs, collapses.*) Jesus fuckin' Christ! (BERT *laughs, as does* TERRY.)

ARTHUR (*laughing*) Get him on his feet, Bert.

(BERT *goes over and lifts up* HIGGS.)

HIGGS I'll just drag it.

BERT Over my dead body. You want people to think yer piss-weak? Upsadaisy, Higgsy. (BERT *places the bag on* HIGGS' *shoulder.*) This time. Come on, yer can do it. Come on. After this, we'll give yer a cool beer. Think of a nice cool beer. (HIGGS *slowly staggers out.*)

ARTHUR Want another beer, Mr Dawson?

GEORGE Love it, but I'd better take Andy home.

ARTHUR He'll be all right here.

GEORGE No, he won't. Andy! (GEORGE *gets the attention of* ANDY, *who has been watching* HIGGS *exit painfully.*) Come on, home. (GEORGE *grabs* ANDY *by the hand and they begin to exit.*)

ARTHUR See you tomorrow, Mr Dawson. Hey, do you want the delivery book?

GEORGE (*without turning*) Tomorrow. (*To* ANDY) What are we going to do with you?

ANDY Is Susan going to read 'The Tiger and the Butter'?

GEORGE No. I'll take you home. Your mum'll be worried.

ANDY Mum said she was going to learn to read 'The Tiger and the Butter' and tell it to me over and over and over . . . (GEORGE *and* ANDY *exit.*)

ARTHUR What a pair! (HIGGS *returns.*)

BERT   Higgsy! Great job. The Army'll be proud of yer.

HIGGS   I'm looking forward to that beer.

BERT   Beer? What beer? Know anything 'bout a beer, Arthur?

ARTHUR   Beer? (*To* TERRY) You know anything about a beer?

HIGGS   (*to* BERT) You said that I'd get a beer if I carried that last sack.

BERT   Did I? Did I say that, Art? (ARTHUR *shakes his head.*) No, see, even the foreman says no. Good job, though. See yer later.

HIGGS   You bastards. (*He turns to exit.* BERT *holds out a bottle of beer.*)

BERT   (*smiling*) Higgsy. (HIGGS *looks back.*) Have a beer.

(*All, including* HIGGS, *laugh. They freeze, disappearing into shadows, while a penny whistle plays the 'Nothing But Wheat' tune.*)

Act II

Scene 1

Daylight. The sound of a crow. Under the shade of a ficus are a long table and chairs facing an unseen cricket ground. CAPTAIN HENRY, SUSAN, LILLIAN *and* GEORGE *sit at the table. They have finished their meal. In the centre of the table is a bowl of small oranges. Everyone drinks lemonade.* SUSAN *rises and walks upstage where she throws the crust of a sandwich onto the ground.*

LILLIAN   (*turning around and spotting what* SUSAN *is doing*) How many times, Susan . . . eat the crusts, you're not a baby.

SUSAN   The birds like them.

LILLIAN   More lemonade, Captain?

CAPTAIN   Thank you. The meal was delicious.

LILLIAN   I'll tell the cook. She'll be . . . tickled pink. (*Looking at the cricket ground*) The soldiers look as though they're getting ready for the game.

CAPTAIN   I think our cook made too much for them.

LILLIAN   I always think that it's better to see food still remaining after a meal, than no food at all. (SUSAN *stares at the unseen* SOLDIERS.) Susan, unless you've got a hat, don't stand in the sun. Come here in the shade. Where is your hat?

SUSAN   (*returning to her chair*) On my chair.

LILLIAN   (*to the* CAPTAIN) Have to be careful. Susan has skin like me. When I

was her age I got sunstroke. I woke to find myself surrounded by a veil of skirts. I had been unconscious for over a minute. (*To* SUSAN) You'll get freckles. (*To the* CAPTAIN) My father planted this ficus nearly fifty years ago – when he first came here. Gigantic, isn't it? (*Slight pause.*) When do you think I should make my speech?

CAPTAIN   We're almost ready, I think. (*Calling*) Sergeant!

GEORGE   How long will the match go for?

CAPTAIN   All afternoon.

SERGEANT   (*entering*) Yes, Sir.

CAPTAIN   Are they ready to start the match?

SERGEANT   Nearly.

CAPTAIN   How was your lunch?

SERGEANT   Delicious. Corporal Grimmett did us proud. (*He picks up an orange and looks astonished as he feels it.*)

LILLIAN   Cotton wool. They're not in season yet.

SERGEANT   Looks like the real thing.

LILLIAN   That's the intention.

CAPTAIN   Sergeant, round up the men in front of here, will you?

SERGEANT   Yes, Sir.

CAPTAIN   Have they picked the captains yet?

SERGEANT   I'll find out. (*He puts the orange back in the bowl and exits.*)

LILLIAN   Sergeant Collins has a ferocious appetite.

CAPTAIN   It's the only ferocious thing about him.

LILLIAN   (*to* GEORGE) Do you wish to address the troops too?

GEORGE   They're only here to play cricket.

LILLIAN   (*to the* CAPTAIN) He has no sense of occasion.

SERGEANT   (*off*) Just about ready, Sir.

LILLIAN   (*looking at unseen troops*) The majority of them going to watch?

CAPTAIN   Cricket has eleven a side, so many have to.

LILLIAN   Though I suppose many of them would enjoy watching rather than playing in this heat.

CAPTAIN   Excuse me, Mrs Dawson.

LILLIAN   Certainly. (CAPTAIN HENRY *stands and addresses the troops.*)

CAPTAIN   Thank you, Sergeant. Before the game begins I would like to thank, on behalf of us all, Mr and Mrs Dawson who provided the flour for your special luncheon. Although I haven't tasted your lunch, Sergeant Collins has assured me that

305

it was excellent. I would also like to thank Mr and Mrs Dawson for the use of their cricket ground. Before the toss of the coin, Mrs Dawson would like to say a few words. (*As* CAPTAIN HENRY *sits,* LILLIAN *stands.*)

LILLIAN Thank you, Captain Henry. Although your Captain has thanked Mr Dawson and myself, I feel we must let you know what a privilege it is for us to have members of the Australian Army here using our playing field. I know you wish to get on with the game, but you must indulge me, for a moment, as it's not often we have soldiers here. In my own way, I want to thank you. I was going to read you parts of Tennyson's *Idylls of a King*, a magnificent and stirring work which, no doubt, some of you may have read, but unfortunately my copy is ruined, having been attacked by some sort of bookworm. (*She pauses and laughs, but as no one else gets the joke, continues.*) However, I remembered an appropriate poem in an anthology called *Seasons of Peace and War*. The poem is called 'Pure at Heart' and I know it off by heart. It has small faults as poetry, but it contains a message which is eternally true.

'Pure at Heart'
Look at the infidels, eyeing us with hate,
Their hearts are full of darkness and
  guile.
Everything they touch, they defile.
To them, we must stand firm like a
  bronze gate.
We stand proudly, our souls sparkling
  clean,
From the infidel we stand apart,
Our morals pure as is our heart,
Our eyes crystal clear and serene.

(LILLIAN *pauses after the word 'serene' and* CAPTAIN HENRY, *thinking it is the end of the poem, begins to applaud and is embarrassed as* LILLIAN *continues.*)

But if the infidels want us to fight
Their black-hearted souls will
Experience our goodness and our might.

(*Silence. The* CAPTAIN *applauds; the* SOLDIERS *follow his lead.*)

CAPTAIN Thank you, Mrs Dawson. The two captains, please. (*Two* SOLDIERS *dressed in khaki shorts and singlets enter.*)

SERGEANT (*announcing them*) Corporal Burke and Private MacDonald.

CAPTAIN (*taking a coin out of his pocket*) Will you toss this, Mrs Dawson?

LILLIAN (*standing*) Certainly.

CAPTAIN (*to* SOLDIERS) Call when Mrs Dawson tosses it.

LILLIAN Ready? Here goes. (*She tosses it into the air.*)

BURKE Heads.

MACDONALD Tails.

LILLIAN I'll wager on heads myself. (*Looking at it*) Ah, yes. King George.

BURKE (*to* MACDONALD) We'll bat.

CAPTAIN Thank you gentlemen. (*The* SOLDIERS *exit.*)

LILLIAN I always thought they dressed in white to play cricket.

CAPTAIN We didn't bring our whites with us. (*Pause.*) Would you like me to explain some of the game to you?

LILLIAN That would be very welcome. Shall we move closer to the game?

CAPTAIN (*nodding*) I can point out a few things to you.

LILLIAN (*taking an umbrella*) Just in case it gets too hot.

(*They move downstage as* SUSAN *and* GEORGE, *sitting behind the table, dissolve into darkness.*)

LILLIAN My father was a great lover of cricket. He built this ground years ago. It used to be an Aboriginals' camp before that. My father clothed them, taught them English, converted them, then one day they just disappeared. Went walkabout. One of the lubras used to sing hymns under my window of a Sunday morning. I was their favourite. 'You're so white, so white', she'd say and gasp over my soft skin and how white it was, as if examining fine silk. (*Reflecting*) Like Mrs Thompson's daughter.

CAPTAIN Excuse me?

LILLIAN Oh, you don't know. A girl called Julie. Some man wronged her and on Thursday she drowned herself in the creek after drinking a whole bottle of whisky. The men who found her called me. I don't know why. She was drained of colour. Colourless, not white. (*Trying not to be melancholic*) After drinking a whole bottle of whisky I'm surprised she managed to walk to the creek.

CAPTAIN Perhaps she drank it on the bank and fell in?

LILLIAN Perhaps. (*A* SOLDIER *on the side of*

the stage starts swinging his bat as if practising.) Isn't that a delightful sound? Dry grass underfoot. Ever since I was a young girl I've hated the sight of dry grass, but loved to hear it underfoot. (*Looking at the ground*) To think that three weeks ago this ground was under water. We thought the wheat crop would be ruined. A dreadful climate. (LILLIAN *and the* CAPTAIN *arrive at a bag containing cricket equipment.*) Your cricket equipment?

CAPTAIN   Loaned to us by the mill workers.

LILLIAN   So much, just for a game. That's a strange piece of equipment. Is it for the knee-cap?

CAPTAIN   (*embarrassed*) No, it's a protector.

LILLIAN   What does it protect? (*She pokes at the box with her umbrella.*)

CAPTAIN   It's . . . how shall I put it . . .

LILLIAN   (*tapping the protector with her umbrella thoughtfully, then realising*) Ah, don't worry yourself, Captain. I have seen the light. I think I was thrown by the size. I should have realised it was a piece of male boasting. (*To herself*) More appropriate to a giant.

CAPTAIN   Excuse me?

LILLIAN   Shall we walk around the ground and you can explain some of the intricacies of the game to me. (*She puts up her umbrella.*)

CAPTAIN   (*spotting* HIGGS *swinging his bat*) Hey, Private. (*Pointing off stage*) Go and practise over there. (*The private doesn't move.*) Private, get away from there.

LILLIAN   He seems unimpressed.

CAPTAIN   Private, did you hear me, get away from there. Practise over there. (HIGGS *looks at him in a surly manner and then wanders off. The* CAPTAIN *speaks to* LILLIAN.) They're generally much better behaved than that. (*The* CAPTAIN *and* LILLIAN *begin to walk off.*)

LILLIAN   I am loquacious, for which I apologise. But I have few intelligent, well-mannered people to talk to here, especially those of the opposite sex. What did you think of that poem I recited?

CAPTAIN   Er . . . interesting.

LILLIAN   I wrote it.

CAPTAIN   I thought I recognised your touch. (LILLIAN *and* CAPTAIN HENRY *dissolve into darkness as lights come up on* SUSAN *and* GEORGE *behind the table.*)

SUSAN   Chasing a ball around! It's silly.

GEORGE   Where did your mother go?

SUSAN   Circling the cricket ground.

GEORGE   Reviewing her troops. (*Taking a mouthful of lemonade*) Terrible stuff. You know I'm proving to you I can be sober.

SUSAN   Miracles can happen. Even if you drank all day you couldn't do worse than the other night when you fell on your face in front of the Captain.

GEORGE   I can't win with you, can I? (SUSAN *sneezes, takes out a handkerchief and wipes her nose.*) Hay fever? (*She doesn't acknowledge she has heard him. Sound of distant yells and applause.*) Someone's out. (*Silence.*) I'm too old to change, Susan. If you only knew how lonely I get. I doubt whether you will ever understand. You'll come back from England knowing less. You're right to admire your mother. My God, I realise my faults, more than you probably know. Put yourself in my position. When I married your mother I had nothing, all this was hers. I think that's why she married me. (*Pause.*) If you only knew how callous and uncompassionate people of your age are. (*Grabbing her hand*) You know how much I care for you. (SUSAN *pulls her hand away.*)

SUSAN   I have to use my handkerchief. (*She wipes her nose lightly.*)

GEORGE   Perhaps I deserve your hatred. Don't look away. (*Sound of distant yells and applause.*) Run out. (*He notices a figure to the left, off stage.*) What's that fellow doing? (SUSAN *looks also.*) Picking at his chest.

SUSAN   Probably drunk.

GEORGE   Probably. (SUSAN *quietly rises and steps behind* GEORGE. *He doesn't turn around, but continues to talk, thinking she is listening.*) Don't go to England. At least not yet. Wait a few years. I feel I can get to know you. (*Sound of 'Catch it, catch it' is heard in the distance.* GEORGE *looks at the game.*) Missed. (GEORGE *continues looking at the game, thinking* SUSAN *is behind him, but* SUSAN *gradually wanders off, after listening to her father's words with a mixture of distaste and confusion.*) You didn't know it, but when you were born and while you were very young, I used to stare at you for hours and wonder how I had brought you into the world. Like an alien. So soft. So fragile. How I loved you. Astonished eyes all the time, you had. But as you grew up and your mother took control over you, I became the stranger. Susan? Do you under – (*He looks behind him and notices she has gone.* CAPTAIN HENRY *and* LILLIAN *enter downstage left.*)

CAPTAIN   You understand?

LILLIAN   Vaguely. Short leg, fine leg, third man, slips and maidens . . . Cricket seems a mixture of bawdy innuendoes and physical deformities.

CAPTAIN   The names can be confusing at first.

LILLIAN   My father tried to teach me and – isn't that rather curious behaviour by that fieldsman over there?

CAPTAIN   Fine leg.

LILLIAN   Whatever. The ball is nowhere near him. Perhaps he's standing on an anthill.

CAPTAIN   (*puzzled*) Perhaps.

LILLIAN   What about that glass of lemonade?

CAPTAIN   I think we need it. (*They go upstage to the table.*)

LILLIAN   (*to* GEORGE *as* CAPTAIN HENRY *takes a long look at the fieldsman in question*) At least look interested. (*Loudly so* CAPTAIN HENRY *can hear*) I've just had a crash course in the rules of cricket. (*Pouring lemonade*) There you are, Captain.

CAPTAIN   Thank you.

LILLIAN   Where's Susan?

GEORGE   Over there with the soldiers watching the game.

LILLIAN   What's she doing over there? (*To the* CAPTAIN) Excuse me a moment. (LILLIAN *exits as we hear yells and applause in the distance.*)

CAPTAIN   Another wicket gone. (*Pause.*) Do you like cricket, Mr Dawson?

GEORGE   Not really.

CAPTAIN   I'm not that fond of it myself, but it makes a nice change for the men. There's been a real improvement in them since we came. Recruits raw as hell in the beginning; now they're soldiers. Have you been in the Army?

GEORGE   No. What for? (*The* CAPTAIN *looks perplexed.*) I don't want to kill anyone.

CAPTAIN   I used to feel like that, but an English major told me you get used to it.

GEORGE   I'm sure you do. I don't know much about it; we're cocooned out here. Wish I had a drink right now . . . (*half to himself*) but you have to keep a tight rein on yourself.

CAPTAIN   You didn't seem to be doing such a good job the other night.

GEORGE   (*light-hearted, like the* CAPTAIN) You teetotallers are all the same. Worse than religious fanatics. If you lived in this country you'd need to drink a lot, Captain. Three years ago we had temperatures of over a hundred, thirty days running. The snow country, that's the place to live. Near the Victorian border. White snow everywhere. A sea of snow covering everything. Now that's serene. Serenity . . . What I wouldn't give for serenity and quietness. Complete silence, except for music, wouldn't that be grand? You can express your soul through music – without words. I believe that. Do you?

CAPTAIN   I like music, but wouldn't put as high a claim on its importance as you.

GEORGE   I wouldn't think a soldier would. I had a wonderful dream once. (*Smiling*) Best part of life, dreams. Everybody had transparent bodies and their hearts pulsated with what they felt and when their bodies pulsated, it created music. No talking, just this serene music . . . This is a fucking lousy country.

CAPTAIN   It's not too bad.

GEORGE   Now, with the wheat growing and the rain just a few weeks back. Live here, then you'll know.

CAPTAIN   I – (*He stops when he notices* LILLIAN *returning with* SUSAN.)

LILLIAN   Lemonade, lemonade, my kingdom for lemonade. It's boiling out of the shade of this ficus. (*She pours herself a drink.*) Just the thing.

(*A* SOLDIER *wearing shorts, cricket pads and singlet, and carrying a cricket bat, enters. He appears confused.*)

CAPTAIN   Where are you going, Private? The way out to the wicket is that way.

PRIVATE   Eh?

CAPTAIN   That way. (*The* PRIVATE *turns and exits the way he came.*)

LILLIAN   Have your men been drinking?

CAPTAIN   Not that I know of.

GEORGE   (*spotting someone off left*) Ah, there he is. (PETER *enters carrying a squeeze box.*) Over here.

LILLIAN   (*spotting* PETER) Always the riff-raff, George.

GEORGE   (*to* PETER) I didn't think you'd come. (*To everyone*) This is my friend, the fellow in the hut, Pete Blackwood. Pete, this is my wife –

LILLIAN   (*coldly*) We've met.

GEORGE   My daughter, Susan.

SUSAN   Pleased to meet you.

GEORGE   And Captain Collins.

CAPTAIN   Captain Henry. Pleased to meet you.

GEORGE   And those are all his men. (*He gestures to the cricket ground, then pulls out a chair, taps it, and motions to* PETER *to sit on it.*)

LILLIAN   Some lemonade, Mr Blackwood?

PETER   Thank you.

LILLIAN   A tiny bit warm.

PETER   Doesn't matter.

LILLIAN   (*half to herself*) I didn't think it would. (*Pause.*) Well, I think I'll go home. I'm feeling partial to a cup of tea. Susan?

SUSAN   I'll stay a little longer.

LILLIAN   Half an hour, no more.

CAPTAIN   I'll escort you home, Mrs Dawson.

LILLIAN   Thank you, Captain. (*To* SUSAN) Don't be long. (*The* SERGEANT *enters.*)

CAPTAIN   Sergeant, I'm escorting Mrs Dawson home. Keep an eye on things.

SERGEANT   Yes, Sir.

LILLIAN   (*to* GEORGE) I suppose you'll be home at an odd hour?

GEORGE   I'll see who wins the match.

LILLIAN   (*to the* CAPTAIN *as they exit*) I have some marvellous tea from India. They say that in hot weather tea cools you down.

GEORGE   (*to* PETER) Aren't you glad you came? (PETER *doesn't seem so impressed.*) You'll get paid double for today.

PETER   I don't want money.

GEORGE   You will when you get it. Come on, let's hear something.

PETER   Sure. (*He starts playing a waltz on the squeeze box.* SUSAN *likes the music. The* SERGEANT *feels the artificial oranges; then, while no one is watching, he steals one.*)

SUSAN   That's a lovely tune, Mr Blackwood.

PETER   (*pleased*) Thank you, Miss.

SERGEANT   Would you like a dance, Miss Dawson?

SUSAN   I –

GEORGE   (*nodding his agreement*) Have some fun.

SUSAN   Thank you, Sergeant.

(*The* SERGEANT *escorts* SUSAN *out into the centre of the stage and they dance. For a bulky man, the* SERGEANT *is quite a good dancer. While they dance,* PRIVATE O'NEILL, *in uniform, enters and watches.*)

SUSAN   You're an excellent dancer.

SERGEANT   You mean, for a man of my build.

(SERGEANT COLLINS *and* SUSAN *dance.* PRIVATE O'NEILL *comes up and taps the* SERGEANT *on the shoulder.*)

O'NEILL   Sergeant.

(SERGEANT COLLINS *refuses to acknowledge him at first, but* SUSAN *is pleased that such a handsome fellow is about to dance with her.*)

SUSAN   I don't think it's polite to refuse, Sergeant. (*The* SERGEANT *nods and lets* PRIVATE O'NEILL *take over.*)

O'NEILL   I'm not a great dancer.

SUSAN   Doesn't matter. Did you get your wagon fixed?

O'NEILL   Uh? Oh, yes.

SUSAN   How come you're not playing cricket?

O'NEILL   Not very good at it.

(*They laugh and keep dancing.* GEORGE *is pleased to see his daughter so happy. Two other* SOLDIERS, *in uniform, enter. One watches the dance, clapping his hands as he does so, while the other, puzzled, goes downstage and looks inside the cricket equipment bag. He takes out two cricket stumps. He starts to bang them together to make noise in rhythm with the music.*)

SOLDIER   (*hitting the stumps*) More noise. (*To* PETER) More. More. Faster. It's not fast enough.

(PETER *starts to play faster.* GEORGE *claps along happily.* SUSAN *and her partner are now dancing much faster as the music goes into a jig. Everybody sings 'She's got a ribbon in her hair'.*)

ALL

    She's got a ribbon in her hair,
    She's got a band on her hand,
    She's got a baby on her lap,
    It's crying 'cos it ain't been fed.

    She's got a husband in her bed,
    She's got a magazine in her hand,
    She's got the city in her head,
    But she's got her husband in her bed.

(*Another* SOLDIER *enters and begins to dance with the* SOLDIER *without the cricket stumps.*)

O'NEILL   Faster. Faster.

(PETER *is enjoying this and is playing as fast as he can.* GEORGE *is growing disturbed by the raucous spectacle, especially the wild way*

PRIVATE O'NEILL *is dancing with* SUSAN. *The* SERGEANT *is also worried: something off stage disturbs him.*)

SERGEANT (*yelling*) Hey, you, stop that!

(*He exits quickly. The noise grows louder as another* SOLDIER *enters. His eyes appear glazed. Two* SOLDIERS, *including the one with the stumps, dance by themselves, shouting and banging.*)

SUSAN Slow down . . . slow down. I can't keep up.

O'NEILL No. Faster. *Faster!* Louder.

GEORGE Susan! Stop. (*To* PETER) Stop that. That'll do.

(*But he can't be heard. One of the* SOLDIERS, *dancing nearby, swings a stump at* GEORGE *and hits him on the back of the head.* GEORGE *falls to the ground, unconscious. No one sees it happen, so immersed or caught up are they in the wild dancing.*)

SUSAN Just slow down for a moment. A breather. Please!

O'NEILL No. Faster. *Faster!*

(*The noise has become tremendous: the dancing feet, the banging sticks, the squeeze box, the yelling, the screams of 'Faster, faster, more noise, louder'.*)

SUSAN Please, slow down. Let me rest for a moment.

O'NEILL No! Faster. Faster. Louder. *Louder. Faster!*

(*The noise and dancing reaches a peak and stops abruptly. Sudden blackout.*)

Scene 2

Twilight. The wheatfields. In the distance we hear yells and the noises of banging objects. PRIVATE HIGGS *wanders on, covered in flour. He resembles a ghost. He stops, puzzled about something. He picks at his chest in sharp, jabbing motions.*

CAPTAIN (*off*) Private! (HIGGS *takes no notice.* CAPTAIN HENRY *and* SERGEANT COLLINS *enter, the latter carrying a long garden rake.*) Private? (HIGGS *looks around, but not at* CAPTAIN HENRY. *He listens to the distant noises which are now fading.* CAPTAIN HENRY *speaks to the* SERGEANT.) What's his name?

SERGEANT Higgs.

CAPTAIN Private Higgs. (HIGGS *doesn't respond to his name.*)

SERGEANT (*as* HIGGS *walks away*) Do you want me to stop him?

CAPTAIN Quickly.

(*The* SERGEANT *jumps in front of the* SOLDIER *and holds the garden rake against his stomach.* PRIVATE HIGGS *stops, confused.*)

CAPTAIN Private Higgs, sit down.

HIGGS Can't. (*Picking at his chest*) They're growing on my chest. Can't turn them out. Can't turn them out.

CAPTAIN Private. Sit!

SERGEANT Down. (*The* SERGEANT *jabs the rake against* HIGGS, *who falls down in a sitting position.*)

HIGGS (*to no one in particular*) Red flowers . . . coming from my chest. (*Picking at his chest*) The red flowers are growing in my chest. Got to get moving. Keep them out. Can't.

(CAPTAIN HENRY *takes some strong twine from his pocket.*)

CAPTAIN (*to* SERGEANT) Hold him. (SERGEANT COLLINS *grabs* HIGGS *as the* CAPTAIN *ties him.*)

HIGGS (*quietly*) They're growing from my chest. In my skin. Red flowers. Red flowers. Cut them out. I'm telling you, cut them out. Turn them out. (*The noise of yelling appears to come closer. The* SERGEANT *finishes tying* HIGGS *while* CAPTAIN HENRY *stands up and looks about him.*)

CAPTAIN I can see some of them near the creek. They must have been in the bins too. (*He bends down and helps the* SERGEANT *complete the tying.*) Hurry. It'll soon be too dark to see. (*They finish and stand up. After looking at* HIGGS, *the* SERGEANT *pushes him into a supine position.*)

HIGGS Must get them. Pick them out. Red flowers. I want you to turn them out. Turn them out. I'm being attacked. Help me, I'm being attacked. (*He continues to mumble as the* CAPTAIN *looks at the sky.*)

CAPTAIN Bugger it. Those clouds are going to cover the moon.

SERGEANT What shall we do with him?

LILLIAN (*off*) Captain. Captain Henry. (LILLIAN *enters with a lantern.*) Captain Henry, have you seen Susan? I can't – (*She stops when she spots* HIGGS.) What's happening here?

CAPTAIN   Wish I knew.

LILLIAN   But this man . . . this soldier . . .

HIGGS   (*mumbling, more loudly than before*) They're all over me. Turn them out. I'm being attacked. Help me. They're digging deeper. The roots are all through me. Please, turn them out, help me, turn them out . . .

SERGEANT   (*jabbing the rake at* HIGGS) *Be quiet.*

LILLIAN   What's the matter with him?

CAPTAIN   We don't know.

LILLIAN   What do you mean? Is he drunk?

CAPTAIN   No. (*Yelling and noises are heard in the distance.*)

LILLIAN   (*looking in the direction of the noise*) Those men . . . like ghosts. (*Motioning to* HIGGS) Like him . . . what's going on?

CAPTAIN   I'm sorry, Mrs Dawson, I don't know. They've taken leave of their senses. Some rolled in the flour bins – like Higgs here.

LILLIAN   They've been down to the mill?

CAPTAIN   The Sergeant tried to stop them, but they turned on him.

SERGEANT   There was nothing I could do. They've gone mad.

LILLIAN   What, all of them?

CAPTAIN   It seems so. (*Motioning to* HIGGS) See his hands . . .

LILLIAN   (*examining them with lantern light*) They're black!

CAPTAIN   We saw one of my men running past us a while ago. He was naked, but his hands and feet were black. Some of the soldiers just lie down on the ground, others seem possessed, like Higgs here. One of them is dead. He beat his head against a tree until it was pulp. Before he died he kept yelling that his head was full of snakes.

LILLIAN   This is . . . I can barely comprehend it all. Is the . . . what would you call it? . . . Is the madness a disease? Is it contagious?

CAPTAIN   We don't know.

LILLIAN   But this can't happen. What about the men who were dancing with my daughter, has this happened to them?

SERGEANT   I don't know.

LILLIAN   What do you mean you don't know?

CAPTAIN   Isn't your daughter home?

LILLIAN   No. Why do you think I'm out here in the fields?

(ARTHUR, *the mill foreman, enters.*)

ARTHUR   Mrs Dawson.

LILLIAN   Arthur, thank goodness. I wanted to see you.

ARTHUR   I couldn't help it. They broke into the bins and then into the mill. They were all crazy. Wild men. They rolled in the flour, screamed and yelled, and then ran off into the fields. Willie tried to stop them, but they attacked him with sticks.

LILLIAN   Is he hurt?

ARTHUR   We pulled him away from them. He should be all right.

LILLIAN   (*to* CAPTAIN) Your men are supposed to protect us, not terrorise us. (*Motioning to* HIGGS) Look at him, mad as a hatter. What kind of men are they? (*To* ARTHUR) Susan is gone, missing somewhere. I can't find her. I want you to get the workers together. Half of them are to be used to protect the mill and the other half to help search for my daughter.

HIGGS   Everywhere. Faceless. Legs cut off. Everywhere.

LILLIAN   Be as quick as possible.

ARTHUR   It'll take hours to round them all up.

LILLIAN   I made you foreman of the mill: prove you're worth it.

ARTHUR   But what about us? We have to protect our families.

LILLIAN   You and your families are my employees. I want Susan found! Is that understood? Now hurry up.

ARTHUR   Yes, missus. (ARTHUR *exits.*)

HIGGS   (*shouting*) Cut them out! Cut them out! They're inside me.

(*The* SERGEANT *pulls out the hand-puppet sock he keeps in his pocket and shoves it into* HIGGS' *mouth.* HIGGS, *still attempting to shout, rolls away a short distance.* GEORGE *enters; the others don't notice. He is drunk and stares, bewildered, at them for a few moments.*)

LILLIAN   I will hold you responsible, Captain, if anything happens to Susan.

CAPTAIN   I will do my best, Mrs Dawson.

GEORGE   Lillian?

LILLIAN   There you are. Where's Susan?

GEORGE   She's at home.

LILLIAN   She's not at home.

GEORGE   Dancing. She was dancing.

LILLIAN (*hitting him across the face*)
Drunken pig! She's not dancing. She's
somewhere out there – in trouble.

GEORGE Susan . . . no, she's – (*spotting*
HIGGS *on the ground*) I saw dozens of ghosts
like him running across the fields yelling
and screaming. One hit me on the head.
(*Feeling the back of his head*) Still hurts.
Had to have a drink. Boy, does it hurt.

LILLIAN Get home.

GEORGE I'll find Susan.

LILLIAN Get home, George. *Get out of the way!*

(GEORGE *looks at* HIGGS *as the* SOLDIER
tries to talk.)

GEORGE Peter had them dancing. He'll
know where Susan is.

LILLIAN George, for the last time – get
home.

GEORGE It's all right, I'll find her.

LILLIAN (*yelling*) Get home! (GEORGE *nods*
and exits. Pause.) I'm sorry, Captain. I must
apologise for that outburst. I must sound
like a harridan. Sometimes my husband
can be so . . . stupid. As you can imagine
. . . I'm a bit flustered at the moment. A bit
lost. Susan is my pride and joy. It's so hot.
(*Wiping a handkerchief across her forehead*)
She could be anywhere.

CAPTAIN I think you should return to the
house.

LILLIAN No, I'll continue looking. I'll be all
right. Look after your men.

CAPTAIN Be careful with that lantern. Some
of them are attracted by the light.

LILLIAN I have a gun at home, I'll get that.
(*She exits.*)

CAPTAIN (*looking at* HIGGS *writhing on the*
ground trying to talk) What's going on in
that skull of his? It's like they're living a
nightmare. What'll we do with him?

SERGEANT What'll we do with him?

CAPTAIN Can't do much at the moment, can
we? Leave him here, I think. He can't do
much harm like that. I wonder if Mrs
Dawson has any more lanterns; we'll need
them. Go with her, Sergeant – get two
lanterns. I'll join you in a moment.

SERGEANT (*exiting hurriedly and yelling*) Mrs
Dawson . . . Mrs Dawson. (*The* CAPTAIN
goes over to HIGGS.)

CAPTAIN Shhh! Calm down. (*He takes the*
sock from HIGGS' *mouth.*)

HIGGS (*shouting*) They're coming. They're
coming. Got to get away. Get moving.

CAPTAIN Shhh! Who's coming?

HIGGS (*more calmly*) The men – that's why
we've got to get up the hill.

CAPTAIN Why do you have to get up the
hill?

HIGGS You fuckin' idiot – I've got to get up
the hill to see the top. All the corpses are
coming down the hill so I've got to get up.
I don't want to die. (*Silence. The* CAPTAIN
stares at HIGGS *as he mumbles.*)

CAPTAIN When you were dancing, did you
see the hill?

HIGGS Of course I did. I danced up it. Light
as a feather, with a body on my back.

(*The* CAPTAIN *stares at* HIGGS, *who*
mumbles as the lights fade. Blackout.)

Scene 3

Night. Fields. LILLIAN *carries a lantern.*

MRS HARRISON (*off*) Andy, Andy . . .

LILLIAN (*calling*) Hello Mrs Harrison.

MRS HARRISON (*entering*) Who's – oh, it's
you, Mrs Dawson.

LILLIAN Have you seen Susan?

MRS HARRISON No. What's happening?

LILLIAN I don't know.

MRS HARRISON I've got to find Andy – he'd
let those soldiers do anything to him.

LILLIAN Andy will be all right – it's Susan
I'm worried about. She ran off with a
soldier while they were dancing. Will you
help me look for her?

MRS HARRISON After I find Andy.

LILLIAN Andy will be all right. Will you
have a look for me down by Hillman's?

MRS HARRISON As soon as I find Andy.

LILLIAN You can look for him near
Hillman's.

MRS HARRISON He won't be there, there's
no trees. He'll be somewhere near the
trees.

LILLIAN He might be near Hillman's – I
can't go everywhere.

MRS HARRISON I'm sorry, Mrs Dawson, he
won't be. I know Andy.

LILLIAN Andy's not like Susan; he's a . . .

MRS HARRISON He's what I live for. I'm
going to find him and I don't give a shit
what you do, Mrs Dawson. When I've
found him, then I'll help you find Susan.

LILLIAN Mrs Harrison, I've done a lot for
you and I will not be spoken to this way by
you. I'm not asking that you give up
searching for Andy, all I'm asking is that
you –

MRS HARRISON   And I'm very grateful for what you've done for us – but Andy comes first.

LILLIAN   Very well. If you do happen to run into Susan, would you be so kind as to tell her I'm looking for her, Mrs Harrison.

(LILLIAN *exits.* MRS HARRISON *watches her go and is not aware that a* SOLDIER *has entered and is behind her. She turns to go and looks startled when she spots him.*)

WATSON   (*staring intently at* MRS HARRISON) Can you tell me? (*Forgetting*) Can you tell me . . . ? (MRS HARRISON *goes to step away. He takes a step forward. She stops in fear.*) I want you to tell me . . . (*He shows her his hands.*) Look my hands. (*He reacts as if* MRS HARRISON *has made a motion towards them, then speaks quietly.*) No, don't touch them. (*Smiling*) I want you to sit down on the bench here and talk to me.

MRS HARRISON   There's no – (*catching herself*) I'm sorry I have to go. I'll be back soon.

WATSON   Can you tell me . . . ? (MRS HARRISON *is about to go when she plucks up enough courage to approach him.*)

MRS HARRISON   Have you seen a boy . . . a seventeen-year-old? Have you been near the trees? He should be near them. (*Silence. It appears he has listened.*)

WATSON   (*smiling*) Can you tell me . . . ? (MRS HARRISON, *realising it is futile, decides to leave.*)

MRS HARRISON   I have to go now. Good night. (*She exits.*)

WATSON   (*parroting her*) Good night. (*Alone for a few moments, the* SOLDIER *smiles to himself. We hear* MRS HARRISON's *cry of 'Andy' slowly fading away. In the distance, we hear* LILLIAN *calling for* SUSAN. WATSON *hears it also. This starts off something in his mind, and he plucks something imaginary from his chest.*) Private. Private. (*His voice becomes sing-song as he falls in love with the sound of the words.*) Private. Private. Private Watson. Private Watson. Watson. Watson. Watson.

(*His name commingles with the faint cry of 'Andy'. Blackout.*)

Scene 4

Night. The remains of the picnic lunch, tables and chairs are seen under the ficus tree. PETER, *in silhouette, is lying near the overturned table.*

In the distance, faint sounds are heard of yelling and other noises. GEORGE *enters, and spots* PETER.

GEORGE   Pete. (*Shaking him roughly*) Pete. Peter.

PETER   Mr Dawson?

GEORGE   Where's Susan?

PETER   Who?

GEORGE   My daughter. (*Pause.*)

PETER   She was dancing.

GEORGE   Where is she?

PETER   They were all dancing. I couldn't keep up. So fast. They kept on saying 'faster, faster'.

GEORGE   Where's Susan?

PETER   She was dancing. The men were wild. Like savages. They smashed up your tables and chairs, then hit each other.

GEORGE   Where's Susan, my daughter?

PETER   Gone.

GEORGE   Where? (*Shaking* PETER) Where? Where did she go?

PETER   Don't do that, Mr Dawson. Please don't do that.

GEORGE   Tell me.

PETER   Don't touch me.

GEORGE   Show me where she went.

PETER   I can't. I can't move. If I move I'll die. One of the soldiers, he was dancing. Oh, shit, shit, shit. He spun around, broke a bottle and stabbed me with it. Then he danced again . . . as if nothing had happened. I've still got my squeeze box. (*Holding it in one hand*) I don't think he knew what he had done. Kept on dancing with the broken bottle in his hand. I pretended I was dead.

GEORGE   Who did she run off with?

PETER   Who?

GEORGE   Susan, my daughter. (*Pause.*)

PETER   The young soldier. He held her in his arms as they danced, almost crushed her, then they ran off together. The others kept dancing.

GEORGE   This way?

PETER   Yes. (GEORGE *jumps up, preparing to leave.*) You going to get help for me?

GEORGE   You sure it's this way?

PETER   Why didn't you leave me in my hut? (*Shouting*) Why didn't you fucking leave me alone!

(GEORGE *exits in the direction* PETER *has indicated. Silence. A* SOLDIER, *in shorts and singlet, covered in flour, enters and advances on* PETER.)

PETER (*quietly*) Go away. (*The* SOLDIER *approaches him and bends down, staring at* PETER *with curiosity.*) Please, go away. (*The* SOLDIER *grabs the squeeze box, but* PETER *won't let go of it.*)

SOLDIER Ta. Say ta.

PETER No, it's mine.

SOLDIER (*threateningly*) Ta. Ta.

(PETER *loosens his grip. The* SOLDIER *takes the squeeze box, stands up, examines it. He then turns back to* PETER. *For a moment he seems ready to attack* PETER, *but he then hears a shout in the distance and exits, slowly, in its direction, still carrying the squeeze box. Blackout.*)

Scene 5

Darkness. On the wheatfield.

LILLIAN (*off*) Susan! Susan! Where are you? (LILLIAN *enters carrying a lantern.*) Susan? (LILLIAN *looks around despairingly.*)

ANDY (*off*) Mrs Dawson. (LILLIAN *is startled by the voice.*) Mrs Dawson.

LILLIAN Who is it? Who's there?

ANDY (*off*) It's me, Mrs Dawson. Up here in the tree. (LILLIAN *looks up at the tree which is just out of view of the audience.*)

LILLIAN Is that you Andy?

ANDY Up here.

LILLIAN You gave me quite a shock. What are you doing up there? Why aren't you home?

ANDY I was going home for tea. I'm hungry.

LILLIAN Come down.

ANDY I can't. The men from the slaughterhouse are here, Mrs Dawson. I can see them way off, running through the fires looking for me.

LILLIAN (*sternly*) Come down, Andy.

ANDY No, they'll put me in the cow again. (*Pause.*)

LILLIAN (*frustrated*) Have you seen Susan?

ANDY Who?

LILLIAN Susan.

ANDY I heard you yelling.

LILLIAN (*irritated*) Susan. Have you seen her? Concentrate, Andy.

ANDY I seen her. Way over there.

LILLIAN When?

ANDY What?

LILLIAN How long ago, Andy? How long ago did you see her?

ANDY Not long.

LILLIAN Where? Where did you see her?

ANDY Near the creek.

LILLIAN Was she with anyone? A soldier . . . ?

ANDY A man. They were being rude.

LILLIAN What do you mean?

ANDY Making babies. (*He giggles.*)

LILLIAN Don't be stupid, Andy. (*Pause.*) I have to go and look for her. I want you to climb down and go home – straight away. Go home to your mother.

ANDY You're looking for Susan . . . (*Laughing*) She's making babies.

LILLIAN Go home, Andy! (LILLIAN *exits hurriedly. Silence.*)

ANDY Mrs Dawson . . . Mrs Dawson, don't go, I'm hungry.

(*Blackout.*)

ANDY Mrs Dawson, the men from the slaughter-yard are here!

Scene 6

Night. In the wheatfields. Yelling in the distance. The noises fade. A SOLDIER, *covered in flour, passes across the rear of the stage mumbling to himself.* CAPTAIN HENRY *enters carrying a lantern.*

SERGEANT (*off*) Captain Henry. Over here. I'm over here. (SERGEANT COLLINS *enters carrying a lantern.*)

CAPTAIN Did you cross the creek?

SERGEANT No.

CAPTAIN The fire jumped the creek a mile back, so both sides are on fire now.

SERGEANT What, all the fields?

CAPTAIN If not all, they soon will be. Where did the fire start?

SERGEANT Don't know.

CAPTAIN Can't the mill workers help us?

SERGEANT Most of them have fled their homes and are sitting in the creek. The winds are blowing the fires towards the mill, they reckon.

CAPTAIN So it's just us?

SERGEANT Looks it. I haven't seen one of our men who isn't affected. I saw two of them rush into the fire. I think its brightness attracted them.

CAPTAIN I don't understand. Why haven't we gone like them? I just can't figure it out. What's possessed them? Soldiers killing one another, running into fires, talking to themselves, hallucinating, believing their heads are full of molten lead, their chests have something growing in them . . . it's . . . what about the mill workers? Are any of them affected?

SERGEANT   No, they were just afraid of the fire and our soldiers.

CAPTAIN   It's unbelievable. Did you manage to wire Sydney?

SERGEANT   I don't know if I got through.

CAPTAIN   Probably take them a day, even more to –

(PRIVATE MILLER *enters. The* SERGEANT *moves towards the* SOLDIER *and holds his lantern up to him. The* SOLDIER *has blinded himself with the stump he still holds in his hand.*)

SERGEANT   He's done it himself.

CAPTAIN   Who is it?

SERGEANT   Private Miller. (*Prodding* MILLER *with his rake*) Over there. Stand over there.

MILLER   My name is Private Miller. I have been dancing. Yes, sir, I have been dancing.

CAPTAIN   Private Miller –

MILLER   Yes?

CAPTAIN   Sit . . . sit down.

MILLER   I don't want to. The light's too bright.

SERGEANT   (*prodding him with the rake*) Sit down.

CAPTAIN   (*to* SERGEANT) You got any twine left?

SERGEANT   No, Sir.

CAPTAIN   We can't do everything by ourselves. Private Miller . . .

MILLER   Yes?

CAPTAIN   Lie down and go to sleep.

MILLER   Better not.

CAPTAIN   It's night. You have to get up early. Go to sleep.

MILLER   Better not. Better not. Got to keep my guard. Keep look out. The enemy is here.

CAPTAIN   There is no enemy.

MILLER   Yes there is. I saw them with my own eyes. They were terrible. A terrible brightness. They were glaring. Too bright. Had to take my eyes out. I saw too much. I can't take off my hands. Can't take them off. They'll rot off. (MILLER *suddenly jumps up.*)

SERGEANT   Look out, Captain!

MILLER   (*swinging the stump*) Keep away. I can see you. (*He stops swinging, then wanders off.*)

SERGEANT   You want me to stop him?

CAPTAIN   Let him go, we can't do anything.

(*The* SOLDIER *stops before exiting, talking to an invisible person.*)

MILLER   Uh? Eh? Come with me then. I'll show you the way. We'll go home with my wife. Be careful, the enemy is everywhere.

(*The* SOLDIER *exits. The* SERGEANT *looks across the wheatfields.*)

SERGEANT   Look at those flames going into the sky.

CAPTAIN   It can't be a house, it must be the mill.

SERGEANT   Must be. (*Pause.*) God, I'm tired. (*He sits and takes out a handkerchief.*) It's becoming hotter. (*He finds two licorice in his pocket.*) Ah good. Want a licorice, Captain?

CAPTAIN   (*preoccupied*) What?

SERGEANT   A licorice all-sort. It's a bit squashed.

CAPTAIN   No thanks.

SERGEANT   Suit yourself. (*The* SERGEANT *wipes his brow, eats the sweet, mumbles something.*)

CAPTAIN   What?

SERGEANT   (*swallowing the licorice quickly*) What do we do next?

CAPTAIN   God knows. If your wire got through, then it will take a day to get help. Otherwise, we can't do anything. It's hopeless.

SERGEANT   (*holding up the other licorice*) Sure you don't want it?

CAPTAIN   No.

SERGEANT   My treat then. (*Chewing it slowly*) Hang on. I might have another. Don't remember getting another . . . (*He pulls out the fake orange he stole at the picnic.*) Wish it were real. I don't suppose you can eat cotton wool?

CAPTAIN   Wouldn't advise it.

SERGEANT   Pity.

CAPTAIN   I admire your ability to be oblivious to your present situation.

SERGEANT   I'm only a sergeant, sir. I've always been of the opinion that it's up to the officers to get excited about things. No sense in everybody getting excited.

(SERGEANT COLLINS *stares at his hands.*)

CAPTAIN   Are you all right?

SERGEANT   Sure. Why?

CAPTAIN   (*noticing something in the distance*) The fire is changing direction, heading this way. We'd better get moving. (*Spotting a silhouette*) Yes? Who is it? (GEORGE *walks downstage.*)

SERGEANT   Mr Dawson.

GEORGE   You got anything to drink?

SERGEANT   Wish we did.

GEORGE   I'm thirsty.

SERGEANT   So are we.

CAPTAIN   I think you'd better go and warn your wife. The fire is turning this way.

GEORGE   Warn that bitch! I was looking for Susan. Couldn't find her. (*Pause.*) You can see the soldiers running in circles near the fire. (GEORGE *goes upstage and watches the fire for a few moments.*) It's hard to tell if they're in panic or dancing with joy.

SERGEANT   What will we do about our men?

CAPTAIN   Nothing. We can't do anything.

SERGEANT   (*referring to* GEORGE) What about him?

CAPTAIN   He can come with us.

SERGEANT   Mr Dawson, we're going back to camp. You can come with us.

GEORGE   I'm staying. I've got to find my daughter.

CAPTAIN   (*to the* SERGEANT) Let him find his own way out. (*They begin to exit right.*)

SERGEANT   Captain! Here. (*The* SERGEANT *shines his lantern on something in front of him: the feet of* SUSAN *are sticking out of a patch of wheat.*)

CAPTAIN   Who is it?

SERGEANT   Mr Dawson's daughter.

CAPTAIN   What?

SERGEANT   Christ, she's been stabbed.

CAPTAIN   (*bending over the corpse, shocked*) Shit . . .

SERGEANT   (*pulling out the knife and giving it to* CAPTAIN HENRY) Probably one of our men. Private O'Neill. He was dancing with her and then went off with her.

CAPTAIN   Where is he now?

SERGEANT   He was one of the two men I saw rushing into the fire. (*Silence. As they stare at the body we hear distant yelling and noise.*)

SERGEANT   Some of the soldiers are attacking one another.

CAPTAIN   Let them go, we can't do anything.

SERGEANT   What about Dawson?

CAPTAIN   Christ . . .

SERGEANT   Shall we tell him?

CAPTAIN   Mr Dawson . . . Mr Dawson . . . will you come here a moment?

GEORGE   I think I'd better be going home, I want a drink.

CAPTAIN   I'm . . . I'm terribly sorry . . . I

have to tell you . . . We found your daughter. She's dead.

GEORGE   Eh?

CAPTAIN   Your daughter. Susan. Here. (*Silence as* GEORGE *looks at corpse.*)

GEORGE   That's not my daughter. (*Pause.*)

CAPTAIN   I'm afraid it is, Mr Dawson.

GEORGE   There's been some mistake. She didn't look like that. You've made a mistake. (GEORGE *looks confused.*)

CAPTAIN   We think one of our soldiers killed her. (GEORGE *shakes his head vigorously.*) I'm sorry.

(GEORGE, *shaking his head, slowly comes to terms with what he sees.*)

GEORGE   No, no. *Impossible.* I – tried to stop her, but she wouldn't listen. (GEORGE *cradles her head in his lap and takes the shirt from her mouth.*) Impossible. (*Stroking her hair, crying*) Oh, God, Susan . . . my darling . . . my darling . . .

(*The* CAPTAIN *nods to the* SERGEANT; *they both move away. The noise of yelling and banging is heard nearby, but it moves away.*)

CAPTAIN   (*referring to* GEORGE) We'll take him with us.

GEORGE   (*rocking his daughter*) My baby . . . my baby . . . I loved you so much . . . why did you hate me?

(SERGEANT COLLINS *abruptly sits and searches his pockets, but can find nothing.*)

CAPTAIN   (*to the* SERGEANT) We'd better hurry.

SERGEANT   What do you reckon the time would be?

CAPTAIN   About midnight or later. Why?

SERGEANT   (*standing up and frantically brushing his trousers free of dirt*) Oh, I was just wondering. (*The* SERGEANT *looks puzzled.*)

CAPTAIN   Mr Dawson?

SERGEANT   Captain?

CAPTAIN   Yes?

SERGEANT   My hands . . . they're numb. (*The* CAPTAIN, *like his* SERGEANT, *is stunned. Silence.*)

CAPTAIN   Perhaps it's pins and needles, you were just sitting down.

SERGEANT   They're grey. They'll go black. I've got it –

CAPTAIN   (*uncomfortably*) Sit down over there, give me time to –

SERGEANT   My hands are going like the others. Look at them. I'll go crazy like them.

CAPTAIN   No you won't. Some of them just slept. It might not be as bad.

SERGEANT   What about your hands?

CAPTAIN   (*examining them*) Nothing. (*Pause.*)

SERGEANT   You're the only one not affected. The only one of us left. (*Silence.*)

CAPTAIN   (*at a loss*) Let's get back to the camp. Come on, the fires will soon be surrounding us.

SERGEANT   You don't understand. I may as well stay here.

CAPTAIN   Don't be ridiculous. Come on. You'll be all right. (*Pause.*) Please, I need you. Please. (*The* SERGEANT *nods.*) You'll be all right. (*Calling*) Mr Dawson, the fire is coming this way. Quickly. Follow us. (*To* SERGEANT) This way. We'll rest on the road over there. We should be safe from the fire there.

SERGEANT   (*grabbing* CAPTAIN) Don't tie me up like the others. Run away from me, but don't tie me up.

CAPTAIN   Eh?

SERGEANT   I mean it.

CAPTAIN   All right. (*Calling*) Mr Dawson. Hurry. Get out of here before it's too late. (CAPTAIN *and* SERGEANT *leave. Silence.*)

GEORGE   (*stroking* SUSAN*'s hair*) I loved you so much.

CAPTAIN   (*off*) Hurry, Mr Dawson. The fire.

(*Two* SOLDIERS, *covered in flour, enter upstage, yelling and piggybacking one another. One of the* SOLDIERS *falls onto the ground and lies there, mumbling incoherently. The other* SOLDIER *yells at him and then strangles him.*)

SOLDIER   Coward, Coward. Kill them. Kill them. Scum. Coward!

(*After killing his fellow* SOLDIER, *the first* SOLDIER *spots* GEORGE. *He goes over to him.* GEORGE, *frightened, bends over his daughter as the* SOLDIER *tries to playfully kick him and his daughter. Soon tired of this game, the* SOLDIER *walks off into the fire.*)

CAPTAIN   (*off*) Private . . . Private . . . You're walking into the fire. *Come back. Come back!*

(GEORGE *stands up, lifting up* SUSAN *with him. He looks confused. The stage grows brighter.*)

CAPTAIN   (*off*) This way, Mr Dawson. Over here – through the break. Through the break! The fire. Quickly, Mr Dawson.

GEORGE   Captain Henry: where are you?

CAPTAIN   (*off*) Over here. To your left. The fire. Get out!

GEORGE   Where?

CAPTAIN   (*off*) Over here. To your – (*Silence.*)

GEORGE   Where are you? (*Silence.*) Answer me. Where are you?

(*Sounds of burning wheat, yelling* SOLDIERS, *banging sticks are heard. The stage grows brighter.* GEORGE, *hanging on to* SUSAN *awkwardly, shields his eyes from the glare with one hand. He looks around for an escape route, but sees none. He then looks lovingly at his daughter.*)

GEORGE   I'm sorry. If you only realised . . . you were the only thing that mattered, the only thing I loved . . . the only thing in this whole world I ever loved. (*Sounds grow louder.* GEORGE *listens, thinking the melange of sounds is a call to him.*) What? What? I can't hear you. (*Looking at* SUSAN, *quietly*) I have nothing left. The only thing I ever loved. (GEORGE *grows angry. He yells orders.*) Burn everything. Drive them out! (*Yelling*) Burn! Burn everything! *Burn!*

(*A sudden brilliance is seen, then a sudden blackout. The noise of the fire grows unbearably loud in the darkness as if the audience is going to be swallowed up by it; then it stops abruptly.*)

Scene 7

Charred ruins of the house. LILLIAN *is searching through the remains. She has the same dress on, but it is torn and dirty.* ARTHUR, *the foreman, enters, carrying* LILLIAN*'s battered umbrella.*

ARTHUR   (*hesitantly*) Mrs Dawson.

LILLIAN   Oh, Arthur, you gave me a fright.

ARTHUR   I found this on the way over.

LILLIAN   Thank you. (*She looks at the umbrella and tries to open it.*) Ruined. But thank you anyway. It's about the only thing I've got left. (*Looking around her*) Everything destroyed. (*Pause.*) Is there any hope of using the mill?

ARTHUR   It will have to be built from scratch. Only Johnson's house escaped being burnt. (*Silence.*) The train has just arrived. It's got tents and food.

LILLIAN (*waking from thought*) Beg your pardon? Yes. I shall be going back with it to Sydney.

ARTHUR You'll be returning?

LILLIAN Of course, but I need a rest first. (*Uncomfortable silence.*)

ARTHUR I came to say how sorry all of us are down at the mill about Susan and Mr Dawson.

LILLIAN Thank you. (*Silence.* ARTHUR *begins to move off.*) Oh, Arthur?

ARTHUR Yes, missus?

LILLIAN Did my husband order you to send that poisoned wheat to the soldiers?

ARTHUR He told me to. He said you wanted it given to them.

LILLIAN No doubt you have heard about my husband's behaviour on Saturday evening. He was mentally unstable. He should have checked the wheat before he gave it to the troops. Would you tell Captain Henry that, if he should ask? There is to be an inquiry. Apparently, the wheat was infected with a fungus and it sent the soldiers mad.

ARTHUR Yes, missus, I'll tell him that. (*Pause.*) Goodbye, Mrs Dawson.

LILLIAN Goodbye, Arthur. Take care.

(*He departs.* LILLIAN *notices she still has the umbrella in her hand. She throws it away in disgust, then bends down to pick up the charred musical box. She opens it. We hear 'Silent Night' – the music in the box has nearly run down. She takes out a biscuit, looks at it, then puts it back in the music box. Sickened by the sight of the rubble around her, she holds her head in her hand and weeps. The* SERGEANT *and the* CAPTAIN *enter.* SERGEANT COLLINS *is wearing socks on his hands; he appears dazed.*)

CAPTAIN (*quietly*) Mrs Dawson. (LILLIAN *is startled for a moment, but quickly composes herself and rises from her haunches.*) Good afternoon, Captain.

CAPTAIN The train has arrived. You still want to go back to Sydney?

LILLIAN There is nothing for me here. Nothing. (*Clapping her hands free of dirt*) Just ashes and dust. (*Pause.*) Were you able to find the bodies of my daughter and husband?

CAPTAIN I'm sorry . . . it will be impossible. The same with my men. The fire made it

impossible to identify anyone. We did find a body wedged in the fork of a burnt tree.

LILLIAN Andy . . . a half-wit. I saw him . . . tried to tell him. He should never have been brought into this world. At least God did the right thing for once – callous but true. (*Pause. She seems nonplussed.*) My husband, he . . . (*She stops herself, turns away and walks over to the charred piano. She opens the lid.*) Worthless. (*Pause. She turns back to* CAPTAIN HENRY.) How many men did you lose?

CAPTAIN Nine.

LILLIAN What about the rest?

CAPTAIN Sick and dazed. I think most will recover. I don't know about some. One of them just counts his fingers over and over and one never stops mumbling about his eyes – he blinded himself. I'm sending them all back on the train.

LILLIAN Are you going back, too?

CAPTAIN I have to stay here for a while. Reinforcements have arrived on the train and I'll direct the clean up.

LILLIAN (*noticing the* SERGEANT) Strange place for your socks, Sergeant.

CAPTAIN (*testily*) He caught the infection. Not as badly as some of the others, but his hands are still tender and black. Unfortunately, Mrs Dawson, we have no supply of gloves. (*Quietly*) I think he's still hallucinating. He'll go back too. (*Staring at the back of the* SERGEANT *who is lost in thought*) I hope they'll recover.

LILLIAN They will.

CAPTAIN I mean, inside their heads. Mentally. Can you go as mad as my men did and fully recover?

LILLIAN Why not? Just as a drunk recovers from his binge.

CAPTAIN No, it's not like drink . . . *yes*, it is. Alcohol releases what's inside of people . . . like the poison in the wheat. The only way I can understand it, Mrs Dawson, is that the terrible things were inside of them, like when people go crazy on drink.

LILLIAN (*slightly testily*) What?

CAPTAIN (*as* LILLIAN *picks up something from the ground and examines it*) It occurred to me while watching my men. What was going on inside of them . . . it would be a mistake to believe that what they experienced – the hallucinations, the horror – wasn't a part of them. What they saw . . . the things that went on in their heads . . . Can they ever see the world the same way they saw it before?

LILLIAN (*throwing away the object she was examining*) Useless. Sorry, what was that?

CAPTAIN Nothing. (*Silence.* LILLIAN *walks through the ruins.*)

LILLIAN How many people admired this house. (*Pause.*) I can't retrieve a thing. All I have is what I wear. Thank goodness I haven't a mirror. (*The* SERGEANT *sits on a charred chair.*) Careful, it might break. (*He pays no attention to her.*) The mill foreman was just here. He confirmed that my husband didn't check the diseased wheat before he sent it to you. I should have done it myself. A strong woman married to a weak man is courting disaster. (*Pause.*)

CAPTAIN Will you ever return here?

LILLIAN No. Never. You can't look back. All you would see is destruction. I think I will be able to get a fair price for the land. The grass will soon grow back – at least the soil is never ruined by fire. The money should be enough for me to be able to live comfortably in England. I have relatives there. It'll be good to be as far away from this place as possible. (*Pause. She looks around at the ruins.*) We must forget all of this. It's too terrible. The strong forget, the weak remember. (*Pause.*)

CAPTAIN Shall we go? I'll take you to the train. (*He nods to the* SERGEANT.) Sergeant.

(CAPTAIN *and* LILLIAN *exit, but the* SERGEANT *stays behind on his chair, staring blankly into the distance, immersed in his own thoughts – a shell of his former self. Slow fade to blackout.*)

14 Jimmy Chi and Kuckles

Bran Nue Dae
Australia

Introduction

Hailed as the country's first Aboriginal musical, Jimmy Chi and Kuckles' *Bran Nue Dae* took Australian theatrical circles by storm after its premiere at the Perth Festival in 1990 where it won a Sidney Myer Award for outstanding achievement in the performing arts. Two national tours to major venues followed, as well as a local tour to Broome, the play's 'birthplace', and other Aboriginal communities in the Kimberley region of Western Australia. *Bran Nue Dae* is widely regarded as a landmark in Aboriginal theatre history, not only because it reached a larger, more differentiated audience than previous work in the field, but also, and more importantly, because its generic innovations and profound rejection of Otherness seemed to open up new possibilities in Aboriginal performing arts. In the 1980s, Aboriginal theatre had largely centred around the monumental achievements of the late Jack Davis, whose primary project had been to dramatise the oppressions of indigenous Australians in the wake of European imperialism. Chi's play does not disavow this history – in fact the colonial legacies of alcoholism, dispossession, and social breakdown are woven into its very fabric – but the emphasis is on celebration and regeneration. In this respect, as the original programme notes put it, *Bran Nue Dae* is indeed 'a play to ease the pain'.

The particular gestation of the play has become something of a legend in Australian theatre circles, in part because it began in the small, isolated, north-western coastal town of Broome, an old pearling port without any real theatrical infrastructure. Chi was born and grew up there, excelling in Catholic secondary schools run by Irish nuns and German priests, before going on to the University of Western Australia to study for an engineering degree. In this new city environment in Perth, his experiences of cultural dislocation and racism precipitated the onset of severe schizophrenia, leading him to abandon his studies and return to Broome to write music. For more than fifteen years before *Bran Nue Dae* was produced, Chi and his band Kuckles (comprising Mick Manolis, Steve Pigram, Pat Bin Amat and Gary Gower) composed and sang songs for local Broome gigs. Much of this music eventually found its way into the play, including the title song, which was purportedly written on the back of a truck during a demonstration to protest the mining of Aboriginal sacred sites in the region. From 1986 to 1989, as Chi's conception of a possible musical drama grew, the idea was developed through several workshopping sessions in Perth and Sydney, with input from such figures as Jack Davis and Aboriginal director Brian Syron. Once a workable script had been devised, the play was rehearsed in Broome with a cast of mainly local actors under the direction of Andrew Ross, whose interpretations of Davis's plays had earned him a reputation for sensitive treatment of Aboriginal works.

The construction of an Aboriginal musical would seem deliberately to appropriate the most Westernised and commercialised of theatre forms – the Broadway production – for oppositional ends: to make a political protest while broadly appealing to the popular imagination. This kind of indigenising experiment has featured widely in postcolonial theatre, notably in the South African township musicals of Gibson Kente, which played an important part in the early cultural struggle against apartheid. Like its counterparts elsewhere, *Bran Nue Dae* presents structurally and thematically as a popular musical, but simultaneously subverts and extends generic conventions, in this case via parody and self-conscious irony in its treatment of the genre itself and both Aboriginal and non-Aboriginal characters and institutions. With its narrative loosely plotted around some twenty songs, the play, subtitled 'a musical journey', draws from the convention of the Aboriginal song cycle as well as from Western musical models. A song cycle, inherently peripatetic in its enactment, is a progression, song by song, along a given track in the country, often using a chorus rising and fading antiphonally to follow the main singer. The physical and spiritual journey of the main characters, Willy and Uncle Tadpole, from Perth to Broome follows this template, recreating a variety of landscapes on the way. Chi keeps the whole flexible enough to become a combination of Aboriginal road movie, romantic comedy, family farce, agitprop revue, and a bid for a new, consciously hybridised, notion of Australian identity.

Bran Nue Dae's narrative focus on the Aboriginal search for a physical and spiritual homeland highlights a common concern of indigenous peoples uprooted by colonial settlement. The Aboriginal quest for cultural renewal is inevitably linked to a demand for land rights, as articulated in the recitative to the title song, but ultimately the play celebrates a nomadic movement through the landscape rather than adhering to dominant notions of land ownership. While Willie and Tadpole's journey from the city to the country activates myths-of-origin thematics, it is more picaresque than pastoral and the text carefully avoids linking the bush to a pre-invasion ideal of Aboriginal essence. This is achieved primarily through a tongue-in-cheek treatment of myths of authenticity that are based on tribal culture. Hence, the appearance of black hunters in loincloths carrying spears is used comically to signal a keen awareness of the ways in which Aborigines have been looked at through the discourses of film, popular theatre, and tourism.

Amid the parody of white 'types', including brutal policemen, demagogue Catholic priests and local hippies trying to find enlightenment in the bush, there is a serious undercurrent in much of *Bran Nue Dae*'s humour. Although the dialogue is generally restrained in its criticisms of white Australian society, many of the lyrics are not; yet, their polemicism is mediated by catchy tunes and pleasant rhythms so that sustained attacks covering a variety of issues are both possible and palatable. Bias against Aborigines within the justice system is one of the more serious issues dramatised with a light but provocative touch. Chi presents as farcical the circumstances of Willie and Tadpole's arrest, and then foregrounds incarceration as simply another of the common vicissitudes of Aboriginal life, so that the spell in jail becomes a ritual initiation into adulthood and a moment of community with the many other Aborigines already there. At the same time, the more ominous aspects of custodial punishment are never entirely absent from this scene, as the haunting melodies of 'Listen to the News' point to atrocities meted out to Aboriginal people in the name of an alien law. For Australian audiences, the travellers' imprisonment in the Roebourne Lockup is especially ominous in view of the highly publicised death in custody of a young Aboriginal man, John Pat, at Roebourne in 1983.

Christian imperialism is also revealed as a major factor in the breakdown of Aboriginal social systems. Early sections of the play show that the overt project of Father Benedictus's teachings is to 'civilise' his young Aboriginal charges according to the norms of white society, a motif extended when Marijuana Annie emerges as one of the 'stolen generation' of part-Aboriginal children raised in missions or white families for the express purpose of assimilation. Notwithstanding his critique of the mission system, Chi's take on Christianity attempts to distinguish between the possible benefits of a largely humanist creed and the particular weaknesses and prejudices of those who have professed to follow it. He carnivalises the authority of church leaders by staging their hypocrisies and excesses, while simultaneously embracing unorthodox and hybridised versions of Christianity. As a result, the contradictions within Christian practice as the Aborigines experience it, and the tensions between Christian doctrine and Aboriginal ways of being, provide much of the dramatic energy driving the text. Ironically, the vision of harmony that emerges at the end of the play is shaped by the same Christian ethos that has been the butt of satire elsewhere in the text. This need not be seen as a sign of ideological confusion but rather as testimony to the power of

Aboriginal peoples to creatively 'contaminate' an imposed religious system to the point where it can serve their own needs.

In performance, much of *Bran Nue Dae*'s exuberant energy derives from a celebration of the sexual/sensual body. A key motif is the search for kuckles (shells said to resemble female genitalia), which Chi enlarges into a preoccupation with sex in general, especially among the younger characters. With roguish humour, the play canvasses issues such as masturbation, contraception, adultery, and religious chastity (or lack thereof). In parts, the dialogue captures the bawdy humour of a Shakespearian comedy, and some of the lyrics are racy, if not raunchy. Puritanical attitudes and behaviour are challenged when sex is foregrounded as creative energy, criticised in its excesses and gently mocked in its gaucheries as the narrative extends the conventional romance trope of the Broadway musical to illustrate what happens after the lovers' first (un)chaste kiss. With such playful representations of untrammelled sexuality, the text points with urbane wit to the prejudices of the entertainment traditions that inform it.

Overall, *Bran Nue Dae*'s governing conception of Aboriginality suggests a culture fully cognisant of its rich historical past but struggling constantly not to be confined to that past. A hybrid vision of life and art informs almost every aspect of the play. The musical score draws on country and western, calypso, reggae, gospel, blues and tribal chants to produce a syncretic text that appropriately reflects the complex genealogies of its characters, most of whom find they are at least part Aboriginal by the end of the play. In his upbeat denouement, Chi, who claims Aboriginal, Chinese, Japanese and Scottish ancestry, celebrates miscegenation as a form of connection between cultures rather than a shameful secret to remain hidden at all costs. All the loose threads of the plot are neatly tied up so that the extended Aboriginal 'family' even includes Father Benedictus, while the multi-racial town of Broome becomes emblematic of a reconceived nation where cultural identity is immensely fluid and eclectic. The implication of the ending is that conceptions of Aboriginality based solely on racial origins are not only untenable (given many Aboriginal people's lack of knowledge about their ancestry because of colonial

assimilation policies) but also unhelpful. It is, paradoxically, the dynamism of hybridised Aboriginal identities, both rural and urban, traditional and contemporary, that best ensures the survival of the culture.

In the wake of *Bran Nue Dae*'s remarkable success, there was some criticism of the production as a piece of mainstream entertainment that pulled its punches to avoid unduly discomforting white audiences. This assessment seems to miss the oppositional tenor beneath an apparently hegemonic form, and it discredits the play's impact as a trailblazer for more recent experiments in Aboriginal musical theatre, notably in Roger Bennett's *Funerals and Circuses* (1992) and Wesley Enoch's *The Sunshine Club* (1999). In terms of performing different kinds of cultural work for Aboriginal people, it is worth noting that the production of *Bran Nue Dae* also launched the careers of actors such as Ningali Lawford and Leah Purcell, both of whom have since devised highly acclaimed autobiographical monodramas that toured within Australia and abroad. Chi's second musical, *Corrugation Road* (1996), a surreal romp loosely based on his own experiences in psychiatric hospitals, continues the project of Aboriginal healing and cultural renewal initiated by *Bran Nue Dae*. Taken together, these two influential works presage a difficult but hopeful future for the reconciliation process between indigenous and non-indigenous Australians.

Production history

Bran Nue Dae, directed by Andrew Ross, premiered on 22 February 1990 at the Octagon Theatre, Perth. Between 1990 and 1993, the play toured to Sydney, Melbourne, Adelaide, Canberra and Brisbane, as well as to various rural venues and Aboriginal communities. An Australian Broadcasting Commission telemovie of the text is currently planned for production in 2001.

Select bibliography

Brady, V. (1991) 'The environment: a *Bran Nue Dae* or a very ancient one?', *Westerly* 36, 4: 100–6.

Davies, C.L. (1993) 'Black rock and Broome: musical and cultural specificities', *Perfect Beat* 1, 2: 48–59.

Gilbert, H. (1998a) *Sightlines: Race, Gender*

and *Nation in Contemporary Australian Theatre*, Ann Arbor, MI: University of Michigan Press, 51–95.

—— (1998b) 'Aboriginality in contemporary Australian theatre', in V. Kelly (ed.) *Our Australian Theatre in the 1990s*, Amsterdam: Rodopi, 71–88.

Lo, J. (2001) 'Tropes of ambivalence in *Bran Nue Dae*', in A. Brewster and H. Webb (eds) *Aboriginal Textual Production*, Perth: Fremantle Arts Centre Press.

Makeham, P. (1996) 'Singing the landscape: *Bran Nue Dae*', *Australasian Drama Studies* 28: 117–32.

Neumann, K. (1992) 'A postcolonial writing of Aboriginal history', *Meanjin* 51, 2: 277–98.

Audiovisual resources

Bran Nue Dae (1991) directed by Tom Zubrycki, Bran Nue Dae Corporation, Broome. Available from Ronin Films, Canberra, Australia: roninfilms@datatrax.com.au

Bran Nue Dae

Jimmy Chi and Kuckles

Characters

ROSIE
WILLIE
UNCLE TADPOLE
FATHER BENEDICTUS
SERGEANT DOOGIE
MARIJUANA ANNIE
SLIPPERY
CONSTABLE GOONGANOONG
PASTOR FLAKKON
AUNTIE THERESA
ENSEMBLE
MUSICIANS
All other characters are played by members
of the ensemble.

Act I

Sun Pictures, Broome

*Two rows of deckchairs face one another across
the forestage. Streeter's Jetty projects towards the
audience, with a pool of water on either side. On
the jetty are small railway lines. There is sand
and coloured Broome rocks. In the back the bare
sand of Kennedy Hill, making three levels of
stage. The Sun Pictures movie screen is the
backdrop.*

SALLY ANNE *enters chewing a Cherry Ripe
chocolate bar. Other members of the* CHORUS –
BERNADETTE, LUCY, RITA, TONI, FRANCES –
enter behind and take seats on either side.

SALLY ANNE   You want some? (*Offering
   Cherry Ripe.*)
BERNADETTE   No, go away Sally Anne.

   (SALLY ANNE *walks over to the other row of
   deckchairs.*)

FRANCES   There your mummy there.
SALLY ANNE   Where's my mummy?

   (WILLIE *and* ROSIE *enter, to sit on opposite
   sides.* CHARLIE *enters stage left with soiled

pants pulled up high and cracked glasses,
reading a PIX magazine.*)

SALLY ANNE   Can I sit down here?

   (SALLY ANNE *plumps herself down between*
   WILLIE *and the rest. This throws* WILLIE *off
   his end of the deckchair row.* LITTLE ABBY
   and PETER *enter.*)

PETER   Hey boy, he tongueing for you.
LITTLE ABBY   Munga dog.

   (*Everyone laughs.* LUCY *calls across.*)

LUCY   Hey Rosie, he wanna sit wit you!
ROSIE   Who?
LUCY   Willie.
ROSIE   He stalebait.
SALLY ANNE   He deadly boy. He come from
   Lombadina.
BERNADETTE   He bin Perth for schooling,
   Rossmoyne.
RITA   That Father Benedictus.
OTHERS   And he going back too.

   (ROSIE *works her way in embarrassment to
   centre stage.*)

ALL   He wanna sit wit you at Sun Pictures.

   (WILLIE *runs to* ROSIE *at base of the jetty as
   the movie begins with the leader countdown
   10 to 1, followed by 'God Save the Queen' with
   Elizabeth II on a horse. The Queen's head
   goes off the screen.* WILLIE *and* ROSIE *are
   transported into the movie.* CHORUS *exits.*)

ROSIE   What, Willie?

   (*Song: 'Light a Light'*)

WILLIE
   Hey girl, you know I've been a dreamer
   following dreams I've dreamed on my
   own.
   Though the dreams are the dream that
   sustain me,
   I'm tired of dreaming alone.

(CHORUS *re-enters from stage right bearing lighted candles.*)

CHORUS

Light a light, leave it in the window,
I'm comin' back, back home to you.
Light a light, leave it in the window
I'll be comin' back home.

There are times when I'm feelin' so
    fearful
times when I'm cut up and crying inside,
those times that find me always remind
    me
of hoping to find you here by my side.

Light a light, leave it in the window,
I'm comin' back, back home to you.
Light a light, leave it in the window,
I'll be comin' back home.

Light a light, leave it in the window,
I'm comin' back, back home to you.
Light a light, leave it in the window,
I'll be comin' back home
I'll be comin' back home.

(*A big refrigerator is wheeled on, with candle holders all around it.* CHORUS *place their candles in the holders.* ROSIE *gives* WILLIE *a friendly glance and wave and leaves him.*)

Rossmoyne Pallottine Aboriginal Hostel

There is an explosion and BENEDICTUS *appears in a cloud of smoke, wearing a black cassock embroidered with Cherry Ripe bars and with a tall mitre and huge crook with a large hook. He wears shoulder pads and built-up shoes, making him larger than life.*

BENEDICTUS (*German accent*) Ah so, Villie! Come een fellow!! Velkom to der city. How are you, my leedle flend?
WILLIE Gud, fada.
BENEDICTUS So fellow, vot haff you been doing? Did you catch any fish vile avay on holidays?
WILLIE No fada.
BENEDICTUS So fellow you must inspect every awailable vacancy at Clontarf to become a successful indaweedal.
WILLIE Yes fada.
BENEDICTUS Villie Villie, ven Joshua valked around Jericho, he did so at the Lord's kommand. You can't get to heaven if you don't go to the sacraments and just sprinkle your arse vit holy vater!

WILLIE Yes fada.
BENEDICTUS Villie, you can go fort and help your people – dey are crying in dere vilderness. You haff so much to gif the vorld! So my leedle flend enjoy your stay wit derfellows; den you can knuckle down to some serious study! Now go – (WILLIE *is half way off.*) Ah Villie! Vill you not be one of my leedle altar boys tomorrow?
WILLIE Okay fada Benedictus. See you fada.

(*Light dims on* BENEDICTUS. *Light comes up on the fridge where* WILLIE *is leading a raid on the tuckshop with the boys* PETER, DARRYL *and* LITTLE ABBY.)

WILLIE Bro no one coming?
LITTLE ABBY Nuh Benny's done his rounds.

(WILLIE *breaks into the tuckshop, opens the fridge revealing Cherry Ripes and Cokes etc.*)

ALL (*exclaiming*) Wahh . . . !!

(WILLIE *takes out a little black book, pretends to be taking orders.*)

WILLIE What you want Bro?
PETER Coke-coke! Cherry Ripe too, Bro! – and Roasted Peanuts!
LITTLE ABBY What you doing bro?
WILLIE Itemising ewery awailable confection unt bewerage purchase, bro.
PETER You think yourself accountant?
WILLIE Yeah, like St Peter, bro. (*They laugh.*)
DARRYL Is Benny looking?
WILLIE Uh – Benny!

(WILLIE *runs up the hill and looks to stage right and comes back.*)

WILLIE No.

(*The boys stuff their shirts as they leave the tuckshop and move to the side and sit down for a feast.*)

WILLIE Yah it is gut to eat at der Lord's table. First ve haff made un inventory ov der spoils. (*He holds the black book up.*) Den ve haff to partake of der fruits ov our labours. Thankyou Lord –
ALL Thankyou Lord!
PETER Und dis is for all der starfing kids in der vorld – (*He bites into a Cherry Ripe bar.*)
DARRYL Like us I bro, us blackies starving.
LITTLE ABBY Yeah bro.
WILLIE Und den der liquid refreshments to make it taste efen bedder!
ALL Ya, ya!

(There is a tinkling of a bell. DARRYL *runs up the hill and whistles a warning.)*

DARRYL Benny, Benny coming –

*(*WILLIE *drops the black book and* LITTLE ABBY *drops an unfinished note to his girlfriend in the confusion of clearing up bottles and wrappers. To the strains of the song 'Calling in the Name',* BENEDICTUS *paces on in stately fashion, passing near the black book and then over it. He leads the* CONGREGATION *on like the pied piper, singing stoutly with crook and mitre. The* CONGREGATION *fans out on either side of the stage,* BENEDICTUS *in the centre, with* WILLIE *on the left side and* DARRYL *on the right staggering under the weight of the missal.)*

CONGREGATION *(sings)*
   Hey listen people
   He is calling in the name
   He is shattering the idols
   Which He scatters on the plain
   He is washing all the nations
   In a spiritual refrain
   And the world keeps on turning
   And will never be the same.

(Kids make fun of BENEDICTUS *behind his back.)*

   There's a new day dawning
   And it's wiping out the tears
   With the task unfolding
   With the passing of the years.
   Take the word upon you
   To the corners of the world
   Lead the people into battle
   With his banners all unfurled.

(Kids dart out, lift and look under his cloak and dart back.)

   See the light arising
   From the east unto the west
   Seeing all the nations being put unto the
     test.
   There's no time to falter, we all have to
     be refined
   Purged of all the coarseness
   And remade to his design.
BENEDICTUS Dere are many evils in der world today. *(The Angelus is rung.)* Countless innumerable abominations to der Lord. However, for now let us just talk about theft und pillage. Und der sins ov der flesh.

(Kids make fun of the sermon, pick their noses and gesticulate. DARRYL *swings the smoking thurible between his legs.)*

My greatest desire is to see der native people be edercarted und trained in der skills ov der modern vorld. To become citerzens ov dis country dat is truly deres. Ve haff to show luff to dese children so dat dey can indeed fulfil der motto: *Lux in tenebris – Light in der darkness!*

(The Angelus is rung. BENEDICTUS *stares meaningfully at* WILLIE. *He closes with benediction.)*

BENEDICTUS *(nasal)* The Lord be wif you.
CONGREGATION *(nasal)* And also wif you.

(The altar boys file past for the last rousing chorus of 'Calling in the Name'. BENEDICTUS *begins swatting his altar boys, whacking each on the hand with a slapstick.)*

CONGREGATION *(sings)*
   See the light arising
   From the east unto the west
   Seeing all the nations being put unto the
     test.
   There's no time to falter, we all have to
     be refined
   Purged of all the coarseness
   And remade to his design.
   Hey listen people
   He is calling in the name –

(A break in the music. WILLIE *pulls his hands away to avoid the whack.)*

BENEDICTUS By hook or by crook I vill vack you!! *(He whacks* WILLIE *on the behind.)*
WILLIE Oohh –
CONGREGATION *(sings)*
   He is shattering the idols
   Which He scatters on the plain
   He is washing all the nations
   In a spiritual refrain
   And the world keeps on turning
   And will never be the same.

*(*CHORUS *as children take up positions either side in the Sun Pictures deck chairs.)*

BENEDICTUS *(exhausted)* Vell working boys und schoolies ve would like to velcome our representatives at Clontarf. Villie back home for turd Sunday as you all know. And ve haff some messages from der little angels . . . Ve need someone to select a message. Abby vill you not come up?

(*Frightened,* LITTLE ABBY *gets up from far right stage and moves to* BENEDICTUS*'s side, centre stage, and kids sing out.*)

CHORUS   Yoh yoh Abby. (*Pointing*) Leg leg –

(LITTLE ABBY*'s right leg is shaking uncontrollably.* BENEDICTUS *points with his crook to* LITTLE ABBY*'s love note that he had dropped during the tuckshop raid. It is right at* BENEDICTUS*'s feet.* LITTLE ABBY *picks it up and* BENEDICTUS *hooks him round the neck and pulls him up close. He takes the note and reads it to assembly.*)

BENEDICTUS   'Hey boy you make me itchy. I'm alvay tongueing for you!'

(LITTLE ABBY *expects the worst but* BENEDICTUS *lets him off, points him back to his seat.* BENEDICTUS *glances severely at* WILLIE.)

Villy! Vill you not come up und see vat ve haff?

(*Drum roll à la madame guillotine –* WILLIE *approaches* BENEDICTUS, *who points with crook to the black book on the floor.* WILLIE *picks it up.* BENEDICTUS *then hooks him round the neck and draws him close up.* BENEDICTUS *takes the book.*)

Ah a present for der good fada. A diary! Vat haff ve now? (*Reads entries.*) Saturday 24th Nowember, 4 bottle Coke (large), 10 pkts Cherry Ripe! 20 pkts Roasted Peanuts. Der list . . . ah der list of omissions! Der list goes on und on! Villy you are a rotten abble in der barrel. You are a blot on der mission and a stain on der celebration of life. (*Ominous strains as* BENEDICTUS *hooks him by the crook, moving him forward and back.*) Stupid kit you are an abomination to der Lord. You are sex und drugs in Chinatown, drinking in der park, looking up der girlies dresses und creeping in der dark.

WILLIE   No fada.

(*Boys cheer.* BENEDICTUS *thinks he is receiving approval from them and he sets* WILLIE *down.*)

BENEDICTUS   You vill never change – You are zer leedle Hitler! You are leading der boys astray. Ve haff no rooms for failures – or ve vant is sucess!

CHORUS   Oooohhhh . . .

(BENEDICTUS *with a sweep of the crook*

hurls WILLIE *to the floor. For a moment he is motionless. The* CHORUS *cheers as he recovers and rises to sing defiantly: 'Nothing I Would Rather Be'.*)

WILLIE
There's nothing I would rather be
than to be an Aborigine
and watch you take my precious land
   away.
For nothing gives me greater joy than to
watch you fill each girl and boy
with superficial existential shit.

(CHORUS *dance on from the side.*)

CHORUS
Now you may think I'm cheeky
but I'd be satisfied
to rebuild your convict ships
and sail you on the tide.

WILLIE
I love the way you give me God
and of course the mining board
for this of course I thank the lord each
   day.
I'm glad you say that land rights wrong
then you should go where you belong
and leave me to just keep on keeping on.

WILLIE and CHORUS
Now you may think I'm cheeky
but I'd be satisfied,
to rebuild your convict ships
and sail you on the tide.

WILLIE
There's nothing I would rather be
than to be an Aborigine
and dream of just what heaven must be
   like,
where moth and rust do not corrupt
when I die I know I'll be going up,
cos you know that I've had my hell on
   earth.

CHORUS
God gave us ten commandments,
ve know ve are informed.

BENEDICTUS   (*sings in slow ominous strains*)
Judgement day is coming,
ve alvays being va-aa-rned.

(*On the back projection is Michaelangelo's 'Creation of Adam'.* WILLIE *and* BENEDICTUS *almost touch their fingers.* WILLIE *is thrown back from the contact.*)

CHORUS
There's nothing I would rather be
than to be an Aborigine

and watch you take my precious land
   away.
No no no no –
And watch you take my precious land
   away.
BENEDICTUS   (*sings*) Ohhhhh no!

(CHORUS *of children exits.*)

By hook or by crook I vill vack you to sort
out dis sordid mess. Clear out of der House
of der Lord, der Temple of der Soul. Clear
out! Go!! Back where you came from, go!!!

(*A scared* WILLIE *exits as if expelled from the
Garden of Eden. Out of one life and into
another.*)

WILLIE   No faaada!

City park at night

TADPOLE *enters from stage right and lights fire.*
CHORUS *of fringe dwellers enters wearing
blankets. Song: 'A Longway Away From My
Country'.*

TADPOLE
   I'm a longway away from my country,
   It's a long time since I've reappeared.
   It's the feeling I feel
   When you're close on the wheel
   And I'm missing the touch of your
      hand.

   It's no good this feeling of sorrow,
   Just go out and face it alone
   And I'm waiting tonight,
   A watch in the night
   And thinking of just going home.

(WILLIE *walks on in a desolate mood, much
the worse for wear. He is attracted by the
singing and the company but hesitates,
unfamiliar with that lifestyle, and disturbed to
find himself a part of it. There is some
movement among the people, a woman getting
up, someone stirring the fire, some drinking,
handing a flagon around, touching and
sharing during the song.* TADPOLE *notices*
WILLIE.)

TADPOLE   Hey boy where you bin come
from? What you name?

(WILLIE *steps over to the campfire.*)

WILLIE   Father bin kick me out. I got
nowhere to stay. I wanna go home to
Broome. (WILLIE *sits dejected, cross legged.
Head in hands, at a loss.*)

TADPOLE   I come from Broome too but you
still never tell me your name yet.
WILLIE   My name William Johnson.
TADPOLE   Yeah eh! You know what? My
name . . . my name Steven Johnson. But
I'm your uncle, Uncle Tadpole! I bin away
for 20 years now. I bin drovin' I bin
drinkin' I bin Christian, I bin everything;
but now its time I gotta go home before I
die. I gotta see old people.
CHORUS   (*sings*)
   So come on you restless young riders,
   Come on you young roving kinds.
   Unless you're prepared
   It's not like you've heard,
   Cos you'll find that you'll run out of
      time.

(WILLIE, *embarrassed by* TADPOLE, *moves
away, afraid of throwing in his lot with him
and ending up like him.* TADPOLE *shuffles
and swings over to* WILLIE.)

TADPOLE   Come on we better piss off eh!
Come on let's go walking down this road
and fuckin' find a place to go home, c'mon.
Yeah my boy, c'mon hurry up, let's go
home. We got no time to muck around!
You know what! You're mother is my uncle
brother and that's my brother but this is
my sister so he call you uncle. That's how
come I'm your sister brother and I'm your
uncle and so I'm your uncle, OKAY!?
WILLIE   Yeah Uncle. But who is my daddy?
TADPOLE   What they bin doing to you my
boy, they bin hit you!
WILLIE   Yeah fada bin hit me. They bin
chuck me out from mission.
TADPOLE   How come? What you bin doing?
WILLIE   Uh I bin . . . uh I bin trying to grab
some tucker.
TADPOLE   Yeah, they always bloody starve
you. They never give you enough tucker
and you never get enough beer . . .

(*Sleepers roll over in park, some men and a
few women embracing.*)

TADPOLE   . . . and you never get enough
woman either and that's your trouble.
WILLIE   Ah no Uncle I'm good man!
TADPOLE   Yeah, I know you, you young
bastards! You fuckin' 'round here, you
fuckin' 'round there, you fuckin' 'round
everywhere. Bloody education that's the
thing to get, not this fuckin 'round. You
wanna end up like your uncle? Yeah I fuck
the sand. I'm here in Perth and I got

fuckin' nowhere to go. What you fuckin' think of this?

WILLIE   Yeah, yeah Uncle, I feel sorry now. I don't know what to tell my mummy!

TADPOLE   Never mind I'll fix up your mummy. Come on then.

(*As they go, the band plays a few bars reprise of 'A Longway Away from My Country' and those left behind sing softly:*)

ALL
Shake off your burdened delusions,
Shake off your dreams that weigh down.
You can follow your dreams
But it's not like it seems
'Cos your heart will just turn you
around . . .

TADPOLE   We'll go back to Lombadina. I got a lot of things to settle in Broome. Ah you'll find out and they'll find out, when we get there. Anyway what we doing here? C'mon we go.

WILLIE and TADPOLE (*downstage in duet*)
You can follow your dreams

But it's not like it seems
'Cos your heart will just turn you around.

A busy city roadside, at traffic lights

CHORUS *become cars and pedestrians in the city.* WILLIE *and* TADPOLE *make a dive to cross the road. They become separated by cars.* WILLIE *beckons* TADPOLE *who nearly gets bowled over, which gives him an idea.*

WILLIE   This big place aye Uncle. Big mob motocar.

(*Song: 'Traffic Lights'*)

CHORUS
If you stop, stop, stop, stop,
Bin roaming around in the city
Yoo yoo yoo yoo,
The peak hour traffic just takes its time
Yoo yoo yoo yoo
Confusions controlled in the city
By traffic lights that sure can blind.

Figure 7 'Traffic Lights'. *Bran Nue Dae*, directed by Andrew Ross, 1990. Photo: David Wilson.

Well you start to move,
but can't get very far,
You're lost in a jungle of cars
White gloved cop is waving at you –

(WILLIE *shouts warning to* TADPOLE.)

CHORUS   (*sings*) While all the traffic lights
tell you what to do.
WILLIE   Uncle! Quickly now.
CHORUS   (*sings*) See a green light –
WILLIE   Move it.
CHORUS   (*sings*) Yellow light –
WILLIE   Slow down!
CHORUS   (*sings*) Red light –
WILLIE   Uncle –
CHORUS   (*sings*) Stop! Don't walk!!

(*A jammed horn blares.* MARIJUANA
ANNIE *and* SLIPPERY *screech to a halt and
back up in their car.* MARIJUANA ANNIE *is a
hippy in her 20s,* SLIPPERY *is a happy
wanderer from Germany in his 20s, on a
perpetual high.*)

M. ANNIE   Old man you alright? Yeh?

(TADPOLE *lies in a crumpled heap giving a
good impression of a moan.*)

SLIPPERY   Mein Gott! Vhat's happening
here?
M. ANNIE   Slippery, come over here and get
this old man into the car, we'll take him to
hospital.
TADPOLE   Don't you fuckin' take me to
hospital, I don't go to no fuckin' hospital.
M. ANNIE   Where do you want to go then?
TADPOLE   I wanna go to fuckin' Broome.
M. ANNIE   You wanta go to Broome?
TADPOLE   Yeah me and this young fella
here, we going to fuckin' Broome. You
bastards gonna take us there or what?
M. ANNIE   It's all right old man, take it easy.
TADPOLE   My name Tadpole. Steven
Johnson Tadpole. They call me Tadpole,
Uncle Tadpole.
M. ANNIE   And who's this one?
TADPOLE   Oh! That's Willy.
M. ANNIE   Oh Willy!
TADPOLE   This my nephew that boy.
M. ANNIE   What a spunk!
TADPOLE   Oh you don't wanna trust him,
that little bastard. Hmph! Willy he bin
fuckin' 'round here, he bin fuckin' 'round
there, he bin fuckin' 'round everywhere,
the little bastard. Well come on, you better
help me up, I better jump inside. I wanna
fuckin' go to Broome! Him too. (*Pointing to

WILLIE*) He wanna come to Broome too!
(WILLIE *and* TADPOLE *climb into the 'car'.*)
M. ANNIE   Slippery, let's go to Broome, let's
take these two blokes to Broome.
SLIPPERY   (*reluctant to take these two 1500
miles overland for free.*) Ah, ah. I don't know
Annie, long way.

(MARIJUANA ANNIE *twists* SLIPPERY *round
her finger, turns on the charm, growing
wistful at the thought of a tropical paradise.*)

M. ANNIE   Why not? It's a good place, I hear
it's good out there. Plenty of fishing, nice
beaches and plenty of people who smoke a
little bit of this and that.
SLIPPERY   Is it the same as Yermany?
WILLIE   Ay?
SLIPPERY   Haff they got forests like in
Yermany?
M. ANNIE   No they haven't got any forests,
but they got 80 mile beaches, and reefs and
places you can nestle away in – I think!

(SLIPPERY *is swayed by the thought of
passion in the tropics.*)

SLIPPERY   Ah yah I think it is gut to go to
Broome. Where you come from old fella,
you come from Broome, do you?
TADPOLE   (*still angry, drunk*) Yeh, what the
fuck, where you come from anyway, you
bastard?
SLIPPERY   I come from Yermany, I am
escaping the army conscription.
TADPOLE   Who? 'Nother Hitler eh?
SLIPPERY   Ya ya. (*Then recollecting himself*) –
Nein nein.
M. ANNIE   I've heard about this Hitler and
all that – he was supposed to have this
spear of Longinus, the one that pierced
Jesus in the side.
TADPOLE   (*real argumentative drunk*) Don't
you talk like that about Jesus Christ, he's
the saviour – everybody always tells me
anyhow – wish the bastard would save us
now.
M. ANNIE   I'm a Buddhist myself.
TADPOLE   Don't you talk about that, that's
proper rude thing to say in our language –
WILLIE   (*a bit tired of this*) You mob knocked
him over, you goin' take us mob back to
Broome or what?
M. ANNIE   Come on, Slippery.

(SLIPPERY *gets into the driver's seat next to*
TADPOLE, MARIJUANA ANNIE *gets in the
back next to* WILLIE *and gives him the eye.*)

SLIPPERY Ah well, I s'pose now that I am in Australia I might as well see it, first hand. And what better experience than to go with you and these two fellows, local people. Aboro-gynal people . . . (*He hesitates at the cool stare* TADPOLE *is giving him.*) Coloured people . . . native people . . . The sort of people that I can relate to in this country, where I am understood, I hope.

(CHORUS *comes down either side of the travellers, miming handline fishing, kuckling, gambling, dreaming, beach relaxing.*)

(*Travel song: 'Feel Like Going Back Home'*)

TADPOLE
>Feel like going back home
>Right now while the mangoes are ripe,
>Frangipanis starting to bloom
>And the Bluebone starting to bite.

CHORUS
>Hey mum I can just taste your fish soup
> and rice,
>I'm coming back home to you,
>Can't hack the pace of the city life,
>Soon I'll be dreaming in Broome.

TADPOLE
>The luggers are in on the spring tide
>And the gambling houses are packed.
>Banker he mukan with sit on
>But Larri we got butta in front.

CHORUS
>Hey dad we gonna rage a little John Hurt
> tonight
>Make Orion sing with the moon.
>Can't hack the pace of the city life,
>Soon I'll be dreaming in Broome.

ALL
>Lazy breeze blowin' through your mind,
>Sky blue sea, catch a feed there any time.

(SLIPPERY *and* MARIJUANA ANNIE *pass a smoke around, which* WILLIE *declines.* SLIPPERY *slips into a daze and the car drifts off the road.* TADPOLE *sees the danger just in time.*)

TADPOLE
>Feel like going back home
>Right now while the mangoes are ripe,
>Jigal tree starting to bloom
>And the Gided starting to bite.

CHORUS
>Hey mum I can just taste your fish soup
> and rice,
>I'm coming back home to you,
>Can't hack the pace of the city life,

>Soon I'll be dreaming in Broome.
>Soon I'll be dreaming in Broome.
>Soon I'll be dreaming in Broome.

The Great Northern Highway, south of Roebourne

M. ANNIE We better stop soon – did you remember to water those plants in the back?

SLIPPERY Ya. But I don't know whether you can keep that stuff here in Australia.

M. ANNIE It's totally necessary Slippery. How do you think I'm supposed to keep my equilibrium and my social outlook together if I don't have this little weed to help me get along?

(*Two khaki-clad northern cops enter and pull them over.*)

COP Pull over there.

M. ANNIE Hey, they're pulling us over –

COP What's this bloody stuff in the back here? Do you realise it's illegal to be in possession of marijew-ahna?

M. ANNIE You can't search our car, you know that's illegal. I've got my rights.

COP Lay-dy, when you carry this stuff around, you've got no rights.

(SLIPPERY *and* MARIJUANA ANNIE *are defiant but* TADPOLE *is used to the situation and influences* WILLIE *to accept it too.*)

M. ANNIE (*as they are hauled off*) You can't – what are you doing with us? You can't – hey!

COP Jump in. Chuck 'em in!

WILLIE Oh Chrije – they gonna put us in jail, Uncle.

TADPOLE That's alright – what the fuck I was a lawyer once, I been in jail many times, but I always get out.

Roebourne Lockup at night

The stage darkens, a steel jail door slams shut, keys rattle. WILLIE, TADPOLE, MARIJUANA ANNIE, SLIPPERY *are led to cells by* SERGEANT DOOGIE.

SLIPPERY Who are these people?

(*Song: 'Linjoo Blues'*)

INMATES
>Some people call them the cops
>Some people call them police,

Back home in Broome
We call them linjoo.

SLIPPERY (*protesting*) I come from Yermany –

COP Where's your passport?

(SLIPPERY *hasn't one.* SERGEANT *grins.*)

SERGEANT What's your name?

SLIPPERY Wolfgang Beuitenmuller.

SERGEANT Jesus. How do you spell that?

SLIPPERY B E U I T E N M U L L E R – my friends just call me Slippery.

SERGEANT I'm not surprised, Slippery.

INMATES (*singing*) Smokin' jokin' with my friends –

WILLIE (*to* MARIJUANA ANNIE) That policeman don't like that green stuff in the back of your car, I?

INMATES (*singing*) Got so stoned it was the end.

COP Listen son, don't get smart with us!

WILLIE Pardon?

INMATES (*singing*) Someone come and knock on the door –

SERGEANT Do you realise that you are being charged with possession of marijew-ahna?

COP Now who is responsible for this stuff?

INMATES (*singing*) Told me not to smoke that gunja no more –

SLIPPERY Yes they did.

TADPOLE I never seen this stuff before. I don't know what this stuff is.

INMATES (*singing*) I got the linjoo blues.

SLIPPERY I don't know – dis feellow who gafe me der car –

INMATES (*singing*) I got the linjoo blues.

SLIPPERY Said if you tek dis stuff to Broome . . . I'll meet you dere!

INMATES (*singing*)
Stop your foolin', stop your foolin'
Stop your messing with my head.

M. ANNIE I found it. I'm taking it to Broome for analysis.

INMATES (*singing*)
Stop your foolin', stop your foolin'
Stop your messing with my head
With my head, with my head.

M. ANNIE I've had enough of this physical harrassment. I know what you police are all about. You just want to lock us all up. Just because we're free spirits and we're trying to have a good time. Everybody wants to lock everybody else up these days. You and me (*to* WILLIE, TADPOLE, *then back to* SERGEANT) well

why don't you lock us all up then. Get rid of us!

SERGEANT (*stares at her*) Yeah, that's right woman. Done!

(SERGEANT *and* COP *throw* MARIJUANA ANNIE *up and over.*)

INMATES (*singing*)
Stop your foolin', stop your foolin'
Stop your messing with my head

(SERGEANT *and* COP *do a cakewalk style strut through figures.*)

TADPOLE This your first time in jail, Willie?

WILLIE Yeah uncle, I'm man now.

TADPOLE Never min' my boy . . . legal aid get you out of here.

WILLIE Uncle, people die in jail I?

INMATES (*singing*)
Now I'm sitting down in this cell
Thinkin' about you baby
Masturbating like hell
Screw come 'round for an early start.

(COP *and* SERGEANT *pounce on* WILLIE.)

COP You come with me feller,
You're here to pull yourself together
Don't pull yourself apart.

INMATES (*singing*)
Stop your foolin', stop your foolin'
Stop your messing with my head.

(*The cops belt* WILLIE.)

TADPOLE (*setting up a commotion*) I wanna see the legal aid. I wanna see the legal aid.

INMATES (*singing*)
Stop your foolin', stop your foolin'
Stop your messing with my head.

CELL VOICE Steven you old bastard – what they got you for?

TADPOLE This bloke here, he got this . . . I don't know, he got plant here, I don't know what kind plant, but they don't like that plant. They chuck us all in. I wanna see the legal aid! My brother's the legal aid in this Roebourne town – I'm the cousin brother but really the brother – where's the legal aid?!

CELL VOICE You tell 'em bro!

TADPOLE Who that?

CELL VOICE I am the legal aid.

TADPOLE Oh fuck 'im.

INMATES (*singing*)
Stop your foolin', stop your foolin'
Stop your messing with my head.

Figure 8 'Listen to the News'. *Bran Nue Dae,* directed by Andrew Ross, 1993. Photo: Jeff Busby.

TADPOLE   Cousin brother! Johnny Johnson!
   What they got you in here for?
CELL VOICE   Ne' mind. I'll get you all out.
   Just tell me what happening.

   (*There's a shout of pain* – WILLIE's *voice.*)

TADPOLE   You better listen you bastard – I'll
   tell you . . .

   (*Song: 'Listen to the News'.* TADPOLE,
   then inmates, joining in. WILLIE *leads the
   dance.*)

TADPOLE
   Man of the gun come shot up the son
   and the girl and the child and the
      mother
   but the child is the son and the son is the
      child
   and the child is the son of the father.
   And the winds sing the song
   of the right and the wrong
   and scatters the tunes and the meaning
   and the passage of time just follows the
      line
   of the law of the land and the dreaming.

ALL
   Listen to the News
   talkin' 'bout the blues
   of our people.
   Listen to the News
   talkin' 'bout the blues
   of our people.
   Everyday everyday
   Discussing a way
   Discussing a way.
TADPOLE   (*with women inmates, in haunting
   harmony*)
   The promises made just spelt out the
      graves
   of the living the dead and the dying
   for the old and the new
   and the words of the few
   just knew that the cycle was changing.
   For the man of the clock
   believed that the lot
   of the people were his for the taking
   though the law was the same
   in his books in his name
   in his words which he kept on
      breaking.

333

Listen to the News
talkin' 'bout the blues
of our people.
Listen to the News
talkin' 'bout the blues
of our people.
Everyday everyday
Discussing a way
Discussing a way.

CHORUS   (*women of the jail only*)
In his eyes all are one
all are sons all begun
all fashioned to bend to his reason
and the mother and child
and the father who smiles
on the world as it carries each season.

For all are the same
just born to the name
of the father whose words have been
   spoken
and the words 'Peace on Earth'
just carry a curse
when the words are so easily broken.

Listen to the News
talkin' 'bout the blues
of our people.
Listen to the News
talkin' 'bout the blues
of our people.
Everyday, everyday
Discussing a way
Discussing a way.

TADPOLE
But a leader will come
from the house of the son
and the man and the gun will be broken
and the word will be heard
when the leader is reared
and the words that he speaks will be
   spoken.
So look to the day
when the sun shines its rays
'cos I know that a new day is dawning
for dawn it will come
when the people as one
shall rise to the light of the morning.

Listen to the News
talkin' 'bout the blues
of our people.
Listen to the News
talkin' 'bout the blues
of our people.
Everyday, everyday
Discussing a way
Discussing a way.

Oo la la la – lalalala – lalalala
Oo la la la la – lalalalala
Oo la la la – lalalala – lalalala
Oo la la la la – lalalalala

Is this the end?
Is this the end of our people?

(*Wail – a woman in the* CHORUS.)

Is this the end?
Is this the end of our people?

(*Wail – a woman in the* CHORUS.)

Is this the end?
Is this the end of our people?

(*Clapsticks, didgeridoo, darkness.*)

Bush and pool Roebuck Plains

Birds calling. The travellers wake up by a pool.
SLIPPERY *meditates. A splash of water –*
WILLIE*'s head emerges from the pool.* TADPOLE
prowls the scene for bush tucker.

M. ANNIE   Jesus it's hot.
TADPOLE   This Roebuck Plains, this country.
M. ANNIE   Fuck is it always this hot up here?
TADPOLE   When you come from this
   country it's not hot. (*Wipes perspiration
   from his face.*)
M. ANNIE   I'm hungry, when do we get to
   Broome?

(TADPOLE *chases behind the hill and then off
stage.*)

SLIPPERY   Vat iss he doing?
WILLIE   (*dully*) Chasing barni.
SLIPPERY   Who iss Barney?
WILLIE   Bungarra.
SLIPPERY   Boong arrows? (*Making motion of
   drawing bow.*)
WILLIE   Jalangardi.

(SLIPPERY *still perplexed.*)

WILLIE   Goanna.
SLIPPERY   Why Anna go?
WILLIE   BEEEEG LIZARD.
SLIPPERY   Big lizard yah? (*Positions hands to
   length of a small lizard.*)

(WILLIE *spreads his hands out to show an
enormous goanna.*)

WILLIE   Wah! (*Splashes the water.*)
SLIPPERY   (*scared*) Fadumpta schizen!

(*Enter* TADPOLE, *and traditional Aboriginal
dancers. Females bear bush tucker in*

bindjins, males have spears and boomerangs. Song: 'Jalangardi')

TADPOLE
Monsoon clouds are coming,

FEMALES
Ngarba yunyarri ngarba yunyarri.

TADPOLE
Gonna bring the barni too.

FEMALES
Ngarba yunyarri ngarba yunyarri.

WILLIE
Magabala Gungkura Gubiny for you
Going down to Roebuck Plains.

(Boisterous dance with hunting and food gathering movements. MARIJUANA ANNIE *is spaced out by it all and entranced by what is happening around her;* SLIPPERY *is frightened of the natives.)*

FEMALES and TADPOLE
Jalangardi, jalangardi
The chase is on
Gotta run, pass 'em gun
The chase is on.

Karrajarri, Yawuru, Nyikina, Bardi
All running, all running
Must have that mungari, mayi,
And wali and arli, and arli, and arli.

TADPOLE
Because it tastes so good,
gotta try it sometime.

CHORUS
The chase is on
Gotta run, pass 'em gun
The chase is on
Jalangardi, jalangardi.

M. ANNIE   Hey this is good.

*(*SLIPPERY *tastes the bush banana and is not so impressed, exclaims, spits out.* TADPOLE *leads a song and dance. Song: 'Everybody Likes a Magabala')*

TADPOLE
Everybody likes a lulb'd goanna
ahha ahha ahha ahha ah-ah

Everybody likes a bush banana
ahha ahha ahha ahha ah-ha

Figure 9 'Everybody likes a Magabala'. *Bran Nue Dae*, directed by Andrew Ross, 1993. Photo: Jeff Busby.

Everybody plucks one
everybody sucks one
everybody's feeling fine.

Everybody knows where
magabala grows yeah
it ripens on the vine, yeah –
it ripens on the vine, yeah –
it ripens on the vine.
Ahha ahha ahha ahha ah-ah

(MARIJUANA ANNIE *and* SLIPPERY *respond to the suggestion of the dance and move up to the hill for lovemaking.* WILLIE *notices them passionately kissing.*)

WILLIE   Uncle, what those two doing there?

TADPOLE   Wah, you don't look that side. You mind your own business.

WILLIE   No Uncle look. He grabbing that thing there!

TADPOLE   Nobody ever tell you about this kind of thing before?

WILLIE   No Uncle. I don't savvy this kind of thing.

TADPOLE   No one bin tell you? Well, when man find a woman you gotta make love to them.

WILLIE   Eh, Uncle!

TADPOLE   I tell you, I tell you – when God made man (*gestures*) when God made man – and he made woman (*gestures*). And he made 'em different and when they find each other . . . they do that thing. You never ever . . . ? Nobody ever tell you about this kind of thing before?

WILLIE   No Uncle.

TADPOLE   Well you better go watch 'em.

(MARIJUANA ANNIE *cradles* SLIPPERY *in her arms and sings.* WILLIE *watches. Song: 'Afterglow'*)

M. ANNIE
Hush a bye little darlin'
won't you lay by my side
and we'll fly together
on a celestial ride.
Close your eyes, little darlin'
I love you don't you know?
And we'll bathe together in the afterglow.

I love you little darlin'
I love you oh so much
and I ride on your rhythm
and move with your touch.
Stay awhile little darlin'
oh please please don't go
and we'll bathe together in the afterglow.

Stay awhile little darlin'
stay awhile with your love
keep me safe in your loving
secure in your touch.
Let us just grow together
as loving must grow
and we'll bathe together in the afterglow.

TADPOLE   Willie, you got girlfriend?

WILLIE   I uncle.

TADPOLE   You like woman? This man got woman, you got woman . . .

WILLIE   Big shame!

TADPOLE   (*pointing with walking stick to* WILLIE's *lower region*) You must feel something dere.

WILLIE   Uh – Uncle, I got this girl Rosie . . . (*confused*) I like 'im but I don't know if he like me. He in Broome now, he bin kicked outta Mission too. He different one from me . . . I don't know if he like me . . .

TADPOLE   And you wanta be a man or what? You gonna be stupid man or you gonna grab 'em or what?

WILLIE   (*realising acutely his own inadequacy*) Ah, I don't know if he like me, Uncle.

TADPOLE   You better go and find 'em and grab 'em. You gotta be man now you not baby anymore – what's wrong with you?!

WILLIE   I don't know if he like me, Uncle.

TADPOLE   Must be proper pretty one, eh?

(*Song: 'If You See Rosie'*)

WILLIE
If you see Rosie
Won't you tell her that I care;
She's the only one that I love
Won't you tell her I'll be there.
Her hair
all a splendour
as she catch the fire's glow,
that's the Rosie I love
and that you love
I suppose.

(*Women and men watch laughing and join the dance routine.* TADPOLE *sits and watches.*)

If you see her smile
You'll know what I feel
to love and kiss and hold her
would make my life unreal
and for her to say she loves me
would make my life complete . . .

TADPOLE
Rosie is the sandwich
and you want to be the meat!

Act II

Chinatown in Broome, outside the Roebuck Bay Hotel

The Roebuck is a legendary bush pub that has seen better days and is trying hard to bring them back. It has big verandahs, for this is the tropics, and a certain tawdry grace. There are no pearling fleets any more but the jade waters of Roebuck Bay are just across the street. The corrugated iron roofs and shacks of Chinatown are white like a pearl, a dust covered pearl.
To the strains of 'Feel Like Going Back Home',
TADPOLE, WILLIE, SLIPPERY *and*
MARIJUANA ANNIE *drive into Broome and arrive outside the Roebuck.*

TADPOLE   Hey boy, we're in Broome now.
ALL   Yeah!
WILLIE   That's the place where I bin used to live before. (*Points*) Kennedy Hill Reserve up there!
TADPOLE   (*getting his walking stick into action*) Turn left over there. We better hit the Roebuck I think.
SLIPPERY   Vats der Roebuck?

(*Faint music in background – opening bars of 'Time Will Heal'.*)

WILLIE   Where all the people drink. Band playing there . . .
M. ANNIE   Let's get some booze.
TADPOLE   That's what you need, everybody needs a drink. If you don't drink you don't shit and if you don't shit, you die!

(*They head for the Branding Iron Bar.*)

Inside the Roebuck – the Branding Iron Bar

Couples at tables. ROSIE, *in white and silver, is the lead singer in a local country and western band. As the travellers enter the bar, the music stops.*

TADPOLE   They real friendly people here.

(*The crowd stares at the new arrivals. Song: 'Time Will Heal'*)

ROSIE
I guess that time will heal
the hurtin' in my heart
but as I contemplate
just how we are apart
I know that I might find

someone to share my life
but I can't understand
the tears I hold inside.

Sometimes I think of you
and wait for someone new
who will engage my dreams
the way you used to do
but now I'm all alone
with memories that I hold
and you are there in these
although you've now grown cold.

(*The music cuts out.* WILLIE *is stunned by* ROSIE's *appearance – before he faints he sees the crowd as if frozen in time.*)

WILLIE   Oh Chrije! That's 'im, that's the woman now I bin tell you about! That's 'im there, now look – he singing . . . Ah I feel funny . . .

(WILLIE *swoons back into* TADPOLE's *arms and sags to the floor.* TADPOLE *revives him with a splash of beer.*)

WILLIE   (*waking up*) Uncle, I don't like beer on me! You crabhole! (*Music resumes.*)
TADPOLE   Oh don't worry. Come on my boy, you gotta friend him up and try grab 'em.

(ROSIE *dances with anyone, hasn't noticed* WILLIE *yet.*)

WILLIE   But I feel big shame. I'm dirty.
TADPOLE   Ah don't worry, we all dirty! (*He drags* WILLIE *along, heads for* ROSIE.)
ROSIE
Sometimes I think of you
And wait for someone new
Who will engage my dreams
The way you used to do
But now I'm all alone
With memories that I hold
And you are there in these
Although you've now grown cold.

And you are there in these
Although you've now grown cold.
And you are there in these
Although you've now grown cold.

(*Raucous applause.*)

M. ANNIE   (*tagging along*) Hey far out!! Wow, wow, this is my kind of scene. Check out the band.

(TADPOLE *fronts* ROSIE *himself.*)

TADPOLE   Hullo my girl. My name Tadpole, Steven Johnson Tadpole, Uncle Tadpole, and this one here my boy. (TADPOLE *feels around for* WILLIE *but he's not there.* ROSIE *reacts to the name.*) He there at the bar. I think he like you too. I just wanna tell you that I think you singing good, that's good, that's deadly.

ROSIE   And what, you wanna have a go old man? (*Invites him to dance.*)

TADPOLE   Ooh, you give me a go with you?

ROSIE   You too old –

TADPOLE   Nah! You better let my young boy have a go with you. I'll have a go at singing. I'll find 'em this woman. I'm good singer. I used to sing before in choir.

ROSIE   (*to band members*) Hey bro! Old man want to get up and play. Sing us a song, what you reckon? Give im a go eh?

TADPOLE   (*as musicians smile at him and tune up*) I wanta sing a country song, I wanta sing a country song.

(*Band cranks up to a fast country number,* TADPOLE *gets ready to sing and tries to pick up the beat but gets left behind. Crowd claps in time and dances around a bit, ending with crescendo as* TADPOLE *brings things to a halt banging his stick.*)

I can't sing a bloody fast song – I'm too old. How can you get a woman singing a fast song. I wanta sing a slow song, real good one like this –

(TADPOLE *taps out the beat with his walking stick, slow and sensual, rocking at the knees. The band starts slower.*)

Yeah, that's 'im –

(*Whistles and stamps as music warms up. Song: 'Is You Mah Baby?'*)

TADPOLE
 Is you mah baby, is you mah baby
 is you?

 Is you mah baby, is you mah baby
 is you?

 When I'm in your warm embrace
 I feel part of the human race
 Oh! . . . is you mah baby, is you mah baby
 is you?

 Is you mah baby, is you mah baby
 is you?

(*During the song he collects the women from the tables. They laugh and whistle and yelp and do a dance routine with him.*)

 Is you mah baby, is you mah baby
 is you?

 You get under mah skin.
 Take off your jowidj and let me in
 Oh! . . . is you mah baby, is you mah baby
 is you?

(*Instrumental with dance routine involving whole female cast. Saloon style piano.*)

TADPOLE
 Is you mah baby, is you mah baby
 is you?
 Is you mah baby, is you mah baby
 is you?

 You wipe me off my face
 let's multiply the Aboriginal race.
 Oh is you mah baby, is you mah baby
 Is you?

 Is you mah baby, is you mah baby
 Is you?

(TADPOLE *is by now surrounded by women.*)

TADPOLE   See, that's how you grab tarts in this country. (TADPOLE *looks around for* WILLIE.)

ROSIE   Hello Willie, how are you?

CHORUS   (*exclaims as they see them together*) Ahhhhaahhh. Oooooooh.

ROSIE   You still deadly, Willie.

WILLIE   Thanks, Rosie . . .

ROSIE   What time low tide? I'm going for kuckle. You want to come?

PUBLICAN   Time please, ladies and gentlemen.

(*The crowd reacts, watching them leave together.*)

CHORUS   Ohhhhhhhhhhhhhhhhhhhh!

Down by the mangroves, Roebuck Bay

Song: 'Everybody Looking for Kuckle'. ROSIE *dances with* WILLIE, MARIJUANA ANNIE *with* SLIPPERY, TADPOLE *with* CHORUS.

ALL
 OOH OOH-OOH! . . . OOH OOH!
 Everybody lookin' for kuckle
 everybody lookin' all day
 everybody lookin' for kuckle
 blackman, whiteman and grey.

 Poppa he lookin' for kuckle
 poppa he lookin' all day

Mumma bin say he got kuckle
poppa bin sing out hooray.

Everybody lookin' for kuckle – OOH!
everybody startin' to itch – OOH!
everybody lookin' for kuckle – OOH!
everybody mussee jirij – OOH!

Just gip me while you rip me
rip me while you gip me
gip me while you rip me
oh yeah – OOH OOH-OOH! . . . OOH
    OOH-OOH!
WILLIE   Hey Rosie.
ROSIE   Yeah Willie?

(*Song: 'Nyul Nyul Girl'*)

WILLIE
    Nyul Nyul girl, walking out at night,
    teeth shining white, nothing else in
        sight . . .
    'Cos I love you, I'll love you until
    there's arrajina Djarindjin hills
    arrajina ungarrabin goolil.

    'Cos I love you, I'll love you until
    there's arrajina Djarindjin hills
    arrajina ungarrabin goolil.

(*Organ music of the Pentecostal Christians,
'All the Way Jesus', takes over and interrupts*
MARIJUANA ANNIE *and* SLIPPERY *in a
passionate embrace. They scramble to their
feet. The Pentecostals enter in procession.*
AUNTIE THERESA *and* PASTOR FLAKKON
in white robes. THERESA *is rapt and does not
notice* WILLIE, *who pulls* ROSIE *away behind
Kennedy Hill.* TADPOLE *stares at* THERESA,
*who hasn't yet seen him. Song: 'All the Way
Jesus'*)

THERESA and CONGREGATION OF
PENTECOSTALS
    All the way Jesus, just all the way Lord
    Bend me and shape me, give me your
        reward.
    Let me lie in your body, when I'm
        wracked in my pain
    And just light up the loving, that always
        remains.
PR. FLAKKON   Tonight is the night of
    miracles!
WILLIE   That my Mummy.
PR. FLAKKON   Do you believe?
CONGREGATION   We believe!!
WILLIE   She don't know I got booted out of
    school yet.
CONGREGATION   We believe!

WILLIE   She think I'm still in Rossmoyne.
PR. FLAKKON   Are you Christians?
ROSIE   Oh shit –
CONGREGATION   (*arms upraised*) Yess!!!
PR. FLAKKON   (*pointing at Tadpole*) Are
    YOUUUU Christian?
TADPOLE
    He's a Christian
    I'm a Christian
    She's a Christian
    We all bloody Christian.

(THERESA *recognises* TADPOLE's *voice, and
is shocked, staring at him.* TADPOLE *slips
away.*)

CONGREGATION   Halleluyah!

(*Frenzy in the assembly, possession on the
floor and tambourines banging.*)

THERESA   Praise the Lord, Halleluyah!
CONGREGATION   Praise the Lord,
    Halleluyah!
PR. FLAKKON   Tonight is the night when a
    great weight will be lifted.
CONGREGATION   Amen! Yea! Amen!
PR. FLAKKON   And in this hour of darkness a
    great light will descend upon us and there
    will indeed be a great revelation.

(WILLIE *watches for a moment in fascination
but* ROSIE *draws him aside to slip away
during the Pentecostal hymn.*)

THERESA
    You may find, if you're true to yourself
    That it's all an illusion, the book's on your
        shelf,
    If you read through the lines, then you'll
        find that it's true
    That there's nobody loving like he's
        loving you.
CONGREGATION
    All the way Jesus, just all the way Lord
    Bend me and shape me, give me your
        reward.
    Let me lie in your body, when I'm
        wracked in my pain
    And just light up the loving that always
        remains.
THERESA
    Now I know, that it's hard on your soul
    When you're down in the gutter, but the
        story unfolds
    How he'll lift you higher, than you've
        ever been
    And he'll show you the glory, that you've
        never seen.

All the way Jesus, just all the way Lord
Bend me and shape me, give me your
  reward.
Let me lie in your body when I'm
  wracked in my pain
And just light up the loving, that always
  remains.

PR. FLAKKON   I can feel someone wants to
testify!

M. ANNIE   I want, I want to testify. I've been
a bad person, I've been bent on sex. I've
had a child out of wedlock and I've been
using drugs and selling myself to get them
and I lost my child. I gave him away after
I lost my boyfriend when I was 19 and he
was shot in the belly in Vietnam . . .
aaaaaahh! And I know I'm not worthy. I'm
a sinner and I'm sorry now –
aahhaahhhaahahah.

PR. FLAKKON   Sing it one more time for the
sister!

CONGREGATION
All the way Jesus, just all the way Lord
Bend me and shape me, give me your
  reward.
Let me lie in Your body, when I'm
  wracked in my pain
And just light up the loving that always
  remains.

(SLIPPERY embraces MARIJUANA ANNIE.
The CONGREGATION gently croons and
sways around the two figures huddled
together.)

SLIPPERY   Annie, Annie don't worry my
dear. I too am evil, I too am a lost
indaweeduwal but you haff me now.
Things are looking better, we can haff
more children, mein lieber.

(Song: 'Marijuana Annie')

SLIPPERY
I know that you're tired and troubled,
  fearful and forlorn,
Tied to your troubles girl that keep on
  keepin' on
But you know I'll never leave ya
  until the morning's dawn,
Marijuana Annie never leave ya
  on your own.

CONGREGATION
Marijuana Annie
Blow your blues away
Stop shooting that shot . . . gun
Strip the night away.
Marijuana Annie

Blow your blues away
Stop shooting that shot . . . gun
Strip the night away.

SLIPPERY
I am tied to troubles too
That sometimes get me down
I'm tired of trying
As I'm slowly highway bound
But you'll always find some peace
Amongst that hustling highway sound
And to find each other
As the world keeps spinning 'round.

CONGREGATION
Marijuana Annie
Blow your blues away
Stop shooting that shot . . . gun
Strip the night away.
Marijuana Annie
Blow your blues away
Stop shooting that shot . . . gun
Strip the night away.
Stop shooting that shot . . . gun . . .

(Organ holds the last note. The
CONGREGATION is stirred in sympathy with
MARIJUANA ANNIE. AUNTIE THERESA
comforts her.)

THERESA   My child, my child, we are sisters
of the spirit. I too have lost my child. I too
have been a sinner –

PR. FLAKKON   Tonight is the night of
miracles, I told you so, do you believe?

CONGREGATION   We do we do believe –

(AUNTIE THERESA starts swaying to music
and heaves with her burden of hidden truth
as all the women join the movement. Song:
'Sweet Sister')

THERESA
Life is just a journey, we're tossed from
  side to side
You know sweet sister, that you can't be
  satisfied.
Till you find the answers
  hidden in the word
And you find the glory
  that lay hidden and unheard.
It's only when you hear and see
  the message in your heart
and realise the truth within
  that can't be pulled apart.
I know that the searching ends
  when you have realised
that the truth remains within
and cannot be denied.

(THERESA *moves from the centre stage towards the pool and baptises* MARIJUANA ANNIE. *They walk towards* PASTOR FLAKKON *on Kennedy Hill.*)

CONGREGATION
Wo ho . . . sweet sister
See you standing down the line
you've had your troubles
but you've left them all behind
Wo ho . . . sweet sister
See you standing down the line
you've had your troubles
but you've left them all behind.

(PASTOR FLAKKON, THERESA, MARIJUANA ANNIE *are at the top of Kennedy Hill.*)

THERESA and M. ANNIE
I feel a strange contentment
when you're standing here by me
the boat keeps rocking tossing
turning on the sea.
I can feel the strength within
the fire deep inside
that knowledge keeps you buoyed
against the surging tide.

ALL
Wo ho . . . sweet sister
See you standing down the line
you've had your troubles
but you've left them all behind
Wo ho . . . sweet sister
See you standing down the line
you've had your troubles,
but you've left them all behind.

THERESA and M. ANNIE
You've had your troubles . . .
but you've left them
all behind.

THERESA   I had a child too, to another man,
to a German missionary. He took my child
away and all I had left to console me was
alcohol and this photo. Look! (THERESA
holds up her photo for all to see.)

CONGREGATION   Benny, oh Benny –

SLIPPERY   Mein fada! Mein fada! (SLIPPERY
produces a matching photograph. He and
THERESA *gaze at one another.*)

THERESA   My son, my son! (*Reeling from the
shock*) My prayers have been answered.

SLIPPERY   (*dazed*) Mein mutter, mein
mutter –

(*They embrace to a reprise of 'Is You Mah
Baby?'*)

SLIPPERY   (*sings*)
Ist you my mutti, ist you my mutti?
Ist you?

THERESA   (*sings*)
Is you my baby, is you my baby,
Is you?

CHORUS
When I'm in your warm embrace,
I feel part of the human race,
Oh is you my – mutti/baby,
is you my – mutti/baby,
is you?

PR. FLAKKON   Hallelujah! Tonight IS the
night! Do you believe?

CONGREGATION   We believe!

TADPOLE   (*entering from the audience*)
Well I got a story to tell if anybody wanna
listen. I had a woman. I bin drinkin', I bin
drovin' and I bin a Christian. But most
of all I bin true to myself. I bin searchin',
searchin' for a long time, searchin' for a
reason why all this happened and how.
Well I come back this time to sort it all
out. I was a young man and I got married
and my wife left me. She left me, so I
turned to drink, and she had a child to
another man. And so I left and I turned to
drink and I bin drovin' and drovin' and
drovin' and I bin drinkin' and drinkin' and
drinkin' and I'm sick of drovin' but I'm not
sick of drinkin' . . . because that's the
woman over there. (TADPOLE *points to*
THERESA.)

THERESA   Ooh, Steben, Steben, I never
meant to do it. It was the debbil's work.
Steben wait for me!

(TADPOLE *storms downstage, off the stage
and up the aisles, followed by* THERESA.)

SLIPPERY   Mutti, my mutti wait for me.
First I yam Cherman, and den I find that
my mutti is Aborigine. Now she iss leaving
me again. Und I vunder vhy?

CONGREGATION   (*looming over him*) Because
we're all born black!

PR. FLAKKON   Go with them my children.
Seek ye first the kingdom of heaven and it
shall be all added unto you! The Lord be
praised –

CONGREGATION   Praise the Lord!

SLIPPERY   Ich bien Ine Aborigine!!

(SLIPPERY *and* MARIJUANA ANNIE *run
forward off stage and up the aisles. The*
CONGREGATION *becomes a* CHORUS
again. ROSIE *emerges from their hiding place*

and runs on to the stage, with WILLIE *in pursuit.)*

WILLIE Hey Rosie, wait –
ROSIE Willie?

(*Song: 'Djarindjin Girl'*)

WILLIE
  Be my Djarindjin girl
  Be the one that I dream of
  Be my Djarindjin girl
  Be the one that I love.
CHORUS
  Don't you ever despair
  I won't let you down
  Be my Djarindjin girl
  Lost but now you're found.
ROSIE
  I wait late in the night
  Waiting and dreaming of you – boy
  You come and lay by my side
  Making my dreams all come true.

(WILLIE, ROSIE *walk arm in arm to the top of the hill, about to kiss –*)

CHORUS Oooooohhh – (*whistles, hoots.*)

(WILLIE, ROSIE *become aware of the* CHORUS *and the audience, and scramble embarrassed behind the hill. The* FEMALE CHORUS *sits on the deck chairs of Sun Pictures.* MALE CHORUS *advances on their counterparts with a proposal. The girls flirt back, leaving their deck chairs. Song: 'Seeds That You Might Sow'*)

BOYS
  She was only 16
  just a child upon the road
  when I moved up to her slowly
  said, I got a heavy load.
  She says
GIRLS
  Maybe, come on baby
  would you like to come on down
  and we'd rock and reel and reel and rock
  all over Chinatown.
ALL
  She says hey boy
  Don't you really go
  I don't feel so mad about the seeds
  that you might sow.
  She says hey boy
  Don't you really go
  I don't feel so mad about
  the seeds that you might sow.

BOYS
  Well I moved up to her slowly
  and I asked her for a go
  and she spoke to me quite softly
  in a voice so sweet and low.
  She said –
GIRLS
  Well I like polony or perhaps a sausage
    roll
  but if you don't use those condoms
  then you cannot pook my hole.
ALL
  She says hey boy
  Don't you really go
  I don't feel so mad about the seeds
  that you might sow.
  She says hey boy
  Don't you really go
  I don't feel so mad about
  the seeds that you might sow.
BOYS
  I am so happy 'cos I did
  what I was told
  for I used those frangers
  and she let me pook her hole.
ALL
  She says hey boy
  Don't you really go
  I don't feel so mad about the seeds
  that you might sow.
  She says hey boy
  Don't you really go
  I don't feel so mad about
  the seeds that you might sow.

(CHORUS *exits stage right, casting condoms into the audience.* TADPOLE *and* THERESA *enter, followed by* MARIJUANA ANNIE *and* SLIPPERY, *who is dressed in Land Rights gear.* THERESA's *pure white gown is astray. So is her hair.*)

THERESA Steben, Steben – wait for me!
TADPOLE I'm going back all the way to Lombadina when I find that boy!
THERESA So am I, Steben, with you. What 'that boy'?
TADPOLE I'm a tracker, I find 'im – up there . . .
SLIPPERY Yeah Uncle Tadpole fada wait for me –
TADPOLE I'm not your fada, that mission fella (*with emphasis*) your Fada!

Kennedy Hill

TADPOLE *climbs Kennedy Hill and* WILLIE
stands up.

WILLIE (*smiling, naked*) Uncle – I'm a man
now.

THERESA (*shocked at seeing* WILLIE *as
nature made him*) Willie! Cover yourself up.
I don't want to see you naked.

TADPOLE And I don't want to see your
noora.

M. ANNIE What have you two been up to
then eh?

SLIPPERY Making da boom boom.

THERESA Whadda yow – you bella bin
coming to us smelling rude yow –

WILLIE (*coming down with* ROSIE) I'm in
heben. That what they tell me when you go
to church. I neber believe them before.

TADPOLE Poo – you bella stink, go wash
your lagurr.

THERESA Stop that William, stop talking like
that. Why aren't you in school, in
Rossmoyne!? Where's you school uniform I
scraped and saved for?

WILLIE Mum – (TADPOLE *is thunderstruck*) –
you been like this ever since I was young. I
can't be like you, I don't wanna be like you,
I can't handle you. You mix me up all the
time so don't know if I'm black or white or
yellow or green or rainbow warrior! And I
don't think you know what you are either.

THERESA My son . . .

TADPOLE Your son?

THERESA And your son!

(TADPOLE *stares at her, then to* WILLIE,
beginning to smile.)

TADPOLE Boy, you my son – I know . . . I
can feel 'im – but how come is my son?

THERESA That time you come to me, before
you go . . .

WILLIE Daddy –

SLIPPERY Brother –

(*Reprise: 'Is You Mah Baby?' They sing
variations.*)

WILLIE/SLIPPERY/TADPOLE/THERESA
(*embracing*)
  Is you my brother/baby, is you my
    brother/baby,
  is you?
  Is you my daddy, is you my daddy,
  is you?

  You wipe me offa my face,

  let's multiply the Aboriginal Race,
  oh is you my brother/baby, is you my
    father/baby,
  is you?

(THERESA *stands in the midst of the
rejoicing.*)

TADPOLE I been drovin', I been drinkin', I
bin Christian, I bin everything, and now
I seen everything and now it's time I gotta
go home, see old people . . .

(THERESA *begins to cry at the resolution
of her past mistakes. Song: 'Town by the
Bay'*)

TADPOLE
  Why are you crying, my pretty Colleen?
  Why are your eyes filled with tears?
  Let me come over and dry your eyes
  and tell you the way that I feel.

THERESA and TADPOLE
  Closer come closer, don't throw me
    away.
  I am so tired and so blue.
  I'm dreaming of someone so far far
    away –
  (*To* TADPOLE) and sharing these
    memories with you.

(CHORUS *enters bearing small boats with
lighted candles. They represent the many
races of Broome. Finally they launch the boats
on the water.*)

ALL
  Just one step closer, don't throw me away
  and carry me back to my town by the
    bay.
  When the darkness is falling at passing of
    days
  won't you cherish the memory of my
    town by the bay?

THERESA
  I still remember the old mission yards,
  the old days the old ways, the times that
    were hard,
  the friends of my childhood, when I was
    young,
  the fathers the brothers, the old Irish
    nuns –

ALL
  So just come one step closer, don't throw
    me away
  and carry me back to my town by the
    bay.
  When the darkness is falling at passing of
    days,

won't you share your new future in my
town by the bay?
When the darkness is falling at passing of
days,
won't you share your new future in my
town by the bay?

TADPOLE   Come on, we gotta go to
Lombadina now, come on you old bitches,
this not our country. Our country up there.
Come on you young bastards, you gotta
come with us too. We family now. Willie –
Rosie!

(*To the strains of 'Nothing I Would Rather
Be'*, MARIJUANA ANNIE, SLIPPERY,
TADPOLE, THERESA, WILLIE *and* ROSIE
all jump in the car and set off.
MARIJUANA ANNIE *puts her hand up.*
SLIPPERY *stops the car and they all look
at her.*)

M. ANNIE   I got 'nother confession to make –
I too am one of you. I was adopted out as a
child – all I can remember is being taken
from a sea of wailing black faces and being
raised in the city, to be white . . . I too am
an Aborigine!

(CHORUS *celebrates with cries. Reprise of
'Nothing I Would Rather Be'.*)

ALL
There's nothing I would rather be
than to be an Aborigine,
and watch you take my precious land
away,
oh no no no –
And watch you take my precious land
away!
Ohhhhhh no.

(*Ethereal music, strains of 'Child of Glory'.
The car stops again.*)

Djarindjin – Lombadina

TADPOLE   There him, there hi. There
Djarindjin hills.
M. ANNIE   Hey, we're in Lombadina.
SLIPPERY   Wahhh – it's just like Goa.

(CHORUS *carries on a statue of the Christ
child in a bindjin followed by the church in
the form of a frame, topped by a cross with
garlands of flowers.*)

M. ANNIE   What's happening?
TADPOLE   Ahh – feast of Christ the King!
Our anniversary, Th'resa.

THERESA   Waddow 'teben!
TADPOLE   Porbella porbella. We hhhhome
now.
WILLIE and ROSIE   (*speaking fast, moved by
the occasion*) Let's join procession, let's join
procession.

(MARIJUANA ANNIE *and* SLIPPERY *stare in
amazement at the procession and are drawn
by the stately movement. They move to join
the slowly measured procession of Christ the
King. Song: 'Child of Glory'.*)

ALL
Child of glory come take me by the hand,
help me, heal me, and make me
understand.
All I survey is there at your command,
Child of glory come take me by the hand.

Though the journey is tortured and so
long,
it's the same path the Christ child trod
upon.
Child of glory come take me by the hand
help me, heal me and make me
understand.

(*The Djarindjin/Lombadina community
greets the new arrivals.* THERESA *is silent.*
BENEDICTUS *appears from within the
framework of the church.*)

BENEDICTUS   Velcome, velcome my long
lost children.
WILLIE   Oh Crije, Benny!
THERESA   (*to* SLIPPERY) That's your father.
SLIPPERY   Mein Gott in himmel – mein
Fada!
TADPOLE   And I'm your father 'nother way.

(BENEDICTUS *covers his embarrassment by
a handy diversion.*)

BENEDICTUS   Villie! Der prodigal son – Ah
Rosie . . . und Tadspole, und Theresa.
SLIPPERY   Und Slippery.
M. ANNIE   Und Annie.
BENEDICTUS   Slippery?
THERESA   Father, this is Wolfgang.
BENEDICTUS   Wolfgang, mein son. Ah
Wolfgang Amadeus Beuitenmuller.

(*They break into one chorus of 'Is You Mah
Baby?' in German.*)

WILLIE   (*cheeky drawl*) Fa-ada!
BENEDICTUS   Ah Villie. Und Slippery und
Annie –Ve are all fallen angels and ve all
haff a multitude of crosses to bear. You haff

Figure 10 'Child of Glory'. *Bran Nue Dae,* directed by Andrew Ross, 1990. Photo: David Wilson.

kom back, und I haff kom back! Der mission is finished! Der Auftrate first ende.

(THERESA *is very still. Everybody lets out one great sigh, a mixture of regret and relief.*)

BENEDICTUS   Ve are all angels und devils. Creatures of darkness and bodies of light . . . *Lux in tenebris!*

TADPOLE   What that, toilet soap?

BENEDICTUS   Dere is no beginning and dere is no end in our long journey through life . . .

TADPOLE   That's what I been tryin' to tell you mob from the beginning, I been drovin' I been drinkin', I been drovin' and drinkin' and drovin' and anyway . . .

(*Song: 'Bran Nue Dae'*)

TADPOLE   (*recitative*) This fella song all about the Aboriginal people, coloured

people, black people longa Australia. Us people want our land back, we want 'em rights, we want 'em fair deal, all same longa white man. Now this fella longa Canberra, he bin talkin' about a Bran Nue Dae – us people bin waiting for dijwun for 200 years now. Don' know how much longer we gotta wait, and boy it's makin' me slack.

(*Sings*) Here I live in this tin shack
Nothing here worth coming back
To drunken fights and awful sights
People drunk most every night.

CHORUS
On the way to a Bran Nue Dae
Everybody everybody say
On the way to a Bran Nue Dae
Everybody everybody say.

TADPOLE   (*recitative*) Other day I bin longa to social security, I bin ask longa job – they

bin say, 'Hey, what's your work
experience?' I bin tell 'em, 'I got nothing'.
They say, 'How come?' I say, 'Cause I can't
find a job.'
   (*Sings*) We've nothing old, an nothing
     new
want us all to be like you,
We've no future we have no past
Hope the sun will shine at last.

CHORUS
   On the way to a Bran Nue Due
   Everybody everybody say
   On the way to a Bran Nue Dae
   Everybody everybody say.

BENEDICTUS Ve are all sinners, mein
children, but I haff vun leedle reward for
der prodigal son –

(BENEDICTUS *throws back the screen of
the church to reveal a huge fridge. The
door swings open and the glowing interior
is filled with stacked red wrapped
confections – Cherry Ripe bars, which*
BENEDICTUS *begins handing out with
abandon.*)

WILLIE Cherry Ripe bro!
BENEDICTUS Line up, mein children! I like
'im too –
ALL
   On the way to a Bran Nue Dae
   Everybody everybody say
   On the way to a Bran Nue Dae
   Everybody everybody say.

(CHORUS *throws Cherry Ripes into the
audience.* BENEDICTUS *remains on
upper level with arms outstretched in
blessing.*)

TADPOLE (*recitative*) They bin talk about
this kind, that kind, anykind, everykind,
but still same kind – and boy make me
slack –
CHORUS (*sings*) Bran Nue Dae. Ooohhh!!!

(BENEDICTUS *describes a crucifix,
performing a blessing with two Cherry Ripe
bars held up as a cross, to absolve all present
from their sins of omission.*)

BENEDICTUS Absolvo Te.

(*The cast assembles as in a portrait, with the
various couples paired:* ROSIE/WILLIE,
TADPOLE/THERESA, MARIJUANA
ANNIE/SLIPPERY. *Song: 'If I Gave My Heart
To You'*)

ROSIE and WILLIE
   If I gave my heart to you
   would you promise to be true
   it would break my heart in two
   if you left me waiting, anticipating.
THERESA and TADPOLE
   That some other magic day
   I may steal your heart away
   but till then I hope and pray
   that my love will break through
   and in time just move you.
M. ANNIE and SLIPPERY
   To a world of different dreams
   where all things aren't what they
     seem
   and then you will take my hand
   and understand me, when you really see
     me.
ALL
   For only truth remains
   for all things are just the same
   for accepting's part of truth
   when I give my heart,
   when I gave my heart
   when I give my heart to you.

(*The cast goes up to heaven, singing 'Bran
Nue Dae'.*)

Glossary

arli fish
arrajina nothing
Bardi language group
barni large goanna
bindjins coolamon; large wooden carrying
  dish
butta second best hand in kudja kudja, a
  gambling game with sticks
dijwun this one
gided fish food, also snapper
goolil turtle
gubiny bush fruit.
gungkura bush fruit
he interchangeably, he or she
I Ay, isn't that so? (as in 'I bro?')
jalangardi goanna
jigal Bauhinia tree
jirij ejaculate; move suddenly
jowidj pants (possibly derived from
  trousers)
Karrajarri language group
lagurr eggs or testicles
lulb'd roasted in the earth
magabala bush fruit
mayi bush food from plants

mukan food (a Malay word)
munga just like, same as
mungari food
mussee must
ngarba water
noora posterior
Nyikina language group

sit on highest hand in kudja kudja
stalebait fishing term, used for people
tongueing longing
ungarrabin young green turtle
wali meat
Yawuru language group
yunyarri coming

15 Briar Grace-Smith

Ngā Pou Wāhine
New Zealand

Introduction

In 1966, the year Briar Grace-Smith was born in Whakatane, New Zealand Opera mounted a nationwide tour of the American musical, *Porgy and Bess,* with an all-Māori cast. From this, the Māori Theatre Trust was formed. Dedicated to providing quality roles for Māori actors, it gave impetus to the development of a vital indigenous theatre tradition, fuelled at various points by key political events. Prominent among these was the 1970s Māori Renaissance, a period characterised by demands for indigenous recognition and land rights. The theatre of this era, as Hone Kouka notes, can be firmly located in the agit-prop tradition as performance born with politics:

> During this period of protest we had found a means of venting our frustrations and victories. In theatre we found a tool that was able to fluently express our ideas and our concerns, and it was all under Māori control – here was tino rangatiratnaga [self-determination] in action – a medium of little cost, with the ability to communicate to many and yet keep the message pure.
>
> (Kouka 1999: 13)

By the 1980s, the Māori voice had become a significant force in the performance culture of Aotearoa/New Zealand, with venues such as The Depot, later renamed Taki Rua (to signify its bicultural aspects), serving as a focal point for the Māori theatre community nationally. Towards the end of the 1980s, Rangimoana Taylor and Jim Moriarty, both leading actors and theatre practitioners, instigated the concept of Theatre Marae. Together, they experimented with ways of changing not only the content and language of Māori-themed plays but, more fundamentally, the nature of the theatrical encounter itself. The basic premise of

Theatre Marae is that European concepts of theatre are secondary to Māori protocols. The welcoming and performative codes of the marae, or meeting house, the heart of Māori community, became the model for this encounter. Thus, for the duration of the performance, the theatre adopts some of the characteristics of a marae: the audience are asked to remove their shoes, and the play-going experience begins with a mihi (chant) and a karanga (call or summon) and ends with a meal that becomes a kind of gathering (hui). Speech-making is an important part of the theatre, with the audience being given the opportunity to reply. Theatre Marae thereby alters the status of the audience from the Western theatrical norm of unacknowledged and silent observers who judge the performance, to that of participants in a ritual, collective experience.

The influence of Theatre Marae is clearly discernible in Grace-Smith's first significant drama, *Ngā Pou Wāhine* , which received the Peter Harcourt award for best short play in 1995. This text's episodic structure recalls the passage through the elements of the marae ritual, as the performance opens with a karanga, and incorporates some stylised movements. The play, however, does not follow Theatre Marae to the letter; rather, it is subtly infused by a sense of the marae to the extent that it becomes a synthesis of the traditional and the contemporary, the Māori and the European. The narrative's structure as a process or journey is reinforced in the title, which translates loosely as 'the posts that mark stages in a woman's life'. Individuated poupou, the carved wooden posts that stand inside a marae, underline the solo actor's transference from one character to another. They also serve to transform the stage and auditorium into a distinctively Māori space, which is made both sacred and personally significant through the consistent association of a character with a particular location. In the original production, according to Grace-Smith's staging notes, each poupou was both contemporary and symbolic of a specific character: the poupou belonging to Lizzie carried a cross, symbolising her faith; Walter's poupou carried a hook, signifying that he was once a great fisherman and hunter. One poupou stood centrally with no platform. This was the poupou belonging to the tupuna, or ancestor, Waiora. Significantly, the stage area in front of the platform occupied by Kura, the play's central character, had no poupou, suggesting the void that initially marks her life (Grace-Smith 1997: 9–10).

The various monologues that make up this text can be seen as analogous to the individual speeches of the marae ritual. Yet, the order in which they take place also presents a range of perspectives on Kura before her character enters, reflecting structurally one of the play's central themes: the necessity of determining one's own identity. We see Kura through the eyes of her Aunty Lizzie, her Uncle Walter, her friend Tia and, in a flashback to the past, or a dream or memory of Kura's, through her mother, Miro. What dominates these perspectives is a repeated insistence that Kura is a dreamer and a fantasist. These assessments have some validity; yet, the play's blurring of the boundaries between dreams and reality suggests that until Kura can understand her dreams and recover knowledge about her past, she will be incapable of living in the reality of the present.

This quest for cultural and personal 'memory' takes place through the invocation of a mythical past. Grace-Smith explains that her inspiration for the play derived from a story told to her by her father about a great tupuna with long red hair. This tupuna, Waiora, was captured and, while being taken out to sea, cut her hair and threw it in the waves, so giving back her mana (strength and power) to her people (Grace-Smith 1997: 8). The Waiora legend has found its way into a number of contemporary Māori plays, notably Hone Kouka's much-lauded 1996 version titled simply *Waiora*. The first scene of *Ngā Pou Wāhine* enacts this mythical past in précis before moving into a contemporary reworking of the myth. Waiora's lament evolves into an emancipatory promise of a

time to come and her red hair becomes a symbol of this covenant. Kura, with her own long red hair, is positioned as the contemporary embodiment of that power. As the play continues, the story of Waiora unfolds in greater depth, as told by Miro, Kura's dead mother. Her account of Takimoana, the greedy man who wanted to rule the Moa people, can be seen as an allegory of colonialism, a project through which Māori culture is captured and desecrated. The myth thus takes on contemporary relevance in a postcolonial context, and the play activates the mythical past for the purposes of empowering Māori in the present. In this way, *Ngā Pou Wāhine* participates in a broader project of cultural reclamation.

As leading feminist theatre practitioner Roma Potiki explains:

> Māori theatre is a theatre that constantly remembers the past. I cannot recall having seen a play by a Māori writer that did not make some reference to tupuna. The emanations of the dead most certainly rattle our bones. It is our ancestors who remind us of who we are, where we belong and why we have been given the gift of life.
>
> (quoted in Kouka 1999: 11)

In *Ngā Pou Wāhine*, this re-establishment of cultural identity is distinctively gendered. The play, which includes the first indigenous woman's monologue in New Zealand theatre, is a reminder of the strength of women in Māori culture. This strength links generations and is passed down from the tupuna, Waiora, through Miro, herself a strong and independent woman, to her daughter Kura, who, in spite of her massive dislocation from her cultural inheritance, still manages to reclaim significant mana through her dreams and recollections. Waiora's strength is also what provokes Takimoana to violence. This violence is played out on a number of levels: in Kura's struggle with TJ and also Miro's struggle with Kepa, both women are pitted against a misogynous and macho culture. Kura's fantasy of Phillip, a member of the peace corps, can thus be seen as a rejection of violence, and an appeal to the possibility of gender harmony.

Questions of gender and power are explored from a different perspective through the character of Aunty Lizzie. Her opening

monologue portrays a bitter Christian woman
governed by ideals of self-sacrifice and
martyrdom that are deeply imbued with
patriarchal values. Not only does she pray to
a masculine god, but also she believes that a
child needs a father, and that Kura just needs
to find a good man. As the plays unfolds,
however, we learn that Lizzie's piety is a
hypocritical cover for her own guilt, and that
taking care of Kura was an attempt to atone
for the death of the unborn child she
conceived with her Pākehā lover Georgie, the
local school-teacher. In Lizzie's dissembling,
Ngā Pou Wāhine reveals the ways in which
the agency of indigenous women has been
compromised by the missionaries'
installation of the patriarchal god of
Christianity and their debasement of both
Māori and women. Lizzie internalises these
beliefs, fostering contempt for her own
culture. The sad irony is that through her
constant need to punish herself for her sins,
she turns out to be incapable of love or
happiness. Her deep-rooted self-hatred,
moreover, is unknowingly racialised: 'Wash
me and I'll be whiter than snow', she says at
one point.

Ngā Pou Wāhine also indicates ways in
which colonisation intersects with, and is
complicated by, issues of class domination.
Class becomes an important factor in the
relationship between Walter and Lizzie as
well as in Kura's attempt to find a place in a
new urban landscape. The play suggests that
the urban drift of contemporary indigenous
culture positions Māori youth in the kind of
unskilled and underpaid factory labour force
of which both Kura and TJ are a part.
Accordingly, Kura's search for her roots
entails a need to see/fantasise something
beyond the alienation of such menial labour.
If, as Miro explains, Waiora's special gift was
foresight, Kura's constant dreaming can be
interpreted as one way of expressing that
legacy. Kura's last vision of her mother,
through which she comes to understand her
connection to Waiora, awakens her to the
potential that she carries inside herself. In
the play's final moments Waiora's poupou is
lit up as Kura moves over each of the
platforms before using her body to make her
own poupou with a strong stylised action, the
Māori pūkana

Grace-Smith, who belongs to the Ngati Hau
Hapu of Hga Puhi, has worked as a journalist,
a weaver and an actor, as well as writing

short stories for both children and adults.
Since *Ngā Pou Wāhine* was first produced, her
output has been prolific, including a number
of important plays that extend her
engagement with Māori myths and/or
philosophies. *Flat Out Brown*, staged in 1996,
dramatises interactions between a group of
urban Māori and features a character
possessed by the spirit of his ancestor.
Waitapu, premiered in the same year, draws
from a myth about the need for atonement to
lift a curse, while *Purapurawhetu*, which won
an award in 1997 for the best New Zealand
play, stages a strange story that unfolds as
two Māori hurry to complete the weaving of a
tukutuku panel. Grace-Smith has also
participated in a number of international
theatre ventures, including the Fourth
International Women Playwright's
conference in Ireland in 1998, and an
exchange with Canada's best known
indigenous company, Native Earth
Performing Arts (1996). Her other plays
include a comedy for youth, *Don't Call me
Bro'* (1996), and *The Sojourns of Boy* (1999),
co-written with Jo Randerson. Grace-Smith's
most recent work is *Haruru Mai*, a tale of
mismatched love, commissioned by New
Zealand International Festival of the Arts
(1999).

Production history

Ngā Pou Wāhine was premiered at Taki Rua
Theatre, Wellington, in May 1995, directed by
Nancy Brunning. In 1997, the play was also
performed in Ireland and at the Festival of
the Dreaming in Sydney.

Select bibliography

Balme, C. (1993) 'Between separation and
integration: contemporary Māori theatre',
CRNLE Reviews Journal 1: 41–8.
—— (1999) *Decolonizing the Stage: Theatrical
Syncretism and Post-Colonial Drama*,
Oxford: Clarendon Press.
Cooke, P. (1997) 'A magical first play', *Theatre
Australasia* 19: 5.
Grace-Smith, B. (1997) *Ngā Pou Wāhine*,
Wellington: Huia.
Kouka, H. (1999) 'Introduction', in H. Kouka
(ed.) *Ta Matou Mangai: Three Plays of the
Nineties*, Wellington: Victoria University
Press, 9–28.
Levy, S. (1991) 'Māori theatre in Pākehā

masks', in C. Schumacher and D. Fogg (eds) *Small is Beautiful: Small Countries Theatre Conference*, Glasgow: Theatre Studies Publications, 203–12.

Potiki, R. (1991) 'Introduction', in S. Garrett (ed.) *He Reo Hou: 5 Plays by Māori Playwrights*, Wellington: Playmarket, 9–13.

—— (1992) 'Confirming identity and telling the stories: a woman's perspective on Māori theatre', in R. Du Plessis (ed.) *Feminist Voices: Women's Studies Texts for Aotearoa/New Zealand*, Auckland: Oxford University Press, 153–62.

Rose, C. (1997) 'Solo wimmin's business bares raw, funny attitude', *Sydney Morning Herald* 19 September: 13.

Ngā Pou Wāhine

Briar Grace-Smith

The Whānau[1]

All roles are played by one female performer.

TE ATAKURA (KURA) Twenty-one years.
  Māori. Lives with her Aunty Lizzie and
  Uncle Walter somewhere in the suburbs.

TIA Twenty-three years. Māori. A student.
  She is Kura's new friend. Tia moves to a
  funky reggae beat.

LIZZIE Fifties. Māori. Married to Walter.
  She has brought up Kura since she was an
  infant. Her prop is a tall-standing silver
  ashtray. She chain-smokes and keeps a
  hanky tucked up her sleeve.

WALTER Fifties. Pākehā. An old fisherman
  and hunter who still clings to the past. Sits
  in an old armchair watching television.

MIRO Late thirties. Māori. Kura's mother.
  She carries a tokotoko (carved walking
  stick). She is seen as a ghost or memory
  brought alive by Kura's imagination. Kura
  is a baby in Miro's scenes; she lies in a
  cradle nearby.

Setting

The opening scene with WAIORA *is set in the
distant past. All the other scenes take place in
1995, except* MIRO'S, *her scenes take place in
1974.*

Scene 1 – Te Ōhākī a Waiora

The actor as WAIORA *stands in front of the
audience. She wears a korowai[2] and has her red
hair in a topknot, bound with a heru (comb).
In this scene we are given a glimpse of the old
story in which* WAIORA, KURA's *tupuna,[3] is
captured. Takimoana has taken* WAIORA *away
from her people and, as the waka[4] heads across
the sea, she sings the following lament, 'Te
Ōhākī a Waiora'. During the course of this, she
becomes physically weaker and by the finish she
is in a kneeling position.*

WAIROA
  Tēnei te moemoeā e te iwi e
  Koia taku haere
  Ka whakangungua koutou
  I te hara kōhuru
  Motumotu rikiriki ngā makawe
  He whero me te toto
  Heoi ehara me te toto
  Kei hea te iringa o te heru
  Motumotu rikiriki e
  I waiho i te iwi e
  He tohu mo te mana
  Tēnā rā te wā
  Inā ia te kore he manako mai hoki
  Ka mutu i konei he raro manako atu ki te
    iwi

(Lifting her head skyward, WAIORA *does the
following karanga:)[5]*

  E ngā atua,
  whakahokia te mana ki te iwi.
  Auē, taukiri eee.

*(*WAIORA, *kneeling, removes the heru, bends
her head forward and makes an action as if to
sever her hair. Lights down on* WAIORA.*)*

Scene 2 – Te Atakura

Actor moves to the space belonging to AUNTY
LIZZIE. *Lights come up on* LIZZIE *in the dining
room of her house.* LIZZIE *lights a cigarette and
takes a long drag. She yells out to* KURA *who is
in another room.*

LIZZIE Kura. Kura. Kura. KURA! Put the jug
  on will you? I know you can hear me
  young lady. What are you doing in there? I
  don't know Kura, you're always dreaming
  when there's work to be done. I've been
  cleaning since eight o'clock this morning.
  I arrived at church to worship, only to find
  that the place had been torn apart by thugs.
  They'd smashed a window and broken one
  of the pews. (*She raises her eyes*

heavenward; dabs her face with her hanky.)
Oh dear lord. How could anyone do such a
thing to a holy place? (*Yells*) Is that jug
boiling yet? Kura? Kura? Kura? Did you
hear me Kura? (*To herself*) She does this for
spite. She just likes seeing me get worked
up. But I won't be ignored in my own
house. I'm not going there, into that room.
She'll trap me with some strange piece of
conversation. Last night it was about the
whales. Something about how saturated
and angry they all were and all I could
think of was the thousands of little holes
those drawing pins were making in my
walls. I've told her so many times, if you
have to put up those posters, use Blu-tac.
But she never listens. (*She speaks to God.*)
Oh, heavenly father. Please give me the
wisdom to understand this girl. Give me the
tolerance to get through the difficult times
that lie ahead of us. Goodness only knows.
Kura's not our own child, but still we have
found room in our hearts for her. We've fed
her and clothed her, and done our best to
protect her, but never once has she
thanked us, never once has she just simply
done what she has been told. That girl is so
sullen, so angry. I am truly at my wit's end.
I pray dear lord that there is a man out
there somewhere who will care for Kura.
A good man, like the one I had . . . the one
I lost. (*She reminisces about her old lover,
Georgie.*) A man who will show her that
there is a time for listening and a time for
speaking. An educated man. (*She stops
herself, blows her nose and yells to* KURA.)
KURA! I want that tea nice and strong.
Two teabags. (*Reassuringly*) Two teabags
nice and strong. Two teabags. (*She tucks her
hanky up her sleeve.*) 'Drink plenty of tea. It
turns the insides of your stomach a golden
brown'. That's what my mother always said
and she was a nurse. She used to ride
around on horseback, crossing flooded
rivers to deliver babies. What a terrible life.
I'll never go back home. WETAS.[6] All I can
see are the wetas. The ground's like hard
clay and full of cracks. At school wetas
would crawl out of cracks and bite my toes.
It's backward there and so are the people.
If I'd stayed I'd have turned out the same.
(*Shivers*) Mark my words. (*Calls out again to*
KURA.) Kura! Make one for your Uncle
Walter too.

(*Lights go down on* LIZZIE. *Actor moves to
the space that belongs to* UNCLE WALTER.

Lights come up. WALTER is *slumped in an
old armchair in the living room, staring
ahead at a television.*)

WALTER   (*to* KURA) Don't forget, Kura. Three
sugars please love. (*Pause.*) Hey Kura. You
still keen on that hunting trip, girl? We'll
have to take a tent, oh, an' plenty of wet
weather gear. You got yourself a good
oilskin? Dogs. We'll have to borrow a couple
from young Charlie. I remember this one
time, Kura. I thought I knew that bush like
the back of me hand, but there was one part
over the eastern ridge . . . ooo . . . I tell ya.
I wandered up there one day – one of me
dogs had gone missing. Normally I would've
let him find his own way home, but he'd
taken a whiff of cyanide on the last hunt
and was still groggy in the head. He was a
bloody good holder but, and I didn't want to
lose him. I dunno how, but I ended up
somewhere on the Eastern Ridge. The sun
was on its way down by this time and me
guts was rumbling, so I sat down to open
me can of baked beans. The bush up there
was first generation for sure. You should've
seen the trunks on them kauris.[7] They were
like this. (*Motions the size with his hands;
pause.*) It felt like no man had ever set foot
in the place. And the birds, they were all so
bloody tame. There they were – tuis,[8]
fantails, and the fattest pigeons you ever
saw, flying around my head like I was an
old mate. (*Pause.*) I felt like I was being
watched. Like God himself was peering
down at me from the top of one of them
kahikateas.[9] (*As the story continues, he
becomes more animated and excited.*) So
there I was, spoon in one hand, can in the
other, shovelling beans down the old
gasper, when I heard this noise. A rasping,
like a lamb having its throat cut. Must be
Charger the dog, I thought, in a bit of strife.
So, I got up to have a jack. I couldn't see
nothing, but I followed the noise anyway.
Well, it was like chasing a bloody rainbow;
it always stayed five steps ahead of me.
Finally, I come to this clearing. Oh Kura, it
was a sight to behold. It looked like a bloody
fairies' garden. The bush flowers hung from
the trees like stars, and inside the trees
was a circle of pongas[10] and fern. And
smack in the centre of that was this spring,
just bubbling away. (*Pause.*) And inside that
spring was the sweetest, most pure water in
the world. I could smell it, and I needed

something to wash down the beans, so I bent down to have a wee drink. (*Pause.*) Then, from outta nowhere, I hear this giggling. It sounded just like little kids playing a trick, but struth, what the hell would kids be doin' way up here? I come from Irish stock, so I know about the little people and how they play tricks on you. This had ta be the same kinda thing. Well, I just about shit meself. It was not the place for a bloke like me to be. I took off outta there like I had a stick of dynamite up me rear end! Hell, I ran so fast I just about broke my neck falling over a ledge. It took me two days to find my way back home and I never saw Charger again. (*Pause.*) Those beans gave me a crook guts too. I was laid up with the runs for a fair while after that. (*Sighs. Realises* KURA *has gone.*) Kura? Kura! Oh Kura, I thought you were dead keen girl. We still gotta talk about the rental car. (*Yells out to her*) Didn't you say Hertz was the best brand? (*Quietly to himself*) I still have the picture in my head. Lizzie walking into the shed with a bundle in her arms. A baby. 'What's her name?' I asked. She said it was Kura. So I picked you up and from the minute I saw you I loved you. (*Smiles.*) You were a wee beauty, with those fat cheeks and that mop of red hair, and you smiled at me. Lizzie told me it was 'cos you had wind and that you were wet. (*Pause.*) But it didn't feel like you'd peed yourself. Then she took you away. (*Pause.*) You know Kura, I . . . aarh . . . forget the tea.

(*Lights down on* WALTER. *Actor moves to* TIA's *space. A funky reggae beat plays and the lights come up.* TIA *is on the street.*)

TIA The first time I saw Te Atakura it was at the bus stop. I saw the hair first. Red as, and piled on top of her head like it might escape. Oh man, she had something serious on her brain that day, scowling away into her chocolate milkshake. There goes MWA, I thought. Māori With Attitude. I didn't want to sit next to her because I thought she might spit on me. Nah. 'Kia ora babe', I said. 'I'm Tia, ko wai tō ingoa?' 'Aye?', she answered. 'It's cool, babe, I just asked you what your name was'. She told me it was Te Atakura. Kura for short. Well, I thought, she's gotta be a special chick to have a beautiful name like that. So, we talked, and she tried to tell me she was a colour analyst at Fine Foods, the tomato sauce factory.

(*Laughs*) I mean, when did tomatoes stop being red? But she didn't stop there. No, not that girl. Then she said that the tomatoes they used were made out of surimi, the same stuff they use for making crabsticks. That's teka,[11] I told her, and you know it. So then she said she was the General Manager there, and she just took the bus to get to know the workers. Oh, my poor sista, I knew straight away that she worked on the factory floor checking sauce cans for defects. Yeah, those bus trips were tūmeke,[12] she'd cram it all in. Her dreams, her out-of-it fantasies, before she'd have to leap off at Fine Foods, and I'd be left with my head spinning all the way to Varsity. Yep. She's well and truly stuck between pō and rangi that dawn child. Pōrangi[13] as. (*To* KURA) You know what girl? Sauce is out. Definitely not cool. I'm the flavour of the month, so you wanna start hanging out with me for a while. (*Clicks her fingers*) Snap snap chick, we're talking action.

(*Lights down on* TIA. *Actor moves to* MIRO's *space, inside a house in a small Northland Community. Lights come up.* MIRO *is sitting leaning on a tokotoko (walking stick). She talks to* KURA, *a young baby in a cradle beside her.*)

MIRO Āe. Kei te maumahara ahau mō te ata i whānau mai koe.[14] The morning you were born Te Atakura. I remember it because the night before, the Howard Morrison Quartet was playing in town and I wasn't gonna miss that for nothing. Not even for you my baby. Gee, it was hard case all right. Me looking like I'd swallowed a pumpkin, wearing your Koro's dungarees, up the front listening to Howie's crooning. (*Sings*) 'Maringi noa ngā roimata, mōu kua wehea nei'.[15] His voice as rich as steam pudding and cream. My sister Ivy was going gaga, she was. (MIRO *sees her neighbour's dog outside. She stands up and yells out.*) Bugger off, you bloody mongrel! Next time he comes around here I'm gonna fix him up with my 44 then leave him to rot on Kepa's front porch. (*She aims her tokotoko out of the window like a rifle.*) I'll tie a bow around its neck with a pretty card. 'HAPPY BIRTHDAY KEPA'. (*Laughs. Then seeing that* KURA *has gone to sleep,* MIRO *puts the tokotoko down and kneels beside her.*) Ah yes, Te Atakura, you dream. And what do you see in your dreams? In mine I see a girl with mana in her hair and magic in her eyes. A girl who'll be a great leader for our people. (*She stands and continues telling her story to a sleeping* KURA.) Oh yes. The morning you were born . . . well, there he was crooning away and then I got this little sharp pain in my back, and I knew it was you wanting to get out, but I chose to ignore it, just kept listening to Howie. And there it was again, only harder. So I gave Ivy a poke in the ribs. 'She's on her way', I said, and off we went back home in Ivy's new Falcon. You were born at half past six the next morning, so we called you Te Atakura. The red dawn. And what a dawn it was.

(*Lights down on* MIRO. *Actor moves to the front of stage, occupying the space in front of the other characters. Lights come up.* KURA *is in her bedroom at* UNCLE WALTER's *and* AUNT LIZZIE's *house.*)

KURA (*angry, replying to* AUNTY LIZZIE) Yes, I heard you. Two teabags. Nice and strong. Nice and strong. (*She quietens down.*) I have this dream. I'm only little and I'm in a hallway that never ends. There are black and white tiles on the floor. And there are these legs in front of me. All I can see are these big huge legs that must go right up to the roof. The legs start walking and I have to follow them, but I have to run because I'm just a little kid and these legs belong to someone giant and beautiful. I think she must be my mother. So, I sprint after the legs and finally I catch them and they stop. Then, I climb up one of them, like it's a big coconut tree. I climb and climb till this arm reaches down and pulls me up the rest of the way. I can't see her face. And she cradles me in her arms like I'm a little kitten. I feel all safe. (*Pause.*) Questions. I have so many questions. But how long do I have to wait for the answers? How long before they see me waiting? I see them now as complete strangers, the same way you see someone you pass on the street, or waiting for the train. Aunty Lizzie, she's just a tight-lipped old bag, standing there. Rigid. In her padded dressing gown. Uncle Walter is nothing but a tired old man. I need to know about my mother, about my home. I need to know.

(*Lights down on* KURA. *Actor moves to* LIZZIE's *space. Lights go up on* LIZZIE. *She lights her cigarette, takes a long drag then dabs her face with her hanky.*)

LIZZIE (*speaking as if to* KURA) Your mother, Miro, was a funny woman. (*Pause.*) Had funny ways, but she would have been pleased you'd come to us, and a child needs a father I always say. When she passed away I did my best by you, Kura. I called the family together, did everything, just like Miro said, just how she wanted it. I even told them she wanted to wear that purple thing and helped dress her. And I told your Aunty Ivy how close Miro and I'd become since the sickness, how I'd helped and how she'd wanted me to take you, Kura. Well, I couldn't let her go with them . . . Ivy's husband, he's a drinker. I mean she'd barely been laid to rest and there he was, in the kitchen with his bottle of Jack Daniel's. *Dabbing her forehead.* No respect for the dead. No. I couldn't let you go to a family like that. Ah, yes, the Lord works in mysterious ways. (*Pause.*) There you were, a cousin's child who needed a home. (*To God*) Oh, and she was such a sweet child. (*Pause.*) But nothing stays the same. I look at Kura now and all I see is this strange, angry young girl standing in my house. I . . . I feel nothing for her, believe me I've tried. I really have tried.

(*Lights down on* LIZZIE. *Actor moves to* WALTER's *space. Lights come up.* WALTER *is slumped in his old armchair.*)

WALTER I remember when I first met you, Lizzie. I'd bring presents for you and your family. One night it'd be salted pork, the next pigeon or salted eel. By the time I'd finished, the old fella was dead keen on having me for a son-in-law. Me and him, we'd yarn away well into the night and you'd be in the kitchen cooking and plucking. We . . . we were something else together, me and you. You were such a pretty thing. The first time I saw you I couldn't keep my eyes off ya. In the middle of nowhere and you looked like you'd just stepped off the page of one of them fashion magazines. Pretty as a picture you were, and god Liz, you could please a man. (*Growls.*) You could've had any one of them bush cowboys, but you chose me, a sharemilker's son from Reporoa. And do you remember that time I went out hunting? I was gone for days. Poor Liz, you were so worried, and then one night I put my head in the door and said to ya, 'Come out here my honey, I gotta surprise for ya'.

I took your wee hand and led you out to the verandah and there it was. 'The Ripper'. The boar every man and his dog had been chasing for the last five years. Your eyes sparkled with pride. I was your Rambo.

(*Lights down on* WALTER. *Actor moves to* KURA's *space. Lights come up.* KURA *has just arrived for work at Fine Foods. She is late. She puts her time card into the machine. There is factory noise.*)

KURA (*as she passes the other workers*) Hi Jimmy. Brenda. Nah. I'm not coming tonight. Yeah? So what about him? Nah. It's history. Which one is she? She's a pog and a sucker. J.T.'s a prick. (KURA *waves to J.T. She takes her place at the conveyor belt. Her head moves from side to side, checking cans. Occasionally, she removes a can and throws it in a bin. She continues to talk and answer questions.*) So, she's the one that ate his neck. Disgusting. No I can't, because I've got other plans. Well, there's this fulla. At the movies. Um Bosnia. In the peace corps. Drives the truck. Look. It's true man. At the movies. The one with Uma Thurman in it. And my mate, Sally. (KURA *abandons the conveyor belt.*) She dared me to say hi to him because he looked so cool. Well, I did, I said 'hi I'm Kura' and he said 'hi I'm Phillip'. (*Yells out to a worker*) PHILLIP! NO, NOT JUST A TRUCK DRIVER, HE'S IN THE PEACE CORPS. So he said, 'how would you like to go out to dinner?' and I said, 'where?' And he said, 'somewhere with a view of the ocean', and I said, 'wonderful'. So, I guess it'll be candles and a white tablecloth. I bet he'll propose. True man. (*Yells out to a nosy worker*) GETTING MARRIED. PHIL. IT HAD UMA THURMAN IN IT. (*Sighs. Goes back to work. She throws a few defected cans off the conveyor belt.*) Defect. Defect. Defect. Defect. (*She starts to fantasise while looking at the cans.*) Defect-ed. Defect-ing. De-fucked. De-moned. Defect Demon. Defected Demon. (*There is eerie lighting and music.*)

(KURA *lives out a fantasy in which she is saving the factory from a defected demon; sometimes she takes on the role of the demon. Then she randomly goes back to checking cans. But the fantasy overcomes her. It is like a silent movie. She is climbing a mountain of cans, escaping from the demon. She pulls out a laser gun and shoots the demon then raises her arms in victory.* KURA *is the hero of the canning factory. Then the fantasy is over and*

she feels deflated. She is left holding a can. She looks around her; people in the factory are staring.)

KURA (*to the curious factory workers*) No, I'm fine thanks. (KURA *starts checking cans again, then boredom sets in. She thinks about her mother.*) I try and I try but I can't remember. Just coloured walls and plastic flowers, and the ticking of a clock. Lots of music and talking . . . all the time I hear talking, but the words run together and melt like butter. Mum, what is it you were telling me? (*Lights down on* KURA.)

Scene 3 – Whakapapa[16]

Actor moves to MIRO's *space. Lights come up.* MIRO *is standing, leaning on her tokotoko and talking to* KURA, *who is in her cradle.*

MIRO Kia ahatia Te Atakura, e pai ana koe? Āe, ka pai. Te wā tēnei mō te moe nei? E hiahia ana ahau, he wāhanga okioki. He maha rawa ā tāua tākaro pōrangi.[17] (*Looks around.*) This place is falling apart. (*She leaves* KURA.) I saw bloody Number 7 wander out of the gate and up to Kepa's place this morning before I had a chance to milk her. I thought, there goes my baby's milk. Just like that. Tipi haere[18] up the road. And you know what bloody Kepa will do with our cow don't you, with Charlie's twenty-first coming up. Throw her in the hāngi[19] with every other bloody living thing he can lay his grubby hands on. The bastard. I tell you, if I wasn't such a light sleeper, he'd have sneaked his way in here, grabbed you and thrown you down the hole with the pigs and chickens. Āhea a Kepa, e mōhio ai. Ahakoa pēhea te nui o te hāngi, e kore ia e mōhio ki te whakatakoto hāngi, kāhore he painga.[20] Yep. He'll be sending all those relations of his home with sore pukus.[21] Good job. (*Pretending to growl at* KURA) Now, stop talking to me would you, and go to sleep. (*She goes to the cradle and strokes* KURA's *hair.*) Āe, tō ātaahua hoki,[22] just like your tupuna, Waiora. She was magic, Kura. She had a mane of red hair that danced around her waist and she had fairy's eyes. She lived in a time when the Moa People walked this land. They were a tall and proud people, an iwi[23] full of kings and queens. Around their necks each of them wore a moa egg. Ko te wairua o te moa tō rātou kaitiaki,[24] and they had nothing but respect for those great birds. Not like Kepa, with his gun blasting the head off every living thing in sight; they only took what they needed. But Waiora didn't belong to them, she was a gift from the Tūrehu, the Fairy People, and she was found in a spring, riding high on a fountain and covered in kōkōwai.[25] You know what that is? It's a powder, the colour of red brick. Māori gold dust I call it. Now, Waiora grew to become a clever girl who loved to play tricks and dance. But her greatest gift was foresight. She knew where the moa were feeding and where the tāmure[26] were schooling and whether the sky was gonna pour down buckets or shine the next day. (*Pause.*) And when their enemies would attack, Waiora kept the Moa People safe. But Waiora had a great pain inside her. She missed the Tāngata Tūrehu,[27] and the spring where she was born. (*The ringing of a cow bell is heard.*) Whakarongo ki tērā, Te Atakura.[28] Sounds like Number 7's bell, ringing its way home. (*She moves to the window and looks out.*) Āe. Kua tae mai ia.[29] The crafty old thing, and look! You wouldn't bloody believe it! Her tits are empty! Hell! She should be bursting. That bloody Kepa! I bet he's having fresh cream on his porridge right now. (*Looking towards* KEPA's *house, she speaks quietly.*) Auē, Kepa. You'll never change. If you got down on your hands and knees and kissed the ground in front of me, I wouldn't marry you. I don't want my baby to be part of you and your koretake[30] ways. Your parties and beer and that long drop with two seats. Too lazy to even wait your turn. You're not bad for a roll in the hay, engari hei tāne, hei pāpā? Kāhore! He koretake rawa koe! I kī mai ngā Rata kua tata mate ahau.[31] That I got cancer. Went into the hospital with whiplash, came out with cancer. They say it's in my spine. Bally hoo. (*Pause.*) And who's that shuffling up the track looking like a flat tyre? Can you believe it? It's cousin Lizzie. He aha rā tana mahi i konei, e Kura?[32] Bet it's something to do with that teacher she fancies. What's his name again? That's it . . . George. George Chambers. Well, Mr George Chambers, what's a young man like you doin' messing round with the local girls? Married ones at that. Georgie Porgie puddin' n pie, kissed cousin Lizzie and made her cry. And poor Walt. She thought he'd give her the fine life because he was a Pākehā and a new face in town. She gotta shock all right! (*She has a laugh, but upon seeing the state* LIZZIE *is in, she stops.*) Auē! Te kino hoki o tōna āhua![33] (*Lights down on* MIRO.)

Scene 4 – Passion

Actor moves to TIA's *space on the street. The lights come up.* TIA's *music plays. She is talking to* KURA.

TIA   Te Atakura, why don't you move in with us, babe? What? You'll think about it? Trouble with you is that you spend too much time dreaming and reality just passes you on by. (*Sighs*) But you're a true sista, okay? And I love you, so this is what I'm gonna do. I'm gonna keep insisting till you stop resisting. You didn't even come to that social the other night. You missed out on a lot of action there, girl. The Waka Taua boys turned up, that could've been you babe. Now, I'm gonna ask you something and I don't want you to get offended, all right? But how many men have you met apart from your Uncle?

(*Lights go down on* TIA. *Actor moves to* KURA's *space. Lights come up on her.*)

KURA   (*replying to* TIA's *question*) After J.T., I'm just not interested. J.T. with his leathers and the only pick up line he knows. (*She speaks as J.T. would.*) 'CHER! You're alright eh? Aw yeah, you into a cruise then? I gotta smoke. CHER'. J.T. and the way he used to ask me for a date. (*As J.T.*) 'Hey, are you into drinking? Wanna come down the clubrooms and skull a few beers after the game? (*Chants*) WARRIORS, WARRIORS (*Pause.*) Aarh, your shout, eh?' For about a month I thought J.T. was the Luke Perry of the sauce factory. He could even pop one eyebrow up by itself. He was beautiful. His dark eyes, his sideways smirk. (*Pause.*) The way he was always chewing Juicy Fruit. Every time he walked into the tearoom my heart would pound in my head like a hammer, and I could hear the blood racing through my veins. I wanted to be his fantasy.

(*Heavy metal music starts to play and the fantasy begins.* KURA *acts the following dialogue out. She is riding a Harley Davidson.*)

My legs would be wrapped in tight leather pants. Dressed in a tasselled jacket and studded belt, I'd come roaring into the tearoom on the meanest, shiniest Harley Davidson he'd ever seen. Cool as, I'd swing my boot over the seat and go to him, mincing all the way. (*She gets off the bike and 'minces' over to an imaginary J.T.*) Then I'd sweep him up into my arms and give him the wettest, longest, hottest kiss ever. (*She dips J.T. and kisses him long and hard.*) Yeah, I'd shove my tongue so hard down his throat he'd choke. The tearoom would be stunned. There'd be wide eyes and cigarettes left hanging in mid-air with the ash just dropping off the end. And finally, after I'd kissed the life out of him, I'd drop him onto the floor and walk. (*She drops J.T. and walks. Then she stops and looks back at him.*) Leaving him a smoking, seething pulp of black leather. (*The fantasy is over.*) Me and J.T. had a few dates outside the clubrooms. There were lots of cuts and bruises and dirt. It was like sumo wrestling downhill. But I believed under the layers of leather and black jersey there was a prince. I thought I was special to him. He said I was 'alright eh'. But then I found out J.T. had sampled most of the women at Fine Foods. J.T. was used goods. What an arsehole. So from across the rows of machines and people I yelled at him 'you fuckin' using prick'. Then I defected a perfectly good sauce can on his head. Only trouble was, he got off on it and I cried for weeks because I thought he loved me. It must have been the same for Aunty Liz and Uncle Walter. With them it must have been one phony burst of passion that burnt them out and left them sick of each other. (*Pause.*) There must have been something that brought them together.

(*Lights down on* KURA. *Actor moves to* LIZZIE's *space. Lights come up.* LIZZIE *lights her cigarette, takes a drag and dabs her forehead with her hanky.*)

LIZZIE 'E moe i te tangata ringa raupā'. Marry a man with calloused hands. Walter's were calloused alright. But the hands I wanted were soft like rose petals, with violinist's fingers and slender wrists. (*She runs her hands over her body, remembering Georgie's touch. The music to 'To Sir with Love' plays tentatively on the piano underneath.*) The only callouses on those hands were from the pressure of his (*pause*) fountain pen. So, so sensitive. Oh Georgie, the hours we would spend lying side by side in our secret spot. You reading to me in that softly-spoken, shy way you had, while I . . . I just floated. 'Someone has stolen the stars from the sky and put them in your eyes', you'd whisper. Oh Georgie, my Georgie. You were always so clean and well dressed. Never any stubble on your face. In fact, your . . . your whole body was hairless. So smooth. Your skin smelt like lavender water and your kisses . . . your kisses tasted like tangerines. (*She sings the lines, 'To Sir with Love'. The music and the dreaming stop sharply and* LIZZIE *snaps back into her reality.*) And I remember you, Walter. Taking me out onto the verandah one night. It was a surprise, you said. You'd been gone for days. It was silly, I knew you'd been out hunting but I thought you had bought me some roses or some chocolates. Instead, there it was. All blood and bristles and (*pause*) dried saliva, with its tusks shining in the moonlight. And it had those horrid little eyes. They had the look of death in them, they did. They just stared at me as if I was to blame. And the next morning there it was again, hanging in the wash house. The blood was dripping on to my new Fisher n' Paykel. How could I live like that, Walter?

(*Lights down on* LIZZIE. *Actor moves to* WALTER's *space. Lights come up on* WALTER *sitting in his chair. He holds up his hands and looks at them sadly.*)

WALTER I wonder how many fence posts I've put in with these hands. How many pigs I've gutted, and how many trees I've felled. They've only ever held one woman though. My Lizzie. My Lizzie with the wind in her hair. Oh Lizzie, you were so . . . but that, all that was a long time ago. (*He sighs.*) What happened to us my honey?

(*Lights down on* WALTER. *Actor moves to* KURA's *space. Lights come up.* KURA *has seen a vision of her mother singing to her as a baby. The oriori (lullaby) her mother sings, tells her of her whakapapa. For the first time,* KURA *begins to realise the potential she carries inside herself. She longs to tell someone. Running to each of the characters' spaces/platforms, she calls to them.*)

KURA Tia!
Uncle Walt!

Aunty Liz!

They are not there. (*She crouches and starts to repeat the song she heard. Singing softly.*)

Te awe o te Waiora . . .

ara ake ana Te Atakura . . .[34]

(*She hums the tune softly. Then slaps the floor with both hands and begins to rise. She does one strong haka action and continues the song, but this time in* MIRO's *space, as* MIRO.)

Scene 5 – Takimoana

Lights on MIRO. *She sings the oriori to* TE ATAKURA. *She sings about whakapapa and the path she wishes* KURA *to follow, as well as her acceptance of her own approaching death.*

MIRO

Auē taku whero

Ka huri taku mata ki aku tūpuna

E okioki mai ana

Māku rawa koe e tuku

Kia tupu ai i raro ngā tohunga o Ngāti Kōkōwai

E noho taha i tō puna wai

Te awe o Te Waiora

E tohu nei e ngā tae

Kei runga i te ao

Ara ake ana Te Atakura

Mai te puna ao roa

Ki te ao mārama e

(*She finishes the oriori and thinks for a moment. Her thoughts are interrupted by* KURA.)

MIRO What was that you said, Kura? Dada? DADA? Ko wai tēnā taurekareka?[35] I don't know any fulla called Dada. (*She feels a sharp pain in her back.*) E hiahia ana rātou kia haere ahau ki te hōhipera.[36] No way. I've seen their medicine. It's electric blue and red and they feed it into your veins. (*Pause.*) You're a special child, and I know whatever it is that you choose to do with your life, you'll be bloody good at it. Just like Waiora. By the time she was a young woman, boy, did she have things under control. The Moa People had always been skilled hunters, fishermen and weavers, but now they were bloody great and they felt great. But not everyone was over the moon about the way things were going. Across the sea another group of the Moa People lived with their leader, Takimoana. Takimoana, he tangata tūkino ia.[37] Yes, he was a greedy man and he had wanted to rule the Moa People, but

they soon gave him the boot and he left with a few of his gang to Motukauri, a nearby island. He hadn't been seen since. But Takimoana hadn't forgotten, and when news of this new rangatira,[38] Waiora, reached the shores of Motukauri, Takimoana was filled with rage. (MIRO *speaks angrily, as* TAKIMOANA.) Waiora. Ko wai ia? Te wāhine e kawe ana te mana o tēnei iwi. I te mate ia, kāhore he iwi. Kāhore he rangatira.[39] (*She laughs evilly.*) Killing Waiora would be his revenge. (*She sighs and rubs her back.*) Ko ahau, ko koe, ko nama Whitu,[40] a few mangy chooks to feed and I'm stuffed by seven o'clock. Must be from that hiding I gave Kepa's pig dog this avo. Chased him around for an hour, I did. He kept skulking round behind those bushes at the back of the house – buggered if I know what he's after. And Lizzie, she's been on my doorstep every day for the past week now. Hapū[41] to her bloody schoolteacher. Four months and she's still wearing them little tight dresses. She thinks I'm the whore of Babylon, so I'll understand. But it's different for me, I've always known just who I wanted in my life. I'm not helping her Kura, she can clean her own dirty washing. She wants me to get rid of the baby. She asked me to give her something to make her bleed. 'Everyone will know it's not Walter's', she says. And she's right. The whole town knows her and the teacher are hot for each other. (*Pause.*) Except for Walter. Poor Walter Jennings. I asked her why she didn't leave him. 'I can't', she answered. 'We're married'. For a minute there, her face got all sad and her lip started drooping and she looked like she wanted to pick you up, girl. Then she changed her mind. Lucky for you. (MIRO *feels a sharp pain, she winces and leans heavily on her tokotoko.*) Aaarh. Come on, Te Atakura. Get up here and give me a hand, would you? (*She laughs then looks down at* KURA.) Te Atakura? Kua ara koe?[42] (TE ATAKURA *is sleeping and* MIRO *is left feeling very alone.*) Auē, Kepa. This is what I get for being so stubborn.

(*Lights down on* MIRO.)

Scene 6 – Standing in the cabbages

Actor moves to TIA's *space. Her music plays. The lights come up.*

TIA   I just got a call from Kura, my imaginary friend. I sometimes wonder if that sista is just a figment of my imagination. I know my mates do. But they'll be pleased to know she's accepted my offer to step into the sun. Yep, she's moving in. I'm gonna paint her room. Something vital. It was gonna be red but red will remind her of sauce for sure, so it's gonna be green. Rejuvenation. She's so tragic.

(*Lights down on* TIA. *Actor moves to* KURA's *space. Lights come up.* KURA *is alone in her room, packing her things.*)

KURA   A few posters, some clothes and my books. That's it. (*She looks around.*) All that's left are the pinholes, some graffiti behind the dressing table and the echoes of my dreams. (*She speaks as if to* LIZZIE *and* WALTER) I'm sorry Aunty Liz, Uncle Walter, but something has changed. (*Pause.*) I heard the words. I saw the memory. Her singing. Telling me of my past, my future. The dreaming has become real and I can't stay here any more. I need to find out where I'm meant to be. (*Pause.*) Uncle Walter, don't miss your moment. I hope that one day you find that kingfish or boar you've been chasing for the last thirty years. And after that? Well, you can find a warm spot with your mates and drink home brew and eat pipis all day long. Aunty Lizzie, for you, I just hope you find out that God's not pissed off all the time. Aunty Lizzie found God when she was four. She said he was seven foot tall and bald and wearing a black cape. He was standing in the cabbages and frowning. (*Pause.*) It was a nice story.

(*Lights down on* KURA. *Actor moves to* LIZZIE's *space. Lights come up.* LIZZIE *is kneeling, taking communion at church. Organ music is playing. She repeats what the minister is saying to her, after taking first the wine, and then the bread.*)

LIZZIE   (*holding her hands open above her to receive the bread*) Take and eat this in memory that Christ died for you. Preserve thy body and soul unto everlasting life. (*She places the bread into her mouth; her hands shake as she accepts the chalice.*) The blood of our Lord Jesus Christ which was shed for you. Preserve thy body and soul unto everlasting life. (*She drinks the wine, then frowns in deep prayer.*) Be merciful to me, God. Wash away my sins because of your great mercy. I have sinned against you, and done what you consider evil, so you are right in judging me. Right in punishing me, leaving me empty. (*Pause.*) Unable to love, unable to feel happiness. A faithful heart is what you want, so fill my mind with your wisdom. Remove my sin and I will be clean. Wash me and I will be whiter than snow. Please. Though I am crushed and broken, let me be happy once more. Close your eyes to my sins and wipe out my evil. Oh, sweet Jesus. Hear my prayer. Amene.

(*Lights down on* LIZZIE. *Actor moves to* WALTER's *space. Lights come up on* WALTER *sitting in his chair.*)

WALTER   Lizzie's at church again. She used to ask me to come with her. Anyway, it's a corker day. The kind of day you should be out fishing. (*He speaks to* KURA) Whaddaya say, Kura? Reckon I should clean up the old *Seagull* and take her out for a blast. They tell me the harbour up north is full of stingrays. You think you've hooked a bloody Kingy, but it's a bloody ray. You can always tell when you've got one of them scoundrels on the line 'cos they don't fight the same way. There's just this Christ almighty thud and your line goes racing out to sea. May as well cut the bastard. That's what happens when you fish out all the snapper. Aw Kura. This is real, isn't it love? I . . . I'm gonna miss ya girl. (*He stands up.*) How would ya feel if I came round for a cuppa some time? (*Lights down on* WALTER.)

Scene 7 – The lure

Actor moves to MIRO's *space. Lights come up.* MIRO *has become very weak, but is doing her best to conceal her pain. She can only move with the help of her tokotoko.*

MIRO   Te Atakura, e kore koe e whakapono ki tēnei.[43] I found out who's been stealing our milk. I saw him, dancing across the field to Number 7. Then, as plain as day he latched onto her udder and had a good long suck. She didn't kick up a fuss either, started mooing away like he was her long lost son, home from the war. Kepa's pig dog. Oh Kura, you know that stupid doctor reckons I'm not long for this world. 'Huh!' I said. 'You've gotta bloody cheek. When did you last look in the mirror?' Sick looking thing he is. (*Pause.*) Trouble is, I'm starting to believe him, Kura. And I don't want people weeping and wailing all over me and treating me like I'm dead while I can still wiggle my toes, so I've only told cousin Lizzie. I know she won't make a fuss. Wouldn't bother her if I kicked the bucket. (*Laughs.*) I've told her Te Atakura, just in case I check out early, that you're to go and live with my sister Ivy, up in Kawakawa. She's got three other kids and a big house and a husband that works hard and thinks with his head. You can take Number 7 with you, and when you're old enough, this house is yours for all it's worth. (*Some guitar music drifts into the house.*) Can you hear that music Te Atakura? Kepa! I'm dying and he's having a bloody party. That'd be right. Hell, I bet he can't wait till the tangi.[44] He'll have a fair hoolie.[45] (*She whispers to* KURA) Hey, if that bastard ever tries to tell you that he's your old man, smack him one in the face for me, would ya? (MIRO *laughs. She stands and joins in with the song that is being played. Then goes back to the cradle to finish the story of* WAIROA, *her farewell to* TE ATAKURA.) So, my baby. Where was I up to with our story? That's right, Takimoana and his gang had come over to join the Moa People. He was as handsome as they come, he was also very vain. He would cover himself in kōkōwai from his topknot to his toes. All red, like Tū Matauenga.[46] When he arrived at the shores of the Moa People, Waiora was there waiting. She had seen Takimoana in her dreams and knew he was a danger to her people. She watched as their waka slid silently into shore. And she looked on in amazement as Takimoana's men lifted him, waka and all, onto the beach. The Moa people had warned Waiora many times of this man's power and she herself had seen him in her dreams. She thought she was prepared. Takimoana felt her watching, and as he stepped out to stretch he turned to meet her gaze. (*Pause.*) In his eyes Waiora saw her own fate, but she couldn't turn away. The kōkōwai that covered Takimoana's lean body sparked and glinted in the sun, reminding her of the spring where she was born and of the Tāngata Tūrehu she missed so much. She was spellbound. Not wanting to hurt her people Waiora convinced Takimoana to

meet her in secret. And after a while he thought to himself, why kill her when he could take her and her power back to Motukauri with him? So late one night he crept inside Waiora's whare.[47] He covered her eyes and dragged her outside. Then he beat her. He beat her just for being strong. Waiora had never felt such hatred and jealousy and for the first time in her life she was afraid. But she didn't fight back and she didn't call for help, if she alerted anyone they too would be in danger (*pause*) and inside she knew that this was something that could not be changed. (MIRO *is breathless; she rests before continuing.*) As they sailed across the moana,[48] towards Motukauri Waiora felt a great shame. She waited until Takimoana was asleep then she pulled out a shiny black flake of obsidian rock, loosened the topknot from her hair, then raising her eyes skyward, she chanted:

E ngā atua,
whakahokia te mana ki te iwi
Auē taukiri e.

She cut her beautiful red hair and, strand by strand, scattered it into the sea. Her mana and her soul danced within the waves, acting as a lure for the greedy white tāmure who were swimming by. She cut and cut and the tāmure snapped up each strand, filling their bellies and turning their scales a brilliant red. And, when the final strand was severed, Waiora fell into a deep sleep. She was never seen again. But her mana was never lost. You see a few months later, the Moa People ate those same sweet tāmure and every now and then a child is born with magic in her eyes and hair the colour of kōkōwai. That is you, Te Atakura. One day you'll understand. (*Quietly and tearfully*) Whakarongo ki te tangi a tō tātou tupuna e karanga mai ana. Whakarongo mai.[49] (*Lights down on* MIRO.)

Scene 8 – Kimihia

Actor moves to LIZZIE's *space. Lights come up.* LIZZIE *is at home,* KURA *has already moved out.* LIZZIE *lights her smoke and dabs her face with her hanky.*

LIZZIE   Kua haere a Kura,[50] she's not coming back. Gone. Gone. They all leave me. (*Memories from the past take over and in her mind she is driving back from Woolies on that day long ago.*) I have to go to town. To Woolies. Flour. Yes, flour. Oh Georgie, yes, soon my love. Soon. Leaving. Walter. Never again. Plucking pheasants. Never again. Bends. These bends and twists and holes. Wetas. Gone soon. (*She smiles to herself.*) Fluttering inside. Feet kicking. My baby. Georgie, baby, white house. Dahlias. All clean. Our baby. Fluttering, kicking, kicking, stabbing, pulling. (LIZZIE *relives the pain, holding her stomach.*) Stabbing, pulling. Stabbing, pulling, leaving. (*She screams out.*) What's wrong? Oh God, what's happening? (*She speaks very clinically.*) There was blood and I had to lie across the back seat. All the time I was praying that no-one would see me or recognise the car. When I saw it, it didn't look like a baby. They didn't look like real hands or feet and it wasn't moving. So I threw it out the window and left it there on the side of the road. I drove to Miro's and she washed me and gave me something bitter to drink and made me sleep. (*Pause.*) I went back and tried to find it, but there was nothing but mud and gravel and tyre marks. (*Upset*) I keep thinking about my baby on the side of the road on the way home and I can't go back there. I can never go back there. (*Pause.*) For one moment I was happy. Just for that one moment I let myself dream of dahlias. I thought taking Kura would make the pain go away, but it didn't. It just made things worse. And it's too late now to go back. But I've paid Miro. I've paid. (*She becomes very upset.*) Kia kite koe nā, ko te pōuri anake e toa ana! Auē! Me mutu rā koutou katoa, me mutu rā![51] (LIZZIE *strikes at her ashtray, knocking it over. She immediately replaces it.*)

(*Lights down on* LIZZIE. *Actor moves to* TIA's *space. Lights come up.* TIA's *music plays.*)

TIA   I took Te Atakura home for a kai tonight. I thought it might do her some good to meet the old man. He's kinda normal. Well, get that girl, not shy, not a problem for her to have three plates of bacon bones and pūhā.[52] Anyway, my old man starts talking to her, wanting to know who her whānau is in case he might know them. (*Sighs.*) You know what those Māoris are like. So then Kura, she blurts out the whole tragically sad story, well what she knows of it and the old man, he looks at

her and goes: (TIA *speaks like her father*) 'E kī ana te kōrero, e kore te maunga e haere ki te tangata, me haere te tangata ki te maunga,[53] or something like that, eh dear?' Which kinda means, if you ain't found the truth by looking at defected cans in a sauce factory in the suburbs, then maybe it lies somewhere else. And Kura, she looked at the old man like she might take that bit of advice on and she might not. Who's she trying to fool? Anyway, I reckon that girl already knows where the answer lies. Just helps to be told. Kinda like how the pot doesn't believe it's black till the kettle tells it. (*Sighs.*) Yeah, Te Atakura's well and truly on her way and once that girl starts moving, everybody better stay clear 'cos she's gonna be scary. True.

(*Lights down on* TIA. *Actor moves to* KURA's *space. Lights come up. Behind her, the poupou representing her tupuna,* WAIORA, *is in light. The others are in darkness.*)

KURA
    The world I live in is rich.
    Its colours are purple and red.
    It joins the earth to the sky and the night
        to the day.
    It is a waking dream.
    Inside me is this spring.
    Its bubbles surge and pop against the
        inside of my skin.
    Through my hair the kōkōwai sparkles.
    It sparkles with life and with mana.
    Hōmai te waiora.[54]

(KURA *spins the pūrerehua*[55] *over each platform. As she does so, the poupou behind light up.* KURA *then does one very strong action with pūkana,*[56] *making her own poupou.*)

Notes

1   Family, in a broad sense.
2   A cloak.
3   Ancestor.
4   A Māori canoe.
5   A call or hail.
6   Large wingless insects of New Zealand.
7   Trees.
8   Parson birds.
9   White pines.
10 Tree ferns.
11 Lying.
12 Too much, fantastic.

13 The phrase puns upon the meanings of the 'dawn child', Te Atakura, whose name can be translated as 'the red dawn'. Pō (night) plus rangi (day) gives Pōrangi, which has meanings such as headstrong, beside oneself, out of one's mind or mad. In Tia's view, Te Atakura is stuck in a liminal zone between night and day, unable to begin the day and hence unable to enter te ao mārama, the world of life and light. Set against Te Atakura's current state of limbo is the birthright and family history that her name symbolises.

14 Yes, I remember the morning you were born.

15 My tears spill forth, for you who has departed.

16 Genealogical table, family.

17 Never mind Te Atakura are you okay? Yes, good. Is this the time to sleep? I want time to rest. We have so many silly things to play.

18 Wander.

19 Pit oven.

20 When will Kepa learn. No matter how big the hāngi is, he will never know how to put it down, it won't be any good.

21 Stomachs.

22 Yes you are so beautiful.

23 Tribe.

24 It was the spirit of the moa that sustained them.

25 Red ochre.

26 Snapper.

27 Fairy people.

28 Listen to that, Te Atakura.

29 Yes, she has returned.

30 Useless.

31 But as a husband, or father. No way! You are too useless. The doctors told me that I was near death.

32 What is she doing here Kura?

33 Goodness, she looks terrible.

34 From the hair of Waiora . . . Arises Te Atakura . . .

35 Who is this slave – mongrel?

36 They want me to go to hospital.

37 Takimoana, he is an evil/cruel man.

38 Leader.

39 Waiora. Who is she? The woman who carries the mana of this tribe. If she dies so will the people. There will be no leader.

40 There is me, you and Number 7.

41 Pregnant.

42 Are you awake?.

43 Te Atakura, you won't believe this.

44 Lamentation, mourning.

45 Slang for party.

46 God of Mankind and War.

47 House, shed.

48 Sea.

49 Listen to the cry of our ancestor calling to us. Listen here.

50 Kura has gone.

51 Just look, there is only grief left. Goodness, you should all end it, all end it.

52 Green vegetables.

53 It is said, the mountain will not go to man, but man should go to the mountain.

54 Give me good health.

55 Bull-roarer, a flat disc on a string that is spun to produce a roar.

56 A wide-eyed stare or glare.

Song translations

The dying speech of Waiora

This then is the dream my people
The reason I have departed
In order for you to be strengthened
by the treacherous deed
Strand by strand I sever my hair
As red as blood
But blood it is not
Where then shall the combs rest?
The severed strands
are left unto the people
A symbol of power and strength
For a future time
If there is no hope
All will be lost my people

Oh spirits,
Return the mane to the people.
Alas!

Oriori – lullaby

Alas my dear one
I turn to face my ancestors
in the final resting place
It will be me that will send you
To learn among our knowledgeable ones
To grow beside the spring
The origin of Te Waiora
That indicates the colours
upon the earth
Rise Te Atakura
From the very depths
Into the world of light

16 Victoria Nalani Kneubuhl _____

The Conversion of Ka'ahumanu
Hawai'i

Introduction

In 1995, when she was presented with Hawai'i's highest award for literary achievement, Victoria Nalani Kneubuhl pointed to her unbroken connection with Pacific island life as the rich well-spring that inspires her work. Born in Honolulu of Samoan, Hawaiian and Caucasian ancestry, and later educated at university in Hawaiian cultural studies, Kneubuhl is ideally positioned as interpreter of her homeland's unique history. She holds a master's degree in drama and theatre studies and has worked extensively on Hawaiian heritage projects, most notably as curator of education at the Mission Houses Museum in Honolulu, where she trained and directed staff in the living history programmes. Such experience has enabled her to develop an extraordinarily rich and detailed knowledge of her region's history, which is imaginatively replayed in a number of dramatic works across genres ranging from historical dramas and pageants to children's plays and contemporary comedies. Kneubuhl has also written documentary scripts for video and television as well as being involved in various community arts organisations, including Kamu Kahua Theatre, which is dedicated solely to the development of local playwrights, directors and performers.

The Conversion of Ka'ahumanu (1988), which charts the early-nineteenth-century beginnings of missionary imperialism in Hawai'i, is one of several Kneubuhl plays to deal with aspects of the region's history. In the year before its premiere, Kneubuhl co-wrote *Ka'iulani*, based on the life of the Hawaiian princess who was heir-apparent to the island kingdom of Hawai'i at the time of its annexation by the United States in 1893. The two plays toured together to the Edinburgh Fringe Festival in 1990 and are in many ways companion pieces, both focusing on legendary women of the Hawaiian royalty at pivotal moments in their kingdom's history. *Ka'iulani* is structurally organised according to Bach's three-movement church cantatas, using music, chant, hula, mime, narrative and Hawaiian symbolism to create a piece of visually arresting theatre. *The Conversion of Ka'ahumanu* unfolds as a more intimate narrative drama that invites compassion for the five very different women whose lives are irrevocably changed by the expansion of Protestant missionary efforts in the Pacific. This play's finely nuanced account of interactions between the missionary wives and the Hawaiian women they seek to convert to Christianity suggests ways in which gender acts as a category that cuts across the discursive field of imperialism.

A favourite wife to King Kamehameha, the historical Queen Ka'ahumanu played a powerful role in Hawaiian politics as kuhina nui (co-ruler) after her husband died, appointing her as guardian to his young heir, Liholiho. One of Ka'ahumanu's first political achievements was to lift the ancient kapu system of religious taboos that severely restricted women's freedoms. Her eventual conversion to Christianity was equally portentous since it paved the way for previously weak mission influences to gain an unprecedented stranglehold on traditional Hawaiian society. While Kneubuhl takes these public events as the historical core and context for her narrative, she is just as interested in revealing her characters' inner lives, their doubts and fears, their prejudices, and above all their respective responses to contact with unfamiliar cultures. The largely domestic focus of the action allows the drama of cultural conflict to be played out at a personal level, while always evoking the social systems, beliefs and attitudes that inevitably shape interactions between the characters. Moments of tenderness or cultural rapprochement, and even risqué humour, are also expressed powerfully at this intimate level. The use of direct audience address consolidates the sense of a living, accessible history whose various protagonists speak through time to activate viewers' own interpretations of the past. Kneubuhl's approach to historical events, both narratively and performatively, thus poses an implicit challenge to the imperial habit of selecting as history the public deeds of so-called great men and presenting them under the guise of ideological neutrality.

The play's even-handed representation of the Euro-American missionaries, Sybil and Lucy, suggests that while colonial women were by no means hapless onlookers of the imperial process in Hawai'i, nor were they as destructive as their male counterparts, sailors and sandalwood traders whose chief legacies are depicted as violence, disease, alcoholism, and land degradation. Developed as a largely sympathetic character, Sybil provides a sharp contrast to the historical figure of her real-life husband, Hiram Bingham, whose puritanical zeal led to the most aggressive kind of Christian proselytising in the region. Within the women's world of the play, Sybil is shown to have forged her own style of missionary work, unlike in most historical accounts of the era, which tend to consign mention of her to a footnote in Bingham's illustrious career. Even the mean-spirited Lucy eventually gains the audience's pity, her ingrained racism mitigated by the ways in which she stoically endures the operation to remove her virulent breast tumour. For their part, the Hawaiian women are not idealised or exoticised but instead developed as complex individuals whose experiences of gender oppression are differentiated by their respective positions in a highly stratified society. As kuhina nui in a patriarchal system, Ka'ahumanu's primary challenges are to maintain her power and lead her people through the catastrophic social changes wrought by imperialism. Hannah's struggles relate to her position as hapa-haole (Hawaiian-Caucasian); she is privileged in some respects but also vulnerable to sexual exploitation by the haole men to whom she is often 'contracted' as payment for her father's gambling debts. Pali, positioned at the very bottom of the social scale and thus subject to all kinds of abuse,

completes the play's portrait of a cross-section of pre-Christian Hawai'i.

The corporeal imagery that runs through *The Conversion of Ka'ahumanu* strikes interesting contrasts with the use of medical motifs in Manjula Padmanabhan's *Harvest*, included in this anthology. Both plays figure disease and medical intervention as metaphorically laden results of colonial–imperial contact, though they harness such images for different ends. In *The Conversion of Ka'ahumanu*, Lucy's cancer appears to signify the sexual frustrations of her libido-denying life as a strict Christian. Ironically, the disease motif also connects Lucy to the natives that so disgust her, those afflicted with the venereal diseases spread throughout the Hawaiian community by the traders and whalers. Lucy's body thus becomes emblematic of the imperial body politic, demonstrating the ways in which the 'cancer' of imperialism – with its harmful physical and psychological effects – infiltrates all levels of the colonial society, even the presumed safe haven of the mission house. Ka'ahumanu's fever dream-sequence indicates the crisis brought on by the impossible decisions she must make about the future direction of Hawaiian society. That she is nursed through her illness by representatives of precisely the colonising American force that threatens her culture's integrity intensifies her conflicts. The play's lurch away from the confines of semi-naturalism at this stage appears to suggest that the fraught contradictions examined in the scene have become too contestatory to be held together via a naturalistic framework.

Christianity is given a complicated treatment in *The Conversion of Ka'ahumanu* rather than simply being dismissed as unequivocally detrimental to the native population. All three Hawaiian women are drawn by the more appealing aspects of missionary Christianity: its emphasis on tolerance and good works, its provision of education, and its relative respect for women. For Pali, as one of the society's kauā (outcasts), the mission also provides a refuge from her own people's cruelty. On the negative side, Kneubuhl chronicles the sexual repression, cultural chauvinism and staunch gender hierarchies undergirded by Christianity. Hence, Hannah chooses to turn her back on the mission because she cannot reconcile her sexuality or her sensual pleasure in life itself with the Christian doctrines of self-denial and guilt. This mixed picture of missionary imperialism does not indicate an ambivalent dramatic perspective; rather, it is a clear-eyed estimation of Christianity's relative merits and weaknesses for a specific society at a given historical place and time. At the end of the play Ka'ahumanu makes a strategic decision to convert, aware that she cannot outgun the traders, and that her people have been too seduced by the material benefits of Western contact ever to reverse the process. While it is ironic that she has disbanded the traditional religion only to accept a similarly prescriptive regime, her sense of survivalism is itself presented as authentically Hawaiian – most indigenous precisely when it is most syncretic.

Another of Knuebuhl's much-praised historical works was the pageant *January 1893* (1993), commissioned for the centennial commemoration of the overthrow of the Hawaiian monarchy. However, her interest in history is not confined to key figures or moments in a verifiable past. In several plays, a sense of historical consciousness is linked to myth and/or to specific characters' felt connections with their ancestors. *The Story of Susanna* (1996) draws on the biblical myth of Susanna in order to give broader resonance to its contemporary protagonist's oppression by a patriarchal justice system. The voice of the past is more personal but no less powerful in *Emmalehua* (1984), where a young woman's grandmother, her Kupuna, manifests in dreams and visions that reshape her life. *Ola Nā Iwi* (*The Bones Live*) (1994) imaginatively brings together different kinds of history meshed by the artifice of theatre. A comedy of sorts, this play includes among its characters an ancestral spirit and two nineteenth-century figures, a physician and a phrenologist, as well as a troupe of modern-day actors who become embroiled in a scheme to recover a Hawaiian woman's bones from a German museum. Such deliberate juxtapositions of past and present poignantly demonstrate Kneubuhl's belief that 'theatre is a conduit into our everyday world through which mystery and magic may still enter' (Kneubuhl 1999: 293).

Production history

The Conversion of Ka'ahumanu was first presented by Kamu Kahua Theatre at Tenney Theatre, Honolulu, on 1 September 1988, directed by Dale Daigle, with Julie Burk as dramaturge.

Select bibliography

Aki, K.F.P. (1993) 'Native Hawaiian writers and barriers to visibility', *Mana* 10, 1: 128–42.

Hadlich, R.L. and Ellsworth, J.D. (eds) (1988) *East Meets West*, Honolulu: Department of European Languages and Literature, University of Hawai'i.

Kneubuhl, V.N. (1999) *The Story of Susanna*, in M.G. D'Aponte (ed.) *Seventh Generation: An Anthology of Native American Plays*, New York: Theatre Communications Group, 291–370.

Sumida, S.H. (1991) *And the View from the Shore: Literary Traditions of Hawai'i*, Seattle, WA: University of Washington Press.

The Conversion of Ka'ahumanu

Victoria Nalani Kneubuhl

Characters

SYBIL MOSELY BINGHAM   thirties, Caucasian
LUCY GOODALE THURSTON   thirties, Caucasian
KA'AHUMANU   forties, Hawaiian
HANNAH GRIMES   twenties, Hapa haole (Hawaiian/Caucasian)
PALI   twenties, Hawaiian

Setting

The set for the play consists of four parts. Downstage centre is the playing area, a free open space. Downstage right, a simple set with a table, benches and a few chairs, including a Boston rocker, suggest the parlour of the Mission House. Behind the playing area, on a slightly raised platform is a lauhala mat with pillows, and perhaps a small Western table, backed by a simple panel to suggest the wall of a hale pili (grass house). This is Ka'ahumanu's house. Downstage left is Hannah's house, represented by a lauhala mat covered with a small Chinese rug, a table with a pretty candelabra, a nice chair, as well as cushions on the mat.

Act I

Scene 1

Spot to SYBIL *in the playing area.*

SYBIL   In 1815, I, Sybil Mosely, felt the calling of our Lord and Saviour Jesus Christ. I confessed my faith before the congregation and now cling to the bosom of the church. Though I am a sinner, I now have hope that God will call me his own and receive me at his right hand.

(*Spot to* LUCY *in the playing area.*)

LUCY   In 1815, I, Lucy Goodale, was washed in the blood of our Lord Jesus. My family rejoiced in my pious calling. I do now truly believe and trust that dear redeemer who tasted death for us all.

SYBIL   In 1819, I am of low spirits. A kindred spirit to whom I was dearly attached has now departed from my life to serve God in another part of the world. I know not where my life is going or what the Lord would have me do. I feel many days of loneliness and sorrow. The joy I once felt at teaching these young girls slowly drains away, and I feel heavy with a weight I can neither understand nor overcome. I read of women who do mission work among the heathen peoples of this earth. I envy them that they have a purpose and service to God. I pray that one day I might find such a purpose.

LUCY   In 1819, my mother died. My dear sister, Persis, was married and left our father's home. My mother, gone! Persis, gone! Wonder not when I say that I more than ever felt myself an orphan. My solitary chamber witnesses my grief as I walk from side to side. My pillow is watered with tears. I apply to the fountain of all grace and consolation for support. I devote my life to the will of the supreme.

SYBIL   My prayers were heard! Today I go to Goshen, Connecticut, to meet one who is perhaps of the same heart and mind as I. A young man about to embark on a life of mission work in the Sandwich Islands seeks a companion for this noble cause. God will guide me.

LUCY   My cousin William visited me today. He gave me information that a mission to the Sandwich Islands was to sail in four to six weeks. He dwelt upon it with interest and feeling. Imagine my surprise to hear him say, 'Will Lucy, by becoming connected with a missionary, now an entire stranger, attach herself to this small band of pilgrims and bring the word of the gospel to a land of darkness?' Now I feel

367

the need of guidance! Oh, that my sister were here!

(SYBIL *and* LUCY *move together.*)

SYBIL   On October 11, 1819, I was joined in Holy Matrimony to the Reverend Hiram Bingham.

LUCY   On October 12, 1819, I was joined in Holy Matrimony to the Reverend Asa Thurston.

SYBIL   On October 23, 1819, we set sail as members of a pioneer company of missionaries to the Sandwich Islands.

LUCY   Like Rebecca, we have said, 'I will go'.

(SYBIL *and* LUCY *wave good-bye as if on a ship. The lights dim and* LUCY *steps out of the light.*)

Scene 2

(*A spot to* KAʻAHUMANU *in the playing area.*)

KAʻAHUMANU   Here is why I Kaʻahumanu, Kuhina nui and widow of Kamehameha have done these things. For many years now we have seen these haole, these foreign men among us. We know that they break the kapu laws. Do the Gods come to punish them? No! Some of the women have gone to the ships and have eaten with these haole men. Do the Gods come to punish them? No! So why should it be that they will come to punish us at all? I think these beliefs are nothing, false. And here is another thing. We know where the punishment comes from. It does not come from Gods. It comes from men. It comes from the priests who grow greedy for power. And who is it who hates most this kapu law of eating? We, women of the aliʻi. We do not want a lowly place any more, and the men of the priesthood will see this! (*She laughs.*) You should have seen the fear in their faces when we sat to eat. Hewahewa made a great prayer to the Gods. Liholiho, the king, approached the women's table. Many of the faces in the crowd became as white as the full moon. Liholiho sat with us to eat. He ate and the people waited in silence, waited for the terrible wrath of the Gods . . . which never came! Then a great cry rose from the women 'Ai noa, 'ai noa! The kapu laws are ended! The Gods are false'.

(*Blackout.*)

Scene 3

The sound of a rough sea. SYBIL *enters.*

SYBIL   What can I say to you my sisters this morning? I can tell you, could your eye glance across the great water and catch this little bark ascending and descending the mountainous waves which contain your dear sister, your hands would be involuntarily extended for her relief, and your cry would be to save her. The sea runs very high, while the wind runs through the naked rigging as you may have heard it in a November's day, through the leafless trees of a majestic forest. The dashing of the waves on deck, the frequent falling of something below, the violent motion of the vessel, going up and then down, would seem to conspire to terrify and distress. Yet, I feel my mind calm as if by a winter's fire in my own land. Is this not the mercy of God?

(LUCY *moves into the light. She is somewhat nervous.*)

SYBIL   Lucy, what are you doing out here?

LUCY   I felt so sick shut up in there!

SYBIL   It's very rough.

LUCY   How long have we been at sea?

SYBIL   About 60 days.

LUCY   And still not half-way there.

SYBIL   Lucy, are you all right?

LUCY   I'm frightened by the sea today.

SYBIL   (*placing her arm around her*) You are safe.

LUCY   What do you think will really happen to us, Sybil?

SYBIL   I don't know, Lucy.

LUCY   (*building*) You know anything, anything could happen to us out here in the sea, in the middle of nowhere. No one would know and no one would care. Why did I come here?

SYBIL   God called you.

LUCY   Suppose they don't want us in their islands? Suppose they aren't friendly? The sailors say –

SYBIL   Don't listen to what the sailors say!

LUCY   I hate the ocean and I hate this ship. (*She sinks down.*)

SYBIL   Now we must lean on Him. Give all your thoughts and all your fears to Him.

LUCY   I'm trying.

SYBIL   And think on the poor heathen, Lucy, whose immortal souls languish in darkness. Who will give them the Bible and tell them of the Saviour if not us? Think of the Hawaiian people who will enjoy that grace because someone such as Lucy Thurston was willing to say 'I will go'.

(*Blackout.*)

Scene 4

Lights to HANNAH*'s house.* HANNAH *sits playing with a ribbon.* PALI *enters from the playing area.*

PALI Hannah, Hannah, have you heard?

HANNAH What?

PALI A war!

HANNAH What are you talking about?

PALI On Hawai'i.

HANNAH Get in here and be quiet.

PALI Why?

HANNAH My father is drinking with some haole men. When they get drunk, they might come looking for me.

PALI I'm glad my father isn't a haole.

HANNAH Hah! You don't even know who your father is.

PALI I do so!

HANNAH Who then, who? . . . See? You don't know.

PALI Well, at least I'm not chased around by haole men.

HANNAH Because you aren't as pretty as me.

PALI No, because I'm not hapa haole. I don't look like them.

HANNAH They aren't so bad. It's only when they're sick with rum.

PALI Are haole men better than a kanaka?

HANNAH I never went with a kanaka. My father would beat me until I couldn't walk. Besides, now I'm Davis's woman.

PALI Will you have another baby with him?

HANNAH Shut up, Pali. You're nothing but a chicken, clucking gossip all over the village. Now, tell me of this battle.

PALI No, you told me to shut up. You think I'm stupid?

HANNAH All right, I'm sorry. Tell me.

PALI No!

HANNAH Come on, Pali. Look, I'll give you this pretty ribbon, see? Everyone will envy you.

PALI What should I do with it?

HANNAH Tie it up in your hair. See how pretty it is?

PALI Where did you get this?

HANNAH I have a lot of them.

PALI You're lucky.

HANNAH Now tell me.

PALI It's because of the free eating and the defying of the kapu. The chief, Kekuaokalani, and his followers don't like the old Gods going. He doesn't like the way Ka'ahumanu has begun to burn the images in the temples. He will fight with Ka'ahumanu and Liholiho.

HANNAH My father said this would happen.

PALI What do you think of the kapu?

HANNAH Lies!

PALI How do you know?

HANNAH I know! There are no such foolish beliefs in other places. I have heard the talk of foreigners.

PALI And there is never any punishment?

HANNAH No! And be quiet! I told you, I don't want them to hear us.

PALI Blood will be spilled.

HANNAH It's a foolish war. A fight over nothing.

PALI Everyone knows Ka'ahumanu will win.

HANNAH I don't care, my life won't change.

(*Lights down.*)

Scene 5

Lights to KA'AHUMANU*'s house.*
KA'AHUMANU *sits on her mats.*

KA'AHUMANU I knew our lives would change forever. I knew that when I did this thing. There was blood spilled. Turmoil rose among the people. Kekuaokalani moved his forces out of Ka'awaloa. We met them at Kuamo'o. We had guns, that is why we won. From Kamehameha, I learned to strike swiftly and with strength. But my heart weeps for the death of Kekuaokalani and his faithful woman, Manono, who fought by his side. Now the old Gods have lost their power, and will go. (*Pause.*) Have I done right? Or have I done great evil? I took down what I knew to be false, but will I, Ka'ahumanu, be able to guide these islands, be able to guide the people? The people now have no Gods, only the ali'i. How will I steer the canoe?

(*Enter* PALI.)

PALI My Ali'i.

KA'AHUMANU Ah, Pali, my pua. You are well?

PALI Yes, thank you. (*Pause.*) A ship has come.

KAʻAHUMANU (sighs) Many ships come. Too many.

PALI This one brings white men and –

KAʻAHUMANU They all bring white men.

PALI And haole women! And they say they are bringing a new God!

KAʻAHUMANU Women?

PALI (excited) ʻAe!

KAʻAHUMANU This is a new sight. Perhaps I will come to see them – after I go fishing. You will come fishing with me?

PALI Well, if it is your wish.

KAʻAHUMANU No, I can see your mind is filled with wondering about these haole women. Go and satisfy this longing.

PALI Oh, thank you, thank you, I will tell you everything that I see.

(Lights down on KAʻAHUMANU's house.)

Scene 6

Lights to SYBIL and LUCY in the playing area.

SYBIL Lucy! Come you can see them!

LUCY There are hundreds, maybe thousands of them.

SYBIL They look so dark. It's hard to see in this blinding light.

LUCY They'll be closer in a minute.

SYBIL How beautiful the mountains are.

LUCY My feet won't know how to walk on solid ground again.

SYBIL Look! Now they're closer. I see a man waving to us.

LUCY Where?

SYBIL In that canoe. Next to the woman holding coconuts.

LUCY Where? Oh, there! (Pause.) Oh Sybil, those are not coconuts!

SYBIL No? Oh, my, no.

LUCY Look at them!

SYBIL Hundreds of them –

LUCY All of them –

SYBIL and LUCY Naked!

LUCY (terribly nervous) What shall we do?

SYBIL (also nervous) Compose ourselves. We must compose ourselves.

LUCY What? They're getting closer.

SYBIL Now, we must try to act naturally.

LUCY Naturally? Yes, we must. But it's disgusting. Even the men.

SYBIL Well, don't look! There, I mean.

LUCY Where? Where shall we look?

SYBIL Lower your eyes and wave politely.

(LUCY and SYBIL lower their eyes and wave politely. They speak straight to the audience.)

LUCY I had never conceived in my life that I would ever see such a sight. To describe the dress and demeanor of these creatures I would have to make use of uncouth and indelicate language. To the civilised eye their covering is revoltingly scanty to say the least. I have never felt such shame or embarrassment as when I first beheld these children of nature.

SYBIL I saw them first as a swarming mass of dark savages, and even as I looked into their eyes I asked myself, 'can they be human?' But the answer came to me: 'Yes! God made these people, they have immortal souls, yes they are human and can be brought to know and love our Saviour.'

LUCY Some of the women are grotesquely large.

SYBIL Mountainous!

LUCY Some chiefesses have Western cloth wrapped about them.

SYBIL In something which resembles a roman toga.

LUCY But is thoroughly immodest.

SYBIL and LUCY (holding hands) Here we will begin God's work.

(LUCY and SYBIL freeze. HANNAH and PALI enter. They walk around the women as if examining objects. LUCY and SYBIL remain frozen.)

HANNAH Look how they cover up their bodies so!

PALI Auē!

HANNAH Look at this white hand.

PALI What puny bodies! What sickly pink skin!

HANNAH (lifting up a dress) Their legs are like sticks.

PALI They look all pinched up in the middle.

HANNAH And wide at the top.

PALI Their eyes are so small.

HANNAH They have no smiles.

PALI I'm sure it's because they are so thin and sickly.

HANNAH Maybe they would improve with bathing in the sea, and lying about in the sun. (She takes PALI aside.) Now we have learned something. This is just why many haole men who come to these islands go so crazy over our women. It is because haole women are so revoltingly ugly. How could a man find any desire for such a creature? Auē! It must be hard for them to get children. I pity them, poor things. I will send them some food.

(SYBIL *and* LUCY *come to life. They approach* HANNAH *and* PALI, *offering them their hands.*)

SYBIL   Aloha.
PALI   (*shaking hands*) Aloha.
LUCY   (*to* HANNAH) Aloha.
SYBIL   (*to* PALI) Aloha.
PALI   Aloha.
HANNAH   Aloha. Aloha.
LUCY   Aloha.
HANNAH   Aloha.

(KA'AHUMANU *enters regally, with an air of disdain.* SYBIL *and* LUCY *timidly approach her.*)

SYBIL   (*offering her hand*) Aloha, your majesty.

(KA'AHUMANU *haughtily extends her baby finger.*)

LUCY   (*stepping back, afraid*) Aloha . . .
SYBIL   (*haltingly*) Your, um, majesty, we bring a message of hope.
KA'AHUMANU   Oh?
LUCY   Of Jesus.
SYBIL   The one true God, the blessed Jehovah –
KA'AHUMANU   (*insistent*) We don't need a new God. Why do you wear so much clothes?
SYBIL   This is the way ladies of America dress.
LUCY   Proper ladies.
KA'AHUMANU   (*fingering their clothes*) I wish to try such clothes. You will make one for me.
SYBIL   Yes, I think we could.
KA'AHUMANU   I will send you cloth.
LUCY   Perhaps you yourself would like to learn to sew.
KA'AHUMANU   Sew?
SYBIL   Yes, it is how we make clothes.
KA'AHUMANU   No! I want you to make it for me.
LUCY   (*flustered*) Oh! Yes! We know, I mean, I only thought that –
KA'AHUMANU   Why do you come to these islands? What do you want?
LUCY   Want?
KA'AHUMANU   Yes. Is it sandalwood? Whale

oil? Your men come for women? What do you want?
SYBIL   (*quickly*) We don't want anything like that.
LUCY   Oh, no.
SYBIL   We want to bring you the good news of our Lord and Saviour Jesus Christ.
KA'AHUMANU   The news of Jesus Christ?
LUCY   Yes.
KA'AHUMANU   Why should I care for news of someone I don't even know?
SYBIL   Well he is God. The blessed son of –
KA'AHUMANU   I do not wish to hear of a God! We have finished with Gods. Pau! I have destroyed many images, burned many heiau. I have forbidden the worship in the old temples. And the king has spoken these things to the people: We want no Gods. The Gods brought only sorrow and unhappiness to our people. We will not have that again. Let us speak of other things. (*A silence.*)
LUCY   Our God is different. He –
(KA'AHUMANU *glares at* LUCY.)
SYBIL   (*loud whisper*) Lucy, please!
KA'AHUMANU   I want clothes which are yellow. I will send yellow cloth.
SYBIL   Yes, we will be happy to do this. You must also come so that we can measure you.
KA'AHUMANU   Measure?
LUCY   So we can cut.
KA'AHUMANU   Cut?
SYBIL   To make your clothes.
KA'AHUMANU   Yes, then I will come. (*To* SYBIL) You have a kind face, but very sad.
SYBIL   (*shyly*) Thank you. When you come, perhaps we will talk a little more.
KA'AHUMANU   Paha, perhaps.
SYBIL   So we may come to know each other's ways.
KA'AHUMANU   Paha.

(*Exit the* HAWAIIAN *women.* LUCY *and* SYBIL *join hands.*)

LUCY *and* SYBIL   Here we will begin God's work.

Scene 7

LUCY *and* SYBIL *move into the Mission house area. They immediately begin to dust, sweep, and go through other actions of housekeeping as they repeat phrases in Hawaiian.*

LUCY   Aloha.

371

SYBIL Aloha kakahiaka.
LUCY Aloha awakea.
SYBIL Aloha 'auinalā.
LUCY Aloha ahiahi.
SYBIL Pehea 'oe?
LUCY Maika'i, pehea 'oe?
SYBIL 'Ano māluhiluhi au.

(HANNAH *and* PALI *enter the playing area as they speak,* SYBIL *and* LUCY *continue to go through the motions of housework while mumbling to themselves in Hawaiian.*)

PALI But why do you think she likes me, Hannah?
HANNAH I don't know.
PALI I know she likes you because you are pretty and smart.
HANNAH (*laughing*) And because I know all of the gossip amongst the foreigners.
PALI But why should she pick me?
HANNAH I don't know. She just picks her favorites. Shall we look in at the mikanele?
PALI Yes.

(HANNAH *and* PALI *look in at the mission women.* SYBIL *is dusting while* LUCY *sews.*)

PALI Look at them. They're always busy.
HANNAH Till their faces make water.
PALI Why do they do that?
HANNAH It's their way. (*She calls out.*) Aloha ē, Mrs Bingham, Mrs Thurston.

(SYBIL *and* LUCY *stop. They come to meet* HANNAH *and* PALI.)

SYBIL Good day, Hannah.
HANNAH Good day.
SYBIL Where are you going?
HANNAH To the house of Ka'ahumanu. (*To* LUCY) Are you making a sail?
LUCY A sail?
HANNAH Yes, like the sailors, with a needle, in and out.
LUCY Why no, this is how we sew. How we make dresses.
HANNAH (*excited*) Are you making a dress? I would like to have a dress!
SYBIL No, Hannah, she's just fixing a tear in her apron.
HANNAH You tore your beautiful clothes? How?
LUCY A fight in the village this morning.
PALI You got into a fight?!
SYBIL Oh, no! She was helping someone.
LUCY A man was being beaten for no reason that I could see.

HANNAH There is always fighting in the village.
LUCY This man had funny marks on his forehead and around his eyes.
PALI A kauā. That's why he was beaten.
HANNAH We despise them. That is why they are marked.
SYBIL Why?
HANNAH I don't know. They're not allowed to live among us. In the old days, they sometimes served as a sacrifice at the heiau. They are filthy people.
LUCY They don't look any different.
PALI That is why they are marked. So people may know them.
SYBIL I don't understand why –
HANNAH I don't know why. They are just no better than animals. There are many who try to pretend they don't belong to the kauā. Some of them try to give away their babies to others so the children will grow up unrecognised. I knew a girl who had a baby by a kauā once. If that happened to me, I would kill it!
SYBIL (*turning away*) How disgusting.
HANNAH They are disgusting.
PALI That is how their blood is hated.
SYBIL I don't want to hear this talk.
LUCY Please, we must go now. We have work to do.

(SYBIL *is obviously disturbed.* HANNAH *and* PALI *think nothing of the conversation and turn to leave.* PALI *turns back to talk to* LUCY.)

PALI This man, he was old?
LUCY (*not very nicely*) Somewhat, he had a limp.
PALI A bad leg? (LUCY *nods.*) Was he killed?
LUCY No, he managed to get away.
PALI (*with sympathy*) Ah!
LUCY Do you –
HANNAH Come on Pali!
PALI (*Leaves fast.*) Aloha!

Scene 8

PALI *runs to meet* HANNAH *at* KA'AHUMANU's *house.* KA'AHUMANU *signals them to come.*

HANNAH Aloha ē, Kuhina nui.
KA'AHUMANU 'Ae, aloha nō. You have brought Pali I see.
HANNAH Yes.
KA'AHUMANU Come Pali, my pua, you comb my hair.

PALI Yes.

KA'AHUMANU You have been well?

PALI Yes, thank you.

HANNAH We stopped in to look at the mikanele.

KA'AHUMANU What were they doing?

HANNAH Running around, taking off dirt.

KA'AHUMANU They always do that!

HANNAH I don't know why they won't get someone else to do the work for them.

PALI Perhaps it is kapu in America.

HANNAH No, it isn't.

PALI How do you know, Hannah?

HANNAH Because Davis told me! (*More slowly*) Once, a long time ago. (*Long pause.*)

KA'AHUMANU What was his sickness?

HANNAH I don't know. My father said he died because he drank too much rum.

PALI You must be lonely for him.

KA'AHUMANU You have a kind heart, Pali.

HANNAH Not very. He was never mean to me, but he was too old. He always smelled like rum. It was my father who made me go with him for a mate. He was as old as my father.

PALI That is not what I would like.

KA'AHUMANU (*slyly*) Well, I hear other eyes are turned your way Hannah Grimes.

PALI Who Hannah? Tell me who!

KA'AHUMANU A younger man whose body speaks for itself when Hannah is near.

PALI Who is it, Hannah?

KA'AHUMANU It will be good for you to go with a younger man, Hannah. The canoe will fit the hālau. (*They laugh.*) I prefer one who is close to me in years.

HANNAH I like the way he touches me, and he does not smell of rum. He likes to laugh.

KA'AHUMANU Jones is better to look at than Davis.

PALI Is it Jones? The haole, the American consul?

HANNAH Yes you clucking hen!

PALI Many women desire him.

KA'AHUMANU But it is Hannah he desires.

(*The* HAWAIIAN *women begin to play cards as they speak.* LUCY *and* SYBIL *enter with a basket. They see the women engaged in a card game and sit on a bench staring forward.* KA'AHUMANU *acknowledges them by a nod of her head, but makes no move to speak to them.*)

KA'AHUMANU When will you find a man for such pleasure, Pali?

PALI I don't want one now, maybe later.

HANNAH (*sassy*) Maybe you've never been with a man.

PALI Maybe.

HANNAH Why?

PALI Because I didn't find one I wanted.

HANNAH Or one who wanted you!

KA'AHUMANU Pali has her own wisdom, Hannah. It is not good to be with a man you don't want. (*To* PALI) Go and tell the mikanele they may join us in cards.

PALI (*going to* LUCY *and* SYBIL) Ka'ahumanu says you may join our game if you wish.

SYBIL I'm sorry we can't play.

PALI Well, I will show you. I'm very good. I won a dollar from a sailor this morning.

LUCY American ladies do not play cards.

PALI You must wait then.

KA'AHUMANU Well?

PALI They said American ladies may not play cards.

KA'AHUMANU Aloha 'ino!

HANNAH No wonder they never look happy. What is the pleasure in their lives?

PALI Many people say the men of the mikanele brought these women only to be cooks and cabin boys to them.

KA'AHUMANU They should learn to throw off their terrible kapu as we did.

(*Lights dim on the card game.* LUCY *is obviously uncomfortable.*)

LUCY Sybil?

SYBIL Yes?

LUCY I, I want to tell you, something . . .

SYBIL Tell me what?

LUCY I feel something, I, I mean I found something.

SYBIL What is it, Lucy?

LUCY It's, it's, well in my –

SYBIL Yes? . . . Lucy?

LUCY Nothing, it's nothing, I'm so silly. I'm sorry.

SYBIL Are you sure?

LUCY (*irritated*) Aren't they finished yet?

SYBIL Not yet.

LUCY Well, this is very rude!

SYBIL It's only rude to us who think it rude to keep people waiting.

LUCY It is rude to keep people waiting!

SYBIL She is used to doing as she pleases.

LUCY It's her heathen manners.

(PALI *is out of the game. She rises and goes to* LUCY *and* SYBIL.)

PALI They are almost finished. Then you will be called.

SYBIL   Thank you.

(PALI *remains and begins to look over* LUCY's *clothing and bonnet. She picks and pulls at* LUCY's *clothing, not in a malicious way, but solely out of curiosity.* LUCY *becomes increasingly irritated.* PALI *looks at her sympathetically and begins to lomilomi* LUCY's *shoulders. Lights go to* KA'AHUMANU *who watches* PALI *and* LUCY. LUCY's *irritation reaches a pitch. Lashing out,* LUCY *violently pushes* PALI *away from her more than once.*)

LUCY   DON'T TOUCH ME!! TAKE YOUR FILTHY HEATHEN HANDS OFF ME!!

SYBIL   Sister Thurston!

(PALI *is stunned and frightened. She runs away.* KA'AHUMANU *strides over.*)

KA'AHUMANU   Why did you do that?

SYBIL   She was frightened. Please forgive her.

LUCY   I, I'm sorry. I just forgot myself.

HANNAH   Pali is a favorite.

LUCY   I'm very sorry.

KA'AHUMANU   (*sternly, moving to the mat*) Come over here now.

SYBIL   Sister Thurston and I have brought something to show you.

KA'AHUMANU   Yes?

SYBIL   (*taking out writing implements*) It is writing.

LUCY   (*taking out a book*) And reading.

KA'AHUMANU   It is the palapala that haole men know?

HANNAH   You know these things?

LUCY   Yes, we do.

SYBIL   In America, many women know these things. We want to teach them to you.

HANNAH   (*excited*) And me? You will show me?

SYBIL   Why, yes, Hannah, if you would like to learn.

KA'AHUMANU   Show me.

SYBIL   (*writing*) We will start with your name, Ka'ahumanu, and yours Hannah. (*She gives them the pens and paper.*) Now try to copy every mark.

KA'AHUMANU   Help me.

SYBIL   (*guides her hand*) There, that is your name.

KA'AHUMANU   Again.

LUCY   Hannah, that is very quick of you.

KA'AHUMANU   (*looking at* HANNAH's) Hers is better. Guide my hand again.

SYBIL   K–A–A–H–U–M–A–N–U.

KA'AHUMANU   Hannah, put away the cards, we will do this now.

SYBIL   Perhaps I could come back tomorrow and begin a lesson.

KA'AHUMANU   (*looking at her, almost yelling*) Not tomorrow, NOW!

(SYBIL *and* LUCY *give each other a frightened look as lights fade to black. Lights to* HANNAH *on the playing area.*)

HANNAH   Many times I have watched the ships sail in and out of the port of Honolulu, and many times the question came to my mind. Who made this great world? Why are people different? Why are there different ways of talking? What does the world look like away from here, far away? These women of the mikanele are the first women of my father's people I have ever seen. They are very different. They work all the time and do not seem to care very much for play or laughter. But there is a way they do things which I like. There is a place for everything in their houses, and it is clean and quiet. There is a fresh feeling. It is a feeling of peace, without the yelling of drunken men and the smell of rum. There is a gentle kindness about Mrs Bingham. And they know how to read and write! To know the palapala is to know many things. Their talk is of a kind god, Jesus. A god to whom women may speak, and a god who will let us in his temple.

(*Fadeout.*)

Scene 9

Lights to the Mission House. LUCY *sits sewing.* SYBIL *enters from the playing area with a basket.*

LUCY   Will this heat ever stop?

SYBIL   The eternal summer?

LUCY   It's so oppressive.

SYBIL   I wish it would rain.

LUCY   Yes. (*Pause.*) Some women came while you were gone.

SYBIL   Did they come in?

LUCY   No, I wouldn't let them.

SYBIL   Why not?

LUCY   They were sick.

SYBIL   Did you tell the doctor?

LUCY   I told them that the doctor couldn't help them.

SYBIL Lucy, why?

LUCY Because he couldn't. It was the venereal distemper.

SYBIL I see.

LUCY They had sores. Open running sores.

SYBIL I'm sorry I wasn't here.

LUCY One was in a great deal of pain, I could tell.

SYBIL We see more of them every day.

LUCY She cried to me, Sybil. Begged me for a medicine to make her well. I told her to go away, there is no medicine. Sometimes I feel as though I couldn't stand to see another face like that – like I won't be able to stand to see another face in pain.

SYBIL This is the gift of men who call themselves Christians and have no knowledge of what that word truly means. Men come to these islands for pleasure, without the love of Christ in their hearts. They are killing them, Lucy. For their own pleasure and their own lust, they are killing these people. They thought Cook was a god? Perhaps he was their angel of death.

LUCY Perhaps God is punishing these people for their sins of idolatry.

SYBIL (*bowing her head*) We are all sinners, sister.

LUCY Yes.

SYBIL It is our job to bring the word of light.

LUCY Yes.

SYBIL And to minister to the needs of these people. But how will we, with so few doctors among us, ever be able to stay the hand of death which every day tightens its grip?

(KA'AHUMANU *approaches.*)

LUCY Aloha, your majesty.

KA'AHUMANU Aloha.

LUCY Come in and be seated.

SYBIL How are you today?

KA'AHUMANU I am well.

LUCY Shall we begin the lesson?

KA'AHUMANU Yes, let's read.

SYBIL I must ask you . . .

KA'AHUMANU Yes?

SYBIL (*uncomfortable*) This sickness that so many women have from the sailors –

KA'AHUMANU You don't have this in America?

LUCY Yes, but . . .

SYBIL (*boldly*) Yes . . . But, well, there are good women and there are bad women, and the good women do not do the things which cause this sickness.

KA'AHUMANU No?

LUCY NO!

KA'AHUMANU Then how is it that they get children?

SYBIL By getting married!

KA'AHUMANU (*amused*) Binamuwahine, that is not what gives you a child.

LUCY What we mean is –

SYBIL We think something should be done.

LUCY To stop these women.

SYBIL They spread the disease.

KA'AHUMANU It is haole men who brought this here.

SYBIL Yes, but these women who go to the ships, they . . . Well, they make it worse.

KA'AHUMANU (*considering*) Perhaps I should make them kapu. All women and men who have this sickness may only go with each other.

LUCY I don't think –

KA'AHUMANU We can mark each person who has the sickness.

SYBIL Perhaps it would be better to forbid people to do . . . what they do.

LUCY If they are not married.

KA'AHUMANU Why?

SYBIL Because it is a sin.

KA'AHUMANU You don't like it?

LUCY Certainly not!

SYBIL It's only for those who are married.

LUCY Only so they may have children.

KA'AHUMANU (*amazed*) You don't do it for the great pleasure of it?

LUCY and SYBIL NO!

KA'AHUMANU Auē! You poor ladies! What do you have to make you happy?

SYBIL We think it is wrong to do without a Christian marriage.

KA'AHUMANU Why do you think this?

LUCY God has said it in his holy commandments.

KA'AHUMANU Oh, him!

SYBIL (*defensive*) If your people followed this commandment, the sickness would not spread through your people. God is the only refuge, the only safe harbor.

KA'AHUMANU These laws you speak of, I will think on them. Perhaps it is a good thing, as the palapala is a good thing. But, I will have no more Gods! There will be no more priests to make me a slave to their power. I have spoken. We will have the lesson now.

SYBIL (*after a pause*) Very well, let us read.

KAʻAHUMANU I will read this that I like. 'Where unto shall we liken the kingdom of God? Or with what shall we compare it? It is the grain of mustard seed, which when it is sown in the earth is less than all the seeds that be in the earth: But when it is sown, it groweth up, and becometh greater than all the herbs, and shooteth out great branches so that all the birds of the air may lodge under the shadow of it'.

Scene 10

Enter HANNAH, *distressed.*

HANNAH (*going to* SYBIL) Please, you will help me?

SYBIL Hannah, what is it?

HANNAH I just put Charlotte in your cellar.

LUCY Why should you put your sister in the cellar?

SYBIL Why does she need to hide?

HANNAH He sold her. My son of a bitch father got drunk again and sold her to Captain Wills of a whaling ship because he got drunk and lost at cards. He said he couldn't pay right away, but Wills just smiled back. 'Sure you can', he says, 'Give me Charlotte. I'll take her up north and bring her back when the ship has a belly full of oil. I'll take good care of her, just for me, no one else'. My father just looked at him and laughed. He called Charlotte and told her that she must now go with this stranger for many months at sea. (*Pause.*) Charlotte is such a good girl, Mrs Bingham. 'Hannah', she said, 'Hannah, what will he do with me?' She is only thirteen.

KAʻAHUMANU The son of a bitch bastard.

HANNAH I hate this way of being treated. I am sick of it. It is like we're nothing but hogs in the yard to sell. What can I do?

SYBIL She's safe here, Hannah. There should be laws so that such things are forbidden.

LUCY Yes, laws to protect women and children!

SYBIL Hannah, if this trouble comes to you or your sisters again, you must come here. Reverend Bingham will stand up for you or any other woman who is forced to such a thing.

LUCY And so will Reverend Thurston, Hannah.

SYBIL Perhaps we should pray for your father, Hannah.

HANNAH HIM?

SYBIL He needs your prayers.

LUCY His heart is dark.

HANNAH (*with emotion*) He is no good.

SYBIL That is why he needs your prayers.

HANNAH (*obedient*) Yes.

SYBIL (*to* KAʻAHUMANU) Will you join our prayers? (KAʻAHUMANU *shakes her head, no.*)

SYBIL Hannah, please lead us in prayer.

HANNAH Me?

SYBIL ʻAe.

HANNAH Please, Jesus, come to my father's sick heart. Make him well again. Make him see the bad things he does to me and my sisters, how he hurts us and makes us suffer. Make him turn away from the evil things he does so his soul will be saved from the place of fires. We ask these things in Jesus' name, Amene.

KAʻAHUMANU (*to* SYBIL) Why do you wish good things for a bad man?

SYBIL It is the Christian way.

KAʻAHUMANU Why?

SYBIL We feel that it is those who do bad things that most need our prayers. That with the help of God they might change their ways.

KAʻAHUMANU (*Pause.*) Perhaps I will hear more of these laws of which you speak. You will advise me.

SYBIL On this matter, you must speak to Reverend Bingham.

KAʻAHUMANU Why? You have a wisdom I like better.

LUCY We are not suited to advise you about laws.

KAʻAHUMANU But you told me about them.

LUCY Yes, but we can't advise you. That would be politics.

SYBIL You see, as ladies it is not a part of our sphere.

LUCY The home is our world.

SYBIL We must not make laws.

KAʻAHUMANU You will not make laws, but you will obey them?

SYBIL We will.

KAʻAHUMANU I feel as if I'm walking through a forest of hau. Come Hannah, I wish to go. Your sister will be safe here. If anyone goes near her, they'll face my anger. Aloha.

LUCY Aloha.

SYBIL Aloha nō.

(KAʻAHUMANU *and* HANNAH *move to the playing area.*)

Scene 11

KAʻAHUMANU   What do you think of these things, Hannah? Laws, and a marriage to only one man.

HANNAH   It would have been good if there was a law that would keep Charlotte safe.

KAʻAHUMANU   Or a marriage that would have kept Jones from leaving you?

HANNAH   You know?

KAʻAHUMANU   ʻAe.

HANNAH   I suppose the whole village knows.

KAʻAHUMANU   It's likely. He's gone for good?

HANNAH   Do we ever know if they're gone for good?

KAʻAHUMANU   He went to America?

HANNAH   If I had been his Christian wife, he would have taken me.

KAʻAHUMANU   You would wish to be as the haole women with a man?

HANNAH   Perhaps.

KAʻAHUMANU   Their god is a man, and their men are gods.

HANNAH   Perhaps it is their love.

KAʻAHUMANU   It's easier to love a man than a god Hannah.

HANNAH   ʻAʻole maopopo iaʻu. (*They enter* KAʻAHUMANU's *house and sit.*)

KAʻAHUMANU   I watched Kamehameha. I saw all the women bow down to him like a god. Do you know why he loved me? (HANNAH *shakes her head, no.*) Because, he knew I was powerful and did not fear him. (*She laughs.*) My own father, Keʻeaumoku told him, 'You have only one person to truly fear in your kingdom. Only one person to take away your rule – your own woman, Kaʻahumanu. For if she chose to rise up against you, the people love her so much, they would follow'. So you see, I stood on the same mountain, looked into the same valley and when I looked at him, I saw a man, not a god.

HANNAH   And what did he see?

KAʻAHUMANU   (*after a pause*) That would be for him to say, Hannah.

HANNAH   You don't like this idea of Christian marriage?

KAʻAHUMANU   I don't care about it. In the old days, if women and men desired each other they joined; if that left, they parted.

HANNAH   But the old days go.

KAʻAHUMANU   Yes, and tomorrow comes with more foreigners and their ideas and their ships and their desires.

HANNAH   Desire. Is that what rules us? I hardly know my own. But the mikanele, they have given me a new kind of desire. A longing to know the things in books and the world outside of here and the ways of God.

KAʻAHUMANU   You believe this God?

HANNAH   Yes, because he is full of mercy.

KAʻAHUMANU   But he keeps a terrible place of fires.

HANNAH   That's for the wicked.

KAʻAHUMANU   Who is wicked?

HANNAH   Those who don't believe.

KAʻAHUMANU   And those who do?

HANNAH   Life everlasting. Where everything is happiness and good.

KAʻAHUMANU   Happiness and good, those are things we need before we die, Hannah.

HANNAH   This life is for tears and sorrow. (KAʻAHUMANU *moves into the free space. Cross-fade to playing area.*)

KAʻAHUMANU   Is this what they teach her? Or is it because of her lover she is sad? Our islands are in the midst of storm, blown every which way by the white men who come here. Laws, these ladies speak of laws, and perhaps their laws are good. The old laws, many of them were foolish and unjust. But perhaps it is good to have the laws which protect the people from harm. As in the old days, if the people see their aliʻi doing good things, they will continue to love and follow us. It would be easy to take this new God and make him steer our canoe through this time, but I can't do it. (*Cross-fade back to* KAʻAHUMANU's *house as* KAʻAHUMANU *goes back to her space.*) I can't trust this haole God.

HANNAH   I know in the days of the kapu, when our hearts were dark, we worshipped the hungry gods. The gods who must be fed with plants and animals and, most terrible, with human flesh that they might live. Men died that the gods might live. But now comes a time of light. A new god who is so full of love that he sends his son to die for men, that they might live.

(*Blackout.*)

Scene 12

Lights to SYBIL *and* LUCY *in the Mission House.*

LUCY   I don't see why you have to chide me for it!

SYBIL   I'm not chiding you, Lucy. I'm simply suggesting –

LUCY   You look down on me for it!

SYBIL   I do not, Sister Thurston.

LUCY   Perhaps you think my feelings don't become a minister's wife . . .

SYBIL   I would never suggest that you weren't a good wife.

LUCY   As a missionary . . .

SYBIL   Lucy, please. I was at fault to mention it.

LUCY   (cooling) Well, I'm not like you, Mrs Bingham. I have never been free with my natural affection.

SYBIL   I'm sure if only you would open your heart, unafraid, you would soon find room for them.

LUCY   I have tried, Sybil. I have. I have told myself that they're people, that they have immortal souls, that I ought to love them as my neighbors at home, but I can't escape the feelings that come over me when I see them in their depravity. I can control the way I look before them, but I can't help the revulsion I feel. I can't bear to be touched by them, by those dark, dirty hands. And I hate the way I am stared at by those great dark eyes. I hate those eyes that stare at me like some animal. I even sometimes feel sickened if there are too many of them in here.

SYBIL   Our work must be selfless, Lucy.

LUCY   It's wicked, I know, but it's true, Sybil. I would change it if I could, but these feelings are beyond my control. But I have made a promise, a promise to God. I promised him that it would never make me falter in my work here in these islands. I can't love these people, but I will work to raise them to a state of Christian civilization. I suppose now you will think me a most unworthy person.

SYBIL   No, I will think no such thing. God gives us our trials, and we must bear them.

LUCY   (breaking) I can't! No! I just don't have the strength!

SYBIL   Lucy! What's wrong?

LUCY   (regaining some composure) I don't know how to tell you. I'm so ashamed.

SYBIL   What is it, Lucy?

LUCY   I've found a hard thing, a lump in my breast.

SYBIL   (after a pause) Have you told Dr Judd?

LUCY   How can I?

(Blackout.)

Scene 13

Lights to the playing area where HANNAH *meets* PALI.

PALI   Where have you been, Hannah? In the house of the mikanele, night and day?

HANNAH   Why don't you come too?

PALI   I think they hate us.

HANNAH   That's not true!

PALI   I think it is. They're not good for us. Their teachings are false and evil. They don't allow you any of the joys you knew before. Come, Hannah, return to the way you were before. Be happy again.

HANNAH   If they hate us, why would they come to teach us?

PALI   I don't know, it's a trick . . .

HANNAH   A trick?

PALI   . . . to make us miserable like them.

HANNAH   They're not miserable.

PALI   Soon your life will leave you, Hannah, and you'll be like them.

HANNAH   No, Pali, they teach me to know more about life. They make new thoughts in my head which weren't there before, and now I may think of many new and wonderful things. I have knowledge and I will have more of it. Before, I was just a pretty thing that men wanted, but now I have a new world of thoughts that is kapu to everyone but myself.

PALI   These things you learn could be lies.

HANNAH   They're not.

PALI   I still say that haole woman hates us!!

(Blackout.)

Act II

Scene 1

SYBIL, LUCY *and* HANNAH *are at the Mission House.* HANNAH *now wears a dress like the mission women.* SYBIL *quizzes* HANNAH *from a book.*

SYBIL   Now Hannah, 'What is sin?'

HANNAH   'Sin is any want of conformity to, or transgression of, the law of God'.

SYBIL   'What is the sin by where our first parents fell?'

HANNAH   'The sin by where our first parents fell was the eating of the forbidden fruit'.

SYBIL   'What is the misery of the estate wherein man fell?'

HANNAH   This one is still hard.

SYBIL   Baptism requires study and diligence.

Now try again. 'What is the misery of the estate wherein man fell?'

HANNAH (*hesitant*) 'All mankind, by their fall, lost communion with God, are under his wrath and curse, and so made liable to all miseries in this life, to death itself, and to the pains of hell forever'.

SYBIL 'Did God leave all men to perish in the estate of sin and misery?'

HANNAH 'No, God, out of his mere good pleasure, has elected some to everlasting life, and will bring these chosen to an estate of salvation by a redeemer, the Lord Jesus Christ'.

(*Enter* PALI.)

PALI Excuse me please.

LUCY Yes?

PALI The doctor wishes you in the village right away. There is some trouble.

LUCY Trouble?

PALI Many people have come down from the mountains where they cut the sandalwood. There is a great sickness among them.

SYBIL No.

PALI (*holding a note*) He asked you to bring these things.

LUCY (*Grabs the note.*) Let me have that. (*To* SYBIL) They are powders from his medical supplies.

SYBIL You get them, Lucy. Hannah, you will study until I return.

HANNAH 'Ae. (*Exit* LUCY *and* SYBIL.)

PALI What are you doing, Hannah?

HANNAH Learning the word of God so I may have baptism.

PALI Oh.

HANNAH 'What does every sin deserve?' 'Every sin deserves God's wrath and curse, both in this life and that which is to come'.

PALI Do you believe this, Hannah?

HANNAH (*halting*) Yes, I want to be baptized.

PALI Why?

HANNAH So I can go to heaven.

PALI This God allows the kanaka in his heaven?

HANNAH Yes.

PALI Even women?

HANNAH Yes, we are all equal in God's sight.

PALI Then why aren't we equal on earth?

HANNAH Be quiet, Pali.

PALI How many haoles do you know who treat us like one of their own? How many

of the aliʻi treat commoners as they do each other?

HANNAH You don't know what you're talking about.

PALI (*building*) No, you don't know Hannah! Things are different for you because you're hapa haole. They treat you so, bring you into their home as a friend because they think you are half like them. You're not like me! You've always had many more things for your comfort in life. You don't know what it is to be poor, and you don't know what it's like to be below everyone else. So don't say your stupid words to me Hannah!

HANNAH (*after a pause, softly*) Pali, what is it? Why are you so angry with me? You could come here too if you wanted.

PALI I'm sorry Hannah. Forgive my words. I don't mean to hurt you.

(*Exit* PALI.)

Scene 2

Lights to the playing area. LUCY *sits,* SYBIL *stands behind her.*

LUCY The greed of men has caused many deaths. Men come from foreign lands wanting ʻiliahi, the scented sandalwood. They bring Western goods and teach the chiefs to covet these things.

SYBIL They ply them with liquor until they are drunk . . .

LUCY Sell them useless things . . .

SYBIL Never worth half of what they charge . . .

LUCY The chiefs pay in sandalwood . . .

SYBIL The makaʻāinana must go to cut the wood . . .

LUCY Holes, the size of ships are dug . . .

SYBIL The commoners must fill them with wood . . .

LUCY Piculs.

SYBIL 133 and 1/3 pounds, one picul.

LUCY The wood grows high in the mountains . . .

SYBIL Many leave their fields unattended . . .

LUCY Kalo rots . . .

SYBIL The sweet potatoes are eaten by worms . . .

LUCY Men, women, mothers with their children go . . .

SYBIL Today, many died . . .

LUCY Tomorrow many more . . .

SYBIL   The people stayed too long. The winds blew too cold. The rain came too hard . . .

LUCY   Not enough food . . .

SYBIL   Exposed to nature's elements . . .

LUCY   Not enough to keep warm . . .

SYBIL   They came down from the green hills crying, for the dead they left behind . . .

LUCY   All for what?

SYBIL   So a few foreigners could increase their wealth . . .

LUCY   Buy lace for their wives . . .

SYBIL   Crystal for their tables . . .

LUCY   Stallions for their sons . . .

SYBIL   (*coming forward*) My dear sisters, if you could only see with what misery and death the foundations of wealthy lives in America, comfortable and safe, are built on! These were once a thriving people. The white men who come here for profits from sandalwood, profits from whale oil or for the pleasure of women, I am ashamed to call my countrymen. If you had seen what I saw today, men, women and children dying, I'm sure you would not hesitate to lay down your beautiful silk dresses, your colored ribbons, your lace gloves and all the finery that surrounds you, to take up a Christian vow of service and poverty so that you would never again prosper by the deaths of others.

Scene 3

Lights to KA'AHUMANU *and* HANNAH *at* KA'AHUMANU's *House.*

KA'AHUMANU   Many chiefs have accepted this new God.

HANNAH   Yes.

KA'AHUMANU   Kaumuali'i wished I would believe, also, Keōpūolani.

HANNAH   Why don't you?

KA'AHUMANU   Some things I like. I think it is good that with this God, women may speak to him. In the old days, only the kahuna spoke to God at the heiau. And I like to see that women may teach things about this God, such as Mrs Bingham teaches. But some things I don't like. I'm afraid that this God would have too much power. That too many things would change. There is something about the mikanele that I do not trust, something which I can't name.

HANNAH   They have been kind teachers to us.

KA'AHUMANU   And they seem to care for the people.

HANNAH   They do many things for us.

KA'AHUMANU   (*bewildered*) Yes. (*Pause.*) You know, Hannah, when I was younger, I felt so strong. That is the good thing about youth, to feel strong in body and purpose. I was not afraid. I saw something to do, and I did it. But everything is changed with the coming of foreigners. Their wealth, ships, guns, these things change everything. They have made the power of the chiefs weak. I make a law against the sale of rum. A ship comes full of men eager for drink. If the captain does not like the kapu, he says, 'Sell us rum or we'll fire our cannon on your town'. Or perhaps he sends an angry mob to fight and make trouble. What am I to do? Keep the law and have destruction? If we engage him in battle more and more ships with guns will come from his country. Should I relent and give him rum, this makes the chiefs look weak. What will I do? In former days, I did not hesitate to act. My mind did not trouble me. The way was clear. I was not afraid to do away with what I knew to be false or to take up what I wished. But now . . .

HANNAH   Everything has changed so much. I know.

KA'AHUMANU   'Ae, the chiefs pass. All the old ones, my counselors and friends, Keōpūolani, gone. My own Kaumuali'i, gone! Kalanimoku grows so old. His strength fades. Our people die. I feel as if I am surrounded by darkness . . . (*The lights go very soft to a spot on* KA'AHUMANU *alone. She chants a kanikau, a mourning chant.*)

'Elua no wahi e mehana ai
O ke ahi lalaku i ke hale
O ka lua o ke ahi, o ka lua kapa
I ka lua poli o ka hoa e mehana'i e
Eia lā, aia lā, eia lā e

(*She lies on the mat.* HANNAH *covers her with a quilt and exits.* VOICES *speak from the darkness rising to confusion and chaos.*)

VOICE 1   Why did you destroy the old ones?

VOICE 2   Why?

VOICE 3   Why?

VOICE 4   Why?

VOICE 1   Your people are dying!

VOICE 2   Why?

VOICE 3   Do something!

VOICE 4   Can't you do anything?

VOICE 1   Too many haole.

VOICE 2   Another warship . . .

VOICE 3   Another government . . .

VOICE 4   Give us sandalwood . . .

VOICE 1   Women. Where are the women?!

VOICE 2   And rum, more rum . . .

VOICE 3   Call for a warship. These chiefs
can't tell us what to do . . .

VOICE 4   I'll do what I like. This isn't
America . . .

VOICE 1   England . . .

VOICE 2   France . . .

VOICE 3   These aren't civilised human
beings.

VOICE 4   Take care of your own people.

VOICE 1   Take care!

VOICE 2   Can't you do anything?

VOICE 3   There's too much sickness . . .

VOICE 4   I need some land . . .

VOICE 1   Send for a warship. I want to be
paid!

VOICE 2   These are only native chiefs . . .

VOICE 3   Stupid savages!

KA'AHUMANU   Why is it so hot?

VOICE 4   There aren't enough children
anymore.

VOICE 1   Why did you leave the old Gods?

VOICE 2   Can't you do something?

KA'AHUMANU   It's too hot.

VOICE 3   What does every sin deserve?

VOICE 4   Everyone will die!

VOICE 1   Die!

VOICE 2   It's too hot!

VOICE 3   Why can't you do anything?

VOICE 4   Why?

ALL VOICES   We're dying! We're all dying.
Do something.

Scene 4

Enter LUCY *and* SYBIL. *They begin to bathe*
KA'AHUMANU*'s face with damp cloths and tend*
her as if she is ill.

LUCY   Is she improved?

SYBIL   Not much, her fever is still very high.

LUCY   You should rest.

SYBIL   I'm fine. It's you I worry over.

LUCY   You've been here all day. You could
become ill yourself.

SYBIL   I've had a little sleep.

(PALI *has softly entered.*)

PALI   Will she die?

SYBIL   (*frightened*) No, she won't die!

PALI   Put her in the stream.

SYBIL   No, Pali, it could make her much
worse.

PALI   She'll burn up inside.

LUCY   Such a stupid belief.

(*Exit* PALI, *quickly.*)

SYBIL   Sister Thurston.

LUCY   I know, I spoke too sharply.

SYBIL   People listen to those whom they feel
to be kind-hearted.

LUCY   It always happens when I feel tired.

SYBIL   (*urgently*) Perhaps you should go back
to the mission and get Reverend Bingham
and the doctor.

LUCY   Is she going?

SYBIL   I don't know. I can't tell if the fever is
breaking or if she's falling into a worse
state.

LUCY   I'll hurry. (*Exit* LUCY.)

KA'AHUMANU   (*mumbling*) No, no. I'm too
hot. Go! Go! Go away . . . I won't go
there . . . No . . . no . . . (*She opens her eyes*
slowly and looks at SYBIL.) Binamuwahine!

SYBIL   (*smiling*) Yes, I'm here.

KA'AHUMANU   I'm very sick?

SYBIL   Yes.

KA'AHUMANU   I had a terrible dream. I saw
that place.

SYBIL   What place?

KA'AHUMANU   The place of fires. (*She tries*
to sit up.)

SYBIL   You must lie down.

KA'AHUMANU   It was a terrible place. I saw
my people burning. It was so hot, great
rivers of lava.

SYBIL   It's all right. You're here now.

KA'AHUMANU   You're so kind to bring me
back from that place.

SYBIL   It is the love of Jesus that has brought
me here.

KA'AHUMANU   It is Jesus who saves us from
this place?

SYBIL   He is the light of the world. It is only
through him that we are saved.

KA'AHUMANU   Perhaps now,
Binamuwahine, I will try one of these
prayers to Jesus.

SYBIL   Now?

KA'AHUMANU   Yes, now, hurry.

SYBIL   Reverend Bingham will be here soon.
Maybe you wish to pray with him.

KA'AHUMANU   No, it's you I wish to share
my first prayer with.

SYBIL   (*touched*) Very well, we will pray as
Jesus taught us to pray, saying: 'Our father
who art in heaven'.

KA'AHUMANU   'Our father who art in
heaven . . .'

(The lights fade as they continue the Lord's Prayer.)

Scene 5

Lights to HANNAH *reading in her house.*

HANNAH 'I opened to my beloved, but my beloved had withdrawn himself and was gone. My soul failed me when he spake: I sought him, but I could not find him. I called him but he gave no answer. The watchman that went about the city found me; they smote me, they wounded me, the keepers of the walls took away my veil from me. I charge you, O daughters of Jerusalem, if ye find my beloved, that ye tell him: I am sick of love'.

(Lights to the Mission House. KA'AHUMANU, SYBIL *and* LUCY *sit.* KA'AHUMANU *now wears a Mu'umu'u.* HANNAH *enters, depressed.)*

SYBIL Good morning, Hannah.
HANNAH Aloha, Binamuwahine. *(To* KA'AHUMANU*)* Pehea 'oe, kupuna?
KA'AHUMANU Maika'i.
SYBIL Are you troubled, Hannah?
HANNAH No.
SYBIL Don't feel bad, Hannah. Reverend Bingham says you may try the examination in another month. Someday you will be baptized.
HANNAH It's all right.
SYBIL Let's continue our work. You may begin reading with Matthew 13.
KA'AHUMANU *(halting)* 'And he spake in many parables to them . . . saying behold a sower . . . went forth to sow: and when he sowed . . . some seeds fell by the wayside and the fowls came and devoured them up'.
SYBIL Hannah, please continue. (HANNAH *is daydreaming.)*
SYBIL Hannah.
HANNAH I'm sorry.
SYBIL Please continue.
HANNAH I don't know the place.
SYBIL You must pay attention, Hannah. Matthew 13, verse 5.
HANNAH 'Some fell upon a stony place where they had not much earth: and forthwith they sprung because they had no deepness of earth . . .'
SYBIL What is wrong with you today, Hannah?

*(*HANNAH *says nothing but looks at her book unhappily.)*

KA'AHUMANU Jones, he came back.
SYBIL I see.
KA'AHUMANU He wants Hannah for his wahine.
HANNAH I told him that I would not come to his bed unless we made a Christian marriage.
SYBIL You are very right, Hannah. God's love and acceptance of you as one of his own requires your virtue.
HANNAH He speaks so nicely to me. He says he loves me.
SYBIL If he won't marry you, Hannah, it's not love, but only a bodily desire for you.
HANNAH If only I could turn my thoughts away from him. I'm trying very hard.
SYBIL Yes, I know, but you must learn to turn away from what is wicked, no matter how sweetly it calls you.
HANNAH Can such kindnesses be wicked?
SYBIL Yes, it is very clear.
KA'AHUMANU I will read now! 'And when the sun was up they were scorched and because they had no root, they withered away'.
SYBIL Hannah.
HANNAH 'And some fell among thorns; and the thorns sprung up and choked them . . .'

(Off stage we hear LUCY *calling to* SYBIL.*)*

LUCY *(off)* Sybil, please, come! Hurry!

*(*SYBIL *exits.* LUCY *and* SYBIL *return helping in* PALI *who has been badly beaten. Her face is black and blue, blood comes from the corner of her mouth.)*

SYBIL How did this happen?
HANNAH Pali!
KA'AHUMANU Who did this to you?
LUCY I found her outside like this. A lady came by and spat at her.
SYBIL Why?
LUCY She called her that name.
SYBIL What name?
LUCY Kauā.
SYBIL She's badly hurt. Lie her down on the mat.

*(*PALI *cries out in pain.)*

PALI I must go away.
SYBIL You're in no state to go anywhere.
LUCY What if those people find you again?
KA'AHUMANU He kauā 'oe?

PALI (*defiantly*) 'Ae!

HANNAH Kūkapilau!

SYBIL Hannah, don't speak like that to her!

KA'AHUMANU But she is kauā!

SYBIL Stop calling her that! She's a person, just like everyone else.

PALI I don't care anymore. I'm tired of always being afraid that someone will find out. My father gave me to a family when I was a baby. He wanted me to grow without the shame. He's been giving this woman food, kapa, pigs, to keep me. He lived poorly so that I might have life. It was him you saw being beaten once in the village. Last night he came to find me, to tell me that my real mother is very ill and wishes once more to see me. Others of the woman's family saw him and forced her to tell the truth. That's why you've found me this way, but I don't care any more! My father is a better man than any in the village whether he has the marks of a kauā or not! He has given everything for me. I would rather stand by him than any other person! Even you Ka'ahumanu!

LUCY Be quiet now.

PALI That woman only liked the food I brought to her table.

HANNAH I must go, now.

PALI I know you will hate me now, Hannah.

SYBIL Hannah doesn't hate you. (*Silence.*) Hannah, where is your Christian charity?

HANNAH (*coldly*) I will *try* not to hate you.

LUCY Perhaps we should move her to the bed in the cellar.

SYBIL Wait until the doctor looks at her.

KA'AHUMANU You will keep her here?

SYBIL Yes, we will.

KA'AHUMANU She will be a filthy thing in your house.

LUCY She needs our help.

(PALI *cries out in pain.*)

KA'AHUMANU Come, Hannah, let's go. (*Exit* KA'AHUMANU *and* HANNAH.)

Scene 6

KA'AHUMANU *and* HANNAH *walk to* KA'AHUMANU'*s house.*

KA'AHUMANU How could she lie and deceive me?

HANNAH She has been in my house many times.

KA'AHUMANU I treated her as one of my own. She should be punished for such lies.

HANNAH Perhaps she is already.

KA'AHUMANU My own favorite. (*They arrive at* KA'AHUMANU'*s house.*)

KA'AHUMANU Have you seen Jones?

HANNAH Only to talk.

KA'AHUMANU And what does Jones say to you?

HANNAH That he loves me and wishes me to share his bed.

KA'AHUMANU You wish this?

HANNAH Yes, but I don't go.

KA'AHUMANU Ah.

HANNAH He comes everyday to my house. Everyday he asks me.

KA'AHUMANU Tell him not to come.

HANNAH You think it's wrong?

KA'AHUMANU The laws of Jehovah say it's wrong.

HANNAH (*confused*) I tell him I can't sin, but he says I think too much about sin. He says that the mikanele worship God in a poison way. He says that God will love us no matter what we do, and if we don't harm others, we don't sin. He says he loves me better than any woman.

KA'AHUMANU Then why doesn't he make a marriage with you? Isn't that the way of his people?

HANNAH (*defensively*) You said yourself that you thought it took more than words to keep a man.

KA'AHUMANU (*peevishly*) Perhaps my thoughts were wrong. (SYBIL *enters.*)

SYBIL I've come to ask you to have pity on Pali.

KA'AHUMANU She's dishonored and deceived me. I chose her for my favorite. I gave her my affection.

SYBIL She only tried to live a life like others.

KA'AHUMANU She comes from a filthy race.

SYBIL Why? Why do you think these people to be so terrible? Have they done great wrongs?

KA'AHUMANU They are what they are.

SYBIL Then think for a moment, your majesty, what if you were to find yourself in such a station in life.

KA'AHUMANU Me! I am ali'i.

SYBIL And what if your own father had suffered to give you a better life. Wouldn't you try to make the most of that life?

KA'AHUMANU (*after a pause*) Perhaps.

SYBIL And, think, if you were this person who looked to her chieftess as the one who should guide and protect you; what would you hope this chieftess would do?

KAʻAHUMANU You think I should change the way these people are treated, is that it?

SYBIL (*exhausted*) I'm not one to advise the Kuhina nui, but I'll tell you what I know from the holy scriptures: '. . . and now abideth faith, hope, and love, these three, but the greatest of these is love'. (*Silence.*)

KAʻAHUMANU Let's take some tea.

SYBIL No, I must go. I have so much work.

KAʻAHUMANU No, you will stay. You look tired. You lie down. I myself will lomilomi.

SYBIL Thank you, but –

KAʻAHUMANU No! You have cared for me when I was sick. Now, I will care for you.

SYBIL Well, perhaps I will try it. (*She lies down.*)

HANNAH You've never tried it?

SYBIL No, I haven't, Hannah.

HANNAH It's very good. Your body will relax and make itself well.

(SYBIL *lies on the mat and* KAʻAHUMANU *begins to massage her.*)

KAʻAHUMANU Before you came we spoke of Jones.

SYBIL Oh?

KAʻAHUMANU He wants Hannah to come to him.

SYBIL Of course, you won't go, Hannah.

HANNAH (*repeating*) Of course, I won't go.

KAʻAHUMANU She thinks he loves her.

SYBIL Christian marriage is how a man proves his love.

HANNAH All your life you will only have one husband?

SYBIL Yes, only if a husband dies can a woman take another husband.

KAʻAHUMANU You have only had one?

SYBIL Yes. (*Pause.*) Although, once, a long time ago, I was engaged to another man.

HANNAH Engaged?

SYBIL (*now very relaxed*) That's when a man and a woman promise that they will marry each other.

KAʻAHUMANU A promise?

SYBIL Then others know they are taken.

HANNAH What was his name?

SYBIL His name?

HANNAH Yes.

SYBIL (*smiling, relaxed*) Levi, Mr Levi Parsons.

HANNAH (*to* KAʻAHUMANU) What's happening?

KAʻAHUMANU Her body and thoughts relax.

HANNAH He was handsome, this man, Parsons?

SYBIL Yes, he was. Like summer.

HANNAH (*to* KAʻAHUMANU, *delighted*) I've never heard her talk like this before!

KAʻAHUMANU (*whispers back*) Auē! Her body is like a shoreline of rocks.

SYBIL It was summertime when I met him. So beautiful. We'd walk and walk and talk about everything.

HANNAH Where is he?

SYBIL He was so kind, and I was so lonely.

HANNAH Where is he?

SYBIL Gone.

HANNAH Where?

SYBIL To be a missionary.

HANNAH (*surprised*) He is one of the mikanele?

SYBIL Not here, in Turkey. Far away. They said he couldn't take a wife. The man must go single.

HANNAH He left you.

SYBIL It was our duty to part.

HANNAH But he, but you loved him, didn't you?

SYBIL Summer. We were so close. Many times I've wished . . .

HANNAH You've wished?

SYBIL Yes, I have wished it so. (SYBIL *stops abruptly. She sits up and looks around in a panic.*) I have to go!

KAʻAHUMANU (*trying to put her gently down*) No, Binamuwahine, you mustn't get up so fast, you are too deep.

SYBIL (*jumping up, almost yelling*) I tell you, I have to go!!

(*Lights down on* KAʻAHUMANU*'s house.* SYBIL *runs to the Mission House. She opens a drawer and snatches up a small hand mirror. She begins to softly touch her face and lips.*)

SYBIL Please, remember me the way I was, not this old woman I've become.

(HANNAH *has approached; unseen she watches* SYBIL *for a moment.*)

HANNAH Binamuwahine are you –

(SYBIL *wheels around and sees* HANNAH. *She throws the mirror into the drawer and slams it shut. She quickly turns on* HANNAH.)

SYBIL (*intense, sternly*) You must choose, Hannah! Between a sensual pleasure of the flesh and what you know to be your Christian duty to God!

HANNAH Please, you've been my teacher and my friend –

SYBIL (*loudly*) Choose!

HANNAH   NO!

(HANNAH *runs from the Mission House to her own space.* SYBIL *moves into the playing area. There is a spot on each.* HANNAH *reads from her Bible.*)

HANNAH   'I sleep, but my heart waketh; it is the voice of my beloved that knocketh saying, open to me, my sister, my love'.

SYBIL   (*to the audience*) She came to our own bosom to be instructed. Mature and meditative, her mind seemed instinctively prepared to receive instruction.

HANNAH   'I am my beloved's and my beloved is mine: he feedeth among the lilies'.

SYBIL   More intelligent, more attractive, more refined; she was our joy. The crown of our school. Rising to a new life, thoroughly instructed in a new system of morals, we even dared to believe that she loved the truth: but the test came . . .

HANNAH   'I am my beloved's and his desire is towards me'.

SYBIL   Official power and wealth, combined, turned the scale. Yet her conscience was so ill at ease. She was on the very point of resisting when she found she had not the strength.

HANNAH   'Many waters cannot quench love, neither can the floods drown it: if a man give all the substance of his house for love . . .'

SYBIL   Here is one of the keenest trials of a mission teacher. We plant a vineyard, when we look that it should put forth grapes, it brings wild grapes.

HANNAH   'Come my beloved, let us go forth into the field'.

SYBIL   I loved her as a child of my own brother or sister.

HANNAH   'Set me as a seal upon thine heart'.

SYBIL and HANNAH   (*They face each other.*) 'O that my head were waters, and mine eyes a fountain of tears, that I might weep for the slain daughters of my people'.

(*Lights to* KA'AHUMANU *who looks at* SYBIL.)

KA'AHUMANU   Faith, Hope and Love, but the greatest of these is Love.

Scene 7

Spot to the playing area. PALI *enters the light.*

PALI   There was, when I was younger, a woman who came to live in the hale nearby who was with child. She was a strange woman with dark looks and knotted fingers. I knew she did not want her baby because many times I saw her gather plants to make a baby go away. But the baby wouldn't go away, and it grew inside her anyway. She had the baby in the dark, by herself, and when we went to see it, she told us to go away, that the baby was sick and would not live. (*Short pause.*) One night, when there was no moon, I saw her steal out with the child all wrapped up. I followed her into the forest. She went far into the night and into the uplands where no one lives but the mountain spirits and the ghosts. I thought the baby had died, and she had come to bury it. I thought perhaps its sickness had made it unbearable to look at, and she wanted no one to see it, even in death. She stopped at a place that was quiet and hidden. I watched her place the white bundle in the ground. She began to walk very quickly back and forth, looking at the bundle. Then she would turn away and pull at her fingers. Over and over again she did this, until finally, she turned and ran. Muttering under her breath, she ran away, and I watched her disappear like a thin ribbon into the night. And there in the forest I began to feel sorry for her. I felt sorry that she had lost her baby and could now see that she now suffered from terrible loss and grief. And from that place I walked away looking through the black branches at the sky. I had gone some distance when I heard the first sound. It was like a small cry, so small I thought it was the far away cry of an owl. But it came again, louder, and a little louder, and louder, and, I knew. She would leave her child while it still had life! The soft crying moved through me. I was sick. I ran back. I ran as fast as I could, toward the sound, but there was nothing there. I heard it again and ran, but nothing. And again and again I would hear and run, searching and searching and finding nothing. For what seemed liked hours, I tried, but I couldn't find it again. Exhausted, I sat down and wept. I cried for everything: for the baby, for myself, my father, for all those like me in the world who had been cast aside and now suffered. I do not know how long I sat there so alone and abandoned and without hope. When all of a sudden it came to me, it was as if loving hands had laid a kihei on my shoulders. Comfort washed over me, and I was quiet. And in the quiet, I heard the voice, the voice of a baby, clear and strong, crying in the night. I stood and walked straight to it. I gathered up the small life I was meant to save. I had made a new life – not from my body, but from a thrown away life that no one wanted. I took the baby far away to a kind woman I knew would care for a child. I had given a new life. And now, that is what the mikanele have given to me, a new life from one that was unwanted, thrown away, and treated like so much rubbish.

(*Cross-fade to the Mission House.* PALI *moves into that space, where she picks up the tea service and serves* SYBIL *and* LUCY *tea.*)

PALI   I have made you some tea.

LUCY   Thank you, Pali.

SYBIL   You are so kind to us.

PALI   No, it is you who have given me kindness.

SYBIL   Do you like it here at the Mission, Pali?

PALI   Yes. Here, I hide nothing.

SYBIL   We have talked it over and would like to know if you will stay and work for us?

PALI   Stay?

LUCY   You will have duties.

SYBIL   We need some help very much . . .

LUCY   But don't expect pay, we have no money . . .

SYBIL   But we can give you food, shelter, clothing . . .

LUCY   And your father may come to visit you here.

PALI   You don't care what I am?

SYBIL   We know what you are, kind, honest and hardworking.

LUCY   We do expect you to study the way of our God.

PALI   Because of your kindness, I will learn the way of God and make him mine.

SYBIL   The doctor says you have mended nicely.

PALI   'Ae. You will let me wash the tea things?

SYBIL   Well, that's a good start, Pali. (*Exit* PALI *with the tea service.*) And what does the doctor say of you, sister?

LUCY   He said we must wait. He said some of these things go away by themselves.

SYBIL   But, if . . .

LUCY   If it doesn't? He will have to operate.

SYBIL   Oh. (*Pause.*) It's past the time that the Queen said she would call.

LUCY   I feel so tired.

SYBIL   Go and rest, Lucy.

LUCY   But the lesson.

SYBIL   I'll do it.

LUCY   I do feel strangely. I think I will take this time to rest, if you don't mind.

SYBIL   Please.

(*Exit* LUCY. *After a beat,* KA'AHUMANU *enters.*)

You've come for your lesson.

KA'AHUMANU   I've brought you some fish.

SYBIL   Thank you so much.

KA'AHUMANU   And some poi, fresh, as you like it.

SYBIL   You'll spoil me.

KA'AHUMANU   If good things aren't for good people, then who are they for?

SYBIL   Well, I guess, I don't know.

KA'AHUMANU   (*sitting*) I've thought more about the church.

SYBIL   You wish to join us?

KA'AHUMANU   I have some thoughts.

SYBIL   (*after a silence*) Do you wish to share them with me?

KA'AHUMANU   I don't wish to make you feel bad.

SYBIL   Make me feel bad? I will listen if –

KA'AHUMANU   But how will you listen? With what ears will you hear and what tongue will you speak? Your own or that of the mission? I wish for you to listen.

SYBIL   (*makes the connection*) I will hear your mana'o.

KA'AHUMANU   There are many things which I am glad to receive from this new God. Jesus Christ, he is a kind God.

SYBIL   Yes.

KA'AHUMANU   He shows us a way of mercy . . . Such as the way you treat Pali.

SYBIL   Yes.

KA'AHUMANU   This is something the great gods in the temples did not teach us. And women may speak to this God, and teach about this God as you do.

SYBIL   That is one of the unusual duties of a mission wife.

KA'AHUMANU   Nevertheless, it is done.

SYBIL   Yes.

KA'AHUMANU   You do many good things for the people.

SYBIL   We want to do good.

KA'AHUMANU   But my heart still holds itself back from your God. You see, I remember the old days. The Gods ruled over us in ways I did not like. So when I saw a chance, I took them down. I did away with them. But this new God, your God; I have seen what happens to those who choose him. He has a strong hold on their hearts. I know if I take this God, the people will follow.

SYBIL   As they have always followed you.

KA'AHUMANU   But I would never be able to change the beliefs of the people once this God took hold.

SYBIL   He is strength.

KA'AHUMANU   He is the God of white men.

SYBIL   Yes.

KA'AHUMANU   And it seems that the haole wish to be God over all. I will never be able to stop them here. There are too many ships, too many guns, too many diseases. If I take up this God perhaps there will be some good, some peace. Other nations will see that we believe in the same God and not think us ignorant savages. I know all the names foreigners have for us, but some will want to protect a Christian people from wrong.

SYBIL   It is a good thought.

KA'AHUMANU   We may be a dying people.

SYBIL   There is still hope that your people will revive themselves. Do not give up that hope.

KA'AHUMANU   You have shown me great kindness, but for some others of your race, I wonder. Will they ever lose their contempt, and will they ever cease to feel that they must be lords over us?

SYBIL   I don't know.

KA'AHUMANU   Our ways are so different.

SYBIL   Yes.

KA'AHUMANU   Perhaps we will never be able to meet without one ruling over another. (*Pause.*) We frightened the very heart of your haole world. Even as I can frighten the very heart of you, Binamuwahine.

SYBIL   Yes.

KA'AHUMANU   The big wave comes, and how will I steer the canoe?

Scene 8

Lights to LUCY *as she stands in the playing area.*

LUCY   The doctor informed me that the tumor was rapidly altering. It approached the surface, exhibiting a dark spot. He said should it become an open ulcer, the whole system would be overcome with its malignancy. He advised immediate operation, warning me that my system would not tolerate any drug to deaden the pain. I agreed to proceed. That night, after everyone had retired, I walked for many hours, back and forth in the yard. Depraved, diseased and helpless, I yield myself up entirely to the will of the holy one. Cold daylight. The doctor now informs me all is in readiness. (LUCY *walks into the Mission House with a cross-fade.*) The chair, the white porcelain wash basins, the dozens of fresh, clean towels, the shiny medical instruments, the strings for tying my arteries, shiny needles to sew up my flesh. I sink into the chair wishing it would swallow me away. The doctor shows me how I must hold my left arm, how to press my feet against the foot of the chair. He looks at me, 'Have you made up your mind to have it cut out?' 'Yes sir'. 'Are you ready now?' 'Yes sir'. My shawl is removed exhibiting my left arm. My breast and side are perfectly bare. I see the knife in the doctor's hand. 'I am going to begin now'. 'Yes sir'. Then comes a gash long and deep, first on one side of my breast and then on another. Deep sickness seizes me, deprives me of my breakfast. This is followed by extreme faintness. My sufferings are no longer local. Agony spreads through my whole system. I feel every inch of me failing. Every glimpse I have of the doctor is only his hand covered to the wrist with blood. It seems like hours that I feel my flesh cut away. I am beneath his hand, cutting, cutting out the entire breast, cutting out the glands, cutting under my arm, tying up the arteries, sewing up the wound. I know it is vanity, but I feel grateful that God has preserved what small dignity I now have. During the whole operation he has granted that I do not lose control of my voice or person. (*Long pause.*) Kindly, the doctor tells me, 'There is not one in a thousand who could have borne it as you have done'. (*Pause.*) Many dangers still lie ahead of me. I am greatly debilitated and often see duplicates of everything my eye beholds. Now, when all is done, a hollowness falls over me. (*Lights *rise a bit and* SYBIL *enters;* PALI *stands apart watching them.*)

LUCY   (*reaching for* SYBIL's *hand*) Sister.

SYBIL   How are you, Lucy?

LUCY   I don't know.

SYBIL   You're still weak.

LUCY   Yes.

SYBIL   Is there any pain?

LUCY   Yes, and a kind of emptiness.

SYBIL   The doctor says I must change the dressing.

LUCY   Oh.

SYBIL   (*cautiously*) I hope that –

LUCY   I know now I'll be nothing but a shame to my husband.

SYBIL   Lucy, don't say that.

LUCY   Everyone knows. That's the first thing that people will think of when they see me. I'll be a shame to him.

SYBIL   Don't think such things.

LUCY   You know it's true.

SYBIL   You must thank God for your life.

LUCY   (*with no conviction*) Yes, I must.

SYBIL   Lucy, I have to change the dressing.

LUCY   Yes.

SYBIL   (*nervous*) Does it look, I mean is it –

LUCY   It's not a pretty sight. I'm sorry, Sybil.

SYBIL   Oh.

LUCY   There's also an odor, not pleasant.

SYBIL   I see, well, I must change it.

LUCY   I'm sorry, Sybil.

(SYBIL *approaches her. She begins to undo* LUCY's *dress.* SYBIL *is obviously in great distress over having to do the task. She several times turns away and then goes back to the work. Her anxiety builds. She becomes visibly nauseated. She struggles with the feeling, but finally turns away.*)

SYBIL   God forgive me, Lucy. (*Silence.*) I can't do it. I can't.

LUCY   I'm sorry.

SYBIL   No, it's I who am sorry and ashamed.

LUCY   Is it very hard to see?

SYBIL   Yes, for me. I want so much to help you but –

LUCY   It's all right, Sybil.

SYBIL   I've tended the sick so many times, I don't understand these feelings . . .

LUCY   You must get the doctor to do it.

SYBIL   It frightens me.

LUCY   It won't happen to you, Sybil.

SYBIL   You were right, anything could happen to us here. (*Pause.*) I'm so sorry.

LUCY   Don't say anymore, please, just get the doctor to see to it.

(*Exit* SYBIL. PALI *who has been watching slowly comes forward. A soft spot rises in* KA'AHUMANU's *house.* KA'AHUMANU *rises, an observer to this scene.* PALI *goes to* LUCY.)

PALI   I wish to do this for you, Mrs Thurston.

LUCY   Pali?

PALI   Yes, I wish to help you.

LUCY   You may feel sickened.

PALI   No. Tell me what to do. (*Silence, then firmly*) You will tell me what to do, and I will do it.

LUCY   First, you must remove the old dressings.

PALI   Yes.

LUCY   Then, you must wash the wound with . . . Pali?

PALI   'Ae?

LUCY   (*taking her hand*) I will remember this kindness all my days.

(*Lights fade on the Mission House for a beat, then slowly rise.* KA'AHUMANU *enters the Mission House.* PALI *is pinning up the hem of a white dress.* PALI *and* KA'AHUMANU *look at each other.* SYBIL *enters and sees them.*)

SYBIL   Good morning.

KA'AHUMANU   Ah, good morning.

SYBIL   So you are resolved to study for baptism?

KA'AHUMANU   Yes.

SYBIL   Pali will be baptized this Sunday.

KA'AHUMANU   She will?

SYBIL   Yes, she has studied very hard.

(*Enter* LUCY, *arm in a sling.*)

LUCY   The Christian path is not the easy one.

SYBIL   But the one which brings salvation.

PALI   I need a needle.

LUCY   You may sit here and sew.

PALI   Perhaps I'm not wanted. (*Silence.*)

KA'AHUMANU   You know these questions for the baptism, Pali?

PALI   'Ae.

KA'AHUMANU   Then you will sit beside me and help me.

PALI   (*sitting*) 'Ae. (SYBIL *gives* PALI *the catechism book and one to* KA'AHUMANU.)

SYBIL   Pali, you will begin the lesson by asking the questions.

PALI   Me? You wish me to ask the questions to –

SYBIL   Yes, you.

PALI   Here is the first question. 'What is sin?'

KA'AHUMANU (*reading back slowly*) 'Sin is any want of conformity to or . . .'

PALI 'or transgression of –'

KA'AHUMANU 'Or transgression of the law of god'.

PALI 'What is the sin by where our first parents fell?'

KA'AHUMANU 'The sin by where our first parents fell . . .' You read it first to me, Pali, my pua.

PALI 'Ae. 'The sin by where our first parents fell was the eating of the forbidden fruit'.

(*At the reading of the questions, the lights start a slow fade to black. Lights to* KA'AHUMANU *and* HANNAH, *who meet on the playing area.* HANNAH *is once again dressed in a kikepa.*)

HANNAH Aloha, nō.

KA'AHUMANU Aloha, Hannah. I hear from the village that you've chosen to live with Jones.

HANNAH Yes, but what will you choose, my ali'i?

KA'AHUMANU Why did you do it, Hannah?

HANNAH I thought this new God, this new way of being, would fill me up full of happiness and purpose, as I thought it did the mikanele, and for a time, it did. But the happiness went farther and farther away, something to wait for after death, and I remembered what you once said to me. That happiness was a thing we need while we are alive. Come away from them, don't join them in their thought that everything which gives pleasure is bad. Come back to the way things were before.

KA'AHUMANU You know things will never be as they were! The world changes before our eyes everyday, and we must change or be lost. Besides, we cannot go back to the way things were before. I will put aside those old ways because the people need a new way for the new world which comes to us. We will have laws. We will be Christian people.

HANNAH This can never be my way. I will believe there is another way.

KA'AHUMANU What way is that?

HANNAH I don't know. I only know that I can't follow the ways of their God, although I know many of their ways to be good. It is something inside that will not be closed off, and this is what will happen to me if I listen to them.

KA'AHUMANU Our lives take us on different journeys then, Hannah.

HANNAH 'Ae.

KA'AHUMANU (*embracing* HANNAH) Aloha, my pua.

HANNAH You will tell Mrs Bingham something for me?

KA'AHUMANU What is it?

HANNAH (*leaving*) Tell her that it is summertime!

KA'AHUMANU (*alone*) Aloha, my pua, and may the old Gods watch over your life.

(*Exit* HANNAH. KA'AHUMANU *moves to a single spot of light downstage centre.*)

KA'AHUMANU (*straight out*) Yes, I have listened to you, my brothers. Now hear my thoughts. The foreigners are among us. Many more will come. Beware, some will come like the hoards of caterpillars, hiding their hunger to devastate the land as we know it, until the time when all the Hawaiian people may be trodden underfoot. We have seen this greed already with the sandalwood trade. We must fight now with our quick thoughts and our grasp of foreign ways. To think too long on the ways of the past is to ignore the hungry sharks that swim among us. I do not look to the past with contempt, but seek to preserve the ways that were good, uniting them with what is good of this new world, that comes to us, *now*.

(*Blackout.*)

17 Tomson Highway

The Rez Sisters

Canada

Introduction

The extraordinary success of Tomson Highway's first major play, *The Rez Sisters* (1986), constituted a turning point in the development of Native Canadian theatre. Prior efforts in the field had largely been confined to fringe and community venues, whereas Highway's earthy comedy about the lives of seven reservation women entered the mainstream in spectacular style. After its warmly received premiere in Toronto in November 1986, where it won a Dora Mavor Moore Award for best new play, *The Rez Sisters* had a sell-out tour of Canada, a season at the 1988 Edinburgh Festival, and a workshop production in New York. This is an impressive achievement by any standards, but perhaps the play's greatest significance stems from its insistence on the inherent theatricality of everyday Native life. By staging 'ordinary' but complex indigenous characters that moved beyond the well-established stereotypes circulated in various white discourses, including drama, Highway had claimed a space in Canadian theatre for Native peoples and Native performance styles. His play initiated a surge of theatrical activity, which has expanded over the 1990s into a substantial corpus of indigenous work that includes contributions by Daniel David Moses, Monique Mojica, Drew Hayden Taylor, Marie Clements and Margo Kane, among others.

Particular details of Highway's background are now well documented by critics, and by the playwright himself in interviews revealing the diverse cultural influences that animate his work. Born in 1951 on a trap-line in northern Manitoba's Brochet Reserve, Highway was the eleventh of twelve children. Cree, his first language, was (forcibly) displaced by English after he was sent, at the behest of the government, to a Catholic boarding school in The Pas with his younger brother, René. Their traumatic acculturation into white society through the residential school system is transformed into magic realist fiction in Highway's best-selling novel, *Kiss of the Fur Queen* (1998). After high school, his studies in classical piano led to an honours degree in music at the University of Western Ontario, where he also gained a bachelor's degree, majoring in English. He abandoned plans for a career as a concert pianist when he realised that playing music for Canada's urban elite would do little to help his own people. Seven years of work on cultural programmes with Native social services organisations followed until, in the early 1980s, he began to bring together his experiences of Native culture and his training in European art forms.

Highway's first theatre pieces, performed largely to Native audiences on reserves and in urban community centres, were works devised for himself and René, who had become a professional dancer. In 1992, Tomson joined the fledgling Native Earth Performing Arts Inc. in Toronto, later becoming the company's artistic director for several years, during which he developed its profile considerably. Over this period, he wrote *Aria* (1987), a solo piece consisting of twenty-two monologues about Native womanhood, collaborated with René on a multimedia work, *New Song . . . New Dance* (1988), and also created, with Bill Merasty, *The Sage, the Dancer and the Fool* (1989), a 'mini-*Ulysses*' dramatising one day in the life of a Native youth in the city. Each of these works figures the Native trickster in some manner, as does *The Rez Sisters* and its companion play, *Dry Lips Oughta Move to Kapuskasing*, which premiered to general acclaim in 1989, consolidating Highway's reputation as a major playwright and earning him more accolades, including the Chalmers award for best Canadian play. *Dry Lips*, the second in a projected cycle of seven 'Rez' plays, dramatises the lives of seven native men on the reservation featured in *The Rez Sisters*. It is a more confronting work than Highway's earlier play and its graphic representation of sexual violence, alcoholism and misogyny has troubled some critics, though Highway defends his material by arguing that the 'poison' must first be exposed before his culture can be healed. His much-awaited third Rez play, *Rose*, a gritty musical about coming to terms with the past, was premiered in 2000 by the University College Drama Program at Guelph.

Highway has spoken frequently about the centrality of the trickster to his artistic work and to the wider indigenous culture that it dramatises. His notes to the published texts of both *The Rez Sisters* and *Dry Lips* explicitly position the trickster as a transformative agent whose presence is essential to the spiritual health of Native societies:

> The dream world of North American Indian mythology is inhabited by the most fantastic creatures, beings, and events. Foremost among these is the 'Trickster', as pivotal and important a figure in the Native world as Christ is in the realm of Christian mythology. 'Weesageechak' in Cree, 'Nanabush' in Ojibway, 'Raven' in others, 'Coyote' in still others, this Trickster goes by many names and many guises. . . Essentially a comic, clownish sort of character, he teaches us about the nature and meaning of existence on the planet Earth; he straddles the consciousness of man and that of God, the great spirit.
> (Highway 1988: xii)

This shape-shifting trickster also transcends gender binaries, adopting either male or female form. Highway's version is Nanabush, who appears in *The Rez Sisters* as a mischievous white seagull, a foreboding black nighthawk and the flamboyant Bingo Master, all performed by a male dancer. These guises suggest movement between the extremes of 'hope and despair, comedy and tragedy, order and chaos, as well as between Native and White cultures' (Nothof 1995: 39). In *Dry Lips*, Nanabush is female and takes the shape of various reservation women, performed by the one actor. While both plays express the concern that Native communities are in danger of forgetting their traditional spiritual

guides, Highway is careful to present the trickster as less a conduit to an irretrievable past than an element of contemporary indigenous life mediated by colonialism.

As a healing force within Highway's fictional Rez community, one of Nanabush's functions is to absorb and transform the pain resulting from atrocities associated with the colonisation of Native lands and cultures. The most compelling, and disturbing, moment in *The Rez Sisters* occurs when Zhaboonigan recounts her rape by a gang of white youths that penetrated her vagina with a screwdriver. While the mentally disabled girl relays her experience with the casual disinterest of a child who understands only a little of what has occurred, Nanabush embodies her trauma by performing the 'agonising contortions' of the rape victim. In this way, the play exposes the violation of the very spirit of Native culture while minimising the pain of Zhaboonigan's memories. The more graphically depicted rape of the female Nanabush in *Dry Lips* similarly suggests the desecration of indigenous spirituality. Here the assault is perpetrated by a Native man suffering from foetal alcohol syndrome, but its cause is located in a broader culture of misogyny that stems in part from colonial intervention in traditional Native social organisation. Though they approach the subject from different angles, both plays aim to refuse the power of rape by subsuming it within the mythological frameworks invoked, since Nanabush is, above all, the great survivor.

The critical role of Nanabush in Highway's dramaturgy distinguishes his project from that of playwrights such as James Reaney and Michel Tremblay, whose contributions to Canadian theatre have significantly influenced his work. *The Rez Sisters* is partly modelled after Tremblay's 1968 play, *Les Belles-Soeurs*, which dramatises the spiritual malaise of seven closely related Québécoise women living in a working-class suburb of Montreal. The two plays show similarities in thematic content, characterisation and narrative texture, and both feature the game of Bingo as the structural pivot around which much of the action revolves. Yet while Bingo figures as an image of shallow consumerism in each text, Highway invests his protagonists' quest with a mythopoeic force that elevates the game from its tawdry and mundane context to a fantastical world where anything can happen. With Nanabush's intervention, the Rez sisters' quest becomes regenerative, not because it might provide the means to alleviate their poverty but rather because they learn from their experiences to value what they have and to use their own energy and ingenuity to solve problems. In this respect, critics regard Highway's play as much more optimistic in outlook than its prototype: 'Les Belles-Soeurs reflects the negativism, nihilism and spiritual void of Western postmodern society; The Rez Sisters, in spite of the similarity of its dramatic matrix, reflects the essential humanism, life-affirming and hopeful world view of Native peoples' (Usmiani 1995: 127).

The mere presence of Nanabush as an embodied character/principle in The Rez Sisters immediately signals the play's efforts to move beyond realism in its portrayal of the petty squabbles, the quiet desperation, the underlying camaraderie and the ebullient hopes of the seven women. Highway further stylises his narrative by featuring a number of spoken and mimed sequences that are carefully choreographed for rhythmic effect. The all-in verbal brawl at the community store, the women's march to the band office, their frantic fundraising activities and the surreal Bingo game are all cases in point. Whereas such highly theatricalised group scenes depict collective activities/concerns, the individual characters are poignantly revealed via introspective 'key-moment' speeches. These are styled as monologues in Act I when each woman describes what she will do if she wins the Bingo jackpot, and duologues in Act II as the women, in turn, 'open up' to one of their 'sisters' during the journey to Toronto. The particular sequencing of both types of scenes within an overall narrative that eventually circles back to its initial points of departure facilitates the sisters' negotiations of individual and communal identities, and affirms their resilience in the face of adversity. With the final image of Pelajia Patchnose hammering the shingles on her roof, the cycle ends where it began, but on a much more optimistic note as Nanabush dances 'merrily and triumphantly' in the background.

Highway's extensive training in music manifests not only in the complex soundscapes of his plays but also in their overall theatrical construction, which tends to follow models of musical composition. A close examination of the particular composition of The Rez Sisters bears out Daniel David Moses' observation that Highway 'uses characters like themes and thinks of character conflict in terms like counterpoint and contrast' (Moses 1987: 88). According to Clay Djubal (1996), the musical model for this play is the classical sonata, which consists of a two-part tonal structure articulated in three main sections: the exposition, the development and the recapitulation, with a short coda at the end. In Highway's exposition, each sister's theme is introduced, along with the dual motifs of home and community. The development section begins with the full-scale riot and continues until Marie-Adele is waltzed off to the spirit world in the arms of the Bingo Master. During this phase, shifts in focus between characters, fragmentation of established motifs and alterations of emotional register create a complex polyphonic texture that rises to a crescendo with the Bingo game, breaking the 'fourth wall' by inviting audience participation. The movement back home to Wasaychigan Hill Reserve for Marie-Adele's funeral constitutes the recapitulation, while a sense of complete closure is realised in the coda, as the opening image is re-presented in a new light (Djubal 1996).

By fusing Native and Western performance aesthetics, Highway's theatre integrates elements of the disparate worlds he has experienced, always invoking indigenous mythology as the scaffolding that bridges gaps and contradictions. He insists that this mythology is a magical force, 'alive, electric, passionate' (Highway 1992: 132), an essential if sometimes suppressed part of his characters' lives. The 'magic' wrought by the Rez sisters' spiritual journey becomes evident at the end of the play in the small but significant changes in each of the women's behaviour. Intimations of a better future are conveyed through Pelajia's determination to improve conditions on the reserve and Veronique's willingness to care for the fourteen Starblanket children, but most of all through Emily Dictionary's pregnancy, and its promise of new life.

Production history

After being workshopped at the De-ba-jeh-mu-jig Theatre Company in West Bay,

Manitoulin Island, *The Rez Sisters* was first produced by the Act IV Theatre Company and Native Earth Performing Arts, Inc. at the Native Canadian Centre of Toronto on 26 November 1986, directed by Larry Lewis. The play subsequently toured across Canada and featured at the 1988 Edinburgh Festival. It was also staged as part of the New York Theatre Workshop's New Directors/New Directions series in 1993.

Select bibliography

Djubal, C. (1996) 'Strategies of subversion: an examination of Tomson Highway's *The Rez Sisters* and its appropriation of sonata form', honours thesis, University of Queensland.

Filewod, A. (1992) 'Averting the colonizing gaze: notes on watching native theater', in P. Brask and W. Morgan (eds) *Aboriginal Voices: Amerindian, Inuit and Sami Theater*, Baltimore, MD: Johns Hopkins University Press, 17–28.

—— (1994) 'Receiving aboriginality: Tomson Highway and the crisis of cultural authenticity', *Theatre Journal* 46, 3: 363–73.

Grant, A. (1992) 'Canadian native literature: the drama of George Ryga and Tomson Highway', *Australian-Canadian Studies* 10, 2: 37–56.

Highway, T. (1987) 'On native mythology', *Theatrum* 6: 29–31.

—— (1988) *The Rez Sisters*, Saskatoon: Fifth House.

—— (1989) *Dry Lips Oughta Move to Kapuskasing*, Saskatoon: Fifth House.

—— (1992) 'The trickster and native theater', interview with W. Morgan, in P. Brask and W. Morgan (eds) *Aboriginal Voices: Amerindian, Inuit and Sami Theater*, Baltimore, MD: Johns Hopkins University Press, 130–8.

—— (1994) 'Twenty-one native women on motorcycles', interview with J. Tompkins and L. Male, *Australasian Drama Studies* 24: 13–28.

Johnston, D.W. (1990) 'Lines and circles: the "Rez" plays of Tomson Highway', *Canadian Literature* 124–5: 254–64.

Maufort, M. (1993) 'Recognising difference in Canadian drama: Tomson Highway's poetic realism', *British Journal of Canadian Studies* 8, 2: 230–40.

Moses, D.D. (1987) 'The trickster theatre of Tomson Highway', *Canadian Fiction Magazine* 60, 1: 83–5.

Nothof, A. (1995) 'Cultural collision and magical transformation: the plays of Tomson Highway', *Studies in Canadian Literature* 20, 2: 134–43.

Preston, J. (1992) 'Weesageechak begins to dance: Native Earth Performing Arts, Inc', *Drama Review* 36, 1: 135–59.

Rabillard, S. (1993) 'Absorption, elimination and the hybrid: some impure questions of gender and culture in the trickster drama of Tomson Highway', *Essays in Theatre* 12, 1: 3–27.

Shackleton, M. (1999) 'Native myth meets Western culture: the plays of Tomson Highway', in J. Kaplan *et al.* (eds) *Migration, Preservation and Change*, Renvall Institute Publications, Helsinki: University of Helsinki, 47–58.

Usmiani, R. (1995) 'The bingocentric worlds of Michael Tremblay and Tomson Highway: *Les Belles-Soeurs vs. The Rez Sisters*', *Canadian Literature* 144: 126–40.

Audiovisual resources

Tomson Highway: Thank You for the Love You Gave (1996) produced by Craig Graham, Cinepro Productions, CBC Life and Times Series. Available Canadian Broadcasting Commission, Toronto: edsales@toronto.cbc.ca

The Rez Sisters

Tomson Highway

Characters

PELAJIA PATCHNOSE 53
PHILOMENA MOOSETAIL 49, sister of Pelajia
MARIE-ADELE STARBLANKET 39, half-sister of Pelajia and Philomena
ANNIE COOK 36, sister of Marie-Adele and half-sister of the other two
EMILY DICTIONARY 32, sister of Annie and ditto
VERONIQUE ST PIERRE 45, sister-in-law of all the above
ZHABOONIGAN PETERSON 24, mentally disabled adopted daughter of Veronique
NANABUSH who plays the Seagull (the dancer in white feathers), the Nighthawk (the dancer in dark feathers) and the Bingo Master

Time

Late Summer 1986.

Place

Wasaychigan Hill Indian Reserve, Manitoulin Island, Ontario. (Note: 'Wasaychigan' means 'window' in Ojibway.)

Act I

It is mid-morning of a beautiful late August day on the Wasaychigan Hill Indian Reserve, Manitoulin Island, Ontario. PELAJIA PATCHNOSE *is alone on the roof of her house, nailing shingles on. She wears faded blue denim men's coveralls and a baseball cap to shade her eyes from the sun. A brightly-coloured square cushion belonging to her sister,* PHILOMENA MOOSETAIL, *rests on the roof beside her. The ladder to the roof is off stage.*

PELAJIA Philomena. I wanna go to Toronto.
PHILOMENA (*from off stage*) Oh, go on.
PELAJIA Sure as I'm sitting away up here on the roof of this old house. I kind of like it

up here, though. From here, I can see half of Manitoulin Island on a clear day. I can see the chimneys, the tops of apple trees, the garbage heap behind Big Joey's dumpy little house. I can see the seagulls circling over Marie-Adele Starblanket's white picket fence. Boats on the North Channel I wish I was on, sailing away somewhere. The mill at Espanola, a hundred miles away . . . and that's with just a bit of squinting. See? If I had binoculars, I could see the superstack in Sudbury. And if I were Superwoman, I could see the CN Tower in Toronto. Ah, but I'm just plain old Pelajia Rosella Patchnose and I'm here in plain, dusty, boring old Wasaychigan Hill . . . Wasy . . . waiting . . . waiting . . . nailing shining shingles with my trusty silver hammer on the roof of Pelajia Rosella Patchnose's little two-bedroom welfare house. Philomena. I wanna go to Toronto.

(PHILOMENA MOOSETAIL *comes up the ladder to the roof with one shingle and obviously hating it. She is very well-dressed, with a skirt, nylons, even heels, completely impractical for the roof.*)

PHILOMENA Oh, go on.
PELAJIA I'm tired, Philomena, tired of this place. There's days I wanna leave so bad.
PHILOMENA But you were born here. All your poop's on this reserve.
PELAJIA Oh, go on.
PHILOMENA You'll never leave.
PELAJIA Yes, I will. When I'm old.
PHILOMENA You're old now.
PELAJIA I got a good 30 years to go . . .
PHILOMENA . . . and you're gonna live every one of them right here beside me . . .
PELAJIA . . . maybe 40 . . .
PHILOMENA . . . here in Wasy. (*Tickles* PELAJIA *on the breasts.*) Chiga-chiga-chiga.
PELAJIA (*yelps and slaps* PHILOMENA's *hand away*) Oh, go on. It's not like it used to be.

PHILOMENA   Oh, go on. People change, places change, time changes things. You expect to be young and gorgeous forever?

PELAJIA   See? I told you I'm not old.

PHILOMENA   Oh, go on. You.

PELAJIA   'Oh, go on. You'. You bug me like hell when you say that.

PHILOMENA   You say it, too. And don't give me none of this 'I don't like this place. I'm tired of it'. This place is too much inside your blood. You can't get rid of it. And it can't get rid of you.

PELAJIA   Four thirty this morning, I was woken by . . .

PHILOMENA   Here we go again.

PELAJIA   . . . Andrew Starblanket and his brother, Matthew. Drunk. Again. Or sounded like . . .

PHILOMENA   Nothing better to do.

PELAJIA   . . . fighting over some girl. Heard what sounded like a baseball bat landing on somebody's back. My lawn looks like the shits this morning.

PHILOMENA   Well, I like it here. Myself, I'm gonna go to every bingo and I'm gonna hit every jackpot between here and Espanola and I'm gonna buy me that toilet I'm dreaming about at night . . . big and wide and very white . . .

PELAJIA   Aw-ni-gi-naw-ee-dick.[1]

PHILOMENA   I'm no good at bingo.

PELAJIA   So what! And the old stories, the old language. Almost all gone . . . was a time Nanabush and Windigo and everyone here could rattle away in Indian fast as Bingo Betty could lay her bingo chips down on a hot night.

PHILOMENA   Pelajia Rosella Patchnose. The sun's gonna drive you crazy. (*And she descends the ladder.*)

PELAJIA   Everyone here's crazy. No jobs. Nothing to do but drink and screw each other's wives and husbands and forget about our Nanabush. (*From off stage* PHILOMENA *screams. She fell down the ladder.*) Philomena! (*As she looks over the edge of the roof*) What are you doing down there?

PHILOMENA   What do you think? I fell.

PELAJIA   Bring me some of them nails while you're down there.

PHILOMENA   (*whining and still from off stage, from behind the house*) You think I can race up and down this ladder? You think I got wings?

PELAJIA   You gotta wear pants when you're doing a man's job. See? You got your skirt ripped on a nail and now you can see your thighs. People gonna think you just came from Big Joey's house.

PHILOMENA   (*she comes up the ladder in a state of disarray*) Let them think what they want. That old cow Gazelle Nataways . . . always acting like she thinks she's still a spring chicken. She's got them legs of hers wrapped around Big Joey day and night . . .

PELAJIA   Philomena. Park your tongue. My old man has to go the hundred miles to Espanola just to get a job. My boys. Gone to Toronto. Only place educated Indian boys can find decent jobs these days. And here I sit all broken-hearted.

PHILOMENA   Paid a dime and only farted.

PELAJIA   Look at you. You got dirt all over your backside. (*Turning her attention to the road in front of her house and standing up for the first and only time.*) And dirt roads! Years now that old chief's been making speeches about getting paved roads 'for my people' and still we got dirt roads all over.

PHILOMENA   Oh, go on.

PELAJIA   When I win me that jackpot next time we play bingo in Espanola . . .

PHILOMENA   (*examining her torn skirt, her general state of disarray, and fretting over it*) Look at this! Will you look at this! Ohhh!

PELAJIA   . . . I'm gonna put that old chief to shame and build me a nice paved road right here in front of my house. Jet black. Shiny. Make my lawn look real nice.

PHILOMENA   My rib-cage!

PELAJIA   And if that old chief don't wanna make paved roads for all my sisters around here . . .

PHILOMENA   There's something rattling around inside me!

PELAJIA   I'm packing my bags and moving to Toronto. (*Sits down again.*)

PHILOMENA   Oh, go on. (*She spies* ANNIE COOK's *approach a distance up the hill.*) Why, I do believe that cloud of dust over there is Annie Cook racing down the hill, Pelajia.

PELAJIA   Philomena. I wanna go to Toronto.

PHILOMENA   She's walking mighty fast. Must be excited about something.

PELAJIA   Never seen Annie Cook walk slow since the day she finally lost Eugene to Marie-Adele at the church nineteen years ago. And even then she was walking a little too fast for a girl who was supposed to be broken-heart . . . (*stopping just in time and laughing*) . . . heart-broken.

(ANNIE COOK *pops up the top of the ladder to the roof.*)

ANNIE (*all cheery and fast and perky*) Hallooo! Whatchyou doing up here?

PELAJIA There's room for only so much weight up here before we go crashing into my kitchen, so what do you want?

ANNIE Just popped up to say hi.

PELAJIA And see what we're doing?

ANNIE Well . . .

PELAJIA Couldn't you see what we're doing from up where you were?

ANNIE (*confidentially, to* PHILOMENA) Is it true Gazelle Nataways won the bingo last night?

PHILOMENA Annie Cook, first you say you're gonna come with me and then you don't even bother showing up. If you were sitting beside me at that bingo table last night you would have seen Gazelle Nataways win that big pot again with your own two eyes.

ANNIE Emily Dictionary and I went to Little Current to listen to Fritz the Katz.

PELAJIA What in God's name kind of a band might that be?

ANNIE Country rock. My favorite. Fritz the Katz is from Toronto.

PELAJIA Fritzy . . . ritzy . . . Philomena! Say something.

PHILOMENA My record player is in Espanola getting fixed.

ANNIE That's nice.

PHILOMENA Good.

ANNIE Is it true Gazelle Nataways plans to spend her bingo money to go to Toronto with . . . with Big Joey?

PHILOMENA Who wants to know? Emily Dictionary?

ANNIE I guess so.

PELAJIA That Gazelle Nataways gonna leave all her babies behind and let them starve to death?

ANNIE I guess so. I don't know. I'm asking you.

PELAJIA and PHILOMENA We don't know.

ANNIE I'm on my way to Marie-Adele's to pick her up.

PELAJIA Why? Where you gonna put her down? (PELAJIA *and* PHILOMENA *laugh.*)

ANNIE (I mean, we're going to the store together. To the post office. We're going to pick up a parcel. They say there's a parcel for me. They say it's shaped like a record. And they say it's from Sudbury. So it must be from my daughter, Ellen . . .

PELAJIA and PHILOMENA . . . 'Who lives with this white guy in Sudbury' . . .

ANNIE How did you know?

PHILOMENA Everybody knows.

ANNIE His name is Ray*mond*. Not *Ray*mond. But Ray*mond*. Like in Bon Bon. (PHILOMENA *tries out 'bon bon' to herself.*) He's French.

PELAJIA Oh?

ANNIE Garage mechanic. He fixes cars. And you know, talking about Frenchmen, that old priest is holding another bingo next week and when I win . . . (*To* PHILOMENA) Are you going?

PELAJIA Does a bear shit in the woods?

ANNIE . . . when I win, I'm going to Espanola and play the bingo there. Emily Dictionary says that Fire Minklater can give us a ride in her new car. She got it through Ray*mond*'s garage. The bingo in Espanola is bigger. And it's better. And I'll win. And then I'll go to Sudbury, where the bingos are even bigger and better. And then I can visit my daughter, Ellen . . .

PELAJIA . . . 'who lives with this white guy in Sudbury' . . .

ANNIE . . . and go shopping in the record stores and go to the hotel and drink beer quietly – not noisy and crazy like here – and listen to the live bands. It will be so much fun. I hope Emily Dictionary can come with me.

PHILOMENA It's true. I've been thinking . . .

PELAJIA You don't say.

PHILOMENA It's true. The bingos here are getting kind of boring . . .

ANNIE That old priest is too slow and sometimes he gets the numbers all mixed up and the pot's not big enough.

PHILOMENA And I don't like the way he calls the numbers. (*Nasally*) B 12, O 64.

ANNIE When Little Girl Manitowabi won last month . . .

PHILOMENA She won just enough to take a taxi back to Buzwah.

ANNIE That's all. (*Both* ANNIE *and* PHILOMENA *pause to give a quick sigh of yearning.*)

PHILOMENA Annie Cook, I want that big pot.

ANNIE We all want big pots.

PELAJIA Start a revolution!

PHILOMENA and ANNIE Yes!

ANNIE All us Wasy women. We'll march up the hill, burn the church hall down, scare the priest to death, and then we'll march all the way to Espanola, where the bingos are bigger and better . . .

PHILOMENA   We'll hold big placards!

ANNIE   They'll say 'Wasy women want bigger bingos!'

PELAJIA   And one will say: 'Annie Cook Wants Big Pot!'

PHILOMENA   . . . and the numbers at those bingos in Espanola go faster and the pots get bigger by the week. Oh, Pelajia Patchnose, I'm getting excited just thinking about it!

ANNIE   I'm going.

PELAJIA   You are, are you?

ANNIE   Yes. I'm going. I'm running out of time. I'm going to Marie-Adele's house and then we'll walk to the store together to pick up the parcel – I'm sure there'll be a letter in it, and Marie-Adele is expecting mail, too – and we'll see if Emily Dictionary is working today and we'll ask her if Fire Minklater has her new car yet so we can go to Espanola for that big pot. (*She begins to descend the ladder.*)

PELAJIA   Well, you don't have much to do today, do you?

ANNIE   Well. Toodle-oo! (*And she pops down the ladder and is gone.*)

PELAJIA   Not bad for someone who was in such a hurry to get her parcel. She talks faster than she walks. (*Noticing how dejected and abandoned* PHILOMENA *looks, she holds up her hammer.*) Bingo money. Top quality. $24.95.

PHILOMENA   It's true. Bingos here in Wasy are getting smaller and smaller all the time. Especially now when the value of the dollar is getting lesser and lesser. In the old days, when Bingo Betty was still alive and walking these dirt roads, she'd come to every single bingo and she'd sit there like the Queen of Tonga, big and huge like a roast beef, smack-dab in the middle of the bingo hall. One night, I remember, she brought two young cousins from the city – two young women, dressed real fancy, like they were going to Sunday church – and Bingo Betty made them sit one on her left, with her three little bingo cards, and one on her right, with her three little ones. And Bingo Betty herself sat in the middle with twenty-seven cards. Twenty-seven cards! Amazing. (PELAJIA *starts to descend the ladder, and* PHILOMENA, *getting excited, steps closer and closer to the edge of the roof.*) And those were the days when they still used bingo chips, not these dabbers like nowadays, and everyone came with a little margarine container full of these bingo

chips. When the game began and they started calling out the numbers, Bingo Betty was all set, like a horse at the race-track in Sudbury, you could practically see the foam sizzling and bubbling between her teeth. Bingo Betty! Bingo Betty with her beady little darting eyes, sharp as needles, and her roly-poly jiggledy-piggledy arms with their stubby little claws would go: chiga-chiga-chiga-chiga-chiga-chiga arms flying across the table smooth as angel's wings chiga-chiga-chiga-chiga-chiga-chiga-woosh! Cousin on the left chiga-chiga, cousin on the right chiga, chiga-eee! (*She narrowly misses falling off the roof and cries out in terror.*)

PELAJIA   Philomena!

PHILOMENA   (*Scrambling on hands and knees to* PELAJIA, *and coming to rest in this languorous pose, takes a moment to retain her composure and catch her breath.*) And you know, to this very day, they say that on certain nights at the bingo here in Wasy, they say you can see Bingo Betty's ghost, like a mist, hovering in the air above the bingo tables, playing bingo like it's never been played before. Or since.

PELAJIA   Amazing! She should have gone to Toronto. (*Blackout.*)

(*The same day, same time, in Wasaychigan Hill.* MARIE-ADELE STARBLANKET *is standing alone outside her house, in her yard, by her fourteen-post white picket fence. Her house is down the hill from* PELAJIA PATCHNOSE's, *close to the lake. A seagull watches her from a distance away. He is the dancer in white feathers. Through this whole section,* NANABUSH (*i.e.* NANABUSH *in the guise of the seagull*), MARIE-ADELE, *and* ZHABOONIGAN *play 'games' with each other. Only she and* ZHABOONIGAN *can see the spirit inside the bird and can sort-of (though not quite) recognise him for who he is. A doll belonging to a little girl lies on the porch floor.* MARIE-ADELE *throws little stones at the seagull.*)

MARIE-ADELE   Awus! Wee-chee-gis. Ka-tha pu-g'wun-ta oo-ta pee-wee-sta-ta-gu-mik-si. Awus! Nee. U-wi-nuk oo-ma kee-tha ee-tee-thi-mi-soo-yin holy spirit chee? Awus! Hey, maw ma-a oop-mee tay-si-thow u-wu seagull bird. I-goo-ta-poo-goo ta-poo. Nu-gu-na-wa-pa-mik. Nu-gu-na-wa-pa-mik.

NANABUSH   As-tum.

MARIE-ADELE   Neee. Moo-tha ni-gus-kee-tan tu-pi-mi-tha-an. Moo-tha oo-ta-ta-gwu-na

n'tay-yan. Chees-kwa. (*Pause.*) Ma-ti
poo-ni-mee-see i-goo-ta wee-chi-gi-seagull
bird come shit on my fence one more time
and you and anybody else look like you
cook like stew on my stove. Awus![2]

(VERONIQUE ST. PIERRE *'passes' by with
her adopted daughter* ZHABOONIGAN
PETERSON.)

VERONIQUE   Talking to the birds again,
Marie-Adele Starblanket?

MARIE-ADELE   Aha. Veronique St. Pierre.
How are you today?

VERONIQUE   Black Lady Halked's
sister-in-law Fire Minklater, Fire
Minklater's husband, just bought Fire
Minklater a car in Sudbury.

MARIE-ADELE   New?

VERONIQUE   Used. They say he bought it
from some Frenchman, some garage.
Cray-*on.*

MARIE-ADELE   Ray*mond.*

VERONIQUE   These Frenchmen are forever
selling us their used cars. And I'm sure
that's why Black Lady Halked has been
baring those big yellow teeth of hers,
smiling all over the reserve recently. She
looks like a hound about to pounce on a
mouse, she smiles so hard when she
smiles. I'd like to see her smile after plastic
surgery. Anyway. At the bingo last night
she was hinting that it wouldn't be too long
before she would be able to go to the bingo
in Espanola more frequently.
Unfortunately, a new game started and you
know how Black Lady Halked has to
concentrate when she plays bingo – her
forehead looks like corduroy, she
concentrates so hard – so I didn't get a
chance to ask her what she meant. So. Fire
Minklater has a used car. Imagine! Maybe
I can make friends with her again. NO! I
wouldn't be caught dead inside her car. Not
even if she had a brand-new Cadillac. How
are your children? All fourteen of them.

MARIE-ADELE   Okay, I guess.

VERONIQUE   Imagine. And all from one
father. Anyway. Who will take care of them
after you . . . ahem . . . I mean . . . when
you go to the hospital?

MARIE-ADELE   Eugene.

ZHABOONIGAN   Is he gentle?

MARIE-ADELE   Baby-cakes. How are you?

ZHABOONIGAN   Fine. (*Giggles.*)

VERONIQUE   She's fine. She went berry-
picking yesterday with the children.

ZHABOONIGAN   Where's Nicky?

MARIE-ADELE   Nicky's down at the beach.

ZHABOONIGAN   Why?

MARIE-ADELE   Taking care of Rose-Marie.

ZHABOONIGAN   Oh.

MARIE-ADELE   Yup.

ZHABOONIGAN   Me and Nicky, ever lots of
blueberries!

MARIE-ADELE   Me and Nicky picked lots of
blueberries.

ZHABOONIGAN   I didn't see you there.

MARIE-ADELE   When?

ZHABOONIGAN   Before today.

MARIE-ADELE   How come Nicky didn't come
home with any?

ZHABOONIGAN   Why?

(MARIE-ADELE *shrugs.* ZHABOONIGAN
*imitates this, and then pretends she is stuffing
her mouth with berries.*)

MARIE-ADELE   Aw, yous went and made
pigs of yourselves.

ZHABOONIGAN   Nicky's the pig.

MARIE-ADELE   Neee.

ZHABOONIGAN   Are you going far?

MARIE-ADELE   I'm not going far.

ZHABOONIGAN   Oh. Are you pretty?

(MARIE-ADELE *embarrassed, for a moment,
smiles and* ZHABOONIGAN *smiles, too.*)

MARIE-ADELE   You're pretty, too.
(ZHABOONIGAN *tugs at* MARIE-ADELE's
shoelaces.) Oh, Zhaboonigan. Now you have
to tie it up. I can't bend too far cuz I get
tired.

(ZHABOONIGAN *tries to tie the shoelaces
with great difficulty. When she finds she can't
she throws her arms up and screams.*)

ZHABOONIGAN   Dirty trick! Dirty trick! (*She
bites her hand and hurts herself.*)

MARIE-ADELE   Now, don't get mad.

VERONIQUE   Stop it. Stop it right now.

ZHABOONIGAN   No! No!

MARIE-ADELE   Zha. Zha. Listen. Listen.

ZHABOONIGAN   Stop it! Stop it right now!

MARIE-ADELE   Come on Zha. You and I can
name the koo-koos-suk.[3] All fourteen of
them.

ZHABOONIGAN   Okay. Here we go.
(MARIE-ADELE *leads* ZHABOONIGAN *over
to the picket fence and* VERONIQUE *follows
them.*)

ZHABOONIGAN   (*to* VERONIQUE) No.
(VERONIQUE *retreats, obviously hurt.*)

MARIE-ADELE   (*taking* ZHABOONIGAN's *hand
and counting on the fourteen posts of her*

white picket fence) Simon, Andrew, Matthew, Janie, Nicky, Ricky, Ben, Mark, Ron, Don, John, Tom, Pete, and Rose-Marie. There. (*Underneath* MARIE-ADELE's *voice,* ZHABOONIGAN *has been counting.*)

ZHABOONIGAN One, two, three, four, five, six, seven, eight, nine, ten, eleven, twelve, thirteen, fourteen. (*Giggles.*)

MARIE-ADELE Ever good counter you, Zhaboonigan.

ZHABOONIGAN Yup.

VERONIQUE This reserve, sometimes I get so sick of it. They laugh at me behind my back, I just know it. They laugh at me and Pierre St. Pierre because we don't have any children of our own. 'Imagine, they say, she's on her second husband already and she still can't have children!' They laugh at Zhaboonigan Peterson because she's crazy, that's what they call her. They can't even take care of their own people, they'd rather laugh at them. I'm the only person who would take Zhaboonigan after her parents died in that horrible car crash near Manitowaning on Saturday November 12 1964 may they rest in peace. (*She makes a quick sign of the cross without skipping a beat.*) I'm the only one around here who is kind enough. And they laugh at me. Oh, I wish I had a new stove, Marie-Adele. My stove is so old and broken down, only two elements work anymore and my oven is starting to talk back at me.

MARIE-ADELE Get it fixed.

VERONIQUE You know that Pierre St. Pierre never has any money. He drinks it all up. (*She sighs longingly.*) Some day! Anyway. Zhaboonigan here wanted to go for a swim so I thought I'd walk her down – drop by and see how you and the children are doing – it will do my weak heart good, I was saying to myself.

MARIE-ADELE Awus!

(*As she throws a pebble at the seagull on the stone,* VERONIQUE, *for a second, thinks it's her* MARIE-ADELE *is shooing away. There is a brief silence broken after a while by* ZHABOONIGAN's *little giggle.*)

VERONIQUE Anyway. I was walking down by that Big Joey's shameless little shack just this morning when guess who pokes her nose out the window but Gazelle Nataways – the nerve of that woman. I couldn't see inside but I'm sure she was only half-dressed, her hairdo was all mixed up and she said to me: 'Did you know, Veronique St. Pierre, that Little Girl Manitowabi told me her daughter, June Bug McLeod, just got back from the hospital in Sudbury where she had her tubes tied and told her that THE BIGGEST BINGO IN THE WORLD is coming to Toronto?'

MARIE-ADELE When?

VERONIQUE I just about had a heart attack.

MARIE-ADELE When?

VERONIQUE But I said to Gazelle anyway: 'Is there such a thing as a BIGGEST BINGO IN THE WORLD?' And she said: 'Yes'. And she should know about these things because she spends all her waking and sleeping hours just banging about in bed with the biggest thing on Manitoulin Island, I almost said.

MARIE-ADELE This bingo. When?

VERONIQUE She didn't know. And now that I think of it, I don't know whether to believe her. After all, who should believe a woman who wrestles around with dirt like Big Joey all night long leaving her poor babies to starve to death in her empty kitchen? But if it's true, Marie-Adele, if it's true that THE BIGGEST BINGO IN THE WORLD is coming to Toronto, I'm going and I want you to come with me.

MARIE-ADELE Well . . .

VERONIQUE I want you to come shopping with me and help me choose my new stove after I win.

MARIE-ADELE Hang on . . .

VERONIQUE They have good stoves in Toronto.

MARIE-ADELE Let's find out for sure. Then we start making plans.

VERONIQUE Maybe we should go back and ask that Gazelle Nataways about this. If she's sure.

MARIE-ADELE Maybe we should go and ask June Bug McLeod herself.

VERONIQUE We can't walk to Buzwah and I'm too old to hitch-hike.

MARIE-ADELE There's Eugene's van. He'll be home by six.

VERONIQUE I want to find out NOW. But what if people see us standing at Big Joey's door?

MARIE-ADELE What do you mean? We just knock on the door, march right in, ask the bitch, and march right out again.

VERONIQUE   Zhaboonigan dear, wait for me over there. (*She waits until* ZHABOONIGAN *is safely out of earshot and then leans over to* MARIE-ADELE *in a conspiratorial whisper.*) Anyway. You must know, Marie-Adele, that there's all kinds of women who come streaming out of that house at all hours of the day and night. I might be considered one of them. You know your youngest sister, Emily Dictionary, was seen staggering out of that house in the dead of night two nights ago?

MARIE-ADELE   Veronique St. Pierre, what Emily Dictionary does is Emily's business.

(ANNIE COOK *enters, walking fast and comes to a screeching halt.*)

ANNIE   Hallooooo! Whatchyou doin'?

VERONIQUE   (*giving* ANNIE *the baleful eye*) How are you?

ANNIE   High as a kite. Just kidding. Hi, Zha.

ZHABOONIGAN   Hi. (*Giggles. She runs toward* MARIE-ADELE, *bumping into* ANNIE *en route.*)

ANNIE   Hey, Marie-Adele.

ZHABOONIGAN   Marie-Adele. How's your cancer? (*Giggles and scurries off laughing.*)

VERONIQUE   Shkanah, Zhaboonigan, sna-ma-bah . . .[4]

MARIE-ADELE   Come on, before the post office closes for lunch.

VERONIQUE   You didn't tell me you were going to the store.

ANNIE   Well, we are. (*To* MARIE-ADELE) Hey, is Simon in? I'm sure he's got my Ricky Skaggs album. You know the one that goes (*sings*) 'Honeee!' (*calling into the house*) Yoo-hoo, Simon!

MARIE-ADELE   He's in Espanola with Eugene.

VERONIQUE   Expecting mail, Annie Cook?

ANNIE   A parcel from my daughter, Ellen, who lives with this white guy in Sudbury . . .

VERONIQUE   So I've heard.

ANNIE   And my sister here is expecting a letter, too.

VERONIQUE   From whom?

ANNIE   From the doctor, about her next check-up.

VERONIQUE   When?

MARIE-ADELE   We don't know when. Or where. Annie, let's go.

ANNIE   They say it's shaped like a record.

VERONIQUE   Maybe there'll be news in that parcel about THE BIGGEST BINGO IN THE WORLD! (*Shouts toward the lake, in a state of great excitement*) Zhaboonigan! Zhaboonigan! We're going to the store!

ANNIE   THE BIGGEST BINGO IN THE WORLD?

VERONIQUE   In Toronto. Soon. Imagine! Gazelle Nataways told me. She heard about it from Little Girl Manitowabi over in Buzwah who heard about it from her daughter June Bug McLeod who just got back from the hospital in Sudbury where she had her tubes tied. I just about had a heart attack!

ANNIE   Toronto?

MARIE-ADELE   We gotta find out for sure.

ANNIE   Right.

MARIE-ADELE   We could go to Big Joey's and ask Gazelle Nataways except Veronique St. Pierre's too scared of Gazelle.

VERONIQUE   I am not.

ANNIE   You are too.

MARIE-ADELE   We could wait and borrow Eugene's van . . .

VERONIQUE   I am not.

ANNIE   . . . drive over to Buzwah . . .

MARIE-ADELE   . . . and ask June Bug McLeod . . .

ANNIE   . . . but wait a minute! . . .

MARIE-ADELE and ANNIE   Maybe there IS news in that parcel about this BIGGEST BINGO IN THE WORLD!

MARIE-ADELE   Come on.

VERONIQUE   (*shouting toward the lake*) Zhaboonigan! Zhaboonigan!

ANNIE   And here I was so excited about the next little bingo that old priest is holding next week. Toronto! Oh, I hope it's true!

VERONIQUE   Zhaboonigan! Zhaboonigan! Zhaboonigan! Dammit! We're going to the store!

(*And the 'march' to the store begins, during which* NANABUSH, *still in the guise of the seagull, follows them and continues to play tricks, mimicking their hand movements, the movement of their mouths, etc. The three women appear each in her own spot of light at widely divergent points on the stage area.*)

ANNIE   When I go to the BIGGEST BINGO IN THE WORLD, in Toronto, I will win. For sure, I will win. If they shout the B 14 at the end, for sure I will win. The B 14 is my lucky number after all. Then I will take all my money and I will go to every record store in Toronto. I will buy every single one of Patsy Cline's records, especially the one that goes (*sings*) 'I go a-walking, after midnight', oh I go crazy every time I hear that one. Then I will buy a huge record player, the biggest one in the whole world. And then I will go to all the taverns and all the night clubs in Toronto and listen to the live bands while I drink beer quietly – not noisy and crazy like here – I will bring my daughter Ellen and her white guy from Sudbury and we will sit together. Maybe I will call Fritz the Katz and he will take me out. Maybe he will hire me as one of his singers and I can (*sings*) 'Oooh', in the background while my feet go (*shuffles her feet from side to side*) while Fritz the Katz is singing and the lights are flashing and the people are drinking beer and smoking cigarettes and dancing. Ohhh, I could dance all night with that Fritz the Katz. When I win, when I win THE BIGGEST BINGO IN THE WORLD!

MARIE-ADELE When I win THE BIGGEST BINGO IN THE WORLD, I'm gonna buy me an island. In the North Channel, right smack-dab in the middle – eem-shak min-stik[5] – the most beautiful island in the world. And my island will have lots of trees – great big bushy ones – and lots and lots and lots of sweetgrass. MMMMM! And there's gonna be pine trees and oak trees and maple trees and big stones and little stonelets – neee – and, oh yeah, this real neat picket fence, real high, long and very, very, very white. No bird shit. Eugene will live there and me and all my Starblanket kids. Yup, no more smelly, stinky old pulp and paper mill in Espanola for my Eugene – pooh! – my twelve Starblanket boys and my two Starblanket girls and me and my Eugene all living real nice and comfy right there on Starblanket Island, the most beautiful incredible goddamn island in the whole goddamn world. Eem-shak min-stik! When I win THE BIGGEST BINGO IN THE WORLD!

VERONIQUE Well, when I win the BIGGEST BINGO IN THE WORLD. No! After I win THE BIGGEST BINGO IN THE WORLD, I will go shopping for a brand-new stove. In Toronto. At the Eaton Centre. A great big stove. The kind Madame Benoit has. The kind that has the three different compartments in the oven alone. I'll have the biggest stove on the reserve. I'll cook for all the children on the reserve. I'll

adopt all of Marie-Adele Starblanket's fourteen children and I will cook for them. I'll even cook for Gazelle Nataways' poor starving babies while she's lolling around like a pig in Big Joey's smelly, sweaty bed. And Pierre St. Pierre can drink himself to death for all I care. Because I'll be the best cook on all of Manitoulin Island! I'll enter competitions. I'll go to Paris and meet what's-his-name Cordon Bleu! I'll write a cookbook called 'The Joy of Veronique St. Pierre's Cooking' and it will sell in the millions! And I will become rich and famous! Zhaboonigan Peterson will wear a mink while she eats steak tartare-de-frou-frou! Madame Benoit will be so jealous she'll suicide herself. Oh, when I win the BIGGEST BINGO IN THE WORLD!

(ZHABOONIGAN *comes running in from swimming, 'chasing' after the other three women, counting to herself and giggling.*)

ZHABOONIGAN One, two, three, four, five, six, seven, eight, nine, ten, eleven, twelve, thirteen, fourteen.

(*At the store.* ANNIE COOK, MARIE-ADELE STARBLANKET, VERONIQUE ST. PIERRE, *and* ZHABOONIGAN PETERSON *have arrived.* EMILY DICTIONARY *makes a sudden appearance, carrying a huge bag of flour on her shoulder. She is one tough lady, wearing cowboy boots, tight blue jeans, a black leather jacket – all three items worn to the seams – and she sports one black eye.*)

EMILY (*in a loud, booming voice that paralyses all movement in the room while she speaks*) Zhaboonigan Peterson! What in Red Lucifer's name ever possessed you to be hangin' out with a buncha' dizzy old dames like this? (*Bag of flour hits the floor with a 'doof'.*)

MARIE-ADELE Emily. Your eye.

EMILY Oh, bit of a tussle.

VERONIQUE With who?

EMILY None of your goddamn business.

MARIE-ADELE Emily, please.

ANNIE (*following* EMILY *about the store while* VERONIQUE *tries, in vain, to hear what she can*) I wasn't able to find out from Pelajia Patchnose or Philomena Moosemeat if Gazelle Nataways is going to Toronto this weekend with . . . Big Joey . . . they didn't know . . . Gazelle did win the bingo last night though.

EMILY Aw shit. Veronique St. Pierre, you old bag. Is it true Gazelle Nataways is takin' off for Toronto with that hunk Big Joey?

VERONIQUE It WAS you coming out of that house two nights ago. I walked by as quickly as I could . . .

EMILY . . . Shoulda come out and nailed your big floppy ears to the door . . .

VERONIQUE . . . and I would have called the police but I was too scared Big Joey might come after me and Zhaboonigan later . . .

EMILY . . . yeah, right.

ZHABOONIGAN Yeah, right.

VERONIQUE . . . and I have a weak heart, you know? Who hit you? Big Joey? Or Gazelle Nataways?

EMILY The nerve of this woman.

VERONIQUE Well?

EMILY (*calls* ZHABOONIGAN, *who is behind the counter, on the floor, playing with the merchandise.*) Zhaboonigan Peterson! Where in Red Lucifer's name is that dozy pagan?

VERONIQUE You keep hanging around that house and you're gonna end up in deep trouble. You don't know how wicked and vicious those Nataways women can get. They say there's witchcraft in their blood. And with manners like yours, Emily Dictionary, you'd deserve every hex you got.

EMILY Do I know this woman? Do I know this woman?

VERONIQUE (*During this speech,* MARIE-ADELE *and* ANNIE *sing 'Honeee' tauntingly.*) I'm sorry I have to say this in front of everyone like this but this woman has just accused my daughter of being a pagan. I didn't call her Zhaboonigan. The people on this reserve, who have nothing better to do with their time than call each other names, they called her that. Her name is Marie-Adele. Marie-Adele Peterson. You should talk. I should ask you where in Red . . . Red . . . whatever, you got a circus of a name like Emily Dictionary.

(EMILY *grabs* VERONIQUE *and throws her across the room.* VERONIQUE *goes flying right into* PELAJIA, *who has entered the store during the latter part of this speech.*)

PELAJIA Veronque St. Pierre! Control yourself or I'll hit you over the head with my hammer.

VERONIQUE (*blows a 'raspberry' in* PELAJIA's *face*) Bleah!

ANNIE No, Pelajia, no.

EMILY Go ahead, Pelajia. Make my day.

ANNIE Down, put it down.

PHILOMENA (*as she comes scurrying into the store*) I have to use the toilet. (*Running to* EMILY) I have to use your toilet. (*And goes scurrying into the toilet.*)

ANNIE (*to* PELAJIA) Remember, that's Veronique St. Pierre and if you get on the wrong side of Veronique St. Pierre she's liable to spread rumours about you all over kingdom come and you'll lose every bit of respect you got on this reserve. Don't let those pants you're wearing go to your head.

PELAJIA (*catching* ANNIE *by the arm as she tries to run away*) Annie Cook! You got a mouth on you like a helicopter.

ANNIE Veronique's mad at you, Emily, because you won't tell her what happened the other night at Big Joey's house. And she's jealous of Gazelle Nataways because Gazelle won the bingo again last night and she hopes you're the one person on this reserve who has the guts to stand up to Gazelle.

VERONIQUE (*making a lunge at* ANNIE, *who hides behind* EMILY) What's that! What's that! Ohhh! Ohhh!

ANNIE Leave me alone, you old snoop. All I wanna know is this big bingo really happening in Toronto?

VERONIQUE Annie Cook. You are a little suck.

EMILY (*to* VERONIQUE) Someday, someone oughta stick a great big piece of shit into that mouth of yours.

PELAJIA (*to* EMILY) And someday, someone ought to wash yours out with soap.

PHILOMENA (*Throwing the toilet door open, she sits there in her glory, panties down to her ankles.*) Emily Dictionary. You come back to the reserve after all these years and you strut around like you own the place. I know Veronique St. Pierre is a pain in the ass but I don't care. She's your elder and you respect her. Now shut up, all of you, and let me shit in peace. (*And slams the washroom door.* VERONIQUE, *scandalised by this, haughtily walks through toward the door, bumping into* PELAJIA *en route.*)

PELAJIA Philomena. Get your bum out here. Veronique St. Pierre is about to lose her life. (*She raises her hammer at* VERONIQUE.)

VERONIQUE (*to* PELAJIA) Put that hammer away. And go put a skirt on, for heaven's sake, you look obscene in those tight pants.

ANNIE Hit her. Go on. Hit the bitch. One good bang is all she needs.

EMILY Yeah, right. A gang-bang is more like it.

(*And a full-scale riot breaks out, during which the women throw every conceivable insult at each other.* EMILY *throws open the toilet door and* PHILOMENA *comes stomping out, pulling her panties on and joining the riot. All talk at the same time, quietly at first, but then getting louder and louder until they are all screaming.*)

PHILOMENA (*to* ANNIE) What a slime. Make promises and then you go do something else. And I always have to smile at you. What a slime. (*To* EMILY) All that tough talk. I know what's behind it all. You'll never be big enough to push me around. (*To* MARIE-ADELE) Fourteen kids! You look like a wrinkled old prune already. (*To* PELAJIA) At least I'm a woman. (*To* VERONIQUE) Have you any idea how, just how offensive, how obnoxious you are to people? And that halitosis. Pooh! You wouldn't have it if you didn't talk so much.

EMILY (*to* PHILOMENA) So damned bossy and pushy and sucky. You make me sick. Always wanting your own way. (*To* VERONIQUE) Goddamned trouble-making old crow. (*To* PELAJIA) Fuckin' self-righteous old bitch. (*To* MARIE-ADELE) Mental problems, that's what you got, princess. I ain't no baby. I'm the size of a fuckin' church. (*To* ANNIE) You slippery little slut. Brain the size of a fuckin' pea. Fuck, man, take a Valium.

VERONIQUE (*to* EMILY) You have no morals at all. You sick pervert. You should have stayed where you came from, where all the other perverts are. (*To* PELAJIA) Slow turtle. Talk big and move like Jell-o. (*To* ANNIE) Cockroach! (*To* PHILOMENA) You big phony. Flush yourself down that damned toilet of yours and shut up. (*To* MARIE-ADELE) Hasn't this slimy little reptile (*referring to* ANNIE) ever told you that sweet little Ellen of hers is really Eugene's daughter? Go talk to the birds in Sudbury and find out for yourself.

PELAJIA (*to* VERONIQUE) This reserve would be a better place without you. I'm tired of dealing with people like you. Tired.

(*To* MARIE-ADELE) You can't act that way. This here's no time to be selfish. You spoiled brat. (*To* PHILOMENA) You old fool. I thought you were coming back to help me and here you are all trussed up like a Thanksgiving turkey, putting on these white lady airs. (*To* ANNIE) Annie Cook. Move to Kapuskasing! (*To* EMILY) 'Fuck, fuck, fuck!' Us Indian women got no business talking like that.

MARIE-ADELE (*to* PELAJIA) You don't have all the answers. You can't fix everything. (*To* ANNIE) White guys. Slow down a minute and see how stupid you look. (*To* EMILY) Voice like a fog-horn. You ram through everything like a truck. You look like a truck. (*To* VERONIQUE) Some kind of insect, sticking insect claws into everybody's business. (*To* PHILOMENA) Those clothes. You look like a giant Kewpie doll. You make me laugh.

ANNIE (*to* MARIE-ADELE) You always make me feel so . . . small . . . like a little pig or something. You're no better than me. (*To* PHILOMENA) Why can't you go to bingo by yourself, you big baby? At least I got staying power. Piss off. (*To* VERONIQUE) Sucking off everybody else's life like a leech because you got nothing of your own. Pathetic old coot. Just buzz off. (*To* EMILY) You call me names. I don't call you names. You think you're too smart. Shut up. (*To* PELAJIA) 'Queen of the Indians', you think that's what you are. Well, that stupid hammer of yours doesn't scare me. Go away. Piss me off.

(*Then* PELAJIA *lifts her hammer with a big loud 'Woah!' And they come to a sudden dead stop. Pause. Then one quick final volley, all at once, loudest of all.*)

PHILOMENA (*to* ANNIE) You slimy buck-toothed drunken worm!

EMILY (*to* VERONIQUE) Fuckin' instigator!

VERONIQUE (*to* MARIE-ADELE) Clutching, clinging vine!

PELAJIA (*to* VERONIQUE) Evil no-good insect!

MARIE-ADELE (*to* VERONIQUE) Maggot-mouthed vulture!

ANNIE (*to* PHILOMENA) Fat-assed floozy, get off the pot!

(MARIE-ADELE, *stung to the quick, makes a vicious grab for* VERONIQUE *by the throat. In a split-second, all freeze. Lights out in store interior. Lights on* ZHABOONIGAN, *who has run out in fright during the riot, outside the store.* NANABUSH, *still in his guise as the seagull, makes a grab at* ZHABOONIGAN. ZHABOONIGAN *begins talking to the bird.*)

ZHABOONIGAN   Are you gentle? I was not little. Maybe. Same size as now. Long ago it must be? You think I'm funny? Shhh. I know who you are. There, there. Boys. White boys. Two. Ever nice white wings, you. I was walking down the road to the store. They ask me if I want ride in car. Oh, I was happy I said, 'Yup'. Took me far away. Ever nice ride. Dizzy. They took all my clothes off me. Put something up inside me here. (*Pointing to her crotch, underneath her dress*) Many, many times. Remember. Don't fly away. Don't go. I saw you before. There, there. It was a . . . screwdriver. They put the screwdriver inside me. Here. Remember. Ever lots of blood. The two white boys. Left me in the bush. Alone. It was cold. And then. Remember. Zhaboonigan. Everybody calls me Zhaboonigan. Why? It means needle. Zhaboonigan. Going-through-thing. Needle Peterson. Going-through-thing Peterson. That's me. It was the screwdriver. Nice. Nice. Nicky Ricky Ben Mark. (*As she counts, with each name, feathers on the birds' wing.*) Ever nice. Nice white birdie you.

(*During this last speech,* NANABUSH *goes through agonising contortions. Then lights change instantly back to the interior of the store. The six women spring back into action.* PHILOMENA *stomps back into the toilet.*)

MARIE-ADELE   (*to* VERONIQUE) Fine. And the whole reserve knows the only reason you ever adopted Zhaboonigan is for her disability cheque.

ANNIE   You fake saint.

(ANNIE, MARIE-ADELE, *and* EMILY *start pushing* VERONIQUE, *round-robin, between the three of them, laughing tauntingly until* VERONIQUE *is almost reduced to tears.*)

VERONIQUE   (*almost weeping*) Bastards. The three of you.

(MARIE-ADELE *grabs* VERONIQUE *by the throat and lifts her fist to punch her in the face. But the exertion causes her body to weaken, almost to the point of collapse, from her illness. At this point,* PHILOMENA *emerges from the toilet.*)

PHILOMENA   (*crinkling her nose*) Emily. Your toilet.

WOMEN   Shhh.

MARIE-ADELE   (*holding her waist, reeling, barely audible*) Oh, shit.

PHILOMENA   I can't get it to flush.

WOMEN   Shhhh.

PELAJIA   (*rushing to* MARIE-ADELE) Marie-Adele. You're not well.

MARIE-ADELE   (*screams*) Don't touch me. (*Complete silence from all while* MARIE-ADELE *weaves and struggles to keep herself from collapsing.* ANNIE *scurries off stage, to the back part of the store, where the post office would be.*)

EMILY   (*to* VERONIQUE) You f'in' bitch!

PHILOMENA   What did I just tell you? Who did that to your eye?

VERONIQUE   Big Joey.

EMILY   (*to* VERONIQUE) Look here, you old buzzard. I'll tell you a few things. You see this fist? You see these knuckles? You wanna know where they come from? Ten years. Every second night for ten long ass-fuckin' years that goddamn Yellowknife asshole Henry Dadzinanare come home to me so drunk his eyes was spittin' blood like Red Lucifer himself and he'd beat me purple.

VERONIQUE   I wish I'd been there to see it all.

EMILY   Yeah, scumbag. I wish you'd been there to watch me learn to fight back like you've never seen a woman fight for her life before. Take a look at this eye. I earned it, Veronique St. Pierre, I earned it.

PHILOMENA   Henry Dadzinanare, Big Joey. They're all the same. Emily, use your brains.

EMILY   Use my brains. Yeah, right. I used them alright the night he came at me with an axe and just about sank it into my spine, I grabbed one bag, took one last look at the kids and walked out of his life forever.

ANNIE   (*from off stage.*) And she took the bus to San Francisco.

PHILOMENA   And gets herself mixed up with a motorcycle gang, for God's sake.

EMILY   (*now addressing all in the room*) Rosabella Baez, Hortensia Colorado, Liz Jones, Pussy Commanda. And me. The best. 'Rose and the Rez Sisters', that's us. And man, us sisters could weave knuckle magic.

VERONIQUE   So why did you bother coming back?

PHILOMENA   You stay out of this.

EMILY   Come back to the Rez for a visit, get all wedged up with that hunk Big Joey one night . . . (*grunts.*)

PHILOMENA   I give up.

EMILY   . . . and I was hooked. Couldn't leave. Settlin' back on a coupla beers with Big Joey the other night when Gazelle Nataways come sashayin' in like she's got half the Rez squished down the crack of her ass. She was high. I was high. Hell, we were all high. Get into a bit of a discussion, when she gets me miffed and I let fly, she let fly, Big Joey let fly, misses that nympho and lands me one in the eye instead.

VERONIQUE   So it was Big Joey.

EMILY   Damn rights. And that's as close as he got cuz I put him out for the night right then and there. Just one of these. (*Brandishing her fist*) One. That's all it took.

(VERONIQUE *runs off to look for* ZHABOONIGAN.)

ANNIE and PHILOMENA   Emily Dictionary. (PHILOMENA *with exasperation,* ANNIE *with adulation, from off stage.*)

ANNIE   You're amazing!

EMILY   Not Dictionary. Dadzinanare. Henry Dadzinanare. The man who made me learn to fight back. Never let a man raise one dick hair against me since.

VERONIQUE   (*calling out to* ZHABOONIGAN) Zhaboonigan. Don't you be talking to the birds like that again. You're crazy enough as it is.

ANNIE   (*as she comes running back in from the post office with her parcel, already unwrapped, and two letters, one for herself, already unfolded, and one still in its envelope*) See? I told you. It's a record. Patsy Cline.

PHILOMENA   Never mind Patsy Cline.

ANNIE   (*as she hands* MARIE-ADELE *the letter in the envelope*) Hey, Marie-Adele.

EMILY   Read your friggin' letter, Annie Cook.

ANNIE   Listen to this. (ZHABOONIGAN *walks back in as* ANNIE *reads her own letter very haltingly.*) Dear Mom: Here is the record you wanted. I thought you'd like the picture of Patsy Cline on the cover. (ANNIE *shows off her record.*) See? It's Patsy Cline. (*Returns to her letter.*) I also thought you might like to know that there is a bingo called THE BIGGEST BINGO IN THE WORLD. Can you fu . . . ture that?

EMILY   (*who has been looking over* ANNIE's *shoulder*) Feature. Feature.

ANNIE   Can you . . . feature . . . that? . . . that's coming to Toronto. The jackpot is $500,000. It's on Saturday, September 8. Ray*mond*'s Mom was in Toronto. Aunt Philomena will hit the roof when she hears this. Much love, your daughter Ellen. (ANNIE *announces the Bingo once more.*)

(*There is a brief electric silence followed by an equally electric scream from all the women. Even* ZHABOONIGAN *screams. Excitement takes over completely.*)

VERONIQUE   So it's true! It's true!

PHILOMENA   The Espanola bingo. Piffle. Mere piffle.

VERONIQUE   My new stove!

PHILOMENA   My new toilet! White! Spirit white!

EMILY   (*grabbing* ZHABOONIGAN *and dancing around the room with her*) I'd take the money, come back to the Rez, beat the shit out of Gazelle Nataways and take you down to Frisco with me. Whaddaya think?

ZHABOONIGAN   Yup.

MARIE-ADELE   (*in the background, where she has been reading her letter quietly to herself*) September 10.

ANNIE   (*taking the letter from* MARIE-ADELE) Look, Pelajia. Marie-Adele's tests are in Toronto just two days after THE BIGGEST. (*There is a brief embarrassed silence.*)

MARIE-ADELE   Kill two birds with one stone. (*To* NANABUSH) I wanna go. (*To* PELAJIA *and* PHILOMENA) I wanna go.

VERONIQUE   Goood!

EMILY   (*mimicking* VERONIQUE) Goood! Now how the hell are you guys gonna get down to Toronto? You're all goddamn welfare cases.

ANNIE   Fire Minklater.

VERONIQUE   Mary, mother of Jesus! I refuse, I absolutely refuse to be seen anywhere near that sorceress! We'll chip in and rent a car.

EMILY   Zhaboonigan Peterson here gonna chauffeur you down?

ZHABOONIGAN   Yup.

VERONIQUE   Don't you make fun of my daughter.

EMILY   What kind of stove you gonna buy, Veronique St. Pierre? Westinghouse? Electrolux? Yamaha? Kawasaki?

VERONIQUE   Oh my god, Marie-Adele, I never thought about it. They will have so many stoves in Toronto, I'll get confused.

ANNIE   If you go to Toronto and leave Wasy for even one day, Emily, you'll lose Big Joey forever . . .

VERONIQUE   To that witch!

ANNIE   . . . and then whose thighs will you have to wrestle around with in the dead of night? You'll dry up, get all puckered up and pass into ancient history.

EMILY   Annie Cook. I don't know what the fuck you're yatterin' on about now but I'd like to hear you say two words of French to that white guy in Sudbury you're so damn proud of.

ANNIE   Oh my god, Marie-Adele, she's right. I won't know what to say to this Ray*mond*. I've never met him. I can't speak French. All I can say in French is Ray*mond* and Bon Bon and I don't even know what that means. I can't go and live with them, not even after I win THE BIGGEST BINGO IN THE WORLD. What am I gonna do? (*She collapses on the floor and rolls around for a bit.*)

EMILY   And Philomena Moosemeat's so fulla shit she'd need five toilets to get it all out.

PHILOMENA   (*going at* EMILY) And just who do you think you're talking to, Miss Dictionary, just who the hell do you think you're talking to? (*With a resounding belly butt from* EMILY, *they begin to wrestle.*)

PELAJIA   (*Banging her hammer on the counter*) Alright, alright. It's obvious we've got a problem here.

EMILY   (*throwing* PHILOMENA *off to the side*) I'll say.

MARIE-ADELE   It's true. None of us has any money.

(*But* VERONIQUE, *standing behind* PELAJIA, *winks at the others and makes a hand motion indicating that* PELAJIA, *for one, does have money. All the other women slowly surround* PELAJIA. *But* PELAJIA *catches the drift and quickly collects herself to meet the onslaught. During* PELAJIA's *speech, the women respond at period intervals with a 'yoah' and 'hmmm', etc., as when a chief speaks at a council meeting.*)

PELAJIA   I say we all march down to the Band Office and ask the Band Council for a loan that will pay for the trip to this bingo. I know how to handle that tired old chief. He and I have been arguing about paved roads for years now. I'll tell him we'll build paved roads all over the reserve with our prize money. I'll tell him the people will

stop drinking themselves to death because they'll have paved roads to walk on. I'll tell him there'll be more jobs because the people will have paved roads to drive to work on. I'll tell him the people will stop fighting and screwing around and Nanabush will come back to us because he'll have paved roads to dance on. There's enough money in there for everyone, I'll say. And if he doesn't lend us the money, I'll tell him I'm packing my bags and moving to Toronto tomorrow.

EMILY   That oughta twist his arm but good.

PELAJIA   And if he still says no, I'll bop him over the head with my hammer and we'll attack the accountant and take the money ourselves. Philomena, we're going to Toronto!

(*The seven women have this grand and ridiculous march to the band office, around the set and all over the stage area, with* PELAJIA *leading them forward heroically, the hammer just a-swinging in the air.* NANABUSH *trails merrily along in the rear of the line. They reach the 'band office' standing in one straight line square in front of the audience. The 'invisible' chief 'speaks': cacophonous percussion for about seven beats, the women listening more and more incredulously. Finally, the percussion comes to a dead stop.*)

PELAJIA   No? (PELAJIA *raises her hammer to hit the 'invisible' chief,* NANABUSH *shrugs a 'don't ask me, I don't know',* EMILY *fingers a 'fuck you, man'.*)

(*Blackout.*)

Act II

All seven women are holding a meeting in the basement of PELAJIA PATCHNOSE's *house. This is a collection of chairs and stools off to the side of the stage area. The only light comes from an old, beat-up twilight pole lamp. Some have tea,* EMILY *and* ANNIE *a beer.*

VERONIQUE   We should have met at the priest's house.

PELAJIA   No! We're gonna work this out on our own. Right here. Emily Dictionary, you chair. (*And she lends* EMILY *her hammer.*)

VERONIQUE   She's good at ordering people around.

PHILOMENA   Shut up.

EMILY   First. When are we leaving? (*She bangs the hammer regularly throughout the meeting.*)

VERONIQUE   How much is the trip going to cost?

EMILY   When are we leaving?

PHILOMENA   How long to Toronto?

ANNIE   Four hours.

EMILY   When are we leaving?

PHILOMENA   The only human being who can make it in four hours is Annie Cook.

VERONIQUE   I'm not dying on the highway.

PHILOMENA   Eight hours.

PELAJIA   No way we're gonna stop at every toilet on the highway.

MARIE-ADELE   Six hours. Eugene's driven there.

VERONIQUE   Maybe we can borrow his van.

ANNIE   Maybe we can borrow Big Joey's van. (*A quick little aside to* PELAJIA) Hey, can I have another beer?

PELAJIA   No.

VERONIQUE   What about Gazelle Nataways?

EMILY   We're gonna borrow his van, not his buns, for Chris'sakes.

MARIE-ADELE   The only thing we have to pay for is gas.

ANNIE   Philomena's got gas.

EMILY   Right! Six hours. Eugene's van.

MARIE-ADELE   We still don't know when we're leaving.

PHILOMENA   Bingo's on Saturday night.

ANNIE   Leave Saturday morning.

VERONIQUE   Oh! I'll be so tired for the bingo. I'll get confused. Wednesday. Rest on Thursday.

ANNIE   And rest again on Friday? Too much resting. I can't go for that.

PELAJIA   And we can't afford such a long stay.

PHILOMENA   Where are we gonna stay?

EMILY   Whoa! (*Pause.*)

PELAJIA   Friday night.

EMILY   Right. Leave Friday night. Next.

PHILOMENA   Coming home right after the bingo.

MARIE-ADELE   And leave me behind? Remember my tests Monday morning.

EMILY   Right. Monday noon, we come back. Next.

VERONIQUE   Don't go so fast. My mind is getting confused.

EMILY   Goood! Next.

MARIE-ADELE   Where are we gonna stay?

ANNIE   The Silver Dollar!

MARIE-ADELE   You can't stay there.

ANNIE   There's rooms upstairs.

PELAJIA   You wanna sleep in a whorehouse?

VERONIQUE   Zhaboonigan! Don't listen to this part.

PELAJIA   There's room at my son's.

PHILOMENA   Two washrooms! He's got a wonderful education.

EMILY   Next.

VERONIQUE   Who's going to drive?

ANNIE   Emily. She can drive anything.

VERONIQUE   I believe it.

ANNIE   But I can drive, too.

VERONIQUE   Oh my god.

ANNIE   Long as I don't have to drive in the city. You drive the city.

VERONIQUE   Me?

ANNIE and MARIE-ADELE   No!

PELAJIA   Long as you don't drive too fast, Annie Cook.

PHILOMENA   And we'll pack a lunch for the trip and then eat in restaurants. Chinese.

PELAJIA   Can't afford it. We chip in, buy groceries and cook at my son's.

VERONIQUE   I'll give $10.

EMILY   You old fossil. You want us to starve?

PHILOMENA $50 a day. Each.

EMILY   Philomena Moosemeat! That's $50 times seven people times four days. That's over $1,000 worth of groceries.

VERONIQUE   Imagine!

MARIE-ADELE   Okay. Veronique St. Pierre. You cook. $20 apiece. Right?

EMILY   Right. Next.

PHILOMENA   Anybody writing this down?

ANNIE   I'm gonna go to Sam the Recordman.

MARIE-ADELE   I'll make the grocery list.

PELAJIA   How much for gas?

VERONIQUE   (*still in dreamland over the groceries*) $1,000!

PHILOMENA   (*flabbergasted*) Nooo! You goose.

ANNIE $40.

EMILY $150. Period. Next.

PELAJIA   We got ten days to find this money.

MARIE-ADELE   What's it cost to get into the bingo?

VERONIQUE   All the Indians in the world will be there!

PHILOMENA $50

ANNIE   And we're gonna be the only Indians there.

PELAJIA   Silence. (*There is a long, thoughtful silence, broken only after awhile by a scream from* ZHABOONIGAN. NANABUSH *has knocked her off her stool. The women laugh.*) Can't think of anything else.

PHILOMENA   Add it up. (*She hands a pencil to* EMILY.)

EMILY   (*calculates*) $1,400. You guys need $200 each.

VERONIQUE   Where am I going to get $400?

EMILY   Make it. End of meeting.

And the women start their fundraising activities with a vengeance. The drive is underlined by a wild rhythmic beat from the musician, one that gets wilder and wilder with each successive beat, though always underpinned by this persistent, almost dance-like pulse. The movement of the women covers the entire stage area, and like the music, gets wilder and wilder, until by the end it is as if we are looking at an insane eight-ring circus, eight-ring because through all this, NANABUSH, *as the seagull, has a holiday, particularly with* MARIE-ADELE's *lines of laundry, as* MARIE-ADELE *madly strings one line of laundry after another all over the set, from* PELAJIA's *roof to* EMILY's *store, etc. For the garage sale,* ANNIE *sells off* PELAJIA's *lamp, chairs, etc., so that* PELAJIA's *'basement' simply dissolves into the madness of the fundraising drive.*

Beat one

PELAJIA *is hammering on the roof.* EMILY *is at the store cash register and rings up each sale as* ANNIE, PHILOMENA, MARIE-ADELE, ZHABOONIGAN, *and* VERONIQUE *stand shoulder to shoulder and pass the following from one side of the stage to the other: seven large sacks marked 'FLOUR', two giant tubs marked 'LARD', one bushel of apples.*

Beat two

ZHABOONIGAN *brings a small table on and puts it stage left.* ANNIE *brings a table on and puts it stage right.* PHILOMENA *brings a basket full of beer bottles to centre and empties it. She has a baby attached to her.* VERONIQUE *comes on with cloth and Windex and starts 'cleaning windows' rhythmically, listening to whatever gossip she can hear.* MARIE-ADELE *strings two lines of clothing across the stage.* PELAJIA *hammers on her roof.* EMILY *brings on several empty beer cases and fills them with* PHILOMENA's *bottles.*

Beat three

ZHABOONIGAN *brings in six quarts of blueberries and then takes over window cleaning*

from VERONIQUE. ANNIE *brings on a basket of old clothes and a broken kitchen chair.* PHILOMENA *brings on another basket full of beer bottles, empties it. She now has two babies attached to her, like a fungus.* EMILY *fills beer cases rapidly, expertly.* PELAJIA *gets down off roof, hammering everything until she is on hands and knees, hammering the floor.* MARIE-ADELE *strings third and fourth lines of laundry across the stage.* VERONIQUE *comes in burdened with seven apple pies and puts them on* ANNIE's *table.*

Beat four

PELAJIA *hammers as she crawls across the floor.* ZHABOONIGAN *washes windows like a person possessed.* EMILY *runs and rings up a sale on the cash register and then brings on more empty beer cases and loads them up.* PHILOMENA *brings on a third load of bottles. Three babies are now attached to her.* ANNIE *brings on an old twilight pole lamp and an old record player, which she opens and stacks alongside the rest of her stuff.* ANNIE *and* EMILY *sing a line of their song with very bad harmony.* MARIE-ADELE *strings fifth and sixth lines of laundry across stage.* VERONIQUE *comes on with seven loaves of bread and puts them neatly by the pies.*

Beat five

PELAJIA *hammers as she crawls across the floor, hammering everything in sight. The women protect their poor feet.* ZHABOONIGAN *washes windows even faster; she's starting to cry.* EMILY *and* PHILOMENA *work together filling the empty beer cases as fast as they can.* EMILY *runs to the register, rings in seven sales and sings a bit of song with* ANNIE, *better this time.* PHILOMENA *now has four kids attached to her body.* ANNIE *comes on with a small black and white TV with rabbit ears and an old toaster.* VERONIQUE *comes on with six dozen buns and dumps them out of their tins all over the table.* PELAJIA *hammers faster and faster.* ZHABOONIGAN *is now working like a maniac and is sobbing.* MARIE-ADELE *strings seventh and eighth lines of laundry across stage.*

Beat six

EMILY *goes to cash register and tallies their earnings; she works the register with tremendous speed and efficiency all this beat.*

ZHABOONIGAN *continues washing windows.*
PHILOMENA *sticks a sign in beer bottles:*
'World's Biggest Bottle Drive'. She now has five
babies attached to her. VERONIQUE *sticks a*
sign on her table: 'World's Biggest Bake Sale'.
ANNIE *sticks a sign up around her stuff:*
'World's Biggest Garage Sale'. MARIE-ADELE
sticks a sign up on ZHA*'s table: 'Big Blueberries*
and Laundry While You Wait'. PELAJIA *begins*
hammering the air. She may have lost her
marbles.

Beat seven

EMILY   Whoa!

The 'music' comes to a sudden stop. The women
all collapse. The women look at each other.
They then quickly clear the stage of everything
they've brought on as PELAJIA *speaks,*
consulting her list. By the end of PELAJIA*'s*
speech, the stage area is clear once more, except
for a microphone stand that one of the women
has brought on as part of the 'clean-up'
activities.

PELAJIA   Bottle drive. Ten cents a bottle,
24 bottles a case, equals two dollars and
40 cents. 777 bottles collected divided by
24 is 32 cases and nine singles that's
32 times $2.40 equals $77.70. Blueberries
equals $90. Good pickin' Zha and the
Starblanket kids. Washing windows at $5.00
a house times 18 houses. Five eights are
40, carry the four and add the five is
90 bucks less two on account of that cheap
Gazelle Nataways only gave three dollars.
That's $88. Household repairs is four roofs
including the Chief's and one tiled floor is
$225. Garage sale brung in $246.95, and
bake sale equals $83 after expenses, we
make 110 bucks on doing laundry, 65 bucks
babysitting, 145 from Emily doing a double
shift at the store and I have generously
donated $103 from my savings. That brings
us to a grand total of $1233.65. So!

(EMILY *and* ANNIE *move forward as the*
music starts up. They are lit only by tacky
floor flood-lighting, and are, in effect, at the
Anchor Inn, Little Current. EMILY *speaks*
into the microphone.)

EMILY   Thank-you. Thank-you, ladies and
gentlemen. I thank you very much. And
now for the last song of the night, ladies
and gents, before we hit the road. A song
that's real special to me in my heart. A

song I wrote in memory of one Rosabella
Baez, a Rez Sister from way back. And Rose
baby, if you're up there tonight, I hope
you're listenin' in. Cuz it's called: 'I'm
Thinkin' of You'. Here goes . . .

(EMILY *and* ANNIE *grab their microphones;*
EMILY *sings lead,* ANNIE *sings backup. And*
it's 'country' to the hilt.)

I'm thinkin' of you every moment,
As though you were here by my side;
I'll always remember the good times,
So darlin' please come back to me.

I'm dreamin' of you every night,
That we were together again;
If time can heal up our partin'
Then love can remove all this pain.

(*Instrumental – dance break.*)

If love is the secret of livin',
Then give me that love, shinin' light;
When you are again by my side,
Then livin' will once more be right.

(*The audience claps.* EMILY *says,*
'Thank-you'. And then she and ANNIE *join*
the other women, who have, during the
song, loaded themselves, their suitcases,
and their lunches into the 'van'. This van
consists of three battered old van seats
stuck to the walls of the theatre, on either
side and up high. The back seat is on the
stage left side of the theatre and the other
two are on the other side, the middle seat
of the van towards the back of the theatre,
the front seat, complete with detachable
steering wheel, just in front and stage right
of the stage area. Each seat is lit by its own
light.)

EMILY   How much did me and Annie take in
singin' at the Anchor Inn?
PELAJIA $330 at the door.
MARIE-ADELE   Solid packed house, eh?
Shoulda charged more.
ANNIE   Fifty bucks for the oom-chi-cha
machine. Twenty bucks for Ronnie's
guitar. That's our only costs.
EMILY   Ha! We're laughin'.

(*A capella reprise of a verse of their song,*
which fades into highway sounds, and they
drive, for a few moments, in silence.
   In the van, driving down the highway to
Toronto, at night. The women have intimate
conversations, one on one, while the rest are
asleep or seated at the other end of the van.

ANNIE *is driving.* EMILY *sits beside her listening to her Walkman, while* MARIE-ADELE *is 'leaning' over* ANNIE'*s shoulder from her place in the middle seat.* VERONIQUE *sits beside* MARIE-ADELE, *sleeping.* PELAJIA *and* PHILOMENA *are in the very back seat with* ZHABOONIGAN *between them.*)

MARIE-ADELE   Nee, Annie, not so fast. (*Pause.* ANNIE *slows down.*) So. You couldn't get Ellen and Raymond to come along? I'd like to meet this Raymond someday.

ANNIE   (*angrily insisting on the correct pronunciation*) Raymond! Ellen says he's got a whole library full of cassette tapes.

MARIE-ADELE   Annie. You ever think about getting married again?

ANNIE   Not really. I can hear the band at the Silver Dollar already.

MARIE-ADELE   Do you still think about . . . Eugene?

ANNIE   What're you talkin' about? Of course, I think about him, he's my brother-in-law, ain't he?

MARIE-ADELE   He made his choice.

ANNIE   Yeah. He picked you.

MARIE-ADELE   Annie. I never stole him off you.

ANNIE   Drop dead. Shit! I forgot to bring that blouse. I mean, in case I sing. Shit.

MARIE-ADELE   If I'm gone and Eugene if he starts drinkin' again. I see you going for him.

ANNIE   Why would I bother? I had my chance twenty years ago. Christ!

MARIE-ADELE   Twenty years ago, I was there.

ANNIE   What would I want fourteen kids for?

MARIE-ADELE   That's exactly what I'm scared of. I don't want them kids to be split up. You come near Eugene you start drinking, messing things up, me not here, I come back and don't matter where you are . . .

ANNIE   I don't want him. I don't want him. I don't want him. I don't want him. I don't want him.

EMILY   Put us all in the fuckin' ditch!

PELAJIA   Hey, watch your language up there.

ANNIE   Shit! I don't care. There's nothing more to say about it. Why don't you take your pills and go to sleep.

(PELAJIA *and* PHILOMENA *begin talking.*)

PHILOMENA   September 8 again.

PELAJIA   Hmmm? What about September 8?

PHILOMENA   You don't remember?

PELAJIA   What?

PHILOMENA   How could you?

PELAJIA   Mama died?

PHILOMENA   No! Remember?

PELAJIA   I can't remember. Got so much on my mind. So many things to forget.

ZHABOONIGAN   (*to* PHILOMENA) You like me?

PHILOMENA   Yes, Zhaboonigan. I like you.

ZHABOONIGAN   I like the birdies.

PHILOMENA   You like talking to the birdies?

ZHABOONIGAN   Yup. (*She falls asleep.*)

PHILOMENA   Zhaboonigan . . . Sometimes I wonder . . .

PELAJIA   It's dark . . . warm . . . quiet . . .

PHILOMENA   Toronto. Had a good job in Toronto. Yeah. Had to give it all up. Yeah. Cuz mama got sick. Philomena Margaret Moosetail. Real live secretary in the garment district. He'd come in and see my boss. Nice man, I thought. That big, red, fish-tail Caddy. Down Queen Street. He liked me. Treated me like a queen. Loved me. Or I thought he did. I don't know. Got pregnant anyway. Blond, blue-eyed, six foot two. And the way he smelled. God! His wife walks in on us. (*Long silence.*) He left with her. (*Long silence.*) I don't even know to this day if it was a boy or a girl. I'm getting old. That child would be . . . 28 . . . 28 years old. September 8. You know what I'm gonna do with that money if I win? I'm gonna find a lawyer. Maybe I can find that child. Maybe I wouldn't even have to let him . . . her . . . know who I am. I just . . . want to see . . . who . . .

PELAJIA   I hope you win.

(ANNIE *and* EMILY, *at the front of the van with* ANNIE *driving, are laughing and singing, 'I'm a little Indian who loves fry bread'. From time to time, they sneak each other a sip of this little bottle of whiskey* ANNIE *has hidden away inside her purse.*)

I'm a little Indian who loves fry bread,
Early in the morning and when I go to
  bed;
Some folks say I'm crazy in the head,
Cuz I'm a little Indian who loves fry
  bread.

Now, some folks say I've put on a pound
or two,

My jeans don't fit the way they used to
do;
But I don't care, let the people talk,
Cuz if I don't get my fry bread, you'll hear
me squawk.

ANNIE So tell me. What's it like to go to a
big bar like . . . I mean like . . . the Silver
Dollar.

EMILY Lotta Nishnawbs.[6]

ANNIE (*disappointed*) Yeah? Is the music
good?

EMILY Country rock.

ANNIE (*screams gleefully*) Yee-haw! Maybe
the band will ask me up to sing, eh? I'll
sing something fast.

EMILY You would, too.

ANNIE (*sings real fast*) 'Well, it's 40 below
and I don't give a fuck, got a heater in my
truck and I'm off to the rodeo. Woof!'
Something like that.

EMILY Yup. That's pretty fast.

ANNIE Hey. Maybe Fritz the Katz will be
there. Never know. Might get laid, too, eh?
Remember Room 20 at the Anchor Inn?
Oh, that Fritz! Sure like singin' with him.
Crazy about the way . . .

EMILY (*Starts singing Patsy Cline's famous
'Crazy . . . Crazy for Feelin' so Lonely . . . '
all the way through* ANNIE'*s next speech.*)

ANNIE . . . he stands there with his guitar
and his ten-gallon hat. Is that what you call
them hats? You know the kind you wear
kind of off to the side like this? That's what
he does. And then he winks at me. (*Sings*)
'Crazy . . . ' Oooh, I love, just love the way
the lights go woosh woosh in your eyes and
kinda' wash all over your body. Me
standing there shuffling my feet side to
side, dressed real nice and going (*sings*)
'oooh darlin' . . . ' with my mike in my
hand just so. Oh! And the sound of that
band behind me. And Fritz. (*Sings*) 'Crazy,
crazy for feelin' so lonely . . . '

EMILY Yeah. You look good on stage.

ANNIE Yeah?

EMILY How come you're so keen on that
guy anyway?

ANNIE Sure Veronique St. Pierre isn't just
pretending to be asleep back there? (EMILY
and MARIE-ADELE *check* VERONIQUE *in the
middle seat.*)

MARIE-ADELE Nah. Out like a lamp.

EMILY Hey, we'll get her drunk at the
Silver Dollar and leave her passed out
under some table. Take two beers to do
that.

ANNIE Hey. Too bad Big Joey had to come
back from Toronto before we got there, eh?

EMILY Man! That dude's got buns on him
like no other buns on the face of God's
entire creation. Whooo! Not to mention a
dick that's bigger than a goddamn
breadbox. (ANNIE *screams gleefully.*) What
about Fritz? What's his look like?

ANNIE (*after an awkward pause*) He's
Jewish, you know.

EMILY (*laughing raucously*) World's first
Jewish country singer!

ANNIE Don't laugh. Those Jews make a lot
of money, you know.

EMILY Not all of them.

ANNIE Fritz buys me jeans and things. I'm
gonna be one of them Jewish princesses.

EMILY What's wrong with being an Indian
princess?

ANNIE Aw, these white guys. They're nicer
to their women. Not like Indian guys.
Screw you, drink all your money, and leave
you flat on your ass.

EMILY Yeah, right. Apple Indian Annie. Red
on the outside. White on the inside.

ANNIE Emily!

EMILY Keep your eye on the road.

ANNIE Good ol' Highway 69.

EMILY Hey. Ever 69 with Fritz?

MARIE-ADELE Neee.

ANNIE White guys don't make you do things
to them. You just lie there and they do it all
for you. Ellen's real happy with her
Raymond. You can tell the way she sounds
on the phone. Maybe someday I'll just take
off with a guy like Fritz.

EMILY Then what? Never come back to the
Rez? (ANNIE *is cornered.* EMILY *then slaps
her playfully on the arm.*) Hey. Know what?
(*Sings*)
When I die, I may not go to heaven,
I don't know if they let Indians in;
If they don't, just let me go to Wasy, lord,
Cuz Wasy is as close as I've been.

ANNIE Lots of white people at this Silver
Dollar?

EMILY Sometimes. Depends.

ANNIE How much for beer there?

EMILY Same as up here. Nah! Don't need
money, Annie Cook. You just gotta know
how to handle men. Like me and the Rez
Sisters down in Frisco.

ANNIE Yeah?

EMILY I'll take care of them.

ANNIE Maybe we can find a party, eh?
Maybe with the band.

411

EMILY Whoa! Slow down, Annie Cook! Easy on the gas!

MARIE-ADELE Annie!

(*Pow. Blackout. They have a flat tire. Everything now happens in complete darkness.*)

VERONIQUE Bingo!

PHILOMENA What was that? What happened?

ANNIE I don't know. Something just went 'poof'!

EMILY Alright. Everybody out. We got a fuckin' flat.

(*They all climb out of the van.*)

VERONIQUE Oh my god! We'll never get to the bingo.

ZHABOONIGAN Pee pee.

PELAJIA I can't fix a flat tire.

ANNIE Emily can.

PELAJIA Get the jack. Spare tire.

ANNIE Philomena's wearing one.

ZHABOONIGAN Pee pee.

PHILOMENA This is all your fault, Annie Cook.

MARIE-ADELE It's in the back.

ANNIE So what do we do?

PELAJIA What's the matter with Zha?

PHILOMENA Gotta make pee pee.

VERONIQUE I knew there was something wrong with this van the moment I set eyes on it. I should have taken the bus.

PHILOMENA Oh shut up. Quack, quack, quack.

ANNIE Don't look at me. It's not my fault the tires are all bald.

PHILOMENA Nobody's blaming you.

ANNIE But you just did.

PHILOMENA Quack, quack, quack.

VERONIQUE Where are we?

ANNIE The Lost Channel. This is where you get off.

VERONIQUE (*groans*) Ohhh!

EMILY Yeah, right.

PHILOMENA Shhh!

PELAJIA Jack's not working too well.

EMILY Okay. Everybody. Positions.

VERONIQUE Not me. My heart will collapse.

EMILY You wanna play bingo?

VERONIQUE (*groans*) Ohhhh!

ANNIE Hurry up! Hurry up!

EMILY Okay. One, two, three lift.
(*Everybody lifts and groans.*)

PELAJIA Put the jack in there.

(*All lift, except* MARIE-ADELE *and* ZHABOONIGAN, *who wander off into the moonlit darkness. Dim light on them.*)

ZHABOONIGAN Ever dark.

MARIE-ADELE You'll be fine, Zhaboonigan.

(*Suddenly a nighthawk –* NANABUSH, *now in dark feathers – appears, darting in the night.*)

ZHABOONIGAN The birdies!

MARIE-ADELE Yes, a birdie.

ZHABOONIGAN Black wings!

(MARIE-ADELE *begins talking to the bird, almost if she were talking to herself. Quietly, at first, but gradually – as the bird begins attacking her – growing more and more hysterical, until she is shrieking, flailing, and thrashing about insanely.*)

MARIE-ADELE Who are you? What do you want? My children? Eugene? No! Oh no! Me? Not yet. Not yet. Give me time. Please. Don't. Please don't. Awus! Get away from me. Eugene! Awus! You fucking bird! Awus! Awus! Awus! Awus! Awus!

(*And she has a total hysterical breakdown.* ZHABOONIGAN, *at first, attempts to scare the bird off by running and flailing her arms at it. Until the bird knocks her down and she lies there on the ground, watching in helpless astonishment and abject terror. Underneath* MARIE-ADELE'S *screams, she mumbles to herself, sobbing.*)

ZHABOONIGAN One, two, three, four, five, six, seven . . . Nicky Ricky Ben Mark . . . eight, nine, ten, eleven, twelve . . . (*until the other women come running. Total darkness again.*)

EMILY What the . . .

ANNIE Marie-Adele!

PELAJIA Stop her! Hold her!

VERONIQUE What's happening?

PHILOMENA Marie-Adele. Now, now . . . come, come . . .

EMILY (*in the background*) Stop that fucking screaming will ya, Marie-Adele!

PHILOMENA Emily. There's no need to talk to her like that now.

PELAJIA Help us get her in the van.

PHILOMENA Come . . . come, Marie-Adele . . . everything's fine . . . you'll be fine . . . come . . . shhh . . . shhh . . . (*and they ease* MARIE-ADELE *back into the van. Once all is beginning to settle down again:*)

PELAJIA Everything okay now?

PHILOMENA   Yes. She's fine now.

PELAJIA   Emily, take over.

VERONIQUE   Yes. I don't trust that Annie Cook. Not for one minute.

EMILY   All set?

MARIE-ADELE   What time is it?

PELAJIA   Twenty after four.

ANNIE   Oh! We're over two hours behind schedule. Hurry up. Hurry up.

VERONIQUE   I'll be exhausted for the bingo tomorrow night. Maybe I should just take fifteen cards.

EMILY   You can rest your heart. And your mouth. All day tomorrow. All set?

(*And she starts up the van. The van lights come back on. The dialogues resume.* MARIE-ADELE *now sits in the front with* EMILY, *who is driving.* ZHABOONIGAN *sits between them.* PELAJIA *and* PHILOMENA *are now in the middle seat,* ANNIE *and* VERONIQUE *in the back.*)

EMILY   You scared the shit out of me out there. (*Silence.*) Don't do that again. (*Silence.*) Feeling better now? (*Silence.*)

MARIE-ADELE   I could be really mad, just raging mad just wanna tear his eyes out with my nails when he walks in the door and my whole body just goes 'k-k-k-k' . . . He doesn't talk, when something goes wrong with him, he doesn't talk, shuts me out, just disappears. Last night he didn't come home. Again, it happened. I couldn't sleep. You feel so ugly. He walks in this morning. Wanted to be alone, he said. The curve of his back, his breath on my neck, 'Adele, ki-sa-gee-ee-tin oo-ma',[7] making love, always in Indian, only. When we still could. I can't even have him inside me anymore. It's still growing there. The cancer. Pelajia, een-pay-seek-see-yan.[8]

PELAJIA   You know one time, I knew this couple where one of them was dying and the other one was angry at her for dying. And she was mad because he was gonna be there when she wasn't and she had so much left to do. And she'd lie there in bed and tell him to do this and do that and he'd say 'Okay, okay'. And then he'd go inside the kitchen and say to me, 'She's so this and she's so that and she's so damned difficult'. And I watched all this going on. That house didn't have room for two such angry people. But you know, I said to her, 'You gotta have faith in him and you gotta have faith in life. He loves you very much but there's only so much he can do. He's only human'. There's only so much Eugene can understand, Marie-Adele. He's only human.

EMILY   Fuckin' right. Me and the Rez Sisters, okay? Cruisin' down the coast highway one night. Hum of the engine between my thighs. Rose. That's Rosabella Baez, leader of the pack. We were real close, me and her. She was always thinkin' real deep. And talkin' about bein' a woman. An Indian woman. And suicide. And alcohol and despair and how fuckin' hard it is to be an Indian in this country. (MARIE-ADELE *shushes her gently.*) No god-damn future for them, she'd say. And why, why, why? Always carryin' on like that. Chris'sakes. She was pretty heavy into drugs. Guess we all were. We had a fight. Cruisin' down the coast highway that night. Rose in the middle. Me and Pussy Commanda off to the side. Big 18-wheeler come along real fast and me and Pussy Commanda get out of the way. But not Rose. She stayed in the middle. Went head-on into that truck like a fly splat against a windshield. I swear to this day I can still feel the spray of her blood against my neck. I drove on. Straight into daylight. Never looked back. Had enough gas money on me to take me as far as Salt Lake City. Pawned my bike off and bought me a bus ticket back to Wasy. When I got to Chicago, that's when I got up the nerve to wash my lover's dried blood from off my neck. I loved that woman, Marie-Adele, I loved her like no man's ever loved a woman. But she's gone. I never wanna go back to San Francisco. No way, man.

MARIE-ADELE   (*comforting the crying* EMILY) You should get some rest. Let Annie take over.

EMILY   I'll be fine. You go to sleep. Wake you up when we get to Toronto.

(EMILY *puts her Walkman on and starts to sing along quietly to 'Blue Kentucky Girl' by Emmylou Harris with its 'I swear I love you . . . ' while* MARIE-ADELE *leans her head against the 'window' and falls asleep. After a few moments,* ZHABOONIGAN, *who has been dozing off between* EMILY *and* MARIE-ADELE *in the front seat, pokes her head up and starts to sing along off-key. Then she starts to play with* EMILY'*s hair.*)

EMILY   (*shrugging* ZHABOONIGAN'*s hand off*) Don't bug me. My favorite part's comin' up.

(*Initiated by* ZHABOONIGAN, *they start playing 'slap'. The game escalates to the point where* EMILY *almost bangs* ZHABOONIGAN *over the head with her elbow.*) Yeah, right. You little retard. (*Mad at this,* ZHABOONIGAN *hits* EMILY *in the stomach.*) Can't hit me there, you little . . . Hey, man, like ummm . . . I'm sorry, Zha.

ZHABOONIGAN Sorry.

EMILY (*Feeling her belly thoughtfully. After a brief silence:*) You gonna have kids someday, Zha?

ZHABOONIGAN Ummm . . . buy one.

EMILY Holy! Well, kids were alright. Aw geez, Zha, that man treated me real bad. Ever been tied to a bedpost with your arms like this? Whoa! (*Grabbing the steering wheel.*) Maybe you should drive.

ZHABOONIGAN Scary.

EMILY Aw, don't be scared. Fuck.

ZHABOONIGAN Fuck.

EMILY Zhaboonigan Peterson! Your ma'll give me a black eye.

ZHABOONIGAN (*Turns her head toward the back seat, where* VERONIQUE *sits sleeping, and says one more time, really loud.*) Fuck!

EMILY Shhh! Look, Zha. You don't let any man bother you while we're down in T.O. You just stick close to me.

ZHABOONIGAN Yup.

EMILY We're sisters, right? Gimme five. (*They slap hands.*) Alright. Bingo!!!

(*Instantly the house lights come on full blast. The* BINGO MASTER – *the most beautiful man in the world – comes running up centre aisle, cordless mike in hand, dressed to kill: tails, rhinestones, and all. The entire theatre is now the bingo palace. We are in: Toronto!!!!*)

BINGO MASTER Welcome, ladies and gentlemen, to the biggest bingo the world has ever seen! Yes, ladies and gentlemen, tonight, we have a very, very special treat for you. Tonight, ladies and gentlemen, you will be witness to events of such gargantuan proportions, such cataclysmic ramifications, such masterly and magnificent manifestations that your minds will reel, your eyes will nictitate, and your hearts will palpitate erratically.

Because tonight, ladies and gentlemen, you will see the biggest, yes, ladies and gentlemen, the very biggest prizes ever known to man, woman, beast, or appliance. And the jackpot tonight? The jackpot, ladies and gentlemen, is surely the biggest, the largest, the hugest, and the most monstrous jackpot ever conceived of in the entire history of monstrous jackpots as we know them – $500,000! Yes, ladies and gentlemen, $500,000 can be yours this very night! That's half a million – A HALF MILLION SMACKEROOS!!!! IF you play the game right.

And all you have to do, ladies and gentlemen, is reach into your programs and extract the single bingo card placed therein. Yes, ladies and gentlemen, the single bingo card placed therein, which bingo card will entitle you to one chance at winning the warm-up game for a prize of $20. $20! And all you have to do is poke holes in that single bingo card. Yes, ladies and gentlemen, just poke holes in that single bingo card and bend the numbers backward as the numbers are called. And don't forget the free hole in the middle of the card. Twenty dollars, ladies and gentlemen, that's one line in any direction. That means, of course, ladies and gentlemen, that the first person to form one line, just one straight line in any direction on their card, will be the very lucky winner of the $20 prize. $20! Are you ready, ladies and gentlemen? Are you ready? Then let the game begin! Under the G 56. Etc. . . .

(*The audience plays bingo, with the seven women, who have moved slowly into the audience during the* BINGO MASTER's *speech, playing along, until somebody in the audience shouts, 'Bingo!'*)

BINGO MASTER Hold your cards, ladies and gentlemen, bingo has been called. (*The* BINGO MASTER *and the assistant stage manager check the numbers and the prize money is paid out.*) And now for the game you've all been waiting for, ladies and gentlemen. Now for the big game. Yes, ladies and gentlemen, get ready for THE BIGGEST BINGO IN THE WORLD! For the grand jackpot prize of $500,000! Full house, ladies and gentlemen, full house! Are you ready? Are you ready? Then let the game begin!

The house lights go out. And the only lights now are on the bingo balls bouncing around in the bingo machine – an eerie, surreal sort of glow – and on the seven women who are now playing bingo with a vengeance on centre-stage, behind the BINGO MASTER, where a long bingo table has magically appeared with ZHABOONIGAN at the table's centre banging a crucifix VERONIQUE has brought along for good luck. The scene is lit so that it looks like 'The Last Supper'.

The women face the audience. The bingo table is covered with all the necessary accoutrements: bags of potato chips, cans of pop, ashtrays (some of the women are smoking), etc. The BINGO MASTER calls out number after number – but not the B14 – with the women improvising responses. These responses – PHILOMENA has 27 cards! – grow more and more raucous: 'B14? Annie Cook? One more number to go! The B14! Where is that B14?! Gimme that B14! Where the fuck is that B14?!!!' etc. until the women have all risen from the table and come running downstage, attacking the bingo machine and throwing the BINGO MASTER out of the way. The women grab the bingo machine with shouts of: 'Throw this fucking machine into the lake! It's no damn good!' etc. And they go running down the centre aisle with it and out of the theatre. Bingo cards are flying like confetti. Total madness and mayhem. The music is going crazy.

And out of this chaos emerges the calm, silent image of MARIE-ADELE waltzing romantically in the arms of the BINGO MASTER. The BINGO MASTER says 'Bingo' into her ear. And the BINGO MASTER changes, with sudden bird-like movements, into the nighthawk, NANABUSH in dark feathers. MARIE-ADELE meets NANABUSH.

During this next speech, the other women, one by one, take their positions around MARIE-ADELE's porch, some kneeling, some standing. The stage area, by means of 'lighting magic', slowly returns to its Wasaychigan Hill appearance.

MARIE-ADELE   U-wi-nuk u-wa? U-wi-nuk u-wa? Eugene? Neee. U-wi-nuk ma-a oo-ma kee-tha? Ka. Kee-tha i-chi-goo-ma so that's who you are . . . at rest upon the rock . . . the master of the game . . . the game . . . it's me . . . nee-tha . . . come . . . come . . . don't be afraid . . . as-tum . . . come . . . to . . . me . . . ever soft wings . . . beautiful soft . . . soft . . . dark wings . . . here . . . take me . . . as-tum . . . as-tum . . . pee-na-sin . . . wings . . . here . . . take me . . . take . . . me . . . with . . . pee-na-sin . . . [9]

(As NANABUSH escorts MARIE-ADELE into the spirit world, ZHABOONIGAN, uttering a

cry, makes a last desperate attempt to go with them. But EMILY rushes after and catches her at the very last split second. And the six remaining women begin to sing the Ojibway funeral song. By the beginning of the funeral song, we are back at the Wasaychigan Hill Indian Reserve, at MARIE-ADELE's grave.)

WOMEN
Wa-kwing, wa-kwing,
Wa-kwing nin wi-i-ja;
Wa-kwing, wa-kwing,
Wa-kwing nin wi-i-ja.[10]

(At MARIE-ADELE's grave. During PELAJIA's speech, the other women continue humming the funeral song until they fade into silence. PELAJIA drops a handful of earth on the grave.)

PELAJIA   Well, sister, guess you finally hit the big jackpot. Best bingo game we've ever been to in our lives, huh? You know, life's like that, I figure. When all is said and done. Kinda' silly, innit, this business of living? But. What choice do we have? When some fool of a being goes and puts us Indians plunk down in the middle of this old earth, dishes out this lot we got right now. But. I figure we gotta make the most of it while we're here. You certainly did. And I sure as hell am giving it one good try. For you. For me. For all of us. Promise. Really. See you when that big bird finally comes for me. (Whips out her hammer one more time, holds it up in the air and smiles.) And my hammer.

(Back at the store in Wasaychigan Hill. EMILY is tearing open a brand-new case of the small cans of Carnation milk, takes two cans out and goes up to ZHABOONIGAN with them.)

EMILY   See, Zha? The red part up here and the white part down here and the pink flowers in the middle?
ZHABOONIGAN   Oh.
EMILY   Carnation milk.
ZHABOONIGAN   Carnation milk.
EMILY   And it goes over there where all the other red and white cans are, okay?
ZHABOONIGAN   Yup.

(ZHABOONIGAN rushes to EMILY and throws her arms around her affectionately. EMILY is embarrassed and struggles to free herself. Just then, ANNIE enters. She's lost *some of her speed and frenetic energy. There's obviously something wrong with her.*)

ANNIE   Hallooo! Whatchyou doing.

EMILY   Red Lucifer's whiskers! It's Annie Cook.

ANNIE   Well, we seem to have survived the biggest bingo in the world, eh? Well . . . ummm . . . not all of us . . . not Marie-Adele . . . but she knew she was . . . but we're okay. (*Laughs.*) . . . us? . . .

EMILY   Annie Cook. Sometimes you can be so godamn ignorant. (*Pause.*) Too bad none of us won, eh.

ANNIE   Philomena Moosemeat won $600. That's something.

EMILY   Yup. That's one helluva jazzy toilet she's got there, eh?

ANNIE   She's got eight-ply toilet paper. Dark green. Feels like you're wiping your ass with moss!

EMILY   Holy!

ANNIE   I'm singing back-up for Fritz weekends. Twenty-five bucks a gig. That's something, eh?

EMILY   Katz's whore . . .

ANNIE   What?

EMILY   You heard me.

ANNIE   The Katz's what?

EMILY   Chris'sakes. Wake up.

ANNIE   I love him, Emily.

EMILY   You been drinkin'.

ANNIE   Please, come with me tonight.

EMILY   Have to wait for the old buzzard to come pick up this dozy daughter of hers and that's not 'til seven.

ANNIE   Okay?

EMILY   Alright. But we're comin' right back to the Rez soon as the gig's over. Hear?

ANNIE   Thanks. Any mail today?

EMILY   Sorry.

ANNIE   That's okay. See you at seven. (*She exits.*)

ZHABOONIGAN   Why . . . why . . . why do you call me that?

EMILY   Call you what?

ZHABOONIGAN   Dozy dotter. (*Awkward silence, broken after a while by* ZHABOONIGAN's *little giggle.*)

EMILY   Look, Zha. Share a little secret with you, okay?

ZHABOONIGAN   Yup.

EMILY   Just you and me, promise?

ZHABOONIGAN   Yup.

EMILY   Gazelle Nataways'll see fit to kill . . . but I'm gonna have a baby.

ZHABOONIGAN   (*Drops the Carnation milk cans she's been holding all this time and gasps.*) Ohhh! Big Joey!

EMILY   (*in exasperation*) This business of having babies . . .

(*And the last we see of them is* ZHABOONIGAN *playfully poking* EMILY *in the belly and* EMILY *slapping* ZHABOONIGAN's *hand away.*

At EUGENE STARBLANKET's *house.* VERONIQUE ST. PIERRE *is sitting on the steps, glowing with happiness, looking up at the sky as though looking for seagulls. She sees none so she picks up the doll that lies under her chair and cradles it on her lap as though it were a child. At this point,* ANNIE COOK *enters.*)

ANNIE   Hallooo! (*surprised to see* VERONIQUE *sitting there*) Veronique St. Pierre. What are you doing here?

VERONIQUE   Annie Cook. Haven't you heard I'm cooking for Eugene and the children these days? It's been four days since the funeral as you know may she rest in peace (*makes a quick sign of the cross without missing a beat*) but I was the only person on this reserve who was willing to help with these fourteen little orphans.

ANNIE   That's nice. But I came to see if Simon Star . . .

VERONIQUE   The stove is so good. All four elements work and there is even a timer for the oven. As I was saying to Black Lady Halked at the bingo last night, 'Now I don't have to worry about burning the fried potatoes or serving the roast beef half-raw'.

ANNIE   Well, I was about to . . .

VERONIQUE   Yes, Annie Cook. I bought a roast beef just yesterday. A great big roast beef. Almost 16 pounds. It's probably the biggest roast beef that's been seen on this reserve in recent years. The meat was so heavy that Nicky, Ricky, Ben and Mark had to take turns carrying it here for me. Oh, it was hard and slippery at first, but I finally managed to wrestle it into my oven. And it's sitting in there at this very moment just sizzling and bubbling with the most succulent and delicious juices. And speaking of succulent and delicious juices, did you come to call on Eugene? Well, Eugene's not home.

ANNIE   Yeah, right. I came to see if Simon had that new record.

VERONIQUE   Why?

ANNIE   I'm singing in Little Current tonight and I gotta practice this one song.

VERONIQUE   (*contemptuously*) That Ritzie Ditzie character.

ANNIE   It's Fritz the Katz, Veronique St. Pierre. FREDERICK STEPHEN KATZ. He's a very fine musician and a good teacher.

VERONIQUE   Teacher?! Of what?! As I was saying to Little Girl Manitowabi and her daughter June Bug McLeod at the bingo last night, 'You never know about these non-Native bar-room types'. I said to them, 'We have enough trouble right here on this reserve without having our women come dragging these shady white characters into the picture'. Before you know it, you will end up in deep trouble and bring shame and disrespect on the name of Pelajia Patchnose and all your sisters, myself included.

ANNIE   Myself included, my ass! Veronique St. Pierre. I wish you would shut that great big shitty mouth of yours at least once a year!

VERONIQUE   (*Stunned into momentary silence. Then*) Simon Starblanket is not home. (*With this, she bangs the doll down viciously.*)

ANNIE   Good day, Veronique St. Pierre (*and exits.* VERONIQUE, *meanwhile, just sits there in her stunned state, mouth hanging open and looking after the departing* ANNIE.)

(*On* PELAJIA PATCHNOSE's *roof. As at the beginning of the play,* PELAJIA *is alone, nailing shingles on. But no cushion this time.*)

PELAJIA   Philomena. Where are those shingles?

PHILOMENA   (*from off stage*) Oh, go on. I'll be up in just a minute.

PELAJIA   (*coughs*) The dust today. It's these dirt roads. Dirt roads all over. Even the main street. If I were chief around here, that's the very first thing I would do is . . .

PHILOMENA   (*coming up the ladder with one shingle and the most beautiful pink, lace-embroidered, heart-shaped pillow you'll ever see*) Oh, go on. You'll never be chief.

PELAJIA   And why not?

PHILOMENA   Because you're a woman.

PELAJIA   Bullshit! If that useless old chief of ours was a woman, we'd see a few things get done around here. We'd see our women working, we'd see our men working, we'd see our young people sober on Saturday nights, and we'd see Nanabush dancing up and down the hill on shiny black paved roads. (ANNIE COOK *pops up at the top of the ladder.*)

ANNIE   Pelajia for chief! I'd vote for you.

PHILOMENA   Why, Annie Cook. You just about scared me off the edge of this roof.

PELAJIA   Someday, we'll have to find you a man who can slow you down. So what do you want this time, Annie Cook?

ANNIE   Well, to tell you the truth, I came to borrow your record player, Philomena Moosemeat . . . I mean, Moosetail. I'm going to practice this one song for tonight. Emily Dictionary is coming to Little Current to watch me sing with the band.

PELAJIA   It's back from Espanola.

PHILOMENA   (*to* PELAJIA) Pelajia Rosella Patchnose! (*To* ANNIE) It's still not working very well. There's a certain screeching, squawking noise that comes out of it every time you try to play it.

PELAJIA   That's okay, Philomena. There's a certain screechy, squawky noise that comes out of Annie Cook every time she opens her mouth to sing anyway.

PHILOMENA   Yes, Annie Cook. You can borrow it. But only for one night.

ANNIE   Good. Hey, there's a bingo in Espanola next week and Fire Minklater is driving up in her new car. There might be room. (*To* PHILOMENA) Would you like to go?

PELAJIA   Does a bear shit in the woods?

PHILOMENA   (*Glares at* PELAJIA *first.*) Yes. (*Then quickly to* ANNIE) Make . . . make sure you don't leave me behind.

ANNIE   I'll make sure. Well. Toodle-oo! (*And she pops down the ladder again, happy, now that she's finally got her record player.*)

PELAJIA   That Annie Cook. Records and bingo. Bingo and records.

PHILOMENA   You know, Pelajia, I'd like to see just what this Fritz looks like. Maybe he IS the man who can slow her down, after all.

PELAJIA   Foolishness! Annie Cook will be walking fast right up until the day she dies and gets buried beside the two of us in that little cemetery beside the church.

PHILOMENA   Oh, go on. (*Pause. As* PHILOMENA *sits down beside her sister, leaning with her elbow on her heart-shaped pillow*) So, Pelajia Patchnose. Still thinking about packing your bags and shipping off to Toronto?

PELAJIA   Well . . . oh . . . sometimes. I'm not so sure I would get along with him if I were

417

to live down there. I mean my son Tom. He was telling me not to play so much bingo.

PHILOMENA His upstairs washroom. Mine looks just like it now.

PELAJIA Here we go again.

PHILOMENA Large shining porcelain tiles in hippity-hoppity squares of black and white . . . so clean you can see your own face, like in a mirror, when you lean over to look into them. It looks so nice. The shower curtains have a certain matching blackness and whiteness to them – they're made of a rich, thick plasticky sort of material – and they're see-through in parts. The bathtub is beautiful, too. But the best, the most wonderful, my absolute most favourite part is the toilet bowl itself. First of all, it's elevated, like on a sort of . . . pedestal, so that it makes you feel like . . . the Queen . . . sitting on her royal throne, ruling her Queendom with a firm yet gentle hand. And the bowl itself – white, spirit white – is of such a shape, such an exquisitely soft, perfect oval shape that it makes you want to cry. Oh!!! And it's so comfortable you could just sit on it right up until the day you die!

(*After a long, languorous pause,* PHILOMENA *snaps out of her reverie when she realizes that* PELAJIA, *all this time, has been looking at her disbelievingly and then contemptuously.* PELAJIA *cradles her hammer as though she'd like to bang* PHILOMENA*'s head with it.* PHILOMENA *delicately starts to descend the ladder. The last we see of her is her Kewpie-doll face. And beside it, the heart-shaped pillow, disappearing like a setting sun behind the edge of the roof. Once she's good and gone,* PELAJIA *dismisses her.*)

PELAJIA Oh, go on! (*Then she pauses to look wistfully at the view for a moment.*) Not many seagulls flying over Eugene Starblanket's house today.

(*And returns once more to her hammering on the roof as the lights fade into blackout.*

Split seconds before complete blackout, NANABUSH, *back once more in his guise as the seagull, 'lands' on the roof behind the unaware and unseeing* PELAJIA PATCHNOSE. *He dances to the beat of the hammer, merrily and triumphantly.*)

Notes

1 Oh, go on (Ojibway).
2 MARY-ADELE Go away! You stinking thing. Don't coming messing around here for nothing. Go away! Neee. Who the hell do you think you are, the Holy Spirit? Go away! Hey, but he won't fly away, this seagull bird. He just sits there. And watches me. Watches me.
  NANABUSH Come.
  MARY-ADELE Neee. I can't fly away. I have no wings. Yet. (*Pause.*) Will you stop shitting all over the place you stinking seagull bird etc. (Cree).
  (Note: 'Neee' is a very common Cree expression with the approximate meaning of 'Oh you'.)
3 The little pigs (Cree).
4 Shush, Zhaboonigan, don't say that (Ojibway).
5 A great big island (Cree).
6 Indians (Ojibway).
7 Adele, I love you (Cree).
8 Pelajia, I'm scared to death (Cree).
9 MARY-ADELE Who are you? Who are you? Eugene? Neee. Then who are you really? Oh. It's you, so that's who you are . . . at rest upon the rock . . . the master of the game . . . the game . . . it's me . . . me . . . come . . . come . . . don't be afraid . . . come . . . come . . . to . . . me . . . ever soft wings . . . beautiful soft . . . soft . . . dark wings . . . here . . . take me . . . come . . . come . . . come and get me . . . wings here . . . take me . . . take . . . me . . . with . . . come and get me . . . (Cree).
10 WOMEN Heaven, heaven, heaven, I'm going there; Heaven, heaven, heaven, I'm going there (Ojibway).

18 Guillermo Verdecchia

Fronteras Americanas (American Borders)
Canada

Introduction

Over the decade that he has been writing for the theatre, Guillermo Verdecchia has earned a reputation as one of Canada's most exciting and innovative dramatists. His overall work is stamped by a strong distrust of naturalism, which, he remarks, 'makes it very difficult to talk about structures of domination, or power, or oppression' because 'it reduces things to the singular, to the unique, the exceptional, an event' (quoted in Harvie 1997: 92). While Verdecchia's plays may begin with a personalised and/or localised event, their canvas is always much broader, sketching not so much the individual experiences of the protagonists but rather the complex social, cultural and political patterns in and through which their everyday life unfolds. The imperative to dramatise the 'big issues' has compelled Verdecchia to create theatre that celebrates and activates an audience's intelligence, that allows people to contend with problems, that implicates both viewers and performers, as well as characters, in the action. This artistic vision is expressed in several experimental works that typically use dialogue, sounds, projected images, music, written text, and/or direct audience address, all bound together to form a rich theatrical matrix through which specific themes are woven. Not surprisingly, such works are marked by a recurrent interest in questions about theatricality itself: how it is understood by audiences, how it mediates our interpretation of a narrative, how it might be used to critique the very processes of representation.

Verdecchia's considerable experience as an actor puts him in an ideal position to interrogate the performative structures through which particular ideologies are communicated to theatre audiences, either implicitly or explicitly. His first major play,

The Noam Chomsky Lectures (1990), written and performed with Daniel Brooks, questions Canada's complicity in US political and military interference in various regions of the world. As a central part of its project, the play, parodically modelled on a series of lectures complete with complicated graphs and diagrams, also questions the ways in which information about global affairs is disseminated. Brooks and Verdecchia's performance is not exempt from this inquiry; in fact, as a section titled 'A Play Within the Play' so clearly demonstrates, understanding the mechanics of representation is essential to avoid being duped by appearances. Towards the end of *The Noam Chomsky Lectures*, the action moves into a different kind of self-reflexivity, directly engaging with issues about theatre as social praxis. At this point, Brooks and Verdecchia discuss the specifics of the Toronto theatre community, taking critics to task for their banal reviews and making an impassioned plea for intelligent theatre that is aware of its own biases. They argue, and demonstrate as performers, that theatrical form is not separable from content, and that theatre must find new forms if it is to survive as 'something other than an expensive alternative to television' (Verdecchia and Brooks 1991: 59). Staged as an integral part of the play's broader investigation of various communication technologies, this metatheatrical discussion is not self-indulgent navel-gazing but rather a demonstration of the ways in which theatre connects to a community, and, by extension, to particular cultural systems.

The conception of theatre as a place for formal experiment – and spirited dissent – could well be seen as a model for Verdecchia's best known play, *Fronteras Americanas/American Borders* (1993). This text is also concerned with globalisation and

US neo-imperialism, but in a way that locates their effects at a very personal level as well as within the context of Canadian national self-fashioning. The play's title signals a central interest in borders or frontiers, those racial, social, geographical and political divisions that inevitably structure human interaction, even in its most intimate moments. According to Mayte Gomez, *Fronteras Americanas* dramatises two main lines of division: the 'continental border' and the 'individual border'. 'The continental border divides the Americas into North and South and is grounded in colonial relations which translate into stereotyped representations of the "other"' (Gomez 1995: 29). This geopolitical division is experienced not only where it putatively exists (between the two continents) but also wherever 'Latinos' or 'Hispanics' come into contact with dominant forms of North American culture: on the street, in the classroom, at the official border, or even in the theatre. Canada, the play suggests, is built upon such divisions in much the same manner as the United States, despite the fact that an official politics of Canadian multiculturalism takes pains to stress the goal of unity within diversity. In this respect, it is difficult to know where Canada's border with its powerful southern neighbour begins and ends.

The individual border zones staged by *Fronteras Americanas* are equally complex and mutable, and they are also inseparable from the socio-political realm. Having been born in Argentina in 1962 and then brought to Canada where his family emigrated during his primary school years, Verdecchia has personally experienced many kinds of borders. He draws on this background to create the stage *persona* of Verdecchia, a quasi-autobiographical character whose cultural positioning as an Argentine–Canadian expresses the multiple and sometimes contradictory sites which the migrant/exile – the hyphenated person – must occupy in an effort to find that elusive space called home. In the course of the play, Verdecchia's various recounted journeys, between continents, across countries, within communities, map out an intensely personal history at the same time as they remap the conceptual cartography of the Americas. This re-imagined cartography uses the border less as a fixed division than as a movable axis, a

line continuously drawn, erased and redrawn for the purposes of orientation. At yet another level, the border/frontera is a productive interstitial space, a site of dialogue between two (or more) sides, a place of resistance *and* mediation.

While Verdecchia (the character) progressively engages with the 'border dialectic' in an effort to locate a sense of self that can live comfortably *in-between* cultures, the play as a whole is deliberately designed to *dislocate* a predominantly 'Saxonian' audience from its privileged position at the centre of the cultural imaginary. This process of disorientation is achieved not only through Verdecchia's dizzying juxtapositions of place/space but more especially by the machinations of his other persona, Wideload, the self-styled Latino stereotype whose chief function is to dismantle all such types by exposing the means by which they are constructed. He does this in at least two ways: first, by patently masquerading as a larger-than-life media icon composed of various popular culture stereotypes, and second, by setting up a number of pseudo-documentary lessons in how to critically interpret a repertoire of media images that perpetuate notions of racial and cultural marginality. The effect of these strategies is that the mediatised image seems to comment on itself, making the play's critique of popular culture mythologies more pointed, even while heightening its comedy.

Wideload alternately beguiles and accuses his audience by means of an extensive theatrical arsenal, including a sustained use of irony, sudden narrative intrusions, witty commentary on projected words and images, and a parodic sales pitch for a third-world theme park that makes explicit the dominant culture's tendency to exoticise difference. His direct address to the audience is reminiscent of stand-up comedy, and shares its tendency towards auto-critique with a regular monitoring of audience response, as in the 'Latin Lover' sequence. The aim of this kind of metatheatricality is to engage viewers and hence provoke critical reflection. But perhaps the play's most powerful weapon against imperial hegemony is its refusal to present a single, fixed sign of Otherness against which the cultural norm might be defined. The monodrama form is crucial in this respect since it allows the solo actor to give life to two very individualised yet *indivisible* characters whose identities are always in flux. Even though Verdecchia and Wideload have their own idiosyncratic gestures, movements and typical modes of appearance, the fact that they are signified by the one performing body means that slippages between the two are inevitable. This blurring of characters, and their dramatisation through transparent processes of role-playing and role-switching, situates Latino identity as always complex and negotiable. Such characterisation is a conscious part of the playwright's agenda to dismantle interpersonal borders as a prelude to the larger cultural project of restructuring community, and even national, relations.

In Canada, as elsewhere, the one-person, semi-autobiographical play has become a powerful mode of expression for the postcolonial subject. Monodramas such as Djanet Sears's *Afrika Solo*, George Seremba's *Come Good Rain*, and Margo Kane's *Moonlodge* also express a deep interest in the processes of cultural dislocation and exile. Like *Fronteras Americanas*, these plays use a type of confessional narrative to trace their respective authors' efforts to find a place within Canadian society. The chosen theatrical form stamps each narrative with a certain authority by using the body of the author-cum-actor as the filter through which all dramatic action is rendered; and yet the purpose is often less to stress the isolation of the protagonist than to reveal the prejudices of the culture in which he or she lives.

The storytelling mode that is so often the central feature of autobiographical monodrama allows for a great degree of flexibility in performance, especially since the author/actor has an immense archive of experience from which to draw images and events relating to the persona being staged. Verdecchia signals this in his preface to the first published edition of *Fronteras Americanas*: 'In performance, changes were made nightly depending on my mood, the public, our location, the arrangement of the planets' (Verdecchia 1993: 13). Because it derives its versatility as well as much of its theatrical power from the presence of an author enacting his/her own stories, an autobiographical monodrama always raises complex questions about who can perform it. Verdecchia is open to alternative interpretations of his text, suggesting that anyone thinking of staging it might 'consider

the possibilities of making (respectful) changes and leaving room for personal and more current responses' (1993: 13). In a 1997 University of Guelph production, Jorge Nef was thus able to make *Fronteras Americanas* his own show, drawing on his Chilean background to personalise the narrative. A recently staged version of the play in Australia (1998) suggests that Verdecchia's particular investigation of cultural stereotyping can resonate even more widely, notwithstanding his specific concern with Latin Americans and the Americas. The concept of 'borderlands', for instance, is immensely transferable, as is the critique of US neo-imperialism and media globalisation.

Verdecchia's dedication to innovative theatre has earned his work a number of well-deserved accolades, including a 1992 Chalmers Award for *The Noam Chomsky Lectures*, as well as the 1993 Governor-General's Award and a 1994 Chalmers Award for *Fronteras Americanas*. In 1996, he won a third Chalmers Award for *A Line in the Sand* (1995), co-written with Marcus Youssef. This savage, haunting play stages an encounter between a troubled Canadian soldier and a teenage Palestinian black-marketeer during the Gulf War. Once again, the focus is on investigating the psychological and cultural roots of racism, which in this case has tragic consequences. Verdecchia's other works include *The Terrible But Incomplete Journals of John D.* (1996), a monodrama that sets the lone actor in dialogue with a cello and a complex soundscape, and *Crucero/Crossroads*, a film adaptation of *Fronteras Americanas*. More recently Verdecchia worked with Daniel Brooks on a new play, *Insomnia* (1998), and published a collection of short stories entitled *Citizen Suàrez*. He currently lives in Toronto, continuing his long-term engagement with the politics of representation via a position as artistic director of Cahoots Theatre Projects, a company dedicated to the creation, development and presentation of new work that reflects Canada's cultural diversity.

Production history

Fronteras Americanas/American Borders was first performed by Guillermo Verdecchia at the Tarragon Theatre Extra Space, Toronto, in January 1993, directed by Jim Warren. Verdecchia has presented the play in several

Canadian cities including Vancouver, Victoria, Winnipeg and Montreal, the latter as part of the 1993 Festival des Amériques. There have also been independent productions in Guelph, Edmonton and Hamilton as well as in Adelaide, Australia.

Select bibliography

Barton, B. (2001) 'Communicating across *Fronteras*: Wideload on the wide screen', *Essays in Theatre*. (forthcoming)

Cottreau, D. (1998) 'Writing for a playwright's theatre: Urjo Kareda on dramaturgy at Tarragon', *Canadian Theatre Review* 97: 5–8.

Gilbert, H. (1998) 'Bodies in focus: photography and performativity in post-colonial theatre', *Textual Studies in Canada* 10–11: 17–32.

Gomez, M. (1995) 'Healing the border wound: *Fronteras Americanas* and the future of Canadian multiculturalism', *Theatre Research in Canada* 16, 1–2: 26–39.

Harvie, J. (1997) 'The nth degree: an interview with Guillermo Verdecchia', *Canadian Theatre Review* 92: 46–9.

Verdecchia, G. (1993) *Fronteras Americanas/American Borders*, Toronto: Coach House.

—— (1997) *The Terrible But Incomplete Journals of John D.*, *Canadian Theatre Review* 92: 50–67.

Verdecchia, G. and Brooks, D. (1991) *The Noam Chomsky Lectures*. Toronto: Coach House.

Verdecchia, G. and Youssef, M. (1997) *A Line in the Sand*, Vancouver: Talon.

Wilson, A. (1996) 'Border crossing: the technologies of identity in *Fronteras Americanas*', *Australasian Drama Studies* 29: 7–15.

Audiovisual resources

Crucero/Crossroads (1993) produced and directed by Ramiro Puerta, written and performed by Guillermo Verdecchia, Snake Cinema Productions. Available Mongrel Media, Toronto. Fax: +1 416 588 6300.

Fronteras Americanas (American Borders)_

Guillermo Verdecchia

Pre-show

(*Music: James Blood Ulmer's 'Show me Your Love America'. Two slides are projected.*)

SLIDE **It is impossible to say to which human family we belong. We were all born of one mother America, though our fathers had different origins, and we all have differently coloured skins. This dissimilarity is of the greatest significance.**
— Simón Bolívar 1819

SLIDE **Fronteras. Borders. Americanas. American.**

Act I

Welcome

(VERDECCHIA *enters.*)

VERDECCHIA   Here we are. All together. At long last. Very exciting. I'm excited. Very excited.

Here we are.

SLIDE **Here We Are**

Now because this is the theatre when I say we I mean all of us and when I say here I don't just mean at the Tarragon, I mean America.

SLIDE **Let us compare geographies**

And when I say AMERICA I don't mean the country, I mean the continent. Somos todos Americanos. We are all Americans.

Now – I have to make a small confession – I'm lost. Somewhere in my peregrinations on the continent, I lost my way.

Oh sure, I can say I'm in Toronto, at 30 Bridgman Ave, but I don't find that a very satisfactory answer – it seems to me a rather inadequate description of where I am.

Maps have been of no use because I always forget that they are metaphors and not the territory; the compass has never made any sense – it always spins in crazy circles. Even gas station attendants haven't been able to help; I can never remember whether it was a right or a left at the lights and I always miss the exits and have to sleep by the side of the road or in crummy hotels with beds that have magic fingers that go off in the middle of the night.

So, I'm lost and trying to figure out where I took that wrong turn . . . and I suppose you must be lost too or else you wouldn't have ended up here, tonight.

I suspect we got lost while crossing the border.

SLIDE **Make a run for the Border / Taco Bell's got your order**

The Border is a tricky place. Take the Mexico–North America border.

SLIDE **Map of Mexico–U.S. border**

Where and what exactly is the border? Is it this line in the dirt, stretching for some 5000 kilometres? Is the border more accurately described as a zone which includes the towns of El Paso and Juárez? Or is the border – is the border the whole country, the continent? Where does the U.S. end and Canada begin? Does the U.S. end at the 49th parallel or does the U.S. only end at your living room when you switch on the CBC? After all, as Carlos Fuentes reminds us, a border is more than just the division between two countries; it is also the division between two cultures and two memories.[1]

SLIDE **Remember the Alamo?**

VERDECCHIA   *Atlantic Magazine* has something to say about the border: 'The border is transient. The border is dangerous. The border is crass. The food is bad, the prices are high and there are no good bookstores. It is not the place to visit on your next vacation'.[2]

To minimize our inconvenience, I've hired a translator who will meet us on the other side.

The border can be difficult to cross. We will have to avoid the Border Patrol and the trackers who cut for sign. Some of you may wish to put carpet on the soles of your shoes, others may want to attach cow's hooves to your sneakers. I myself will walk backwards so that it looks like I'm heading north.

Before we cross, please disable any beepers, cellular phones or fax machines and reset your watches to border time. It is now Zero Hour.

El Bandito

(*Music: 'Aquí vienen los Mariachi'*)

SLIDE **Warning: gunshots will be fired in this performance . . .**

SLIDE **Now**

(*Gunshots. The performer appears wearing a bandito outfit. He has shifted into his other persona,* WIDELOAD.)

WIDELOAD   Ay! Ayayayay! Aja. Bienvenidos. Yo soy el mesonero acá en La Casa de La Frontera. Soy el guía. A su servicio. Antes de pasar, por favor, los latinos se pueden identificar? Los 'latinoamericanos' por favor que pongan las manos en el aire . . . (*He counts.*) Que lindo . . . mucho gusto. . . Muy bien. Entonces el resto son . . . gringos. Lo siguiente es para los gringos:

Eh, jou en Méjico now. Jou hab crossed de border. Why? What you lookin' for? Taco Bell Nachos wif 'salsa sauce', cabrón? Forget it gringo. Dere's no pinche Taco Bell for thousands of miles. Here jou eat what I eat and I eat raw jalopeño peppers on dirty, burnt tortillas, wif some calopinto peppers to give it some flavour! I drink sewer water and tequila. My breath keells small animals. My shit destroys lakes. Jou come dis far south looking for de authentic Méjico? Jou looking for de real mezcal wit de real worm in it? I'll show you de real worm – I'll show jou de giant Mexican trouser snake. I will show you fear in a handful of dust . . .

Jou wrinklin' jour nose? Someting stink? Somebody smell aroun here? Si, I esmell. I esmell because I doan bathe. Because bad guys doan wash. Never.

Bandito maldito, independista, Sandinista, Tupamaro, mao mao powpowpow.

(WIDELOAD *removes bandito outfit.*)

Ees an old Hallowe'en costume. Scary huh?

Introduction to Wideload

WIDELOAD   Mi nombre es Facundo Morales Segundo. Algunos me llaman El Tigre del Barrio. También me dicen El Alacran porque . . .

(*Music: 'La Cumbia del Facundo' by Steve Jordan*)

My name ees Facundo Morales Segundo. Some of you may know me as de Barrio Tiger. I am de guy who told Elton John to grow some funk of his own. I am de heads of Alfredo Garcia and Joaquin Murrieta. I am a direct descendent of Túpac Amaru, Pancho Villa, Doña Flor, Pedro Navaja, Sor Juana and Speedy Gonzalez.

Now when I first got here people would say, 'Sorry what's de name? Fuckundoo'?

'No mang, Fa – cun – do, Facundo.'

'Wow, dat's a new one. Mind if I call you Fac?'

'No mang, mind if I call you shithead?'

So, you know, I had to come up with a more Saxonical name. And I looked around for a long time till I found one I liked. And when I found the one I wanted I took it. I estole it, actually from a TV show – *Broken Badge or* something like that.

I go by the name Wideload Mckennah now and I get a lot more respect, ese.

SLIDE **Wideload**

I live in the border – that's in Parkdale for you people from outta town. Ya, mang, I live in de zone – in de barrio – and I gotta move. Is a bad neighbourhood. Like today on my way here somebody first tried to sell me some drugs, den somebody tried to rip off my wallet, den de police picked me up to take me in for questioning about somefing I had nothing to do with, den somebody stabbed me, den I got caught in some cross-fire – and when I got to my car it was estolen so I had to esteal somebody else's car but it didn't have a tape deck and den it exploded about six blocks from da theatre so I had to walk the rest of the way. So I gotta move . . .

But first I gotta make some money. I want to cash in on de Latino Boom. Ya, dere's a Latino Boom, we are a very hot commodity right now. And what I really want to do is get a big chunk of toxic wasteland up on de Trans-Canada Highway and make like a third-world theme park.

You know, you drive up to like big barbed wire gates with guards carrying sub-machine guns and you park your car and den a broken-down Mercedes Benz bus comes along and takes you in, under guard, of course. And you can buy an International Monetary Fund Credit Card for seventy-five bucks and it gets you on all de rides.

And as soon as you're inside somebody steals your purse and a policeman shows up but he's totally incompetent and you have to bribe him in order to get any action. Den you walk through a slum on the edge of a swamp wif poor people selling tortillas. And maybe like a disappearing rainforest section dat you can actually wander through and search for rare plants and maybe find de cure to cancer and maybe find . . . Sean Connery . . . and you rent little golf carts to drive through it and de golf cart is always breaking down and you have to fix it yourself. And while you're fixing de golf-cart in de sweltering noonday sun, a drug lord comes along in his hydrofoil and offers to take you to his villa where you can have lunch and watch a multi-media presentation on drug processing.

I figure it would do great. You people love dat kinda *shit*. And I can also undercut dose travel agencies dat are selling package tours of Brazilian slums. Dis would be way cheaper, safer and it would generate a lot of jobs – for white people too. And I would make some money and be able to move out of the barrio and into Forest Hill.

Ya, a little house in Forest Hill. Nice neighbourhood. Quiet. Good place to bring up like fifteen kids. Course dis country is full of nice neighbourhoods – Westmount in Montreal looks good, or Vancouver you know, Point Grey is lovely or Kitsilano. Or de Annex here in Toronto – mang, I love de Annex: you got professionals, you got families, you got professional families. Ya. I could live dere. Hey mang, we could be neighbours – would you like dat? Sure, I'm moving in next door to . . . you . . . and I'm going to wash my Mustang every day and overhaul de engine and get some grease on de sidewalk and some friends like about twelve are gonna come and stay with me for a few . . . Years.

You like music? Goood!

Ya, how 'bout a Chicano for a neighbour? Liven up de neighbourhood.

SLIDE

Chicano: a person who drives a loud car that sits low to the ground?
a kind of Mexican?
a generic term for a working class Latino?
a wetback?
a Mexican born in Saxon America?

Technically I don't qualify as a Chicano. I wasn't born in East L.A. I wasn't born in de southwest U.S.A. I wasn't even born in Méjico. Does dis make me Hispanic?

SLIDE

Hispanic: someone who speaks Spanish?
a Spaniard?
a Latino?
root of the word spic?

Dese terms, Latino, Hispanic, are very tricky you know but, dey are de only terms we have so we have to use dem wif caution. If you will indulge me for a moment I would like to make this point painfully clear:

De term Hispanic, for example, comes from the Roman word, Hispania, which refers to de Iberian peninsula or eSpain. eSpain is a country in eEurope. Many people who today are referred to as Hispanic have nothin to do wif Hispain. Some of dem don't even speak Hispanish.

De term Latino is also confusing because it lumps a whole lot of different people into one category. Dere is a world of difference between de right wing Cubans living in Miami and exiled Salvadorean leftists living in Canada; between Mexican speakers of Nahuatl and Brazilian speakers of Portuguese; between a Tico and a Nuyorican (dat's a Puerto Rican who lives in New York) and den dere's de Uruguayans. I mean dey're practically European. As for me, let's just say . . . I'm a pachuco.[3]

(*Music: 'Pachuco', Maldita Vecindad*)

It starts

VERDECCHIA Okay, I just want to stop for a second before we get all confused.

I've known that I've been lost for quite some time now – years and years – but if I can find the moment that I first discovered I was lost, there might be a clue . . .

This all starts with Jorge. After I'd been in a therapy for a few months, Jorge suggested I go see El Brujo. I wasn't keen on the idea, being both sceptical and afraid of things like curanderos but Jorge was persuasive and lent me bus fare enough to get me at least as far as the border . . .

It actually starts before that. It starts in France, Paris, France, the Moveable Feast, the City of Light where I lived for a couple of years. En France où mes étudiants me disaient que je parlais le français comme une vache Catalan. En France où j'étais étranger, un Anglais, un Argentin-Canadien, une faux touriste. Paris, France where I lived and worked illegally, where I would produce my transit pass whenever policemen asked for my papers. In France, where I was undocumented, extralegal, marginal and where for some reason, known perhaps only by Carlos Gardel and Julio Cortázar, I felt almost at home.

Or it starts before the City of Light, in the City of Sludge: Kitchener, Ontario. There in Kitchener, where I learned to drive, where I first had sex, where there was nothing to do but eat donuts and dream of elsewhere. There in Kitchener, where I once wrote a letter to the editor and suggested that it was not a good idea to ban books in schools, and it was there in Kitchener that a stranger responded to my letter and suggested that I go back to my own country.

No. It starts, in fact, at the airport where my parents and my grandparents and our friends couldn't stop crying and hugged each other continually and said good bye again and again until the stewardess finally came and took me out of my father's arms and carried me on to the plane – forcing my parents to finally board –

Maybe. Maybe not.

Maybe it starts with Columbus. Maybe it starts with the genius Arab engineer who invented the rudder. Maybe a little history is required to put this all in order.

History

SLIDE **An Idiosyncratic History of America**

VERDECCHIA Our History begins approximately 200 million years ago in the Triassic Period of the Mesozoic Era when the original super-continent, Pangaea, broke up and the continents of the earth assumed the shapes we now recognize.

SLIDE **map of the world**

5000 B.C.: The first settlements appear in the highlands of Mexico and in the Andes mountains.

1500 B.C.: The pyramid at Teotihuacán is built.

SLIDE **photo of pyramid**

At the same time, the Pinto build settlements further north.

Early 1400s A.D.: Joan of Arc

SLIDE **statue of Joan of Arc**

is born and shortly thereafter, burned. At the same time, the Incas in Peru develop a highly efficient political system.

1492: Catholic Spain is very busy integrating the Moors. These Moors or Spaniards of Islamic culture who have been in Spain some 700 years suffer the same fate as the Spanish Jews: they are converted, or exiled, their heretical books and bodies burned.

SLIDE **portrait of Columbus**

Yes, also in 1492: this chubby guy sails the Ocean Blue.

1500: Pedro Cabral stumbles across what we now call Brazil – Portugal, fearing enemy attacks, discourages and suppresses writing about the colony.

1542: The Spanish Crown passes the Law of the Indies. This law states that the settlers have only temporary concessions to these lands while the real owners are the Native Americans. Curiously, the Spanish Crown does not inform the Natives that the land is legally theirs. An oversight no doubt.

1588: The invincible Spanish Armada is defeated. Spain grows poorer and poorer as gold from the New World is melted down to pay for wars and imported manufactured goods from the developed northern countries. El Greco finishes *The Burial of Count Orgaz.*

SLIDE *The Burial of Count Orgaz*

Lope de Vega writes *La Dragontea.* Caldéron de La Barca and Velázquez are about to be born.

1808: Beethoven writes Symphonies 5 and 6. France invades Spain and in the power vacuum, wars of independence break out all over New Spain. Goya paints

SLIDE **Executions of the Citizens of Madrid**

Executions of the Citizens of Madrid.

1812: Beethoven writes Symphonies 7 and 8 and a war breaks out in North America.

1832: Britain occupies the Malvinas Islands and gives them the new, silly name of the Falklands.

1846: The U.S. attacks Mexico.

1863: France attacks Mexico and installs an Austrian as emperor.

1867: Mexico's Austrian emperor is executed, volume one of *Das Kapital* is published, and The Dominion of Canada is established.

1902: Gorki writes *The Lower Depths*, the U.S. acquires control over the Panama Canal and Beatrix Potter writes *Peter Rabbit.*

SLIDE **illustration of Peter Rabbit**

1961: Ernest Hemingway kills himself,

SLIDE **photo of Hemingway**

West Side Story

SLIDE **photo of the 'Sharks' in mid-dance**

wins an Academy Award, a 680-pound giant sea-bass is caught off the Florida coast,

SLIDE **photo of large fish**

and the U.S. attacks Cuba.

SLIDE **photo of Fidel Castro**

1969: Richard Nixon

SLIDE **photo of Richard Nixon**

is inaugurated as president of the U.S., Samuel Beckett

SLIDE **photo of Samuel Beckett**

is awarded the Nobel Prize for Literature, the Montreal Canadiens

SLIDE **photo of the 1969 Canadiens team**

win the Stanley Cup for hockey and I attend my first day of classes at Anne Hathaway Public School.

Roll call

(*Music: 'God Save the Queen'*)

VERDECCHIA   I am seven years old. The teacher at the front of the green classroom reads names from a list.

'Jonathon Kramer?'

Jonathon puts his hand up. He is a big boy with short red hair.

'Sandy Nemeth?'

Sandy puts her hand up. She is a small girl with long hair. When she smiles we can see the gap between her front teeth.

'Michael Uffelman?'

Michael puts his hand up. He is a tall boy

with straight brown hair sitting very neatly in his chair.

My name is next.

Minutes, hours, a century passes as the teacher, Miss Wiseman, forces her mouth into shapes hitherto unknown to the human race as she attempts to pronounce my name.

'Gwillyou – ree – moo . . . Verdeek – cheea?'

I put my hand up. I am a minuscule boy with ungovernable black hair, antennae and gills where everyone else has a mouth.

'You can call me Willy', I say. The antennae and gills disappear.

It could have been here – but I don't want to talk about myself all night.

Wideload's terms

WIDELOAD   Thank God.

I mean I doan know about you but I hate it when I go to el teatro to de theatre and I am espectin to see a play and instead I just get some guy up dere talking about himself – deir life story – who cares? Por favor . . . And whatever happened to plays anyway – anybody remember plays? Like wif a plot and like a central character? Gone de way of modernism I guess and probaly a good thing too. I mean I doan know if I could stand to see another play about a king dat's been dead for 400 years –

Anyway –

The Smiths

WIDELOAD   When I first got to América del Norte I needed a place to live and I diden have a lot of money so I stayed wif a family. The Smiths – Mr. and Mrs. and deir two kids Cindy and John. And it was nice you know. Like it was like my first contact with an ethnic family and I got a really good look at de way dey live. I mean sure at times it was a bit exotic for me, you know de food for example, but mostly I just realized they were a family like any other wif crazy aunts and fights and generation gaps and communication problems and two cars, a VCR, a microwave, a cellular phone and a dog named Buster dat ate my socks.

Dey wanted to know all about me so I told dem stories about my mafioso uncle El Gato and how he won a tank and his wife in a poker game, and stories about my aunt, the opera singer, Luisa la Sonrisa, and about my cousin, Esperanza, about her border crossings and how she almost fell in love.

I came here because I wanted some perspective – you know working for a mafioso gives you a very particular point of view about de world. You know, we all need a filter to look at de world through. Like standing in Latin America I get a clear view of Norteamérica and standing on Latin America while living in Norf America gives me a new filter, a new perspective. Anyway, it was time to change my filter so I came here to estudy. Sí, thanks to mi tío El Gato and my cousin Esperanza who always used to say, 'You should learn to use your brain or somebody else will use it for you', I practically have a doctorate in Chicano estudies. Dat's right – Chicano estudies . . . Well not exactly a doctorate – more like an M.A. or most of an M.A., cause I got my credits all screwed up and I diden finish – my professors said I was ungovernable. I lacked discipline. You know instead of like doing a paper on de historical roots of the oppression of La Raza I organized an all night Salsa Dance Party Extravaganza. I also organized de month-long 'Chico and de Man' Memorial Symposium which I dedicated to my cousin, Esperanza, back home.

Going Home

VERDECCHIA I had wanted to go home for many years but the fear of military service in Argentina kept me from buying that plane ticket. Nobody was certain but everybody was pretty sure that I had committed treason by not registering for my military service when I was sixteen, even though I lived in Canada. Everybody was also reasonably sure that I would be eligible for military service until I was thirty-five. And everybody was absolutely certain that the minute I stepped off a plane in Buenos Aires, military policemen would spring from the tarmac, arrest me and guide me to a jail cell where they would laugh at my earrings and give me a proper hair cut.

I phoned the consulate one day to try to get the official perspective on my situation. I gave a false name and I explained that I wanted to go HOME for a visit, that I was

now a Canadian citizen and no, I hadn't registered for my military service. The gentleman at the consulate couldn't tell me exactly what my status was but he suggested that I come down to the consulate where they would put me on a plane which would fly me directly to Buenos Aires where I would appear before a military tribunal who could tell me in no uncertain terms what my status actually was.

'Well I'll certainly consider that', I said.

And I waited seven years. And in those seven years, the military government is replaced by a civilian one and I decide I can wait no longer; I will risk a return HOME. I set off to discover the Southern Cone.

To minimize my risk I apply for a new Canadian passport which does not list my place of birth,

SLIDE **passport photos**

and I plan to fly first to Santiago, Chile and then cross the border in a bus that traverses the Andes and goes to Mendoza, Argentina.

After an absence of almost fifteen years I am going home. Going Home. I repeat the words softly to my self – my mantra: I Am Going Home – all will be resolved, dissolved, revealed, I will claim my place in the universe when I Go Home.

(*Music: 'Vuelvo al Sur', Roberto Goyeneche*)

I have spent the last fifteen years preparing for this. I bought records and studied the liner notes. I bought maté and dulce de leche. I talked to my friends, questioned my parents and practiced my Spanish with strangers. I befriended former Montonero and Tupamaro guerrillas and people even more dangerous like Jorge: painter, serious smoker, maître de cafe. Jorge the Apocryphal, Jorge of the savage hair. Jorge who moved to Italy and left me alone with my memories. I've spent the past fifteen years reading newspapers, novels and every Amnesty International report on South America. I tracked down a Salvador Allende poster, found postcards of Che and Pablo Neruda. I drank Malbec wines and black market Pisco with a Chilean macro-economist whose cheques always bounced. I learned the words and sang along with Cafrune and Goyeneche.

I saw *Missing* three times.

Santiago

VERDECCHIA   Santiago, Chile.

Chile, your Fodor's travel guide will tell you, immediately strikes the visitor as very cosmopolitan and is known for its award-winning wines and excellent seafood. Chileans, Fodor's tell us, are a handsome, stylish people known for their openness and hospitality. My 1989 Fodor's Guide also tells me that under Pinochet, Chile enjoys a more stable political climate than it did in the early seventies but reports persist of government-sponsored assassinations, kidnappings and torture. (Tell me about it man, I saw *Missing*.)

Well, it is now 1990 and the horrific Pinochet dictatorship is a thing of the past. I ride a comfortable bus into Santiago and continue reading my Fodor's: unfortunately, South America's democracies seem to have higher street-crime rates than the police states. I guess it all depends on how you define street crime. I look out the window and read the graffiti: Ojo! La derecha no duerme. I count all the policemen, one per block it seems. What was it like under Pinochet? A policeman in every house?

(*Music: 'Jingo', Carlos Santana*)

Tired from a ten-hour flight I check into the Hotel de Don Tito, listed on page 302 of your Fodor's as a moderate, small hotel with six suites, eight twins, eight singles, bar, homey atmosphere, and it's located on one of the main streets in Santiago on Huérfanos at Huérfanos 578. (Huérfanos – Spanish for orphans.) I shower, shave and take an afternoon nap.

Three blasts from the street wake me up and pull me to the window.

There, three stories below, directly in front of the moderate and homey Hotel de Don Tito, there on the road, directly below my window, there a man in a suit, his shirt soaked an impossible red, lies writhing as an enormous crowd gathers. I reach for my camera and begin to take photographs. I take photographs with a 135 mm. telephoto and then change lenses to get a sense of the crowd that has built up. I take photographs of the man who was shot on the first day of my return home after an absence of almost fifteen years, as more policemen arrive pulling weapons from their jean jackets. I take photographs as the man in the suit, his lower body apparently immobilized, reaches wildly for the legs that surround him, as the motorcycle police expertly push the crowd away from the Hotel de Don Tito, moderate in Fodor's, Huérfanos 578, homey, page 302. I take photographs as still more policemen arrive waving things that look like Uzis. I take photographs with a Pentax MX and a 35 mm. F 2.8 lens as the dying man, one of his shoes lying beside him, his gun on the road, gives up reaching for the legs around him. I take photographs from my room in the Hotel de Don Tito, Huérfanos 578, moderate in Fodor's, as the press arrives and NO AMBULANCE EVER COMES. I take photographs, 64 ASA Kodachromes, as he dies and I take photographs as the policemen (all men) talk to each other and I wonder if anyone has seen me and I take photographs as the policemen smoke cigarettes and cover him up and I take photographs and I realize that I have willed this to happen.

Dancing

WIDELOAD   Oye, you know I do like you Saxons. Really you guys are great. I always have a very good time whenever we get together. Like sometimes, I'll be out with some friends from de Saxonian community and we'll be out at a bar having a few cervezas, you know, vacilando, and some music will be playing and *La Bamba* will come on. And all de Saxons get all excited and start tappin' deir toes and dey get all carried away and start doing dis thing with deir heads . . . and dey get dis look in deir eyes like it's Christmas an dey look at me and say, 'Hey Wideload, *La Bamba*'.

'Ya mang, la puta bamba'.

'Wideload man, do you know de words?'

'Do I know de words? Mang, do I have an enorme pinga? Of course I know de words: pala pala pala la bamba . . . Who doesn't know de words?'

(*Music: 'Navidad Negra', Ramiro's Latin Orchestra*)

Espeaking of music I haf to say dat I love de way you guys dance. I think you Saxons are some of de most interesting dancers on de planet. I lof to go down to the Bamboo when my friend Ramiro is playing and just watch you guys dance because you are so free – like nothing gets in your way: not de beat, not de rhythm, nothing.

What I especially like to watch is like a Saxon guy dancing wif a Latin woman. Like she is out dere and she's smiling and doing a little cu-bop step and she's having a good time and de Saxon guy is like trying really hard to keep up, you know he's making a big effort to move his hips independently of his legs and rib cage and he's flapping his arms like a flamenco dancer. Generally speaking dis applies just to the male Saxon – Saxon women seemed to have learned a move or two . . .

Of course part of de problem is dat you guys wear very funny shoes for dancing – I mean like dose giant running shoes with built-in air compressors and padding and support for de ankles and nuclear laces – I mean you might as well try dancing wif snowshoes on. Your feet have got to be free, so dat your knees are free so dat your hips are free – so dat you can move your culo wif impunity.

So dere dey are dancing away: de Saxon guy and de Latin woman or de Saxon woman and de Latin guy and de Saxon, you can see de Saxon thinking:

Wow, he/she can really dance, he/she can really move those hips, he/she keeps smiling, I think he/she likes me, I bet he/she would be great in bed . . .

Now dis is important so I'm going to continue talking about it – even though it always gets real quiet whenever I start in on this stuff.

Now dere are two things at work here: the first is the fact that whenever a Latin and a Saxon have sex it is going to be a mind-expanding and culturally enriching experience porque nosotros sabemos hacer cosas que ni se imaginaron en la *Kama Sutra*, porque nosotros tenemos un ritmo, un calor un sabor un tumbao de timbales de conga de candomble de kilombo. Una onda, un un dos tres, un dos. Saben . . . ?

Dat's de first factor at work and for dose of you who want a translation of dat come and see me after de show or ask one of de eSpanish espeakers in de audience at intermission.

De second component is the Exotica Factor. De Latin Lover Fantasy. And I'll let you in on a little secret: Latins are no sexier dan Saxons – well maybe just a little.

De difference is dis: we like it. A lot. And we practise. A lot. Like we touch every chance we get.

Now I doan want you to get de impression I'm picking on you Saxons. Nothing could be further from my mind . . . I have de greatest respect for your culture . . . and you know, every culture has its own fertility dances, its own dance of sexual joy – you people hab de Morris Dance

SLIDE **Morris dancers in mid-dance**

and hey, you go to a Morris Dance Festival and it's de Latinos who look silly. You have de Morris Dance – very sexy dance – you know a bunch of guys hopping around wif bells on and every once in a while swinging at each other. Now, I am not doing de dance justice and I am looking for a Morris Dance teacher so if you know of one please pass deir name along. You have de Morris Dance and we have de mambo, de rumba, de cumbia, de son, son-guajiro, son-changui, de charanga, de merengue, de guaguanco, de tango, de samba, salsa . . . shall I continue?

Latin lover

WIDELOAD   Latin Lovers.

SLIDE   **photo of Antonio Banderas**

Dis is Antonio Banderas. He is a Spanish actor, a Spaniard from Spain. Dat's in Europe. Some of you may know him from Almódovar films like *Tie Me Up*, *Tie Me Down* and some of you may know him from de Madonna movie where he appears as de object of her desire and some of you may know him from *De Mambo Kings* based on de excellent book by Oscar Hijuelos. Now according to *Elle* magazine (and dey should know)

SLIDE   ***Elle* magazine cover**

Antonio Banderas is de latest incarnation of de Latin Lover. It says right here: 'Antonio Banderas – A Latin Love God is Born'.

De Latin Lover is always being re-incarnated. Sometimes de Latin Lover is a woman – Carmen Miranda for example.

SLIDE   **photo of Carmen Miranda**

She was Brazilian. Poor Carmen, smiling, sexy even with all dose goddamned bananas on her head – do you know she ended up unemployable, blacklisted because a certain Senator named McCarthy found her obscene?

SLIDE **photo of Delores del Rio**
Dere was also Delores del Rio,

SLIDE **photo of Maria Montez**
Maria Montez, some of you may remember her as Cobra Woman,

SLIDE **photo of Rita Moreno**
den Rita Moreno, today we have Sonia Braga . . .

SLIDE **photo of Sonia Braga**

SLIDE **photo of Rudolph Valentino**
For de men dere was Rudolf Valentino,

SLIDE **photo of Fernando Lamas**
Fernando Lamas,

SLIDE **photo of Ricardo Montalban**
Mr. Maxwell House and of course . . .

SLIDE **photo of Desi Arnaz**
Desi Arnaz whom we all remember as Ricky Ricardo from Ricky and Lucy those all-time great TV lovers. Now Ricky may not exactly live up to de steamy image of unbridled sexuality we expect from our Latin Lovers but you have to admit he's a pretty powerful icon. Funny, cute, musical and more often dan not, ridiculous.

Let's see what *Elle* magazine has to say about Latin Lovers:

'He's short dark and handsome, with lots of black hair from head to chest. He's wildly emotional, swinging from brooding sulks to raucous laughter and singing loudly in public. He's relentlessly romantic, with a fixation on love that looks to be total: he seems to be always about to shout, "I must have you"'.

SLIDE **I must have you**
'He is the Latin Lover, an archetype of masculinity built for pleasure'.

The article begins by explaining the myth of the Latin Lover and then uses the myth to explain Banderas. Banderas cannot explain himself apparently because his English is too limited.

In *Mirabella,*

SLIDE ***Mirabella* cover**
another glossy magazine, there is another article on Banderas and it describes how Banderas pronounces the word LOVE. He pronounces it 'Looov–aaa'. Ooooh isn't dat sweet and sexy and don't you just want to wrap him up in your arms and let him whisper filthy things in your ear in Spanish and broken English? Especially when, as also described in the *Mirabella* article, he wipes his mouth on the tablecloth and asks, 'What can I done?' Don't you just want to fuck him? I do. I

wonder though if it would be quite so disarming or charming if it was Fidel Castro wiping his mouth on the tablecloth?

SLIDE ***Gentleman's Quarterly* cover**
Dis is Armand Assante.

He plays Banderas's brother in de movie, *Mambo Kings.*

He is an Italo-American.

The subtitle here says *De Return of Macho*. Did macho go away for a while? I hadn't noticed. Anyway, it has returned for dose of you who missed it.

According to dis article in *GQ*, Signor Assante almost did not get de part in de movie because de estudio, Warner Brothers, wanted a name – dey wanted a big-name A-list actor – like Robin Williams to play a Cuban. But, according to de article the director of the movie had the 'cajones'

SLIDE **cajones**
to buck the studio and give the part to Assante. Cajones . . .

Now the word I think they want to use is cojones,

SLIDE **cojones**
which is a colloquial term for testicles. What they've ended up with in *GQ* magazine is a sentence that means the director had the crates or boxes to buck the studio.

SLIDE **cojones = testicles**
SLIDE **cajones = crates**
Could be just a typo but you never know.

Now I find it really interesting dat all of the advance publicity for dis movie was concentrated in de fashion-magazine trade. When a Hollywood trade-magazine and major newspapers tell me de movie feels authentic and when the movie is pre-sold because its stars are sexy Latino love gods and macho and cause dey wear great clothes, I begin to suspect dat dis movie is another attempt to trade on the look, the feel, de surface of things Latin.

It goes back to this thing of Latin Lovers being archetypes of men and women built for pleasure. Whose pleasure mang? Your movie-going pleasure? The pleasure of de Fashion-Industrial-Hollywood complex? Think about it –

In dose movies we can't solve our own problems, we can't win a revolution without help from gringos, we can't build the pyramids at Chichén Itzá without help from space aliens, we don't win the Nobel

Prize, no, instead we sing, we dance, we fuck like a dream, we die early on, we sleep a lot, we speak funny, we cheat on each other, we get scared easy, we amuse you. And it's not just in de movies – it's in –

(*A loud buzzer goes off.*)

Dere goes de buzzer – indicating dat some forty-five minutes of de show have elapsed and dat less dan fifteen minutes remain till intermission. Unofficial tests indicate dat audiences grow restless at de forty-five-minute mark so we are going to take de briefest of breaks and give you de opportunity to shift around in your seats and scratch your culo and whisper to the person next to you.

And during dis break we are gonna see some clips from a mega-musical spectacular dat will be opening here soon. It's called *Miss Tijuana*. Dey are gonna be building a special theatre to house *Miss Tijuana* cause it's a very big show wif lots of extras. It's going to be an adobe theatre wif Adobe Sound.

Here's de break.

(*Video: clips of cartoons and movies featuring, among other things: Latinos, Hispanics, dopey peasants, Anthony Quinn and a certain mouse. Cheesy music plays. Then the loud buzzer goes off again.*)

Travel sickness

VERDECCHIA   When I travel I get sick. I've thrown up in most of the major centres of the Western world: Paris, Rome, Madrid, New York, London, Venice, Seaforth, Ontario, Calgary . . . And it's not just too much to drink or drugs, sometimes it's as simple as the shape of the clouds in the sky or the look on someone's face in the market or the sound my shoes make on the street. These things are enough to leave me shaking and sweating in bed with a churning stomach, no strength in my legs and unsettling dreams.

Well, I'm in Buenos Aires and so far I haven't thrown up. So far, Everything's Fine.

We meet in Caballito. And Alberto and I have dinner in a bright, noisy restaurant called The Little Pigs and Everything's Fine. And now we're looking for a place to

hear some music, a place in San Telmo to hear some contemporary music, not tango and not folklore. Alberto wants to go see a band called Little Balls of Ricotta and Everything's Fine, but first we have to get the flat tire on his Fiat fixed. We stop at a gomería, a word which translated literally would be a 'rubbery', it's a place where they fix tires. I'm feeling like I need some air so I get out of the car and Everything's Fine, I'm looking at Alberto in the gomería there's this weird green light in the shop and I'm leaning over the car and suddenly I feel very hot and awful and just as quickly I suddenly feel better. I wake up and I'm sitting on the road and somebody's thrown up on me, then I realize the vomit is my own and I'm in Buenos Aires and I'm sick and I've thrown up and we're in a tricky part of town and the cops will be passing by any minute and I haven't done my military service –

Alberto puts me in the back of the car. From the gomería, Alberto brings me half a Coke can whose edges have been carefully trimmed and filed down – a cup of water. I lie in the back of Alberto's uncle's Fiat as we pull away. There's a knock at the window and I'm sure it's the police saying, 'Excuse me but have you got a young man who hasn't done his military service in there, a degenerate who's vomited all over the street?' – but no, it's the guy from the gomería – he wants his Coke-can cup back.

We drive back to my apartment, not mine actually, my grandmother's but she's not there for some reason and I'm using it. I'm feeling a little better but weak, can't raise my head, I watch Buenos Aires spin and speed past and around me, through the back window, like a movie I think, ya that's it I'm in a Costa Gavras film.

I'm on the toilet in my grandmother's apartment, I leave tomorrow, back to Canada, and I ruined this last evening by getting sick, I can't fly like this all poisoned and I have to throw up again and the bidet is right there, and for some reason I remember Alberto telling me how by the end of the month people are coming to his store on the edge of the villa, on the edge of the slum, and asking if they can buy one egg or a quarter of a package of butter or a few cigarettes, and I think yes, in a few years we will kill for an apple, and I throw

up in the bidet and I just want to go home
– but I'm already there – aren't I?

Eventually, I crawl into my
grandmother's bed and sleep.

(*Music: 'Asleep', Astor Piazzolla and Kronos Quartet*)

I dream of Mount Aconcagua, of Iguaçú,
of Ushuaia and condors, of the sierras,
yellow and green, of bay, orange,
quebracho and ombu trees, of running,
sweating horses, of café con crema served
with little glasses of soda water, of the
smell of Particulares 30, of the vineyards of
Mendoza, of barrels full of ruby-red vino
tinto, of gardens as beautiful as Andalusia
in spring. I dream of thousands of emerald-
green parrots flying alongside my airplane
– parrots just like the ones that flew
alongside the bus as I travelled through the
interior.

The Other

VERDECCHIA   I would like to clear up any
possible mis-impression. I should state now
that I am something of an impostor. A fake.
What I mean is: I sometimes confuse my
tenses in Spanish. I couldn't dance a tango
to save my life.

All sides of the border have claimed and
rejected me. On all sides I have been
asked: How long have you been . . . ? How
old were you when . . . ? When did you
leave? When did you arrive? As if it were
somehow possible to locate on a map, on
an airline schedule, on a blueprint, the
precise coordinates of the spirit, of the
psyche, of memory.

(*Music: 'El Mal Dormido', Atahualpa Yupanqui*)

As if we could somehow count or
measure these things.

These things cannot be measured – I
know I tried.

I told the doctor: 'I feel Different. I feel
wrong, out of place. I feel not nowhere, not
neither'.

The doctor said, 'You're depressed'.

I said, 'Yes I am',

The doctor said, 'Well . . . '

I said, 'I want to be tested. Sample my
blood, scan my brain, search my organs.
Find it'.

'Find what?'

'Whatever it is'.

'And when we find it?'

'Get rid of it'.

SLIDES   **x-rays, brain scans**

They didn't find anything. Everything's
absolutely normal, I was told. Everything's
fine. Everything's where it should be. I
wasn't fooled. I am a direct descendant of
two people who once ate an armadillo –
armadillo has a half-life of two thousand
years – you can't tell me that isn't in my
bloodstream. Evita Perón once kissed my
mother and that night she felt her cheek
begin to rot. You can't tell me that hasn't
altered my DNA.

El Teatro

WIDELOAD   Okay,

(*The house lights come up.*)

let's see who's here, what's everybody
wearing, let's see who came to El Teatro
dis evening. What a good-looking bunch of
people. What are you doing here tonight? I
mean don't think we doan appreciate it, we
do. We're glad you've chosen to come here
instead of spending an evening in front of
the Global Village Idiot Box.

Are you a Group? Do you know each
other? No, well, some of you know de
person next to you but collectively, you are
strangers. Estrangers in de night. But
perhaps by the end of the evening you will
no longer be strangers because you will
have shared an experience. You will have
gone through dis show together and it will
have created a common bond among you, a
common reference point.

That's the theory anyway. That the
theatre is valuable because a bunch of
strangers come together and share an
experience. But is it true? I mean how can
you be sharing an experience when you
are all (thankfully) different people? You
have different jobs, different lives, different
histories, different sexual orientations. You
are all watching dis show from a different
perspective. Most of you, for example,
have been awake.

Maybe the only thing you have in
common is dat you are all sitting here right
now listening to me speculate about what
you have in common and dat you all paid
sixteen dollars to hear me do so. But not
everybody paid sixteen dollars, my friends

get in free. So do theatre critics. Weird, huh?

People do end up in the weirdest places. I mean some of you are from Asia, some from el Caribe, some from Africa, some of you are from de Annex and you ended up in dis small room with me. And me, I left home to escape poverty and I ended up working in de theatre? Weird. Let's take a break, huh?

It's intermission ladies and gentlemen. Get your hot chocolate and Wideload wine gums outside.

(*Music: 'La Guacamya', Los Lobos*)

Act II

SLIDE **Every North American, before this century is over, will find that he or she has a personal frontier with Latin America.**

This is a living frontier, which can be nourished by information, but, above all, by knowledge, by understanding, by the pursuit of enlightened self-interest on both parts.

Or it can be starved by suspicion, ghost stories, arrogance, ignorance, scorn and violence.
– Carlos Fuentes[4]

(*Music: 'Peligro', Mano Negra*)

Call to arms

VERDECCHIA (*voice-over*) This play is not a plea for tolerance. This is not a special offer for free mambo lessons nor an invitation to order discount Paul Simon albums. This is a citation, a manifesto. This is a summons to begin negotiations, to claim your place on the continent.

Of ferrets and avocado

WIDELOAD NEVER GIVE A FERRET AVOCADO!
SLIDE **photo of a ferret**
De ferret ees a Northern European animal – known also as de polecat and related to de bear and de wolberine. Dey are fierce little creatures, used to kill pests like rabbits. De ferret can be domesticated. Some of you may have a ferret of your own which you have affectionately named

Blinky or Squiggly or Beowulf. Ferrets, as you ferret owners will attest, are excellent pets: intelligent, playful, affectionate, cute as all-get-out. It takes four generations to domesticate a ferret but only one generation for the ferret to revert to a feral state – dat means to go savage. Interesting huh?

De avocado is a fruit from de Southern hemisphere – known variously as avocado, aguacate and, for some reason known only to themselves, as palta to Argentinians. De avocado is a rich, nutritious fruit which can be used in all sorts of ways – as a mayonnaise, in guacamole, spread some on some pork tenderloin for a sanwich Cubano. Avocados make lousy pets. Dey are not playful and do not respond at all to commands.

Never give a ferret avocado.

Because it will blow up. Deir northern constitutions cannot process de rich southern fruit.

Think about dat.

(*Music: Fela Kuti's 'Shalaode', performed by Wganda Kenya*)

Correction

WIDELOAD I want to draw some attention to myself. Some more attention. I want to talk about dat nasty 's' word: estereotype. I would like to set the record straight on dis subject and state dat I am by no means an estereotype. At least I am no more of an estereotype dan dat other person in de show: dat neurotic Argentinian. And I know dere's a lot of confusion on dis subject so let me offer a few pointers.

If I was a real estereotype, I wouldn't be aware of it. I wouldn't be talking to you about being an estereotype. If I was a real estereotype, you would be laughing at me, not with me. And if I was a real estereotype, you wouldn't take me seriously. And you do take me seriously. Don't you?

I'm the real thing. Don't be fooled by imitations.

Border crossings

VERDECCHIA (*speaking to Customs Agent*) 'Los Angeles. Uh, Los, Las Anngel – Lows Anjelees, uh, L.A.

'Two weeks.

'Pleasure.

'I'm a Canadian citizen.

'Pleasure'. (*To audience*) Didn't I just answer that question?

(*To Customs Agent*) 'I'm . . . an . . . actor actually.

'Ever seen "Street Legal"?

'Well, I'm mostly in the theatre. I don't think . . . Okay uh, the Tarragon uh, Canadian Stage, the –

'I'm not surprised.

'Yes, that's my book. Well, it's not *mine*. It's a novel. That I'm reading.

(*To audience*) Oh, Jeeezzuz.

(*To Customs Agent*) 'A guy, you know, who has a kind of identity problem and uh –

'I told you: pleasure. Come on what is this? I'm a Canadian citizen – we're supposed to be friends. You know, Free Trade, the longest undefended border in the world . . . all that?' (*To audience*) I had less trouble getting into Argentina.

(*To Customs Agent*) 'No, I'm not unemployed. I'm an actor. I'm between jobs, I'm on holidays.

'Thanks'.

(*To audience*) Some borders are easier to cross than others. Try starting a conversation in Vancouver with the following statement: 'I like Toronto'.

Some things get across borders easier than others.

SLIDE **large, angry bee**

Killer Bees for example.

(*Music: 'Muiñeira de Villanova', Milladoiro*)

Music. Music crosses borders.

My grandfather was a gallego, from Galicia, Spain. This music is from Galicia and yes, those are bagpipes. Those of us with an ethnomusicological bent can only ask ourselves, 'How did the bagpipes ever end up in . . . Scotland?'

Ponte guapa que traen el haggis!

The bandoneon, cousin to the concertina and step-brother to the accordion, came to the Río de la Plata via Germany. Originally intended for organless churches, the bandoneon found its true calling in the whore-houses of Buenos Aires and Montevideo playing the most profane music of all: the Tango.

Banned by Pope Pius X, the tango was, at first, often danced only by men because its postures were considered too crude, too sexual for women – it was, after all, one of the first dances in which men and women embraced.

King Ludwig of Bavaria forbade his officers to dance it and the Duchess of Norfolk explained that the tango was contrary to English character and manners, but the tango, graciously received in the salons of Paris, soon swept London's Hotel Savoy and the rest of Europe. Finally, even polite society in Argentina acknowledged it.

The tango, however, has not been entirely domesticated. It is impossible to shop or aerobicize to tango . . . porque el tango es un sentimiento que se baila.

And what is it about the tango, this national treasure that some say was born of the gaucho's crude attempts to waltz?

(*Music: 'Verano Porteño', Astor Piazzolla*)[5]

It is music for exile, for the preparations, the significations of departure, for the symptoms of migration. It is the languishing music of picking through your belongings and deciding what to take. It is the two a.m. music of smelling and caressing books none of which you can carry – books you leave behind with friends who say they'll always be here when you want them when you need them – music for a bowl of apples sitting on your table, apples you have not yet eaten, apples you cannot take – you know they have apples there in that other place but not these apples, not apples like these – you eat your last native apple and stare at what your life is reduced to – all the things you can stick into a sack. It will be cold, you will need boots, you don't own boots except these rubber ones – will they do? You pack them, you pack a letter from a friend so you will not feel too alone.

Music for final goodbyes, for one last drink and a quick hug as you cram your cigarettes into your pocket and run to the bus, you run, run, your chest heaves, like the bellows of the bandoneon. You try to watch intently to emblazon in your mind these streets, these corners, those houses, the people, the smells, even the lurching bus fills you with a kind of stupid happiness and regret – music for the things you left behind in that room: a dress, magazines, some drawings, two pairs of

shoes and blouses too old to be worn any
more . . . four perfect apples.

Music for cold nights under
incomprehensible stars, for cups of coffee
and cigarette smoke, for a long walk by the
river where you might be alone or you
might meet someone. It is music for
encounters in shabby stairways, the music
of lovemaking in a narrow bed, the
tendernesses, the caress, the pull of strong
arms and legs.

Music for men and women thin as bones.
Music for your invisibility.

Music for a letter that arrives telling you
that he is very sick. Music for your arms
that ache from longing from wishing he
might be standing at the top of the stairs
waiting to take the bags and then lean over
and kiss you and even his silly stubble
scratching your cold face would be
welcome and you only discover that you're
crying when you try to find your keys –

Music for a day in the fall when you buy
a new coat and think perhaps you will live
here for the rest of your life, perhaps it will
be possible, you have changed so much,
would they recognize you? Would you
recognize your country? Would you
recognize yourself?

WIDELOAD   Basically, tango is music for
fucked up people.

VERDECCHIA   Other things cross borders
easily. Diseases and disorders. Like
amnesia. Amnesia crosses borders.

Drug war deconstruction

WIDELOAD   Hey I want to show you a little
movie. It's a home movie. It came into my
home and I saved it to share with my
friends. It's called *The War On Drugs*. Some
of you may have seen it already so we're
just gonna see some of de highlights.

(*An edited drug-war TV movie plays without
sound.* WIDELOAD *explains the action.*)

Dis is de title: It says DE WAR ON
DRUGS. In BIG BLOCK LETTERS. In
English. Dis is another title: *The Cocaine
Cartel*. Dey're talking about de Medellin
Cartel in Colombia.

Dis is de hero. He is a Drug Enforcement
Agent from de U.S. who is sent to Colombia
to take on de Medellin Cartel. He is
smiling. He kisses his ex-wife. (*As character
on-screen turns away*) Oh . . . he is shy.

Dis woman is a kind of judge – a
Colombian judge and she agrees to
prosecute de Medellin cartel, to build a case
against de drug lords even though her life is
being threatened here on de phone even as
we watch. Watch. (*On-screen, the judge
speaks into the phone;* WIDELOAD *provides
the dialogue.*) 'But . . . I didn't order a pizza'.

Dis guy is a journalist, an editor for a big
Colombian newspaper. He is outspoken in
his criticism of the drug lords. He has
written editorial after editorial condemning
de Cartel and calling for de arrest of de
drug lords. He is a family man as we can
tell by his Volvo car and by de presents
which he loads into de car to take to his
loved ones.

Okay, dis is a long shot so can we
fast-forward through this part? (*The tape
speeds up.*)

He's going home after a hard day at de
office. He is in traffic. He is being followed
by two guys on a motorcycle. Dey come to
an intersection. (*The tape resumes normal
speed.*)

Dey estop. De light is red. De guy gets off
de motorcycle. Dum-dee-bumbe-dum. He
has a gun! Oooh! And de family-man editor
is killed and as we can see he is driving one
of dose Volvos wif de built-in safety feature
dat when de driver is killed, de car parks
itself automatically. Very good cars Volvos.

Dis is de Medellin Cartel. Dese are de
drug lords. Dey are de bad guys. We know
dey are bad because dey have manicured
hands, expensive jewellery, even more
expensive suits and . . . dark hair. Dere's a
lot of dem, dey are at a meeting, talking
business. And dis guy is de kingpin, Pablo
Escobar, head of de Medellin Cartel, de
baddest of de bad. We know he is bad
because he has reptilian eyes.

Okay, lemme put dis on pause for a
second – Dis movie shows us a lot of
things. It shows us dat drugs wreck families
– in dis case de family of de nice white guy
who is trying to stop de drug dealers –
nobody in his family uses drugs – it's just
he spends so much time fighting drugs dat
his family falls apart.

De movie shows us dat de drug lords are
nasty people who will not hesitate to kill
anybody who gets in deir way. And de big
guy, de kingpin, Pablo Escobar who is now
dead, was, according to *The Economist*
magazine, one of the richest men in de

world. Now Señor Escobar is not only a giant in free-market capitalism, he was also very big in public works, especially public housing. Interesting huh? De movie doesn't show us dat.

What else doesn't de movie show us?

It does not show us dat, for example, profits from de sale of cocaine are used to fund wars like de U.S. war on Nicaragua which left some 20,000 Nicaraguans dead. Dis movie does not show us dat right wing Miami-based terrorists, major U.S. drug traffickers, de Medellin Cartel, Syrian drug and arms dealers, de CIA, de State Department and Oliver North all worked together to wage war on Nicaragua. It does not show us that charges against major U.S. drug traffickers – dose are de people who bring de drugs on to dis part of de continent – charges against dose people were dropped once they became involved in the Contra war against Nicaragua.

Some of you are, naturally, sceptical and some of you have heard all dis before because you have read de Kerry Sub-Committee report. Allow me to recommend it to those of you who haven't read it. It is incomplete at 400 pages but it does outline dese things I'm talking about. It makes excellen' bedtime or bathroom reading. I urge you to pick up a copy. And if you have any questions gimme a call.

So de next time a blatant piece of propaganda like dis one comes on, I hope we will watch it sceptically and de next time we stick a straw up our nose I hope we will take a moment to make sure we know exactly where de money we give our dealer is going.[6]

Audition

VERDECCHIA   It's two o'clock on a wintry afternoon and I have an audition for a TV movie. (*A dialect tape plays.*)

The office has sliding glass doors, hidden lighting fixtures and extravagant windows. There are four or five people seated behind a table including a guy with very expensive sunglasses.

(VERDECCHIA *sits down in front of a video camera. A close-up of* VERDECCHIA *appears on a monitor. In the following section, he sometimes speaks to the camera and sometimes off-camera to the audience.*)

(*on-camera*) Hi, I'm Guillermo Verdecchia. I'm with Noble Talent.

(*off-camera*) For those of you who aren't in the business this is called slating. And when I say the Business I do mean the Industry. Slating is the first thing you do when you audition for a part on a TV show or a movie – you put your face and your name and your agent's name on tape before you read the scene.

(*on-camera*) I'm 5'9". On a good day.

(*off-camera*) That's called a little joke. Always good to get the producers and director laughing.

(*on-camera*) I'm from Argentina, actually. My special skills include driving heavy machinery, tango dancing, scuba diving, polo playing and badminton. I speak three languages including English and I specialize in El Salvadorean refugees, Italian bob-sledders, Arab horse-thieves and Uruguayan rugby players who are forced to cannibalize their friends when their plane crashes in the Andes.

(*off-camera*) Actually, I've never played a horse-thief or a rugby cannibal but I have auditioned for them an awful lot.

(*on-camera*) No. I've never been on 'Really-True-Things-That-Actual-Cops-Do-As-Captured-By-Totally-Average-Citizens-With-Only-A-Video-Camera' before. It's a pleasure to be here. I'm reading for the part of Sharko.

(*off-camera*) An overweight Hispanic in a dirty suit it says here. I'm perfect for it.

(*on-camera*) Here we go.

(*Music: 'Speedy Gonzales Meets Two Crows from Tacos', Carl Stalling*)

(*Reads on-camera*) A black Camaro slides into the foreground, the engine throbbing like a hard-on from hell. Cut to close-up on trunk opening to reveal a deadly assault rifle. We hear Sharko's voice.

(VERDECCHIA *slips on a red bandanna*)

(*off-camera*) That's me.

(*Reads Sharko's part on-camera.*) There it is man. Is a thing of great beauty, no?

Sure man, I got what you ordered: Silencer, bullets. I even got you a little extra cause I like doing business wif you. A shiny new handgun.

Come on man, it's like brand-new. I got it off some old bag who used it to scare away peeping toms.

Ah man, you take all this stuff for two grand, and I'll throw in the pistol for a couple of hundred. If you don't like it, you can sell it to some school kids for twice the price.

You already got one, hah? It was a present . . . I see. A present from who?

From your Uncle Sam. Dat's nice. I diden know you had got an Uncle . . .

(*with dawning horror*) You're a cop?

(*off-camera*) Well that's that. I should've done it differently. I could've been funnier.

(*on-camera*) Uh, would you like me to do the scene again? I could do it differently. I have a blue bandanna.

Okay. Thanks very much.

Nice to meet you.

SLIDE **Ay ay ay ay I am the Frito Bandito**

(*Music: 'Cielito Lindo', Placido Domingo*)

Santiago two

VERDECCHIA I went back to Santiago and looked for some sign of the man who had been shot on the first day of my return. I looked for a stain, a scrape, anything, his shoe perhaps had been left behind. Nothing.

I wondered who he might have been. I remembered the redness of his shirt, the brightness of the sun. It was five o'clock.

A las cinco de la tarde.

Eran las cinco en punto de la tarde.

Un niño trajo la blanca sábana

a las cinco de la tarde.[7]

I saw someone die, I watched him die – that's what it looks like. That's where they end up – gun men, bank robbers, criminals and those brave revolutionaries and guerrillas you dreamed of and imagined you might be, might have been – they end up bleeding in the middle of the street, begging for water.

They end up dying alone on the hot pavement in a cheap suit with only one shoe. People die like that here. Ridiculous, absurd, pathetic deaths.

I came for a sign, I came because I had to know and now I know.

SLIDE **photos of shooting**

¡Que no quiero verla!

Que mi recuerdo se quema.

¡Avisad a los jazmines

con su blancura pequeña!

¡Que no quiero verla![8]

At the hotel they told me he was a bank robber. The papers said the same thing – a bank robber, died almost immediately in a shoot out, name of Fernando Ochoa, nationality unknown, not interested. Case closed. Dead gone erased.

I told them I was a Canadian writer/journalist/film maker. They believed me. They let me look at the files, they let me talk, very briefly, to the cops who shot him, and since no one had shown up to claim them, they let me go through his personal effects. There wasn't much. A Bic lighter, with a tiny screw in the bottom of it so it could be refilled, an empty wallet. A package of Marlboros, with two crumpled cigarettes. There was a letter to someone named Mercedes. It read 'Querida Mercedes: It is bitterly cold tonight in my little room but I can look out the window and see the stars. I imagine that you are looking at them too. I take comfort in the fact that you and Ines and I share the same sky'. There was also a newspaper from August 2nd, the day I arrived, the day he was shot. The headline claimed that former president Pinochet and the former Minister of the Interior knew nothing about the bodies that had been found in the Río Mapocho. I asked about his shoe – the one I saw on the road – no one knew anything about a shoe although they knew he wore size forty-two just like me –

Decompression

VERDECCHIA I'm sitting in the bar at Ezeiza, I'm in the bar at Heathrow, in the bar at Terminal sixty-two at LAX and I'm decompressing, preparing to surface. I'll arrive at Pearson at Mirabelle at Calgary International and I know that nothing will have changed and that everything will be different. I know that I've left some things behind – a sock in a hotel in Mendoza, a ring in a slum in Buenos Aires, a Zippo lighter in a lobby in Chile, a toenail in Ben's studio in Pougnadoresse, a combful of hair in the sink in the washroom at Florian in Venice.

These vestiges, these cells are slowly crawling towards each other. They are crossing oceans and mountains and six-lane expressways. They are calling to each other and arranging to meet in my sleep.

The therapist

VERDECCHIA   So . . . I went to see a
Therapist. He trained in Vienna but his
office was in North York. I didn't tell him
that I was afraid my toenails were coming
after me in my sleep – I told him how I
felt, what was happening. I have memories
of things that never happened to me – I
feel nostalgia for things I never knew – I
feel connected to things I have no
connection with, responsible, involved,
implicated in things that happen thousands
of miles away.

My Therapist asked about my family. If
I'd been breast-fed. He asked about my sex
life, my habits. He asked me to make a list
of recurring dreams, a list of traumatic
events including things like automobile
accidents. I answered his questions and
showed him drawings.

SLIDE   **drawings**

My Therapist told me I was making
progress. I believed him. (Who wouldn't
believe a Therapist trained in Vienna?) At
about the same time that I started doing
what he called 'deep therapy work', or
what I privately called reclaiming my inner
whale, I began to lose feeling in my
extremities. It started as a tingling in the
tips of my fingers and then my hands went
numb. Eventually, over a period of
months, I lost all feeling in my left arm and
I could hardly lift it.

My Therapist told me to see a Doctor.

The Doctor told me to rest and gave me
pills.

Jorge made me go see El Brujo.

I said, 'Jorge, what do you mean brujo?
I'm not going to somebody who's gonna
make me eat seaweed'.

Jorge said, 'No, che loco, por favor,
dejate de joder, vamos che, tomate un
matecito loco y vamos . . . '

Who could argue with that? 'Where is
this Brujo, Jorge?'

'En la frontera'.

'Where?'

'Bloor and Madison'.

El Brujo

(*Music: 'Mojotorro', Dino Saluzzi*)

SLIDE   **The West is no longer west. The
old binary models have been replaced
by a border dialectic of ongoing flux.**

**We now inhabit a social universe in
constant motion, a moving cartography
with a floating culture and a
fluctuating sense of self. – Guillermo
Gómez-Peña**[9]

VERDECCHIA

Porque los recién llegardos me
  sospechan,
porque I speak mejor Inglish que
  eSpanish,
porque mis padres no me creen,
porque no como tripa porque no como
  lengua,
porque hasta mis dreams are subtitled.

I went to see El Brujo at his place on
Madison and you know I'd been to see a
palm reader before so I sort of knew what
to expect. And he's this normal guy who
looks sort of like Freddy Prince except with
longer hair. And I told him about my
Therapist and about the numbness in my
body and El Brujo said, 'He tried to steal
your soul', and I laughed this kind of
honking sputtering laugh. I thought maybe
he was kidding.

El Brujo asked me, 'How do you feel?' and
I said, 'Okay. My stomach is kind of upset'.

And he said, 'Yes it is', and I thought, 'Oh
please just let me get back to reclaiming
my inner whale'.

El Brujo said, 'You have a very bad
border wound'.

'I do?'

'Yes', he said, 'and here in Mexico any
border wounds or afflictions are easily
aggravated'.

I didn't have the heart to tell him that we
were at Bloor and Madison in Toronto. El
Brujo brought out a bottle and thinking this
would be one way to get my money's
worth, I started to drink.

El Brujo said, 'I remember the night
Bolivar burned with fever and realized
there was no way back to the capital; the
night he burned his medals and cried,
"Whosoever works for the revolution plows
the seas"'.

'You *remember* that do you?' I said. 'That
was what 1830 or something?' And I
laughed and had another drink. And El
Brujo laughed too and we had another
drink and another drink and another.

El Brujo said, 'I remember the Zoot Suit
Riots. We were beat up for our pointy shoes
and fancy clothes. I still have the scar'. And
he lifted up his shirt and showed me a

gash. It was ugly and ragged and spotted with freshly dried blood. And that's when I first suspected that maybe we weren't at Bloor and Madison. You see, the Zoot Suit Riots were in 1943.

'What do you remember?' he asked.

'Not much'.

'Try'.

'I remember the Alamo?'

'No you don't'.

'No, you're right I don't'.

El Brujo said, 'Your head aches'.

'Yes it does'.

'Because your left shoe is too tight. Why don't we burn it?' And maybe because I was drunk already or maybe because I really thought that burning my shoe would help my headache, we threw it in the bathtub, doused it in lighter fluid and watched it burn this wild yellow and a weird green when the plastic caught on.

'What do you remember now?' he asked.

'I remember the French Invasion of Mexico; I remember the Pastry War.

'I remember a bar of soap I had when I was little and it was shaped like a bear or a bunny and when it got wet, it grew hair, it got all fuzzy.

'I remember a little boy in a red snow suit who ran away whenever anyone spoke to me in English. I remember la machine queso.

'I remember a gang of boys who wanted to steal my leather jacket even though we all spoke Spanish, a gang of boys who taught me I could be a long-lost son one minute and a tourist the next.

'I remember an audition where I was asked to betray and insult everything I claim to believe in and I remember that I did as I was asked.

'I remember practising t'ai chi in the park and being interrupted by a guy who wanted to start a fight and I remember thinking, "Stupid drunken Mexican". I remember my fear, I taste and smell my fear, my fear of young men who speak Spanish in the darkness of the park, and I know that somewhere in my traitorous heart I can't stand people I claim are my brothers. I don't know who did this to me. I remember feeling sick, I remember howling in the face of my fear . . .

'I remember that I had dreamt I was playing an accordion, playing something improvised, which my grandmother recognized after only three notes as a tango from her childhood, playing a tango I had never learned, playing something improvised, not knowing where my fingers were going, playing an accordion, a tango which left me shaking and sweating.

'And I remember that I dreamt that dream one night after a party with some Spaniards who kept asking me where I was from and why my Spanish was so funny and I remember that I remembered that dream the first time one afternoon in Paris while staring at an accordion in a stall at the flea market and then found 100 francs on the street'.

As I passed out El Brujo said, 'The border is your . . . '

(*Music: 'Nocturno a mi Barrio', Annibal Troilo*)

SLIDE **Cuándo, cuándo me fui?**

The other America

VERDECCHIA The airport is clean clean clean. And big big big. The car that takes me back into the city is big and clean. We drive through big clean empty land under a big, fairly clean sky. I'm back in Canada. It's nice. I'm back in Canada . . . oh well . . .

Why did I come back here?

This is where I work I tell myself, this is where I make the most sense, in this Noah's ark of a nation.

I reach into my pocket expecting to find my Zippo lighter and my last package of Particulares, but instead I find a Bic lighter with a tiny screw in the bottom of it so it can be refilled and a package of Marlboros with two crumpled cigarettes in it. And written on the package is a note, a quote I hadn't noticed before. It says:

No estoy en el crucero:
elegir
es equivocarse.[10]

SLIDE

I am not at the cross roads.
to choose
is to go wrong.
– Octavio Paz

And then I remember, I remember what El Brujo said, he said, 'The Border is your Home'.

I'm not in Canada; I'm not in Argentina. I'm on the Border.

I am Home.

Mais zooot alors, je comprends maintenant, mais oui, merde! Je suis Argentin–Canadien! I am a post-Porteño neo-Latino Canadian! I am the Pan-American Highway!

Latin invasion

WIDELOAD   It's Okay, mang. Everybody relax. I'm back. Ya, I been lying low in dis act but let me tell you I'm here to stay.

And it's quiz time. Please cast your memories way back and tell me who remembers José Imanez?

Ah-ha.

Who remembers de Frito Bandito? Who remembers Cheech and Chong?

Who remembers de U.S. invasion of Panama?

Dat's okay, dat was a trick question.

Who remembers de musical *De Kiss of de Spider Woman*? I do because I paid forty-two bucks to see it: a glamorous, musical celebration of the torture and repression of poor people in a far-away place called Latin America where, just over the walls of the prison, there are gypsies and bullfights, women with big busts and all sorts of exotic, hot-blooded delights. Dat's one of de hit songs from de show, *Big Busted Women*, some of you may recall . . .

Who remembers de ad dat Macdonald's had for deir fajitas not too long ago, featuring a guy called Pedro or Juan, and he says dat he's up here to get some McFajitas because (*reciting with supreme nasality*) 'Dese are de most gueno Fajitas I eber ate'. What de fuck ees dat?

Can you imagine an ad dat went like: 'Hey Sambo, what are you doing here?' 'Well, Mistah, I come up here to get some o' yo' pow'ful good McGrits. Mmmmm-mmm. Wif a watahmelon slice fo' deesert. Yassee'.

I mean, we would be offended.

So, what is it with you people? Who do you think you are? Who do you think we are?

Yes, I am calling you you – I am generalizing, I am reducing you all to de lowest common denominator, I am painting you all with the same brush. Is it starting to bug you yet?

Of course, it is possible dat it doesn't really matter what I say. Because it's all been kind of funny dis evening.

Dat has been my mistake. I have wanted you to like me so I've been a funny guy.

(*Silence.*)

Esto, en serio ahora –

Señoras y señores, we are re-drawing the map of America because economics, I'm told, knows no borders.

SLIDE   **Somehow the word 'foreign' seems foreign these days. The world is smaller, so people are thinking bigger, beyond borders. – IBM advertisement**

Free Trade wif Méjico – dis is a big deal and I want to say dat it is a very complicated thing and it is only the beginning. And I wish to remind you, at this crucial juncture in our shared geographies, dat under dose funny voices and under dose funny images of de frito bandito and under all this talk of Money and Markets there are living, breathing, dreaming men, women and children.

I want to ask you please to throw out the metaphor of Latin America as North America's 'backyard' because your backyard is now a border and the metaphor is now made flesh. Mira, I am in your backyard. I live next door, I live upstairs, I live across de street. It's me, your neighbour, your dance partner.

SLIDE   **Towards un futuro post-Columbian**

Consider

WIDELOAD and VERDECCHIA   Consider those come from the plains, del litoral, from the steppes, from the desert, from the savannah, from the fens, from the sertão, from the rainforest, from the sierras, from the hills and high places.

Consider those come from the many corners of the globe to Fort MacMurray, to Montreal, to Saint John's to build, to teach, to navigate ships, to weave, to stay, to remember, to dream.

Consider those here first. Consider those I have not considered. Consider your parents, consider your grandparents.

Consider the country. Consider the continent. Consider the border.

Going forward

VERDECCHIA   I am learning to live the border. I have called off the Border Patrol.

I am a hyphenated person but I am not falling apart, I am putting together. I am building a house on the border.

And you? Did you change your name somewhere along the way? Does a part of you live hundreds or thousands of kilometres away? Do you have two countries, two memories? Do you have a border zone?

Will you call off the Border Patrol?

Ladies and gentlemen, please reset your watches. It is now almost ten o'clock on a Friday night – we still have time. We can go forward. Towards the centre, towards the border.

WIDELOAD   And let the dancing begin!

(*Music: 'Bacalao con Pan', Irakere*)

Notes

1 Carlos Fuentes' 1984 Massey Lectures, published as Fuentes (1985) *Latin America at war with the Past* (Toronto: CBC Enterprises), elegantly explores, in greater detail, the divisions expressed by the Mexico–North America border.

2 William Langewiesche (1992) 'The Border', *Atlantic Magazine*, 269, 5: 56. This excellent article deals specifically with the Mexico–U.S. border: border crossings, border patrol, drug traffic, economics, etc.

3 The term Latino has its shortcomings but seems to me more inclusive than the term Hispanic. Hispanic is a term used in the United States for bureaucratic, demographic, ideological and commercial purposes. Chicano refers to something else again. Chicano identity is based in the tension of the border. Neither Mexicans nor U.S. Americans, Chicanos synthesize to varying degrees Mexican culture and language – including its indigenous roots – and Anglo-American culture and language.

4 Fuentes, *Latin America at war with the Past*, p. 8.

5 Strictly speaking, Piazzolla's music is not tango with a capital T. Many purists would hotly contest my choice of music here, arguing that Piazzolla destroyed the tango. I would respond that Piazzolla reinvented and thereby rescued the tango from obsolescence. There is no foreseeable end to this argument.

6 For a thorough analysis of the actual parameters of the War on Drugs, see Peter Dale Scott and Jonathon Marshall *Cocaine Politics* (1991) University of California Press.

7 Federico Garcia Lorca (1948) 'La cogida y la muerte', in *Poema del cante jondo / Llanto por Ignacio Sánchez Mejías*, Buenos Aires: Editorial Losada, p. 145.

8 Federico Garcia Lorca (1948) 'La sangre derramada', in *Poema del cante jondo / Llanto por Ignacio Sánchez Mejías*, Buenos Aires: Editorial Losada, p. 148.

9 Guillermo Gómez-Peña (1991) 'The world according to Guillermo Gómez-Peña', *High Performance*, 14, 3: 20. A MacArthur fellow, Gómez-Peña has been a vital contributor to the U.S. debate on 'multiculturalism', urging a rigorous reappraisal of terms such as assimilation, hybridization, border-culture, pluralism, and coexistence. A former member of Border Arts Workshop, he continues to explore notions of identity and otherness in his writings, and in performances such as *Border Brujo* and *The Year of the White Bear*, a collaboration with Coco Fusco.

10 Octavio Paz (1979), from 'A la mitad de esta frase', in *A Draft of Shadows*, edited and translated by Eliot Weinberger, New York: New Directions, p. 72.

19 Charabanc Theatre Company _____

Somewhere Over the Balcony
Northern Ireland

Introduction

The Charabanc Theatre Company drew its
name from a benched open-air wagon used in
Ireland early in the twentieth century for day
trips. For the five out-of-work actresses who
borrowed the term to name their newly
formed company, 'charabanc' was chosen to
connote a collective female endeavour with a
good deal of humour thrown in. The
company was formed in 1983 when Carol
Scanlon, Eleanor Methven, Marie Jones,
Maureen Macauley and Brender Winter, fed
up with the paucity of good roles available for
women in Northern Ireland, came together to
create their own theatre. Their first play, *Lay
Up Your Ends* (1983), about the 1911 strike of
women mill workers in Belfast's linen
industry, was developed from research,
community interviews and workshop
material and scripted with the aid of Martin
Lynch, an established playwright. So
successful was this venture that the group
were encouraged to apply their talents to
further projects of its kind. In fairly rapid
succession, they developed such 'social
history' plays as *Oul' Delf and False Teeth*
(1984), focusing on market dealers hoping for
post-war prosperity, *Now You're Talking*
(1985), about women in a 'reconciliation
centre' dealing with sectarian issues, and
Gold in the Streets (1986), three one-act plays
tracing Irish emigration to England from
early in the twentieth century. Later works
included *Weddins, Weeins and Wakes* (1989)
and *The Blind Fiddler of Glenadauch* (1990), as
well as *The Girls in the Big Picture* (1987), an
uncharacteristically rural drama focusing on
the claustrophobic lives of three unmarried
women in a small community.

Like Sistren in Jamaica, Charabanc adopted
a collaborative process in preparing the
plays, initially using taped interviews for
script material, conducting round-table
discussions on the storyline and sometimes
seeking outside help with writing and
directorial tasks. Later on, this modus
operandi appears to have changed, with
Marie Jones doing the actual writing after the
group had pooled ideas and brainstormed
potential approaches. Typically, the character
roles, whether male or female, were played
by female members of the company, with
props kept to a minimum to reduce costs and
facilitate touring. Often the group auditioned
for directors for specific projects, nicely
inverting the usual hierarchy in the theatre
world. Punchy, topical, written in vernacular
idioms and firmly rooted in everyday
Northern Irish culture, Charabanc's plays
were designed to both entertain and confront.
As standard practice, the company toured
their work widely in both Northern Ireland
and the Irish Republic, often playing at
unconventional venues in order to reach
audiences beyond the urban middle classes.

As a group that worked collectively on
projects examining the lives of ordinary
women in their local constituency,
Charabanc clearly had much in common with
self-declaredly 'feminist' theatre groups
internationally. However, members of the
company were cagey about using the term to
describe themselves, on practical grounds,
because they feared it would alienate the
audiences they sought to address; and on
theoretical/political grounds, because, for
the group, 'feminism' tended to connote
middle-class careerist individualism, which
compromised important class and religious
affiliations/oppressions central to the
political situation in Northern Ireland.
Instead, Charabanc saw their 'feminism' as
inhering in the practice of writing from a
female point of view, stressing that this was
not so much through adherence to feminist
doctrine as simply a natural starting place.
Company members explain this position in

an interview discussing their position within feminist theatre in Ireland:

> we in Northern Ireland live in a military or paramilitary state. That affects our lives and work in very fundamental ways. We have to approach our work from a woman-centred position whilst in a state of war . . . So, in our early work, we felt ourselves to be feminist but we had to begin from a more general, politicised place: we couldn't jump right in and examine one woman's conflict with her sense of family or self, as first we needed to consider her sense of safety in a community and culture. We had to look at the effects of the political situation on women generally, rather than individually.
>
> (Goodman 1996: 280–2)

As a result of their dramaturgical approach, Charabanc was able to create female characters that moved beyond the mythopoeic stereotypes common in a long tradition of patriarchal Irish theatre. These stereotypes, as Maria Delgado explains, are inflected differently by the schism in Irish religion/politics: 'In Catholicism we see woman as angelic virgin figure reworked by the nationalist movement into Mother Ireland; in Protestantism, woman as loyal steadfast servicer and nurturer of men willing to die for Queen and country' (quoted in Trotter 1999: 2). While such representations were also being challenged by various Irish women playwrights, notably Anne Devlin and Christina Reid, Charabanc's work constituted a major break from established patriarchal conventions, not only in terms of character portraits but also because the group, comprising both Catholic and Protestant members, crossed sectarian lines in its very working methods.

Charabanc's work has only recently begun to attract scholarly interest as theatre that intervenes in nationalist discourses and/or wider Irish cultural and political debates. Maria DiCenzo argues that this is because 'the violent nature of domestic life is generally denied the political value assigned to acts of military or terrorist violence' (1993: 182). Hence critics saw male companies of the time – Field Day, which included high-profile playwright Brian Friel, is a case in point – as interested in political rather than gender issues, while they categorised Charabanc as a group preoccupied with women's concerns

(see Lojek 1999). In this context, the company's black farce, *Somewhere Over the Balcony* (1988), claims a place in the annuals of Irish drama for focusing exclusively on *women's* accommodation to life in a war zone. It is the one Charabanc play to dramatise the 'Troubles' in Northern Ireland, although all of the company's work insists upon the inextricable intermeshing of politics and daily existence.

Somewhere Over the Balcony signals its position as political drama in a number of ways; so deftly is the action crafted that the audience never loses sight of the larger politico-cultural landscape, even when the protagonists convey their most personal experiences. Set on balconies of adjoining council flats in a Catholic ghetto in Belfast on the eve of Internment Day (the anniversary of the 1971 instigation of a British policy allowing imprisonment without trial), the play portrays a series of outrageously improbable events in order to suggest that life in Northern Ireland has taken on surreal aspects as violence becomes the norm. These events, including a helicopter hijacking aided by the efforts of a one-eyed dog that bites British soldiers, are vividly described by the three women rather than being presented on stage. In this way, the women are positioned as filters through whom the outside street action is relayed, a dramaturgical manoeuvre that suggests ways in which they might live out their lives amid the clamour of violence and political mayhem. By not staging the political conflict explicitly, the play also works against the commodification of violence, a theme taken up in the parody of the German tourist who is looking for souvenirs to attest to his visit to the 'war zone'.

Charabanc's Eleanor Methven explains that *Somewhere Over the Balcony* is especially black as 'there is little that has not happened in Belfast short of a siege in the Cathedral, so it is difficult to exaggerate the conditions and events' (quoted in DiCenzo 1993: 181). This kind of world is aptly conveyed by the play's fashioning of the street action as a surrealist farce; nevertheless, the sheer ridiculousness of its plot suggests that the political situation cannot and should not be accepted as normal, even if the characters appear to take it in their stride. The women's narrative incorporates many of the conventional elements of farce – the complicated twists in the plot, the fortuitously timed encounters, the absurd disguises – to create a riveting tale that is made even more entertaining by the popular songs and hilarious rhyming couplets incorporated into the text. To narrate rather than enact a farce, which conventionally depends on precisely timed visual cues and situations in which the audience can see what the characters cannot, presents interesting challenges for the audience as well as the performers. As Rebecca Pelan argues,

> [This] staging creates a peculiar complexity of audience reaction: on the one hand, there is a sense in which the women are fortified – high up and aware of their surveillance, they bombard the army above them and their fellow residents below them with batterings made of words. But on the other hand, there is an equal sense of siege on the part of the women who clearly use their words as a means of staying on top of the immense isolation, loneliness and desperation that is their everyday condition.
>
> (Pelan 2000: 9)

At another level, Charabanc's narration technique sets up a dialectic between *perceived* and *conceived* space that reflects the play's tension between hilarity (elicited in the ways in which the women respond to the action) and horror (at the anarchy their descriptions evoke).

Against the rollicking farce that unfolds through the women's live commentary are juxtaposed extended monologues that reveal much more mundane aspects of their lives: Kate's preoccupation with religious rituals, Ceely's resentment towards her father, Rose's exhaustion from caring for her demanding twins. These monologues allow the women a degree of distance and self-awareness not available in naturalistic characterisation. They also underline the sense of their isolation, a motif stressed by Ceely's suggestion that Rose might enjoy being interrogated because it will get her out of the flat for a while. Together, the continuities and disjunctions between the two levels of action suggest the absurdity of the political stalemate that shapes all the strata of the society.

Before they folded in 1995, Charabanc created over twenty stage pieces, and developed a considerable international reputation during visits to London, Moscow, Leningrad, Munich, Toronto and various cities in the United States. Their determinedly non-sectarian politics (while being daily enmeshed in sectarianism) led them to experiment both thematically and stylistically in order not to be pigeon-holed into representing one ideological position. For the production of *Now You're Talking*, for instance, the company regularly changed the finale, depending on their audience make up and their own evolving ideas about the play itself. While the group preferred non-sectarian performance venues for its touring, it also played in venues strongly associated with one political side or the other. Asked in interview how playing to trenchantly sectarian audiences works in practice, Marie Jones responds that 'the more sectarian they are, the more they laugh' (quoted in Martin 1987: 94). This extraordinary ability to move their audiences out of the binary politics of Irish nationalism, and to make them laugh while doing so, surely situates Charabanc's theatre praxis as a model to emulate.

Production history

Somewhere over the Balcony premiered at the Drill Hall Arts Centre, London, in 1987, directed by Peter Sheridan. Its highly successful 1988 tour to the United States featured productions in Baltimore, San Francisco, Houston, St Paul and Boston. The play has also been performed in Dublin, Belfast, Brighton, Atlanta and Amherst.

Select bibliography

DiCenzo, M.R. (1993) 'Charabanc Theatre Company: placing women center-stage in Northern Ireland', *Theatre Journal* 45, 2: 175–84.

Goodman, L. (1996) 'Charabanc Theatre Company on Irish women's theatres', in L. Goodman and J. De Gay (eds) *Feminist Stages: Interviews with Women in Contemporary British Theatre*, Amsterdam: Harwood Academic, 278–82.

Harris, C. (ed.) (forthcoming 2001) *Five Plays by Charabanc Theatre Company: Reinventing Woman's Work*, London: Colin Smythe. This book features a detailed introduction to the company, a comprehensive glossary and the following scripts: *Lay Up Your Ends*, *Now You're Talkin'*, *Gold in the Streets*, *The Girls in the Big Picture*, and *Somewhere over the Balcony*.

Lojek, H. (1999) 'Playing politics with Belfast's Charabanc Theatre Company', in J.P. Harrington and E.J. Mitchell (eds) *Politics and Performance in Contemporary Northern Ireland*, Amherst, MA: University of Massachusetts Press, 82–102.

Martin, C. (1987) 'Charabanc Theatre Company: "quare" women "sleggin" and "geggin" the standards of Northern Ireland by "tappin" the people', *Drama Review* 31, 2: 88–99.

Pelan, R. (1999) 'In a class of their own: women and theatre in contemporary Ireland', in H. Gilbert (ed.) *(Post)Colonial Stages: Critical and Creative Views on Drama, Theatre and Performance*, Hebden Bridge, UK: Dangaroo, 243–52.

—— (2000) 'Dramatic tiers: contemporary women's drama from Northern Ireland', in *Proceedings from the Eleventh Irish–Australian Studies Conference*, Sydney: Crossing Press.

Pilkington, L. (1998) 'Irish theater historiography and political resistance', in J. Colleran and J.S. Spencer (eds) *Staging Resistance: Essays on Political Theater*, Ann Arbor, MI: University of Michigan Press, 13–30.

Sullivan, E.B. (1998) 'What is "left to a woman of the house" when the Irish situation is staged', in J. Colleran and J.S. Spencer (eds) *Staging Resistance: Essays on Political Theater*, Ann Arbor, MI: University of Michigan Press, 213–26.

Trotter, M. (1999) 'Other voices: women playwrights in Northern Ireland', in E. Aston and J. Reinelt (eds) *The Cambridge Companion to British Women Playwrights*, Cambridge: Cambridge University Press.

Wilmer, S. (1991) 'Women's theatre in Ireland', *New Theatre Quarterly* 7, 28: 353–60.

Somewhere Over the Balcony _____

Charabanc Theatre Company

Marie Jones, Eleanor Methven, Carol Moore and Peter Sheridan

Characters

KATE TIDY   devout Catholic in her thirties
CEELY CASH   irreverent widow in her
   thirties
ROSE MARIE NOBLE   mother of twins in her
   thirties

Setting

Balconies in tower block council flats, Belfast.

Act I

Lights up on KATE TIDY, *a woman in her early thirties. She is wearing a night-dress and dressing gown and carrying a large tin rubbish bin. It is the first light of the day.* KATE *plonks the bin down and sits on it. Pause as she takes in the silence of the morning.*

KATE   See this bin . . . thank God for it . . . (*pause*) . . . Oh, the peace and quiet. If it wasn't for me having my own bin I wouldn't know peace and quiet. They all used to laugh at me in these flats . . . 'Look at Kate Tidy with a bin . . . we have rubbish chutes, nobody needs bins in here'. But I was one step ahead of them. I get up at five o'clock every morning when there is not a sinner about and I can carry my bin out 'til my heart's content. (*Listens.*) There's not a peep . . . it's Heaven. (*Stares up as if looking at something.*) . . . I remember when the British Army moved into that tower block . . . my Frank says 'Them bastards are watching us'. Says me, 'They must have bloody good eyesight cos they are fifteen floors up'. 'Cameras', he says. 'Close-up cameras'. And lo and behold that very next day there was five soldiers hokin' around in my rubbish . . . but I don't care cos I never done nothin' as long I can't see them looking at me. So I just bought myself a new dressing gown and ignored them . . .

'They can hear you too', says he . . . Big deal (*realises she might be heard and changes to whisper*) 'Big deal', says me, 'sure them English can't understand us anyway'. (*Pause.*) I wonder how many videos they have of me and my bin? Hundreds over the years. I'll be doing them a favour cos they'll have nothin' to look at soon . . . Only four families left in that block. (*Indicates block of flats opposite.*) The army won't be wasting any more film on them. We're the next block to be demolished, I can't wait. Wonder what they'll do then. Ach, I suppose they'll just get bored and go back to England.

(*SFX of early morning sounds – e.g. traffic, helicopters, the signature tune of an early morning soap,* Neighbours. *Lights up on balcony.* CEELY *and* ROSE *enter and climb onto balcony. They are women in their thirties. They are also dressed in nightwear.* KATE *joins them. SFX of helicopter becomes the dominant sound. The three women look up at the sky.* KATE *and* ROSE *pretend to bring chopper to land with hand signals while* CEELY *looks at it through army binoculars. SFX of chopper landing on roof of nearby tower block. SFX of music fades in for song. The following dialogue takes place during the introductory music for the song.*)

ROSE   (*tongue in cheek*) British Airways. They'll be staying in the Penthouse.
CEELY   I love it when a new tour comes in. All them wee pink arses not tanned yet.
KATE   (*mock horror*) Ceely Cash, have you been fraternising with the foreigners?
CEELY   No, just spying on them from the balcony with my binoculars.
KATE   It's them that spy on us from the tower with their cameras. (*Said loud as if army can hear. They all wave and give rude signs.*)

ROSE They'll be on the rampage tonight. Rape and pillage, getting drunk, projectile vomiting from the fifteenth floor, drowning the natives.

CEELY (*sarcastically*) Sure, aren't they on their holidays?

ROSE Oh, is that what they call it?

KATE Sure, everybody deserves a wee holiday.

CEELY Everybody has a right to a holiday.

ROSE (*ironically*) Aye, holidays. (*They all sing 'Why Do You Watch Me?'*)

ALL

> Why do you watch me? I won't do no wrong.
> Just mind my own business and wish you were gone.
> You hear every whisper, each move that I make.
> And when I am sleeping you're always awake.
> You're there every morning every hour of the day.
> I've nowhere to run to, I just gotta stay.
> I can't see your eyes, I can't look on your face,
> but I feel your presence all over this place.
> Why don't you leave me for my peace of mind?
> You don't belong here, not one of my kind.
> Go back where you came from, I'm tired of your stare.
> I can't have my freedom until you're not there.

(KATE *climbs off balcony and sits on her bin while* ROSE *and* CEELY *stare up at look-out post on tower block.*)

ROSE (*Holding a child's bath sponge, e.g. animal shape. To* CEELY) The water is off again.

CEELY (*to tower*) The water's off again. Plenty of water in 1969 when yous all came lookin' cups of tea. (*To* ROSE) To think I made a cup of tea for a Brit.

ROSE My ma made tea for the Brits.

CEELY Everybody's ma made tea for the Brits. Except for Mena Mackle over there. (*Reciting the rest of dialogue as if it is a well-known poem*) She never gave in. She stood all alone and rattled her bin. When biscuits and cream buns were passed all around, she warned us beware of that vile English crown . . . She is famous. That's the only woman on the Falls Road never to make a cup of tea for a Brit.

ROSE How am I going to wash my twins?

CEELY (*shouts up at army*) How is she going to wash her twins? (*To* ROSE) Sure you washed them yesterday.

(*SFX of helicopter as if flying just above them.*)

ROSE (*screams*) I wish the British Army would get silencers for their choppers.

CEELY (*looking through binoculars*) Jesus look at that soldier. (*Incredulously*) He's joggin'!

ROSE (*grabs binoculars.*) On the tower block? They'll be sunbathing up there next.

CEELY (*fantasising*) Oh, he'll be all hot and sweaty now.

ROSE (*shocked*) Ceely Cash, he's a Brit.

CEELY (*snaps at her*) He'll still be all hot and sweaty.

(KATE *appears on balcony. She has a clothes peg on her nose.*)

KATE Flies, wasps, ants, cockroaches . . . It is like a flippin' jungle in my flat. (*Shouts up at army post*) My toilet is blocked up again. (*To* ROSE *and* KATE *as she takes clothes peg from her nose*) I'm nearly stunk out. Has anybody seen my Pepe?

CEELY (*shouts up at army post*) Have yousins got her dog?

ROSE I seen him playing over in the empty flats with Rambo McGlinchy. He'll get the mange, that dog is stinkin'.

KATE Pepe! Pepe! (*SFX of dogs barking as if they come running past them on the balcony and almost knock them over as they all shout 'Get down', 'Go away', etc. Then they look across to the flats opposite as if that is where the dogs have gone.*) Pepe, come you down out of those empty flats. That place is dangerous.

ROSE I don't know why they just don't pull that oul' buildin' down and chuck all them squatters out. Look, you can see right through to the other side.

CEELY Aye, but you get a lovely view of the City Hall.

ROSE It is an eyesore. A death trap.

KATE (*calling to Pepe*) No, just stay where you are. Ach, he'll be safe with Rambo. That dog has ate more soldiers' legs than dog biscuits, and him with only one eye.

CEELY   He used to be the quietest wee dog in Belfast, until he got shot with a plastic bullet.

ROSE   (*sarcastically*) Oh aye, a legend in his own lifetime.

(CEELY *begins to sing very reverently and* KATE *joins in to the tune of 'The Holy Ground'.*)

Oh, Rambo McGlinchey, you've only got one eye.
You're fearless and brave, and for us you would die.
You take on the British with no weapons at all,
And when Ireland at last is free you will hang on our wall.

CEELY   Fine dog y'are.

KATE   Ceely, you know the state of my walls. Would you tell your ones to keep their ghetto blasters down a wee bit? I don't mind one, but four going at the same time . . .

CEELY   Why don't you tell them to keep their choppers down?

KATE   It's terrible. Every time I sneeze they tremble. I've done four novenas, lit six candles, Mena Mackle is doing a daily vigil to St. Teresa, the two wee holy sisters from the tower block are doin' 'Our Lady of Perpetual Succour', and wee Bridie is coming round the night to rub them down with Padre Pio's mitt.

ROSE   Padre Pio's mitt! For your walls?

CEELY   It's good for getting phlegm up.

ROSE   My Tucker could maybe do something. He is awful good with his hands.

KATE   Just ask him to put them together in prayer for me.

ROSE   Plasterin'? He has a quare straight eye, great snooker player.

KATE   (*indignantly*) My walls are in the hands of St. Jude. (KATE *exits to ground level and sits on her bin.*)

ROSE   She cud start a Fruit Shop with fungus growing out o' her walls.

CEELY   Fungus! . . . Jesus, that reminds me. (*Shouts over balcony*) Tucker! Come on up here and shave your granda. Tucker! Tucker! (*Sees* JOLENE.) Jolene, go and find our wee Tucker for me. Tell him to come up and shave his granda before these foreign visitors come. (*To* ROSE) Can you take two of the 'Troops Out' movement?[1]

ROSE   I can't take no movements . . . the twins are too strange . . . they wouldn't like it.

CEELY   No wonder they're strange . . . sure the poor wee articles never see the light of day.

ROSE   Anyway, you can't talk to them people . . . going on about Marx and Lenin and all.

CEELY   You don't haft to talk to them. All you have to do is give them a fry.

ROSE   Aye, then they think we're stupid. Anyway, I've no room.

CEELY   (*shouts over balcony*) Jolene! (*Sees* CRYSTAL.) Crystal, love, will you go and find our wee Tucker for me? (*To* ROSE) No room, my arse. I've my seven kids, old Granda Tucker, and I can find room.

ROSE   Where are you goin' to find the water to shave Granda Tucker?

CEELY   Our Lady of Lourdes . . . (ROSE *is disgusted.*) I'll pour it back when the water comes on.

ROSE   I'll bet you their water never gets turned off.

CEELY   Hey, Rose Marie, that is a new batallion that just flew in. They haven't got our photographs yet. Come on . . . (*Strikes provocative pose for army.*)

ROSE   I will not.

CEELY   (*striking several sexy poses*) Come on. They're free.

ROSE   Don't. That gives me the creeps. (*Tries to leave.*) I'm away to help my Tucker wash our car.

CEELY   There's no water.

ROSE   We'll polish it, then.

CEELY   The two of yous isn't right in the head.

ROSE   What is wrong with keeping it clean?

CEELY   It doesn't go.

ROSE   It is temporarily broke down.

CEELY   Then get it fixed.

ROSE   So the Hoods can drive it away and wreck it?

CEELY   Hoods!

ROSE   Hoods.

CEELY   That happens to be my children you are talking about.

ROSE   I know.

(SFX *of fire brigade, getting louder.* KATE *gasps as she looks on from her bin. The others rush to the end of the balcony.*)

CEELY and ROSE   Who is it?

KATE   One of the wee O'Neills has fallen out of the empty flats. But as luck would have it, he has landed on Mena Mackle's aerial.

CEELY and ROSE   Thanks be to God!

KATE   He's swingin' two floors up and them ones is taking photos of him.

CEELY and ROSE   Who?

KATE   Some big German photographers that are here for the internment anniversary.[2] They asked wee O'Neill to hang out of an empty flat with a tricolour in his hand while they took his photo.

ROSE   (sarcastically) Oh, aye, right enough. All them empty flats was missin' was a tricolour.

CEELY   And a child swinging from an aerial.

KATE   The worst of it is, Mena Mackle was sittin' watchin' the last ten minutes of Neighbours and her reception went.

CEELY and ROSE   (sympathetically) Ach, no.

KATE   She is now climbing up that German photographer's back trying to get at wee O'Neill . . . I think his name is Tucker.

ROSE   Aye, that is big Tucker's wee one.

KATE   (laughing) He is telling the Fire Brigade not to rescue him, and Mena is raging. She's the only flat not blocked up on her row, and he goes and lands on her aerial.

CEELY   (shouts) That will put the climbing out of you. (Suddenly) Kate, here's one of them big Germans coming over here.

ROSE   He's got his cheque book out.

KATE   (jumps off her bin suspiciously) Ten pounds? For my bin lid? Away and feel your head. That was the first bin lid ever banged on internment morning . . . was handed down from my granny. It is a collector's item. It's worth . . .

CEELY and ROSE   (whisper to her) Two hundred pounds.

KATE   Two hundred pounds.

CEELY and ROSE   (to German) A bargain.

KATE   (looks disappointed) A photograph? Aye, all right. (Poses with bin lid.)

ROSE   The authorities should issue the kids round here with parachutes.

CEELY   The least they could do is have twenty-four hour security on that oul' building. God knows there is enough lazy bastards out of work. (To ROSE) Look at your Tucker.

ROSE   Aye, just look at my Tucker.

CEELY   Aye, just look at your Tucker.

ROSE   Look at your Tucker.

CEELY   My wee Tucker?

ROSE   No, your big Tucker.

CEELY   He's dead.

ROSE   I know he's dead. I'm just sayin' . . .

CEELY   Just sayin' what?

ROSE   Just sayin' he's dead . . . Look at him when he was livin'.

CEELY   What about my big Tucker when he was livin'?

ROSE   He was a lazy bastard, too.

CEELY   He wouldn't stand and wash a car that didn' go.

ROSE   Oh, is that right?

CEELY   Aye, just right.

ROSE   Aye, right.

CEELY   Right!

ROSE   Right! (shouts) Tucker! Go you over and guard them empty flats. You polished the car this mornin' . . . you hung your ma's curtains yesterday . . . You don't need a crash helmet . . . Just go. (Changing her tone) I'll bring your sandwiches over to the site, pet.

(SFX of ambulance driving off at top speed.)

KATE   Ach, no . . . I told that ambulance man not to get out of the driver seat.

ROSE   (over the balcony) Mister, stop moaning. They'll burn it; you'll get your insurance.

CEELY   (shocked) Look at my Tucker.

ROSE   (proudly) Look at my Tucker.

KATE   Where is my Pepe?

CEELY   That's him with Tucker.

ROSE   My Tucker?

CEELY   No, my Tucker.

KATE   Your Tucker?

CEELY   Aye, my wee Tucker.

ROSE   Just look at my Tucker.

KATE   My wee Pepe with your wee Tucker?

CEELY   Aye, my wee Tucker.

KATE   Where?

CEELY   In the passenger seat of the ambulance.

KATE   (horrified) Oh no! My Pepe is a joyrider!

CEELY   It's okay. My Tucker is experienced.

ROSE   Look at the tourists.

KATE   (delighted) They are taking photos of my Pepe.

ROSE   No, my big Tucker.

CEELY   No, my wee Tucker.

KATE   My wee Pepe with your wee Tucker.

CEELY   Action pictures . . . five pounds a shot.

KATE   Joyriding poodles . . . we've the lot.

ROSE   Snap my Tucker guardin' the flats.

CEELY   My wee Marty chasin' rats.

KATE   Want a bin lid, two hundred pound?

ROSE   A photo of my Tucker marchin' round?

CEELY   Rubber bullets? Antique collection?

ROSE   Avoid the chutes, you'll get infection.

CEELY   Plastic ones are going cheap.

ROSE   Chase them kids from the rubbish heap.

CEELY   Gas masks, riot gear, souvenirs.

KATE   Collected with care over many years.

ROSE   Take them home for your living room wall.

KATE   And if you want a riot, just give us a call. (*Pause.*)

CEELY   (*calling over balcony*) Tucker, give that wee man back his ambulance . . . give it back immediately, or I will break your two legs. And come up here now and shave your granda . . . (*To* KATE *and* ROSE) That wee fella of mine is getting out of control.

KATE   Pepe! Put your paws up for the cameras. Dat a good boy.

ROSE   (*exasperated*) No, Tucker . . . stay there. It is not a part-time job; you have to stay all day.

(*SFX of helicopter hovering above through scene change.*)

CEELY   (*as lights fade*) Quiet sort of a morning.

(*They come off the balcony, which pushes back and becomes part of the set, and the rest of the play is played on floor level apart from three high chairs which they use for monologues. Lights up on* CEELY, *who is perched on high chair with large headphones on her head with an attached mouthpiece.*)

CEELY   Good morning, are yis all tuned in?

ROSE and KATE   (*from darkness*) Aye.

CEELY   After me . . . I promise.

ROSE and KATE   I promise.

CEELY   Not to tell.

ROSE and KATE   Not to tell.

CEELY   On Ceely Cash.

ROSE and KATE   On Ceely Cash.

CEELY   Who has an illegal pirate radio station. Oh, God, I am all eights and nines this mornin'. What with all these foreign visitors here and then I couldn't get oul' Granda Tucker to ate his boiled eggs . . . he never ates on internment anniversary. Says I, 'I'll put you back into gaol and you will be glad of a boiled egg'. Ach, you wanna see him, he is sitting here wrapped up in my good pink duvet waitin' for a foreign photographer to take his picture.

The laugh is he was never 'On the Blanket';[3] they threw him out of Long Kesh before that.[4] Oul' eejit. Well, how are yis all this morning? Did you see the big limousine arriving for Charlene MacAldooney's wedding? Dead exciting, isn't it? Oh, frig, I hope somebody told the driver not to get out of it. So how is everybody over in the MacAldooneys'? Up to high doh, eh? Mona, take you a wee brandy, love. It is not every day your daughter gets married. Oh, yes, that was the first thing that cured me at my big Tucker's funeral. Of course, I drank the whole bottle and near fell in the grave beside him. Right! I have a whole heap of good luck wishes for Charlene and Danny, but before I do that I have a bone to pick with all yousins out there and yis are sittin' on your arses and you know rightly what it is, and you are not lettin' on. There are sixteen visitors sittin' over in that chapel, two arms the one length, and they still haven't bin claimed yet. Now, I want them out and lodged before Charlene and Danny get married, right? Two 'Troops Out' from Manchester men, middle-aged. Two Basque Separatists; they want to stay together. Six of the Communist Party of Great Britain; they don't mind what way they're split up. Two Nicaraguan freedom strugglers and two 'Rock Against Racism' for anybody that likes a wee bit of a dance. And guess who? Vladimir the wee 'Solidarity' Polish fella. That cratur has been coming here on internment anniversary for three years, and he hasn't got a bed yet. Are yis gonna let the poor soul kip in the chapel again this year? I know nobody can be bothered because he doesn't speak any English, but still he is very, very interesting. By the way, where the hell is Nicaragua? I'll bet you oul' Granda Tucker knows. He knows everything. He's very deep. Jesus, that reminds me, Annie McGorman's flat was flooded out again last night.

ROSE and KATE   Ach, no. Not again.

CEELY   Yes, again. Can anybody take Annie and the kids in? They are over in the chapel too. Ach, look on the bright side, Annie. You are the only one in this complex that has any water. Now, I'd like to play a wee request for Charlene and Danny. It's very sentimental to me. Reminds me of my wedding. (*SFX of introductory music for song.*) This is for you,

Charlene and Danny, and please God and his holy Mother your wee reception goes off without any oul' trouble. (*They sing in turn 'The Wedding Song'.*)

CEELY
I had a beautiful wedding
My bridesmaids were all in pink.

(*Lights up on* ROSE *and* KATE.)

We spent our honeymoon night
With him throwin' up in the sink.

KATE
He was on the rebound
It was my mate he wanted instead.

ROSE
You'll never want for nothing,
That's what my poor Tucker said.

ALL   (*singing chorus*)
For poorer, not richer
In sickness, not health
It might have been better
To stay on the shelf.
Good times are coming,
Is that what they say?
Well, I'm still here waiting
Since my white wedding day.

(KATE *and* ROSE *climb off chairs and go to* CEELY. *The following lines are spoken.*)

ROSE   Right!
KATE   Right!
CEELY   I've changed my mind.
ROSE   Altar!
KATE   Altar!
CEELY   I'm too scared!
KATE   Too bad.
CEELY   I'm too young.
ROSE   Too late.

(*They pull* CEELY *off of chair and put her white dressing gown over her head in the shape of a veil. The following lines are sung.*)

KATE
She never loved him like I did,
I jumped to his every whim.

ROSE
Married bliss and a lovely new semi
With babies, a freezer and him.

CEELY
A waster and a drunkard,
But eyes that could break my heart.

KATE
I cooked, I cleaned and I mended,
Perfect at playing my part.

(*The chorus is repeated. During chorus and introduction to next verse the following dialogue and action take place.* KATE *and* ROSE *go behind a screen which is set at the back of the high chairs. The screen has several shelves on it containing several pieces of military equipment and a sign which reads 'Ceely's Souvenir Shop'.* KATE *and* ROSE *change into their day clothes.* CEELY *remains in her nightwear throughout the play. The following lines are spoken.*)

CEELY   Hey! Did yous keep the light on?
KATE   I kept my nightie on.
ROSE   He kept his socks on.

(*The following lines are sung.*)

CEELY
I said every night I was leaving
Then he'd smile and my legs would go weak.

ROSE
As the bills got higher and higher
The business went right down the creek.

KATE
I did all the things I should,
But he still walked out the door.

CEELY
Then he died, the ungrateful bugger,
But I yearn for his touch once more.

(*Chorus is repeated.* KATE *and* ROSE *are now dressed and seated on chairs also.*)

CEELY
Then we moved to this luxury apartment,
It was just like a villa in Spain.

ROSE
Kitchen, bathroom, and through-lounge,

KATE
Designed to soak up the rain.

ALL
I still have my lucky black cat,
My horseshoe and my rabbit's foot,
That little piece of blue ribbon
That was sewn to my stocking foot.
I had all the things you need,
So I'd never have bad luck again,
But I thought they might be suspect,
As I stood there in the rain.

(*Chorus is repeated. End of song.*)

CEELY   (*speaking into headset*) Anybody that has seen the last ten minutes of *Neighbours* for Jesus sake go over and tell Mena Mackle what happened. She's ready to kill dead things.

(*Lights out on* CEELY *and a spot on* KATE, *who is speaking into a tape recorder. She is enveloped in a cloud of smoke.*)

KATE   (*to tape and wearing a gas mask*) To whom it may concern. This is Kate Tidy of 19 . . . I repeat, 19 Dooney Row. My damp dividing walls are about to crumble before my two eyes, and my flat will soon be aptly named. (*Switches off tape and removes mask.*) Wee 'Child of Prague', you've been hangin' there for 12 years, if that wall goes you've had it. Your wee head will fall off and I will have bad luck til the day I die. I know what you are sayin' . . . 'Why don't you take me down, then?' I can't. If I do I'll have bad luck til the day I die. You helped my wee Dustin pass his eleven plus, don't let them fall, wee child. (*Switches on tape.*) Will this walless pot hole be fit for a young boy with a bad chest who is going to grammar school? (*Switches off tape.*) Wee St. Francis, don't let my wee Pepe run away from me. He won't stay in the house. The children put the rubbish chute beside me on fire and it smokes us out. He doesn't like it. Wee St. Jude, (*whispers*) you are my wee favourite. You won't let my walls fall. Ceely Cash and Rose Marie Noble still have theirs, and they don't even have you hangin' up. Is it just me? (*Switches on tape.*) It's a plot to get me out, cos I have no man and only one child left. (*Switches off tape. To herself*) My wee Coreen gone. It wasn't my fault she slipped. (*Not allowing herself to get morbid*) Maybe I should have bought bigger statues. I don't think these ones are workin'. Wee Bridie has a five foot St. Brigid in her hall, and she always wins at bingo. Yes, that's what's wrong, but then Ceely Cash uses Our Lady of Lourdes water when ours gets turned off, she never goes to the chapel, and nothing ever happens to her. God! Will you speak to the British Army for me? Every time an army chopper flies by, my heart is in my mouth for my wee walls just can't take it. God! My wee Dustin is an altar boy in the chapel, servin' at his first weddin', I'm never out of the confession box. I collect for the missions in Africa. I even have my neighbours prayin', ones that don't usually, so that's good isn't it? Don't let them fall on me, God. (*Switches on tape.*) My Dustin will be going to grammar school in a wet uniform and mouldy books smelling of smoke. Is this to be the life of a young boy who could well be the brains of the future? Yours, Kate Tidy. (*Switches off tape as lights fade on her and up on* ROSE, *who is attaching the heads of plastic flowers to their stems. She talks as if she is speaking to the twins.*)

ROSE   Here, stop that! Give it back to him . . . I said give it back. You think I'm not wise? You wore that saucepan the whole way through *Playschool*. It's his turn now . . . He looks no more stupid in it than you did . . . Anyway, it's not a saucepan, it's a helmet . . . It was a helmet the whole way through *Playschool* . . . You can just leave them other pots alone . . . Only one helmet allowed at a time, you haft to learn to share . . . Hey, boy, turn that T.V. down a bit. My head is opening . . . Down! . . . You will feel the back of my hand . . . Well, if you can't hear it you'll haft to take your saucepan off . . . No, you can't . . . It's still his helmet even when he is not wearin' it . . . Stop that . . . It's not nice . . . Turn that T.V. back . . . Turn it back . . . Stop playin' with the knobs; you will break the bloody thing . . . Right! . . . Right! Off . . . Off! If yous can't learn to watch it without fightin' it goes off. NO . . . that is not on until five past two . . . No, I'm busy . . . Plenty of stories in your books . . . Then make one up out of your heads; that's what your imaginations are there for . . . Leave me in peace . . . All right . . . all right . . . (*aggressively*) sit down the two of yis . . . Once upon a time there were two wee Princes . . . who lived in a lovely wee blue castle on a hill . . . with their ma and da, the King and Queen. Now outside this castle was a cave with a big, big, ugly, slimy, pig of a dragon livin' in it . . . Now up above the castle on a mountain lived thousands of knights who were supposed to be brave and protect the wee princes . . . yella big ghetts . . . they stayed up on the mountain gawkin' down. No, the King wasn't afraid of the dragon; he just stayed out of his road . . . He is brave . . . cos he's a King and Kings are brave . . . He just made sure the Queen and the wee princes had nothin' to do with the dragon . . . Oh, yes, he could knock his shite in if he wanted to . . . because he just doesn't . . . That's why . . . Because . . . A coward? . . . He is not a coward . . . For frig sake, doesn't he protect the Queen and the wee princes? . . . What more do yis want? . . . He stands guard at the mouth of the dragon's cave . . .

Yes, just like they have in the big shops down the town . . . a security guard . . . Well, he is a security King . . . The villagers all love the King, cos he makes sure their children never go near the dragon . . . Cos the King just stands there and here he is, 'Right, I am the King around here . . . Get it? And all you cheeky wee skitters can just frig off home . . . ' Yes, there are children who get through security . . . and the big dragon just goes 'Whoosh! . . . Whoosh!' and burns the arses off them, and nobody sheds one tear for them dirty wee ghetts. Then the King becomes so famous for fightin' dragons that he gets invitations from all over the world to come and fight other people's dragons . . . with his own two bare hands . . . Then one day the King comes to the Queen and the two wee princes and he says, 'Now that I am a brave and noble fightin' warrior we are gonna shift . . . get a new wee castle on the ground . . . with a wee bit of a garden and real roses for your ma the Queen' . . . Yes, the two wee princes would be on the ground . . . Aye, they could play in the street . . . No, that wouldn't matter, they could fall all they wanted to; they would be on the ground . . . We'll be goin' soon . . . No, not tomorrow . . . Because . . . Just because . . . That's why . . . Ask your da . . . Because he is a King . . . He is a King if I say he's a King . . . I am a Queen, his wife. He is a King, my husband, and yous are two gurny wee shites! (*Sound of helicopter overhead. Sharply*) No! . . . You can't go out and play on the balcony.

CEELY (*on balcony, looking up at army post on the tower and talking to herself*) Just look at him, joggin' round and round. I wonder is he the same one that looked at me on the stairs yesterday. He did . . . cos I would know that chemistry anywhere. Must be cold up there . . . he'll be warm, though . . . I wonder what he is like out of that uniform. Sexy . . . Jesus, Ceely Cash, he is a Brit. I would get done. Ach, sure I'm just lookin', that's all, just lookin'. (CEELY *stares dreamily over the balcony, then suddenly notices something. She runs to her chair and puts head set on.*) May Day! May Day! Slimy the dole snooper is in the area. He is disguised as a paratrooper with a foot patrol. Anybody doing the 'double', down tools immediately. The foot patrol are just passing the empty flats. (*Comes out onto balcony.*) Tucker, tell that snooper over there that you are voluntary . . . he *is* a snooper. He's a snooper dressed as a soldier so he doesn't look like a snooper . . . Just tell the snooper dressed as a soldier . . . No, not that soldier, that is a real soldier. The other soldier who is not a soldier, who is a snooper dressed as a soldier. Hey! Hey! Mister, don't you report him; he's not workin' . . . He is just doin' a job that's not a job. It's just a job until he gets a job, but it's not a job like a real job, like your job. Tucker! Punch that snooper in the gub. I said punch him in the gub. No! Not that gub, that is the wrong gub. That is a real soldier's gub. Mister, don't arrest him. He thought you were a soldier dressed as a snooper. No, I mean a snooper dressed as a soldier. Mister, don't arrest him. (KATE *has appeared and is watching her getting excited and tongue tied. She is holding her bin lid in her hand.*)

KATE Stand back! (*Shouts*) Rambo! Pepe! Brits!

(*SFX of dogs growling and barking.* KATE *and* ROSE *watch as soldiers scatter.*)

ROSE Tucker, stay at your post!

KATE (*holding her bin lid in front of her like a riot shield*) Your Tucker is gonna need protection. I saw a dark figure trying to drop a toilet bowl on his head!

ROSE Dark figure?

KATE From the whisperin' stairs in the empty flats.

ROSE Whisperin' stairs?

KATE Two soldiers . . . Glorious Gloucesters . . . got blew up over there. They come back to haunt . . . I've seen them many a night floating about on the balcony and whisperin' like this. (*Mimics ghostly whisper.*) Then they throw things out and try to land them on people's heads. You think wee Tucker O'Neill fell? (*Nods her head mysteriously.*) They are getting their own back. Ever hear them chitterin'?

ROSE I wouldn't go near them empty flats.

KATE Won't be content until the whole buildin' is demolished . . . then they are going to come over here.

ROSE Are they responsible for your walls?

KATE Oh, no! I got Father McCann to exorcise me. (*Offers bin lid to* ROSE.) Yes, your Tucker is gonna need protection.

ROSE Ceely's souvenirs?

KATE Yes.

ROSE   I don't like going into her flat. That oul' man . . .

KATE   Oul' Tucker! Ach, he is a harmless oul' crater.

ROSE   Never talks. Just stares.

KATE   He used to talk years and years ago. Then he got interned. He was fifty-six years of age . . . too old . . . nearly killed him. Threw him out of the helicopter and it only six inches off the ground. Hasn't spoke from the day and hour they let him out. (*Looks up at army post.*) Cos of themmins listening. Claims they even bug the confession boxes.

ROSE   Are they bugged?

KATE   Oh, no doubt. I used to whisper to Father McCann, but he couldn't hear me, so I write it down on a wee piece of paper, slip it through the grill. He forgives me, and then I take it home and burn it.

(*They turn to walk into* CEELY*'s. They go behind screen.* CEELY *is on her chair and speaking into radio.*)

CEELY   Has anybody seen my wee Johnny? I hear he is throwing toilet bowls out of them empty flats. Attention! Anybody going to the MacAldooney wedding, watch yourselves passing them empty flats. You are liable to get flattened. Oh, Mona, all this reminds me of my wedding day. Mickey McGlade our best man, he forgot what day it was and we had to go and get him out of bed, so my Tucker goes to the hire shop for the suits . . . suits that must have been for bloody big rugby players, and Mickey McGlade and my Tucker no bigger than two ducks' arses. Mona, I was affronted. It took me an hour and a half to find my Tucker's hand in the chapel. The chapel, never let me forget it til God calls me. My da goes without his teeth, so my ma sends him out in the middle of the Mass to go and get them. Then the priest asks, 'Who is bringing up the offerings?' And isn't it my da who is on his way over here like two men and a wee lad for his choppers . . . Silence . . . The Priest asks again, 'Who is bringing up the offerings?' Well, my wee aunt Beattie, (*whispers*) she is a wee Protestant, she didn't know what he was talking about . . . She walked the whole length of that aisle and handed the Priest a set of pink His and Hers towels, and the whole congregation bursted out laughin'. I was cut to the bone . . . Then we get to the community centre for the reception and get a phone call. The caterer's van has been highjacked and a bomb put in it, so we wait. Then BOOM! Forty-five roast turkey dinners and sherry trifles splattered all over Great Victoria Street. So my da, the toothless wonder, phones up the Chinese on the Falls Road, forty-five curry chips . . . two hours later . . . forty-five stone cold curried chips, the van was held up in a bomb scare. Of course by this time Mona, everybody is paralytic drunk and they ate them anyway. My da tries to touch up Tucker's aunt from America, so my ma beats her up, throws his teeth down the toilet and flushes it. As for me and my big Tucker, my weddin' dress was covered in curry sauce where he threw up on me. Then we couldn't get home here cos the Brits had this place cordoned off while they were raidin'. Oh, a day to remember all right, Mona. But then, that was in 1969 durin' all the trouble . . . It's all different now.

(ROSE *and* KATE *come from behind the screen.* ROSE *is wearing a police riot helmet and carrying the bin lid and a baton.* KATE *is wearing an army shirt.*)

ROSE   (*takes off riot helmet and sniffs it.*) Jesus, Ceely, where did you get this?

CEELY   It fell off the back of a police Landrover.

ROSE   Was the policeman still in it at the time?

CEELY   It will cost you fifteen pounds. (*To* KATE) And two pounds for that shirt. (*To* ROSE) I'll throw in the baton as well.

ROSE   Will you take it out of my Christmas club?

CEELY   Aye. (*SFX of clapping and cheering.*) Quick, everybody out on the balcony for the wedding.

KATE   Look at the size of Mona's hat. They'll haft to put her in the lift sideways.

CEELY   Charlene, your dress is a wee beauty. (*To* KATE) You wouldn't know she was pregnant.

KATE   Look at all the wee flower girls. Ach, and the wee page boys. They are like wee . . .

ALL   Angels!

KATE   That's why there's nobody about to stone the army.

ROSE   Yoo hoo, Danny!

CEELY   Ach, Danny and his wee best man.

ROSE   That is not right . . . the groom seeing the bride before the wedding. Bad luck.

KATE   Look at their wee blonde tips and their walkin' sticks.

ROSE   Ach, now, that is not right. Charlene, the ma, the da . . . bridesmaid, flowergirls, pageboys, all comin' out at the one time with their walkin' sticks . . .

ALL   (baffled) Walkin' sticks?

KATE   (also baffled . . . then realising there is something afoot) The whole family is lame.

CEELY   Curse put on them since birth.

(SFX of helicopters hovering above.)

ROSE   That best man does not look like himself.

CEELY   (realises what is going on.) That's because he is not himself.

ROSE   Who is he?

CEELY   Tootsie O'Hare disguised as big Tucker O'Neill.

KATE   On the run disguised as Tootsie O'Hare.

ROSE   Why?

CEELY   Cos Danny didn't want Tucker, he wanted Tootsie.

KATE   So Tootsie is Tucker, and Tucker is Tootsie!

ROSE   Why is Tucker 'on the run' when he didn't do nothin'?

KATE and CEELY   So Tootsie could do best man . . . For fuck sake!

ROSE   Right!

KATE and CEELY   Aye, right!

ROSE   Aye, just right!

KATE and CEELY   Aye, just right indeed.

(SFX of helicopter as if hovering right above.)

ROSE   (realises) They're gonna arrest the whole weddin' party.

KATE   Quick, Mona, get into the lift.

CEELY   Mona, take your bloody hat off.

KATE   She is that stubborn.

CEELY   Push her, Charlene.

ROSE   Put her in feet first and set her at an angle.

CEELY   They're in!

ROSE   The Brits will get them when they come out of the lift.

KATE   (confidently) That lift will never open.

CEELY   Who has been jammin' lifts in these flats since he was in nappies?

ROSE   Tucker O'Neill.

KATE   No . . . Tootsie O'Hare.

ROSE   And then what?

ALL   (singing)
Hear, see, and speak no evil
Cos that's the jungle law.
We just swing from our branches
And see what we never saw.
Hear, see, and speak no evil
Don't think we monkeys are scared,
We're too busy gathering berries
To see what we never saw
Or hear what we never heard.

Hear, see, and speak no evil
We eat bananas instead.
The lion's never gonna catch us
We don't say what was never said
Or see what was never saw
Or hear what was never heard
Or see what was never seen
Or heard what we never did hear
Or see what we never heard
Or say what was never seen
Or hear what we never said
Or see what was never heard.

CEELY   (during musical break) Marty! Marty! Run away over to the chapel. Shimmy up the drainpipe and borrow a priest's vestments for Tootsie . . . quick!

(Last section of song is repeated. End of song. They are looking across to the lift.)

ALL   And the lift doors are opening . . . Good morning, Father!

(SFX of army jeeps etc. driving into square.)

KATE   Look at all the flowers.

ROSE   Beautiful.

CEELY   Charlene, you're like a scene out of Dynasty. (SFX of shouting and screaming.) They're liftin' Tootsie. (Shouts) Imagine arrestin' a man of the cloth.

ROSE   Pack of heathens.

KATE   Yous will all be struck by lightnin'.

CEELY   Shove your walkin' sticks up their . . .

ROSE   Mona is fit to kill. She is beatin' the head of that paratrooper with her handbag.

CEELY   Charlene! Stuff your bouquet down his throat.

ROSE   Best dressed riot I have ever seen.

KATE   Mona! Beat him with your stilettoes. Pepe! You stay out of it.

CEELY   Knock his shite in, Father.

ROSE   Look at that big pig of a soldier. He's throwin' him into the saracen. Made a lovely wee priest, too.

KATE   Danny, pull Mona off the saracen. She'll be piggin'.

(*SFX of saracen driving off.*)

CEELY   They got him! Pigs!

ROSE   That's not right. Mona, the da, Charlene, Danny, bridesmaids, pageboys, flowergirls, all barricadin' themselves in the chap . . .

ALL   In the chapel!

KATE   Look at your Tucker.

ROSE   My Tucker?

KATE   No, her wee Tucker.

CEELY   My wee Tucker?

KATE   With my wee Pepe!

CEELY   Where?

KATE   Drivin' the saracen.

CEELY   (*delighted*) With Tootsie O'Hare disguised as a priest and my Tucker dressed as a soldier . . . (*shocked*) . . . My Tucker dressed as a soldier?

KATE   I know where he got the uniform from. See that dole snooper who was disguised as a para! He's hiding in the empty flats disguised as a streaker.

ROSE   Tucker! Knock his shite in.

KATE   Hold on tight, Pepe!

CEELY   Tucker, put your seatbelt on . . . you'll get arrested!

(CEELY *and* KATE *exit stage right.* ROSE *follows, then runs back into her flat for a can of polish. As she re-emerges onto the balcony she stops short. The following is played as in a conversation with an invisible soldier.*)

ROSE   What? . . . offensive weapon . . . no it's only polish . . . look. (*Sprays at the imaginary soldier.*) Ooops sorry . . . It's just to clean this riot helmet . . . no not a real riot, it's in case of toilet bowls . . . oh, you mean *this* is an offensive weapon? (*Indicating truncheon*) . . . No it's not . . . well, I suppose it would be if you were to be offensive with it, but it's not goin' to offend nobody . . . it's just for my man's work, and this is only an oul' bin lid I brought out to polish . . . for I'm sure you know yourself how dirty your bin can get . . . it's just for my husband's head and the soldiers on the whispering stairs – no, not live soldiers, dead soldiers. No, not real dead soldiers . . . ghosts . . . throwin' toilet bowls . . . Here mister, you can't arrest me. I've two wee twins not washed yet. (*She exits.*)

KATE   What a day, Ceely. My Dustin under seige. My wee Pepe on the run. And now Rose Marie arrested.

CEELY   And it's only half eleven.

KATE   It wasn't fair arrestin' her. All she was doin' was polishing Tucker's riot gear.

CEELY   What do you expect? She was standin' out in the middle of the balcony with a can of Pledge and half the British Army lukin' up at her.

KATE   She's never been interrogated before.

CEELY   She'll love it. Isn't it getting her out of the house for a couple of hours?

(*SFX of jeeps and saracens.*)

KATE   Oh, no! Here's more reinforcements.

CEELY   Poor Mona. Surrounded.

KATE   She'll be goin' daft. It's near time for your radio bingo, and she's only waitin' on two numbers for the jackpot.

CEELY   Wish we could make contact.

KATE   Oul' Paddy! He's in the chapel. Mona's da. He's deaf. (CEELY *doesn't know what she is on about.*) Isn't he always complaining cos he can pick your station up on his hearing aid.

CEELY   (*delighted*) Kate, if you had brains you would be dangerous. (*She runs to the head set.*) Calling Mona MacAldooney in the chapel. Calling Mona MacAldooney in the chapel. Mona, are you tuned in?

(*SFX of chapel bell; tolls four times.*)

KATE   She can hear you.

CEELY   Mona, love, don't you take them barricades down. Don't you give in to them pigs. You didn't know when you got up this mornin' that you had all this excitement in front of you. We've had our own excitement here on the balcony. They have arrested Rose Marie Noble in her riot gear. It's all go. Mona, I hope you brought that brandy in with you in your beg. Take a double. You're surrounded by three hundred Brits and fifteen army jeeps, but don't you take them barricades down til they give in to your demands. God knows! A Priest, thirty chicken salads and a three piece band is no big deal.

KATE   (*grabs mouthpiece*) Thirty chicken salads? Mona MacAldooney, are you gonna keep them visitors hostage and not feedin' them? What happened to the Ireland of the Welcomes? (*Jumps off chair and runs to the balcony.*) Calling the British Army! Hey you! Mona MacAldooney changes that to forty-five chicken salads.

(*SFX of continuous dog crying.*)

CEELY (*into headset*) The residents of the area would like to apologise to all our foreign guests held hostage in the chapel. We hope that you look on it as doing your 'Wee Bit for Ireland' . . . (*comes out to balcony to* KATE, *who appears to be looking down at Rambo crying.*)

KATE Poor Rambo. He is crying his eyes out cos he didn't get goin' on the run with my Pepe.

CEELY (*getting emotional*) I'm all excited so I am . . . When wee Tucker was wee, big Tucker used to say to him, 'Son, what do you wanna be when you grow up?' And he would a said, 'On the run, daddy'. Oh, God, if he was alive the day he would be so proud of him. He's probably in Bundoran by now.

KATE (*upset*) It's well for you, Ceely. My Dustin wants to become a computer scientist.

CEELY My wee Tucker was just lucky, Kate. He happened to be in the right place at the right time.

KATE I don't know if my wee Dustin can make it what with me and my walls.

CEELY You should have let him go to America with my Dwane and the rest of the Deprived Children of the Area.

KATE I was too scared. I heard if them Americans like your children they don't allow them to come home. They try and adopt them.

CEELY Not my Dwane. Dr. Barnardo wouldn't even take him.

(*SFX voice over: 'Attention! Attention! Would all residents please leave their homes immediately as we have reason to believe there is a suspect device in the area'. The same message is repeated through the following dialogue.*)

CEELY Bloody army. That is gonna interfere with my radio bingo!

KATE It's just an excuse so they can raid the place.

CEELY (*on headset*) Mona, pay no heed to themmins. Only tryin' to get you to surrender.

KATE The Brits have surrounded Rose Marie Noble's car.

CEELY (*casually*) Probably gonna blow it up.

KATE And it only polished, too.

CEELY (*shouts*) Tucker! The Brits are gonna blow up your wee motor. Tucker! . . .

Doesn't realise . . . too busy guardin' that naked snooper.

(CEELY *goes to exit and* KATE *stops her.*)

KATE What about Granda Tucker and the tortoise?

CEELY It would take more than a bomb to shift them two. But if they get blew up, they needn't come runnin' crying to me. (*To* KATE) Come on. (*They are about to exit and* CEELY *stops. Calls back*) And if my good duvet gets smoke damaged it's comin' out of your pension. (*Stops and looks over balcony. To* KATE) That is a beautiful day, isn't it?

KATE That's what I love about this place. On a day like today you could be anywhere. (*They pause and take in the sun.*) Ceely, are you not going to put some clothes on?

CEELY Sure, I'm only going to the Falls Road.

(*As they exit . . . SFX of bomb exploding. Blackout.*)

Act II

ROSE *and* CEELY *are seated on their chairs.* KATE *is seated on a toilet bowl covered by a sheet. She is dressed in army boots, trousers, and camouflage jacket. She speaks through the sheet.*

KATE When I woke up this mornin', had my fry, give Dustin his syrup of figs, I thought to myself something is afoot, for when I looked to my walls my wee St. Francis was slanty. 'An omen', I says to myself, 'an omen'. And I was right. (*Throws off sheet to reveal toilet bowl.*) Today, August 8th, 1987, as a result of a controlled explosion, my walls finally crumbled.

(*Lights up on* CEELY.)

CEELY I am never speaking to Granda Tucker ever again. He is one miserable oul' decrepit pig. He sat there and let the Brits lift my wee pirate radio station, my only pleasure. And he just let them walk in and take it away. Jealousy, that's what it is, not gettin' enough attention. I wouldn't mind if he was company. Company! I'd rather live with Psycho . . . at least he spoke.

(*Lights up on* ROSE.)

ROSE Arrested! Me arrested! And I never even done nothin'. I says, 'Mister, I'm only polishing my man's workin' clothes, his riot shield and his helmet'. Next thing I'm led down to a saracen with my two wee twins dukin' over the balcony shoutin', 'Is that the brave knights come to rescue us?' Says I, 'Mister, will you tell them wee boys that you're the King's messengers and we're away to look for a new wee castle?' They thought I was mental, and the shape of me tryin' to get up into the saracen. I couldn't. Kate's bin lid kept jammin' in the door, and then I hear Kate shouting from the balcony at the soldiers, 'Hey, watch my bin lid. That is a family heirloom'. I was prayin' they would ignore her, cos I heard if you complained you got beat up . . . And my poor Tucker and the twins were wavin' like I was goin' on a bus trip to Portrush. Oh, God, and the thing was speedin' . . . and this big ginger one . . . she was a woman, too . . . she kept sayin', 'Hold on tight'. But I was fallin' on top of her, and then fallin' back on the wee soldier with his rifle. Here's me, 'If that thing goes off I am dead', but I couldn't help it.

KATE Welcome to my through–lounge and open–plan kitchen and bathroom. Frank said when he left me, 'Kate, no good will come of you'. And he was right, for all I am left with is Ceely Cash's walls on one side and a rubbish chute on the other. How could any of that be my fault? (*Suddenly realises*) Dustin can watch me goin' to the toilet. I won't be able to.

CEELY Twelve miserable years I put up with him sittin' there. (*Sarcastically*) 'Commandant Cash, Communications Officer' . . . communications my arse. No wonder the fifties campaign was a friggin' disaster. Our wee Dwane's tortoise has more sense. The people were dependin' on that radio the day for the bingo. Big jackpot game. Mona and everybody under seige in the chapel were going to play. The whole district. What has he left them with? (*Produces empty bean can, with string attached to one end, from back of her chair. Pulls string and speaks.*) Kate, Rose, will yous play bingo?

(KATE *and* ROSE *also produce bean cans, but are more concerned with their own dilemmas and are half-hearted about it.*)

CEELY Testing! Testing! One . . . two . . . single line across and then a full house.

ROSE They get me into this room. 'Do you wanna be examined by a doctor?' I says, 'Mister, I'm not sick'. 'Take your belt off', they said. Here's me, 'What for?' 'In case you hang yourself'. 'Oh no, I wouldn't do that', I says, 'I am heart scared of heights'. Then here they were, 'We know your twins throw stones at us. Who taught them to do that? Your husband?' Here's me, 'What?' I near had a fit, but I had to calm myself cos the big ginger woman was dead scary lookin'. I said, 'My husband and my children would not lift their hand to nobody, we just mind our own business. Anyway', I says, 'my husband has a bad chest'. Here they are, 'We know!'

CEELY (*through bean can*) Eyes down . . . look in . . . Two rubber bullets, 22. Armalite gun, 21. On the run, 31. Unlucky for some, 13.

KATE That's it, some people are lucky with their walls and some aren't. Ceely and Rose still have theirs, so it must be my fault. I get the blame for everything. That was Frank, everything was my fault. (*Mimics* FRANK.) 'Kate, keep the kids in; there's rats'. Not my fault. 'Kate, them sewers is stinkin'. My fault? 'Kate, it's rainin'. (*Looks bemused.*) He still thinks our wee Coreen slipped on my rubbish on the stairs, but I've always had my own bin, handed down from my granny. I brought it here when we got married, carried it up these stairs myself cos the lift was broke. That was the start of things going wrong. 'Kate, the lift is broke'.

CEELY I could have been somebody if it hadn't been for lookin' after him . . . Not even my friggin' da . . . could be calling out numbers in the Silver Star Bingo, makin' somethin' of myself. Oh, but I know what he wants . . . me to shut up too so that nobody says nothin' to nobody ever again, but I am a communicator, that's me, that's my way. My big Tucker used to say that to me when he had a few drinks in him. 'Ceely, you're a Mouth'. Two weeks before he died he went out and he stole me all my radio equipment. He knew he was dying and he wanted to leave me somebody to take his place. Not many men will leave you a whole district. (*Indicates* GRANDA TUCKER) I wish to hell they had never let him out of gaol. (*Back to bean can.*) Doin' time, 29. Two dead men, number 10. Two fat peelers, 88.

ROSE Two big skinny ones they were, and

one of them had a stutter. I tried to finish his sentences for him, but the big ginger one was givin' me dirty looks, so I just sat there. 'Do you wi . . . wi . . . want a' (*Mimes cigarette.*) But I wouldn't in case they were drugged, and they made me sign a statement. Then the other one says, 'What does your husband use his car for?' Here's me, 'Nothin'. It doesn't go. It is temporarily broke down'. Then the other one says, 'What would his poor invalid mother think of him bein' mixed up with smugglin' wea . . . wea . . .' I finished it for him cos I was gettin' annoyed. Here's me, 'Weapons!' And the big ginger one, her glasses started steamin' up. Here's me, 'Weapons! Me and him is not like that. We have two wee children . . . Wea Wea Weapons'!

CEELY (*in bean can*) Prods are dirty, number 30. Pope's a Mick, 26.

KATE Check! 'Not my rubbish', I says to Frank. 'Correen did not slip on my rubbish. Cos I examined it afterwards'. I said, 'Frank, none of us eat custard. We don't even like it'. But it was still my fault. I shud have watched her, but I've only got two eyes. Not my fault. 'No excuse', he said. 'But you will be repaid', and he was right. But what he doesn't know, my Dustin is going to grammar school. (*Switches on tape and speaks into it.*) This is the last will and testament of Kate Tidy of 19 Dooney Row. In the event of my ceiling falling down and suffocating me, Don't! I repeat, Don't! let Granny Tidy take my Dustin or my poodle Pepe. (*Switches off tape.*) My wee altar boy under seige. Ach, he'll be safe in the chapel, not even the soldiers would storm it, cos I'm sure most of them are Catholics too, and the statues barricading the chapel doors are their statues too. God, my wee statues are all broken, and the chapel statues are being used as a barricade. It's not their day either.

CEELY Eyes down for your full house. Two big choppers, 77. Sniffin' glue, 62. Brits are thick, 36.

ROSE Then they says to me, 'Why do you want to move, Mrs. Noble? Is it not safe there anymore because your man is doin' a bit of toutin'?' Here's me, 'How did yous know? I mean, how did you know that we wanted to move, not that he's a tout, cos he's not a tout. I meant how did yous know?' Oh, God, and then I got all confused and I started stutterin' too. The big ginger one thought I was makin' fun of the big skinny one. It was awful. Here's me, 'I want my mammy', and they says, 'She is in the Isle of Man for her holidays'. I couldn't believe it.

CEELY Oh, God, if I knew then what I know now I wouldn't be here, but then he knows what he did to me, and what's more he knows I know he knows what he did to me. But he doesn't know I know what to do. He just thinks he knows I don't know what to do, but he doesn't know that I know what to do. But then he who thinks he knows best . . . knows fuck all! (*Into bean can*) Valium heaven, number 7. Blocked up loo, 42. Great position, 69.

KATE Yes, Frank, you would be havin' a quare laugh if you were here now. You're probably up there with them army ones, laughin' at me. That's where you have been all these years. Now yous can all sit and watch me goin' to the toilet. But my wee Pepe doesn't blame me, so there! He'll come back, so he will, and my Dustin will be all right in the chapel, so you see, you didn't get it all your own way. I still have them. You thought the rats would get me. (*Points to her army boots smugly.*) You thought I would freeze to death because of my walls. (*Points to battle jacket.*) Oh, yes, you can laugh, Frank Tidy, but it is my brains that Dustin has. You couldn't even do the *Daily Mirror* crossword, but I could. I could do it. But don't think you can come runnin' back when Dustin is clever and I have walls, for you won't get in . . . But you're hopin' my walls don't get built cos it was my fault. But I had the nicest walls in our row. Beautiful pink with roses. All my wee saints. Four walls like in *Playschool* 'one . . . two . . .'

CEELY (*through bean can*) Kate!

KATE Aye.

CEELY (*has taken her slipper off and sees that the sole is falling off*) What colour were your walls?

KATE Pink.

CEELY With roses?

KATE Aye.

CEELY (*She looks dismayed . . . her slipper is pink with roses.*) Jesus!

ROSE Then this peeler says . . . 'Where is your buggy . . . the pink one?' Here's me, 'Stole!' 'Where from?' 'From outside our door'. 'Not report it?' Says I, 'Mister, are you wise? Wouldn't I look sick reportin' a stolen buggy when there is people gettin' murdered out there?' 'Exactly!' he says. Do you know what they arrested me for? That peeler that was shot at the corner of Leeson Street by a woman with a twin buggy. Here's me, 'Mister, could you see me, puttin' my twins in a buggy, danderin' up to Leeson Street, shootin' a peeler, danderin' back home and makin' my Tucker his tea as if nothin' had happened?' Here's me, 'Mister, are you mental? Anyway', I says, 'I am not the only woman in Belfast with twins'. Then he said, 'What would happen them two wee boys if we were to arrest your husband as well? Put them in an orphanage?' 'Oh, no, Mister, don't do that', I said. 'You see, they are a wee bit strange cos I am scared to let them out. Don't do that, Mister'. Then I turned to the big ginger one, I says, 'Missus, you're a woman, don't let them take my wee children'. And you talk about hard . . . here she was, 'What do you think of a United Ireland?' 'Oh, no', I says, 'I don't want a United Ireland, I couldn't afford a United Ireland. I would haft to move to England'. Then the big skinny one says, 'You can g . . . g . . . go . . . ' I thought he was never gonna say it . . . Then the big ginger one says, 'Do you want to be examined by a doctor?' Here's me, 'No . . . ' Well, we'd no water this morning and I wasn't even washed!

CEELY   I should have escaped in that saracen with our wee Tucker . . . Set up my own radio station in Bundoran, all them men on the run would be glad of me for the company . . . 'Ceely, the Volunteers' Sweetheart'. I could poison him . . . No, the lift is broke I would never get his oul' coffin down the stairs . . . I know! I'll tell the Brits he has been gun runnin' and get him arrested. Brilliant! (*Fantasising*) I could be sittin' down the town in one of the big bingo halls, callin' out numbers over a microphone . . . There would be silence, hundreds of people waitin' for me to speak. I'd put a frock on every single day. People would be stoppin' in the streets (*mimics whispering*) 'There's Ceely Cash the Bingo Caller. She looks great in real life'. (CEELY *speaks through bean can as if it is a microphone.*) Ladies and Gentlemen, do we not have any sweats yet? (*Gets very excited.*) And it's . . . Sniper McKee, 53. Paisley's drum, 51. Hide your gun, 61. Lock your door, 74. Duck and dive, 55. In a state, 68. Keyhole Kate, 78!

KATE   (*screams*) Check! (*Then to herself*) Look at the state of my ceiling . . . very dicey. (*Gets army camouflage helmet from under her chair and puts it on.*) Maybe Father McCann didn't exorcise me properly . . . maybe the Glorious Gloucesters are beyond exorcism . . . maybe Frank snuck in one night and did somethin' to it . . . maybe I was just doomed since birth . . . maybe it was the time I broke my rosary when I jammed it in the lift door. (*In tears*) No, it was cos Coreen slipped and I wasn't there. Oh, my God, how am I ever gonna get washed again?

CEELY   And that is a full house check for Kate Tidy!

(*They begin to sing 'Hey St. Jude'*)

ROSE   (*singing*)
Hey, St. Jude, won't you hear my plea,
Got nothing left, I'm in misery.
Hey, St. Jude, I'm a desperate case,
Can't you see when you look on my face?
KATE
Hey, St. Jude, I'm down on my knees,
I'm a lost cause, so help me please.
I put your statue on my bedroom wall
With Jesus and Mary, St. Peter and Paul.
ALL   (*singing chorus*)
Don't want silver, don't want gold,
Want to win just once
Before I get old.
Dear ole Jude from the promised land,
Save my soul from the final demand.
CEELY
Hey, St. Jude, I'm all alone,
No one to lean on to call my own.
Just someone to talk to
I don't want much,
Or you're back in the cupboard
With my old cracked cups.

(*Chorus is repeated. At end of song they are all out on the balcony looking towards the chapel.*)

KATE   (*gasps*) Look what Rambo is about to do in front of the chapel doors. Rambo! Bad Boy! No shame, that dog, imagine shiting (*she mouths word*) in front of three-hundred soldiers.
ROSE   The chapel doors are opening!
CEELY   (*shouts*) Mona, don't surrender. (*They all watch.*)

KATE Ach . . . it's only Vladimir the wee Pole.

ROSE Mona is taking this all very seriously. That's what they do on the TV Let one hostage go at a time . . . gesture of good will.

CEELY They are arrestin' him.

KATE At least he'll get a proper bed for the night . . . It's an ill wind.

ROSE That's my pot he has on his head. Hey! That is my Mark's helmet.

KATE He is attacking that soldier with your saucepan. Don't struggle, Vladimir. Why is he shoutin' 'Fuck the Brits?'

CEELY Because the youngsters told him that was English for 'Thanks very much'.

ROSE Hey, look! Our car is away. Tucker must have got it to go. (KATE and CEELY *move away from her quickly.*) Ach, isn't that nice . . . he wanted to surprise me. Must have the twins away for a wee drive. It's an ill wind blows somebody some good right enough. (*Looking very pleased.*)

KATE (*tentatively*) Rose Marie! (KATE and CEELY *are now at far side of the balcony.* ROSE *comes over.*) See that big lump of red metal over there? Her Jolene is tap dancing on . . . Tucker's car.

CEELY (*pleased*) I never knew our Jolene could tap dance.

ROSE Tucker! Tucker!

KATE There he is in one of the empty flats . . . He is pullin' it apart.

CEELY He is supposed to stop the youngsters doin' that.

ROSE Tucker! I'm back . . . all in one piece . . . more than I can say for our car. Where's the twins? Tucker, answer me, I said where's the twins? Children, remember? Two wee boys, brown hair, blue eyes . . . you'll know them if you see them, they'll be callin' you daddy. Shush! . . . Shush! . . . don't you tell me to shush, you have lost my children. Tucker speak to me. Why won't he speak to me?

CEELY He is pullin' that empty flat apart plank by plank. Probably throwin' a wobbler cos the Brits blew up his motor.

KATE Tucker! Keep me the walls, will you?

ROSE All right . . . All right . . . Don't speak, just nod. Have you got the twins? No! No? No, you didn't mean no, you meant yes, didn't you? No! No, you did mean no, or no you meant yes? Yes . . . yes? Does that mean you meant no the first time? Tucker, speak to me.

KATE I think he means he hasn't got them.

CEELY Stupid ghett! Losin' two children.

ROSE Tucker, take the saucepan off your head and you'll hear me.

CEELY Ach . . . he never got wearin' his wee new R.U.C. riot helmet.

ROSE Take off your helmet! Off . . . (*gives up on him.*) My other pot was lyin outside the chapel. (*Delighted*) The twins, they're in the chapel . . . they're safe. (*Horrified*) No, they're not, they're under seige . . . (*panics*) Mona! Mona!

KATE She won't hear you.

ROSE I'm away to look for them.

CEELY The army won't let you out.

ROSE (*grabs bean can*) Mona! Mona!

CEELY (*laughs*) Are you daft? Mona has to have one of them to hear you back. (*To* KATE) What school did she go to?

ROSE Give me yours and I'll take it down to her.

KATE Oh, aye. Dander down through 300 Brits, five army jeeps, break down the chapel doors and hand that to Mona.

ROSE Aye, very funny.

KATE Aye, very bloody funny.

ROSE Aye, I'm laughin' my leg off . . . Aye . . . oh . . . ho, ho.

KATE Ha, bloody ha . . .

(CEELY *begins to sing as if something is dawning on her. The other two stop and look at her. Through the song she is trying to indicate that she has thought of an idea.*)

CEELY (*As she sings she looks up at the army post as if the song is a code.*)
They were just newly wed.
They went upstairs to bed.
He turned the lights down low
Cos she was rather shy.
He said come here my dear
She said no fuckin' fear.
I'd rather stay down here
Among my souvenirs.

(*The word souvenirs prompts them into action.* KATE *runs behind the screen and appears with a C.S. gas gun.*)

ROSE The Brits will see us.

CEELY No, they won't. (CEELY *grabs* KATE's *sheet to shield her while* ROSE *puts the bean can into the spout of the gun.*) Right, Kate, you're aimin' for the belfry.

KATE Where is the belfry?

ROSE Where they keep bells, bats, hunchbacks . . . for Christ sake, just shoot!

KATE (*annoyed*) Right!

ROSE Aye, right!

KATE Aye, just right!

CEELY (*breaking them up*) Right!

KATE (*aiming*) I can't. There is a wee pigeon sittin' on it.

CEELY (*shouts*) Clear off.

ROSE Shoot for god sake.

KATE I can't kill a wee innocent pigeon.

(CEELY *and* ROSE *start screaming at her to shoot. Then suddenly, SFX of can being shot, landing on belfry. They are all on the ground covering their ears, then SFX of chapel bells tolling four times. They all jump up delighted. They grab a chair and bring it on to the balcony.* CEELY *gets the other bean can and climbs up onto the chair.*)

CEELY (*through bean can*) Calling Mona MacAldooney in the belfry . . . calling Mona MacAldooney in the belfry. Is that a big ten-four? (*Holds can tentatively to her ear . . . delighted.*) She can hear us. Mona, love, how is it over there? Is everybody okay? (*Listens. To others*) Mona is panicking. She has reduced her demands. A priest and forty-five egg and onion sandwiches.

KATE Mona, don't surrender. (*To* CEELY) Tell her about my walls.

ROSE The twins! The twins!

CEELY (*to can*) What is wrong? Why do you not want the three-piece band? (*Listens.*)

ROSE The twins!

CEELY Oh, that is stickin' out Mona! (*To others*) You know Seamie McKee? The wee man that races the greyhounds and sings round in the club? He is singin' and playin' the organ. (*To can*) Mona, Seamie only sings when he is drunk. (*Listens.*) Oh, the communion wine . . . that was handy. (*Listens as if she can hear the singing in the chapel and begins to sing along, and* KATE *joins in.*)

CEELY and KATE (*singing*) I am prayin' for rain in California . . .

ROSE (*getting frustrated with them*) The twins! The twins!

CEELY (*snaps*) Ach, how many bloody twins have you? (*To can*) Mona, have you got Rose Marie Noble's twins in there? (*Listens.*) Only Annie McGorman's kids? Are you sure, Mona?

ROSE (*takes can*) Mona, check the confession boxes. They're very strange. (*Listens.*) No, not the boxes, my twins. (*Hands can back to* CEELY. KATE *and*

CEELY *are singing along to Seamie in the chapel as* CEELY *holds the can up to their ears.* ROSE *just stares up at Tucker.*) Tucker, our wee twins are under seige!

KATE (*rocking to and fro as* CEELY *hums*) Mona, is my wee Dustin all right?

ROSE My Tucker is on the roof now! Tucker, please speak to me.

KATE (*listening into can*) My wee Dustin is servin' up the hosts now. Everybody is starvin' . . .

ROSE (*over balcony*) There's a nun . . . Sister! Sister! Are there two wee twins in that chapel?

KATE (*still rocking and humming*) Mona, I hope they are not consecrated.

ROSE Sister! Sister!

KATE Mona, get my Dustin to sing 'Edelweiss' . . . over the mike . . . he's brilliant.

ROSE Sister, is there two wee . . . (*stops and looks shocked.*)

KATE Rose Marie, come and hear my wee Dustin. He is gonna sing 'Edelweiss' in the chapel.

(KATE *notices the nun. They both stare at her.*)

ROSE That is the strangest lookin' nun I have ever seen.

KATE It's a lovely wee shampoo and set she has. Wonder where she got it done?

ROSE Kate, she has pink high heels underneath her habit.

KATE Well, they just do not go with that outfit.

ROSE She is the spittin' image of your mother-in-law.

KATE (*pause*) That *is* my mother-in-law. Granny Tidy, what are you doing here dressed up as a nun? (ROSE *slinks away and goes to* CEELY. *They just watch in disbelief.*) Dustin? He's a wee altar boy in the chapel. The seige was not my fault. No, you can't take him . . . It could have happened to any wee altar boy . . . he is safe . . . nobody is gonna hurt him in a chapel. Anyway, he is havin' a good time. (*Indicating sheet*) I can go to the toilet. No, you cannot take him away. I *can* look after even a dog . . . Go away . . . I'll tell the army you're not a real nun, that you're really an old cow. *I* look stupid? What do you think *you* look like? You are the first nun I ever knew had six children and a beer belly. I'm not a fit mother? Ceely! She says that I am not a fit mother . . . are you a fit granny? Clear off, you're not gettin' my son . . . Frank? Frank who? My Frank! Your Frank? Dustin's daddy? Here? For Dustin. (*Laughs in disbelief.*) To steal my Dustin . . . you just tell that slimy good for nothin' pig if he lays one finger on him I will break his neck . . . (*summons* CEELY *over.* CEELY *holds can up to* KATE's *mouth.*) Mona, don't surrender.

(CEELY *and* KATE *stick their tongues out at* GRANNY TIDY, *and run back to* ROSE *who is looking very dismayed.* CEELY *feels sorry for her.*)

CEELY (*to can*) Mona, are you sure you haven't got Rose Marie Noble's twins in there?

(CEELY *listens.*)

ROSE Ask her to check under the pews . . . in the crypt.

(CEELY *is listening intently to what* MONA *is saying. She looks shocked and then crosses herself, then looks at* ROSE.)

CEELY Annie McGorman's youngsters are going buck mad, they have put moustaches on all the statues with their felt tips. They have put Mina Dumphy's Robin Hood hat on the Virgin Mary. (*To can*) Mona, that is terrible . . . what a day . . . and I am awful sorry about the bingo game. I knew how much everybody was looking forward to it. The Brits came in and raided me, took my wee radio station . . . terrible loss to the whole community. (*Listens, begins to look very hurt at what* MONA *is saying.*) Oh, is that right, Mona? (*Choked up*) Well, I am sure that is great for you. (*Brings can down and can hardly speak she is so upset.*) Mona has her own bingo game going on over in the chapel. Danny's ma is callin' out the numbers over the mike . . . (*angry*) I hate that Bridie Hagan! She is a part-time caller down in the Silver Star Bingo, and now she thinks she is somebody . . . typical . . . my wee radio station is not away a meal hour and not one sinner gives a damn. (*Gives can to* ROSE *and climbs up on her chair.*)

ROSE (*to can*) Mona, have you definitely not got them? (ROSE *hands can back to* CEELY; *has given up.* CEELY *refuses to accept, she is still upset.* ROSE *hands it to* KATE, *looks up at* TUCKER.) Tucker! Our wee children are lost. He just keeps sayin' shush. He has

went mad. The controlled explosion has flipped his lid. He must have went cuckoo, he has never disobeyed me in his life . . . never! Ceely, look at what they have done to my husband, turned him into a lunatic.

KATE (*has been listening into the can*) Oh, that is awful, burstin' to go to the toilet in a chapel . . . that's that oul' cheap communion wine . . . runs right through you. What are you gonna do? (*Tries to hand can to* CEELY *who refuses it.* KATE *persists and* CEELY *takes it.*)

CEELY (*smugly*) Serves you right, Mona MacAldooney. You know there are no toilets in a chapel . . . (*then feels sorry for her.*) Ach, what are they gonna do?

ROSE Who gives a damn! I have lost my children.

CEELY Will you give over . . . There is a wee bride and groom in there . . . (*points into bean can*) . . . trying to get married before their wee child is born . . . Three-hundred British soldiers not lettin' them, forty-five people that can't go to the toilet and a bingo game going on without me, and all you're concerned about is two snattery-nosed wee blurts.

KATE And my child is about to be snatched by a demented nun. (*Addresses the army*) Hey, if you see a terrorist disguised as a demented nun, don't let her into the chapel . . . Right! . . . Aye, right! . . . Aye, just right!

CEELY And give Mona MacAldooney a priest and a Portaloo. (*To can*) Hey, Mona, what about the holy water fonts? (*Listens.*) Annie McGorman's youngsters are paddling in them.

ROSE (*losing control and screaming*) Tucker, Tucker, Tucker! (CEELY *and* KATE *indicate to her to keep quiet. They are listening into the can and humming 'Edelweiss'.*) What is Tucker playing at? He has all the kids on the roof of the empty flats. (KATE *and* CEELY *continue to hum.*) They are carrying planks . . . what the hell is going on? (*Starting to go mad also*) Tucker, speak to me . . . I am your wife, mother of your lost children . . . Don't you shush and shrug me . . . What are you doing with all them kids on the roof carrying Union Jacks . . .

CEELY (*Stops singing abruptly and looks up in horror.*) My Union Jacks, from my souvenir collection. I was savin' them up to make my aunt Beattie a bedspread, (*Whispers to* KATE) She's a wee Protestant. (*To* ROSE) Your Tucker is a thievin' pig. (*Jumps off chair and goes over to her.*) It's bad enough gettin' raided by the British Army, but when your own next door neighbour is doin' it . . . (*Glares at* ROSE. KATE *has been ignoring this and is still listening to 'Edelweiss' in the bean can, offers it to* CEELY *to listen to cheer her up. She accepts.*)

CEELY (*as* KATE *hums*) Wish my wee Dwane was here, he would love all this action, if he comes back from America with an accent I'll murder him . . . Wee Tucker O'Neill was sent home after three weeks, he is talkin' like John Wayne. If my Dwane lasts six weeks without gettin' into trouble, it will be a bloody miracle. (*Suddenly*) Jesus, I forgot to feed his tortoise.

KATE (*shocked*) Starsky! (KATE *and* CEELY *get on their knees and start frantically searching for the tortoise.*)

CEELY Starsky . . . Starsky . . .

ROSE (*to herself*) Try up at the altar or behind the statues.

CEELY Starsky, where the hell are you?

KATE (*urgently*) Ceely!

CEELY (*still searching*) Starsky!

KATE (*More urgently, she is now looking back into flat.*) Ceely, where is Granda Tucker?

CEELY Hiding underneath my duvet ashamed to show his sleekit face . . . Starsky!

KATE (*screams*) Ceely! Ceely! (CEELY *jumps up.*) The duvet is there, but Granda Tucker isn't in it. (CEELY *turns tentatively round. They both gasp in horror.* CEELY, ROSE *and* KATE *all face front, horror stricken, as if they'd seen a ghost.*) Your duvet was pink with roses . . . like my walls . . .

CEELY (*can hardly get the words out*) My slippers . . .

ROSE (*also shocked*) My buggy . . .

KATE An omen! (*They all shiver.*)

CEELY (*tearful*) Old Granda Tucker . . . gone . . . he hasn't left that house in twelve years. (*They are all in tears.*)

KATE When did you last see him?

CEELY I don't know. I never look for him because . . .

ALL He's always there.

CEELY (*Suddenly stops crying.*) Wait a minute! (ROSE *and* KATE *also stop.*) Just before the controlled explosion he wouldn't come out, remember?

KATE The raid!

CEELY (*suspiciously*) No granda . . . No radio . . .

KATE No Starsky!

ROSE No buggy!

ALL The Brits! (*They all march to the end of the balcony.*)

CEELY Right, you . . . (*pointing out*) . . . No, not you . . . you! Right, you big English ghett . . . Where is Granda Tucker? Speak to me, I said where is oul' Granda Tucker? (*Holding back her tears*) You walked into my house and arrested an old man with one foot in the grave and a wee tortoise . . . suppose you're gonna try and interrogate the two of them. (*Puts her head on* KATE'*s shoulder.*) This will kill oul' Tucker.

KATE (*bravely*) Don't let them see you cry, Ceely.

CEELY Don't yous be beatin' him up . . . he never done nothin' . . . When yous can walk into a house, lift an old man out of a duvet and a wee tortoise out of a shoe box, yous are capable of murderin' your own mothers! (*Puts her hand out for the can and* KATE *hands it to her.*) Mona! They have arrested Granda Tucker and our wee Starsky, and they are gonna arrest you too, so you may as well stay in the chapel as Castlereagh . . . (*Holds can up so that army can hear.*) No surrender!

KATE and ROSE No surrender!

CEELY (*listening into can*) Oh, frig! Mona wants a priest and a midwife. (*To army*) Satisfied? Satisfied? There is a wee child about to be born in there (*points into can*) out of wedlock . . . in a chapel.

ROSE Born in a chapel! Hope my twins aren't in there . . .

KATE Ach, you want them in, you want them out, what the hell do you want? (*Over balcony*) Well, I hope you are all well satisfied now . . . yous have arrested an old man and a wee tortoise, you're lettin' a wee child be born in that chapel and his ma and da aren't even married yet.

ROSE And turned my husband into a lunatic.

KATE And blew up my walls.

ROSE Stole my buggy.

CEELY And took my wee radio.

ROSE And yous just stand there and laugh. (*All begin to sing, 'Out There Somewhere'.*)

ROSE

Out there somewhere, there's gardens with fences and little oak benches.

CEELY

Women with husbands, loving and caring

KATE

Children in college, reading and learning

ALL   (*singing chorus*)
Out there on the ground
They're all sleeping sound tonight
Out there on the ground.

ROSE
Out there somewhere, they dine on steak
dinners
Always back winners.

CEELY
Planning a future and talking together

KATE
Warm and cosy whatever the weather

ALL   (*singing chorus*)
Yes, they're all sleeping sound tonight
Yes, they're all sleeping sound tonight.
Over here in the air
The army are spyin'
Cameras are pryin'
Touts they are lyin'
Choppers are flyin'
But we are defiant
Over here in the air
It's hard to sleep sound tonight
Yes, it's hard to sleep sound tonight.

(*At end of song, they all just sit and stare out.*)

CEELY   Poor Mona, she prayed day and night
for that wee child to be born proper.

KATE   Her first grandchild was born in gaol
. . . the second was delivered by a part-time
soldier in the U.D.R.

CEELY   The next two wee ones were born on
the run.

ROSE   That last wee one was the worst . . . it
was born in England.

CEELY   Poor Mona, she hasn't had a normal
grandchild in two years. (*To can*) Mona,
how fast are the contractions comin'? All
the time. (*To others*) All the time. It was all
the excitement. (*To can*) Was it the bingo
game? (*To others*) It was the bingo game.
(*To can*) Did she win the jackpot game?
(*To others*) She won the jackpot.

KATE and ROSE   (*delighted*) Charlene won
the jackpot. (CEELY *jumps off the chair as
something dawns on her.*)

CEELY   (*suspiciously, into can*) She won the
jackpot. Oh, well, I suppose you could say
this was all your fault, Mona. I have told
you before you go far too slow with your
numbers and the people aren't prepared
for checking . . . you see, Mona, what I do
is, I start off slow and then build gradually
and gradually so that the tension actually
builds with the person. (CEELY *is getting
carried away.*) Oh, no, Mona, you will

never be a full-time professional bingo
caller because you have not made yourself
aware of the whole psychology of it like I
have. (*Pulls can away from her ear as if
hearing* MONA *screaming through it.*) All
right, Mona, keep your hair on.

ROSE   (*looking up at* TUCKER) What is he
doing? I can't cope.

CEELY   (*over balcony to soldiers*) Give Mona
MacAldooney a priest and a midwife.

ROSE   Look at him . . . He's puttin' the
planks across from the empty flats to the
chapel roof.

KATE   The soldiers don't know what the hell
is goin' on.

ROSE   That makes three hundred and one of
us.

CEELY   Well, they can't touch them children
because they are not carrying no weapons.

KATE   They can't touch them children
because Rambo is standin' guard. He would
ate them soldiers if they came near.

CEELY   They can't touch them children
because they are carryin' my friggin' Union
Jacks. I'll kill your Tucker.

ROSE   If he doesn't kill himself first. (*Baffled*)
He's carrying the kids on his back across
the planks onto the chapel roof. (*Shouts*)
Quasifuckinmodo!

CEELY   And the British Army are just
standing looking.

ROSE   (*losing control*) Tucker! Tucker! Tucker!

KATE   Shush . . . There is a Priest tryin' to
get into the chapel. Quick, Father, before
the wee child is born . . .

CEELY   (*excitedly into can*) Mona! Mona!
There is a priest pleadin' with the army to
let him in. (*There is obviously no response
from can.*) Mona! (*Bangs can.*) Mona, speak
to me.

ROSE   She has been struck dumb too. Frig
me!

CEELY   (*panicking*) Mona! Mona! (*Takes can
calmly away from her mouth*) Pigs! They
have cut communication. (*They all cross
themselves.*)

SFX   (*of priest speaking through megaphone*)
This is Father Mulcahey here. I appeal to
you to come out.

KATE   He should be appealin' to go in.

SFX   This is a sin against your church.

KATE   (*weakly*) Dustin! (*She is helpless and
begins to cry.*)

SFX   You are dancing in the aisles.

ROSE   You look like a British soldier . . . go
down there and tell them.

SFX   This is a sin against your church.

KATE   But I can't speak like one. They speak English. (*Weakly*) Mona! (*Realises there is no longer communication.*)

SFX   I appeal to you to come out.

ROSE   Tucker, do something.

SFX   I implore you to come out.

CEELY   (*suddenly*) Our Dwane!

SFX   I beseech you to come out.

ROSE   He's in America. Big deal!

SFX   Come out or be damned!

CEELY   But his catapult isn't. (CEELY *runs behind screen and produces catapult.*)

SFX   I will pray to Our Lady for your forgiveness.

CEELY   (*aims*) Right, Kate, he is gonna get this in the scone. (KATE *has composed herself.*)

SFX   You are singing lewd songs on the organ.

KATE   (*takes catapult*) Stand back! Right, Frank Tidy, this is curtains.

SFX   I appeal to you to give yourselves up in the name of God.

ROSE   Okay . . . left a bit . . . right . . . right.

KATE   (*aggressively*) Right!

SFX   I appeal to you, Mona MacAldooney.

KATE   That pigeon is sitting on the megaphone.

ROSE and CEELY   (*scream*) Fire!

SFX   I appeal to you for the sake of the little children under seige.

ROSE   (*She is guiding* KATE*'s arm.*) Right, he is on his knees.

CEELY   He's getting up again . . .

SFX   I appeal to you, Danny Hagan and Charlene MacAldooney . . .

ROSE   Fire!

SFX   I appeal to you . . . Aaaaagh . . . (*SFX of priest scream and thud. Immediately, SFX of ambulance. They all watch.*)

ROSE   God, that was quick!

CEELY   Quick when they want to be quick.

ROSE   Not quick when we want them to be quick.

CEELY   Quick when it suits them to be quick.

KATE   (*aims catapult*) Quick . . . There's Granny Tidy.

CEELY   (*grabs her arm*) Kate, she is an oul' woman.

KATE   She's an oul' whore.

CEELY   (*aims* KATE*'s arm*) Right enough!

KATE   Aye . . . Too right!

ROSE   (*grabbing* KATE *violently and directing her arm*) Kate, get a soldier. Get them all.

Get Tucker, so I can go down there and get my twins.

CEELY   The ambulance has stopped. The driver is asking your Tucker if he is gonna jump.

ROSE   That is why my Tucker is on the roof. He is gonna commit suicide.

CEELY   Jump if you're gonna jump. Stop keeping the ambulance man waiting.

KATE   Is he insured?

ROSE   Well . . . Well . . . Well . . . What a day . . . no children, no car . . . no man, and no insurance . . . but I am sure there are plenty of people worse off than me.

KATE   Yes . . . Wee Charlene is about to have a wee child out of wedlock.

CEELY   In a chapel.

ROSE   Jump . . . go on . . . Jump . . . don't just stand there. At least you're local; they usually come from outside to do it up there. I am glad it was one of our own.

KATE   Have you flipped?

CEELY   Smell! Do you smell it? Do you feel it? The tension . . . Yes, the Brits are gonna storm the chapel any minute. I know that feeling . . . it's like when somebody is waitin' on one number for a big Saturday night scoop . . . You know it's gonna happen . . . you can't stop it . . . you just haft to go with it.

KATE   All them children are wavin' Union Jacks when they should be stoning soldiers, and your Tucker is egging them on.

ROSE   Jump! I'll pick up your bits . . . you will look lovely on top of my T.V.

CEELY   I can't look. They're movin' in, I can feel it.

ROSE   Wee bits of Tucker all over the house. Some people have a china collection. I'll have a Tucker collection.

KATE   Them youngsters are all burnin' your Aunt Beattie's bedspread.

ROSE   Tucker's Last Rights . . .

KATE   Whose side is who on any more? Them kids are lighting up the chapel roof to land that army chopper, and your Tucker is waving it in.

(*SFX of army helicopter.*)

ROSE   Tucker, don't die a traitor, don't leave me to live with the shame of it. Think of your wee children.

KATE   Sure they're lost.

CEELY   Yes, there is gonna be a check any minute. Everybody is sweatin'.

(*SFX of helicopter as if it is right overhead.*)

KATE (*looks up*) All right. All right. We know what you're gonna do. (*SFX of helicopter as if it swoops right over their heads. They all scream and fall to the ground.*) Is that chopper driver drunk?

ROSE No, it's all right. My Tucker is gonna show them where to land. He's turned all them wee children into Brit lovers too.

KATE They're not gonna land . . . they're throwin' out a rope.

CEELY A rope! A rope! OH NO! They are gonna land a top marksman on the belfry. (*She turns away in despair.*)

KATE Mona, surrender!

ROSE He has all them wee children dancin' up and down on the chapel roof. He's put them all away in the head too. (*She also turns away in despair.*)

KATE (*She is staring at the chopper, then grabs* CEELY.) The chopper . . . the chopper. (*She is jumping up and down and can hardly get the words out. She grabs* CEELY.) The chopper. The chopper.

CEELY Yes, it's a chopper. We know it's a chopper.

KATE No, the chopper, the chopper.

CEELY No, it's not a chopper? It is a chopper.

KATE (*getting very excited*) No, the chopper driver, the chopper driver!

CEELY (*horrified*) There's no chopper driver? (*To* ROSE) There's no chopper driver.

ROSE (*screams*) There's no chopper driver!

KATE No! No! Look at the ch . . . ch . . . chopper . . . the chopper. (KATE *has to scream over the top of them to make herself clear.*) LOOK AT THE CHOPPER! (*They all stop and stare up at the helicopter.*)

CEELY (*quietly*) Jesus, Mary and Holy St. Joseph . . . that is my wee Tucker!

KATE And Granda Tucker!

ROSE In the Chucker!

CEELY How the hell . . .

ROSE (*staring at the helicopter*) Kate . . . Ceely . . . Who is that in the . . . behind your . . . is it . . . is it . . . (*in disbelief*) It is . . . my wee twi . . .

KATE And my Pe . . . Pe . . . (*She can't get the words out.*)

ROSE and CEELY Your Pepe!

CEELY If oul' Tucker was here . . . and my wee Tucker was with Tootsie . . .

KATE Disguised as a . . .

ROSE Driving the stolen sara . . .

CEELY How the hell did oul' Tucker make contact?

KATE He took your . . .

CEELY (*delighted*) Radio . . . my wee radio.

ROSE Stationed my Tucker on the roof.

KATE To bring in the ch . . .

ALL With burning . . . Jacks.

CEELY It all fits.

KATE Where's Starsky! (*Pause. They all look towards the helicopter.*)

ROSE What is that my Mark has on his head?

ALL A tortoise.

CEELY My Starsky is in the helicopter.

SFX (*of* GRANDA TUCKER *speaking from megaphone in helicopter. They all stand and listen in disbelief.*) Attention the enemy. This is Commanding Officer Tucker Allouisis Cash of the Twenty-first Ardoyne Batallion.

CEELY (*in shock*) He hasn't spoke in twelve years.

SFX My comrades and I are holding Major Devenport of the Gloucesters as hostage.

ALL Hostage!

SFX We are about to lower a British Army Chaplain. We demand that the wedding of Charlene Macaldooney and Danny Hagan be consecrated immediately. Tiocfaidh ar la!

(*SFX of cheering and clapping. They all stand waving at the helicopter.*)

CEELY (*shouts*) Tucker, put your seatbelt on. (*A long pause as if everything is now back to normal.*)

ROSE Wonder is the water back on.

CEELY Well, there's one good thing, Rose Marie. You won't have to wash Tucker's car ever again.

KATE They got a great day for the wedding.

ROSE Just in time . . . look . . . they are bringing wee Susie Quinn's coffin out to the chapel.

KATE Is it half past four already?

CEELY Oh, great, I forgot about the funeral.

KATE That's what I love about this place. On a day like today you could be anywhere.

(*All sing 'The Sun is Shining'*)

ALL
> The sun is a shinin' and the bees are a hummin'
> Flowers are a bloomin' and the Lord is a comin'
> Yes, the Lord is a comin'
> Yes, the Lord is a comin'.

Kids are a playin' and the dogs are a
barkin'
Mothers are a laughin' and the Saints are
a marchin'
Yes, the Saints are a marchin'
Yes, the Saints are a marchin'
Yes, the Saints are a marchin'!

Hey, Mister Maker, we know you care
Cos we're nearer to heaven than the folks
down there.
Yes, the Lord is a comin'
And the Saints are a marchin'
And the Lord is a comin'
And the Saints are a marchin.'
Hey, Mister Maker, we know you care.
Cos we're nearer to heaven than the folks
down there.

(*Blackout.*)

Notes

1   Troops Out, a British pressure group in
support of British withdrawal from
Northern Ireland and of the Republican
movement, arrived in Belfast at Divis
flats on the anniversary of the Eve of
Internment every year for a
demonstration.

2   On 9 August 1971, the British government
introduced internment to Northern
Ireland, allowing the arrest and
imprisonment without trial of many
Catholics who were suspected members
of the IRA. In the early hours of the
morning, army raids were carried out in
Nationalist areas and thousands of men
were 'lifted' for internment. Internment
Day is now marked, on the anniversary of
introduction, every year in Nationalist
areas with bonfires. Various British and
Nationalist support groups visit areas
such as Divis on the anniversary.

3   A campaign against the criminalisation of
political prisoners. Nationalist prisoners
protested for special status (i.e. political
status) in 1980–1, one form of which was
wearing only blankets instead of ordinary
criminal prison uniform.

4   Long Kesh is a prison also known as the
Maze. It lies outside of Belfast and
contains the H-blocks where the hunger
strikes of 1981 took place. The prison
served as a camp for those imprisoned
during the internment.

Glossary

beg bag
charabanc an open top bus used for
excursions; a trip on a charabanc
represented leisure for the working class
CS riot control gas gun
doing the 'double' the illegal practice of
working while drawing state wefare
dukin' peeping
frig it/frigging derogatory exclamation
ghett bad rascal, jerk, brat, pest (derogatory
remark)
gurney wee shites whiny little shits
hokin' looking
Holy Ground, the Irish sea shanty
Oul' Nick the Devil
peeler police
piggin' dirty, filthy
quare real, very, a good many, a lot,
exceptional
R.U.C. Royal Ulster Constabulary (Northern
Ireland police force)
saracen protected army vehicle
skitter derogatory name
snattery snotty
Tiocfaidh ar la 'Our day will come';
pronounced Chukkie r la
tricolour the national flag of the Republic
of Ireland
Tucker nickname very popular in Divis
Flats, short for Tommy, i.e. 'little Tommy
Tucker'
U.D.R. Ulster Defence Regiment, a locally
recruited regiment of the British Army;
the majority of the members are part time
wains wee ones, children
wheen many, a lot